XI

The Last Word

MATTHEW ARNOLD

THE LAST WORD

Edited by R. H. Super

ANN ARBOR   THE UNIVERSITY OF MICHIGAN PRESS

Second printing 1978
Copyright © by The University of Michigan 1977
All rights reserved
ISBN 0-472-11661-4
Library of Congress Catalog Card No. 60-5018
Published in the United States of America by
The University of Michigan Press and simultaneously
in Rexdale, Canada, by John Wiley & Sons Canada, Limited
Manufactured in the United States of America

3Ø8Ø96Ø

Editor's Preface

Arnold survived his retirement from his post with the Education Department by less than two years—a period marked by heavy commitments to friends, editors, and chairmen of speakers' committees for discourses on a wide variety of subjects. The present volume includes his final work as a public servant—the report on certain aspects of Continental education done for the Education Department in Whitehall—and the wide range of essays that followed in what may well be his most prolific biennium, essays on education, politics, literature, religion, and society. The report on Continental education was reprinted in his lifetime; four of the other essays were gathered into *Essays in Criticism, Second Series* in the year of his death, and the two essays on American subjects, "General Grant" and "Civilisation in the United States," were pirated in America in the same year. Nearly all the contents of this volume except the *Essays in Criticism* has been reprinted within the last twenty-five years in editions that had an academic origin: ten essays, letters, and speeches in Fraser Neiman's *Essays, Letters, and Reviews by Matthew Arnold* (Cambridge, Mass.: Harvard University Press, 1960), of which volume they constitute nearly a third part; two in Kenneth Allott's *Five Uncollected Essays of Matthew Arnold* (Liverpool: University Press, 1953), "General Grant" in a separate edition by John Y. Simon (Carbondale and Edwardsville: Southern Illinois University Press, 1966), and *Elementary Education in Germany, &c.*, (mistitled "Cross Commission Report") in Paul Nash, ed., *Culture and the State: Matthew Arnold and Continental Education* (New York: Teachers College [Columbia University] Press, 1966). The only essays here republished for the first time, then, are the very brief Preface Arnold wrote for the American edition of Mary S. Claude's *Twilight Thoughts* and the much longer and quite significant survey of English elementary and secondary education in the reign of Queen Victoria written for a Jubilee volume edited by the husband of Arnold's niece, T. Humphry Ward. To these are added reports of public lectures and brief notes by Arnold in the public press.

All but one of these works exist in a single authoritative text; the only variants to be recorded in the Textual Notes for most of them, then, are editorial emendations. The report on Continental schools uses the text of the reprint Arnold authorized in 1888.

The aim of the Critical and Explanatory Notes is here, as in the preceding volumes of this edition, to give some account of the circumstances under which each essay was written, to identify so far as I have been able the sources of Arnold's quotations and information, and to explain the force of his allusions. In this task I have been assisted by Dr. Victor N. Boutellier of Zurich, by Dr. Park Honan, Mr. David A. Roos, Mrs. Sue Bonner Walcutt, and by my former students Drs. James Berlin, Mark Greenberg, James Rosenberg, Lynn Willing Weisberg, and Jeffrey Welch, to all of whom I owe a great debt. I am also indebted to Miss Marjorie G. Wynne of the Beinecke Rare Book and Manuscript Library of Yale University and Mr. E. V. Quinn, librarian of Balliol College, Oxford. It remains to be said, of course, that if the notes do not supply the information the reader wants, the reason may be editorial oversight, but is at least as likely to be the editor's inability to find what was needed. The notes commonly give cross-references to similar ideas or phrases in other writings of Arnold; where these are insufficient, the Index may help.

A final volume in an edition may need two features that its predecessors did not require—a title index of all the works included in the entire edition, and (for a fallible editor) pages of additions and corrections to the earlier volumes. The Title Index tries to include all the titles by which a work was known in Arnold's lifetime, not merely the title adopted for this edition. Materials for the Additions and Corrections have been gleaned from comments of keen-eyed reviewers and from generous suggestions privately transmitted by other Arnold scholars, some friends, some not personally known to the editor. Among these should be named, with gratitude, Roger L. Brooks, P. H. Butterfield, Sidney M. B. Coulling, J. C. Maxwell, John H. Raleigh, Patrick G. Scott, Geoffrey Tillotson, and especially David J. DeLaura. It must be said, however, that most of the additions and corrections are the fruit of my own constant work with these volumes, not systematically re-examined, but used and re-used as the editing progressed.

"Perhaps no extensive and multifarious performance was ever effected within the term originally fixed in the undertaker's mind. He that runs against Time has an antagonist not subject to casualties," remarked Johnson in an essay Arnold re-published. It is now sixteen years since the first volume of this edition appeared, and nearly two decades since the task was undertaken. Among its earliest encouragers some at least—Arnold's grandson Professor Arnold Whitridge, Professors Douglas Bush and Warner G. Rice—will see the task completed. Arduous as the work has been, tedious as the infinite collating, proofreading, checking of references, and indexing have been, the lively mind of Arnold himself and the range of his interests have prevented the task from lapsing into routine dullness. The editor's aim has always been the usefulness of the edition to the reader and scholar. Though the length of some of the notes in this final volume begins to suggest the garrulousness of advancing years, I still hope not to have incurred the criticism Arnold made of an edition he himself was once reviewing: "All knowledge may be in itself good, but this kind of editing seems to proceed upon the notion that we have only one book to read in the course of our life, or else that we have eternity to read in." I have tried firmly to restrict myself to the immediate illumination of the text.

Making Arnold's work available, as well as comprehensible, has inevitably seemed to me to mean making it available within a reasonable period of time. Although the edition has indeed taken longer than I fancied it would at the beginning, I have determinedly kept it moving. Moreover, making it available has seemed to me to involve keeping the price as low as possible for the reader; to that end, the editor has waived all royalties and all payments whatsoever from the publisher. No part of the purchase price of these volumes has gone to the editor. The generous support, therefore, of fellowships and grants from the American Council of Learned Societies, the John Simon Guggenheim Memorial Foundation, and the Horace H. Rackham School of Graduate Studies of the University of Michigan is the more welcome.

One strongly-worded criticism of the edition may need a reply. The text adopted, as announced at the outset, has been the latest text Arnold may have supervised, and substantive variants from earlier versions have been recorded in the Textual Notes to each volume; a very few necessary emendations have been made by the editor. On this principle, for the bulk of volumes I, III, and V to IX (and for pp. 3–29 of volume II), the copy sent to the printer has been the so-called New York edition, printed in Edinburgh for Arnold's publisher Macmillan, for distribution in America at the time of Arnold's lecture tour of 1883–84; this edition was published with Arnold's consent and he saw proofs of it. It was also the basis of the posthumous De Luxe edition published in London in 1903–4. A recent commentator in *Notes and Queries* (November, 1972, and July, 1974) has written: "The choice of the New York edition as copy-text is unjustifiable," on the ground that the nature and number of the substantive variants peculiar to that edition do not persuade him that the author "worked over the text with the care that would allow an editor to assume that Arnold acquiesced in its innovations." He may be right, of course, though he would have been more constructive had he demonstrated, even in a sample, what choice would have been the correct one and how significant the differences were from mine. As regards substantive variants, the total number of instances in which I have preserved a unique "New York" reading has been about thirty-six in the entire eleven volumes, most of them single words, and counting such alterations from earlier editions as "farther" into "further," "as far as" into "so far as," "an unique" into "a unique," "while" into "whilst," "we shall" into "we will." As regards accidentals, my critic is, it seems to me, entirely misleading: "The New York edition introduces about five punctuation changes per (Michigan) page for the sections I have checked." No perfectly scrupulous bibliographer, I think, would be content with such a statement; it can, of course, hardly be tested, since he mentions neither which "sections" he has checked, nor against which editions. But since he goes on to hold up the 1875 edition of *Essays in Criticism* as one to which he conceives Arnold gave appropriate and detailed attention, I must quite simply assert that there are almost no changes in punctuation between that and the New York edition—not five per (Michigan) page, but scarcely one in ten pages. I am grateful to my critic for making me re-examine my text and leading me to catch some errors, but with all allowance for an editor's blunders (and the pages of errata will show that I am not oblivious to them), the text of the present edition will not be significantly faulted. What may be expected—indeed what has already occurred in some instances (as the Additions and Corrections show)—is that as Arnold's manuscripts turn up they will reveal occasional single words the compositor misread, his plausible substitutions for which escaped the eye of all successive proofreaders.

There remain a few very important acknowledgments to be made. My son David was early involved with helping to check the indexes, and my wife Rebecca spent infinite hours with me correcting the proofs. Of the many excellent works of scholarship that have been useful, one stands out especially, the Lowry, Young, and Dunn edition of Arnold's *Note-Books*. It can not detract from my sense of the contributions of all departments of the University of Michigan Press if I acknowledge especially the help of the successive editors there with whom I have worked, Walter A. Donnelly, Philip Krapp, and Elnor C. Parker, and mention Fred D. Wieck, the Director who sought out and began the publication of this edition. And finally, there are few libraries in this country or in the world so well equipped and so easy to use for a wide-ranging task like this one as the Library of the University of Michigan.

Contents

* *Essays in Criticism*, Second Series.

Special Report on Certain Points
Connected with Elementary Education
in Germany, Switzerland, and France

PREFACE

When it was proposed to reprint for popular use the following Report, made originally to the Education Department, I was asked whether I wished to alter or expand what is said in it. I replied that I did not; that I thought the Report would be more useful in its original state than altered or expanded. But I wish ⁵ to indicate three points to which those for whose use the Report is now designed will do well, I think, to direct their minds.

The first of these points is the need that those who use the popular school should arrive at clear and just notions of what ¹⁰ they want their own school to be, and should seek to get it made this. At present their school is not this, but is rather what the political and governing classes, establishing a school for the benefit of the working classes, think that such a school ought to be. ¹⁵

The second point is, that our existing popular school is far too little formative and humanizing, and that much in it, which its administrators point to as valuable *results*, is in truth mere machinery.

The third and last point is, that religious instruction, which ²⁰ politicians making or administering the popular school seek to exclude as embarrassing, if not futile, is a formative influence, an element of culture of the very highest value, and more indispensable in the popular school than in any other. Political pressure tends to exclude this element of culture; clerical pressure ²⁵ tends to give it a false character. The interest of the people

is to get a true character imparted to it, and to have it firmly
planted, with this character, in the popular school.

MATTHEW ARNOLD

February, 1888

5   NOTE.—*The Council of the Education Reform League, considering
that this Report is of great importance to the working classes, resolved
to reprint it in as cheap a form as possible, and through the courtesy of
the author they are enabled to add the [above] Preface, which has been
specially written by* MR. MATTHEW ARNOLD *for this edition.*

SPECIAL REPORT ON CERTAIN POINTS
CONNECTED WITH ELEMENTARY EDUCATION
IN GERMANY, SWITZERLAND, AND FRANCE

May, 1886.

SIR,

In November last I received instructions from the Education Department to visit Germany, Switzerland, and France, for the purpose of making inquiry on certain points connected 5 with elementary education in those countries. My attention was to be more particularly directed to Germany and Switzerland.

The points were these:—

1. Free education. 10
2. Quality of education.
3. Status, training, and pensioning of teachers.
4. Compulsory attendance and release from school.

To perform the task entrusted to me I left England on the 11th of November, and proceeded to Northern Germany, 15 where I remained until just before Christmas. I came back to England for the Christmas holidays, during which all schools are closed, and on the 21st of January in the present year I again went abroad, and spent two months in visiting schools in France, Switzerland, and Bavaria. On my way home I again 20 passed through Northern Germany, and gave a few days to the schools there.

I had thus at disposal, for my inquiry, about fourteen weeks, of which five were spent in Prussia, two in Saxony, two in Bavaria, two in Switzerland, and three in France. I received 25 every kindness and assistance from Her Majesty's representatives abroad, and from the functionaries of public instruction to whom I was through their means introduced and recommended. I must particularly mention my obligations to Dr.

Schneider and Dr. Tyszka at Berlin, Dr. Bornemann and Mr.
Eichenberg at Dresden, Mr. Von Auer at Munich, Mr. Küttel
at Lucerne, Mr. Hirzel at Zurich, M. Buisson and M. Gaillard
in Paris. All facilities were given me for seeing schools, and I
5 was furnished with all documents which were thought likely
to be of service to me.

In 1859, and again in 1865, I was sent to inquire into the
systems of education in use in certain foreign countries, and to
make a report on them. On the present occasion I have had to
10 deal with certain points only in foreign systems of education,
not to give an account of the systems in their entirety. This is
to be borne distinctly in mind in reading my report. My time
was altogether too short to make a full study of the systems of
education with which I was dealing, changed as these systems
15 are since I last saw the schools of foreign countries. I feel very
strongly that it was too short to allow me to make even a study
of them fully adequate for the purposes of my present inquiry
and report. On previous occasions I remained many months on
the Continent, and was able, after seeing schools, to read on the
20 spot the documents with which I was furnished, and to ask
those who furnished them to explain anything which I did not
understand, anything which I found it hard to reconcile with
what I had actually seen and heard. On the present occasion I
could not do this. All my time was required for what is the
25 really important part of a mission such as that entrusted to me:
for seeing the schools with my own eyes, and for hearing what
those concerned with them had to tell me. The documents I
have been obliged to read in great measure at home since my
return, and I do not feel so sure of my ground as if I had been
30 able to read them, as on former occasions, on the spot, and with
my guides and expounders at hand. Not only, therefore, does
the following report make no pretensions to be a complete account of the systems of elementary education in the countries
to which it relates, not only must it omit much in those systems
35 which is of interest to many persons, but it may probably
also, I am afraid, even on those points with which it deals, be
less thorough and satisfactory than I could wish it to be. However, I shall deal with the matters referred to me as well as
I can.

I take them in their order, and first:—

Free Education.—Under this head I was directed to ascertain whether gratuitous education is confined to elementary schools or extends to other schools or colleges; what reasons induced the State to establish the gratuitous system; in what way (directly or indirectly) the lower classes of society are made to feel the weight of the expenditure on education; in what way the dirty and neglected children in large towns are dealt with, and especially whether all descriptions of children are mixed in the same schoolroom; whether there is a legal prohibition against charging fees in public schools even if parents and children are willing to pay; whether the attendance of children has increased or diminished since the establishment of free schools.

Free Education in Prussia.—Prussia has no general school law, although such a law has long been projected, and has indeed been actually drafted. Elementary education is governed by a number of orders and regulations emanating from the local as well as from the central government, and by a number of laws directed to special points. But in the Prussian Constitution of 1850 there is this provision: *In der öffentlichen Volksschule wird der Unterricht unentgeltlich ertheilt.* "In the public popular school the instruction is given gratuitously." A further provision is: "The means for erecting, maintaining, and enlarging the public popular school are supplied by the communes, and in case of proved inability the deficiency is made good by the State." Another article of the Constitution, however, permits the *Gemeinden,* or communes, to decide for themselves whether they will make their schools free or will charge school fees, only their decision must have the sanction of the *Regierung,* the provincial government.

The obligation on parents in Prussia to send their children to school from the age of five to that of fourteen was established by a general regulation in 1763, completed by further law and regulation in 1794 and 1825.

The provision in the Constitution of 1850, for making instruction in the popular schools gratuitous throughout Prussia, has hitherto remained inoperative. The popular school is to be supplied and maintained by the *Gemeinde,* the municipal unit or commune, and the communes have not in general found

themselves able to dispense with the resources furnished by school fees. Neither has the State found itself able to undertake the expense for gratuitous schooling, which the communes have been unable or unwilling to bear. Several communes in
5   different parts of the country have, however, made their popular schools gratuitous. Some of them are small places. Düsseldorf is an instance of an important and wealthy place which has made its popular schools free. But the great instance is Berlin itself, the capital.

10   The municipality of Berlin paid for its communal schools in the year 1821 the sum of 3000 marks (the mark answers to our shilling). In the year 1879 it paid more than 4,000,000 marks for them, in 1885 more than 6,000,000. The schools were in 1837 taken over by a municipal school board (*Schul-deputation*)
15   from the administrators for the poor, the municipal officers who had hitherto had charge of them. At the end of 1869 the municipality resolved to make from the beginning of 1870 the instruction in its communal schools gratuitous for all scholars. In 1869, before this introduction of free schooling, the munici-
20   pality had 49 communal schools, with 31,752 scholars. In 1885 it had 146 communal schools with 132,889 scholars. This is a sufficient answer to the question whether school attendance has increased or diminished since the abolition of school fees, although it should be added that school attendance increases
25   everywhere in Germany, in localities which retain school fees as well as in those which have abolished them.

The *Gemeinde-schulen*, or communal schools, are the only body of schools in Berlin, or in other localities in Prussia, where school fees are not paid. But I will append a table of the
30   schools in Berlin, showing what is the provision, not only of popular schools there, but also of public secondary or intermediate schools, the schools for the middle and upper classes.*
It will be seen from that table what a provision for the education of these classes is made by the municipality or the State. In

35   * See Table A. In Table B. the same thing is shown for a whole country, Saxony, which in Table A. is shown for the city of Berlin only. In Table C. is shown how the cost of the Saxon schools is distributed. [The tables are not included in the present edition—Ed.]

higher schools, or universities, the same aid is continued, and this is the important thing for us in England to know and remember. We are misled if we are merely told that the schools for the lower classes in Berlin are free, while those for the middle and upper classes charge school fees. What would the schools for these classes be in Berlin, or, indeed, anywhere in Germany, if they had merely their school fees to depend upon? The schools are built and maintained, their teachers are paid, by the State or the municipality; the school fees of the pupils, always very moderate according to our notions, are merely a contribution in aid of the expense of admirable schools provided really, like the elementary schools, by the public.

If it is asked what induced the municipality of Berlin or of other places to make popular education gratuitous, the first answer will be that the Prussian Constitution says that it shall be gratuitous, and that the word of the Constitution ought not to remain a dead letter. The municipalities with sufficient means at their disposal comply with the rule of the Constitution. The difficulty of collecting fees is said also to have been a strong motive with the Berlin municipality for making its schools free. Opinion in Prussia is greatly divided as to whether or no it is an advantage to make them free. I found the Minister of Education, Mr. Von Gossler, warmly in favour of making them so; it is commonly asserted that Prince Bismarck is of the same way of thinking. Free schooling he is said to consider a particularly safe and useful form of public aid to the working classes. The weight of opinion, however, among Government functionaries, teachers, and the general public I found to be on the other side. Why should not the parents who can afford it pay, say excellent and experienced teachers; it would be good for them, and they would pay quite willingly. At any rate, however, free schooling will not, I am told, be made universal in Prussia just yet; the communes cannot support the charge, and the State is not disposed to relieve them of it. If the thing is to be done, the State will have to do it, as the State is doing it in France. In view of this contingency it is well to remark that the proportion of the expense of schools which is supplied

by the present low school fees is not very considerable. Its relinquishment would be a heavy loss for the communes to bear, but not, perhaps, for the State. It appears from some very careful statistics issued in 1882 that in the year 1878 of the cost
5   of teaching in the popular schools (which is 70 per cent. of the total cost for them) the school fees, which are entirely applied to meet this charge, furnished little more than one-fifth part. On an average for the whole kingdom school fees meet 20.58 per cent. of the cost of teaching in the Prussian
10 popular schools, endowments 12.02 per cent., the municipalities 55.26 per cent., and the State 12.14 per cent.

In towns where the popular schools are not generally free, provision has been made for giving free instruction to poor children in schools for themselves. This is done, for instance,
15 at Cologne, where the municipality has town schools for children who can pay, and who are charged from 1s. to 1s. 6d. a month, according to the taxes paid by their parents; and free schools for the poor, where everything is found, sometimes even clothes. But in Berlin all the children of what we call the
20 working class, and very many of the middle class, use the schools together, and are all alike exempt from school fees. I was informed that there is no specially poor quarter of Berlin like the *East End* of London; of course there is poverty, but the working classes live in the basement storeys of the houses
25 in all quarters of Berlin, and are numerous in the quarters inhabited by the Court and rich people, as well as in others. Their children, therefore, are equally distributed through the schools, and certainly I found no groups of dirty and miserable-looking children in the schools which I visited. All the children
30 I saw were decently clad, and I was told that in all the Berlin schools I should find them so. But then they were no more dirty and ragged-looking in a poor school for Catholics which I visited at Cologne than in the Berlin schools.

The only distinction made on the ground of poverty at
35 Berlin is that school books and school material are supplied gratuitously where it is represented that the child cannot well afford to buy them, and the teacher finds this to be really the case. In general the children buy them.

It is evident that the question of permitting the payment of fees does not arise in cases where a municipality, as at Berlin and other places in Prussia, thinks proper to make its schools free. The State may give municipalities permission to levy fees in spite of a constitutional rule to the contrary; but there can be no room for such a permission when the municipality of its own accord establishes free schools.

Free Education in Saxony.—In Saxony free schooling, as a rule for the whole school, is confined to certain foundation schools and schools maintained by charitable associations. In the ordinary popular schools children whose parents are paupers are paid for out of the local *Armen-kasse* or poor-chest. But for the children in general who attend these schools the Saxon School Law of 1873 expressly imposes the payment of a school fee. The managers are to levy it, and to adapt it to the means and condition of the parents. It therefore varies surprisingly in amount; in country schools from 3*s*. 1½*d*. a year (for in Germany the school fee is in general paid quarterly and reckoned by the year) to 10*s*. 6*d*.; in town schools from 3*s*. or 4*s*. a year to £3 or £4, and the variation commonly occurs, both in town and country, in the same school. In a list of ten towns for which Dr. Bornemann, the Director of Elementary Education in Saxony, has given me the rates of school fees, I find one town only, Langefeld, where there is a uniform fee in the popular school for all payers; the fee is 15*s*. a year. In the other nine the scale varies from 6*s*. a year to 36*s*. in one case, from 6*s*. to 60*s*. in another, 6*s*. 9*d*. to 54*s*. in a third, 4*s*. to 32*s*. in a fourth, 20*s*. 10*d*. to 88*s*. 2½*d*. in a fifth, and so on. In the secondary or intermediate schools, which are also public schools, the *Gymnasien*, *Real-schulen*, and Higher Schools for girls, the fee for schooling is £6 a year.

From the Minister of Education, Dr. Von Gerber, downwards, I found opinion in Saxony against the abolition of school fees. The families, it was said, have the first and greatest interest in their children's education; they ought, therefore, to contribute towards paying for it. On the other hand the *Gemeinde*, the local community, also gets benefit by the children being educated; the *Gemeinde*, therefore, ought to contribute too.

Why is it harder, it was said again, upon an artisan with £50
a year to have to pay 6s. a year for his child's schooling than
upon an officer or a civil servant, with £200 or £300 a year, to
have to pay £6?

5   Dr. Bornemann was of opinion that the general establishment
of gratuitous popular instruction in Germany, though everywhere a good deal discussed at the present moment, will not
actually come. If it does come, he said, it will lead to a great
development of private schools. Poor children cannot learn so
10   much as the better off, who have more means for preparation
at home; the schools will drop to the level of the poorer
children, and the better off will go to private elementary
schools.

Free Education in Bavaria.—In Bavaria it is as in Prussia;
15   certain municipalities have made their popular schools gratuitous, but payment of a school fee is the general rule. Bavaria
has not in its Constitution any declaration respecting free
schooling such as that which the Prussian Constitution contains, but it resembles Prussia in having no one general school
20   law. Such a law was drafted and brought in twenty years ago,
but did not obtain the assent of Parliament. Orders, regulations,
and laws on special points govern popular education in Bavaria
as in Prussia.

The general rule in Bavaria is to levy school fees, which are
25   regarded as the natural provision for the teacher of the popular
school. The public school fee has to be paid for every child
of school age in the *Gemeinde*, whether such child attends the
public school or a private one. Only when the legal amount
of the teacher's salary is completely supplied from endowment,
30   or in other ways, is it allowable not to levy school fees.

The fee is fixed by law at a minimum of 8d. and a maximum
of 1s. 4d. per quarter. Where, however, higher fees were levied
before 1862, the date of the school dotation law, they may be
levied still. The poor are paid for out of the poor-chest.

35   I found two important instances in which, the teachers'
salaries being provided in the "other ways" allowed by the
law, school rates are not levied. They were Munich and
Nuremberg. I might add a third, Fürth; but Fürth may be

regarded as a manufacturing extension of Nuremberg, from which it is only ten minutes distant by rail. I could hear of no other instances in Bavaria. In both Munich and Nuremberg a wealthy municipality had solved the difficulty of collecting fees by abolishing them altogether and taking upon itself the cost for the schools and the teachers' salaries. In Nuremberg the abolition took place quite recently, not more than a year and a half ago. The results of the change cannot yet be perfectly judged, but where the change has been so recent one has the advantage of finding the previous state of things, and the reasons which led to its being altered, still full in people's recollection. The burgher-master of Nuremberg told me that in Nuremberg and Fürth fees had been abandoned because of the difficulty of collecting them, the teachers, on whom the task of collection was thrown, objecting to perform it. He added that, with a shifting population, the obtaining of the fees of children of new-comers from their own communes, in which, and not in Nuremberg, the fees for these children were chargeable, led to much intricate account keeping and troublesome correspondence. The attendance had increased since the change, but it is increasing everywhere in Germany, whether school fees are charged or no. Before the change Nuremberg had three classes of popular schools—schools in which all the scholars paid, schools in which a part of them paid, schools in which none paid. The schools in which all paid were, the burgher-master said, undeniably much the best; the schools in which a part paid were the next best; the free schools were the worst. In the present schools there is a much greater mixture of classes than in the schools before the change; the majority of the municipality, said the burgher-master, thought this mixture a good thing; he himself did not.

In the popular schools of Munich I found this mixture of classes thoroughly established; much more so than in North Germany. In South Germany the obligation to attend daily school ends when the child is 13, a year sooner than in North Germany. I was told that in Munich the boys who do not attend the popular school up to the age of 13 are hardly more than 1 per cent.; afterwards the sons of wealthier parents go to

secondary schools. The proportion of girls who attend, up to
13, other than the public popular schools, is a good deal larger;
still, many girls of the wealthier classes do attend them.

The result, then, as to Prussia, Saxony, and Bavaria, of my
5 inquiry concerning school fees is this: payment is the rule, free
schooling is the exception. The popular school in these countries is a municipal thing; it is maintained, so far as it is not
self-supporting, out of municipal resources and municipal taxes.
A special school rate is not levied. If a Prussian or Bavarian
10 municipality choose to abolish school fees and maintain the
schools out of municipal resources and taxes, they can do so.
In Prussia and Bavaria municipalities have in some cases done
so. In Saxony they have to charge school fees in all public
popular schools. In Hamburg, a free town, I found the pay-
15 ment of school fees required by law, and poor children are
to be admitted free. This, I say, is the general rule in Germany—
a school fee charged where the scholar can afford to pay it,
remitted where he cannot. In those countries of Germany
which I did not visit, the general rule, I am informed, is the
20 same, although in those countries also there are to be found
cases in which the municipalities have made instruction in the
popular schools gratuitous.

Free Education in Switzerland.—In Switzerland the question
of school fees is determined by the Federal Constitution, which
25 bears date the 29th of May 1874. Article 27 of this Constitution
says, "Primary instruction is obligatory and in the public
schools gratuitous."

The Swiss cantons are jealous of their independence in their
local affairs, and a proposal to appoint a federal secretary of
30 education was rejected by a large majority. But all the cantons
have complied with the article of the Constitution which declares primary instruction to be obligatory and in public
schools gratuitous. Many people are in favour of also supplying
books and school materials gratuitously; but this has not yet
35 been done.

I visited, as specimens of the Swiss schools, the schools of
Canton Zurich and Canton Lucerne; one of them a Protestant
and industrial canton, the other a mountain canton and Catholic.

Each canton has its school law. In Lucerne the child must come to school at seven years old, and may come at six; his day-school course lasts till he is 14, and he has then, unless he goes to some higher school, to attend a *Fortbildungs-schule*, or continuation school, for two years more, until he is 16. In Zurich the child must come to school at six years old; his day-school course lasts for six years, until he is 12. A proposal to lengthen it was rejected in a general meeting of the canton by an immense majority. But he has three years of obligatory attendance at an *Ergänzungs-schule*, or completion school, after he is 12, besides an hour a week at a singing school.

All these schools are free. In Canton Lucerne the higher schools are free also.* In Canton Zurich the *Secundär-schulen*, schools taking the pupil when he leaves the primary school, and giving him four years more of schooling, are free; but fees are charged in the cantonal *Gymnasium, Real-schule*, and higher school for girls. These fees are of about the same amount in the boys' schools as the fees in the corresponding schools in Dresden; in the higher schools for girls they are lower, only £4. An entrance fee of 2 francs and a small fee for lessons in book-keeping and foreign languages are also charged in the evening school, or trade school (*Gewerbeschule*) as it is called, which takes young men from the age of 17 to that of 20; the other matters of instruction in this school are free.

But as in Germany, so in Canton Zurich, a whole system of intermediate schools exists by public establishment so much better and cheaper than could exist without it, that the class using them, though it may have to pay school fees, has yet its full and fair share of benefit from public expenditure on education, as well as the class for whom the popular schools are provided. Above the intermediate schools Zurich has, as establishments for higher education, the University of Zurich, a cantonal institution, and the Polytechnicum or Technical University, a federal one.

---

* In the United States secondary instruction is incompletely organized, but it is worth remarking that at Boston not only are the common schools free, but also the Latin school and the high schools.

In other countries it is a political or governing class which
establishes popular schools for the benefit of the lower classes.
But in Switzerland we have the spectacle of a country where
the community establishes the popular school for its own
5 benefit. The same may be said, I suppose, of the institution of
the popular school in the United States. Every one who knows
Switzerland has seen the general equality of conditions which
prevails there, and which determines the habits of life for the
nation at large. A rich man at Zurich, the greatest employer of
10 labour in Switzerland, told me that he sent his own children,
both girls and boys, without hesitation to the popular school.
They went afterwards to higher schools, of course. His wife
told me that she thought the contact in the *Gymnasium* or
classical school more objectionable, that there was more dif-
15 ficulty in letting her son bring home with him his class-mates
there than had been the case when he was in the popular school.
When the popular school is thus freely used by all classes, and
a convenience, if not a positive need, for all, it is natural to
make its establishment and maintenance a corporate charge.
20 This is what the Swiss Constitution has done; and the cantons
and communes have willingly followed the ruling of the Constitution, and made the popular school rest for support on
municipal tax, not on school fee.

I was told, too, that it was found convenient in enforcing
25 school obligation in a democratic country like Switzerland,
where the action of public authority is less strong and stringent
than in Germany, to be able to allege the gratuitousness of the
schooling imposed. "You have nothing to pay, you can have
no difficulty on that score, your child must attend"—is found,
30 the school authorities told me, to be a good and effectual line
of remonstrance with careless or uncomplying parents.

The article of the Swiss Constitution which establishes the
obligatoriness and gratuitousness of the popular school goes
on to say next: "The public schools shall be capable of being
35 attended by adherents of all confessions without injury to their
freedom of faith and conscience." Whoever has seen the divisions caused in a so-called logical nation like the French by
this principle of the neutrality of the popular school in matter

of religion might expect difficulty here. None whatever has arisen. The Swiss communities, applying the principle for themselves, and not leaving theorists and politicians to apply it for them, have done in the matter what they find suitable to their wants, and have in every popular school religious instruction in 5 the religion of the majority, a Catholic instruction in Catholic cantons like Lucerne, a Protestant in Protestant cantons like Zurich. There is no unfair dealing, no proselytizing, no complaint. In the German countries generally I have been struck with the same thing. In Germany the schools are confessional, 10 or, as we say, denominational; that is (for the sect ramifications of Protestantism are not regarded) they are Evangelical, Catholic, or Jewish. When there are enough children of the confession of the minority, a separate school is established for them, but where there are not enough and they are taught with 15 the children of the confession of the majority, there is, so far as I could learn, no unfair dealing and no complaint. In Saxony, where the Catholics are a small minority (in round numbers, 73,000 to nearly 3,000,000 of Protestants), there are confessional schools for Catholics; but, of course, many scattered Catholic 20 children are attending the Protestant schools. Of these children, the elder ones must stay away from the religious instruction; the younger ones may follow it if their parents please, and often do follow it. In the great town school of Lucerne I found about 400 Protestant children in class with 2900 Catholics; the 25 Catholic children receive their religious instruction at the school, the boys from the director of the institution, the girls from a priest; the Protestant children receive theirs out of school and out of school hours. But at the large country school of Krientz, near Lucerne, I found that even in the head classes 30 the few Protestant children were receiving religious instruction along with their Catholic school-mates, the parents approving. The only case of religious difficulty which came to my notice was at Zurich, where some excellent people, evangelical Protestants, considering the Protestantism of the public training 35 college and schools too broad and too lax, had founded, by private subscription, a more strictly evangelical college and school, which have been very successful.

What has been said of the general equality of conditions in Switzerland supplies an answer as to the question whether there are separate schools for dirty and neglected children. There is no such class of children; provision, however, is made for giv-
5   ing school books and materials free to children whose parents cannot provide them.

To the question whether the attendance at school has increased or diminished since the instruction was made gratuitous, I can give no answer so complete as a confrontation of the
10   numbers at present actually attending the town school of Lucerne just now mentioned, with the numbers attending it 15 years ago. They are now 3300; they were then 1500. I regard free schooling, however, rather as a part and sign of the movement of advance in popular education than as itself the
15   cause of the movement.

Free Education in France.—The law of June 16, 1881, when M. Jules Ferry was Minister of Public Instruction, abolished the payment of fees in the public primary schools, the infants' schools, and the normal schools of France.

20   Attendance at school was made obligatory by the law of March 28th in the year following, M. Jules Ferry being still Minister. Article 4 of this law says:—"Primary instruction is obligatory for children of both sexes between the ages of six years complete and 13 years complete."

25   In France, as in Germany and Switzerland, intermediate and higher instruction are established and aided by the State, although for instruction at these stages fees are paid. But in the great towns, and above all in Paris, there is a whole system of schools and appliances connecting themselves with the primary
30   school, and completing or continuing it, which are also made gratuitous. The municipality of Paris has thus not only its infants' schools and elementary schools, it has also its evening classes for adults and apprentices, its establishments of superior primary instruction, and its establishments of professional in-
35   struction, all of them for young people of both sexes, and all of them gratuitous.

If the creators of this great gratuitous system are asked what moved them to establish it, they will reply with entire frankness, *l'idée démocratique*, the democratic idea. In a democratic society, they will say, the distinction between the school child who can afford to pay fees for his schooling and who pays them, and the school child who cannot and does not, is wounding and improper. I am not quoting journalists and irresponsible declaimers, but Ministers and responsible functionaries. Democracy in France is moreover at war with clericalism, and therefore, so far as the wishes of the local population as to its school might give an opening for clerical influences, they are over-ridden by democracy. There is no religious instruction allowed in the primary schools; the buildings may not be used for such instruction even out of school hours; the chaplaincies attached to the normal schools were suppressed by decree in 1883; a Bill is now being passed forbidding the communes, even if they desire it, to employ members of the teaching religious orders as schoolmasters or schoolmistresses in communal schools. So many feelings and interests are hurt by this mode of proceeding that free schooling in France and Paris is quite a different thing from free schooling in Switzerland, Berlin, or Munich. It provokes bitter complaint, and calls forth the establishment by private effort of rival schools. I have before me a speech made last year by M. Charles Robert, a very leading Protestant, whom I knew as chief assistant to M. Duruy at the Ministry of Public Instruction in 1865, and who is now at the head of a great insurance company, in which he exhorts the French Protestants to maintain their schools zealously, because "moral education and the formation of the judgment and the character are too often neglected by the new official pedagogy." The Catholics prove the sincerity of their dislike of the new schools in the strongest manner by having raised for their schools in Paris more than 15,000,000 of francs in the last six years, and by educating at the present moment in their schools, supported through voluntary effort solely, one-third of the school children of Paris.

With all this discontent it would be difficult, if not impossible, to make the local communities throughout France defray the heavy and increasing charge of the popular schools, and the burden is being assumed by the Central Government, the

State. The finance of French public instruction is, by the confession of the functionaries themselves who administer it, extremely complicated. But the facts of the case will be made
sufficiently intelligible by the following statement. The com-
5   munes had formerly to maintain their primary schools out of
their own resources, supplemented, if necessary, by an addition
of four centimes to the four direct taxes for the commune,
further supplemented, if still necessary, by an addition of four
centimes to the four direct taxes for the department, supple-
10 mented finally, if still necessary, by grant from the State. These
eight centimes for the commune and department have now
been made regular and fixed taxes paid to the State. Since 1882
the State has relieved of all further charge for their primary
schools those communes which could not meet such charge
15 out of their own resources. Only the five chief cities of France
have undertaken so to meet it: Paris, Lyons, Marseilles, Bor-
deaux, Lille. In all the other communes of France the cost of
primary instruction is met out of the public taxes by the State.

When therefore it is asked how the lower classes feel the
20 weight of the expenditure on education, the answer must be: so
far as they feel their share in the general taxation of the country
to be increased by it. And this probably they do not feel at all.

It would be entirely contrary to "the democratic idea" to
form separate schools for dirty and neglected children. As at
25 Berlin so at Paris, I was surprised to find how little difference
there was in the appearance of school children in different
quarters of the city. The wealthier classes use the public
primary schools, I think, very little at present, but I saw no
groups of children who could be called dirty and neglected.
30 The Paris municipality provides, in connexion with all its
infants' schools and primary schools, a system of penny dinners,
which makes undoubtedly the frequentation of these schools in
decent attire an easier matter for the children of the poor. To
send them decently dressed is more possible to them the less
35 they have to spend on their food. And the rule of the municipality is that to children really poor the penny dinner shall be
given free. All school children have also their school books and
materials provided for them by the municipality free of cost.

The increase both in the outlay on primary schools and in
the number of children attending them has been enormous
since I saw the schools in 1859. I see that in 1856, the latest
year for which I then could obtain full returns, of 42,297,332
francs raised for primary instruction there were furnished, in
round numbers, 9¾ millions by school fees, 22 millions by the
communes, 5¼ millions by the departments, 5¼ millions by
the State. At present nothing is received from school fees, and
M. Buisson informs me that the State bears nine-tenths of the
annual expense of primary instruction, and spends over 80
millions of francs on it. As to attendance, the municipality of
Paris had, in 1871, 94 infants' schools, with places for 16,111
children; in 1884 it had 128 infants' schools, with places for
20,215 children. Of boys' and girls' schools it had, in 1871,
243, with places for 73,579 scholars; in 1884 it had 361, with
places for 121,798 scholars.

2. *Quality of Education.*—I was further directed to ascertain,
so far as I could, the quality of the education furnished in the
elementary schools of the countries I visited, particularly in
the case of children between the ages of 10 and 14. It was suggested that I should ask the teachers to set papers in dictation
and arithmetic, on the model of those which are set in our
schools under the Code, and should bring the papers away
with me so that they might be compared with the papers
worked in our schools. The curriculum or course of school
study followed in the foreign schools was also to be compared
with the curriculum set forth in our Code.

In order to procure specimens of examination papers worked
under the same conditions as ours, I took abroad with me a
number of the arithmetic cards in use in my own district, and
would have set them to children of the same age as the children
who have to work them here at home. But there was first of
all the difficulty that most sums on our cards deal with our
English money, weights, and measures, not familiar to foreign
children. And even when I found sums in vulgar and decimal
fractions, where this difficulty did not exist, the whole spirit
and course of teaching in a foreign school was, I found, opposed to setting in school hours a number of sums and leaving

the children to do them by themselves. Our notion is to give children the rule for doing a sum and then test them by seeing if by that rule they can do so many sums right. The notion of a German teacher is that the school hour for arithmetic is to
5   be employed in ascertaining that the children understand the rule and the processes to which it is applied. For each branch of their instruction there is in the plan of instruction a *Lehrziel*, an aim and object prescribed for the teacher to have in view; in teaching arithmetic, says the Saxon programme, "the instruction
10 is to render the pupils capable of solving, independently and with certainty, the calculations which are likely to come before them in their ordinary life." It is thought that this aim is best attained by oral teaching and questioning. When, therefore, in order to test a class I put a sum in vulgar fractions upon the
15 black-board, the teacher, as a matter of course, asked me to call up children to the black-board and let them work it before me, giving their reasons for every stage in the process. The same with dictation: if I gave a passage for dictation, the teacher's notion was that in school time children were to be
20 tested in writing from dictation by being brought up one after the other to the black-board, writing what was dictated, and being questioned on punctuation and other matters as they wrote. The children acquitted themselves very well, both in their sums and in their writing from dictation, but I secured in
25 this way no bundle of exercises to carry off with me, and I found that without uncivil persistency I could not make the teachers depart from the methods natural to them. Here and there I laid hold of an exercise done in my presence, by which I was struck, and I have received, through the kindness of Mr.
30 Hirzel, the director of elementary education at Zurich, to whom I explained the comparison which I wished to institute, a number of written exercises worked in the Zurich schools in the examination at the end of the school year held since I left Zurich. The best test, however, of school work is afforded, in
35 my opinion, by what one oneself sees and hears the scholars do; for that reason I looked upon it as the essential part of my business to be as much as possible in the classes while they were at work, and I spent there every hour I could. The im-

pression which I thus obtained of the quality of the school
work as compared with ours I will describe presently. But first
I had better make clear what the school course in a foreign
school really is, that this too may be compared with what we
have in our schools at home.   5

I will take the school course in good schools, and the good
schools of one place, the free town of Hamburg. I will premise
that school hours and school courses are by no means the same
in all the schools which I visited abroad. But I shall have an
opportunity later of speaking of country schools with short   10
hours and reduced school course; the course of a good and
fully equipped school in German countries, at any rate, will
be more intelligible if, premising that there are variations, we
take one school course as a type, and follow it steadily, than
if we take a number of school courses together, and tire our   15
attention by passing from one of them to the other and
enumerating their variations.

The school course in the popular schools of the town of
Hamburg, then, is a seven years' course, corresponding to the
seven years which, by the Hamburg school law of 1870, the   20
child has to pass at school. He cannot enter before he is six;
he is entered on the first school day in April after he has completed his sixth year. On an average let us suppose that a child
enters at the age of 6½; then, if he goes through a class, which
is the rule, in each year, he will be in the seventh class (the   25
lowest) from the age of 6½ to 7½; from 7½ to 8½ he will
be in the sixth class; from 8½ to 9½ in the fifth class; from 9½
to 10½ in the fourth class; from 10½ to 11½ in the third class;
from 11½ to 12½ in the second class; from 12½ to 13½ in the
first or head class. His obligation to attend school expires on   30
the last day of March, at the end of the seventh year of his
schooling. A select class is formed in certain picked schools
in which the more capable and diligent scholars of all the
popular schools of Hamburg can continue their schooling, if
they please, after their seven years' time is ended.   35

The school course is issued on the authority of the
Oberschulbehörde, the "supreme school authority" of Hamburg. This authority has for its president a *Schulrath*, or

"Councillor for Education," and for its members representatives of the Senate of Hamburg, the clergy, the teachers, and the body of the citizens. It has the direction of all the schools of Hamburg, and forms itself into sections for the different

5   classes of schools. The school course which I am about to describe is drawn up and issued by the *Section für das Volksschulwesen*, the "Section for Popular Schools."

The fixed matters of the school course are Religion, German Language, English Language, Object Lessons, History, Geog-

10 raphy, Natural History, Arithmetic and Algebra, Geometry, Writing, Drawing, Singing, and Gymnastics. This school course has a special interest for English people, in that it includes the English language as one of the fixed matters of instruction. In general, foreign languages are optional matters,

15 and French has the preference. In Hamburg English must be taught in the popular schools from the third class upwards, and French comes in as an optional matter (the only one), and to take it the consent of the *Oberschulbehörde* is required.

The two lower classes have each of them 26 hours of school-

20 ing a week, the class next above them has 28, the four higher classes have 32 each. Some of the popular schools in Hamburg, like those in Berlin, meet once a day only. In summer the schools meet at 8 in the morning, and the different classes go on till 12, 1, or 2 on different days in the week, so that each

25 class shall make its proper number of weekly hours. In winter they meet at 9 and go on an hour later. When I was there the higher classes were going on till 3 on Wednesdays and Saturdays. No week-day is a holiday like the Saturday with us and the Thursday with the French. Other schools have two daily

30 meetings, from 8 to 11 or 12, and from 2 to 4, the proper number of hours for each class being again always made. Local convenience determines whether the school shall have two daily meetings or one. The pressure which the long attendance from 8 to 2 or from 9 to 3 would seem likely to exercise is

35 remedied by an arrangement which I found general in German countries, and which works very well. At the end of each hour the class disperses to the corridors and playground, and the teachers to the teachers' meeting room. In 10 minutes a bell

rings and the classes and teachers re-assemble refreshed. How much the work of a long morning is lightened by this simple plan may be observed by any one of school experience who will pass a morning in a German or Swiss school.

I will not go through the matters taught and the hours allotted to them in all the classes of a Hamburg popular school, but I will give them for the seventh or lowest class, where we may take the average age of the children as six years and a half; for the fourth class, a class in the middle of the school, where the average age will be nine years and a half; and for the first or highest class, where the children will be aged from thirteen to fourteen. The seventh class has, it will be remembered, 26 school-hours a week; the fourth and first have 32 hours each.

Each class has its teacher, the number of scholars to each teacher is 50, and in large schools such as those which I saw there are several parallel classes.

The seventh class has two hours a week for religion, nine for German, four for object lessons, five for arithmetic, two for drawing, two for singing, and two for gymnastics. Writing does not begin till the child reaches the sixth class; in his first year he learns drawing only.

The religious confession of the great majority at Hamburg is Lutheran, and the religious instruction in schools there, except in a very few special cases, is according to the Lutheran form. The general *Lehrziel*, or aim prescribed for this instruction by the programme is, "to get the saving facts and saving doctrines of Christianity apprehended and appropriated by the school-child." Nothing can be better. The instruments to be used are Scripture, the Lutheran catechism, and the church hymns. Bible stories and the learning of Bible sentences and of verses of hymns by heart are the religious instruction of the seventh class.

As to the nine hours for German, it is to be observed that the German child has to learn to read three sets of letters, the Latin letters, the Gothic letters, and finally the letters of that bane of Germany, a legacy from the monks, the *Cursiv-schrift* used in handwriting. It is often urged by Germans that our

spelling increases a child's labour in learning to read English;
let it be considered how the German child's reading labours
are increased by his three alphabets.

The *Anschauungsunterricht*, for which I have given the
5 unsatisfactory equivalent of object lessons, demands a word of
notice. Our object lessons give us little idea of it. The funda-
mental maxim with German teachers is *Von der Anschauung
nach dem Begriff!* from the intuition to the notion, from concretes to abstracts, and not, as was formerly the common rule
10 in teaching, from abstracts to concretes. The lessons specially
designed to give effect to this maxim deserve great attention
from us; they show what good methods may do to found
habits of clear apprehension and clear expression.

Class 4 (children from 9 to 10) have three hours a week for
15 religion, eight for German, two for history, two for geography,
two for natural history, five for arithmetic, one for geometry,
three for writing, two for drawing, two for singing, and two
for gymnastics; in all, 32 hours a week.

The instruction in religion takes the children through Bible
20 history down to the end of the Acts of the Apostles, and they
are taught the exposition given by the Lutheran catechism to
the Decalogue and the Lord's Prayer. But the most valuable
portion of the religious instruction is still, in my opinion, the
Bible passages and church hymns learnt by heart. In German
25 grammar they learn the declension of nouns, the comparison
of adjectives, and the conjugation of verbs. In history, where
the prescribed aim is to make the scholar acquainted with the
prominent persons and events in the development of mankind
in general and of the German nation in particular, biographical
30 notices are the matter for this class. In arithmetic they have
vulgar and decimal fractions; in geometry they have the elements of geometrical forms, the teaching basing itself upon
intuition, or what they can see with their eyes. In singing they
begin to learn their notes.

35 Class 1 (boys from 13 to 14) have two hours a week for
religion, five for German, four for English (classes two and
three have each five hours for English), two for history, two
for geography, one for natural history, four for natural

philosophy, four for arithmetic and algebra, two for geometry, one for writing, two for drawing, one for singing, and two for gymnastics; 32 hours in all, like class 4.

In religion, parables and hymns are still learnt and said by heart; a further useful part of the instruction here is the acquaintance given with the literary history and translation of the Bible. In German the class has classical works of some considerable length from German literature (in a school which I visited in Hamburg I found class one reading Schiller's *Wilhelm Tell*), composition, and grammar briefly presented in a general view. In English (which I heard) they had English grammar, letter writing, reading, and translation from English into German. In history they had modern history with special reference to Germany, and a general view of history. In geography they had the geography of Germany in detail, the geography of the principal non-German nations, and the main points in mathematical geography. In natural philosophy they had the mechanical phenomena of solid, fluid, and aëriform bodies, the theory of light, and the principal elements and combinations in chemistry. In arithmetic and algebra they had difficult problems in practical arithmetic, and easy quadratic equations. In geometry they had measurement of solids, measurement of flat surfaces, and problems. In writing they had mercantile writing and formulas. They drew from models; in music they learnt times and expression marks, and also part-singing.

I should add that the books in use were chosen by the teachers but approved by the *Oberschulbehörde*. Everywhere in Germany I thought the school books good; in general each German country has its own.

The school buildings at Hamburg, as in general everywhere now in towns in Germany, Switzerland, and France, were spacious and handsome. In staircases, landings, and corridors, they had the advantage of ours; in England it seems impossible to an architect not to pinch his staircases and his passages. I suppose it would be admitted that in sanitary arrangements England is still ahead of the Continent: but the improvement in respect of these since my last visit struck me very much in

the foreign schools, particularly in France. Certainly ventilation is more cared for with us, and it is more the habit to open windows; at Hamburg, however, I observed more attention than anywhere else to the state of the air in the schoolroom.
5   The Hamburg schoolrooms too were always so arranged that the light came from the left to the children as they sat at work. The number of children in a class I found to be generally within two or three of 50, the number fixed by the law. The discipline and quietude in these large classes, and even in classes
10   a good deal larger, is uniformly good, so far as I saw, in Germany and in German Switzerland; in France it is not quite so good, but wonderfully improved since my former visit, and better, I think, than with us. That is to say, it is more independent of the personal character and force of will of the
15   teacher; the children are more interested in their work itself.

As to length of school time, the weekly number of hours for a Hamburg child between the ages of 10 and 14 is, as I have said, 32; with us, under the Code, for a child of that age, it is 20. That is to say, for the instruction assigned and planned
20   by the Code, and for which alone we take any guarantee, the Code fixes a legal and necessary school time of 20 hours a week; the Hamburg Code fixes for the like instruction a legal and necessary school time of 32 hours. I will notice hereafter cases in which, in Germany, this rate of school time is much
25   reduced, but in general in the towns and in large schools a rate of from 25 to 32 hours prevails.

The Hamburg child remains at school until he is 14. Under special circumstances a boy of 13 who has gone through the school course may be released, but even this is not common in
30   Germany. To release a child, as we do, from school at 10 or 11, because he can pass the Fifth Standard, would be thought in Germany absurd and most injurious. It cannot be seriously supposed that to be able to pass a certain examination in reading, writing, and arithmetic is the same thing to a child as a
35   year or two of schooling, or an adequate substitute for it. To put the thing on no higher ground, the matters acquired for examination may so rapidly be forgotten and lost! Whereas, if the child remains at school he is still securing his hold on what he has already learnt, and also learning more.

The boys in the upper classes of a Hamburg school have, as
the obligatory matters of their 32 hours of weekly instruction,
religion, German, English, history, geography, natural history,
natural philosophy, arithmetic and algebra, geometry, writing,
drawing, singing, and gymnastics, 13 matters in all. In one of
our schools under the Code the boys in the upper classes have
as obligatory matters three—English, writing, and arithmetic.
Of the optional matters they generally take, in fact, four, singing and geography (for what is called English in our programme is really to be reckoned, like German in German
schools, as one matter with reading), and as *specific subjects*,
say algebra and physiology, or French and physiology. This
makes in all, for their school week of 20 hours, seven matters
of instruction.

Along with the fuller programme and longer course of German schools, I found, also, a higher state of instruction than in
ours. I speak of what I saw and heard and of the impression
which it made upon me after seeing English schools for more
than 30 years. The methods of teaching in foreign schools are
more gradual, more natural, more rational than in ours; and
in speaking here of foreign schools I include Swiss and French
schools as well as German. I often asked myself why, with
such large classes, the order was in general so thoroughly
good, and why with such long hours the children had in
general so little look of exhaustion or fatigue; and the answer I could not help making to myself was, that the cause
lay in the children being taught less mechanically and more
naturally than with us, and being more interested. In the
teaching of arithmetic, geometry, and natural science I was
particularly struck with the patience, the clinging to oral
question and answer, the avoidance of over-hurry, the being
content to advance slowly, the securing of the ground. This
struck me the more because in these matters, in which I
am not naturally quick, I always had, as a learner, the sense
of being over-hurried myself by my teachers, and in the foreign schools I constantly felt that if I had been taught these
matters in the way in which I heard them taught there I could
have made progress. I am told that young men studying for
Woolwich, who go to Germany to learn the German language,

are at first struck in the schools there with the mathematics being much less advanced than at home; but presently they find
that the slower rate of advance is more than compensated by
the thoroughness of the teaching and the hold gained upon the
5   matter of study. I speak with hesitation, however, on these
matters, and often I wished for some of my more competent
colleagues to be with me that I might have pointed out to them
what struck me, and have asked them if they could help own-
ing that it was so. At any rate the impression strongly made
10   upon me was such as I have described.

The same thing in teaching the elements of writing and reading, and in training children to answer questions put to them;
the same patience, the same care to make the child sure of his
ground. A child asked a question is apt to answer by a single
15   word, or a word or two, and the questioner is apt to fill out
the answer in his own mind and to accept it. But in Germany
it is a regular exercise for children to be made to give their
answers complete, and the discipline in accuracy and collected-
ness which is thus obtained is very valuable.

20   But the higher one rises in a German school the more is the
superiority of the instruction over ours visible. Again and again
I find written in my notes, *The children human*. They had been
brought under teaching of a quality to touch and interest them,
and were being formed by it. The fault of the teaching in our
25   popular schools at home is, as I have often said, that it is so
little formative; it gives the children the power to read the
newspapers, to write a letter, to cast accounts, and gives them
a certain number of pieces of knowledge, but it does little to
touch their nature for good and to mould them. You hear often
30   people of the richer class in England wishing that they and
their children were as well educated as the children of an elementary school; they mean that they wish they wrote as good
a hand, worked sums as rapidly and correctly, and had as many
facts of geography at command; but they suppose themselves
35   retaining all the while the fuller cultivation of taste and feeling
which is their advantage and their children's advantage over
the pupils of the elementary school at present, and they forget
that it is within the power of the popular school, and should

be its aim, to do much for this cultivation, although our schools accomplish for it so very little. The excellent maxim of that true friend of education, the German schoolmaster, John Comenius, "The aim is to train generally all who are born men to all which is human," does in some considerable degree govern the proceedings of popular schools in German countries, and now in France also, but in England hardly at all.

No one will deny that religion can touch the sources of thought, feeling, and life, and I had not been prepared for the seriousness with which the religious instruction is given in Germany, even in Protestant Germany, and for the effect which it produces. Little or nothing was said in Lutheran schools, about the church and its authority, about the clergy and their attributes, but I was surprised to find with what energy and seriousness points raised by the catechism—for example, the question in what sense it can be said that God tempts men—were handled, and with what intelligence and interest the children followed what was said and answered the questions put to them. The chief effect of the religious teaching, however, certainly lies in the Bible passages, and still more in the evangelical hymns, which are so abundantly learnt by heart and repeated by the children. No one could watch the faces of the children, of the girls particularly, without feeling that something in their nature responded to what they were repeating, and was moved by it. It is said that two-thirds of the working classes in the best educated countries of Protestant Germany are detached from the received religion, and the inference is drawn that the religious teaching in the schools must be a vain formality. But may it not happen that chords are awakened by the Bible and hymns in German schools which remain a possession even though the course of later life may carry the German adult far away from Lutheran dogma?

Passing from the question of religious instruction, I will say that in the specially humanizing and formative parts of the schoolwork I have found in foreign schools a performance which surprised me, which would be pronounced good anywhere, and which I could not find in corresponding schools at home. I am thinking of literature and poetry and the lives

of the poets, of recitation and reading, of history, of foreign
languages. Sometimes in our schools one comes across a child
with a gift, and a gift is always something unique and admirable. But in general in our elementary schools when one
5 says that the reading is good, or the French, or the history,
or the acquaintance with poetry, one makes the mental reservation, "good, considering the class from which children and
teachers are drawn." But in the foreign schools lately visited
by me I have found in all these matters a performance which
10 would be pronounced good anywhere, and a performance not
of individuals, but of classes. At Trachenberge, near Dresden,
I went with Mr. Grüllich, the inspector, into a schoolroom
where the head class were reading a ballad of Goethe, *Der
Sänger;* Mr. Grüllich took the book, asked the children ques-
15 tions about the life of Goethe, made them read the poem,
asked them to compare it with a ballad of Schiller in the same
volume, *Der Graf von Habsburg,* drew from them the differences between the two ballads, what their charm was, where
lay the interest of the Middle Age for us, and of chivalry,
20 and so on. The performance was not a solo by a clever inspector, the part in it taken by the children was active and
intelligent, such as would be called good if coming from children in an altogether higher class of school, and such as proved
under what capable teaching they must have been. In Ham-
25 burg, again, in English, and at Zurich, in French, I heard children read and translate a foreign language with a power and
a pronunciation such as I have never found in an elementary
school at home, and which I should call good if I found it in
some high-class school for young ladies. At Zurich, I remem-
30 ber, we passed from reading and translating to grammar, and
the children were questioned about the place of pronominal
objects in a French sentence. Imagine a child in one of our
popular schools knowing, or being asked, why we say *on me
le rend* but *on le lui rend,* and what is the rule on the subject!
35   The instruction is better in the foreign popular schools than
in ours, because the teachers are better trained, and of the
training of teachers I shall have to speak presently. This is
the main reason of the superiority, that the teachers are better
trained. But that they are better trained comes from a cause

which acts for good upon the whole of education abroad, that
the instruction as a whole is better organized than with us.
Indeed, with us it is not and cannot at present be organized
as a whole at all, for the public administration, which deals
with the popular schools, stops at those schools, and takes into   5
its view no others. But there is an article in the Constitution of
Canton Zurich which well expresses the idea which prevails
everywhere abroad of the organization of instruction from top
to bottom as one whole: *Die höhern Lehranstalten sollen mit
der Volksschule in organische Verbindung gebracht werden;*   10
the higher establishments for teaching shall be brought into
organic connexion with the popular school. And men like Wilhelm von Humboldt in Germany and Guizot or Cousin in
France have been at the head of the public administration of
schools in those countries, and have organized popular instruc-   15
tion as a part of one great system, a part in correspondence
of some kind with the higher parts, and to be organized with
the same seriousness, the same thorough knowledge and large
views of education, the same single eye to its requirements, as
the higher parts.   20

We may imagine the like in England if we suppose a man
like Sir James Mackintosh at the head of the Education Department having to administer the public school system for
intermediate and higher education as well as the popular
schools, in continual intercourse with the representatives of   25
that system as well as with representatives of the popular
schools, and treating questions respecting popular instruction
with a mind apt for all educational questions and conversant
with them, aided, moreover, by the intercourse just spoken of.
Evidently questions respecting codes and programmes would   30
then present themselves under conditions very different from
the present conditions. The popular school in our country is
at present considered by the Minister in charge of it not at
all as one stage to be co-ordered with the other stages in a
great system of public schools, and to have its course surveyed   35
and fixed from the point of view of a knower and lover of
education. Not at all; the popular school is necessarily, for
him, not so much an educational problem as a social and political one; as a school dealing with a few elementary matters,

simple enough; and the great thing is to make the House of Commons and the public mind satisfied that value is received for the public money spent on teaching these matters. Hence the Code which governs the instruction in our popular schools.

5 And I have always felt that objections made in the pure interest of good instruction and education to the Code had this disadvantage, that they came before a man, often very able, but who, from his circumstances, would not and could not consider them from the point of view of a disinterested knower

10 and friend of education at all, but from a point of view quite different.

In this report I have not space for showing the many ways in which abroad the higher education of the country is in continual correspondence with the popular education, helping

15 and strengthening the work of the training colleges, advising the Minister by commissions of experts on educational questions requiring study, and so forth. But it will be at once evident how directly schools like the *Höhere Volksschulen* of Saxony, the *Secundär-schulen* of Zurich, the *École Turgot* at

20 Paris, under one public administration with the ordinary popular schools, and receiving boys from them to be prepared for commercial and industrial pursuits, and to continue up to the age of sixteen or seventeen the education commenced in the popular school, it will be at once evident, I say, how this con-

25 tinuation and correspondence must naturally affect the programme of the popular school. That programme cannot be treated as something isolated and quite simple, having merely to satisfy, not those who look well into the matter, but the so-called practical man and the public mind.

30 3. *Status, Training, and Pensioning of Teachers.*—Under this head I was directed to inquire from what class of society the teachers in the countries which I visited come; how, where, and for how long they are trained; whether the teachers in all public schools are certificated; their annual emoluments; and

35 whether they are entitled to retiring pensions, and upon what conditions.

As to the first point, I believe that teachers in Germany, Switzerland, and France come from the same class of society

as teachers in England. A boy in an elementary school has aptitude for teaching, or, at any rate, he and his friends wish him to be a teacher; he trains himself for the office, and becomes a teacher accordingly.

As to the training of teachers, I will follow the same course which I have followed as to the hours and programme of study in schools. Instead of giving details for each country, when I should have to be either frequently repeating the same thing or else recording variations of little or no importance, I will take the training system of a single country of Germany and the training system of France. The training school in German Switzerland does not materially differ from that of Germany. As in the case of Hamburg for popular schools and their course, I will take for the training schools a good representative of Germany; I will take a country which must always have a special interest for Anglo-Saxon people; I will take Saxony.

The training school course there lasts six years. But a youth enters at the age of about fourteen, with the attainments required for passing an examination for the *Entlassungs-zeugnis,* or certificate of discharge, from a *Mittlere Volksschule,* or popular school of the second grade, a school which in Saxony must be organized in at least four classes, with a two years' course for each. In the training school, instruction and lodging are free; a small sum is paid for board, but a certain number of free boarders, "gifted poor children," are admitted. In the Friedrichstadt training school at Dresden, which I visited, there were more day students than boarders, only 88 out of 216 being boarders. But this is not the usual proportion; students, however, are permitted to live at home or with families chosen by their parents, and there being much pressure for admission to the Friedrichstadt school, many, for whom there is not room as boarders, attend as day students rather than not attend at all. The training school at Dresden for schoolmistresses takes no boarders; all the students live at home or in private families.

To the training school is attached a practising school, organized as a *Mittlere Schule,* a middle school with four classes and 155 scholars. In this school the students see and learn the

practice of teaching. Their own instruction they receive in small classes which may not have more than twenty-five scholars. Their hours in class may not exceed thirty-six a week, not counting the time given to music. The matters of instruction
5 are religion (the Friedrichstadt school is Protestant), German language and literature, Latin, geography, history, natural science both descriptive and theoretical, arithmetic, geometry, pedagogy including psychology and logic, music, writing, drawing, and gymnastics. All of these matters are obligatory,
10 but after the first year students of proved incapacity for music are no longer taught it.

Article 64 of the law for training schools, a law dating from the year 1876, provides that one-third of the teaching staff of the training school may be distinguished elementary teachers
15 without university training, but this proportion is never to be exceeded. Each teacher, exclusive of the director, is bound to give twenty-six hours of teaching in the week. There are half-yearly examinations; the six years' term may be lengthened by one year for a student who is deemed not ripe for the leaving
20 examination, which comes at the conclusion of the course. On the other hand, students can be admitted up to the age of eighteen, or even later by permission of the Minister, if they can pass in the first case an examination showing them qualified to take the work of the third year, in the second case that of the
25 fourth. But in general the full course is preferred, as the youth who means to enter the training school (always in Germany called *Seminar*) must be at school somewhere, and he had better be at school in the *Seminar* itself. The younger students have opportunities given to them from time to time of witness-
30 ing work and model lessons in the practising school; in the fifth and sixth year every student has to pass in the practising school four hours a week.

At the end of the course, when the student is about twenty years old, he undergoes the *Schulamtskandidaten-Prüfung* or
35 examination for office. The examination is both oral and in writing, and turns upon the work of the student's course in the training school. The examining commission is composed of

the Minister's commissary, a church commissary, and the whole staff of the training college. The staff conduct the examination, the Minister's commissary presides and superintends.

If the student passes he receives his *Reifezeugnis*, or certificate of ripeness, and is now qualified to serve as assistant in 5 a public popular school, or as a private teacher where his work has not to go beyond the limits of popular school instruction. After two years of service as assistant, at the age of about 22, the young teacher returns to the training school and presents himself for the *Wahlfähigkeits-Prüfung* or examination for de- 10 finitive posting. For this examination the commission is composed of the Minister's commissary, a church commissary, the director of the *Seminar*, and either two of its upper teachers, or else other approved schoolmen named by the Minister. This examination again is both written and oral. I attended the oral 15 part on two days at the Friedrichstadt training school, and heard and saw candidates examined in religion, music, German language and literature, the history of education, pedagogy, psychology, logic, and school law. The Minister's commissary was the inspector for Dresden, Mr. Eichenberg; he took an 20 active part in the examination. The church commissary listened in silence, but his signature is required for the certificate. Of a batch of 10 students whom I heard examined together in the history of education I observed that seven wore spectacles. But in general the students gave me the impression of being 25 better and more fully educated than ours, under a better planned system, and by better trained instructors. The school synod at Hamburg unites all the teachers of the city, and something of this union of the lower members of the teaching profession with the higher exists throughout Germany and is of 30 great value. I found that Mr. Grüllich, the inspector for the country district round Dresden, a very accomplished and able man, held periodical conferences with the teachers of his district. The conferences were not fewer than six in the year, lasted a whole afternoon, and turned on matters settled by pro- 35 gramme beforehand, matters of interest to those engaged in education. The *Lehrziel*, or aim to guide the teaching of the students' several subjects, which is given in the Saxon *Semi-narordnung*, or regulation for ordering of training schools, is in itself an instructor's manual full of counsel and suggestiveness.

5 The training school course for Saxon schoolmistresses resembles in general that for schoolmasters, but it lasts for five years only instead of six. The obligatory matters are the same as for students of the other sex, except that French is substituted for Latin, and needlework is added. English and instrumental music are optional subjects. The rules for examination and certificate
10 granting are similar.

Training schools for schoolmistresses are, however, much less numerous in Germany than those for schoolmasters, because in German countries women are much less used in teaching than men. In Prussia, for instance, there are 115 training schools for
15 schoolmasters, but only 10 for schoolmistresses. In Saxony there are 16 for schoolmasters, one of the 16 being for Catholics; there are only two for schoolmistresses. It is held to be beyond question that certain matters of instruction in the upper classes of the popular school women cannot teach satisfactorily. In
20 general a woman may in boys' or mixed schools teach only the lower classes. The Hamburg school law directs that in the popular schools for girls in that city the head teacher and one other teacher at least shall always be men. At Zurich I found a very capable and pleasing schoolmistress, who had been employed
25 at Versailles by the French Education Department (what a lesson for our Department!) during the year of the last Paris Exhibition, to conduct a primary school and show French teachers practically what the methods of a good Swiss school were. At Zurich she was teaching a lower class, and complained
30 much that she could not rise higher. The French Education Department would gladly have retained her in France, and if it had not been for home duties she would gladly, she said, have stayed; the career for a schoolmistress was so much better there.

35 In Saxony we have the German training school at its best, but the general system of training, studies, examinations, and certificates is the same in all German countries. In Prussia and Bavaria *Präparanden-schulen* or special schools for those pre-

paring to be teachers take the place of the earlier classes of
the Saxon *Seminar*, and are distinct from the training school
itself. In Canton Zurich the age for admission to the *Seminar*
is 15, and the candidate must pass a satisfactory examination in
the third year matters of the *Secundär-schule*. The course in   5
the *Seminar* itself lasts four years. French and not Latin is the
obligatory second language. But I heard at Zurich the students
of the training school for schoolmistresses take English, as they
take other lessons also, with the pupils of the higher school for
girls; the performance was very good, and the beautiful reading   10
to them by their German teacher which followed, of *Wallen-
stein's Tod*, was a thing to remember. At Munich I heard with
pleasure, in the training school for schoolmistresses there, the
lessons in botany and French. This school is maintained by the
province, and the State maintains another at Aschaffenburg;   15
in Zurich the *Seminar* for schoolmistresses was maintained by
the municipality. At Munich it was a five years' course, the
classes for the first three years being called *Secundär-schule*.
In the training school for masters the same. But the practising
school was as distinct from the *Secundär-schule* as from the   20
lower classes of the *Seminar* at Dresden. I mention these things
to show that there are varieties of detail, but the general system is the same.

The French training schools require separate notice. Not that
the forms of the system established by the Training School   25
Law of 1879, when M. Jules Ferry was Minister of Instruction, and organized by the decree of 1881, differ very greatly
from those in Germany. Boarding is more generally the rule,
and board, lodging, and instruction are all of them gratuitious;
but the age of admission is 15, though candidates are received   30
up to 18. The candidate must have the *certificat d'études pri-
maires*, or certificate that he has passed the leaving examination
of the primary school, and he must engage himself to serve for
10 years as a functionary of public instruction. His time passed
in the training school, however, after the age of 18 has been   35
reached by him, counts towards the fulfilment of this engagement. The training school course lasts three years; at the end
of the first year the student has to pass his examination for the

"elementary brevet of capacity," or certificate as we call it; at the end of the third year that for the "superior brevet." The examination turns upon the obligatory matters of the training school course, which are moral and civic instruction, reading,
5   writing, the French language and elements of French literature, history and geography, those of France in particular, and so on; a programme less strong than that of a German training school, but taking the same line of subjects, except as to religion. One or more modern languages may be taken, but this is optional.
10 To each training school a practising school is attached as in Germany.

Every French department has now a training school for masters in compliance with the law of 1879, but only 15 departments have as yet established one for schoolmistresses,
15 though other departments are building. The delay has arisen from the preference shown by many communes for the employment of sisters of a teaching religious order; the sisters are of use in the communes for many purposes, and the communes have, therefore, persisted in using them much more than
20 in using the Congreganist Brothers. The employment of sisters has, of course, caused fewer lay schoolmistresses to be employed, and fewer training schools for them, therefore, have been necessary. But while I was in Paris a law was being passed which among other provisions contains one forbidding the
25 communes to employ any teachers belonging to a religious order; and many more posts will, in consequence, be opened to lay schoolmistresses.

Much may be said against the economy and against the judiciousness of this wholesale exclusion of the religious orders
30 from the public schools. There is no doubt that the Government is actuated by political motives in excluding them; it believes the religious to be hostile to the Republic and its institutions, and is determined to have at any rate made the lay character of the schools an accomplished fact before the
35 counter-revolution arrives, if it is to arrive. It is doubtful, I say, whether the haste, the harsh measures, the interference with old habits, the heavy expenditure, to which the Republican Government commits itself with this aim, are judicious;

whether the irritation caused does not do more in favour of reaction than the bulwarks set up do against it. The strength of voluntary effort in the Catholic Church and its hold upon the parents turn out to be much greater than might have been expected; and if the Catholic Church were not misled by its own strength, and by its capacity for resistance, if it were more flexible and could better adapt itself to the age in which we live, and the change which is irresistible, it would, in my opinion, have a future more promising than that of the Governments which attack it.

At the same time the school expenditure of the Republican Government is not all due, as its enemies would have us believe, to a hatred of religion; it is due also to a belief in the value of sound and full popular instruction, which is one of the best articles of the democratic creed, and to a conviction that this sound and full instruction is not and cannot be given by the religious. If many of the establishments of the religious are, as in fact I thought them, quite as well taught as those of the State, this is in part due, no doubt, to the wholesome necessity which competition with the State imposes on the religious to make also their secular instruction as good as that of the State. The State in France shows at present a genuine and most effective zeal for instruction, whatever other motives and feelings may be mixed with the zeal; and even the much abused municipality of Paris deserves a like praise, in this respect, with the State.

In the training schools the good effects of the present zeal and liberal expenditure for improved popular instruction are especially visible. I saw no school institution on the Continent better than the training school for masters at Auteuil. I doubt whether I saw any so good, certainly I saw none so interesting, as the training school at Fontenay aux Roses for directresses and teachers of training schools for schoolmistresses. The students in both seemed to me to be excellent material; a Frenchman who takes his vocation seriously and is properly prepared makes a good teacher, a Frenchwoman makes one of the best in the world. Then too the merit which I have noticed as distinguishing the foreign administration of popular schools

from our own, that popular instruction is placed in vital correspondence and contact with higher instruction, is eminently characteristic of French administration. Besides the regular professors and masters of the training school, *"auxiliary pro-*
5 *fessors and special masters,"* says the decree of 1881, "named or delegated by the Minister, give instruction in the training schools." The students thus come in contact with men of real distinction and with teaching of the highest order.

I will particularly mention the classes in modern languages,
10 English and German, at Auteuil. These languages are *facultative* or, as we say, optional matters, and the study of modern languages is, as is well known, a point in which the French are weak. But both the teaching of the professors and the performance of the students in these matters at Auteuil was much
15 superior to what we should find in training schools at home.

Fontenay aux Roses was yet more interesting than Auteuil. It has been established but a year or two; 70 young women are being trained there for employment in normal schools; the course is of three years' length for examination for the post
20 of directress in such schools, two years' for that of teacher. The place is delightful, the students are good material, and the superintendent, a widow lady, Madame Feldberg, excellently chosen. But the soul of the place is the director, M. Pécaut, a man now between 60 and 70, whom I had already had the
25 pleasure of meeting when I was in France twenty years ago. When I hear it said that all which the French Republican Government is doing for popular education is being done out of hatred to religion, I think of Fontenay aux Roses and of M. Pécaut, of the work being done at Fontenay, and of the
30 cordial confidence and firm support given by the Minister of Public Instruction to M. Pécaut who does it, and I render justice to the Republican Government. Of course the question of religious and moral training is of great interest in connexion with the French public schools just now. All direct
35 religious instruction, Catholic or Protestant, is entirely banished from them, and the "moral and civic instruction," which is the substitute, seemed to me, so far as I could judge from the manual of it which I perused, and from the many lessons

in it which I heard, of little or no value. What I heard was in general decorous and dull; the most effective thing I heard owed its effectiveness, perhaps, chiefly to the shock of surprise which it occasioned. The thing was this. A child was asked the question, so common in the training of the young, to whom do you owe all that you are enjoying here, this fine school-room, these pictures, these books, this splendid city, all that gives security, comfort, and pleasure to your life; who gives it all to you? I listened languidly at first, but my interest awoke as it occurred to me: surely all this can be leading up to but one answer, the established answer, *God*, and that answer may not be given here. And it was not given; the answer at last to the question put to the child, Who is your benefactor? was this: *Et bien, c'est le pays;* "Your benefactor is your country." The force of civic instruction, whatever we may say as to moral, could hardly, perhaps, further go.

The young women at Fontenay were in general Catholics, going to church on Sundays. The director, M. Pécaut, was originally a Protestant pastor, afterwards an inspector-general of primary instruction. The lessons of pedagogy in his hands become (and this is the point to which I wish to call attention) a treatment of this subject really and truly moral and religious, and yet neither Catholic nor Protestant. He takes with his class some writer on education, Locke, Rousseau, Pestalozzi; the day I was at Fontenay it was Bishop Dupanloup, whose book, *L'École*, raises what are called burning questions in every page. They were treated, I say, in a manner deeply moral and perfectly religious, and yet neither Catholic nor Protestant; and not only did M. Pécaut so treat them himself, but he had trained his pupils, who were called upon one after another either to discuss their author extempore or to read short papers which they had prepared, so to treat them also. If M. Pécaut could be multiplied and placed in every normal school in France, the foundation of a moral instruction, not futile as at present, but seriously and religiously effective, though independent of the established confessions, would be made possible in the French schools. At present it is at Fonte-nay only that I found an instruction of the kind, but what is

accomplished at Fontenay is of the highest value. All the instruction which I heard given there was of sound and good
character, but this particular instruction was unique.

It remains to speak of teachers' emoluments and pensions.
5 Here, again, it is easy to quote from printed laws and orders;
but there is so much of local usage and regulation affecting
the matter that what one finds done in cases with which one
has personally become acquainted is more interesting and important, perhaps, than the bare provisions of the law. These
10 vary very much. In Hamburg, of which I have said so much,
and where the standard and expense of life most resembles,
perhaps, that of England, salaries are by law regulated as follows:—The head master of a popular school there has a house
rent free, or else £25 a year in lieu of a house, and a salary
15 of £100 a year rising after five years to £125, and after another
five years to £150. A teacher fully posted has a salary of £75,
rising after five years to £87 10s., and after five years more to
£100. An assistant master has a salary fixed by the Education
Department at a sum between £30 and £60 a year. A school-
20 mistress fully posted has from £40 to £50 a year; an assistant
schoolmistress from £20 to £30.

In Prussia it appears from Mr. Petersilie's volume of statistics, published in 1878, that the average salary of a schoolmaster was then £51 12s. a year for the whole country to-
25 gether, £68 5s. in towns, and £43 14s. in the country. Lodging
and fuel are provided besides. In Berlin the average salary was
£103 3s. At present in Berlin, as appears from a return issued
by the municipality, the average salary of a *Rector*, or head
master of a communal school, is £175; of an ordinary master,
30 £111 15s.; of a schoolmistress, £73 2s.; of an assistant master,
£60.

In Bavaria the salaries are lower. They are composed of a
communal minimum with augmentations. In communes with
more than 10,000 inhabitants the minimum of salary for a
35 schoolmaster is fixed by law at £42 17s. 2d., in communes
with from 2500 to 10,000 inhabitants at £38 11s. 6d., in communes with less population at £35. This salary is augmented by
the State to £38 11s. 6d. in these last-named communes, to

£42 17s. 2d. in communes with from 2500 to 10,000 inhabitants. The Bavarian schoolmaster has, moreover, an augmentation, after 10 years of service, of £4 10s. a year for each period of five years since he left the training school. The salaries of assistants are lower still.

In Canton Zurich the minimum for the master of a lower popular school (*Primärschule*) is £48 a year; for the master of a higher popular school, £72, with lodging and fuel. The canton joins with the commune in augmenting the lower of these salaries to £60 a year, and the higher to £80. The canton pays a further augmentation, after five years of public service, of £4 for each succeeding period of five years, so that a teacher who has served over 20 years has an augmentation grant of £20 a year. In Lucerne the primary schoolmaster has from £32 to £44 a year, with lodging and fuel, the primary schoolmistress from £24 to £36, according to length of service. The master of a *Secundär-schule* has from £48 to £64, the mistress from £40 to £52.

In the French primary schools there are four classes of salaries for men and three for women. Every teacher begins in the lowest class, and can only rise to the next after five years' service. A master's salary in the lowest class is £36, in the third class £40, in the second class £44, in the highest class £48. The salary of a schoolmistress in the lowest class is £28, in the second class £32, in the highest class £36. The rates for assistants are lower still, from £32 for a village assistant master, as the highest rate, to £24 for a village assistant mistress, as the lowest. Every teacher who obtains the complete brevet becomes entitled to a yearly augmentation of £4, and there are further augmentations, obtainable either as prizes or on the ground of local circumstances, which may increase the salary by from £2 10s. to £12 a year more. In the higher primary schools a director at his lowest stage has a minimum salary of £80, at his highest of £112; an assistant at his lowest stage has £48, at his highest £72.

These are minima; they are often exceeded, in the country through the addition of other employment, in towns through the liberality of the municipal authority. In Germany generally

the office of village schoolmaster is partly a church office; in
some cases the duties of sexton, choir master, and organist
have to be performed by him without addition to his salary,
in others he is paid extra for them; but in all cases he is paid
5   extra for clerk work, whether for church or commune, which
he is required to do. In a village school sixty miles from Berlin,
in the province of Brandenburg, I found that the teacher had
£50 a year, with a good house and fuel; but he received an
addition for clerk work which he did for the great landowner
10   of the place, in whose company I visited the school. At another
village school, in Silesia, I found the master in receipt of £75
a year, with house and fuel; he was over sixty years of age, was
Cantor as well as schoolmaster, and had an addition to his salary
both as *Cantor* and for length of service. His income was thus
15   composed: school fees (from a school of 148 children in a
village with 800 inhabitants), £37; gratuity added by the
Gemeinde, £8; augmentation from the State for length of service, £15; payment as *Cantor*, £15 more. In a town school six
or seven miles from Berlin I found that the salaries of the
20   teachers, male and female, began at £45 a year, and were to
rise in fifteen years, those of the masters to £105 a year, those
of the mistresses to £75. The married masters had an allowance
of £15 a year for lodging, bachelors and schoolmistresses half
that sum. If a schoolmistress in Germany marries she loses her
25   situation. In a small country school on the mountain behind
Zurich I found that the master had from the *Gemeinde* a
salary of £24, with a house and an allowance of £8 a year for
fuel and garden stuff; from the canton he had besides £32 a
year; he was paid for his services as organist, and made some
30   money by giving private lessons.

In Hamburg, Berlin, and Paris I found incomes of masters of
popular schools reaching £150 and exceeding it, but none, so
far as I could learn, reaching £200 a year. In Munich the
salaries of full teachers are said, in an official work, to range
35   from £87 a year to £123, with an augmentation, for head-
masters, of £45.

Everywhere, in the countries which I visited, the teachers
have retiring pensions, to establish which there is a deduction

made from their salary. In France the pension can be claimed at the age of fifty-five after twenty-five years of service, is calculated on an average of the six years when the salary was highest, can in no case exceed three-fourths of that average salary, or fall below £24 a year for a master and £20 a year for a mistress. Exceptional pensions are granted in cases of premature break-down of health; the widows of teachers who have served for twenty-five years, whether they were fifty-five years old at death or not, receive a pension of £8 a year. In Canton Zurich teachers after thirty years of service receive a pension of not less than one-half or more than two-thirds of their salary at the time of retiring. In Prussia a teacher can claim a pension after ten years' service, if a break-down of health forces him to retire; his pension is then fifteen-sixtieths of his salary. For each year of service after the tenth another sixtieth is added until forty-five sixtieths are reached, after which the pension increases no further. It is not necessary to give the details for every country visited; the above will suffice.

4. *Attendance.*—I was finally directed to ascertain in the countries visited by me "whether any law exists to enforce attendance; the nature of this law; whether it requires attendance every time the school is open; how many times the school must be open, and especially whether it is necessary for a child to pass a particular standard of examination before being allowed to go to work, and whether the right to labour is simply a question of age; also what penalties are prescribed for breaking the law, and if it is rigorously enforced; and lastly, what excuses for non-attendance may be pleaded."

Some of these questions have been already answered in what has preceded; but to make it clear of what nature is the law in foreign countries as to school attendance, and how what is there done in this matter differs from what is done amongst ourselves, it may be convenient to quote the exact words of the Saxon law on the subject, and to mention what has been ruled as to questions arising under them.

Section IV., paragraph 1, of the Saxon School Law of 1873 is as follows:—

"Every child has to attend, for eight years uninterruptedly, the common popular school in the school district where it resides; as a rule, from the completion of the sixth year of its age to the completion of its fourteenth."

5   Then come provisions with respect to children who may be sent elsewhere than to the common popular school, the provisions having for their object to secure that such children shall receive at least as good an instruction as that of the popular school, and for as long a time.

10   It has been ruled that "at the close of each school year, shortly before Easter, an examination of the whole school shall take place under the direction and presidency of the local inspector; the examination, however, need not extend to all the matters of instruction in each class." Each child has then a

15   report furnished to him on his conduct and school work for the year; these reports or certificates, however, "may never stand in lieu of the *Entlassungs-zeugnis*, or certificate of discharge, to be obtained by him at the end of his whole school course."

20   Paragraph 6 of Section IV. says: "Only in specially urgent cases, and, as a rule, not until the child's fourteenth year is completed, can, after a *seven* years' attendance at school, discharge from the common popular school be granted by the district inspector, on the recommendation of the teacher and

25   the local inspector." It has been ruled that no child can receive this earlier discharge whose performance in the principal matters of instruction has not gained at least the mark of *genügend*, "satisfactory," and that the parent's wanting the child to go to work is not one of the *urgent cases* contemplated.

30   In paragraph 7 it is added: "Children who by the end of their eighth school year do not attain due proficiency in the principal matters of instruction—that is to say, in religion, the German language, reading, writing, and arithmetic—have to attend school a year longer."

35   The holidays for the popular schools in Saxony are fixed by law, and amount to forty-four days in the year. In general the school meets for a minimum of three hours in the morning and of two hours in the afternoon. "Parents and guardians are

bound," says Section V. of the law, "to keep children of
school age to a regular attendance in school hours. As a general
rule, only illness of the child, or serious illness in the child's
family, is ground of excuse for its missing school."

Absences, with their causes, are entered daily by the teacher
in the school registers. At the end of every month he hands a
list of them to the managers, whose chairman has to bring,
within eight days after the end of the month, all punishable
absences to the notice of the magistrate, if he has not previously
brought the parents to their duty by an admonition, or had
the child fetched to school by the school beadle, to whom a
small fee is due from the parent for his trouble. If, however,
the matter goes before the magistrate, this functionary inflicts
a fine, which may go as high as 30s., and if the fine is not paid
the penalty is changed to one of imprisonment.

This is the Saxon law, and, without going into details for
each country, it will sufficiently serve to show how in general
the law as to attending school, and as to the penalties for missing school, stands in each.

A very competent and well-informed Englishman, settled
at Weimar, has supplied the Education Department with statistics as to entrances, attendances, absences, and fines in popular
schools in Germany, which give all the information of this
kind which is necessary. He mentions, what the authorities
told me also, that returns are not at present made in Germany,
as with us, comparing the number of attendances with the
number of children on the school-books. Local testimony in
single cases, therefore, as to regularity or irregularity of attendance becomes of the greater importance.

Wherever I inquired, in Germany and Switzerland, inspectors and teachers assured me that they had not to complain of
the parents; that the children were sent to school regularly. By
looking at the registers I was able to assure myself how few of
the absences were entered as contumacious. A contumacious
absence, I was told, was never passed over; and on one occasion
I was myself present when the school officer was despatched
to fetch an offender, a girl, and fetched her. But in general the
children have the habit of coming to school as a matter of

course, and the parents have the habit of acquiescing, as a
matter of course, in their children's going. This is the great
matter. I was told that the magistrates, when cases came before
them, were apt to be lenient; and, indeed, a local landowner
5 and magistrate in a Silesian village, when I asked him, pointing
to a passing villager and his boy, "But if that man was summoned and declared to you that he kept his boy from school
because he was too poor to do without his labour, what would
you say?" answered me in English: "*I would remain silent.*"
10 But in that very village the master of the school told me that
not a case for summoning a child had arisen for the last ten
years. Even more palpable was the evidence of regular attendance in the little Zurich school already mentioned by me.
I arrived there wholly unannounced and unexpected, and asked
15 to see the registers. I found forty-eight children entered, I
counted forty-six present in school before me, and learnt that
the two absentees were kept away because of infectious fever
in their family. In great cities there is less regularity of attendance than in the country; the Berlin municipality, in 1884,
20 with 134,411 children in school, inflicted penalties on 1181
heads of families.

   In France the attendance is a good deal less regular than in
Germany; in the country, I am told, especially. The established
habit of school-going has not yet had time to be formed there.
25 But the law itself in France gives a surprising license for
periodical absences from school. At the age of 11 the child can
leave school if he has obtained the certificate of being up to
the mark in the work of a primary school; but, moreover,
before that age, the law of 1882 allows managers to give three
30 months' leave a year, besides the holidays, to a child living at
home, and to permit a child employed away from home to
come to school for half the day only. In Germany the school
obligation is much more serious. But even in Germany and
German Switzerland the school time is not universally what
35 from reading the provisions which I have quoted from the
Saxon law might be supposed. In the first place the holidays
are in general a good deal more than the 44 days given by the
Saxon law. In the Lucerne school law the school year—the

annual term for which the child must be at school—is fixed at 40 weeks.* This makes 12 weeks of holidays instead of 6 weeks and two days. In general in Germany and Switzerland the holidays occupy, I think, at least eight or ten weeks of the year. And it is wholesome and right that this should be so; few people would be disposed to find fault with it.

But many people might look with less favour on another abridgment of school time which happens even in the best educated German countries. In Saxony the law prescribes that the number of scholars in a class shall not exceed 60, and that the number of scholars to one teacher shall not exceed 120. In schools with from 60 to 120 children, therefore, if the commune is not rich enough to do more in the way of providing teachers than the law actually requires, two classes are formed, and a reduction of school time takes place for each, in order to allow the one master to conduct them separately.

The same thing in Prussia. There the law allows 70 children to a class, 80 children to a teacher; but where there are more than 80 children to a teacher the commune may have recourse to the half-day system, by which one division of children has school in the morning, the other in the afternoon. Not till there are 120 children do the Government regulations prescribe a second teacher; and the school is then to be organized in three classes, with 12 hours a week for the lowest class, 24 for the middle class, and 28 for the highest. This regulation dates from 1872, and was meant to ensure a full school time for the elder children at any rate. But the authorities were to respect the wishes of the localities in carrying the regulation into effect, as in general local habits and wishes are far more respected by the Prussian Government than we in England suppose. And it was found that the rural population greatly preferred the *half-day*

---

* Just the number of weeks for which I found a rural school in New York State to be open. But the school law there only required a school year of twenty-eight weeks; such a child's obligation to attend school is satisfied by an attendance of but fourteen weeks, eight of .which must be consecutive. In the teacher's salary the difference from foreign rates was striking. The teacher, a young mistress, with about thirty scholars, was receiving £100 a year.

school, as it is called, for all the children, because they had thus the elder children at their disposal for half the day.

In a great country like Prussia, with more than twenty-seven millions of inhabitants, a system like that of the half-day school
5 affects a very large number of schools and children. In 1882, the last year for which I have a return, there were 2989 half-day schools in Prussia, schools in which all the children had but half a day's schooling, and 1847 schools with two teachers and three classes, schools in which a large part of the children
10 had only half a day's schooling.

The Silesian school which I have mentioned was a half-day school. I passed a whole school day in it, and saw both divisions at work. The division of elder children, 86 in number, had three hours in the morning; the division of younger children,
15 62 in number, had two hours in the afternoon. The local school inspector, the Lutheran minister of the parish, had represented, as was his duty, to the inspector of the *Kreis* or district in which the school is situated, who was also a Lutheran minister, and lived in a parish about four miles off, that the school
20 ought to have a second teacher. The district inspector had summoned the commune to provide a second teacher; the commune had replied that its means were insufficient, and that things did very well as they were. The district inspector had forwarded this answer to the authority of the province, the
25 *Provinzial Schul Collegium,* representing the Minister, and when I was in the place the answer had just arrived from the provincial authority to say that the commune's objections could not be admitted, and that a second master there must be.

Besides calling attention to the half-day system, both entire
30 and partial, I ought also to say that there are a number of schools in Prussia with what the Government report calls *Anomale Frequenz-verhältnisse,* that is to say, in which the rules as to the number of children to a teacher and the distance of school from the child's home are not observed. The rule as
35 to the number of children to one teacher has been given; the rule as to distance of school from the child's home is that it ought not to exceed 3¾ kilometres. But tables are given to show that there are many whole *Kreise* or districts, and even two whole provincial government divisions (*Regierungs-*

Bezirke) in which the proportion of 100 children to a teacher
is on an average exceeded throughout the schools; and further
lists are given showing in all the provinces single cases where
there is but one teacher to 200 children and more, and where
there are populations distant five and six kilometres and more
from the school. To such an extent do these breaches of the
rule prevail, that while in Prussia there are 2,275,616 children
in schools which the Government report calls normally constituted—in which, that is, the rules as to staff of teachers and
distance are observed—there are in schools abnormally constituted—in which, that is, these rules are not observed—no
less than 2,064,113 children.

No doubt the inequalities in school provision between town
and country and between district and district, the insufficiency
of the resource of school fees, the difficulties of communes,
are temptations to a Government to sweep away school fees
and municipal responsibility for schools, and to take the charge
upon itself, upon the State, as is being done in France. Yet the
best and most observant judges are still of opinion that the
payment of school fees is wholesome, and that the popular
school is rightly a municipal institution; that school fees should
be retained therefore, and that the State should come in with
grants in aid to the commune, and should not supersede it.

What chiefly struck me, however, in the German and Swiss
schools which I watched working under what we should call
unfavourable conditions—the half-day school in Silesia, with
one master, over 60 years of age, to 150 scholars; the school at
Krienz, a large and busy *Gemeinde* near Lucerne, with 63
scholars in the seventh or head class, 80 in the sixth, 68 in the
fifth, 80 in the fourth, 96 in the third, 97 in the second, and
the first or lowest class not coming at all in winter; the school
on the Zürich-berg, with 48 children organized in six classes
under a single master—what most struck me, I say, was not
their deficiencies (except in point of ventilation), but much
rather the good instruction of the children and their good
behaviour.

I was sent to make inquiries, and I have tried to give, as
succinctly as I could, the result of them. That I should add

recommendations was not in my commission, but I may be allowed, perhaps, to put forward one or two remarks which are very present to my mind in consequence of what I have seen.

In the first place, the retention of school fees is not a very important matter. Simply from the point of view of a friend of education there are advantages in their retention, and advantages in their abolition, and the balance of advantage is decidedly, in my opinion, on the side of retention. But we must remember, on the other hand, that there are some questions which it is peculiarly undesirable to make matters of continued public discussion; questions particularly lending themselves to the mischievous declamation and arts of demagogues, and that this question of gratuitous popular schooling is one of them. How often, if the question becomes a political one, will declaimers be repeating that the popular school ought to be made free because the wealthier classes have robbed the poor of endowments intended to educate them! The assertion is not true, indeed; what we call "popular education" is a quite modern conception; what the pious founder in general designed formerly was to catch all promising subjects and to make priests of them. But how surely will popular audiences believe that the popular school has been robbed, and how bad for them to believe it, how will the confusion of our time be yet further thickened by their believing it! I am inclined to think therefore that sooner than let free popular schooling become a burning political question in a country like ours, a wise statesman would do well to adopt and organize it. Only it will be impossible to organize it with the State limiting its concern, as its does now, to the popular school only; and this can be so palpably shown to be a matter of common justice that one need not despair of bringing even the popular judgment to recognize it.

Secondly, there is a danger, perhaps, lest when we have got very elaborate and complete returns, and these returns show a very satisfactory proportion between scholars in daily attendance and scholars on the books, a very satisfactory limit to the number of scholars allowed to each teacher, and a very satisfactory percentage of passes in the established matters of instruction, we should think that therefore we must be doing

well with our popular schools, and that we have no cause to
envy the popular schools abroad, and nothing to learn from
them. On the contrary, the things on which we pride ourselves
are mere machinery; and what we should do well to lay to
heart is that foreign schools with larger classes, longer holidays,   5
and a school-day often cut in two as we have seen, nevertheless,
on the whole, give, from the better training of their teachers,
and the better planning of their school course, a superior popular instruction to ours.

And this brings me thirdly and finally to the point raised at   10
the end of my first remark, and urged by me so often and so
vainly ever since my mission abroad in 1859: our need to
organize our secondary instruction. This is desirable in the
interest of our secondary and higher instruction, of course,
principally; but it is desirable, I may say it is indispensable, in   15
the interest of our popular instruction also. Every one now
admits that popular instruction is a matter for public institution
and supervision; but so long as public institution and supervision stop there, and no contact and correlation are established
between our popular instruction and the instruction above it,   20
so long the condition of our popular instruction itself will and
must be unsatisfactory.

> I remain, Sir,
>   Your obedient servant,
>   (Signed)   MATTHEW ARNOLD   25

The Secretary, Education Department, Whitehall

The Nadir of Liberalism

'Demas hath forsaken me'—so the deserted and dejected Muse of Literature may say—'Demas hath foresaken me, having loved this present world, and hath betaken himself to this or that constituency.' It is now more than fifteen years since I exhorted
5 my young literary and intellectual friends, the lights of Liberalism, not to be rushing into the arena of politics themselves, but rather to work inwardly upon the predominant force in our politics—the great middle class—and to cure its spirit. From their Parliamentary mind, I said, there is little hope; it is in
10 getting at their real mind, and making it work honestly, that all our hope lies. For from the boundedness and backwardness of their spirit, I urged, came the inadequacy of our politics; and by no Parliamentary action, but by an inward working only, could this spirit and our politics be made better. My ex-
15 hortations were as fruitless as good advice usually is. The great Parliamentary machine has gone creaking and grinding on, grinding to much the same result as formerly. But instead of keeping aloof, and trying to set up an inward working on the middle-class spirit, more and more of one's promising young
20 friends of former days have been tempted to put their hands to the machine; and there one sees them now, helping to grind —all of them zealous, all of them intelligent, some of them brilliant and leading.

What has been ground, what has been produced with their
25 help? Really very much the same sort of thing which was produced without it. Certainly our situation has not improved, has not become more solid and prosperous, since I addressed to my friends, fifteen years ago, that well-meant but unavailing advice to work inwardly on the great Philistine middle class, the
30 master-force in our politics, and to cure its spirit. At that time

I had recently been abroad, and the criticism which I heard abroad on England's politics and prospects was what I took for my text in the first political essay with which I ventured to approach my friends and the public. The middle class and its Parliament were then in their glory. Liberal newspapers heaped   5
praise on the middle-class mind, 'which penetrates through sophisms, ignores commonplaces, and gives to conventional illusions their true value;' ministers of State heaped praise on 'the great, the heroic work' performed by the middle-class Parliament. But the foreigners made light of our middle-class mind,   10
and, instead of finding our political performance admirable and successful, declared that it seemed to them, on the other hand, that the era for which we had possessed the secret was over, and that a new era, for which we had not the secret, was beginning. Just now I have again been abroad, and under pres-   15
ent circumstances I found that the estimate of England's action and success under a Liberal Government had, not unnaturally, sunk lower still. The hesitancy, imbecility, and failure of England's action abroad, it was said, have become such as to delight all her enemies, and to throw all her friends into conster-   20
nation. England's foreign policy, said some clever man, reminds me of nothing so much as of Retz's character of the Duke of Orleans, brother to Louis the Thirteenth: 'There was a wide distance, with him, between wishing and willing, between willing and resolving, between resolving and the choice of means,   25
between the choice of means and the putting them in execution. But what was most wonderful of all, it frequently happened that *he came to a sudden stop even in the midst of the putting into execution*.' There, said the speaker, is a perfect prophecy of England in Egypt! At home we had Ireland; to   30
name Ireland is enough. We had the obstructed and paralysed House of Commons. Then, finally, came the news one morning of the London street-mobs and street-riots, heightening yet further the impression of our impotence and disarray. The recent trial and acquittal of the mob-orators will probably   35
complete it.

With very many of those who thus spoke, with all the best and most important of them at any rate, malicious pleasure in our misfortunes, and gratified envy, were not the uppermost

feelings; indeed, they were not their feelings at all. Do not
think, they earnestly said, that we rejoice at the confusion and
disablement of England; there may be some, no doubt, who do;
perhaps there are many. We do not. England has been to us a
5   cynosure, a tower, a pride, a consolation; we rejoiced in her
strength; we rested much of our hope for the Continent upon
her weight and influence there. The decline of her weight and
influence we feel as a personal loss and sorrow. That they have
declined, have well-nigh disappeared, no one who uses his eyes
10 can doubt. And now, in addition, what are we to think of the
posture of your affairs at home? What is it all coming to? It
seems as if you were more and more getting among the break-
ers, drifting towards the shoals and the rocks. Can it really be
so? and is the great and noble ship going to break to pieces?
15   No, I answered; it is not going to break to pieces. There are
sources, I trust, of deliverance and safety which you do not
perceive. I agree with you, however, that our foreign policy
has been that of people who fumble because they cannot make
up their mind, and who cannot make up their mind because
20 they do not know what to be after. I have said so, and I have
said why it is and must be so: because this policy reflects the
dispositions of middle-class Liberalism, with its likes and dis-
likes, its effusion and confusion, its hot and cold fits, its want of
dignity and of the steadfastness which comes from dignity,
25 its want of ideas and of the steadfastness which comes from
ideas. I agree, too, that the House of Commons is a scandal,
and Ireland a crying danger. I agree that monster processions
and monster meetings in the public streets and parks are the
letting out of anarchy, and that our weak dealing with them
30 is deplorable. I myself think all this, and have often, too often,
said it. But the mass of our Liberals of the middle and lower
classes do not see it at all. Their range of vision and of knowledge is too bounded. They are hardly even conscious that the
House of Commons is a scandal or that Ireland is a crying dan-
35 ger. If it suited their favourite minister to tell them that neither
the one nor the other allegation is true, they would believe
him. As to foreign policy, of course it does suit him to tell
them that the allegation that England has lost weight and in-

fluence is not true. And when the minister, or when one of his
ardent young officials on their promotion, more dauntless than
the minister himself, boldly assures them that England has not
at all lost weight and influence abroad, and that our foreign
policy has been sagacious, consistent, and successful, they joy-   5
fully believe him. Or when one of their minister's colleagues
assures them that the late disturbances were of no importance,
a mere accident which will never happen again, and that monster processions and monster meetings in the public streets and
parks are proper and necessary things, which neither can be   10
prohibited nor ought to be prohibited, they joyfully believe
him. And with us in England, although not in the great world
outside of England, those who thus think or say that all is well
are the majority. They may say it, replied the speaker already
mentioned, who has a turn for quotation; they may say it. But   15
the answer for them is the answer made by Sainte-Beuve to
M. Rouher asserting that all was well with the Second Empire
in its closing years: 'He may say so if he pleases, but he deceives himself, and he thinks contrary to the general opinion.'

Yet surely there must be something to give ground to our   20
prevalent notion of Mr. Gladstone as a great and successful
minister. Not only the rank and file, the unthinking multitude,
of the Liberal party, have it and proclaim it, but the leaders,
the intelligent and educated men, embrace it just as confidently. Lord Ripon speaks of 'the policy we might expect from   25
the glorious antecedents of Mr. Gladstone.' Professor Thorold
Rogers calls him 'that veteran statesman with fifty years of
victory behind him.' Mr. Reginald Brett says that any scheme
for Ireland which he produces will be 'a scheme based on his
unrivalled experience of the art of government.' Mr. John   30
Morley says that 'in his great abilities and human sympathy
will be found the only means capable of solving the great Irish
question.' Sir Horace Davey 'will not hesitate to say that he has
confidence in Mr. Gladstone, and that he believes the country
also has confidence in Mr. Gladstone. The Liberals of England   35
would not soon withdraw their confidence from that illustrious
statesman, who had so often led them to victory.' Surely there
must be some foundation or other for this chorus of eulogy

and confidence. Surely there must have been great success of some kind, surely there must have been victory.

Most certainly there has been victory. But has there been success? The two things are often confounded together, and 5   in the popular estimate of Mr. Gladstone we have a signal instance of the confusion. He has been victorious, true; he has conquered, he has carried his measures. But he has not been successful. For what is success for a statesman; is it merely carrying his measures? The vulgar may think so, but a mo- 10   ment's reflection will tell us that the vulgar are wrong; that success for a statesman is succeeding in what his measures are designed to do.

This is the test of a statesman's success, and the great and successful statesmen are those whose work will bear trying by 15   it. Cavour and Prince Bismarck are statesmen of our own time who are really great, because their work did what it was meant to do. Cavour's design was to make a united Italy, Prince Bismarck's to make a strong Germany; and they made it. No minor success, no success of vanity, no success of which the issue 20   is still problematical and which requires other successes for its accomplishment, will suffice to assure this title of *successful* to a statesman. To some people Prince Bismarck seems great because he can snub all the world, and has even been enabled, by an incredible good fortune, to snub the proudest of countries 25   and the one country against which, above all others, he was powerless—England. These successes of vanity are nothing. Neither is he to be called a successful statesman because he carried the May laws, for it is as yet uncertain whether the end which those laws were designed to attain they will accom- 30   plish. But let us see, then, what it is which does indeed make Prince Bismarck a great and successful statesman, a statesman whose 'antecedents,' to take Lord Ripon's phrase, are indeed 'glorious.' He is successful because, finding his country with certain dangers and certain needs, he has laboured for forty 35   years, at first as a subordinate, but for the far greater part of the time as principal, to remove the one and to satisfy the other.

Germany had needs, she found impediments or she found perils to her national life, on the side of Denmark, Austria,

Russia, France. First her needs on the side of Denmark were satisfied, in spite of the opposition of France and England. Graver difficulties had to be faced next. A strong Germany was impossible without a strong Prussia. But Prussia seemed to be one of the Great Powers only in name; Austria, thwarting and supercilious, checked her movements at every turn, frustrated all efforts to consolidate Germany. Except by Prussia's beating Austria, the consolidation of Germany could not go forward; but a war with Austria—what a difficult war was that for a Prussian minister to make! Prince Bismarck made it, and the victory of Sadowa gave Prussia free action in Germany. But except free action in Germany, Prince Bismarck demanded nothing from Austria; no territory, no indemnity—not a village, not a shilling.

Russia had saved Austria from the Hungarians, why did she not save her from the Prussians? Because the Prussian Government, foreseeing the future, foreseeing the inevitable struggle with Austria, had refused to take part with the Western Powers in the Crimean War—a foolish and prejudicial war for England, but which would have been still more foolish and prejudicial for Prussia. Austria had in a half-hearted way taken part with the Western Powers; Russia's neutrality in Austria's war with Prussia was Prussia's reward for the past and Austria's punishment.

Meanwhile at Prussia's success France looked on, palpitating with anger and jealousy. A strong Germany was a defiance to all French traditions, and the inevitable collision soon came. France was defeated, and the provinces required to give military security to Germany were taken from her. Why had not Austria now sought to wreak her revenge on Prussia by siding with France? She had Russia to still reckon with in attempting to do so. But what was of yet more avail to stay her hand was that Prince Bismarck, as has been already mentioned, had with admirable wisdom entirely forborne to amerce and humiliate her after Sadowa, and had thus made it possible for the feelings of German Austria to tend to his side.

For the last fifteen years he has constantly developed and increased friendly relations with Austria and Russia. As regards

France, whose friendship was impossible, he has kept Germany
watchful and strong. Those legitimate needs and that security
of Germany, which thirty years ago seemed unattainable for
her, he has attained. Germany, which thirty years ago was
5   hampered, weak, and in low esteem, is now esteemed, strong,
and with her powers all at command. It was a great object, and
the great *Reichskanzler* has attained it. Such are Prince Bismarck's victories.

I observe that Mr. John Morley, like many people in this
10   country, speaks of the work of Prince Bismarck as something
extremely precarious, and likely to crumble away and vanish
as soon as the Emperor William dies. 'When the disappearance
of Kaiser Wilhelm dissolves the fabric of the Triple Alliance,
new light will be thrown on the stability of governments which
15   are anti-democratic.' In my opinion, Mr. Morley deceives himself. Advanced Liberals are always apt to think that a condition
of things where the people cannot hold whatever meetings and
processions they like, and wherever they like, is an unnatural
condition and likely to dissolve. But I see no signs which show
20   that Prince Bismarck and his policy will disappear with the
Emperor William. The Crown Prince is too judicious a man to
desire it; even if he desired it, I doubt whether he could bring
it about. The state of Germany is, unless I am much mistaken,
more solid than our own. Prince Bismarck commits errors, the
25   German character has faults, German life has deficiencies; but
the situation there is a great deal more solid, and Prince Bismarck far more fixed in the national affections, than our Radicals suppose.

But now let us come to the victories of Mr. Gladstone. Are
30   they not victories only, but successes? that is, have they really
satisfied vital needs and removed vital dangers of the nation?
Sir Robert Peel's abolition of the Corn Laws may be said to
have removed a risk of social revolt. But the general development of Free Trade cannot absolutely, as we are all coming
35   to see, be said to have satisfied vital needs and removed vital
dangers of the nation; free trade is not, it is now evident, a
machinery making us by its own sole operation prosperous
and safe; it requires, in order to do this, many things to sup-

plement it, many conditions to accompany it. The general
development of free trade we cannot, therefore, reckon to
Mr. Gladstone as a success of the sort which stamps a statesman as gloriously successful. The case was one not admitting
of a success of the kind. On foreign affairs I shall not touch;   5
his best friends will not allege his successes there. But at home
for a success of the kind wanted, a true and splendid success,
Mr. Gladstone has had three great opportunities. He had them
in dealing with the Irish Church, with the Irish land question,
with obstruction in Parliament. In each case he won a victory.   10
But did he achieve not only a victory, but that which is the
only real and true success for a statesman? did he, by his victory, satisfy vital needs and remove vital dangers of his country? Did he in the case of the Irish Church? The object there
for a statesman was to conciliate the Catholic sentiment of   15
Ireland; did his measure do this? The Liberal party affirmed
that it did, the Liberal newspapers proclaimed it 'a great and
genial policy of conciliation,' and one of Mr. Gladstone's colleagues told us that the Ministry had 'resolved to knit the
hearts of the empire into one harmonious concord, and knitted   20
they were accordingly.' True, there were voices (mine was
one of them) which said differently. 'It is fatal to the English
nation,' I wrote in *Culture and Anarchy*, 'to be told by its flat-
terers, and to believe, that it is abolishing the Irish Church
through reason and justice when it is really abolishing it   25
through the Nonconformists' antipathy to establishments; fatal
to expect the fruits of reason and justice from anything but
the spirit of reason and justice.' This was unpopular language
from an insignificant person, and was not listened to. But who
doubts now that the Catholic sentiment of Ireland was not in   30
the very least conciliated by the measure of 1868, and that
the reason why it was not and could not be conciliated by it
was that the measure was of the nature above described?

The Irish Land Act, in like manner, was a victory but not a
success. It was carried, it was applauded; the Liberal party duly   35
extolled it as 'a scheme based on Mr. Gladstone's unrivalled
experience in the art of government.' But did it satisfy vital
needs and remove vital dangers? Evidently not; the legislation

now proposed for Ireland is impregnable proof of it. Did the victory, again, achieved in the reform of procedure, achieved by Mr. Gladstone wielding a great majority and spending the time of Parliament without any stint, did this victory succeed?

5   Did it satisfy the nation's needs and remove the nation's dangers as regards obstruction in the House of Commons? Why, the Conservatives have had to devise a fresh scheme, and the Liberal Government has had to adopt it from them and is at this moment working in concert with them to mature it!

10 Well then, 'our veteran statesman with his fifty years of victory behind him,' with his 'glorious antecedents,' with his 'unrivalled experience in the art of government,' turns out, in the three crucial instances by which we can test him, not to have succeeded as a statesman at all, but on the contrary to

15 have failed. 'Let me try again,' he is now saying. And Mr. Morley assures us that in 'Mr. Gladstone's great abilities and human sympathy will be found the only means capable of solving the great Irish problem.' The mass of Liberal voices chime eagerly in with Mr. Morley. I do not deny the great

20 abilities and the human sympathy; I admit them to the fullest extent. I do not even say that Mr. Gladstone is to be blamed for not having succeeded. But succeeded, in the true sense of the word, he has not; his work as a statesman has hitherto failed to satisfy the country's vital needs, to remove the coun-

25 try's vital dangers. When, therefore, he proposes, in a most critical condition of things, to fall to work again on a bigger scale than ever, we may well feel anxious. We may well ask ourselves what are the causes which have kept him back from a statesman's true success hitherto, and whether they will not

30 also keep him back from it in what he purposes to do now.

The reason why Mr. Gladstone has not succeeded hitherto in the real and high work of a statesman is that he is in truth not a statesman, properly so called, at all, but an unrivalled parliamentary leader and manager. A little development is

35 needed to bring out clearly what I mean.

Mr. Gladstone is the minister of a party and a period of expansion, the minister of the Liberals—the Liberals whose work it should be to bring about the modern development of

English society. He has many requisites for that leadership. Everybody will admit that in effectiveness as a public speaker and debater he cannot be surpassed, can hardly be equalled. Philosophers may prefer coolness and brevity to his heat and copiousness; but the many are not philosophers, and his heat 5 and copiousness are just what is needed for popular assemblies. His heat and copiousness, moreover, are joined with powers and accomplishments, with qualities of mind and character, as admirable as they are rare. The absence in him of aristocratical exclusiveness is one of the causes of his popularity. But not 10 only is he free from *morgue*, he has also that rarest and crowning charm in a man who has triumphed as he has, been praised as he has: he is genuinely modest. Every one should read in proof of this a beautiful and touching letter from him in Hope Scott's Life, a letter so deeply modest, and yet breathing, at 15 the same time, the very spirit of sincerity. If one could be astonished at anything in political partisans, I should be astonished at the insensibility of his opponents to the charm of Mr. Gladstone. I think him an unsuccessful, a dangerous minister; but he is a captivating, a fascinating personality. 20

Why then, with all these gifts and graces, does he fail as a statesman? Probably because, having to be the minister of the modern development of English society, he was born in 1809. The minister of a period of concentration, resistance, and war, may be spiritually rooted in the past; not so the minister of a 25 work of civil development in a modern age. I once ventured to say to Lord Salisbury, before he became the leading personage he is now, that he interested me because, though a Conservative, he was reared in a post-Philistine epoch and influenced by it. I meant that his training had fallen on a time when a man of his 30 powers and cultivation must needs get a sense of how the world is really going, a sense which the old time of routine and fictions was without. Lord Salisbury is a Conservative leader; his business is to procure stability and permanence for that which already exists, much of it undeniably precious. He may have a 35 sense in his own inner mind of what is mere survival of routine and fiction from the past and of how the modern world is really going, but that knowledge has not to be the grand spring

and motor of his public action. A Liberal leader here in England is, on the other hand, a man of movement and change,
called expressly to the task of bringing about a modern organisation of society. To do this, he should see clearly how the
world is going, what our modern tendencies and needs really
are, and what is routine and fiction in that which we have inherited from the past. But of how few men of Mr. Gladstone's
age can it be said that they see this! Certainly not of Mr. Gladstone. Some of whom it cannot be said may be more interesting
figures than those of whom it can; Cardinal Newman is a more
interesting figure, Mr. Gladstone himself is a more interesting
figure, than John Stuart Mill. But a Liberal leader of whom
it cannot be said that he sees how the world is really going is
in a false situation. And Mr. Gladstone's perception and criticism of modern tendencies is fantastic and unsound, as his
criticism of Homer is fantastic and unsound, or his criticism
of Genesis. But he loves liberty, expansion; with his wonderful
gifts for parliamentary and public life he has naturally an irresistible bent to political leadership; he will lead the Liberal
party. And he will lead it, he will lead this great party of movement and change, by watching their mind, adapting his programme to it, and relying on their support and his own inexhaustible resources of energy, eloquence, and management, to
give him the victory.

But the task of providing light and leading is thus shifted
upon men yet more incompetent for it than Mr. Gladstone. It
is thrown upon the middle class in English society, the class
where lay the strength of the Liberal party until the other day,
and upon the working class, which conjointly with the middle
class makes its strength now. Both are singularly bounded, our
working class reproducing, in a way unusual in other countries,
the boundedness of the middle. Both have invaluable qualities,
closely allied, as generally happens, with their defects. The
sense for conduct in our middle class is worth far more than the
superior intellectual lucidity to be found in divorce from that
sense among middle classes elsewhere; the English workman, as
a great Swiss employer of labour testified to me the other day,
is still the best in the world; the English peasant is patient,

faithful, respectful, kindly, as no other. But range of mind, large and clear views, insight—we must not go to our middle and lower classes for these. Yet it is on our middle and lower classes that the task is really thrown, Mr. Gladstone's gifts and deficiencies being what they are, of determining the pro- 5 gramme of Liberal movement for our community, and indeed of determining the programme of our foreign policy also; while Mr. Gladstone finds the management and talents for insuring victory to the programmes so determined. Thus it is that our foreign policy has been what we have seen it; thus 10 it came about that the Irish Church was abolished by the power of the Dissenters' antipathy to Church Establishments. And so we find that precisely the reverse happens of what Mr. Frederic Harrison bids us expect; the minister, says he, initiates, the un- trained elector simply finds a good minister. 'Now very plain 15 men know how to find the set of ministers who wish them well and will bring them good.' But we see that in fact our Liberal electorate has the task thrown upon it not only of choosing a good minister, but also of determining what the good shall be which this minister is to bring us. 20

Such, then, is our situation. A captivating Liberal leader, generous and earnest, full of eloquence, ingenuity, and re- source, and a consummate parliamentary manager—but without insight, and who as a statesman has hitherto not succeeded, but failed. A Liberal party, of which the strength and substance is 25 furnished by two great classes, with sterling merits and of good intentions, but bounded and backward. A third factor in our situation must not be unnoticed—an element of Jacobinism. It is small, but it is active and visible. It is a sinister apparition. We know its works from having seen them so abundantly in France; 30 it has the temper of hatred and the aim of destruction. There are two varieties of Jacobin, the hysterical Jacobin and the pedantic Jacobin; we possess both, and both are dangerous.

At such a moment Ireland sends eighty-five Home Rulers to the House of Commons; and the Irish question, which had 35 previously given to Mr. Gladstone so much occasion for show- ing how he can conquer without succeeding, must be dealt with seriously at last. What grand scope is here offered for the

talents of the great Parliamentary manager! The thing is, to
have the eighty-five Home Rulers voting solid with the Liberal
party. How is it to be effected? The generous and ardent feelings of Mr. Gladstone rush to his aid. Ireland has been abomi-
5 nably governed! True. Ireland desires autonomy more hotly
than any other part of these islands desires it! Very naturally.
Why then should we not give to the Irish what they so hotly
desire? Why not indeed? responds the Liberal party. Only
there must be no endowment of religion, no endowment, above
10 all, of Popish superstition! There shall be none, says Mr. Gladstone. In that case, replies his Liberal following, go on and
prosper! Let the Irish have what the majority of them like. It
is the great blessedness for man to do as he likes; if men very
much wish for a thing, we ought to give it them if possible.
15 This is the cardinal principle of Liberalism; Mr. Fox proclaimed it.

Yes, Mr. Fox proclaimed it—the brilliant and generous schoolboy! But what would Burke have said to it? Nay, even a sagacious woman, who had closely watched a time of civil trouble,
20 knew better. 'Quand les hommes se révoltent, ils y sont poussés
par des causes qu'ils ignorent; *et, pour l'ordinaire, ce qu'ils
demandent n'est pas ce qu'il faut pour les apaiser.*' Men are
driven to revolt by causes not clearly known to them; and in
general the thing they call for is not the thing requisite to
25 content them. The observation is profoundly just and true.

The project of giving a separate Parliament to Ireland has
every fault which a project of State can have. It takes one's
breath away to find an English statesman propounding it. With
islands so closely and inextricably connected together by na-
30 ture as these islands of ours, to go back in the at least formal
political connexion attained, to make the political tie not
closer but much laxer, almost to undo it—what statesmanship!
And when, estranged from us in feeling as Celtic Ireland unhappily is, we had yet in Ulster a bit of Great Britain, we had
35 a friend there, you propose to merge Ulster in Celtic Ireland!
you propose to efface and expunge your friend! Was there
ever such madness heard of?

Those Irishmen, who may happen to know anything about so unimportant a person as I am, will know that I am no enemy of Ireland. They will therefore, I hope, have patience with me while I tell them the truth. The more intensely the Irish desire a separate Parliament, the more it proves that they ought not to have one. If they cry out for a separate Irish Parliament when Scotland and Wales do not cry out for a Scotch or Welsh Parliament, that is not a reason for giving such a Parliament to Ireland rather than to Scotland or Wales, but just the contrary. The Irish desire it so much because they are so exasperated against us. The exasperation is good neither for us nor for themselves. The thing is to do away with the sense of exasperation by removing its causes, to make them friends. The causes of the exasperation are not in our political tie with them, but in our behaviour and treatment. Amend the behaviour and treatment by all means. But simply to cut the Irish adrift in their present state of feeling, to send them away with the sense of exasperation rankling, with the memory of our behaviour and treatment fresh in their minds, what is it but to leave the sense of exasperation to last for ever, and to give them more full and free scope for indulging it? No gratitude for a measure which its supporters are already recommending by the ignoblest appeals to our fears will prevent this. To our fears the measure will be imputed; and to our fears or our foolishness, and to no more worthy or winning motive, will it indeed be due. Every guarantee we take, every limit we impose, will be an occasion for fret and friction. The temptation to the Irish legislature *ampliare jurisdictionem*, to extend and enlarge its range of action, will be irresistible; the very brilliancy and verve of Irishmen necessitate it. The proper public field for an Irishman of signal ability is the Imperial Parliament. There his faculties will find their right and healthful scope; he is good for us there, and we for him. But he will find scope for his faculties in an Irish Parliament only by making it what it was not meant to be, and what it cannot be without danger. It will be a sensation Parliament—a Parliament of shocks and surprises.

Ask those 'thoughtful Americans' who in conjunction with his own terrors are the mighty pursuaders of Mr. Whitbread's mind, ask them what they would think of a proposal to make the South one homogeneous political body distinct from the North, and with a separate Congress in Richmond. They will laugh. The South, they will say, is certainly much inferior in strength and population to the North. But such a Congress would inevitably come to regard itself as a rival to the Congress at Washington, the Southern States which are in sympathy with the North would be swamped by those which are not; it would be a perpetual stimulus to secession. And then let Mr. Whitbread, if his tremors have left him any voice, ask his 'thoughtful Americans' what it is which they are so thoughtfully and kindly exhorting him to do in Ireland!

This brings me to the challenge constantly thrown out to those who condemn Mr. Gladstone's plan of an Irish Parliament, to produce an alternative policy of their own. Why, really such a policy, in its main lines, which are all the state of the case at present requires, produces itself! Let us give to our South, not a single central Congress, but provincial legislatures. Local government is the great need for us just now throughout these islands; the House of Commons is far too large a body, and is weighted with much work which it ought not to have. But in Great Britain we have this difficulty: the counties would give us local legislatures too numerous, and not strong enough; and we have no provinces. The difficulty may be overcome, but a difficulty it is. But in Ireland it does not present itself; Ireland has four provinces. Ireland's strong desire for local government is no good reason for giving Ireland an Irish Parliament; but it is a good reason for seizing as promptly as possible any fit means for organising local government there, and for so organising it even before we organise it in Great Britain; and such means the Irish provinces supply. Munster and Connaught may probably be considered as of one character, and some of western Ulster, as being of the same character, might go naturally with them. But we have at least three divisions in Ireland, each of them with a distinct stamp and character of its own, and affording, each of them, materials for a separate provincial assembly: Ulster proper, or British Ireland; Leinster, or metropolitan Ireland; Munster and Connaught, or Celtic Ireland. Evidently the assembly representing British Ireland would be one thing, the assembly representing Celtic Ireland quite another. Perhaps Leinster, the old seat of the capital and of metropolitan life, would give us an assembly different in character from either. So much the better. Each real and distinct part of Ireland would have its own legislature, and would govern its own local affairs; each part would be independent of the others, neither of them would be swamped by the others. The common centre would be the Imperial Parliament at Westminster. There the foremost Irishmen would represent Ireland, while for the notables of each province the provincial legislatures would afford a field.

It is deemed enough to say, in condemnation of any scheme of this kind, that it is not what the majority of the Irish are demanding, and that the eighty-five members who follow Mr. Parnell would not accept it. But carry it, and what would happen? Would not Ulster accept it? It is just what Ulster desires, while a general Irish Parliament is just what Ulster fears. Would Leinster, Munster, and Connaught, metropolitan and Celtic Ireland, refuse to accept? How would they carry their refusal into effect? They could only do so by the majority abstaining from the election of members for the provincial legislatures. But this would leave those assemblies to be elected by the minority, who would assuredly elect them gladly enough, but how would that suit the majority? No, the Home Rulers may say that nothing less than an Irish Parliament will they accept, and no wonder that, with Mr. Gladstone's offer before them, they should say so; but once carry a plan for establishing provincial legislatures, and they will come into it before long.

And indeed one cannot but at first feel astonishment that Mr. Gladstone should have preferred to such a plan his plan for an Irish Parliament. Last year I was often and often inclined to say as to Egypt: With one tenth of the ingenuity and pains which Mr. Gladstone spends to prove, what neither he nor any one else ever *can* prove, that his Egyptian policy

has been sagacious, consistent, and successful, he might have
produced an Egyptian policy sagacious, consistent, and successful. So one may say now as to Ireland: With one tenth of
the ingenuity and pains which Mr. Gladstone is expending
5   upon a bad and dangerous measure for Ireland, he might have
produced a good and safe one. But alas, he is above all a great
Parliamentary manager! Probably he is of the same opinion
with Cardinal de Retz, who has been already mentioned; he
thinks 'that it takes higher qualities to make a good party-
10 leader than to make a good emperor of the universe.' The
eighty-five Parnellite members added to the Liberal majority,
and enabling him, as he hopes, to defy opposition and to carry
his measure victoriously, are irresistible to him. To the difficult work of a statesman he prefers the work for which he has
15 such a matchless talent—the seemingly facile but really dangerous strokes of the Parliamentary tactician and party manager.
    Not that he himself foresees danger from it. No, that is the
grave thing. He does not foresee danger. Statesmen foresee,
Mr. Gladstone does not. He no more foresees danger from his
20 Irish Parliament than he foresaw that his abolition of the
Irish Church would not conciliate Catholic sentiment in Ireland, or that his Land Act would not conciliate the Irish peasant. He has no foresight because he has no insight. With all
his admirable gifts he has little more real insight than the rank
25 and file of his Liberal majority, people who think that if men
very much want a thing they ought to have it, and that Mr.
Fox's dictum makes this certain. It is this confiding majority
under this unforeseeing leader which makes me tremble. Will
anything ever awaken either the leader or the followers to a
30 sense of danger? When the vessel of State is actually grinding
on the rocks, will Mr. Gladstone be still cheerfully devising
fresh strokes of management; and, when not engaged in ap-
plauding him, will Mr. Illingworth be still prattling about
disestablishment and Mr. Stansfeld about contagious disease?
35   I have long been urging 'that the performance of our Liberals
was far less valuable than they supposed, that their doings
wanted more of simple and sincere thought to direct them, and

that by their actual practice, however prosperous they might fancy themselves, they could not really succeed.' But now they do really seem to have done what the puzzled foreigners imagine England altogether has done—to have reached the nadir. They have shown us about the worst that a party of 5 movement can do, when that party is bounded and backward and without insight, and is led by a manager of astounding skill and energy, but himself without insight likewise. The danger of our situation is so grave that it can hardly be exaggerated. People are shocked at even the mention of the con- 10 tingency of civil war. But the danger of civil war inevitably arises whenever two impossible parties, full of hatred and contempt for each other, with no mediating power of reason to reconcile them, are in presence. So the English civil war arose when, facing and scornfully hating one another, were two 15 impossibilities: the prerogative of the King and the license of the Cavaliers on the one side, the hideousness and immense *ennui* of the Puritans on the other. The Vendean war arose out of a like collision between two implacable impossibilities: the old *régime* and Jacobinism. Here lies the danger of 20 civil war in Ireland, if the situation cannot find rational treatment; Protestant ascendency is impossible, but the Ulster men will not let bunglers, in removing it, drag them down to a lower civilisation without a struggle. Nay, the like danger exists for England itself. Change we must; but if a Liberal 25 party with no insight, led by a victorious manager who is no statesman, brings us to failure and chaos, the existing England will not let itself be ruined without a struggle.

Therefore at the present time that need for us, on which I have so often and so vainly insisted, to let our minds have 30 free and fair play, no longer to deceive ourselves, to brush aside the claptrap and fictions of our public and party life, to be lucid, to get at the plain simple truth, to see things as they really are, becomes more urgent, more the one thing needful for us, than ever. That sentence of Butler, which I have more 35 than once quoted in past times, acquires now a heightened, an almost awful significance. '*Things are what they are, and*

*the consequences of them will be what they will be; why then
should we desire to be deceived?'* The laws which govern the
course of human affairs, which make this thing salutary to a
nation and that thing pernicious, are not of our making or
5   under our power. Our wishing and asserting can avail nothing
against them. Lord Ripon's calling Mr. Gladstone's antecedents glorious cannot make them other than what they are—
Parliamentary victories, but a statesman's failures. Mr. Morley's 'great triumph' in the election of '330 Liberal members,
10   more or less, who without excessive arrogance may be taken
to be the best men in the way of intelligence and honesty that
the Liberal party can produce,' cannot make the Liberal party,
both in and out of Parliament, other than what it is—a party
of bounded and backward mind, without insight. Deluders and
15   deluded, the utterers of these phrases may fancy them solid
while they utter them, the hearers while they hear them. But
solid they cannot make them; and it is not on the thing being
asserted and believed, but on its being really true or false, that
our welfare turns.

20   Whatever may be the faults of the Liberal party, 'the Conservative party at any rate,' say Mr. Bradlaugh, 'is blind;' and
here, too, of course, there is danger. The Conservative party
is the party of stability and permanence, the party of resistance to change; and when the Liberal party, the party of
25   movement, moves unwise and dangerous changes, recourse will
naturally be had, by sensible men, to the Conservative party.
After all, our country as it is, as the past has made it, as it
stands there before us, is something; it is precious, it shall
not lightly be imperilled by the bungling work of rash hands.
30   Burke from such a motive threw himself on the Conservative
forces in this country to resist Jacobinism. But no solution of
the problems of national life is to be reached by resting on
those forces absolutely. Burke would have been far more edifying for us to-day if he had rested on them less absolutely.
35   What has been said of the urgent need of seeing things as
they really are is of general application, and applies to Conservative action as well as Liberal. If Conservative action is

blind, we are undone. True, for the moment our pressing danger is just now from the Liberal party and its leader. If they cannot be stopped and defeated, the thing is over, and we need not trouble ourselves about the Conservative party and its blindness. But supposing them defeated, the Conservative programme requires to be treated just like the Liberal, to be surveyed with a resolutely clear and fair mind.

Now there is always a likelihood that this programme will be just to maintain things as they are, and nothing further. Already there are symptoms of danger in the exhortations, earnestly made and often repeated, to keep faith with the Irish proprietor to whose security England, it is said, has pledged herself; to secure the Irish landowners and to prevent the scandal and peril of Catholic supremacy in Ireland.

As to Catholicism, it has been the great stone of stumbling to us in Ireland, and so it will continue to be while we treat it inequitably. Mr. Gladstone's Bill treats it inequitably. His Bill withholds from the Irish the power to endow or establish Catholicism. That, he well knows, is the one exception which his Liberal followers make to their rule, borrowed from Mr. Fox, that if men very much wish to do a thing we should let them do it. To endow Catholicism they must not be permitted, however much they may wish it. That provision alone would be fatal to any sincere and lasting gratitude in Ireland for Mr. Gladstone's measure. If his measure is defeated it would be fatal to repeat his mistake. Why should not the majority in Ireland be suffered to endow and establish its religion just as much as in England or Scotland? It is precisely one of those cases where the provincial legislatures should have the power to do as they think proper. Mr. Whitbread's 'thoughtful Americans' will tell him that in the United States there is this power, although to the notions and practice of America, sprung out of the loins of Nonconformity, religious establishments are unfamiliar. But even in this century, I think, Connecticut had an established Congregational Church, and it might have an Established Church again to-morrow if it chose. Ulster would most certainly not establish Catholicism.

If it chose to establish Presbyterianism it should be free to do so. If the Celtic and Catholic provinces chose to establish Catholicism, they should be free to do so. So long as we have two sets of weights and measures in this matter, one for Great
5   Britain and another for Ireland, there can never be concord.

The land question presents most grave and formidable difficulties, but undoubtedly they are not to be got rid of by holding ourselves pledged to make the present Irish landlords' tenure and rents as secure as those of a landlord in England. We
10   ought not to do it if we could, and in the long run we could not do it if we would. How greatly is a clear and fair mind needed here! and perhaps such a mind on such a subject the Conservatives, the landed party, do not easily attain. We have always meant and endeavoured to give to the Irish landlord
15   the same security that the English has. But the thing is impossible. Why? Because at bottom the acquiescence of the community makes the security of property. The land-system of England has, in my opinion, grave disadvantages; but it has this acquiescence. It has it partly from the moderation of the
20   people, but more from the general conduct and moderation of the landlords. If many English landlords had borne such a reputation as that which the first Lord Lonsdale, for instance, acquired for himself in the north, the English landed system would not have had this acquiescence. In Scotland it has it
25   in a less degree, and is therefore less secure; and, whatever the Duke of Argyll may think, deservedly. Let him consult the Tory Johnson for the past, and weigh, as to the present, the fact that Mr. Winans is possible. But it has it in a considerable degree, though in a lower degree than England. Ire-
30   land has it in the degree to be expected from its history of confiscation, penal laws, absenteeism—that is to say, hardly at all. And we are bound in good faith, we are pledged to obtain, by force if necessary, for the Irish landlord the acquiescence and security which in England come naturally!
35   We are bound to do it for a landed system where the landowners have been a class with whom, in Burke's words, 'the melancholy and invidious title of grantees of confiscation was

a favourite;' who 'would not let Time draw his oblivious veil over the unpleasant means by which their domains were acquired;' who 'abandoned all pretext of the general good of the community'! But there has been great improvement, you say: the present landowners give in general little cause for complaint. Absenteeism has continued, but ah! even if the improvement had been ten times greater than it has, Butler's memorable and stern sentence would still be true: 'Real reformation is in many cases of no avail at all towards preventing the miseries annexed to folly *exceeding a certain degree.* There is a certain bound to misbehaviour, which being transgressed, there remains no place for repentance in the natural course of things.' But a class of altogether new and innocent owners has arisen. Alas! every one who has bought land in Ireland has bought it with a lien of Nemesis upon it. It is of no use deceiving ourselves. To make the landowner in the Celtic and Catholic parts of Ireland secure as the English landowner is impossible for us.

What is possible is to bear our part in his loss; for loss he must incur. He must incur loss for folly and misbehaviour, whether on his own part or on that of his predecessors, *exceeding a certain degree.* But most certainly we ought to share his loss with him. For when complaints were addressed to England, 'the double name of the complainants,' says Burke, 'Irish and Papist (it would be hard to say which singly was the more odious), shut up the hearts of every one against them.' All classes in Great Britain are guilty in this matter; perhaps the middle class, the stronghold of Protestant prejudice, most. And, therefore, though the Irish landlords can, I think, be now no more maintained than were the planters, yet to some extent this country is bound to indemnify them as it did the planters. They must choose between making their own terms with their own community, or making them with the Imperial Parliament. In the latter case, part of their indemnity should be contributed by Ireland, part, most certainly, by ourselves. Loss they must, however, expect to suffer, the landowners of the Celtic and Catholic provinces at

any rate. To this the English Conservatives, whatever natural
sympathy and compassion they may entertain for them, must
clearly make up their minds.

   On the reasonableness of the Conservative party our best
5   hope at present depends. In that nadir of Liberalism which
we seem to have reached, there are not wanting some signs
and promise of better things to come. Lord Rosebery, with
his freshness, spirit, and intelligence, one cannot but with
pleasure see at the Foreign Office. Then the action of Lord
10   Hartington and Mr. Trevelyan inspires hope: that of Mr.
Chamberlain inspired high hope at first, but presently his attitude seemed to become equivocal. He has, however, instincts
of government—what M. Guizot used to call 'the govern-
mental mind.' But the mass of the great Liberal party has
15   no such instincts; it is crude and without insight. Yet for
the modern development of our society, great changes are
required, changes not certainly finding a place in the programme of our Conservatives, but not in that of our Liberals
either. Because I firmly believe in the need of such changes,
20   I have often called myself a Liberal of the future. They must
come gradually, however; we are not ripe for them yet. What
we are ripe for, what ought to be the work of the next few
years, is the development of a complete and rational system
of local government for these islands. And in this work all
25   reasonable Conservatives may heartily bear part with all reasonable Liberals. That is the work for the immediate future,
and besides its own great importance, it offers us a respite
from burning questions which we are not ripe to treat, and
a basis of union for all good men. The development of the
30   working class amongst us follows the development of the
middle. But development for our bounded and backward middle class can be gained only by their improved education
and by the practice of a rational, large, and elevating system
of local government. The reasonableness and co-operation of
35   the Conservatives are needed to attain this system. By reasonableness, by co-operation with reasonable Liberals, they
have it in their power to do two good things: they can keep off

many dangers in the present, and they will be helping to rear up a Liberalism of more insight for the future.

But is it possible, and is there time? Will not the great Parliamentary manager, with his crude Liberal party of the present, sweep everything before him now? The omens are not good. At Munich a few weeks ago I had the honour to converse with a wise and famous man, as pleasing as he is learned, Dr. Döllinger. He is an old friend of Mr. Gladstone. We talked of Mr. Gladstone, with the interest and admiration which he deserves, but with misgiving. His letter to Lord de Vesci had just then appeared. 'Does it not remind you,' Dr. Döllinger asked me, 'of that unfortunate French ministry on the eve of the Revolution, applying to the nation for criticisms and suggestions?' Certainly the omens are not good. However, that best of all omens, as Homer calls it, ourselves to do our part for our country, is in our own power. The circumstances are such that desponding and melancholy thoughts cannot be banished entirely. After all, we may sometimes be tempted to say mournfully to ourselves, nations do not go on for ever. In the immense procession of ages, what countless communities have arisen and sunk unknown, and even the most famous nation, perhaps, is only for its day. Human nature will have in dark hours its haunting apprehensions of this kind. But till the fall has actually come, no firm English mind will consent to believe of the fall that it is inevitable, and of 'the ancient and inbred integrity, piety, good-nature, and good-humour of the English people,' that their place in the world will know them no more.

The Political Crisis

Sir,—All next week, while the moment for the great vote draws near, I shall be on the sea, going to visit our American kinsmen, who abstained from setting up a Southern Parliament themselves, but are so anxious, it seems, that we should set up an Irish one.

Suffer me to say, before I depart, that the mind of the country, which is slowly but surely waking up on this Irish question, will not be satisfied unless the vote is taken on a clear issue and accompanied by a distinct engagement.

The vote is not taken on a clear issue if it is taken on any question but that of a separate national Parliament for Ireland. Mr. Chamberlain and Mr. Trevelyan may be so committed that they prefer to have the vote taken on some other issue than this. They deserve every consideration. They had the merit of opening their eyes when they saw where Mr. Gladstone was going, instead of shutting them tighter and tighter like Mr. Campbell-Bannerman. An indirect issue may suit the convenience of other members also. But a clear, direct issue is what will alone suit the mind of the country.

A separate Parliament for Ireland is Mr. Gladstone's irreducible *minimum*. Ireland is a nation, says Mr. Parnell menacingly, Mr. Stansfeld gushingly; a nation should have its national Parliament.

Ireland has been a nation, a most unhappy one. Wales too, and Scotland, have been nations. But politically they are now nations no longer, any one of them. This country could not have risen to its present greatness if they had been. Give them

separate Parliaments, and you begin, no doubt, to make them
again nations politically. But you begin also to undo what
has made this country great.

Do not let us be preposterously alarmist. Perhaps, if it
suits Mr. Gladstone's purposes, Scotland, Wales, and Ireland   5
may all of them, to Mr. Stansfeld's delight, become politically
nations again, and yet this country, such is its force, may still,
by new and untried ways, continue great. But it will be a
plunge into the unknown, and surely such a plunge is a dangerous thing, not to be risked without absolute necessity.   10

In the case of Austria-Hungary, there was such necessity.
Hungary was the bigger of the two. But what was done there
was a plunge into the unknown and a very grave one. Who will
say that the Austria of to-day is as strong and solid a Power
as the Austria of the end of last century, or that by the end   15
of next century Austria's German provinces will not have
gravitated to Germany?

But the necessity for making Ireland a separate nation some
people find in our ill-treatment of her, and in the failure of
coercion. We have let Scotland have her schools and Church   20
to her mind, says Sir Lyon Playfair, we have not let Ireland;
therefore we must make Ireland a separate nation! The Northern States could not go on ruling the South by coercion, says
Mr. Bryce; therefore we must make Ireland a separate nation!
But the North did not give the South a national Parliament;   25
Scotland has not a national Parliament. The course taken has
not been to make them separate nations. Scotland had the just
and due control of her own affairs left to her; the South was
suffered to resume such control. This, then, is what the analogy
requires for Ireland, this and this only; the just and due con- 30
trol of her own affairs.

Why should a national Parliament be the only possible cure
for Irish discontent? Read Madame de Sévigné's letters from
Brittany in 1675. Four thousand soldiers were quartered on
the province, the Parliament had been banished, men were   35
broken on the wheel and hanged by scores; the population was
seething with turbulence and hatred. What has changed Brit-

tany—separate institutions? No, but a rational and equitable system of government.

Twenty years after Madame de Sévigné wrote, Duke Hamilton was praising Scotland to William III., and the King answered him, "My lord, I only wish it was a hundred thousand miles off, and that you was King of it!" What has changed Scotland—a separate Parliament? No, but a rational and equitable system of government.

And this is what the awakening mind of the country demands for Ireland. Not that we should give her a separate Parliament, but that we should seriously engage and set ourselves to give her a rational and equitable system of government. Lord Salisbury's bad and arbitrary temper (I mean, of course, as a politician, a home politician) is as great a misfortune to the country as Lord Randolph Churchill's intriguing. A separate Parliament for Ireland is a dangerous plunge into the unknown, and not necessary; but not necessary on condition only that we do really at last give Ireland a rational and equitable system of government; and Lord Salisbury can talk of nothing but coercion. Let us refuse a separate Parliament for Ireland with all firmness; but with equal firmness let us insist on the condition which alone justifies our refusal. Lord Hartington has a good temper (I mean, again, as a politician) and is no intriguer; Mr. Goschen has made local government his special study. They may be trusted, I hope, to make the necessary refusal firmly, and the necessary engagement emphatically. Nothing less will satisfy that which it is indispensable to satisfy, the mind of the country.

The passionate supporters of Mr. Gladstone in his operations are the political Dissenters and the Radical workmen in the great towns. I agree with Mr. Labouchere that aristocracies are not, in general, the best of guides in politics. But I have too much respect for his undoubted lucidity to believe him capable of really thinking the political Dissenters and the Radical working men to be on a question like that of Ireland any better guides, or even so good. They know little and prize little beyond the one their dissent, the other their union for trade or politics. In the past they would have applauded Cromwell's dealings with Ireland, or William the Third's, as they applaud Mr. Gladstone's now. It is on the country as a whole, and on the mind of the country, that we must rely.

I am, Sir, your obedient servant,   5
MATTHEW ARNOLD

After the Elections

Sir,—When I was leaving England two months ago you printed a letter from me on the Irish question. In my letter I expressed the conviction that the country was minded to reject Mr. Gladstone's Irish policy, but also to give the Irish the due control of their own affairs.

I write now from the United States, where the conviction that Mr. Gladstone would be victorious has been universal. Everything favourable to him has been current here; nothing unfavourable. However, my faith in the country which, with all its shortcomings, has yet more of solid political sense than any other country has been justified. Mr. Gladstone is defeated. The American newspapers are now crying out that the defeat is but momentary; that his speedy and complete success is certain. Mr. T. P. Gill writes to them that "the situation looks first-rate;" Mr. John Morley predicts that "within a year Mr. Gladstone's Irish proposals will carry with them Parliament and the country;" Mr. Gladstone exults that he has "the civilized world" with him.

All this confidence would be more impressive if its entertainers had not been equally confident of Mr. Gladstone's success in his late appeal to the country. They were wrong in their confidence then; why should they be right in their confidence now? But in a matter of this gravity one cannot be too prudent. Let us see, then, how the case really stands now that the elections are over.

And, first, as to the unanimity of the civilized world in Mr. Gladstone's favour. This would be important if true. I suppose in no country is the unanimity in his favour stronger than in the United States. And yet, even here, if you weigh opinions instead of counting them, the balance of opinion is against Mr. Gladstone's Irish policy. High intelligence and wide knowledge are rare everywhere; they are rare in America. Moreover, it is notorious that in no country do the newspapers so little represent the best mind of the country as they do here. But yet, even here, whenever you meet with a man of high intelligence and wide knowledge, you will almost certainly find him a disbeliever in the wisdom of Mr. Gladstone's Irish policy. "I admire Mr. Gladstone," he will probably say, "but I think he is making a mistake in Ireland." I have myself found but one stanch supporter here of Mr. Gladstone's Irish policy whom I should call a man of high intelligence and wide knowledge—Mr. Godkin, the well-known editor of the *Evening Post* and the *Nation*. And Mr. Godkin is an Irishman.

The general American public knows that over here the several States have the control of their own affairs, and that Ireland has been badly governed. It hears that Mr. Gladstone proposes to give to Ireland Home Rule. It inquires no further, but says,—"Mr. Gladstone is right; by all means let Ireland have Home Rule." The Americans are glad to be able safely to do a pleasure to the Irish, who live among them in large numbers and have great influence on elections and journalism. This is the main motive. Some ill will there may be in the masses, some pleasure in abetting embarrassments to a country which unaccountably goes on attracting more of the world's attention and interest than "the greatest nation on earth." But the main motive is the temptation to do the Irish a pleasure safely. The weighty opinion is not that of the general public who yield to this temptation; it is that of men who resist it and who look deeper into the matter. Of these serious people in America the opinion is, I repeat, against Mr. Gladstone, and I strongly suspect that the same thing is true of the rest of "the civilized world" also.

Nevertheless, the Americans do sincerely think, one and all, that the Irish ought to have the control of their own local affairs. They cannot understand its being disputed. The same feeling prevails on the Continent of Europe. And, therefore,

I return to the second point of my former letter—that the English nation is now minded, at the same time that it rejects Mr. Gladstone's policy, to give the Irish the due control of their own affairs.

5   The newpapers here keep repeating Mr. Gladstone's declaration that his principle is "to give Ireland an effective government by Irishmen." But this is, I believe, as much the principle of the English nation as of Mr. Gladstone. The question is, how can it be properly done? Mr. Gladstone says,

10   "By establishing a legislative body in Ireland for the management of exclusively Irish affairs." Change one word in this, for "body" read "machinery," and you pass from what is supremely dangerous to what is supremely expedient. A legislative body in Ireland means a national Irish Parliament. With

15   the history of Ireland, and the character and bent of Irishmen before our eyes, any prudent man can see the dangers from such a Parliament. Place what restrictions upon it you will, it will, by the law of its nature, be for ever striving to pose as an independent Parliament; to make Ireland count as

20   an independent nation. The case is precisely parallel with that of the South over here. If a Southern Congress had been conceded, you might have guarded your concession by what restrictions you pleased, but it would still have been a perpetual source of danger. The remembrance of past enmity, the

25   traditions of the political talents and weight of men like Clay and Calhoun, would inevitably have made a Southern Congress always seek to pose as an independent Parliament, to erect the South into an independent nation.

What the Americans did, therefore, was not to establish

30   in the South a legislative body for the management of local affairs, but a legislative machinery. They let the localities manage their own affairs. In this there was great advantage and no danger. And this is what we have to do in Ireland.

A legislative machinery by which the localities can manage

35   their own affairs is as much wanting in Great Britain as in Ireland. Even that basis of all local government, a municipal machinery, is wanting. We have isolated municipalities in towns; but the country as a whole in regard to municipal

government is in the condition of France before the Revolution. This is because our people, being conservative, and both
they and our aristocracy moderate in temper, the existing state
of things has worked on without our feeling its defects to be
intolerable. Local government culminates in local Legislatures.   5
But our Parliament at Westminster has had to act both for
the localities and for the nation; it is, to use the American
terms, Congress and State Legislatures in one. On the whole,
Parliament has done, both in England and in Scotland, what
the majority wanted. Its size is now unwieldy, its work is un-   10
wieldy; moreover, we are without a safeguard and an education which organized local government affords to those who
possess it; there is great need to organize it for us also.

But the need to organize it in Ireland is most urgent of all.
For undoubtedly the Parliament at Westminster has not been   15
that tolerable though imperfect substitute to Ireland for local
Legislatures which it has been to England and Scotland. It has
not done what the majority in Ireland wanted, it has done
what either the minority in Ireland wanted, or the British
Philistine. The situation is only made hopeless by denying this   20
or by shutting our eyes to it. Ireland is treated, say many, precisely like England and Scotland. And they say this with the Established Churches of England and Scotland before their eyes;
with the Universities of Oxford and Cambridge before their
eyes, Edinburgh and Glasgow. Of all details of local govern-   25
ment, where what takes place in Ireland differs widely from
what takes place in Great Britain, they may be ignorant; but
what is done in Church and education cannot surely be invisible to them. The allegation that Ireland is treated just
like England and Scotland must to Irishmen be almost mad-   30
dening. And therefore I have never inveighed against Mr.
Parnell and his followers, irritating as much in their language
and proceedings is, bad for Ireland as I think their policy,
firmly as I would resist it, rigorously as I would suppress, if
necessary, their seditious meetings and incendiary newspapers.   35
What they do is often most evil and dangerous, but I consider the provocation they have received. To have Parliament
treating the local affairs of Ireland as the Irish minority or the

British Philistine desire, and then to be told that Ireland is on the same footing as England and Scotland! It needs an Irishman of Burke's calibre to be a reasonable politician under such circumstances.

5 The dangers of this state of things are nearly as great as those of Mr. Gladstone's proposed plan of dealing with it. Of this the country is becoming conscious. It rejects Mr. Gladstone's plan, but it would give the Irish the control of their own local affairs. If the Conservatives cannot see this, if they

10 think they have only to keep order in Ireland, if they let things drift, then the present great opportunity is lost and we are given over to Cleon and his democracy.

If, on the contrary, the Conservatives do as the country wishes and produce a suitable plan of local self-government,

15 for Ireland first, then for Great Britain also, the situation, to borrow Mr. T. P. Gill's phrase, "looks first-rate." To establish such a plan the Unionists can work in perfect concert with Lord Salisbury. It matters little whether their leaders enter the Government or not, though the leaders of one con-

20 tingent of them should certainly not enter it without the leaders of the other. What is important is that the Unionists should not allow themselves to be divided, that they should determine resolutely to postpone all other questions to those of procedure and local government, and that on these, and

25 till these are settled, they should act with Lord Salisbury. The future will shape itself, will take care of itself. Sufficient for the day are the needs thereof.

Lord Salisbury may perfectly well frame a good plan of local self-government. But he must weigh his words as well

30 as his measures. He complains of those who say that he has nothing to propose but coercion. He ought, on the contrary, to be grateful to them. When he said that what Ireland required was governing he did not mean, he tells us, that all she required was a firm hand over her; he meant that she

35 needed good government of all kinds. Be it so. But his mode of expressing himself was unfortunate, and he ought to thank those who by seizing on his expression, call his attention to what is his side of weakness and danger. Perhaps all public

men have such a side, and we critics, were we in public life, should show ours fast enough. Lord Hartington's is some want of flexibility and fertility, Mr. Goschen's some want of sympathy with men's instinct of expansion, Mr. Chamberlain's some want of respect for the past. Lord Salisbury's is an imperious and scornful treatment of popular wishes. *Beati mansueti.* There never was a moment which tried tempers more than the present moment, or where more was to be gained by controlling them. What is the use of being irritated by the exaggeration, violence, and hatred of the Irish members, or by the lively nonsense of Mr. Labouchere? To good temper, good sense, and honesty all things are possible—to negotiate with the Irish members without intriguing with them or surrendering to them, and to make Mr. Labouchere laugh at his own nonsense. Do not let us assume that the Liberals of the nadir must of necessity find a lower nadir still, or that Mr. Gladstone must become more and more of a Cleon. Of Mr. Gladstone's recent performances it is indeed difficult to speak without grave and stern reprobation. The desperado burning his ship, the gambler doubling and trebling his stakes and mortgaging the future as luck goes against him, are the images which come irresistibly to one's mind. This Prime Minister's passionate tirades against a social fabric intrusted to his charge and against a union which it is his duty to maintain, have centupled the difficulties of mending either the one or the other. But wisdom, we are told, is justified of her children, and I suppose unwisdom must needs be justified of hers also. Yet of one with such gifts and graces as Mr. Gladstone I, for my part, will never despair. If Lord Salisbury produces a good scheme of local government for Ireland I should not be surprised if Mr. Gladstone supported it. The important thing is that Lord Salisbury should do as the country wishes and produce it.

I am, Sir, your obedient servant,

MATTHEW ARNOLD

July 24

Common Schools Abroad*

I think I have mentioned somewhere or other how much I was struck with a remark made to me more than twenty years ago at Rome by Cardinal Antonelli. I was visiting popular schools on the Continent. "So you have come to see our
5   schools," he said, "our popular schools; and many people would tell you that our popular education is nothing at all, or next to nothing, and that you will not be able to find anything worth reporting to your government about it. But you may tell your government this," continued the Cardinal: "that il-
10 literate as the Italian population is said to be, and I suppose is, yet, if you mix with the people at any festival and listen to their criticism of what they see,—*è brutto, è bello* (that's ugly, that's fine!),—you will find their criticism to be almost invariably right. And a people," he concluded, "of whom that
15 can be said must surely be allowed to have a certain sort of education."

    I thought of the stolid insensibility to ugliness, the inability to discern between good and evil where the beautiful is concerned, which so easily besets our Anglo-Saxon race, and I
20 acquiesced in what the Cardinal said. And at the same moment there rose to my memory the admirable sentence of a Moravian school-master in the seventeenth century, John Comenius, fixing the universal scope and aim for education. "The aim is," says Comenius, "to train generally all who are born men
25 to all which is human." Surely, to be offended by ugliness, to be delighted and refreshed by beauty, is eminently human; just as, on the other hand, it is a proof that our humanity

---

* Address delivered before the University of Pennsylvania.

is raw and undeveloped if we confound the two together or are indifferent to them. For we are then "in bondage," as Goethe says, "to the common and inferior"; out of that bondage we have to rise, and to know that, however general it may be around us, it is not less a bondage and an evil. 5

Almost immediately after my arrival the other day in this country, I happened to come across a speech by one of your politicians, whom I hope I may venture to call a friend of mine, Senator Hawley of Connecticut. He was praising the system of government of the United States, and he praised it 10 as being "a government of, by, and for the average man." I will not dispute whether or no in politics this is a benefit; but remember that in our education and culture it is precisely the slough of "the common and average and inferior thing," *das Gemeine*, as Goethe calls it, which we have to cast off and 15 rise out from. The common and average thing is our danger; it is comparatively easy of attainment, but no true friend of education will be satisfied so long as this is attained and nothing more.

In popular education, at present, "the common and average 20 thing" is the ability to read, write, and calculate, and the possession of a certain amount of what is called useful knowledge. This is what, in progressive nations, we nowadays expect the whole population to attain, and what they do attain. If we ask for the educative result of this, we shall find it to be, in 25 the main, that the whole population learns to read the newspapers, is formed by the newspapers. This is what modern popular education really leads up to, and many of us are apt to congratulate ourselves when this result has been achieved, and to think that here we have indeed a triumph of progress 30 and civilization.

But then, Cardinal Antonelli points to an illiterate people able to discern much more justly than the English, and probably than the Americans either, between beauty and ugliness, and suggests how far distant, therefore, the popular education 35 of our progressive nations still is from Comenius's ideal of a training of all to all which is human. And when our attention has once been called to the matter we may go further, and

consider how entirely the popular education actually now
given, in England at any rate, often fails to awaken and train
not only the sense of beauty, but the soul and feelings generally. Therefore, what interests me in popular training abroad,
5   which I have formerly had opportunities of studying, and have
again been studying very recently, is especially to ascertain
how far it succeeds in doing more than impart a certain amount
of useful knowledge, how far it reaches the soul and feelings,
and trains its pupils to that which is really human.

10   I am not sure to what extent your common schools in America resemble ours in their deficiencies; but I hope you will
listen to me while I mention some points in which the common schools of Germany and France seem to me to succeed
better than common schools in England in training their
15   pupils to what is really human. You will then be able to judge
for yourselves whether your common schools in America are
more in the case of our English schools, or in that of the
schools of France and Germany.

I will take first what is certainly a main agent in touching
20   man's soul and feelings—religion. In England, religion is excluded from the official programme of the popular schools.
If it is taught, it is taught outside of the official school-hours,
and subject to private and local regulation. Religious liberty,
it is said, requires this. If religion is taught at the public ex-
25   pense, what religion is it to be? If it is the religion of the
majority, the minority are aggrieved. Religion, therefore, must
not be a prescribed school matter at all.

Well, in Germany they no more hesitate to make the religion approved by the majority a school matter for fear the
30   minority should object, in the name of religious liberty, to
its being taught, than they hesitate to make the literature
approved by the majority a school matter, for fear the minority should object, in the name of intellectual liberty, to its
being taught. In German countries—for German Switzerland
35   is much the same as Germany in this respect—religion stands
as one of the foremost subjects of instruction in the popular
school. Instead of being, as in England, a subject not laid out
or noticed in official programmes, a subject which inspectors

and official people are told to avoid, it is a subject laid out with the greatest care, and in which inspectors examine with special diligence and interest.

In general, one may say that three religious denominations, and no more, are recognized in German schools,—the Evangelical or Protestant, the Catholic, and the Jewish. Between Catholics and Protestants the public authority deals, both in theory and in practice, with absolute fairness. There is no persecution and no proselytism. So fair is the action of the administration, so complete is the confidence of the people in its fairness, that in the lower classes of Evangelical or Catholic schools you not unfrequently find the Evangelical or the Catholic minority taking the religious instruction, by the parents' consent, along with the majority. In the upper classes, the law requires the minority in these mixed schools to be separated, and to receive religious instruction from teachers of their own communion.

With us the difficulty of including religion in the school programme is caused by the sects of Protestantism. Everybody knows how our Protestantism breaks into sects. There is an instructive list of them in "Whitaker's Almanack." One might say that amongst our Anglo-Saxon race a new sect often arose from the mere pleasure of making one. And these sects in England would cry out against a religious instruction based on the formularies of the established church, or in America, where you have no established church, of any one great body of Protestants; but throughout Protestant Germany the religious instruction in Protestant schools is based on the Lutheran catechism, the Evangelical hymn-book, and the Bible, and all denominations are expected to follow it. With us, the individual judges what degree of diversity among religionists renders separate religious instruction necessary; in Germany, the law.

I do not think that in Germany, where the spirit of sect has been less carefully cultivated than amongst ourselves, Protestants in general feel the obligatory religious instruction of the public school to be any hardship. I could not hear of any complaints on the subject. But I was very curious to learn

how the working classes in the German cities, who are said
to be greatly estranged from the Christian religion, took the
obligatory religious instruction of their children. In the capital
of Saxony, the country which is reported to be the stronghold

5   of socialism, I asked an inspector what proportion of the working classes he thought were socialist and opposed to the established religion. "At least two-thirds," he answered. "Well,
then," said I, "how do they like all this Lutheran religion for
their children?" "They do not like it at all," he replied, "but

10 they have to submit to it." He added that the religious instruction did the children good; that the mothers in general
could perceive this, and some even of the secularist fathers.

I spoke on the same subject, when I was at Berlin, with a
man whose name will be received with respect in any univer-

15 sity,—Professor Mommsen, the celebrated historian. I told him
how surprised I had been to find, after all I had heard of the
decay of religion in Protestant Germany, how important a
place it still held in the programme of the public schools. He
agreed that it did so, and he, too, thought that this was a

20 good thing. He said that the actual religious instruction given
was too dogmatic, and that it was a fault of the persons in
power that they made it more and more strictly so. But in
general, he thought the school instruction in religion a good
thing. He quoted to me words of Goethe which I remem-

25 bered: "He who has art and science, has religion." But he
quoted them with an addition which I had forgotten: "He
who has not art and science, let him have religion." The popular school is for those, he said, who have not art or science;
to leave religion out of its programme would therefore be a

30 great mistake.

Imagine, in a country where government is, as Senator
Hawley declares, of, by, and for the average man, imagine
recommending that a religious instruction should be imposed
upon the common school because the classes frequenting it,

35 not having art or science, require religion! Every term in the
proposition is to the average man either unmeaning or else
offensive. But I doubt whether the religious feeling of England
would not be as much shocked as the democratic feeling of

America by the notion of teaching religion in the popular schools as a thing which uncultivated people require, though cultivated people do not. And therefore, while the spirit of sect makes it in one way impracticable to introduce religion into the programme of our popular schools in England, the spirit of religion makes it impracticable in another.

Nevertheless, I wish to report things as I have actually found them, and as they are. The religious instruction in the popular schools of German countries seems to me one of the best and most effective parts of the school work. I have had a long experience of school-teachers and school-children, but seldom have I seen teachers and children to more advantage than once when in a Saxon school I heard them dealing with a theological problem raised in the Lutheran catechism,—the question in what sense men can be said to be tempted of God. In spite of the necessary ambiguity of terms which attends all such questions, in spite of their perhaps necessary insolubleness, they are eternally interesting when handled with thought and earnestness; and so they were handled in this instance.

But if one might have doubts as to the profitable effect, in the common school, of these theological questions, one could have none as to the good effect of what is, after all, the chief and the best part of the religious instruction in German schools: the learning by heart of Bible sayings and parables, and of the Evangelical hymns. I lay stress on the hymns in particular, because such hymns are a form of literature of which I keenly feel the defects, and of which I have more than once spoken disparagingly. The German hymns, however, are better than ours; and no one who watched the serious and touched expression which often came over a child's face at a moving verse, could doubt that here the soul and feelings were reached in a way of which we get no experience with the secular programme and with the useful knowledge of our own common schools.

It is said that the alienation of the working classes in Germany from the Christian religion proves that all the religious instruction of the popular schools is of very little use. I believe that the alienation is exaggerated. But even admitting it

to be as great as any one chooses to suppose, I feel sure that
on the religious German nature sentiments and impulses raised
by the religious instruction of school often and often continue to work, even though from positive Christianity a man
5   may have become quite estranged.

Well, then, in the religious instruction of the German
schools I find an educative force of much value, which in our
English common schools is wanting and perhaps impossible.
You will know whether it is wanting in your schools also.

10   But curiously enough I unexpectedly found in France likewise, in a public school, a type of religious instruction which
seemed to me of high interest and value, and which also would
be in the public schools of England quite impossible.

Not that religion holds the place in the programmes of
15   the French public schools which it holds in those of Germany.
Twenty years ago, when I had last seen the French schools,
it did, but it does so no longer. The chaplains are gone from
the public schools, and religion is gone from their programmes;
it may no longer be taught in the public school-rooms out of
20   school hours even. True, moral and civic instruction has a
place in the school programmes, and regulations and high functionaries say that the schools are to teach the existence of a
God, "in accordance with that spiritualist philosophy which
is the glory of Descartes and of France." But in Paris, the
25   center of that great development of popular education which
undoubtedly is now going forward in France, in Paris the municipality, which provides and maintains the popular schools,
will not have the name of God introduced in their teaching,
and has even sanctioned a school manual altogether hostile to
30   religion and contemptuous of it. It has not been possible, indeed, to bring the book into use; but the action of the Paris
municipality, in regard to religion, is undoubtedly violent and
blameworthy. That municipality has a sincere zeal for instructing the people, and from jobbery and corruption it is,
35   I am told, perfectly free. But it has pushed forward school
establishment so fast, and on such a scale as to expense, that
the complaints of its extravagance are loud; and so intemperately as to religion, that it outruns the wishes of even that

not very religious population, the population of Paris. The religious teaching orders, banished from the public schools, have been enabled, wonderful to relate, to give to their own schools—which are now maintained by private contributions only, and that in a country where voluntary effort is supposed 5 not to flourish—an immense development, so that these orders now actually educate, in private schools, one-third of the school-children of Paris.

As to the moral and civic instruction of the French schools, it seemed to me to be poor stuff, and I saw no signs of its 10 touching the soul or mind of anybody receiving it. Moral teaching for young people, except when it is indirectly conveyed in stories, as in Miss Edgeworth's immortal "Parents' Assistant," is in general dull; and when it is conveyed in stories, the story may interest, but the moral is apt to be lost sight 15 of. As to civic teaching, the most remarkable specimen of it which I met with I will mention, for it is worth mentioning. "Who gives you," said the questioner to the children, "all the benefits you are enjoying: these fine school-buildings with all their appliances, your instructors, this beautiful city where 20 you live, everything in which the comfort and security of your life consists?" I was attentive, for I said to myself: Surely the child must be going to answer what children have from time immemorial been taught to answer to the like question, "God gives me all this"; and yet the name of God must not 25 be used in a school of the Paris municipality. But the civic instruction proved equal to the occasion, and a legitimate answer came from the child: "It is our country gives us all this." *Eh bien, c'est le pays!* The force of civic instruction, I think, could hardly go further. 30

All this seems futile enough; but I am bound to record, too, that in a French training college I found, in connexion with the teaching of pedagogy, what was really a religious instruction of the most serious and effective kind. I am disposed to say that I should call it, in view of our modern situation and 35 needs, the best religious instruction which I have ever yet heard. The college is at Fontenay-aux-Roses, a few miles out of Paris. It was instituted a year or two ago by the French

government in order to train directresses and teachers for the
normal colleges for lay school-mistresses, which are now to be
established throughout France. At the head of it was placed
a man between sixty and seventy years old, who was originally
5   a Protestant pastor and afterwards an inspector-general of primary schools, M. Pécaut. The choice was indeed an admirable
one. M. Pécaut has the very gifts requisite for the delicate and
difficult post to which he has been called. Whoever wishes to
find a success achieved in the teaching of that much-talked-of
10   but in general most unsatisfactory thing, undogmatic religion,
should go to Fontenay and hear M. Pécaut in his morning hour
with his students. He is fortunate in their quality; the Frenchwoman, under good teaching, makes one of the best students
and school-mistresses in the world: so quick is she, so clear,
15   with such perfect presence of mind, such a keen and true sense
for excellence. Most of the girls at Fontenay are Catholics, and
attend Catholic service on Sundays. But I heard them taking
with their director, paragraph by paragraph, Bishop Dupanloup's book on school, "L'École," a book in which all sorts
20   of questions of religion in connexion with education are
raised; and really these girls were led to treat them in the
same large and free, but at the same time tolerant, sympathetic, and pious, spirit, in which M. Pécaut treated them himself. A German expert in schools, who has lately been report-
25   ing to his government on female education in France, is as
much struck with admiration at Fontenay and its inmates as
I am.

Now here again we have a success which in England would
hardly be possible. A government setting up a training college
30   like Fontenay, with a man like M. Pécaut at the head of it,
and with a religious instruction like that given by M. Pécaut,
would run the risk of being accused of wishing to start a new
religion of its own; and no English government in our day
would ever, I suppose, run such a risk as that!

35   I pass on now to other matters of teaching. Here too I had,
of course, our English popular schools constantly in my mind
while I was observing the foreign schools, and the comparison
thus established was highly instructive. In general I thought

the methods of teaching better in the foreign schools than with us, and the results of the teaching better. And they are better because the teachers are better trained.

To take the scientific branches of instruction first. Anybody can construct a pretentious and showy school programme. Such a programme is the habitual instrument of unsound schools and superficial teachers. The limitations of a programme are often a proof of wisdom. In arithmetic and mathematics a hasty observer might at first, perhaps, be disposed to wonder that the common schools abroad, and particularly in Germany, do not go further and faster than they do. But in my opinion they prove the goodness of their methods just by not going too far and too fast, by directing their efforts above all to making sure that the average learner shall master every step of the process which he is following. I take myself to have been barely an average learner in arithmetic and mathematics, and I have the most distinct recollection that in these matters I was taken too far and too fast. Either the rule was propounded to us as a kind of trick, and then we had to bring sums right by following it, whereby we got no real insight into arithmetical principles at all; or else the principle of the rule was explained, but not sufficiently developed and dwelt upon for the average learner, who was too rapidly hurried forward before he had fully grasped it.

Again, the use of the blackboard and of oral teaching for arithmetic will often in German schools strike an English observer as excessive. It seems as if a German child in his schooltime was never to be left to work sums quietly on his slate by himself; but the sum is put on the blackboard and one child after another is called up to bear part in working it, with continual questioning as to his reasons for what he does. This certainly takes time; but the teacher's aim and endeavor is, not to make his pupil bring sums right (as the phrase is) in as many rules as possible, but to train him to understand the principles of arithmetic.

In teaching natural science and physics, the Germans show a like care not to outrun their scholar, to insure his comprehending all that is said and shown to him. I heard a lesson on

electricity given to a class of girls in a Berlin school. I should
call it an ambitious lesson in one sense; namely, that it went
much beyond anything that I have known attempted in a popular school for girls in England. But what I felt, as I listened
5   to it, was how thoroughly the lesson was within the girls'
comprehension, and how I myself, if I had been taught in this
fashion, could have been interested in electricity, though I have
no bent for studies of this kind. The answering of the class
proved how the girls were interested by their teacher's treat-
10 ment of his subject, and how intelligently they followed it.

But the literary branches of the instruction were what interested me most. These are eminently the humanities, these
are what train us to all which is human; and I find occurring
frequently in my notes on the foreign schools this entry: *the*
15 *children human.* I can best explain what I meant by saying
frankly what is the impression generally made upon me by
the literary performances—reading, reciting, foreign languages,
literary history and criticism—in popular or common schools.
Often I have to praise the performance as good; but I feel
20 almost always bound in conscience to add secretly to myself:
good, considering the class from which the children come,
considering that they come from the uncultivated class.

In fact, for the production of good reading and reciting,
really good reading and reciting, reading and reciting with
25 proper intonation, pronunciation, and expression, it seems requisite generally to have been brought up in a certain atmosphere of refinement, in the company of people whose speech
has these characters. Of course, raw people may call their
own speech proper if they choose, but the good judges will
30 not go with them, and this is a case which turns on what "the
judicious," as Aristotle says, would decide.

For foreign languages, again, some advantage of travel, of
mixing with foreigners, is in general necessary, if proficiency
is to be attained; and this advantage can seldom fall to the lot
35 of those from whom the common schools are mostly recruited.

For conversance, once more, of any genuine sort with literary history or criticism, to have lived with cultivated people
and to have heard their talk and their judgments seems in

general necessary. There may be individuals of genius who have such astonishing natural aptitudes for declamation, or languages, or literature, that they seem to be self-made; but in general, good reading and reciting, and proficiency in foreign languages, and conversance with literary history and criticism, are produced as I have said, or, if they are produced in a class of learners otherwise, then we conclude that there must have been very superior teaching.

I repeat, therefore, that when I call the reading, or the declaiming, or the French, or the literature in a common school *good*, I usually mean good when all due allowances have been made, good considering that the children come from an uncultivated class. And I can hardly remember a case where I have not had to make such a secret reservation in praising these matters in English common schools, except now and then when I have found myself in presence of an eminent and charming natural gift for declamation.

But in popular schools on the Continent of Europe, I have found whole classes whose reading and reciting might be called good without any such allowance or reservation whatever, called good just as absolutely as we can call reading and reciting of children of the cultivated classes good; reading and reciting with proper intonation, pronunciation, and expression, and which it was a pleasure to listen to. I recall particularly the reading and reciting of Lamartine's poetry by a class of girls in a primary school in Paris, and the reading of Schiller's "Wilhelm Tell" by a class of boys in a primary school at Lucerne.

Foreign languages are not in general obligatory matters in popular schools abroad, and it is not judicious, I think, in schools of that kind to make them obligatory. But in the popular schools in Hamburg English is obligatory, owing probably to the commercial intercourse of Hamburg with England; and in the popular schools of German Switzerland French is obligatory, because Switzerland is a bilingual nation. In Hamburg one could praise the performance of an English class, in Zurich that of a French class, without any mental reservation, just as one might praise the performance of a French

class in a good and expensive school for young ladies in England. The performance was not limited to a few pages of
vocabulary and exercises, as in an elementary school in England; the class turned English or French fluently into Ger-
5   man, and German fluently into English or French; they knew
the grammar of their foreign language, and the way to pronounce it.

Finally, in literary history and criticism, I found in the
common schools abroad entire classes familiar with the biog-
10   raphy of the great authors their countrymen; capable of comparing and discussing their productions, and of indicating the
sources whence these productions draw their power to move
and delight us. I found classes trained to that which is human—to follow still the formula of Comenius—to this remark-
15   able extent, a thing unexampled, so far as my experience goes,
in popular schools at home.

I cannot enable you to hear the reading, or reciting, or the
French and English, of these foreign classes, and thus to make
a comparison of it with what you have in America. But I can
20   give you two instances to show you, first, what degree of
grammatical proficiency in a foreign language I have found
in a common school abroad, and next what degree of proficiency in literary history and criticism.

Visiting one day the French class in a school at Zurich, I
25   asked the master what his pupils were doing. He handed to
me the book he was using, and went on with his lesson. His
subject was the place of the pronominal objects in a French
sentence. Many people who think they know French well
are not sound on this point, though it is one where no French
30   person will ever make a mistake. In a popular school in England, to deal with such a point at all would be ridiculous.
The point is that in an indicative sentence the pronoun of the
first or second person, used datively, always precedes the
pronoun of the third person used accusatively: *on me le donne.*
35   But if both pronouns are in the third person, the accusative
comes first: *on le lui donne.* There are further rules as to the
order of the pronouns in imperative sentences, both affirma-
tive and negative. The point is rather a nice one for a for-

eigner who has not the instinct of custom to guide him; but
again and again the Zurich pupils, to my surprise, displayed
their firm hold upon the rules in question, and applied them
unerringly. This is a matter of detail, but to any one who
knows what common schools are, and what modern languages 5
in them are, it will have great significance.

My second instance has a wider range. At Trachenberge,
near Dresden, I entered the common school with the inspector, and found the upper class at their reading lesson. The inspector took the book; the children were reading a well- 10
known ballad by Goethe, "Der Sänger," and he began to
question them about Goethe's life. They answered as no children in a similar school in England would answer about the
life of Milton or of Walter Scott. Then the ballad was read,
and the children were asked to compare it with a ballad by 15
Schiller which they had been reading lately, "Der Graf von
Habsburg." They were asked what gave to each of these ballads its charm; what the Middle Age was, and whence is
the attraction it has for us; what chivalry was, what the career of a minstrel, and so on. They answered in a way in which 20
only children of the cultivated class, children who had had all
manner of advantageous influences to mold them, would answer in England; and which led me to write in my note-book
the remark which I have already mentioned: the children
human. 25

You will judge whether you have in your common schools
a like soundness of performance in these matters; whether you
really have it, I mean, and are not merely said by patriots
and newspapers to have it. I do not think it has much to do
with the form of government. One learns, as one grows older, 30
to assign causes with more and more caution. I do not see
any necessary connexion between government of, by, and
for the average man, and an educational superiority such as
I have been describing.

No, that superiority is due to a more direct and simple 35
cause. That cause has powerfully affected and benefited popular education in Germany for a long time past, and is now
showing its power for good in France also. It has expression

well given to it by an article in the constitution of Canton
Zurich, which declares that "there shall be an *organische Verbindung*, an organic connexion, between all the schools of the
Canton, from the lowest to the highest." It is this connexion,
5 this vital connexion of popular with higher instruction, which
produces its superiority.

America has been severely blamed by foreigners,—by foreigners I do not mean Englishmen; I never speak of Englishmen as foreigners to America, nor of Americans as foreigners
10 to England,—but by foreigners America has been severely
blamed for contenting herself generally with instituting a
good public system of common schools, and leaving intermediate and higher instruction to chance. When one sees colleges such as Harvard, and Yale, and Columbia, one may be
15 inclined to say that in America higher instruction seems able
to take good care of itself. But the question will still remain:
What connexion does it hold with popular education, what
influence does it exercise upon *that?* In England we inherit
from the past splendid seats of higher instruction, where some
20 great branches of knowledge are undeniably taught with high
success; but our higher instruction has no relations whatever
with our popular instruction. In Germany, France, and Switzerland the case is otherwise.

There the Ministry of Public Instruction represents the
25 community, in its collective and corporate character, dealing
with education as one whole. Higher schools and universities
are for the most part state institutions. With them the minister
is most directly concerned. Often he is himself a personage
distinguished in the higher instruction; thus Guizot and Cousin
30 have been education ministers in France, Wilhelm von Humboldt in Prussia. At any rate, he is always surrounded by representatives of the higher instruction, and in close communication
with them.

The popular school is naturally and properly a municipal
35 thing. The minister's dealings with it will be less direct than
with the higher schools. But he has the supervision of it, he
has the responsibility for its being kept efficient and complying
with the school-law of the country. Above all, he has under

his direct care the training colleges, where the teachers of
the popular schools are formed.

Now observe what effect this naturally has upon popular
education. The minister is, I say, often a man who himself
has borne a leading part in the highest and best instruction of 5
the country,—in that which is most opposed to charlatanism,
vulgarity, and unsoundness in learning, least apt to be satisfied
with the common and average and inferior thing. At all events,
he is surrounded by representatives of that higher instruction,
he is constantly feeling their influence, he has them at his dis- 10
position to be consulted and used at any moment. In all those
questions so important to the popular school, questions as to
studies, methods, school-books, examinations, he takes their advice. They are his delegates and commissaries in his dealings
with the popular schools. In the training colleges a certain pro- 15
portion only of the teachers may be taken from the popular
school; the rest must be representatives of the higher instruction. The minister can also depute special professors to give important parts of the training-college teaching; in France especially this is done. At Fontenay, which I have already 20
mentioned, and at Auteuil, the training college of Paris for
school-masters, I found the young men and women thus coming under some of the very best and most stimulative instruction to be had now in all France.

You can understand how this action of superior instruc- 25
tion upon the teachers of the common schools must affect
them; how it must tend to raise their work above that "common and average thing" which the school work of institutions
fed from the least cultivated classes, and taught by instructors
drawn from those classes, would of itself tend to become. 30
You will understand how it produces results upon the training of the scholars of the common school which again and
again moved me, as I have told you, to write in my notes:
"The children *human*."

In England things are very different. There no branch of 35
education is publicly administered except popular education.
The education minister is charged with one branch of national education only, and that the lowest and simplest, as it

is thought. When, moreover, the English Government found itself at last compelled to assume the responsibility for popular education, it approached it from the point of view of the politician rather than that of the knower and lover of edu-
5   cation. Popular instruction had to be recognized as a public charge; it must necessarily be costly, and the great thing, therefore, was to satisfy the House of Commons and the public mind that the public had value for its money. Hence our system of *payment by results*, as it is called,—a vicious system
10   educationally. But then our education minister does not see education as a whole; he is not surrounded by representatives of the higher instruction, men who look to the effect on education of plans adopted in schools, not to the effect on the House of Commons. A friend of education, who can merely
15   urge interests of education against a plan for schools which is likely to please the House of Commons and the public mind, must feel that he is listened to with polite inattention. "It is all very fine," the minister is saying in his heart, "but my business is not to satisfy educationists; it is to satisfy the newspapers
20   and the House of Commons."

If we could have for education minister in England a man like Sir James Mackintosh or Mr. Hallam, and surround him with the representatives of all the higher instruction of the country, then we should have a minister living in an atmosphere
25   of what one may call *educational opinion*, and induced to give effect to it when the common schools and their studies are concerned. Such a minister we have never had in England, but in Germany and France they have; and the common schools of those countries have felt the benefit of it in their methods
30   and studies, in the training of their teachers and the humanization of their school-children.

Therefore I say that what is most to be desired for the common school is an *organic connexion*, to borrow the phrase of the Zurich Constitution, with higher instruction,—a vivifying
35   relation and contact with it. But for this purpose public instruction must be organized as one whole. We have not yet so organized it in England, and I do not think that in America you have yet done so either, although in your State govern-

ments you have the very machinery best suited for the purpose, a machinery which is lacking at present to us in Great Britain no less than in Ireland, where its absence attracts just now universal attention. Intermediate and higher instruction would themselves, in my opinion, be great gainers by such an organi-   5
zation. But the great gainer of all would be popular education. I can conceive no worthier ambition than that of training all who are born in a country like this of yours to all which is human. But it will not be done unless we can impart to popular instruction the contempt for charlatanism and vulgarity,   10
the sound standard of excellence, by which all serious higher instruction is characterized. Bring, therefore, popular instruction in America into organic connexion with higher instruc-
tion. Universities and higher schools would do a gracious, a patriotic, and a wise thing by advocating this; and let me say   15
that such advocacy could come from no university with more grace and more force than from the university of Franklin.

Sainte-Beuve

SAINTE-BEUVE, Charles Augustin (1804–1869), the most notable
critic of our time, was born at Boulogne-sur-Mer on 23d
December 1804. He was a posthumous child,—his father, a
native of Picardy, and controller of town-dues at Boulogne,
5 having married in this same year, at the age of fifty-two,
and died before the birth of his son. The father was a man
of literary tastes, and used to read, like his son, pencil in hand;
his copy of the Elzevir edition of Virgil, covered with his
notes, was in his son's possession, and is mentioned by him in
10 one of his poems. Sainte-Beuve's mother was half English,—
her father, a mariner of Boulogne, having married an Englishwoman. The little Charles Augustin was brought up by his
mother, who never remarried, and an aunt, his father's sister, who lived with her. They were poor, but the boy, hav-
15 ing learnt all he could at his first school at Boulogne, persuaded his mother to send him, when he was near the age of
fourteen, to finish his education at Paris. He boarded with
a M. Landry, and had for a fellow-boarder and intimate friend
Charles Neate, afterwards fellow of Oriel College and member
20 of parliament for the city of Oxford. From M. Landry's
boarding-house he attended the classes, first of the Collége
Charlemagne, and then of the Collége Bourbon, winning the
head prize for history at the first, and for Latin verse at the
second. In 1823 he began to study medicine, and continued
25 the study with diligence and interest for nearly four years,
attending lectures on anatomy and physiology and walking
the hospitals. But meanwhile a Liberal newspaper, the *Globe*,
was founded in 1824 by M. Dubois, one of Sainte-Beuve's
old teachers at the Collége Charlemagne. M. Dubois called

to his aid his former pupil, who, now quitting the study of
medicine, contributed historical and literary articles to the
Globe, among them two, which attracted the notice of Goethe, on Victor Hugo's *Odes and Ballads*. These articles led
to a friendship with Victor Hugo and to Sainte-Beuve's con-   5
nexion with the romantic school of poets, a school never entirely suited to his nature. In the *Globe* appeared also his
interesting articles on the French poetry of the 16th century,
which in 1828 were collected and published in a volume, and
followed by a second volume containing selections from Ron-   10
sard. In 1829 he made his first venture as a poet with the
Vie, Poésies, et Pensées de Joseph Delorme. His own name
did not appear; but Joseph Delorme, that "Werther in the
shape of Jacobin and medical student," as Guizot called him,
was the Sainte-Beuve of those days himself. About the same   15
time was founded the *Revue de Paris*, and Sainte-Beuve contributed the opening article, with Boileau for its subject. In
1830 came his second volume of poems, the *Consolations*, a
work on which Sainte-Beuve looked back in later life with a
special affection. To himself it marked and expressed, he said,   20
that epoch of his life to which he could with most pleasure
return, and at which he could like best that others should see
him. But the critic in him grew to prevail more and more and
pushed out the poet. In 1831 the *Revue des Deux Mondes* was
founded in rivalry with the *Revue de Paris*, and from the first   25
Sainte-Beuve was one of the most active and important contributors. He brought out his novel of *Volupté* in 1834, his
third and last volume of poetry, the *Pensées d'Août*, in 1837.
He himself thought that the activity which he had in the meanwhile exercised as a critic, and the offence which in some   30
quarters his criticism had given, were the cause of the less
favourable reception which this volume received. He had long
meditated a book on Port Royal. At the end of 1837 he quitted France, accepting an invitation from the academy of Lausanne, where in a series of lectures his work on Port Royal   35
came into its first form of being. In the summer of the next
year he returned to Paris to revise and give the final shape
to his work, which, however, was not completed for twenty

years. In 1840 M. Cousin, then minister of public instruction, appointed him one of the keepers of the Mazarin Library, an appointment which gave him rooms at the library, and, with the money earned by his pen, made him for the first time in
5 his life easy in his circumstances, so that, as he afterwards used to say, he had to buy rare books in order to spend his income. A more important consequence of his easier circumstances was that he could study freely and largely. He returned to Greek, of which a French schoolboy brings from
10 his *lycée* no great store. With a Greek teacher, M. Pantasides, he read and re-read the poets in the original, and thus acquired, not, perhaps, a philological scholar's knowledge of them, but a genuine and invaluable acquaintance with them as literature. His activity in the *Revue des Deux Mondes* continued, and
15 articles on Homer, Theocritus, Apollonius of Rhodes, and Meleager were fruits of his new Greek studies. He wrote also a very good article in 1844 on the Italian poet Leopardi; but in general his subjects were taken from the great literature which he knew best, that of his own country,—its litera-
20 ture both in the past and in the contemporary present. Seven volumes of "Portraits," contributed to the *Revue de Paris* and the *Revue des Deux Mondes*, exhibit his work in the years from 1832 to 1848, a work constantly increasing in range and value. In 1844 he was elected to the French Academy as suc-
25 cessor to Casimir Delavigne, and was received there at the beginning of 1845 by Victor Hugo.

From this settled and prosperous condition the revolution of February 1848 dislodged him. In March of that year was published an account of secret-service money distributed in
30 the late reign, and Sainte-Beuve was put down as having received the sum of one hundred francs. The smallness of the sum would hardly seem to suggest corruption; it appears probable that the money was given to cure a smoky chimney in his room at the Mazarin Library, and was wrongly entered
35 as secret-service money. But Sainte-Beuve, who piqued himself on his independence and on a punctilious delicacy in money matters, was indignant at the entry, and thought the proceedings of the minister of public instruction and his of-

ficials, when he demanded to have the matter sifted, tardy
and equivocal. He resigned his post at the Mazarin and accepted an offer from the Belgian Government of a chair
of French literature in the university of Liége. There he gave
the series of lectures on Chateaubriand and his contemporaries 5
which was afterwards (in 1861) published in two volumes.
He liked Liége, and the Belgians would have been glad to
keep him; but the attraction of Paris carried him back there
in the autumn of 1849. Louis Napoleon was then president.
Disturbance was ceasing; a time of settled government, which 10
lasted twenty years and corresponds with the second stage
of Sainte-Beuve's literary activity, was beginning. Dr. Véron,
the editor of the *Constitutionnel*, proposed to him that he
should supply that newspaper with a literary article for every
Monday; and thus the *Causeries du Lundi* were started. They 15
at once succeeded, and "gave the signal," as Sainte-Beuve himself says with truth, "for the return of letters." Sainte-Beuve
now lived in the small house in the Rue Mont-Parnasse (No.
11) which he occupied for the remainder of his life, and
where in 1850 his mother, from whom he seems to have 20
inherited his good sense, tact, and finesse, died at the age of
eighty-six. For three years he continued writing every Monday for the *Constitutionnel;* then he passed, with a similar
engagement, to the *Moniteur*. In 1851 his Monday articles
began to be published in volumes, and by 1862 formed a col- 25
lection in fifteen volumes; they afterwards were resumed under the title of *Nouveaux Lundis*, which now make a collection
of thirteen volumes more. In 1854 M. Fortoul nominated him
to the chair of Latin poetry at the College of France. His
first lecture there was received with interruptions and marks 30
of disapprobation by many of the students, displeased at his
adherence to the empire; at a second lecture the interruption
was renewed. Sainte-Beuve had no taste for public speaking
and lecturing; his *frontis mollities*, he said, unfitted him for
it. He was not going to carry on a war with a party of tur- 35
bulent students; he proposed to resign, and when the minister
would not accept his resignation of his professorship he resigned its emoluments. The *Étude sur Virgile*, a volume pub-

lished in 1857, contains what he had meant to be his first
course of lectures. He was still a titular official of public instruction; and in 1858 his services were called for by M.
Rouland, then minister of public instruction, as a lecturer
5   (*maître de conférences*) on French literature at the École
Normale Supérieure. This work he discharged with assiduity
and success for four years. In 1859 he was made commander
of the Legion of Honour, having twice previously to 1848
refused the cross. During the years of his official engagement
10   his Monday contributions to the *Moniteur* had no longer been
continuous; but in 1862 an arrangement was proposed by
which he was to return to the *Constitutionnel* and again supply an article there every Monday. He consented, at the age
of fifty-seven, to try this last pull, as he called it, this "dernier
15   coup de collier"; he resigned his office at the École Normale
and began the series of his *Nouveaux Lundis*. They show no
falling off in vigour and resource from the *Causeries*. But the
strain upon him of his weekly labour was great. "I am not
a *monsieur* nor a gentleman," he writes in 1864, "but a work-
20   man by the piece and by the hour." "I look upon myself as
a player forced to go on acting at an age when he ought to
retire, and who can see no term to his engagement." He had
reason to hope for relief. Except himself, the foremost literary men in France had stood aloof from the empire and
25   treated it with a hostility more or less bitter. He had not been
hostile to it: he had accepted it with satisfaction, and had
bestowed on its official journal, the *Moniteur*, the lustre of
his literature. The prince Napoleon and the princess Mathilde were his warm friends. A senatorship was mentioned;
30   its income of £1600 a year would give him opulence and
freedom. But its coming was delayed, and the strain upon
him continued for some time longer. When at last in April
1865 he was made senator, his health was already seriously
compromised. The disease of which he died, but of which the
35   doctors did not ascertain the presence until his body was
opened after his death—the stone—began to distress and dis-
able him. He could seldom attend the meetings of the senate;
the part he took there, however, on two famous occasions,

when the nomination of M. Renan to the College of France came under discussion in 1867 and the law on the press in the year following, provoked the indignation of the great majority in that conservative assembly. It delighted, however, all who "belonged," to use his own phrase, "to the diocese 5 of free thought"; and he gave further pleasure in this diocese by leaving at the beginning of 1869 the *Moniteur*, injudiciously managed by the Government and M. Rouher, and contributing to a Liberal journal, the *Temps*. His literary activity suffered little abatement, but the attacks of his mal- 10 ady, though borne with courage and cheerfulness, became more and more severe. Pain made him at last unable to sit to write; he could only stand or lie. He died in his house in the Rue Mont-Parnasse on the 13th of October 1869. He had inherited an income of four thousand francs a year from his 15 mother, and he left it six thousand; to the extent of eighty pounds a year and no further had literature and the senatorship enriched him. By his will he left directions that his funeral was to be without religious rites, quite simple, and with no speeches at the grave except a few words of thanks 20 from one of his secretaries to those present. There was a great concourse; the Paris students, who had formerly interrupted him, came now to do honour to him as a Liberal and a champion of free thought—a senator they could not but admit—undeniably, alas, a senator, but *oh, si peu!* Yet his own 25 account of himself is the best and truest,—an account which lays no stress on his Liberalism, no stress on his championship of free thought, but says simply: "Devoted to my profession as critic, I have tried to be more and more a good, and, if possible, an able workman." 30

The work of Sainte-Beuve divides itself into three portions —his poetry, his criticism before 1848, and his criticism after that year. His novel of *Volupté* may properly go with his poetry.

We have seen his tender feeling for his poetry, and he 35 always maintained that, when the "integrating molecule," the foundation of him as a man of letters, was reached, it would be found to have a poetic character. And yet he declares, too,

that it is never without a sort of surprise and confusion that
he sees his verses detached from their context and quoted in
public and in open day. They do not seem made for it, he
says. This admirable critic knew, indeed, what a Frenchman
5 may be pardoned for not willingly perceiving, and what even
some Englishmen try to imagine that they do not perceive,
the radical inadequacy of French poetry. For us it is extremely
interesting to hear Sainte-Beuve on this point, since it is to
English poetry that he resorts in order to find his term of
10 comparison, and to award the praise which to French poetry
he refuses. "Since you are fond of the poets," he writes to
a friend, "I should like to see you read and look for poets
in another language, in English for instance. There you will
find the most rich, the most dulcet, and the most new poetical
15 literature. Our French poets are too soon read; they are too
slight, too mixed, too corrupted for the most part, too poor
in ideas even when they have the talent for strophe and line,
to hold and occupy for long a serious mind." And again: "If
you knew English you would have treasures to draw upon.
20 They have a poetical literature far superior to ours, and, above
all, sounder, more full. Wordsworth is not translated; these
things are not to be translated; you must go to the fountain-
head for them. Let me give you this advice: learn English."

But, even as French poetry, Sainte-Beuve's poetry had faults
25 of its own. Critics who found much in it to praise yet pronounced it a poetry "narrow, puny, and stifled," and its style
"slowly dragging and laborious." Here we touch on a want
which must no doubt be recognized in him, which he recognized in himself, and whereby he is separated from the spirits
30 who succeed in uttering their most highly inspired note and
in giving their full measure,—some want of flame, of breath,
of pinion. Perhaps we may look for the cause in a confession
of his own: "I have my weaknesses; they are those which gave
to King Solomon his disgust with everything and his satiety
35 with life. I may have regretted sometimes that I was thus
extinguishing my fire, but I did not ever pervert my heart."
It is enough for us to take his confession that he extinguished
or impaired his fire.

Yet his poetry is characterized by merits which make it readable still and readable by foreigners. So far as it exhibits the endeavour of the romantic school in France to enlarge the vocabulary of poetry and to give greater freedom and variety to the alexandrine, it has interest chiefly for readers 5 of his own nation. But it exhibits more than this. It exhibits already the genuine Sainte-Beuve, the author who, as M. Duvergier de Hauranne said in the *Globe* at the time, "sent à sa manière et écrit comme il sent," the man who, even in the forms of an artificial poetry, remains always "un penseur 10 et un homme d'esprit." That his Joseph Delorme was not the Werther of romance, but a Werther in the shape of Jacobin and medical student, the only Werther whom Sainte-Beuve by his own practical experience really knew, was a novelty in French poetical literature, but was entirely characteristic of 15 Sainte-Beuve. All his poetry has this stamp of direct dealing with common things, of plain unpretending reality and sincerity; and this stamp at that time made it, as Béranger said, "a kind of poetry absolutely new in France." It found, therefore, with all its shortcomings, friends in men so diverse as 20 Béranger, Lamartine, Jouffroy, Beyle. Whoever is interested in Sainte-Beuve should turn to it, and will be glad that he has done so.

It has been the fashion to disparage the criticism of the *Critiques et Portraits Littéraires*, the criticism anterior to 1848, 25 and to sacrifice it, in fact, to the criticism posterior to that date. Sainte-Beuve has himself indicated what considerations ought to be present with us in reading the *Critiques et Portraits*, with what reserves we should read them. They are to be considered, he says, "rather as a dependency of the elegiac 30 and romanesque part of my work than as express criticisms." "The *Revue des Deux Mondes*," he adds, which published them, was young in those days, "mixed a good deal of its wishes and its hopes with its criticism, sought to explain and to stimulate rather than to judge. The portraits there of 35 contemporary poets and romance-writers can in general be considered, whether as respects the painter or as respects the models, as youthful portraits only; *juvenis juvenem pinxit*."

They have the copiousness and enthusiasm of youth; they
have also its exuberance. He judged in later life Chateaubri-
and, Lamartine, Victor Hugo, more coolly, judged them differently. But the *Critiques et Portraits* contain a number of
5   articles on personages, other than contemporary French poets
and romance-writers, which have much of the soundness of
his later work, and, in addition, an abundance and fervour of
their own which are not without their attraction. Many of
these are delightful reading. The articles on the Greek poets
10 and on Leopardi have been already mentioned. Those on
Boileau, Molière, Daunou, and Fauriel, on Madame de la Fay-
ette and Mademoiselle Aïssé, may be taken as samples of a
whole group which will be found to support perfectly the
test of reading, even after we have accustomed ourselves to
15 the later work of the master. Nay, his soberness and tact
show themselves even in this earlier stage of his criticism, and
even in treating the objects of his too fervid youthful enthusiasm. A special object of this was Victor Hugo, and in the
first article on him in the *Portraits Contemporains* we have
20 certainly plenty of enthusiasm, plenty of exuberance. We
have the epithets "adorable," "sublime," "supreme," given to
Victor Hugo's poetry; we are told of "the majesty of its
high and sombre philosophy." All this is in the vein of Mr.
George Gilfillan. But the article next following this, and writ-
25 ten only four years later, in 1835, is the article of a critic, and
takes the points of objection, seizes the weak side of Victor
Hugo's poetry, how much it has of what is "creux," "sonore,"
"artificiel," "voulu," "théâtral," "violent," as distinctly as the
author of the *Causeries* could seize it. "The Frank, energetic
30 and subtle, who has mastered to perfection the technical and
rhetorical resources of the Latin literature of the decadence,"
is a description never to be forgotten of Victor Hugo as a
poet, and Sainte-Beuve launches it in this article, written
when he was but thirty years old, and still a painter of "por-
35 traits de jeunesse" only.

   He had thus been steadily working and growing; nevertheless, 1848 is an epoch which divides two critics in him of
very unequal value. When, after that year of revolution and

his stage of seclusion and labour at Liége, he came back to Paris in the autumn of 1849 and commenced in the *Constitutionnel* the *Causeries du Lundi*, he was astonishingly matured. Something of fervour, enthusiasm, poetry, he may have lost, but he had become a perfect critic—a critic of measure, not 5 exuberant; of the centre, not provincial; of keen industry and curiosity, with "Truth" (the word engraved in English on his seal) for his motto; moreover, with gay and amiable temper, his manner as good as his matter,—the "critique souriant," as, in Charles Monselet's dedication to him, he is called. 10

Merely to say that he was all this is less convincing than to show, if possible, by words of his own, in what fashion he was all this. The root of everything in his criticism is his single-hearted devotion to truth. What he called "fictions" in literature, in politics, in religion, were not allowed to 15 influence him. Some one had talked of his being tenacious of a certain set of literary opinions. "I hold very little," he answers, "to literary opinions; literary opinions occupy very little place in my life and in my thoughts. What does occupy me seriously is life itself and the object of it." "I am accus- 20 tomed incessantly to call my judgments in question anew, and to re-cast my opinions the moment I suspect them to be without validity." "What I have wished" (in *Port Royal*) "is to say not a word more than I thought, to stop even a little short of what I believed in certain cases, in order that my 25 words might acquire more weight as historical testimony." To all exaggeration and untruth, from whatever side it proceeded, he had an antipathy. "I turn my back upon the Michelets and Quinets, but I cannot hold out my hand to the Veuillots." When he was writing for the *Moniteur* he was asked by the 30 manager of the paper to review a book by an important personage, a contributor; his answer is a lesson for critics and paints him exactly. "I should like to say yes, but I have an insurmountable difficulty as to this author; he appears to me to compromise whatever he touches; he is violent, and has 35 not the tradition of the things he talks about. Thus his article on Condorcet, which the *Moniteur* inserted, is odious and false; one may be severe upon Condorcet, but not in that

tone or in that note. The man has no *insight*—a defect which
does not prevent him from having a pen with which at a given
moment he can flourish marvellously. But, of himself, he is
a gladiator and a desperado. I must tell you, my dear sir, that
5   to have once named him with compliment in some article of
mine or other is one of my self-reproaches as a man of letters.
Let me say that he has not attacked me in any way; it is a
case of natural repulsion."

But Sainte-Beuve could not have been the great critic he
10   was had he not had, at the service of this his love of truth
and measure, the conscientious industry of a Benedictine. "I
never have a holiday. On Monday towards noon I lift up my
head, and breathe for about an hour; after that the wicket
shuts again and I am in my prison cell for seven days." The
15   *Causeries* were at this price. They came once a week, and to
write one of them as he wrote it was indeed a week's work.
The "irresponsible indolent reviewer" should read his notes
to his friend and provider with books, M. Paul Chéron of
the National Library. Here is a note dated the 2d of January
20   1853: "Good-day and a happy New Year. To-day I set to
work on Grimm. A little dry; but after St François de Sales"
(his Monday article just finished) "one requires a little relief
from roses. I have of Grimm the edition of his *Correspondence* by M. Taschereau. I have also the *Memoirs* of Madame
25   d'Épinay, where there are many letters of his. But it is possible that there may be *notices* of him mentioned in the bib-
liographical book of that German whose name I have forgotten. I should like, too, to have the *first editions* of his
Correspondence; they came out in successive parts." Thus
30   he prepared himself, not for a grand review article once a
quarter, but for a newspaper review once a week.

His adhesion to the empire caused him to be habitually
represented by the Orleanists and the Republicans as without
character and patriotism, and to be charged with baseness and
35   corruption. The Orleanists had, in a great degree, possession
of the higher press in France and of English opinion,—of
Liberal English opinion more especially. And with English
Liberals his indifference to parliamentary government was in-

deed a grievous fault in him; "you Whigs," as Croker happily says, "are like quack doctors, who have but one specific for all constitutions." To him either the doctrine of English Liberals, or the doctrine of Republicanism, applied absolutely, was what he called a "fiction," one of those fictions which "always end by obscuring the truth." Not even on M. de Tocqueville's authority would he consent to receive "les hypothèses dites les plus honorables,"—"the suppositions which pass for the most respectable." All suppositions he demanded to sift, to see them at work, to know the place and time and men to which they were to be applied. For the France before his eyes in 1849 he thought that something "solid and stable" —*un mur*, "a wall," as he said—was requisite, and that the government of Louis Napoleon supplied this wall. But no one judged the empire more independently than he did, no one saw and enounced its faults more clearly; he described himself as being, in his own single person, "the *gauche* of the empire," and the description was just.

To these merits of mental independence, industry, measure, lucidity, his criticism adds the merit of happy temper and disposition. Goethe long ago noticed that, whereas Germans reviewed one another as enemies whom they hated, the critics of the *Globe* reviewed one another as gentlemen. This arose from the higher social development of France and from the closer relations of literature with life there. But Sainte-Beuve has more, as a critic, than the external politeness which once at any rate distinguished his countrymen: he has a personal charm of manner due to a sweet and humane temper. He complained of *un peu de dureté*, "a certain dose of hardness," in the new generation of writers. The personality of an author had a peculiar importance for him; the poetical side of his subjects, however latent it might be, always attracted him and he always sought to extricate it. This was because he had in himself the moderate, gracious, amiably *human* instincts of the true poetic nature. "Let me beg of you," he says in thanking a reviewer who praised him, "to alter one or two expressions at any rate. I cannot bear to have it said that I am the *first* in anything whatever, as a writer least of all; it is not a thing which can be admitted, and these ways of classing people give offence." Literary man and loyal to the French Academy as he was, he can yet write to an old friend after his election: "All these academies, between you and me, are pieces of childishness; at any rate the French Academy is. Our least quarter of an hour of solitary reverie or of serious talk, yours and mine, in our youth, was better employed; but, as one gets old, one falls back into the power of these nothings; only it is well to know that nothings they are."

Perhaps the best way to get a sense of the value and extent of the work done in the last twenty years of his life by the critic thus excellently endowed is to take a single volume of the *Causeries du Lundi*, to look through its list of subjects, and to remember that with the qualities above mentioned all these subjects are treated. Any volume will serve; let us take the fourth. This volume consists of articles on twenty-four subjects. Twenty of these are the following:—Mirabeau and Sophie, Montaigne, Mirabeau and Comte de la Marck, Mademoiselle de Scudéry, André Chénier as politician, Saint-Évremond and Ninon, Joseph de Maistre, Madame de Lambert, Madame Necker, the Abbé Maury, the Duc de Lauzun of Louis XVI.'s reign, Marie Antoinette, Buffon, Madame de Maintenon, De Bonald, Amyot, Mallet du Pan, Marmontel, Chamfort, Ruhlière. Almost every personage is French, it is true; Sainte-Beuve had a maxim that the critic should prefer subjects which he possesses familiarly. But we should recognize more fully than we do the immense importance and interest of French literature. Certain productions of this literature Mr. Saintsbury may misjudge and overpraise; but he is entirely right in insisting on its immense importance. More than any modern literature it has been in the most intimate correspondence with the social life and development of the nation producing it. Now it so happens that the great place of France in the world is very much due to her eminent gift for social life and development; and this gift French literature has accompanied, fashioned, perfected, and continues to reflect. This gives a special interest to French literature, and an interest independent even of the excellence of individual French writers, high as that often is. And nowhere shall we find such interest more completely and charmingly brought out than in the *Causeries du Lundi* and the *Nouveaux Lundis* of the consummate critic of whom we have been speaking. As a guide to bring us to a knowledge of the French genius and literature he is unrivalled,—perfect, so far as a poor mortal critic can be perfect, in knowledge of his subject, in judgment, in tact, and tone. Certain spirits are of an excellence almost ideal in certain lines; the human race might willingly adopt them as its spokesmen, recognizing that on these lines their style and utterance may stand as those, not of bounded individuals, but of the human race. So Homer speaks for the human race, and with an excellence which is ideal, in epic narration; Plato in the treatment at once beautiful and profound of philosophical questions; Shakespeare in the presentation of human character; Voltaire in light verse and ironical discussion. A list of perfect ones, indeed, each in his own line! and we may almost venture to add to their number, in his line of literary criticism, Sainte-Beuve.

Preface

[TO MARY S. CLAUDE's *Twilight Thoughts: Stories for Children and Child-Lovers*]

How can I refuse a word of preface to these stories? They carry me back to the fells and rills of Westmoreland, to long-past days when Westmoreland was the Westmoreland of Wordsworth and Hartley Coleridge, and when the authoress
5   of these stories moved in her youth and spirit and grace through that beautiful region, herself a vision worthy of it.

    She was connected with Germany; and the soul of Northern Europe, of the Germany of Jean Paul Richter, of the Denmark of Hans Christian Andersen, is in her stories, lend-
10   ing to them its familiar treatment of nature, its facile attribution to animals and plants and pebbles and clouds, of the life and feelings of man. Many a stroke of playful humour, many a moral and deeply humane suggestion, she owes to this genius—inextricably allied in her, however, with the En-
15   glish sadness.

    But it is the neighbour and hearer of Wordsworth who appears in such stories as the "Notice to Trespassers," "The Meadow," "The Stream"; of Wordsworth pleading against the invasion of the beautiful romance of nature by improve-
20   ments, and of the liberty of the peasant and the child by encroachments. "I have no respect whatever for the Whigs," he said most truthfully to Crabb Robinson, "but I have a great deal of the Chartist in me." And just this Wordsworthian Chartism inspires the "Notice to Trespassers."
25   For me, however, the main charm of the stories is in the breath of Westmoreland which blows through them, in the touch which reminds one that there indeed they were born. The cold little new-born rill "creeping softly through the long, drooping moss among the pale and tiny flowers," then

"sleeping in quiet pools while the wag-tail and the stone-chat flit restlessly from stone to stone, or a mountain lamb bleats piteously, afraid to ford the shallow wave," then reaching "the small grey cottages in the shadow of the sycamore, the hanging alders, the broad grey stepping-stones"—this is   5
Westmoreland, rendered with what truth, with what beauty!

And so there is nature and fable and humour and pathos and morality and Chartism in these stories—something for every taste; and it is well that America, too, should possess them and read them. May they give pleasure there as they have given   10
pleasure here; and may they not be suffered, as they have here, to become rare or to go out of print!

The Zenith of Conservatism

There was a favourite saying of Ptolemy the astronomer, which Lord Bacon quotes in its Latin version thus: *Quum fini appropinquas, bonum cum augmento operare*—'As you draw near to your latter end, redouble your efforts to do good.' From time to time I have ventured to criticise the action of our great political parties. The professional politicians are always apt to be impatient of the intervention in politics of a candid outsider, and he must expect to provoke contempt and resentment in a good many of them. Still the action of the regular politicians continues to be, for the most part, so very far from successful, that the outsider is perpetually tempted to brave their anger and to offer his observations, with the hope of possibly doing some little good by saying what many quiet people are thinking and wishing outside of the strife, phrases, and routine of professional politics. Declining years supply a motive, Ptolemy tells us, to an aged outsider for more than ever trying to do this, and so, at the present moment of crisis, I find myself drawn back to politics. Before the defeat of the Liberals I criticised the performance and situation of the Liberal party under Mr. Gladstone, and said that this great party seemed to have at that moment pretty well reached its *nadir*, or lowest. The other great political party, the party of the Conservatives, might on the contrary before the recent sudden surprise of Lord Randolph Churchill's resignation have been said to stand at its zenith, or highest. Before Parliament meets, and it is decided whether the fortunes of Conservatism shall remain prosperous or shall take a turn to decline and fall, I want to inquire how things look to plain people outside of the rivalry of parties, and on what the standing or falling of the Conservative fortunes seems to depend.

When one thinks of the weakness of the Conservatives in the last Parliament, of the confidence of Mr. Gladstone and his followers that in the elections for the present Parliament they would sweep the Conservatives from the field, and how this confidence proved false and the Conservatives from very weak in Parliament became very strong; when one thinks, next, of the prophesying of the Liberals that the alliance between the Conservatives and the Liberal Unionists would instantly dissolve, and how false, too, this prophesying proved; when one considers, finally, how the Conservatives in their resistance to Mr. Gladstone had and have the mind of the country with them, or at least the mind of England, of the far greatest, most civilised, and most influential part of the country, the part, too, where the mere trade or game of politics least absorbs men, where there is to be found the largest number of people who think coolly and independently—when one considers all this, one must surely own that the Conservatives might until just now have been said to be at their zenith.

Certainly there have been appearances of danger. We heard at one time that Mr. Chamberlain was consenting to an attack on the Home Secretary's seat at Birmingham, at another that Sir George Trevelyan was going himself to contest a Conservative seat at Brighton. Then, too, there was Mr. Gladstone's friendly proposal that the Liberal Unionists should join with him to force the hand of the Conservative leaders at the beginning of this coming session, and to make them at once produce their plans for dealing with Ireland. But these former appearances of danger passed off. Mr. Chamberlain was staunch, Sir George Trevelyan was staunch. Mr. Gladstone's friendly call to co-operation was received by Lord Hartington with a coldness which reminds one irresistibly of the attitude of the prince in *Rasselas:* 'His old instructor officiously sought opportunities of conference, which the prince, having long considered him as one whose intellects were exhausted, was not very willing to afford.'

Now, however, has come the startling surprise of Lord Randolph Churchill's resignation. Of course, that resignation is a
grave event, throwing a very serious responsibility upon Lord
Randolph Churchill, a very serious responsibility upon Lord
5 Salisbury. So long, however, as the Liberal Unionists continue
staunch, and the majority remains unimpaired, the gravity of
the event is ministerial and parliamentary, rather than national.
But the attitude of Mr. Chamberlain, agitated by Lord Randolph Churchill's resignation, has become equivocal. More
10 than ever is it important that the mind of the country, the
great power of quiet reasonable opinion in England, should
make its force felt. Parliaments, parties, and politicians, are
more or less discredited; that force is at bottom sound, and
affords our best guarantee of national strength and safety. It
15 placed the Conservatives in office, and, if not alienated, it will
for the present keep them there. Questions of persons sink
into insignificance beside the paramount question, whether
Ministers will, by their policy on two or three matters, now of
main concern, carry the mind of the country with them. It is
20 favourable to them at present, in spite of Lord Randolph
Churchill's defection and of Mr. Chamberlain's signallings to
the enemy. It is favourable to them at present, and shows no
signs of withdrawing from them its goodwill. But how are
they to keep it favourable? How are they to retain the goodwill
25 of that great body of quiet reasonable people, who thought the
course attempted by Mr. Gladstone and his Liberals a false and
dangerous one, and rejoiced at the success of the Conservatives
in stopping it?

Well, what the Conservatives, having been themselves suc-
30 cessful, have now above all to do, is to make their country too,
in its turn, *succeed*. There can be no doubt that for this good
while past our country has not been, in the judgment of any
cool-headed person, succeeding; that it has seemed somehow,
as has been said, to flounder and to beat the air; to be finding
35 itself stopped on this line and on that, and to be threatened with
a sort of standstill. People carried away by party spirit will say
anything; they will say that Mr. Gladstone succeeded in Egypt,
that he was successful with his Land Act, successful with pro-

cedure. But that great body of plain reasonable people, whose goodwill at present makes, I say, the strength of the Conservative Government, know better. Perhaps party writers on the Tory side will say that Lord Salisbury's Government, since it has been in power, has already been succeeding; but dispassion- 5 ate observers will hardly agree to that either. The Conservatives have done little or nothing hitherto, since they came into power, to make their country *succeed*, to make things go happily for us, any more than the Liberals did. I do not say that the Conservatives are to be blamed for this; perhaps they 10 have not had time, perhaps they have been reserving themselves for the meeting of Parliament. But the fact remains; they have not yet made their country visibly recover itself and succeed, and to make it do this is what is wanted of them. If they are to remain at the zenith, they must do it; and both for their 15 own sake and for the sake of the country it is most important for them, and now since Lord Randolph Churchill's defection more important than ever, to consider by what sort of proceedings when Parliament meets, since they seem to be waiting for the meeting of Parliament, they are likely to do it. 20

Soon enough will the occasions come to the Conservative Government, the occasions for standing or falling; and in what fashion soever they may meet them they will have plenty of party foes sure to tell them that they do ill, and plenty of party friends to tell them that they do well. But the verdict which 25 will decide whether they and the great Conservative party led by them shall really stand or fall is, I repeat, the great force of fair and reasonable English opinion independent of party. This force is what they must keep in view and seek to satisfy. It will go with them in not permitting questions to be raised which 30 ought to be postponed to matters more urgently pressing now. But with three matters of urgent present importance the Government will, as every one knows, have to deal: procedure, the state of Ireland, local government. It is probable also that some branch or other of the question of Church disestablishment will 35 force itself under the notice of Parliament and compel discussion. On perhaps four matters, therefore, the Government will, we may expect, have to declare itself: procedure, the state of

Ireland, local government, Church disestablishment. On these
it will have to carry with it, if it is to stand and not to fall, the
great body of independent reasonable opinion in England.

Let us take procedure first. Probably no member of Parliament quite knows how scandalous and intolerable the present
state of the House of Commons appears to the great body of
quiet reasonable people throughout the country. Party men
may find their account, one way or another, in that state of
things; the excitement of it, and self-importance, may make
many members of Parliament blind to the actual truth. But the
actual truth is that plain reasonable people outside the House
of Commons regard the confusion into which it has fallen, and
its apparent helplessness to extricate itself, with ever deepening
disgust and shame; it is a relief to them when Parliament is not
sitting; they are uneasy and apprehensive as soon as it meets
again, for they know that the time for humiliation has returned.
A Minister said solemnly, after a scandalous scene: 'The
country will judge;' the *Times* sounded its eternal warning: 'If
this sort of thing continues, it will become necessary to apply
some very stringent remedy.' The country *has* judged, judged
and condemned. It has judged that the stringent remedy ought
to have been long before now applied, and has condemned the
House of Commons of impotence for not applying it. Factious
men in the House of Commons may from party interest oppose
a stringent reform of procedure, vain men may oppose it in the
interest of their own importance; pedants, both inside and outside the House of Commons, may oppose it on the strength of
stock phrases which perhaps had force and truth once but
which have them no longer. But the body of quiet reasonable
opinion throughout the country is in favour of a most stringent
reform; and this opinion will heartily approve the Government
if it undertakes such a reform and carries it through, will be
displeased and alienated if it does not. Plain people will not be
impracticable and insist on having closure by a bare majority,
if the Government finds that time and labour are saved through
accepting closure by a majority of three-fifths, or of two-
thirds; but the more stringent a closure the Government can
carry, the better will plain people be pleased. I presume it will

hardly now be Lord Randolph Churchill who will propose closure; but to imagine that we should have been so stiff as not to accept closure from Lord Randolph Churchill because he of old intemperately inveighed against it, is to think us foolish indeed. The *Saturday Review* objects to my quoting Bishop Wilson, but really I have a maxim of his which fits Lord Randolph Churchill's duty in this matter exactly: 'Let us not afflict ourselves with our failings; our perfection consists in opposing them.'

The subject of Ireland I will leave to the last, because it requires to be treated at most length. We come next, therefore, to the question of local government. It cannot be said that the opinion which the Conservative Ministry is so concerned to satisfy, the opinion of quiet reasonable people throughout the country, has as yet much addressed itself to this question of local government, or feels a keen interest in it. Such people are indeed bent, as I believe, on giving to the Irish the due control of their own local affairs, just as the Scotch have it, or the English themselves. Through the Parliament at Westminster Scotchmen and Englishmen do in the main get this control, though by an imperfect and inconvenient method; Irishmen, however, fail to get it, and a plan of local government is necessary in order to give it to them. The necessity is recognised; it is known, moreover, that other nations have reformed their system of local government to meet modern needs, whilst ours remains chaotic and inefficient. And the more the advantage of the reforms effected elsewhere comes to be understood, the greater will be the impatience at our unreformed chaos. Difficulties are raised, it is objected that a thorough system of local government, such as we see, for instance, in the United States, implies a federal organisation of the people concerned. But the kingdom of Prussia is not organised federally any more than the kingdom of Great Britain; and in Prussia the Liberals have reformed almost the whole system of the local governments, and established a system new and thorough; it is the one success of the Prussian Liberals. Prussia has thirteen Provinces and four hundred and sixty-nine Circles or Districts, each with its assembly elected by a very simple and wide suffrage; after

these come all the municipalities, urban and rural, each of them
with its own elective assembly too. The system works well. I
have most examined it in connexion with the elementary
schools. These have far more to do with the district and pro-
5   vincial governments than with the central government. They
are gainers thereby, they are managed with less of what we call
red tape, with much more understanding of local needs. Fur-
thermore, in monarchical Prussia just as in republican and federal America, the district and provincial assemblies afford a
10 wholesome training in public affairs to their members, a training which both informs and raises them, and of which the
middle class in our country is destitute. The more that all this
comes to be known and considered, the more will the force of
quiet reasonable opinion here be engaged in favour of creating
15 a thorough system of local government. At present our people
do, as I have already admitted, chiefly think of it as a remedy
for the Irish difficulty. Whether as a system for Ireland only,
or for the entire kingdom, it is important that it should be
built on sufficiently large lines, not too complicated, not fan-
20 tastic, not hesitating and suspicious, not taking back with one
hand what it gives with the other. Why? Because a measure of
that kind cannot possibly win general and cordial acceptance,
cannot, therefore, really succeed; and *success*, clear and broad
success, is what the general sentiment demands from measures
25 produced by the Government. People are become very impatient of seeing their country fumble and fail, the efforts of government turn awry, our affairs go amiss. If Ministers do not see
their way to producing a full and frank measure of local government at the present moment, they would surely do well to
30 put off the production of their measure rather than produce a
lame one; most especially if, as is rumoured, Ireland is thought
to be not in a proper state for the immediate introduction there
of any such measure at all.

Next we have the question of Church disestablishment, which
35 is likely to come under discussion in connexion with Wales.
Here it is above all important that Ministers should not only
think of defeating their party opponents and of gratifying their
party supporters, but also of carrying with them the mind of

the country, the force of quiet reasonable opinion in the nation. Admit reforms they must; but Conservatives are always saying that it is their principle to make needful reforms, only without destroying. I will add that they can afford to disregard entirely their adversaries' reproach of stealing the Liberal reforms. The important reforms which the Liberal party, the party of movement and change, has bought about, are almost entirely reforms demanded—legitimately, I will add, demanded—by the instinct of expansion in our community, reforms among which the extension of the suffrage, with the ballot, may stand as chief. But these are reforms of machinery, requiring not much insight or thought to make them; comparatively easy, and tempting in proportion to their ease. For the more vital and constructive kinds of reform the Liberal party has shown, except in the single and doubtful case of Free Trade, little disposition and no faculty. What is the Liberal policy in Ireland? Throwing up the game there, the virtual abandonment of the Union. What is the Liberal policy with regard to the Church? Mere destruction of a great and old national agency. What with regard to the House of Lords? Very much the same thing. Sir George Trevelyan seems inclined, Unionist though he is, to make the Liberal party his religion, just as the religion of Gambetta, Mr. Frederic Harrison tells us, was France; and I must say that neither the one nor the other object for religion seems to me adequate. When the Liberal party proposes to reform without destroying, its proposals are commonly childish. Take the well-known Liberal proposition to expel the bishops from the House of Lords. One can hardly imagine sensible men planning a Second Chamber which should not include the Archbishop of Canterbury for the time being, or which should include the young gentlemen who now flock to the House of Lords when pigeon-shooting is in question. But our precious Liberal reformers are for retaining the pigeon-shooters and for expelling the Archbishop of Canterbury.

No: if the Conservatives can produce vital and constructive reforms, there is no fear of our finding them to be plagiarisms from the Liberals. But vital and constructive reforms, such as may so properly come from the party of stability and perma-

nence—reforms which possess, as Burke finely says, 'all the benefits which may be in change without any of the inconve-
niences of mutation,' these the Conservatives must produce, or
must at least show themselves capable of producing; and no-
5   where more than in Church matters.

Twenty years and more have now gone by, since in a lecture at Oxford I quoted the declaration of a member of Parliament, a friend of mine, that a thing's being an anomaly was in
his opinion no objection to it whatever, and I remarked that at
10 any rate, perhaps, the labours of the friends of light might be
trusted to prevail so far as this: that in twenty years' time it
should be thought, even in England, an objection to a thing that
it is absurd. And this is what has really come about. The epoch
of concentration has ended for us, the ice has broken up, things
15 are no longer looked upon as a part of the order of creation
merely because we find them existing. If they are absurd, this
is now a positive objection to them; they become impossible
as well, and have to be got rid of. Apply this to Church matters.
The American newspapers have all been saying with wonder
20 lately, and our newspapers have repeated it after them, that the
present Earl of Lonsdale has forty Church livings in his gift,
and nominates their incumbents. Perhaps he has not really so
many as forty, but certainly he has a good number. Well,
twenty years ago, if a like thing had been mentioned, the stale
25 old hacks in politics and religion, whose business it was to talk
plausibly on these topics but to prevent all innovation, would
have uttered their decorous platitudes, would have said that the
thing was unfortunate, but that it could not possibly be helped,
and our society at large would have gravely acquiesced. But
30 now the mention of a thing of this kind startles people, raises
their impatience. They feel that Lord Lonsdale's having the
presentation to these livings is an absurdity. The body of quiet
reasonable people throughout the country, whose goodwill is
so essential to the Government, have come, I say, to perceive,
35 when a thing of this kind is brought to their notice, that it is
absurd; it is felt to be absurd, and its long continuance henceforth, therefore, becomes impossible. The Government must
in questions of Church patronage be in concert with this force

of reasonable opinion, not lagging behind it or in conflict with
it.

The same as to the maintenance of the Church establishment
on its actual footing, under circumstances such as those which
we see presenting themselves in Wales. To maintain the estab- 5
lishment in Wales for the sole benefit of a small minority of the
population is an absurdity there, just as it was in Ireland. When
it comes before the mind of reasonable people, it is felt by them
to be an absurdity. The thing being felt to be an absurdity, its
long continuance becomes impossible. Does that necessitate 10
disestablishment, secularisation of Church revenues, giving to
roads and bridges what was meant for religion? Not by any
means. The sterile programme of our actual party Liberalism
has no better solution than this to offer, but a better solution
may be found, and it is the business of a truly Conservative 15
government to find it. The mind of the country will be heartily
with them if they can produce and apply it.

And now I come, lastly, to that which is, after all, both the
great opportunity and the great danger for the Conservatives
at present—Ireland. If they succeed here, they will be at the 20
zenith beyond all doubt or question, and whatever Lord Randolph Churchill or Mr. Chamberlain may do or say; if they
fumble and fail, if their efforts go awry and affairs in Ireland
go amiss, then inevitably must come the turn of Cleon and his
democracy, who will resume in triumph the game which the 25
country cut short once, but will then reluctantly leave them
free to pursue. All that will be left for the Conservatives will be
to cry out, like the Abbé Sieyès: *Ruit irrevocabile vulgus.*

Now, however, Ministers have the mind of the country
thoroughly with them in resisting Home Rule—Home Rule as 30
Mr. Gladstone and his followers understand it. There prevails,
apparently, in the ideas of many people who think and talk
about Home Rule, the most astonishing laxity and confusion.
Home Rule, for many people, means just the same thing as local government. Whoever is for local government, for giving 35
the Irish people the control of their own local affairs, is for
Home Rule, only his opposition to Mr. Gladstone makes him
choose a different form of expression! I have seen Sir Redvers

Buller called a Home Ruler because he is, or is supposed to be, for putting pressure on harsh and impracticable landlords. But Home Rule has for Mr. Gladstone and his followers a certain definite, fixed meaning, which they have again and again declared to us, and it is this: *A separate Parliament for Ireland, with an Irish executive responsible to that Parliament.* I know they reserve Imperial affairs, and withhold them from the control of the Irish Parliament and Irish executive. But the point is, that by Home Rule they mean one separate Parliament for the Irish, with a separate executive responsible to it. Local government may mean many things, but Home Rule has now come to mean this particular, definite thing, which Mr. Gladstone and his followers declare themselves to understand by it. And the question is, is the thing expedient, or is it dangerous and to be resisted? There can be no doubt that the Conservatives think it dangerous and to be resisted, that the mind of the country has gone with them in their resistance to it hitherto, and still goes with them in resistance to it now.

Treatises might be written—treatises *are* written, treatises very ingenious, very elaborate, and very long—on the dangers of Home Rule as Mr. Gladstone and his followers understand it. But I have here in view the opinion and disposition of the great body of plain reasonable people throughout the country, whose favour has brought the Conservatives to their zenith, and must be retained if they are to stay there. For general use by plain reasonable people the apparatus of argument employed against Home Rule is excessive; it is much too full and too vast. And it is not required; a single apposite and clear illustration brings the state of the case home to their minds better than scores of long speeches and treatises, with all their elaborate apparatus of argument. This is why I have so much insisted on an illustration afforded by the United States of America. Lord Spencer, having apparently, in his strange courses of late, got hold of a formula of Jacobinism by mistake for a formula of Whiggery, asks with earnestness: 'Is there not a mandate from the Irish people to the British Parliament to give Home Rule?'—and seems to think that this settles the matter. Ireland

could address no stronger mandate to Parliament to give Home
Rule than the Southern States addressed to the North to give
them a separate Congress and a separate executive. If that mandate ought to have settled the matter for the Americans, then
the Irish mandate ought to settle the matter for us. If it would 5
have been the same thing for the United States to grant to the
South a separate Southern Congress and executive at Richmond as to grant them provincial governments at Montgomery,
Atlanta, and all the rest of the Southern chief towns, then to
grant Gladstonian Home Rule to Ireland is the same thing as 10
granting local government to it. If it would have been dangerous to grant a Southern Congress and a Southern executive,
then it would be dangerous to grant an Irish Parliament, and an
executive responsible to it. If a Southern Congress, with whatever restrictions you might have surrounded it, would have 15
been sure to pose sooner or later as an independent Parliament
and to threaten and embarrass the North, so would an Irish
Parliament—take what securities now you please, devise and
apply every safeguard you can—inevitably act towards Great
Britain. It is in the nature of things that it should be so, and in 20
the case of Ireland even more than in the case of the Southern
States of America. If these States were left confronting the
North, after their bitter conflict, with feelings of irritation and
estrangement, what were those feelings compared with the
rage, hatred, and scorn with which the Irish, as they themselves 25
are every day telling us, regard Great Britain? To be a thorn
in Great Britain's side, to make alliance with its rivals, to turn
against it in a crisis of danger, would be more tempting to the
Irish by far (I judge them, again, simply from what they themselves say) than a similar conduct towards the Northern States 30
would have been to the South. The abundance of political talent
and energy in the South, however, would have of itself been
enough, without fierce hatred to help it, to impel a Southern
Parliament to make itself independent and formidable. The
love for the game of politics, and the talent for it, are as strong 35
in the Irish as in the men of the South; Bishop Berkeley long
ago remarked the 'general parturiency in Ireland with respect

to politics and public counsel.' And to make Irishmen extend
the scope, importance, and power for mischief of their Parliament, they have all the stimulus of fierce hatred as well.

What has been here said touches only, an Irishman may
urge, the interest of Great Britain in the matter. A separate
Parliament may still, he will say, be for the advantage of Ireland, and an Irishman may desire it, though it might prove embarrassing to Great Britain. Burke, we now continually hear
it alleged, was for retaining the Irish Parliament, and against
such a union with Great Britain as was afterwards established.
It is most important to have Burke's very words on this matter.
Thus he writes in 1792:

> I have heard a discussion concerning such a union amongst all
> sorts of men ever since I remember anything. For my own part
> I have never been able to bring my mind to anything clear and
> decisive upon the subject. There cannot be a more arduous ques-
> tion. As far as I can form an opinion, it would not be for the
> mutual advantage of the two kingdoms. Persons, however, more
> able than I am, think otherwise.

Was ever disapprobation more cautious, more candidly doubtful of itself? I have so much respect for Burke's judgment that
I am willing to share his doubt whether in 1792 the projected
Union may have been advisable. But I am quite sure that to go
back upon it in 1886, after it has been established for nearly a
hundred years, and to return to a separate Parliament for Ireland, is a retrograde step inexpedient and dangerous, and for
Ireland not less than for England; and I am sure that Burke
would have thought so too. For in our present circumstances,
and with tempers as they are now, a separate Parliament for
Ireland would assuredly, as we have seen, of itself supply fresh
occasions for conflict between Ireland and Great Britain, and
increase the alienation and distrust already too prevalent. And
'the closest connexion between Great Britain and Ireland is
essential,' Burke thought, 'to the wellbeing, almost to the very
being, of the two kingdoms.' He thought that 'by the separation of Ireland Great Britain, indeed, would be ruined; but as
there are degrees even in ruin, it would fall the most heavily

on Ireland. By such a separation Ireland would be the most completely undone country in the world, the most wretched, the most distracted, and, in the end, the most desolate part of the habitable globe.'

The Irish mandate for Home Rule, therefore, on which Lord   5
Spencer relies, is really a mandate for increased alienation; and increased alienation means increased misery, for Ireland above all. If the Irish have set their affections on this, it is surely a case for telling them, with Shakespeare, that

> . . . your affections are   10
> A sick man's appetite, who desires most that
> Which would increase his evil;—

for telling them, in the words of the Frenchwoman who observed the troubles of the Fronde, that *ce qu'ils demandent n'est pas ce qu'il faut pour les apaiser*, 'what they ask for is not what   15
is wanted to bring them peace.' Mr. Gladstone may fail to perceive this, because, with all his wonderful gifts, he yet lacks so signally the crowning gift of wisdom and insight. Mr. Morley may fail to acknowledge it, because he despairs of the English people and Parliament. But the mind of the country at once   20
instinctively perceived it, instinctively felt that the separate Irish Parliament and Irish executive means a lull for an instant, to be followed by increased contention and misery in the near future. Lord Hartington's sound judgment is shown by his having from the first signalised this proposal of Mr. Glad-   25
stone as the specially dangerous one, and never wavered in doing so. The Conservative party, as a whole, has staunchly taken and held the same view. The mind of the country is with them in it, the great body of quiet reasonable opinion in England wishes them continued success in their resistance to Glad-   30
stonian Home Rule.

But what, now, shall we say of the set and disposition of this great force of opinion, in the questions which arise as to acts of firm government in Ireland? It is entirely favourable to such acts. The language of certain eager and impassioned Liberal   35
newspapers on this topic is such as to show a sheer absence of

all instinct of government, and finds no response at all in the
mind of plain reasonable Englishmen generally. 'What might
be a fair rent to pay?' Mr. Sheehy asks an Irish crowd. 'A voice
responded, *"Nothing!"* followed by a burst of laughter and
5   applause. "I like your music," says Mr. Sheehy, "and I hope that
many will learn it."' 'We will march on from victory to victory,' says Mr. O'Brien, 'until we shall have liberated this land
from the two curses of landlordism and English rule.' 'In the
day of our power we will remember the police,' says Mr. Dil-
10 lon. O'Connell was prosecuted in 1824 for saying: 'If Parliament
will not attend to the Catholic claims, I hope that some Bolivar
will arise to vindicate their rights.' That was excess on the side
of government. But now we have changed all that, and if Mr.
Dillon and Mr. O'Brien are prosecuted when they use language
15 such as that which I have just quoted, the *Pall Mall Gazette* exclaims that this is 'arbitrary interference with the ordinary liberties of the subject.' Surely this is excess on the side of anarchy.
It finds, I say, no response in the minds of quiet reasonable
Englishmen generally. Rather they are indisposed by what
20 looks like weakness, hesitation and pedantry enfeebling the
mind and hand of the executive government, suffering disorder
to grow to a height, and the public authority to be scorned and
set at naught. Far from thinking that the interference of
Government with Irish liberty of speech and action has been
25 excessive, the majority of fair-minded and peaceable Englishmen think that it has been insufficient. It is fatal for the Irish
themselves to acquire the habit of setting government and law
at defiance. Merely to break down this habit of defiance is not
all that we have now to do in Ireland; that is quite true, and
30 most important it is to insist upon it. But the habit of defiance
must not be allowed to establish itself, must be quelled when it
seeks to establish itself. Whatever fanatics or party politicians
may say, the mind of the country is clear and firm on this matter, and will uphold Government in quelling anarchy.
35   But there must be *success* in quelling it. The executive must
not give to the world, and to the Irish themselves, in trying to
quell it, the spectacle of fumbling and failure, of efforts going
awry, of justice defeated, of authority made ridiculous. Days

spent by a sheriff and his men in vainly trying to get possession
of a barricaded house, the sheriff's men maltreated and blinded,
the crowd jeering and yelling, with a force of police and
soldiers looking on and doing nothing—this is not quelling anarchy. Bringing offenders before juries who are delighted to   5
show their enmity to Government by acquitting them, is not
quelling anarchy. In general, administrative action is what is
now required against anarchy in Ireland, not recourse to proceedings at law. 'Trial by jury in Ireland,' said Sir James Graham as long ago as 1844, 'is the weak place which renders the   10
civil government of that country all but impossible.' Changing
the venue to England would be at least as odious to the Irish
as firm administrative action. Administration may do a great
deal; 'he who administers, governs,' says Burke; but then the
administration must not be punctilious, dilatory, and vacillating. 15
There are surely some kinds of speeches, some kinds of meetings, some kinds of newspaper-writing, which in the present
circumstances of Ireland should not be permitted there and
should be stopped. Political adversaries will of course reproach
the administration with being, in Mr. Morley's phrase, 'so ready   20
to go before the law instead of waiting to see what the law is!'
But there is no doubt what the law is. The judges have just pronounced the Plan of Campaign to be 'an absolutely illegal organisation.' It was perfectly well known to be so, Mr. Morley
himself knew it to be so, before this last pronouncement of the   25
judges. It was perfectly well known, Mr. Morley himself knew
it, that such language as that used by Mr. Dillon, Mr. O'Brien,
and Mr. Sheehy is, as the judges now again tell us, language
'liable to lead to crime and outrage.' The thing is, for the administration to act with firmness, intelligence, and consistency,   30
on this very clear knowledge. I remember saying to Mr. Forster
that it was utterly useless to be shutting up 'village ruffians,' or
even Mr. Parnell himself, while *United Ireland* was inflaming
and infuriating the Irish people all day long with impunity. Of
course only the administration can deal with such an incitement   35
to crime and outrage as *United Ireland;* an Irish jury at present
will not. But administrative action, steady and resolute, in repressing this and other undoubted incitements to crime and

outrage in Ireland, the great body of plain reasonable opinion in England would see with hearty approval.

What, however, as to Mr. Dillon's contention that he is 'endeavouring to bring pressure to bear upon bad landlords to get rack-rents reduced, and to save the tenants, who cannot possibly pay them, from destitution and misery'? The answer, for whoever is not infected with the Jacobinical temper and passions, is clear. Grant that there are bad landlords in Ireland, and rents which ought to be reduced; grant also that concessions have often been wrung from government only by the fear of disturbance, crime, and outrage. Never, for all that, let us forget or deny for a moment that unswerving firmness in repressing disturbance, crime, and outrage, or whatever plainly leads to them, is always a government's duty. If there is wrong to be redressed, and the government, after repressing disorder, does not redress it, the government leaves a part, a great part, of its duty undone. Let us diligently train ourselves, and train public opinion, to make government do this part of its duty also; but do not let us ever approve of its leaving the other part of its duty, the quelling of anarchy, undone. The temper of the English people is not Jacobinical; more than most communities, the body of quiet people here are capable of grasping and holding firm the indispensable truth that under no circumstances may a government be irresolute in repressing disorder.

Still the redressing of wrong is assuredly part of a government's duty as well as the repressing of disorder. And there are very bad landlords in Ireland. So there are, it may be said, everywhere. But, in Ireland, they represent, as I have often urged, a system; they represent to the Irish a system which has made peace and prosperity impossible, and which strikes at the root of order. The Duke of Wellington, with his deep practical good sense, warned the Irish landlords, warned them earnestly; Croker says, in his valuable Sketch of the State of Ireland, that it was 'concocted with Sir Arthur Wellesley,' then Irish Secretary. And let us hear Croker, that most unsuspected witness, on the cause of 'the constant warfare between the landlords and their tenants by which for fifty years past Ireland has been disturbed and disgraced.' Here is the cause:—

A landlord is not mere land-merchant; he has duties to perform as well as rents to receive; and from his neglect of the former springs his difficulty in the latter, and the general misery and distraction. The combinations of the peasantry against this short-sighted monopoly are natural and fatal. Whoever assembles the Irish, disturbs them; disturbance soon coalesces with treason.

But we were then, and for long afterwards, living in an epoch of concentration. Nothing could be done. The Duke of Wellington himself seems to say mournfully under his breath: *Non possumus!* The stale old hacks, plausible and proper as usual, protested that it was unfortunate, but that nothing could by any possibility be done. Ministers left the sufferers to 'general sympathy.' But general sympathy was then timid and hide-bound, at any rate where the land was concerned, and the land, moreover, with Papists to occupy it. But now there has come a change. We are living in an epoch of expansion; with the loss of some salutary restraints, there has been gain in an enlarged and heightened power of sympathy; with the fading of the theological and distant view of Christianity, the practical and direct view of it has certainly strengthened, and has quickened our sense of sympathy. The nature, rights, and duties of property are freely canvassed; those of property in land above all. Well, the change has gone so far that at this moment, not to the populace only, not to Jacobins, not to socialists, not to newspaper declaimers, not to Radical demagogues, not to these only, but to the great body of quiet reasonable people throughout the country, Lord Clanricarde with his fifty thousand acres in Galway is, like Lord Lonsdale with his forty livings in the Church, an absurdity. Lord Clanricarde, 'mere land-merchant,' living, we are told, in the Albany, contemptuous and neglectful, never going near his tenants, never hearing what they have to ask or say, doing nothing at all for them, is an absurdity, and therefore cannot now long be maintained. Being felt to be absurd, he is become, or is fast becoming, impossible. That same great force of reasonable opinion in this country which is now favourable to Ministers, and makes their chief force, will not suffer this sort of landlord to be long maintained. True, if his tenants are evicted, they are to be evicted without the spectacle

of a siege in which the sheriff's people are maltreated and
scalded all day amid the yells of a mob, while the police and
soldiers are kept looking on, doing nothing. But that he should
be long maintained is impossible.

5   Ministers should consider that the general opinion is not
without sympathy for Mr. Dillon personally, and for much
which he thinks and says, although it wishes his defiance of law
to be firmly stopped. If Lord Clanricarde's tenants are evicted,
it wishes them evicted without rioting; but it has its own
10 thoughts about Lord Clanricarde. Lord Salisbury's figure of the
highwayman, Mr. Goschen's of the garrotter, are smart rhetoric
rather than sound statesmanship, if the tenants in conflict with
Lord Clanricarde do not really at all present themselves to the
mind of the country as highwaymen and garrotters, and cannot
15 be made so to present themselves. Samson's pulling down of the
court-house at Gaza upon himself and the Philistine lords was
a violent, irregular, and unlawful proceeding. But we do not in
the least think of Samson as a garrotter and highwayman, nor
will quiet people in general think of Lord Clanricarde's tenants
20 under this figure. Garrotters and highwaymen have only to be
brought under the strong hand of the law; Lord Clanricarde's
tenants have to be firmly stopped, indeed, from rioting, but
then something further has to be done for them, some relief
afforded. The land question has indeed to be dealt with, and
25 there can be no peace in Ireland until it has been dealt with successfully; that is most true.

The Land Act of 1881 unsettled everything; it introduced
or confirmed a divided ownership full of inconvenience, full
of elements of dispute. But its chief fault was that whereas the
30 Irish tenant had two grievances, a material grievance and a
moral grievance, the Land Act, which dealt after a fashion with
the material grievance, left the moral grievance, the grievance
of bad landlordism carried to lengths hardly exampled elsewhere and striking at the root of order, wholly untouched.
35 How very great a force moral grievance has in human affairs
we all know. But the Land Act recognised no difference whatever between good landlords and bad, between landlords who
had always done their duty and landlords who had never done

it at all. I insisted, at the time when the Land Act was passing, upon this its capital defect; I urged that the great and passionately felt moral grievance of the Irish peasantry could be met and wiped out best, could be met and wiped out only, by a direct moral satisfaction, by some measure distinguishing between good landlords and bad, and telling on the bad with severity. I said that if we liked to suppose one of our chief judges and one of our chief philanthropists authorised to establish, on due inquiry, the distinction demanded, and then a measure of expropriation founded on the distinction so reached, that would give us the sort of equity, the sort of moral satisfaction, which the case needed. By Mr. Gladstone's recent Purchase Bill the landlords were to be bought out; but again no distinction was recognised between good and bad landlords, all were to get the same terms. The Purchase Bill is said to have reconciled Lord Spencer to the Home Rule Bill; the majority of Mr. Gladstone's followers would probably have rejected it after they had carried Home Rule. But the Purchase Bill, like the Land Act before it, left the moral grievance of the Irish tenantry wholly untouched; and it may be confidently affirmed that no bill for buying out the Irish landlords will really *succeed* which does not touch this grievance, does not distinguish between good landlords and bad, does not give better terms to the good landlords, worse to the bad.

The mind and conscience of the country, not only Irish malcontents and their Liberal allies, will demand this, and would be alienated, I most sincerely believe, by the Government's declaring against it. Meanwhile Ministers have promised to put what pressure they can upon bad landlords in order to make them reasonable. Administrative action is here again of extreme value and importance. Sir Michael Hicks-Beach and Sir Redvers Buller have been sharply attacked on the supposition that they were putting pressure on bad landlords. Under present circumstances they perform a high public duty in applying it; and they are, moreover, the very best persons by whom it can be applied. Their own interests are known to be naturally with the landlords; what they do to press them will therefore be done simply for the public safety. It is asked, why may Sir

Michael Hicks-Beach put pressure on bad landlords, when Mr.
Morley might not? I have often expressed my high esteem for
Mr. Morley, and wherever his course may lead him I shall always feel for him regard and affection. But in despair of the
5   good sense and justice of England he has surrendered to Mr.
Parnell and his party; and to complain of its being thought unsafe to let Mr. Morley put pressure on the landlords, is like
complaining of its being thought unsafe, in the War of Secession, to let Mr. Jefferson Davis put pressure on the abolitionists.
10 The same as to Mr. Dillon and Mr. Parnell. Why not let Mr.
Dillon put pressure on bad landlords, since pressure on them is
needed? why not have accepted Mr. Parnell's bill for putting
it? Why? Because Mr. Parnell and Mr. Dillon are Separatists
and Home Rulers, and it is not consistent with public safety
15 to let them usurp the functions of government in Ireland, in
the midst of a struggle whether Home Rule and separation are
or are not to be conceded. But functionaries who are the strong
opponents of Home Rule and separation, and whose interests,
too, are naturally with the landlords, are just the people whom
20 we may well trust, if they put pressure upon landlords, to put
it so far as the public good imperatively requires, and no further.

May they to that extent put it freely, and may Government
uphold them in putting it, as the general opinion of the country
25 most certainly will! May Government also, when it comes to
deal by legislation with the land question in Ireland, make good
the Land Act's great omission, and regard equity! May the
Conservative leaders also produce a good measure of local government, and rescue procedure from chaos; may they likewise
30 be reasonable on Church questions; then the opinion and favour
of the country will remain with them, as that opinion is with
them now. Let them therefore be strong and of a good courage.
A government not brilliant, but with an open mind, and quite
honest and quite firm, may serve our present needs much better
35 than a government far more brilliant, but which is not perfectly
honest or not perfectly firm. But on no account must Ministers
give cause for saying, as Mr. Chamberlain has hastened to say
already, that Lord Randolph Churchill's retirement marks the

victory, in the Conservative Government, of the stupid and noxious Toryism opposed to all serious improvement. They must 'be up and doing, and doing to good purpose;' they must keep friends with the mind of the country. And in the present unripe state of the Liberals of the nadir, we Liberals of the future, who happen to be grown, alas, rather old, shall then probably have to look forward to the Conservative Ministry, whether with or without Lord Randolph Churchill, lasting at least our time, and shall be able to look forward to this without much repining or dissatisfaction.

General Grant

I have heard it said, I know not with what degree of truth, that while the sale in America of General Grant's *Personal Memoirs* has produced three hundred thousand dollars for the benefit of his widow and family, there have not in England been sold of
5   the book three hundred copies. Certainly the book has had no wide circulation here, it has not been much read or much discussed. There are obvious reasons for this. The book relates in great detail the military history of the American Civil War, so far as Grant bore part in it; such a history cannot possibly have
10   for other nations the interest which it has for the United States themselves. For the general reader, outside of America, it certainly cannot; as to the value and importance of the history to the military specialist, that is a question on which I hear very conflicting opinions expressed, and one on which I myself can
15   have, of course, no opinion to offer. So far as the general European reader might still be attracted to such a history, in spite of its military details, for the sake of the importance of the issues at stake and of the personages engaged, we in Europe have, it cannot be denied, in approaching an American recital
20   of the deeds of "the greatest nation upon earth," some apprehension and mistrust to get over. We may be pardoned for doubting whether we shall in the recital find measure, whether we shall find sobriety. Then, too, General Grant, the central figure of these *Memoirs*, is not to the English imagination the
25   hero of the American Civil War; the hero is Lee, and of Lee the *Memoirs* tell us little. Moreover General Grant, when he was in

England, did not himself personally interest people much. Later he fell in America into the hands of financing speculators, and his embarrassments, though they excited sorrow and compassion, did not at all present themselves to us as those of "a good man struggling with adversity." For all these reasons, 5 then, the *Personal Memoirs* have in England been received with coldness and indifference.

I, too, had seen General Grant in England, and did not find him interesting. If I said the truth, I should say that I thought him ordinary-looking, dull and silent. An expression of gentle- 10 ness and even sweetness in the eyes, which the portraits in the *Memoirs* show, escaped me. A strong, resolute, businesslike man, who by possession of unlimited resources in men and money, and by the unsparing use of them, had been enabled to wear down and exhaust the strength of the South, this was what 15 I supposed Grant to be, this and little more.

Some documents published by General Badeau in the American newspapers first attracted my serious attention to Grant. Among those documents was a letter from him which showed qualities for which, in the rapid and uncharitable view which 20 our cursory judgments of men so often take, I had by no means given him credit. It was the letter of a man with the virtue, rare everywhere, but more rare in America, perhaps, than anywhere else, the virtue of being able to confront and resist popular clamour, the *civium ardor prava jubentium*. Public opinion 25 seemed in favour of a hard and insolent course, the authorities seemed putting pressure upon Grant to make him follow it. He resisted with firmness and dignity. After reading that letter I turned to General Grant's *Personal Memoirs*, then just published. This man, I said to myself, deserves respect and atten- 30 tion; and I read the two bulky volumes through.

I found shown in them a man, strong, resolute and business-like, as Grant had appeared to me when I first saw him; a man with no magical personality, touched by no divine light and giving out none. I found a language all astray in its use of *will* 35 and *shall*, *should* and *would*, an English employing the verb *to conscript* and the participle *conscripting*, and speaking in a despatch to the Secretary of War of having *badly whipped*

the enemy; an English without charm and without high breeding. But at the same time I found a man of sterling good-sense
as well as of the firmest resolution; a man, withal, humane, simple, modest; from all restless self-consciousness and desire for
5   display perfectly free; never boastful where he himself was
concerned, and where his nation was concerned seldom boastful, boastful only in circumstances where nothing but high
genius or high training, I suppose, can save an American from
being boastful. I found a language straightforward, nervous,
10   firm, possessing in general the high merit of saying clearly in
the fewest possible words what had to be said, and saying it,
frequently, with shrewd and unexpected turns of expression.
The *Memoirs* renewed and completed the impression which the
letter given by General Badeau had made upon me. And now
15   I want to enable Grant and his *Memoirs* as far as possible to
speak for themselves to the English public, which knows them,
I believe, as imperfectly as a few months ago I myself did.

General Grant was born at Point Pleasant, in the State of
Ohio, on the 27th of April, 1822. His name, *Ulysses*, makes one
20   think of *Tristram Shandy;* but how often do American names
make one think of *Tristram Shandy!* The father of the little
Ulysses followed the trade of a tanner; he was a constant reader
both of books and newspapers, and "before he was twenty
years of age was a constant contributor," his son tells us, "to
25   Western newspapers, and was also, from that time until he
was fifty years old, an able debater in the societies for this
purpose, which were then common in the West." Of many and
many an American farmer and tradesman this is the history.
General Grant, however, never shared the paternal and national
30   love for public speaking. As to his schooling, he never, he tells
us, missed a quarter from school, from the time he was old
enough to attend till the time when he left home, at the age of
seventeen, for the Military Academy at West Point. But the
instruction in the country schools at that time was very poor:—
35   "A single teacher—who was often a man or a woman incapable of teaching much, even if they imparted all they knew—
would have thirty or forty scholars, male and female, from the

infant learning the A B C, up to the young lady of eighteen and the boy of twenty studying the highest branches taught—the three R's. I never saw an algebra, or other mathematical work higher than the arithmetic, until after I was appointed to West Point. I then bought a work on algebra in Cincinnati; but, having no teacher, it was Greek to me."

This schooling is unlike that of our young gentlemen preparing for Sandhurst or Woolwich, but still more unlike theirs is Grant's life out of school-hours. He has told us how regularly he attended his school, such as it was. He proceeds:

"This did not exempt me from labour. In my early days, every one laboured more or less in the region where my youth was spent, and more in proportion to their private means. It was only the very poor who were exempt. While my father carried on the manufacture of leather and worked at the trade himself, he owned and tilled considerable land. I detested the trade, preferring almost any other labour; but I was fond of agriculture and of all employments in which horses were used. We had, among other lands, fifty acres of forest within a mile of the village. In the fall of the year choppers were employed to cut enough wood to last a twelvemonth. When I was seven or eight years of age I began hauling all the wood used in the house and shops. I could not load it on the wagons, of course, at that time, but I could drive, and the choppers would load and some one at the house unload. When about eleven years old, I was strong enough to hold a plough. From that age until seventeen I did all the work done with horses, such as breaking up the land, furrowing, ploughing corn and potatoes, bringing in the crops when harvested, hauling all the wood, besides tending two or three horses, a cow or two, and sawing wood for stoves, &c., while still attending school. For this I was compensated by the fact that there never was any scolding or punishing by my parents: no objection to rational enjoyments, such as fishing, going to the creek a mile away to swim in summer; taking a horse and visiting my grandparents in the adjoining county, fifteen miles off; skating on the ice in winter, or taking a horse and sleigh when there was snow on the ground."

The bringing up of Abraham Lincoln was also, I suppose, much on this wise; and meagre, too meagre, as may have been the schooling, I confess I am inclined on the whole to exclaim: "What a wholesome bringing up it was!"

I must find room for one story of Grant's boyhood, a story which he tells against himself:—

"There was a Mr. Ralston living within a few miles of the village, who owned a colt that I very much wanted. My father had offered twenty dollars for it, but Ralston wanted twenty-five. I was so anxious to have the colt, that, after the owner left, I begged to be allowed to take him at the price demanded. My father yielded, but said twenty dollars was all the horse was worth, and told me to offer that price; if it was not accepted, I might offer twenty-two and a half, and if that would not get him, might give the twenty-five. I at once mounted a horse and went for the colt. When I got to Mr. Ralston's house, I said to him: 'Papa says I may offer you twenty dollars for the colt, but if you won't take that, I am to offer twenty-two and a half, and if you won't take that, to give you twenty-five.' It would not require a Connecticut man to guess the price finally agreed upon. I could not have been over eight years old at the time. This transaction caused me great heart-burning. The story got amongst the boys of the village, and it was a long time before I heard the last of it."

The boys of the village may well have been amused. How astounding to find an American boy so little "'cute," so little "smart." But how delightful also, and how refreshing; how full of promise for the boy's future character! Grant came in later life to see straight and to see clear, more than most men, more than even most Americans, whose virtue it is that in matters within their range they see straight and see clear; but he never was in the least "smart," and it is one of his merits.

The United States Senator for Ohio procured for young Grant, when he was seventeen years old, a nomination to West Point. He was not himself eager for it. His father one day said to him: "Ulysses, I believe you are going to receive the appointment." "'What appointment?' I enquired. 'To West

Point; I have applied for it.' 'But I won't go,' I said. He said he thought I would, *and I thought so too, if he did*. I really had no objection to going to West Point, except that I had a very exalted idea of the acquirements necessary to get through. I did not believe I possessed them, and could not bear the idea of failing." 5

He did go. Although he had no military ardour he desired to see the world. Already he had seen more of it than most of the boys of his village; he had visited Cincinnati, the principal city of his native State, and Louisville, the principal 10 city of the adjoining State of Kentucky; he had also been out as far as Wheeling in Virginia, and now, if he went to West Point, he would have the opportunity of seeing Philadelphia and New York. "When these places were visited," he says, "I would have been glad to have had a steamboat or railroad 15 collision, or any other accident happen, by which I might have received a temporary injury sufficient to make me ineligible for awhile to enter the Academy." He took his time on the road, and having left home in the middle of May, did not arrive at West Point until the end of the month. Two weeks later he 20 passed his examination for admission, very much, he tells us, to his surprise. But none of his professional studies interested him, though he did well in mathematics, which he found, he says, very easy to him. Throughout his first year he found the life tedious, read novels, and had no intention of remaining in the 25 army, even if he should succeed in graduating at the end of his four years' course, a success which he did not expect to attain. When in 1839 a Bill was discussed in Congress for abolishing the Military Academy, he hoped the Bill might pass, and so set him free. But it did not pass, and a year later he would have 30 been sorry, he says, if it had passed, although he still found his life at West Point dull. His last two years went quicker than his first two; but they still seemed to him "about five times as long as Ohio years." At last all his examinations were passed, he was appointed to an infantry regiment, and, before joining, 35 went home on leave with a desperate cough and a stature which had run up too fast for his strength.

In September 1843 he joined his regiment, the 4th United States infantry, at Jefferson Barracks, St. Louis. No doubt his training at West Point, an establishment with a public and high standing, and with serious studies, had been invaluable to him. But still he had no desire to remain in the army. At St. Louis he met and became attached to a young lady whom he afterwards married, Miss Dent, and his hope was to become an assistant professor of mathematics at West Point. With this hope he re-read at Jefferson Barracks his West Point mathematics, and pursued a course of historical study also. But the Mexican war came on and kept him in the army.

With the annexation of Texas in prospect, Grant's regiment was moved to Fort Jessup on the western border of Louisiana. Ostensibly the American troops were to prevent filibustering into Texas; really they were sent as a menace to Mexico in case she appeared to comtemplate war. Grant's life in Louisiana was pleasant. He had plenty of professional duty, many of his brother officers having been detailed on special duty away from the regiment. He gave up the thought of becoming a teacher of mathematics, and read only for his own amusement, "and not very much for that;" he kept a horse and rode, visited the planters on the Red River, and was out of doors the whole day nearly; and so he quite recovered from the cough, and the threatenings of consumption, which he had carried with him from West Point. "I have often thought," he adds, "that my life was saved, and my health restored, by exercise and exposure enforced by an administrative act and a war, both of which I disapproved."

For disapprove the menace to Mexico, and the subsequent war, he did. One lingers over a distinguished man's days of growth and formation, so important for all which is to come after. And already, under young Grant's plain exterior and air of indifference, there had grown up in him an independent and sound judgment. "Generally the officers of the army were indifferent whether the annexation was consummated or not; but not so all of them. For myself, I was bitterly opposed to the measure, and to this day regard the war which resulted as one of the most unjust ever waged by a stronger against a weaker nation."

Texas was annexed, a territory larger than the Austrian Empire; and after taking military possession of Texas, the American army of occupation, under General Taylor, went on and occupied some more disputed territory beyond. Even here they did not stop, but went further on still, meaning apparently to force the Mexicans to attack them and begin war. "We were sent to provoke war, but it was essential that Mexico should commence it. It was very doubtful whether Congress would declare war; but if Mexico should attack our troops, the Executive could announce: 'Whereas war exists by the acts of, etc.,' and prosecute the contest with vigour. Once initiated, there were few public men who would have the courage to oppose it."

Incensed at the Americans fortifying themselves on the Rio Grande, opposite Matamoras, the Mexicans at last fired the necessary shot, and the war was commenced. This was in March 1846. In September 1847 the American army entered the city of Mexico. Vera Cruz, Puebla, and other principal cities of the country, were already in their possession. In February 1848 was signed the treaty which gave to the United States Texas with the Rio Grande for its boundary, and the whole territory then included in New Mexico and Upper California. For New Mexico and California, however, the Americans paid a sum of fifteen millions of dollars.

Grant marks with sagacity and justness the causes and effects of the Mexican war. As the North grew in numbers and population, the South required more territory to counterbalance it; to maintain through this wide territory the institution of slavery, it required to have control of the national Government. With great energy and ability, it obtained this control; it acquired Texas and other large regions for slavery; it proceeded to use the powers of Government, in the North as well as in the South, for the purpose of securing and maintaining its hold upon its slaves. But the wider the territory over which slavery was spread, and the more numerous the slaves, the greater be-

came the difficulty of making this hold quite secure, and the stronger grew the irritation of the North to see the powers and laws of the whole nation used for the purpose. The Fugitive Slave Law brought this irritation to its height, made it uncon-
5   trollable, and the War of Secession was the result. "The Southern rebellion," says Grant, "was largely the outgrowth of the Mexican war. Nations, like individuals, are punished for their transgressions. We got our punishment in the most sanguinary and expensive war of modern times."

10 The part of Grant in the Mexican war was of course that of a young subaltern only, and is described by him with characteristic modesty. He showed, however, of what good stuff he was made, and his performances with a certain howitzer in a church-steeple so pleased his general that he sent for Grant,
15 commended him, and ordered a second howitzer to be placed at his disposal. A captain of voltigeurs came with the gun in charge. "I could not tell the general," says Grant, "that there was not room enough in the steeple for another gun, because he probably would have looked upon such a statement as a
20 contradiction from a second lieutenant. I took the captain with me, but did not use his gun."

When the evacuation of Mexico was completed, Grant married, in August 1848, Miss Julia Dent, to whom he had been engaged more than four years. For two years the young couple
25 lived at Detroit in Michigan, where Grant was now stationed; he was then ordered to the Pacific coast. It was settled that Mrs. Grant should, during his absence, live with her own family at St. Louis. The regiment went first to Aspinwall, then to California and Oregon. In 1853 Grant became captain. But he
30 had now two children, and saw no chance of supporting his family on his pay as an army officer. He determined to resign, and in the following year he did so. He left the Pacific coast, he tells us, very much attached to it, and with the full intention of one day making his home there, an intention which he
35 did not abandon until, in the winter of 1863-4, Congress passed the Act appointing him Lieutenant-General of the armies of the United States.

His life on leaving the army offers, like his early training, a curious contrast to what usually takes place amongst ourselves. First he tried farming, on a farm belonging to his wife near St. Louis; but he could not make it answer, though he worked hard. He had insufficient capital, and more than sufficient fever 5 and ague. After four years he established a partnership with a cousin of his wife named Harry Boggs, in a real estate agency business in St. Louis. He found that the business was not more than one person could do, and not enough to support two families. So he withdrew from the co-partnership with Boggs, 10 and in May 1860 removed to Galena, Illinois, and took a clerkship in a leather shop there belonging to his father.

Politics now began to interest him, and his reflexions on them at the moment when the War of Secession was approaching I must quote: 15

"Up to the Mexican war there were a few out and out abolitionists, men who carried their hostility to slavery into all elections, from those for a justice of the peace up to the Presidency of the United States. They were noisy but not numerous. But the great majority of people at the North, where 20 slavery did not exist, were opposed to the institution, and looked upon its existence in any part of the country as unfortunate. They did not hold the States where slavery existed responsible for it, and believed that protection should be given to the right of property in slaves until some satisfactory way 25 could be reached to be rid of the institution. Opposition to slavery was a creed of neither political party. But with the inauguration of the Mexican war, in fact with the annexation of Texas, the inevitable conflict commenced. As the time for the Presidential election of 1856—the first at which I had the 30 opportunity of voting—approached, party feeling began to run high."

Grant himself voted in 1856 for Buchanan, the candidate of the Slave States, because he saw clearly, he says, that in the exasperation of feeling at that time, the election of a Republi- 35 can President meant the secession of all the Slave States, and the plunging of the country into a war of which no man could foretell the issue. He hoped that in the course of the next four years—the Slave States having got a President of their own choice, and being without a pretext for secession—men's passions would quiet down, and the catastrophe be averted. Even if it was not, he thought the country would by that time be better prepared to receive the shock and to resist it.

I am not concerned to discuss Grant's reasons for his vote, but I wish to remark how completely his reflexions dispose of the reproaches addressed so often by Americans to England for not sympathising with the North attacking slavery, in a war with the South upholding it. From what he says it is evident how very far the North was, when the war began, from attacking slavery. Grant himself was not for attacking it; Lincoln was not. They, and the North in general, wished "that protection should be given to the right of property in slaves, until some satisfactory way could be reached to be rid of the institution." England took the North at its word, and regarded its struggle as one for preserving the Union, and the force and greatness which accrue from the Union, not for abolishing slavery. True, far-sighted people here might perceive that the war must probably issue, if the North prevailed, in the abolition of slavery, and might wish well to the North on that account. They did so; coldly, it is true, for the attitude of the North was not such as to call forth enthusiasm, but sincerely. A great number of people in England, on the other hand, looking at the surface of things merely, clearly seeing that the North was not meaning to attack slavery but to uphold the power and grandeur of the United States, thought themselves quite free to wish well to the South, the weaker side which was making a gallant fight, and to favour the breaking up of the Union.

Here was the real offence. The Americans of the North, admiring and valuing their great Republic above all things, could not forgive disfavour or coldness to it; could only impute them to envy and jealousy. Far-sighted people in England might perceive that the maintenance of the Union was not only likely to bring about the emancipation of the slave, but was also on other grounds to be desired for the good of the world. Our artizans might be in sympathy with the popular and unaristocratic institutions of the United States, and be therefore averse to any weakening of the great Republic. And these feelings prevailed here, as is well known, so as to govern the course taken by this country during the War of Secession. Still, there was much disfavour, and more coldness. Americans were, and are, indignant that the upholding of their great Republic should have had in England such cold friends, and so many actual enemies. It is like the indignant astonishment of George Sand during the German war, "to see Europe looking on with indifference to the danger of such a civilization as that of France." But admiration and favour are uncompellable; we admire and favour only an object which delights us, helps us, elevates us, and does us good. The thing is to make us feel that the object does this. Self-admiration and self-laudation will not convince us; on the contrary, they indispose us. France would be more attractive to us if she were less prone to call herself the head of civilization and the pride of the world; the United States, if they were more backward in proclaiming themselves "the greatest nation upon earth."

In 1860 Lincoln was elected President, and the catastrophe, which Grant hoped might have been averted, arrived. He had in 1860 no vote, but things were now come to that pass that he felt compelled to make his choice between minority rule and rule by the majority, and he was glad, therefore, to see Lincoln elected. Secession was imminent, and with secession, war; but Grant confesses that his own views at that time were those officially expressed later on by Mr. Seward, that "the war would be over in ninety days." He retained these views, he tells us, until after the battle of Shiloh.

Lincoln was not to come into office until the spring of 1861. The South was confident and defiant, and in the North there were prominent men and newspapers declaring that the government had no legal right to coerce the South. It was unsafe for Mr. Lincoln, when he went to be sworn into office in March 1861, to travel as President-elect; he had to be smuggled

into Washington. When he took on the 4th of March his oath
of office to maintain the Union, eleven States had gone out of
it. On the 11th of April, Fort Sumter in Charleston harbour
was fired upon, and a few days after was captured. Then the
5   President issued a call for 75,000 men. "There was not a State
in the North of a million inhabitants," says Grant, "that would
not have furnished the entire number faster than arms could
have been supplied to them, if it had been necessary."

As soon as news of the call for volunteers reached Galena,
10 where Grant lived, the citizens were summoned to meet at the
Court House in the evening. The Court House was crammed.
Grant, though a comparative stranger, was called upon to
preside, because he had been in the army, and had seen service.
"With much embarrassment and some prompting, I made out
15 to announce the object of the meeting." Speeches followed;
then volunteers were called for to form the company which
Galena had to furnish. The company was raised, and the officers and non-commissioned officers were elected, before the
meeting adjourned. Grant declined the captaincy before the
20 balloting, but promised to help them all he could, and to be
found in the service, in some position, if there should actually be
war. "I never," he adds, "went into our leather store after that
meeting, to put up a package or do other business."

After seeing the company mustered at Springfield, the capital
25 of Illinois, Grant was asked by the Governor of the State to
give some help in the military office, where his old army experience enabled him to be of great use. But on the 24th of May he
wrote to the Adjutant-General of the Army, saying that, "having been fifteen years in the regular army, including four at
30 West Point, and feeling it the duty of every one who has been
educated at the Government expense to offer their services for
the support of the Government," he wished to tender his services until the close of the war, "in such capacity as may be
offered." He got no answer. He then thought of getting ap-
35 pointed on the staff of General McClellan, whom he had
known at West Point, and went to seek the General at Cincinnati. He called twice, but failed to see him. While he was at

Cincinnati, however, the President issued his second call for troops, this time for 300,000 men; and the Governor of Illinois, mindful of Grant's recent help, appointed him colonel of the 21st Illinois regiment of infantry. In a month he had brought his regiment into a good state of drill and discipline, and was then ordered to a point on a railroad in Missouri, where an Illinois regiment was surrounded by "rebels." His own account of his first experience as a Commander is very characteristic of him:

"My sensations as we approached what I supposed might be 'a field of battle,' were anything but agreeable. I had been in all the engagements in Mexico that it was possible for one person to be in; but not in command. If some one else had been colonel, and I had been lieutenant-colonel, I do not think I would have felt any trepidation. Before we were prepared to cross the Mississippi River at Quincy, my anxiety was relieved; for the men of the besieged regiment came straggling into the town. I am inclined to think both sides got frightened and ran away."

Now, however, he was started; and from this time until he received Lee's surrender at Appomattox Court House, four years later, he was always the same strong man, showing the same valuable qualities. He had not the pathos and dignity of Lee, his power of captivating the admiring interest, almost the admiring affection, of his profession and of the world. He had not the fire, the celerity, the genial cordiality of Sherman, whose person and manner emitted a *ray* (to adopt, with a very slight change, Lamb's well-known lines)—

> "a ray
> Which struck a cheer upon the day,
> A cheer which would not go away—"

Grant had not these. But he certainly had a good deal of the character and qualities which we so justly respect in the Duke of Wellington. Wholly free from show, parade, and pomposity; sensible and sagacious; scanning closely the situation, seeing things as they actually were, then making up his mind as to the

right thing to be done under the circumstances, and doing it;
never flurried, never vacillating, but also not stubborn, able to
reconsider and change his plans, a man of resource; when, however, he had really fixed on the best course to take, the right
5   nail to drive, resolutely and tenaciously persevering, driving
the nail hard home—Grant was all this, and surely in all this he
resembles the Duke of Wellington.

The eyes of Europe, during the War of Secession, were
chiefly fixed on the conflict in the East. Grant, however, as we
10 have seen, began his career, not on the great and conspicuous
stage of the East, but in the West. He did not come to the East
until, by taking Vicksburg, he had attracted all eyes to the
West, and to the course of events there.

We have seen how Grant's first expedition in command
15 ended. The second ended in much the same way, and is related
by him with the same humour. He was ordered to move against
a Colonel Thomas Harris, encamped on the Salt River. As
Grant and his men approached the place where they expected
to find Harris, "my heart," he says, "kept getting higher and
20 higher, until it felt to me as if it was in my throat." But when
they reached the point from which they looked down into the
valley where they supposed Harris to be, behold, Harris was
gone! "My heart resumed its place. It occurred to me at once
that Harris had been as much afraid of me as I had been of him.
25 This was a view of the question I had never taken before, but I
never forgot it afterwards. I never forgot that an enemy had as
much reason to fear my forces as I had his. The lesson was valuable."

But already he inspired confidence. Shortly after his return
30 from the Salt River, the President asked the Congressmen from
Illinois to recommend seven citizens of that State for the rank
of brigadier-general, and the Congressmen unanimously recommended Grant first on the list. In August he was appointed to
the command of a district, and on the 4th of September assumed
35 command at Cairo, where the Ohio River joins the Mississippi.
His first important success was to seize and fortify Paducah, an
important post at the mouth of the Tennessee River, about fifty

miles from Cairo. By the 1st of November he had 20,000 well-drilled men under his command. In November he fought a smart action at Belmont, on the western bank of the Mississippi, with the object of preventing the Confederates who were in strong force at Columbus in Kentucky, on the eastern bank, from detaching troops to the West. He succeeded in his object, and his troops, who came under fire for the first time, behaved well. Grant himself had a horse shot under him.

Very important posts to the Confederates were Fort Henry on the Tennessee and Fort Donelson on the Cumberland River. Grant thought he could capture Fort Henry. He went to St. Louis to see General Halleck, whose subordinate he was, and to state his plan. "I was received with so little cordiality that I perhaps stated the object of my visit with less clearness than I might have done, and I had not uttered many sentences before I was cut short as if my plan was preposterous. I returned to Cairo very much crest-fallen."

He persevered, however, and after consulting with the officer commanding the gunboats at Cairo, he renewed, by telegraph, the suggestion that, if permitted, he "could take and hold Fort Henry on the Tennessee." This time he was backed by the officer in command of the gunboats. Next day, he wrote fully to explain his plan. In two days he received instructions from headquarters to move upon Fort Henry, and on the 2nd of February, 1862, the expedition started.

He took Fort Henry on the 6th of February, and announcing his success to General Halleck, informed him that he would now take Fort Donelson. On the 16th, Fort Donelson surrendered, and Grant made nearly 15,000 prisoners. There was delight in the North, depression at Richmond. Grant was at once promoted to be major-general of volunteers. He thought, both then and ever after, that by the fall of Fort Donelson the way was opened to the forces of the North all over the southwest without much resistance, that a vigorous commander, disposing of all the troops west of the Alleghanies, might have at once marched to Chattanooga, Corinth, Memphis, and Vicksburg, and broken down every resistance. There was no such commander, and time was given to the enemy to collect armies and fortify new positions.

The next point for attack was Corinth, at the junction of the two most important railroads in the Mississippi Valley. After Grant had, after a hard and bloody struggle of two days, won the battle of Shiloh, in which a ball cut in two the scabbard of his sword, and more than 10,000 men were killed and wounded on the side of the North, General Halleck, who did not love Grant, arrived on the scene of action and assumed the command. "Although next to him in rank," says Grant, "and nominally in command of my old district and army, I was ignored as much as if I had been at the most distant point of territory within my jurisdiction." On the advance to Corinth, "I was little more than an observer. Orders were sent direct to the right wing or reserve, ignoring me, and advances were made from one line of intrenchments to another without notifying me. My position was so embarrassing, in fact, that I made several applications to be relieved." When he suggested a movement, he was silenced. Presently the Confederate troops evacuated Corinth in safety, carrying with them all public property. On the side of the North, there was much disappointment at the slackness with which the enemy had been pressed, and at his success in saving his entire army.

But Corinth was evacuated; the naval forces of the North took Memphis, and now held the Mississippi River from its source to that point; New Orleans and Baton Rouge had fallen into their possession. The Confederates at the West were now narrowed down, for all communication with Richmond, to the single line of road running east from Vicksburg. To dispossess them of Vicksburg, therefore, was of the highest importance. At this point I must stop for the present. Public attention was not yet fixed upon Grant, as it became after his success at Vicksburg; and with his success there a second chapter of his life opens. But already he had shown his talent for succeeding. Cardinal Mazarin used to ask concerning a man before employing him, *Est-il heureux?* Grant was *heureux.*

[PART II*]

We left Grant projecting his attack upon Vicksburg. In the autumn of 1862, the second year of the war, the prospect for the North appeared gloomy. The Confederates were further advanced than at the beginning of the struggle. Many loyal people, says Grant, despaired at that time of ever saving the 5 Union; President Lincoln never himself lost faith in the final triumph of the Northern cause, but the administration at Washington was uneasy and anxious. The elections of 1862 had gone against the party which was for prosecuting the war at all costs and at all risks until the Union was saved. Voluntary enlist- 10 ments had ceased; to fill the ranks of the Northern armies the draft had been resorted to. Unless a great success came to restore the spirit of the North, it seemed probable that the draft would be resisted, that men would begin to desert, and that the power to capture and punish deserters would be lost. It was 15 Grant's conviction that there was nothing left to be done but *"to go forward to a decisive victory."*

At first, however, after the battle of Shiloh and the taking of Corinth, he could accomplish little. General Halleck, his chief, appears to have been at this time ill-disposed to him, and to 20 have treated him with coldness and incivility. In July 1862, General Halleck was appointed general-in-chief of all the armies of the North, with his headquarters in Washington, and Grant remained in Tennessee in chief command. But his army suffered such depletion by detaching men to defend long lines 25 of communication, to repair ruined railroads, to reinforce generals in need of succour, that he found himself entirely on the defensive in a hostile territory. Nevertheless in a battle fought to protect Corinth he repulsed the enemy with great slaughter, and being no longer anxious for the safety of the territory 30 within his command, and having been reinforced, he resolved on a forward movement against Vicksburg.

* Personal Memoirs of U. S. Grant. (2 vols.; Sampson Low, Marston, & Co.).

Vicksburg occupies the first high ground on the Mississippi below Memphis. Communication between the parts of the Confederacy divided by the Mississippi was through Vicksburg. So long as the Confederates held Vicksburg, and Port
5   Hudson lower down, the free navigation of the river was prevented. The fall of Vicksburg, as the event proved, was sure to bring with it the fall of Port Hudson also. Grant saw nearly his whole force absorbed in holding the railway lines north of Vicksburg; he considered that if he moved forward, driving
10 the enemy before him into Southern territory not as yet subdued, those lines in his rear would almost hold themselves, and most of his force would be free for field operations. But in moving forward he moved further from his bases of supplies. One of these was at Holly Springs, in the north of the State of
15 Mississippi; the enemy appeared there, captured the garrison, and destroyed all the stores of food, forage, and munitions of war. This loss taught Grant a lesson by which he, and Sherman after him, profited greatly: the lesson that in a wide and productive country, such as that in which he was operating, to cling to
20 a distant base of supply was not necessary; the country he was in would afford the supplies needed. He was amazed, he says, when he was compelled by the loss of Holly Springs to collect supplies in the country immediately around him, at the abundant quantity which the country afforded. He found that after
25 leaving two months' supplies for the use of the families whose stores were taken, he could, off the region where he was, have subsisted his army for a period four times as long as he had actually to remain there. Later in the campaign he took full advantage of the experience thus gained.

30   The fleet under Admiral Porter co-operated with him, but all endeavours to capture Vicksburg from the north were unavailing. The Mississippi winds and winds through its rich alluvial valley; the country is intersected by *bayous* or water-courses filled from the river, with overhanging trees and with narrow
35 and tortuous channels, where the bends could not be turned by a vessel of any length. To cross this country in the face of an enemy was impossible. The problem was to get in rear of the

object of attack, and to secure a footing upon dry ground on the high or eastern side of the Mississippi—the side on which Vicksburg stands—for operating against the place. On the 30th of January, 1863, Grant, having left Memphis, took the command at Young's Point in Louisiana, on the western bank of the Mississippi, not far above Vicksburg, bent on solving the problem.

It was a wet country and a wet winter, with high water in the Mississippi and its tributaries. The troops encamped on the river bank had, in order to be out of the water, to occupy the levees, or dykes, along the river edge, and the ground immediately behind. This gave so limited a space, that one corps of Grant's army, when he assumed the command at Young's Point, was at Lake Providence, seventy miles above Vicksburg. The troops suffered much from malarial fevers and other sickness, but the hospital arrangements were excellent.

Four ineffectual attempts were in the course of the winter made to get at the object of attack by various routes. Grant, meanwhile, was maturing his plan. His plan was to traverse the peninsula where he lay encamped, then to cross the Mississippi, and thus to be able to attack Vicksburg from the south and east. Above Young's Point, at Milliken's Bend, begins a series of bayous, forming, as it were, the chord of an immense bend of the Mississippi, and falling into the river some fifty miles below Vicksburg. Behind the levees bordering these bayous were tolerable roads, by which, as soon as they emerged from the waters, Grant's troops and wagon-trains could cross the peninsula. The difficulties were indeed great: four bridges had to be built across wide bayous, and the rapid fall of the waters increased the current, and made bridge-building troublesome; but at work of this kind the "Yankee soldier" is in his element. By the 24th of April Grant had his headquarters at the southern extremity of the bend. The navy under Admiral Porter, escorting steamers and barges to serve as ferries and for the transport of supplies, had run fourteen miles of batteries, passed Vicksburg, and come down the river to join Grant. A further march of twenty-two miles was still necessary in order to reach

the first high ground, where the army might land and establish itself on the eastern shore. This first high land is at Grand Gulf, a place strongly held at that time by the Confederates, and as unattackable from the river as Vicksburg itself. Porter ran the
5   batteries of Grand Gulf as he had run those of Vicksburg; the army descended the river a few miles, and on the 30th of April was landed at Bruinsburg, on the eastern shore, without meeting an enemy.

Grant's plan had succeeded. He was established on the east-
10 ern bank, below and in rear of Vicksburg. Though Vicksburg was not yet taken, and though he was in the enemy's country, with a vast river and the stronghold of Vicksburg between him and his base of supplies, yet he "felt a degree of relief scarcely ever equalled since. I was on dry ground on the same side of the
15 river with the enemy."

And indeed from this moment his success was continuous. The enemy had at Grand Gulf, at Haines Bluff north of Vicksburg, and at Jackson, the capital of the State of Mississippi, in which State all these places are, about 60,000 men. After fight-
20 ing and losing an action to cover Grand Gulf, the Confederates evacuated that place, and Grant occupied it on the 3rd of May. By the 7th of May Sherman joined him at Grand Gulf, and he found himself with a force of 33,000 men. He then determined at once to attack the enemy's forces in the rear of Vicksburg,
25 and then to move on the stronghold itself. In order to use Grand Gulf as his base of supplies for these operations, he must have constructed additional roads, and this would have been a work of time. He determined therefore merely to bring up by the single road available from Grand Gulf, what rations of
30 biscuit, coffee, and salt he could, and to make the country he traversed furnish everything else. Beef, mutton, poultry, molasses, and forage were to be found, he knew, in abundance. The cautious Halleck would be sure to disapprove this bold plan of almost abandoning the base of supplies, but Grant counted on
35 being able to obtain his object before he could be interfered with from Washington.

The nature of the ground making Vicksburg easily defensible on the south, Grant determined to get on the railroad running east from Vicksburg to Jackson, the State capital, and to approach the stronghold from that side. At Jackson was a strong Confederate force, the city was an important railway centre, and all supplies of men and stores for Vicksburg came thence; this source of aid had to be stopped. But in order to reach Jackson, Grant had to abandon even that one road by which he had partially supplied his army hitherto, to cut loose from his base of supplies altogether. He did so without hesitation. After a successful action he entered Jackson on the 14th of May, driving out of it the Confederates under General Johnston, and destroyed the place in so far as it was a railroad centre and a manufactory of military supplies. Then he turned westward, and after a severe battle shut up Pemberton in Vicksburg. An assault on Pemberton's defences was unsuccessful, but Vicksburg was closely invested. Pemberton's stores began to run short, Johnston was unable to come to his relief, and on the 4th of July, Independence Day, he surrendered Vicksburg, with its garrison of nearly thirty-two thousand men, ordnance and stores. As Grant had foreseen, Port Hudson surrendered as soon as the fall of Vicksburg became known, and the great river was once more open from St. Louis to the sea.

In the north the victory of Gettysburg was won on the same day on which Vicksburg surrendered. A load of anxiety was lifted from the minds of the President and his ministers; the North took heart again, and resolved to continue the war with energy, in the hope of soon bringing it to a triumphant issue. The great and decisive event bringing about this change was the fall of Vicksburg, and the merit of that important success was due to Grant.

He had been successful, and in his success he still retained his freedom from "bounce" and from personal vanity; his steadfast concern for the public good; his moderation. Let us hear his account of being under fire during a fruitless attack by Admiral Porter's gunboats on the batteries of Grand Gulf:

"I occupied a tug, from which I could see the effect of the battle on both sides, within range of the enemy's guns; *but a small tug, without armament, was not calculated to attract the fire of batteries while they were being assailed themselves.*"

He has to mention a risk incurred by himself; but mentioning it, he is at pains to minimise it.

When he assumed command in person at Young's Point, General McClernand, from whom the command now passed to
5   Grant, his senior and superior, showed temper and remonstrated:

"His correspondence with me on the subject was more in the nature of a reprimand than a protest. It was highly insubordinate, *but I overlooked it, as I believed, for the good of the*
10 *service*. General McClernand was a member of Congress when the Secession War broke out; he belonged to that party which furnished all the opposition there was to a vigorous prosecution of the war for saving the Union; but there was no delay in his declaring himself for the Union at all hazards, and there
15 was no uncertain sound in his declaration of where he stood in the contest before the country."

To such a man Grant wished to be forbearing when he could say to himself that, after all, it was only his own dignity which was concerned. But later, when an irregularity of the same
20 General was injurious to good feeling and unity in the army, Grant was prompt and severe:

"I received a letter from General Sherman, and one from General McPherson, saying that their respective commands had complained to them of a fulsome congratulatory order pub
25 lished by General McClernand to the 13th Corps, which did great injustice to the other troops engaged in the campaign. This order had been sent north and published, and now papers containing it had reached our camps. The order had not been heard of by me; I at once wrote to McClernand, directing him
30 to send me a copy of this order. He did so, and I at once relieved him from the command of the 13th Army Corps. The publication of his order in the press was in violation of War Department orders, and also of mine."

The newspaper press is apt to appear to an American, even
35 more than to an Englishman, as part of the order of nature, and contending with it seems like contending with destiny. Grant had governing instincts. "I always admired the South, as bad

as I thought their cause, for the boldness with which they silenced all opposition and all croaking by press or by individuals within their control." His instincts would have led him to follow this example. But since he could do nothing against the newspaper nuisance, and was himself the chief sufferer by it, he bore it with his native philosophy:

"Visitors to the camps went home with dismal stories. Northern papers came back to the soldiers with these stories exaggerated. Because I would not divulge my ultimate plans to visitors, they pronounced me idle, incompetent, and unfit to command men in an emergency, and clamoured for my removal. They were not to be satisfied, many of them, with my simple removal, but named who my successor should be. I took no steps to answer these complaints, but continued to do my duty, as I understood it, to the best of my ability."

Surely the Duke of Wellington would have read these *Memoirs* with pleasure. He might himself have issued, too, this order respecting behaviour towards prisoners: "Instruct the commands to be quiet and orderly as these prisoners pass, and to make no offensive remark." And this other, respecting behaviour in a conquered enemy's country: "Impress upon the men the importance of going through the State in an orderly manner, abstaining from taking anything not absolutely necessary for their subsistence whilst travelling. They should try to create as favourable an impression as possible upon the people."

But what even at this stage of the war is very striking, and of good augury for the re-union which followed, is the absence, in general, of bitter hatred between the combatants. There is nothing of internecine, inextinguishable, irreconcilable enmity, or of the temper, acts, and words which beget this. Often we find the vanquished Southerner showing a good-humoured audacity, the victorious Northerner a good-humoured forbearance. Let us remember Carrier at Nantes, or Davoust at Hamburg, and then look at Grant's picture of himself and Sherman at Jackson, when their troops had just driven the enemy out of this capital of a "rebel" State, and were destroying the stores and war-materials there:

"Sherman and I went together into a manufactory which had not ceased work on account of the battle, nor for the entrance of Yankee troops. Our entrance did not seem to attract the attention of either the manager or the operatives, most of whom were girls. We looked on for a while to see the tent cloth which they were making roll out of the looms, with "C.S.A."* woven in each bolt. Finally I told Sherman I thought they had done work enough. The operatives were told they could leave, and take with them what cloth they could carry. In a few minutes the factory was in a blaze. The proprietor visited Washington, while I was President, to get his pay for this property, claiming that it was private."

The American girls coolly continuing to make the Confederate tents under the eye of the hostile generals, and the proprietor claiming afterwards to be paid by Congress for them as private property, are charming.

It was one of Grant's superstitions, he tells us, never to apply for a post, or to use personal or political influence for obtaining it. He believed that if he had got it in this way he would have feared to undertake any plan of his own conception, for fear of involving his patrons in responsibility for his possible failure. If he were selected for a post, his responsibility ended, he said, with "his doing the best he knew how."

"Every one has his superstitions. One of mine is that in positions of great responsibility every one should do his duty to the best of his ability, where assigned by competent authority, without application or the use of influence to change his position. While at Cairo I had watched with very great interest the operations of the Army of the Potomac, looking upon that as the main field of the war. I had no idea, myself, of ever having any large command, nor did I suppose that I was equal to one; but I had the vanity to think that, as a cavalry officer, I might succeed very well in the command of a brigade. On one occasion, in talking about this to my staff officers, I said that I would give anything if I were commanding a brigade of cavalry

* Confederate States Army.

in the Army of the Potomac, and I believed I could do some good. Captain Hillyer suggested that I should make application to be transferred there to command the cavalry. I then told him that I would cut my right arm off first, and mentioned this superstition."

But now he was to be transferred, without any solicitation on his own part, to "the main field of the war." At first, however, he was appointed to the command of the "Military Division of the Mississippi," and after fighting a severe and successful battle at Chattanooga in November (1863), relieved that place and Knoxville, which the Confederates were threatening. President Lincoln, who had daily, almost hourly, been telegraphing to him to "remember Burnside," to "do something for Burnside," besieged in Knoxville, was overjoyed. "I wish," he wrote to Grant, "to tender you, and all under your command, my more than thanks, my profoundest gratitude, for the skill, courage and perseverance with which you and they, over so great difficulties, have effected this important object. God bless you all!" Congress voted him thanks and a gold medal for his achievements at Vicksburg and Chattanooga.

In the dead of the winter, with the thermometer below zero, he made an excursion into Kentucky, and had the pleasure of finding the people along his route, both in Tennessee and Kentucky, in general intensely loyal to the Union:

"They would collect in little places where we would stop of evenings, to see me. The people naturally expected to see the commanding general the oldest person in the party. I was then forty-one years of age, while my medical director was grey-haired, and probably twelve or more years my senior. The crowds would generally swarm around him, and thus give me an opportunity of quietly dismounting and getting into the house."

At the beginning of the next year, 1864, a Bill was passed through Congress for restoring the grade of Lieutenant-General in the army. Grant was nominated to that rank, and having been summoned to Washington he received his commission from the President on the 9th of March, in the presence of the

Ministers. Before he came to Washington, he had meant to return to his command in the West even after being made lieutenant-general; but at Washington he saw reason to change his mind. The important struggle was now between the Army

5   of the Potomac and Lee. From what he saw, Grant was convinced that in that struggle no one except himself, with the superior rank he now bore, could, probably, "resist the pressure that would be brought to bear upon him to desist from his own plans and pursue others." He obtained, therefore, the nomina-

10   tion of Sherman to succeed him in command of the Military Division of the Mississippi. On the 12th of March orders were published by the War Department, placing Grant in chief command of all the armies.

The position of General Meade, who was at that time in com-

15   mand of the Army of the Potomac, and who had won the important battle of Gettysburg in the previous summer, underwent a grave change through Grant's promotion. Both Meade and Grant behaved very well. Meade suggested to Grant that he might wish to have immediately under him Sherman, who

20   had been serving with Grant in the West. He begged him not to hesitate in making the change if he thought it for the good of the service. The work in hand, he said, was of such vast importance, that the feelings and wishes of no one person should stand in the way of selecting the right men. He was

25   willing himself to serve to the best of his ability wherever placed. Grant assured him that he had no thought of moving him, and in his *Memoirs*, after relating what had passed, he adds: "This incident gave me even a more favourable opinion of Meade than did his great victory at Gettysburg the July

30   before. It is men who wait to be selected, and not those who seek, from whom we may always expect the most efficient service." He tried to make Meade's position as nearly as possible what it would have been had he himself been away in Washington or elsewhere; he gave all orders for the movements

35   of the Army of the Potomac to Meade for execution, and to avoid the necessity of having to give direct orders himself, he established his headquarters close to Meade's whenever he

could. Meade's position, however, was undoubtedly a somewhat embarrassing one; but its embarrassment was not increased by soreness on his part, or by want of delicacy on Grant's.

In the West, the great objects to be attained by Sherman were the defeat of Johnston and his army, and the occupation of Atlanta. These objects he accomplished, proceeding afterwards to execute his brilliant and famous march to Savannah and the sea, sweeping the whole State of Georgia. In the East, the opposing forces stood between the Federal and Confederate capitals, and substantially in the same relations to each other as when the war began three years before. President Lincoln told Grant, when he first saw him in private, that although he had never professed to know how campaigns should be conducted, and never wanted to interfere in them, yet "procrastination on the part of commanders, and the pressure from the people at the North and Congress, *which was always with him*, forced him into issuing his series of Military Orders. He did not know but they were all wrong, and did know that some of them were. What he wanted," he continued, "was a general who would take the responsibility and act; he would support him with all the power of the Government." He added that he did not even ask to know what Grant's plans were. But such is human nature, that the next moment he brought out a map of Virginia, showed Grant two streams running into the Potomac, and suggested a plan of his own for landing the army between the mouths of these streams, which would protect its flanks while it moved out. "I listened respectfully," says Grant, with dry humour, "but did not suggest that the same streams would protect Lee's flanks while he was shutting us up."

In Grant the President had certainly found a general who would take the responsibility, would act, and would keep his plans to himself. To beat Lee and get possession of his army, was the object. If Lee was beaten and his army captured, the fall of Richmond must necessarily follow. If Richmond were taken by moving the army thither on transports up the James River, but meanwhile Lee's army were to remain whole and unimpaired, the end of the war was not brought any nearer.

But the end of the war must be reached soon, or the North might grow weary of continuing the struggle. For three years the war had raged, with immense losses on either side, and no decisive consummation reached by either. If the South could succeed in prolonging an indecisive struggle year after year still, the North might probably grow tired of the contest, and agree to a separation. Persuaded of this, Grant, at the beginning of May 1864, crossed the Rapidan with the Army of the Potomac, and commenced the forty-three days' Campaign of the Wilderness.

The Wilderness is a tract north of Richmond, between the Rapidan and the James River, much cut up with streams and morasses, full of broken ground, densely clothed with wood, and thinly inhabited. The principal streams between the Rapidan and the James River are the branches of the Anna, uniting in the Pamunkey, and the Chickahominy. The country was favourable for defence, and Lee was a general to make the most of its advantages. Grant was in an enemy's country, but, moving by his left flank, was in connection with the sea, of which the Northerners were masters, and was abundantly supplied with everything. Of artillery, in particular, he had so much that he was embarrassed by it, and had to send some of it away. Overwhelmingly superior in numbers and resources, he pressed steadily forward, failing and repulsed sometimes, but coolly persevering. This campaign, of which the stages are the battles of Chancellorsville, Spottsylvania, North Anna and Cold Harbour, was watched at the time in Europe with keen attention, and is much better known than the operations in the West. I shall not attempt any account of it; for its severity let the losses of Grant's successful army speak. When he crossed the Rapidan the Army of the Potomac numbered 115,000 men; during the forty-three days' campaign reinforcements were received amounting to 40,000 men more. When the army crossed the James River, it was 116,000 strong, almost exactly the same strength as at the beginning of the campaign. Thirty-nine thousand men had been lost in forty-three days.

A yet greater loss must have been incurred had Grant attacked Lee's lines in front of Richmond; and therefore, crossing the James River, he invested, after failing to carry it by assault, Petersburg, the enemy's important stronghold south of Richmond. Winter came and passed. Lee's army was safe in its lines, and Richmond had not yet fallen; but the Confederates' resources were failing, their foes gathering, and the end came 5 visibly near. After sweeping Georgia and taking Savannah in December, Sherman turned north and swept the Carolinas, ready to join with Grant in moving upon Lee in the spring. Sheridan made himself master of the Shenandoah Valley, and closed to the Confederates that great source of supply. Finally 10 Grant, resuming operations in March 1865, possessed himself of the outer works of Petersburg, and of the railroad by which the place was supplied from the south-west, and on the 3rd of April Petersburg was evacuated. Then Grant proceeded to possess himself of the railroad by which Lee's army and Rich- 15 mond itself now drew their supplies. Lee had already informed his government that he could hold out no longer. The Confederate President was at church when the despatch arrived, the congregation were told that there would be no evening service, and the authorities abandoned Richmond that afternoon. 20 In the field there was some sharp fighting for a day or two still; but Lee's army was crumbling away, and on the 9th of April he wrote to Grant, requesting an interview with him for the purpose of surrendering his army. Grant was suffering from sick headache when the officer bearing Lee's note reached him, "but 25 the instant I saw," he says, "the contents of the note, I was cured."

Then followed, in the afternoon of that same day, the famous interview at Appomattox Court House. Grant shall himself describe the meeting: 30

"When I had left camp that morning I had not expected so soon the result that was then taking place, and consequently was in rough garb. I was without a sword, as I usually was when on horseback in the field, and wore a soldier's blouse for a coat, with the shoulder-straps of my rank to indicate to the army 35 who I was. When I went into the house I found General Lee. We greeted each other, and, after shaking hands, took our seats.

"What General Lee's feelings were I do not know. As he was a man of much dignity, with an impassible face, it was impossible to say whether he felt inwardly glad that the end had finally come, or felt sad over the result and was too manly to
5   show it. Whatever his feelings, they were entirely concealed from my observation; but my own feelings, which had been quite jubilant on the receipt of his letter, were sad and depressed. I felt like anything rather than rejoicing at the downfall of a foe who had fought so long and valiantly, and had
10 suffered so much for a cause, though that cause was, I believe, one of the worst for which a people ever fought.

"General Lee was dressed in a full uniform which was entirely new, and was wearing a sword of considerable value, very likely the sword which had been presented by the State
15 of Virginia. In my rough travelling suit, the uniform of a private with the straps of a lieutenant-general, I must have contrasted very strangely with a man so handsomely dressed, six feet high and of faultless form. But this was not a matter that I thought of until afterwards.

20 "We soon fell into a conversation about old army times. He remarked that he remembered me well in the old army (of Mexico); and I told him that as a matter of course I remembered *him* perfectly, but from the difference in our rank and years (there being about sixteen years' difference in our ages)
25 I had thought it likely that I had not attracted his attention sufficiently to be remembered by him after such a long interval. Our conversation grew so pleasant that I almost forgot the object of our meeting. After the conversation had run on in this style for some time, General Lee called my attention to the
30 object of our meeting, and said that he had asked for this interview for the purpose of getting from me the terms I proposed to give his army. I said that I meant merely that his army should lay down their arms, not to take them up again during the continuance of the war unless duly and properly exchanged."

35 Lee acquiesced, and Grant, who throughout the interview seems to have behaved with true delicacy and kindness, proceeded to write out the terms of surrender. It occurred to him,

as he was writing, that it would be an unnecessary humiliation to the officers to call upon them to surrender their side-arms, and also that they would be glad to retain their private horses and effects, and accordingly he inserted in the terms that the surrender of arms and property was not to include the side-arms, horses and property of the officers. Lee remarked that this would have a happy effect on the army. Grant then said that most of the men in Lee's ranks were, he supposed, small farmers; that the country had been so raided by either army that it was doubtful whether they would be able to put in a crop to carry themselves and their families through the next winter without the aid of the horses they were then riding; that the United States did not want them, and he would therefore give instructions to let every man of the Confederate army, who claimed to own a horse or mule, take the animal to his home. Again Lee remarked that this would have a happy effect.

At half-past four Grant could telegraph to the Secretary of War at Washington: "General Lee surrendered the army of Northern Virginia this afternoon." As soon as the news of the surrender became known, Grant's army began to fire a salute of a hundred guns. Grant instantly stopped it.

The war was at an end. Johnston surrendered to Sherman in North Carolina. President Lincoln visited Richmond, which had been occupied by the Army of the Potomac the day after the Confederate Government abandoned it. The President on his return to Washington invited Grant, who also had now gone thither, to accompany him to the theatre on the evening of the 14th of April. Grant declined, because he was to go off that evening to visit his children who were at school in New Jersey; when he reached Philadelphia, he heard that the President and Mr. Seward had been assassinated. He immediately returned to Washington, to find the joy there turned to mourning. With this tragic event, and with the grand review in the following month of Meade's and Sherman's armies by the new President, Mr. Johnson, the *Memoirs* end.

Modest for himself, Grant is boastful, as Americans are apt to be, for his nation. He says with perfect truth that troops

who have fought a few battles and won, and followed up their
victories, improve upon what they were before to an extent
that can hardly be counted by percentage; and that his troops
and Sherman's which had gone through this training, were by
the end of the war become very good and seasoned soldiers.
But he is fond of adding, in what I must call the American vein,
"*better than any European soldiers.*" And the reason assigned
for this boast is in the American vein too: "Because they not
only worked like a machine, but the machine thought. European armies know very little what they are fighting for, and
care less." Is the German army a machine which does not think?
Did the French revolutionary armies know very little what
they were fighting for, and care less? Sainte-Beuve says charmingly that he "cannot bear to have it said that he is the *first* in
anything; it is not a thing that can be admitted, and these
ways of classing people give offence." German military men
read Grant's boast, and are provoked into replying that the
campaigns and battles of the American Civil War were mere
struggles of militia; English military men say that Americans
have been steady enough behind breastworks and entrench-
ments against regulars, but never in the open field. Why cannot
the Americans, in speaking of their nation, take Sainte-Beuve's
happy and wise caution?

The point is worth insisting on, because to be always seeking
to institute comparisons, and comparisons to the advantage of
their own country, is with so many Americans a *tic*, a mania,
which every one notices in them, and which sometimes drives
their friends half to despair. Recent greatness is always apt to
be sensitive and self-assertive; let us remember Dr. Herman
Grimm on Goethe. German literature, as a power, does not
begin before Lessing; if Germany had possessed a great literature for six centuries, with names in it like Dante, Montaigne,
Shakespeare, probably Dr. Herman Grimm would not have
thought it necessary to call Goethe the greatest poet that has
ever lived. But the Americans in the rage for comparison-mak-
ing beat the world. Whatever excellence is mentioned, America
must, if possible, be brought in to balance or surpass it. That

fine and delicate naturalist, Mr. Burroughs, mentions trout, and instantly he adds: "British trout, by the way, are not so beautiful as our own; they are less brilliantly marked and have much coarser scales, there is no gold or vermilion in their colouring." Here superiority is claimed; if there is not superiority there must be at least balance. Therefore in literature we have "the American Walter Scott," "the American Wordsworth"; nay, I see advertised *The Primer of American Literature*. Imagine the face of Philip or Alexander at hearing of a Primer of Macedonian Literature! Are we to have a Primer of Canadian Literature too, and a Primer of Australian? We are all contributories to one great literature—English Literature. The contribution of Scotland to this literature is far more serious and important than that of America has yet had time to be; yet a "Primer of Scotch Literature" would be an absurdity. And these things are not only absurd; they are also retarding.

My opinion on any military subject is of course worth very little, but I should have thought that in what Napier calls "strength and majesty" as a fighter, the American soldier, if we are to institute these comparisons, had his superiors; though as brave as any one, he is too ingenious, too mental, to be the perfection of a fighting animal. Where the Yankee soldier has an unrivalled advantage is in his versatility and ingenuity; dexterous, willing, suggestive, he can turn his hand to anything, and is of twenty trades at the same time with that of soldier. Grant's *Memoirs* are full of proofs of this faculty, which might perhaps be of no great use in a campaign in the Low Countries, but was invaluable in such campaigns as those which Grant and Sherman conducted in America. When the batteries at Vicksburg were to be run with hired river steamers, there were naturally but very few masters or crews who were willing to accompany their vessels on this service of danger. Volunteers were therefore called for from the army, men who had had any experience in river navigation. "Captains, pilots, mates, engineers, and deck-hands, enough presented themselves," says Grant, "to take five times the number of vessels we were moving." The resource and rapidity shown by the troops in the repair of railroads wrecked by the enemy were marvellous. In Sherman's Atlanta campaign, the Confederate cavalry lurking in his rear to burn bridges and obstruct his communications had become so disgusted at hearing trains go whistling by, within a few hours after a bridge had been burned, that they proposed to try blowing up some of the tunnels. One of them said on this: "No use, boys; old Sherman carries duplicate tunnels with him, and will replace them as fast as you can blow them up; better save your powder!"

But a leader to use these capable and intelligent forces, to use all the vast resources of the North, was needed, a leader wise, cool, firm, bold, persevering, and at the same time, as Cardinal Mazarin says, *heureux;* and such a leader the United States found in General Grant.

He concludes his *Memoirs* by some advice to his own country and some remarks on ours. The United States, he says, are going on as if in the greatest security, "when they have not the power to resist an invasion by the fleets of fourth-rate European Powers for a time until we could prepare for them." The United States "should have a good navy, and our sea-coast defences should be put in the finest possible condition. Neither of these cost much when it is considered where the money goes and what we get in return."

The tone and temper of his remarks on England, and on her behaviour during the war, are in honourable contrast with the angry acrimony shown by many who should have known better. He regretted, he said, the exasperation. "The hostility of England to the United States, during our rebellion, was not so much real as it was apparent. It was the hostility of the leaders of one political party. England and the United States are natural allies, and should be the best of friends."

The *Memoirs* stop, as I have said, in 1865, and do not embrace Grant's Presidency, his journey to Europe, his financial disaster, his painful illness and death. As to his financial disaster, I will repeat what one of Grant's best friends, a man of great business faculty and of great fortune, remarked to me. I had been saying, what one says so easily, that it was a pity Grant had suffered himself to be drawn in by speculators. "Yes," answered his friend, "it was a pity. But see how it happened, and put yourself in Grant's place. Like Grant, you may have a son to whom you are partial, and like Grant, you have no knowledge of business. Had you been, like Grant, in a position 5 to make it worth while for a leader in business and finance to come to you, saying that your son had a quite exceptional talent for these matters, that it was a thousand pities his talent should be thrown away, 'give him to me and I will make a man of him,' would you not have been flattered in your parental pride, 10 would you not have yielded? This is what happened to Grant, and all his financial misfortunes flowed from hence." I listened, and could not deny that most probably I should have been flattered to my ruin, as Grant was.

Grant's *Memoirs* are a mine of interesting things; I have but 15 scratched the surface and presented a few samples. When I began, I did not know that the book had been reprinted in England; I find that it has,* and that its circulation here, though trifling indeed compared to that in America, has been larger than I supposed. But certainly the book has not been read here 20 anything like so much as it deserves. It contains a gallery of portraits, characters of generals who served in the war, for which alone the book, if it contained nothing else, would be well worth reading. But after all, its great value is in the character which, quite simply and unconsciously, it draws of Grant 25 himself. The Americans are too self-laudatory, too apt to force the tone and thereby, as Sainte-Beuve says, to give offence; the best way for them to make us forgive and forget this is to produce what is simple and sterling. Instead of Primers of American Literature, let them bring forth more Maxims of Poor 30 Richard; instead of assurances that they are "the greatest nation upon earth," let them give us more Lees, Lincolns, Shermans, and Grants.

* By Messrs. Sampson Low, Marston & Co.

A 'Friend of God'

There has lately been published[1] a pretty little volume entitled *The Following of Christ, by John Tauler; done into English by J. R. Morell.* It is not certain that the work is by Tauler; the weight of authority and of probability is, it seems to me, against his being its author. The book has many repetitions, and a manner formal and sometimes tiresome of conducting its argument. Mr. Morell's translation is written in an English occasionally slovenly and even inaccurate. Still, this little volume—which is cheap, let me say, as well as pretty—should certainly not be suffered to pass unnoticed. If it does not proceed from Tauler himself, it proceeds from one of that remarkable group of German mystics—'Friends of God,' as they called themselves—amongst whom the great Dominican preacher of Strassburg lived and worked. And the contents of the little book, notwithstanding its forms and repetitions, are full of value. Therefore we may well say in this case with the *Imitation,*—which itself, also, issued from the deep religious movement felt in the Germanic lands along the Rhine in the fourteenth century:—'Ask not who wrote it, but attend to what it says.' Mr. Morell's translation, finally, in spite of its occasional inaccuracy and slovenliness, is on the whole a sound and good one, with the signal merit of faithfully reproducing the plain and earnest tone characteristic of the original.

Every one is familiar with the *Imitation*, attributed to Thomas à Kempis. Tauler however, and his immediate group, are to most of us names and nothing more. *Tauler's History and*

[1] By Burns & Oates, London and New York.

Life and Twenty-five of his Sermons, translated by Miss Winkworth, were published in 1857, with a preface by Charles
Kingsley. The book is out of print and can hardly be obtained.
Some of the sermons are interesting, but in general the book,
even if obtained, will disappoint, I think, those who have been   5
attracted to it by Tauler's reputation, and to reprint it as it
stands would be unadvisable. Much more interesting is the
Theologia Germanica, also translated by Miss Winkworth, a
work not by Tauler himself, but by one of his group who
shared his spirit. On this short book Luther set the very highest   10
value, and justly. But this book likewise is out of print, and
scarcely obtainable.

Its merit is of like kind with that of the book translated by
Mr. Morell to which I now wish to call attention. Each of the
two is an answer of the sincere and deeply religious German   15
nature to the need felt, by itself and by others, in a time such
as was the middle of the fourteenth century, a time 'of famine'
(to use the words of the prophet Amos) 'of hearing of the
words of the Eternal.' We read in the *Following of Christ:* 'It
is often said, He who suffereth a man to die of bodily hunger   20
when he might have helped the sufferer, would be guilty of the
death of that man. Much more is a man guilty towards souls
when he letteth them die of hunger. For just as the soul is
much nobler than the body, so much more are you guilty if
you allow the soul to suffer hunger.' To this hunger and suffer-   25
ing of the soul the *Following of Christ* is a response, but a response with a special character of its own. The *Imitation* is also
a response to the same hunger, but a response of a different
character. 'No way to life and peace but the way of the cross!'
that, in sum, is the response of the *Imitation.* Tauler and his   30
group would have sincerely professed that they likewise
adopted it; and yet the real and characteristic response of the
'Friends of God' and of such works as the *Following of Christ*
and the *Theologia Germanica* is far rather this, which I quote
from the first-named work: 'Sin killeth nature, but nature is   35
abhorrent of death; therefore sin is against nature, therefore
sinners can never have a joy.' That is the negative side of the

response, and its positive side is this: 'They who have left sins and come to grace have more delight and joy in one day than all sinners have ever gained.'

It is the natural truth of religion and of Christianity which occupies these 'Friends of God.' The truly natural thing is virtue, Christian virtue; and that it is so is proved by the peace and happiness ensuing from it. 'It is much more according to nature to work virtue than vice; for virtue places nature firmly and supports it, while vice displaces it. A thoroughly natural man is a pure man. That which maketh nature impure is a faulty accident of nature and is not the essence of nature.' But in order to be 'a thoroughly natural man,' one who 'enters into himself, listens to the eternal word, and has the life full of ecstasy and joy,' a man must 'set aside all things and follow Christ. Christ is the everlasting aim of all men.'

I have mentioned Luther as a lover of the *Theologia Germanica*. Luther too, some hundred and fifty years after our mystics, had to provide for 'a famine of the words of the Eternal.' Vinet has said with perfect truth that 'the reformers did not separate morals from dogma; Calvin, the most dogmatic of them all, is the one who most efficaciously and most constantly preached morals.' Undoubtedly the reformers preached morals; undoubtedly, too, Calvin and Luther produced an immeasurably greater effect than Tauler and his group. But how was the effect obtained? After laying down the *Following of Christ*, I took up Luther's famous *Commentary on Galatians*. The Commentary deserves its reputation; it has clearness, force, unction. But on what thought does Luther rest with all his weight, as Tauler rests with all his weight on the thought: 'Sin is against nature; they who have left sins have more delight and joy in one day than all sinners have ever gained'? Luther rests with his whole weight on the article of justification, that Gospel doctrine which, he says, is *suavissima et consolationis plenissima*. 'All heretics have continually failed in this one point, that they do not rightly understand or know the article of justification; do not see that by none other sacrifice or offering could God's fierce anger be appeased, but by the precious blood of the son of God.'

The article of justification has been made arid and obnoxious by formalists; let us take it from the mouth of this man of genius, its earnestly convinced and unrivalled expositor. *Christ has been made a curse for us!*—that is the point; Christ has assumed, in our stead, the guilt and curse of sin from which we could not otherwise be delivered, but are delivered by believing in his having so done. 'When the merciful Father saw us to be so crushed under the curse of the law, and so bound by it, that we could never through our own strength get free from it, he sent his only begotten Son into the world and laid on him the sins of all men, saying: "Be thou that Peter the denier, that Paul the persecutor, that David the adulterer, that sinner who ate the apple in Paradise, that thief on the cross; in a word, be thou the person who has done the sins of all men; consider then how thou mayest pay and make satisfaction for them." Then comes in the law and says: "I find him a sinner, and a sinner who has taken unto himself the sins of all men, and I see no sin besides except in him, therefore let him die on the cross!" and so the law falls upon him and slays him. By this transaction the whole world has been purged and purified of all sins, and at the same time, therefore, been set free from death and from all evil.' By giving our hearty belief to this transaction we are admitted to its benefits.

Here we have the *Cabala vera*, says Luther, the true mystery of Christianity—here, in the transaction just recorded. I will not now discuss the misunderstanding of St. Paul which Luther's message of comfort involves. I will not discuss its faults as a religious conception. I will admit that it has indeed been a message of comfort to thousands, and has produced much good and much happiness. I will simply point out that it is mythology, and that this is daily becoming more and more evident; as sheer mythology, at bottom, as Saturn's devouring his children or Pallas springing from the head of Zeus. The transaction between the magnified and non-natural man, whom Luther calls 'the merciful Father,' and his Son, never really took place; or what comes to the same thing, its having taken place can no more be verified, and has no more real probability in its favour, than Saturn's devouring his children or Pallas springing from the head of Zeus. This character of mythology is a disadvantage to Luther's message of comfort now. But it was an advantage to it when the message was delivered. It gave to it an immense superiority in effectiveness over such a message of comfort as Tauler's. The one leavened a group, and individuals; the other created the Protestant Churches.

To the mass of those who seek religion, an element of mythology in it, far from being an objection, has hitherto been a recommendation and attraction; and they hold to this element as long as ever they can. Only, to moral and serious people, such as were the Germanic races who made the Reformation, it must be a moral mythology, and moreover a mythology receivable and approvable by them in the intellectual stage at which they are then arrived. The serious Germanic races, visited by that *soul-hunger* which Tauler describes, could easily be brought to recognise that much of the mythology presented to them by mediæval religion, with its machinery of Virgin and saints, Pope and priest, was unscriptural and immoral; and that good works in the current conception of them as 'fasts, pilgrimages, rosaries, vows'—to adopt Luther's list— were unfruitful. A powerful spirit who went to the Bible and produced from it a new and grave mythology with a new and grave conception of righteousness, was the man for that moment. Luther's doctrine of justification, Calvin's doctrine of election, were far more effective to win crowds and found churches than Tauler's *Following of Christ* just because the doctrines of Calvin and Luther are mythology, while the doctrine of Tauler is not. Luther's doctrine and Calvin's were a mythology appealing directly and solely to the Bible for support, and they professed, also, to deepen men's conception of righteousness; they were therefore acceptable to thousands of serious people in the intellectual and moral stage of that time. They were, however, a mythology. But as such they enlisted in their favour those forces of imagination, wonder, and awe, which men love to feel aroused within them; and they enlisted these in an immeasurably greater degree than Tauler's doctrine of the *Following of Christ*, which is not a mythology at all.

Hence their immeasurably greater scale of effect and number of adherents.

And so it has been ever since, up to this day. Let us confine our view to our own country. Hitherto an element of mythology, the stronger and the more turbid the better, has been a help rather than a hindrance to what are called religious causes. To the Calvinists, to the Methodists, to the Revivalists, to the Salvation Army, have been the striking effects and the heavy numbers; to the Latitude Men, to Leighton, to Erskine of Linlathen, as to Tauler and his friends in the fourteenth century, action on a group merely, or on individuals. Men such as Butler, or Wilson of Sodor and Man, who have had far wider influence in our religious world than the mystics, and who yet at the same time were true 'Friends of God' at heart, have owed their wide influence not to this character but chiefly to something else. The true grandeur of Butler is in his sacred horror at the thought 'of committing the dreadful mistake of leaving the course marked out for us by nature, whatever that nature be;' his reputation is from his embarrassed and unsatisfying apologetic. The true glory of Wilson is his living and abiding sense that 'sin is against nature, therefore sinners can never have a joy;' his reputation is as the most exemplary of Anglican Churchmen.

The immense, the epoch-making change of our own day, is that a stage in our intellectual development is now declaring itself when mythology, whether moral or immoral, as a basis for religion is no longer receivable, is no longer an aid to religion but an obstacle. Our own nation is not specially lucid, it is strongly religious, we have witnessed in the Salvation Army the spectacle of one of the crudest and most turbid developments of religion with the element of mythology in full sway; and yet it is certain that, even amongst ourselves, over all which is most vigorous and progressive in our population mythology in religion has lost or is fast losing its power, and that it has no future. The gross mob has ever been apt to show brutality and hostility towards religion, and demonstrations of this spirit we have often enough still. But mingled with the mere ignoble and

vicious enmity against any discipline to raise, restrain, and transform, there is also in the common people now a sense of impatience and anger at what they think futile trifling with them on the part of those who offer to them, in their sore need,
5 the old mythological religion—a thing felt to be impossible of reception and going if not quite gone, incapable of either solving the present or founding the future.

This change is creating a situation much more favourable to the mystics. Whole libraries of theology have lost their inter-
10 est when it is perceived that they make mythology the basis of religion, and that to take seriously this mythology is impossible. But for those groups and individuals, little regarded in their day, whom their heart prompted to rest religion on natural truth rather than on mythology, the hour of hearing and of
15 well-inclined attention has at last come. For a long while it was heavily against them that they merely preached the following of Christ, instead of the article of justification, the article of election; now at last it is in their favour.

Let me be candid. I love the mystics, but what I find best in
20 them is their golden single sentences, not the whole conduct of their argument and result of their work. I should mislead the reader if I led him to suppose that he will find any great body of discourse in the work attributed to Tauler, *The Following of Christ*, which Mr. Morell has translated, of like value with
25 the detached sentences from it which I have quoted above. But the little book is well worth reading if only for the sake of such sentences. The general argument, too, if not complete and satisfying, has an interest of its own from the natural, or, as we nowadays say, the *positive* point of view taken by the author,
30 without regard to mythology, or conventions, or *shams*, in Carlyle's phrase, of any kind.

For instance, the book developes the idea of following Christ, and teaches how for him who would follow Christ, poverty, both inward and outward, is necessary. Christ's is emphatically
35 a '*poor* life.' Yet to follow him and his life is really to follow nature, to be happy. And to enter into the kingdom of heaven is really nothing else than this following him, this following

nature, this being happy. When Jesus said: 'How hardly shall they that have riches enter into the kingdom of heaven,' this was, in our mystic's view, but another way of saying: 'How hardly shall they that have riches follow me and my life, live naturally, be happy.' The life poor in external goods, as Christ's was, is therefore, concludes our mystic, the happy, natural life, the life to be preferred.

But the official and current religion interprets Christ's words, as we all know, in quite another fashion, and makes him in fact say: 'If you trust in riches, if you make a bad use of riches, you cannot enter after death into the paradise above the sky.' Now I do not at present inquire whether the doctrine of our mystic is right or wrong, adequate or inadequate. But it is well to re-mark how much nearer, at any rate, he comes to the mind of Christ, how much more sincerely and faithfully he interprets it, than our official religion does. For undoubtedly what Jesus meant by the kingdom of God or of heaven was the reign of saints, the ideal future society on earth. 'How hardly shall they that have riches be fit for the society of the future,' was what he in fact said. One who is unfit for this ideal society does not follow Christ; he is also in conflict with nature, cannot be happy. This is the doctrine of Jesus, and our mystic has rightly seized it. Jesus threw out the doctrine and left it to bear fruit. It has worked in many and many an individual mind since, and will work more and more. The worldly themselves have to deal with it. They can free themselves from all concern about the paradise above the sky, but from concern about the society of the future they cannot. It will arrive, its beginnings are even now. No one yet, however, has disengaged the doctrine from difficulty, has so set it forth as to make it useable and service-able; certainly our mystic has not. But to have rightly seized it is something.

Christ's sentence on riches is but a corollary from what we call his *secret:* 'He that loveth his life shall lose it, he that will lose his life shall save it.' Now the infinite progress possible in Christianity lies in the gradually successful application, to doc-trines like this secret of Jesus and the corollary from it, of

what we call his *epieikeia*, his temper of sweet reasonableness,
consummate balance, unerring felicity. Although the application has here not yet been successfully made, and the mystics
have not made it, yet the secret and its corollary are increas-
5   ingly felt to have in them something deeply important, and to
be full of future; at the same time that mythology, like Luther's
article of justification or Calvin's article of election, is felt to
be passing quite away and to have no future at all. The mystics,
then, have the merit of keeping always before their minds, and
10   endeavouring earnestly to make operative on their lives, just
that in Christianity which is not perishable but abiding.

But I ought before I end to let our mystic, whether he be
indeed Tauler as Mr. Morell thinks, or another, to speak for
himself at more length than I have let him speak hitherto. I
15   have mentioned his insistence on external poverty; let us hear
him on internal poverty, poverty of spirit, 'a going out of yourself and out of everything earthly.' A man 'must perceive and
listen to the eternal word, and this hearing bringeth him to everlasting life.'

20   Through the outer word that men hear, they attain to the
inner word, which God speaketh in the essence of the soul.
They who have not come to this should hear preaching, and
learn and follow what they hear or read; thus they come to
the real truth, and to life, which is God. Even if a man is so
25   advanced that he hear the word in himself, he is yet not at all
times prepared for it, for bodily nature cannot bear it, and a
man must sometimes turn to his senses and be active; but he
ought to direct this work of the senses to the best end. If preaching is useful to him, he can hear it; if an outward virtue is useful
30   to him, he can work it; and he ought to exercise himself in what
he recognises as the best. But this by no means hindereth him
from hearing the everlasting word, but it furthers him to what
is best. And he should drop and drive out with violence all that
hindereth him in this. Then he doeth as Jesus did in the Temple,
35   when he drove out buyers and sellers and said: 'My house is a
house of prayer, but ye have made it a den of thieves.' A pure
heart is a temple of God; the tradesmen whom Jesus drove out

are the worldly furniture and goods that rust in the heart and are
hurtful to it. If now the heart keepeth the useless thoughts and
tarrieth over them, it is no longer a house of prayer but a den
of thieves, for the evil thoughts drive out God from his dwelling
and murder him. But the man who resisteth all thoughts that 5
keep him apart from God, receiveth from God living, divine
power. This inpouring is God's inspeaking, and that is the life
full of ecstasy and joy.

The reader will recognise the strain of homage which from
age to age successive generations of mystics have ever loved 10
to uplift to 'the eternal word.' I will not say that it is entirely
satisfying, but at least it is always refreshing, consoling, and
ennobling.

Whoever turns to the little volume which Mr. Morell has
translated will find plenty in this strain to give him refreshment. 15
But he will find more than this, he will find sentences such as
those of which I spoke in beginning, and to which in ending I
would return; isolated sentences fitted to abide in the memory,
to be a possession for the mind and soul, to form the character.
'Sin killeth nature, but nature is abhorrent of death; therefore 20
sin is against nature, therefore sinners can never have a joy.'
'They who have left sins and come to grace have more delight
and joy in one day than all sinners have ever gained.'

Up to Easter

Professor Huxley told us in this Review last month, that in his eyes the chief good is, in brief, freedom to say what he pleases, when he pleases. Singular ideal for so clear-sighted a man! It is the ideal of Mr. Dillon, and Mr. W. O'Brien, and apparently of the Gladstonian Liberals generally: if Mr. Dillon and Mr. W. O'Brien please to say 'disagreeable things,' it is monstrous and intolerable, says Mr. John Morley, that they should be prevented. For my part, as I grow old, and profit, I hope, by the lessons of experience, I think the chief good, that which above all makes life worth living, is *to be of use*. In pursuit of this good, I find myself from time to time brought, as almost every one in the present critical juncture must be brought, to politics. I know the objections to meddling with them; I know and can perfectly understand the impatience and irritation which my intervention in these matters causes to many people. Nothing I should like better than to feel assured that I should never have occasion to write a line on politics again. I write on other subjects with much more pleasure; and it is true, quite true, that there are springs of movement in politics which one must be in the game to perceive and estimate fully—which an outsider, as he is called, cannot duly appreciate.

But on the other hand there is in practical politics a mass of insincerity, of phrase, fiction, and claptrap, which can impose, one would think, on no plain reasonable man outside of politics. This insincerity is found useful for purposes of party or faction; but there are moments when it is expedient for plain reasonable people, who have nothing to gain by it and everything to lose, to say to one another how hollow it all is. There are happily thousands of such people in this country, and they

are the greater force here in England because to their plain reasonableness, which is a thing common enough where men have not interest to blind them, they add courage. They want nothing for themselves in politics, they only demand that the politician shall not bring the country into danger and disaster. 5
To them, as one to whom some of them are not ill-disposed to listen, I speak; as one of themselves, as one who wants nothing for himself through politics, who is too old, and of habits and tastes too formed, to wish to enter the House of Commons even if he could; whose one concern with politics is that the poli- 10
ticians should not bring the country into danger and disaster.

The force of which I have been speaking has defeated Mr. Gladstone; but the call upon its activity and watchfulness is not yet over. It is very far from being over, although the prospects of a happy issue, if this great force remains active and watch- 15
ful, are favourable. From time to time those who compose it should ask themselves how things stand at the moment to which we are come, what has been accomplished; what still remains to be accomplished; what is likely to lead us to success, what to failure: and this, at the short pause brought by Easter, I now 20
propose to do.

When Parliament met there were three questions making evidently the first and chief demand upon its attention: the questions of procedure, Ireland, local government. Procedure has been dealt with. The debate on the Address was proof 25
enough, if any proof had been wanted, how urgent was the need of some power to stop debating prolonged for the pur- pose of delay and obstruction. The amiable leader of the House of Commons expressed his profound regret at having to propose the creation of such a power; he ought rather to 30
have expressed profound regret at its not having been pro- posed long ago. Long ago the country had made up its mind that to pretend 'discussion' to be the object of such debates as those which have gone on in the House of Commons during the last few years was an absurdity; a conspicuous instance of 35
that inveterate trick of parliamentary insincerity of which one is inclined to ask with Figaro, 'Who is being taken in by it?' It matters not what party it is which may seek to profit by

such 'discussion,' whether Conservatives, or Radicals, or Par-
nellites: it should be made impossible. The state of the House of
Commons, since such 'discussion' grew to prevail there, had
become a scandal and a danger. Mr. Gladstone seems now
5   doomed to live, move, and have his being in that atmosphere
of rhetorical and parliamentary insincerity of which I have
spoken; to him, therefore, it may be vain to urge that the state
of the House of Commons alone was perhaps a change more
serious for evil than all his catalogued jubilee-host of Liberal
10 reforms was a change for good. Instinctively, however, the
country felt how grave was the danger, and was deeply relieved when the power of closure was carried.

It is a step of incalculable importance; a step restoring to the
House of Commons free action, dignity, all that enables it to be
15 a blessing to the country and not a bane. The form in which
the power is conferred is a thing of minor importance as compared with the attainment of the power itself. Perhaps closure
by a majority of three-fifths would have been a better form
than that which has been adopted. That which has been adopted
20 is in itself good and reasonable enough, and no one really
doubts that the Speaker's leave will be given or refused with
perfect fairness. But parliamentary insincerity is to be reckoned
with, which certainly will never hesitate to denounce the
Speaker's action as unfair, so often as it finds its own interest
25 in doing so. This, however, is an inconvenience which we must
now make up our minds to face, along with the other incon-
veniences of parliamentary insincerity. The great matter is that
we have at last got the desired, the salutary, the indispensable
power of closure. May it be applied wisely, but resolutely!
30 The debates on the Address and on Procedure were full of
Ireland, but since those debates ended Ireland occupies the
attention of Parliament with hardly an admixture of anything
else. There is the Bill for making good certain shortcomings
in the Land Act of 1881 which have become apparent, and
35 there is the Crimes Bill. The first of these two Bills need not
long detain us. The Act of 1881 may be a bad one, but if it
exists and has to be worked, manifest shortcomings in it ought
to be repaired. The Crimes Bill—the eighty-seventh Coercion

Bill, so its enemies are fond of telling us, the eighty-seventh of
our Coercion Bills, and the most savage and odious of them all—
is the important matter in question just now. How is the
country likely to take it? how ought the country to take it?
I have repeatedly urged that we might need a much more   5
thorough repression of disorder than any we have had hitherto,
but that much more thorough remedial measures were needed
as well. Lord Spencer, a man who deserves all our respect, tells
us that he has come to believe in Home Rule, because he found
that 'repressive measures, accompanied though they had been   10
by remedial measures, had not succeeded, though they for a
time put down crime.' But surely the defect may have lain in
the remedial measures. If they had been better, they might
have succeeded; but unless crime is put down, and if law and
government are powerless, your remedial measures, even   15
though thorough and good, cannot.have the chance of succeeding. Therefore whoever obstructs the repression of disorder,
obstructs remedial measures. Meanwhile, as to the past, it is
something to have put down crime, even if your remedial measures have turned out to be not yet what is right and sufficient.   20

Many Conservative candidates at the last election declared
against coercion. They said with Mr. Pitt that they wished the
Irish to live under equal laws with the English and Scotch, and
they added that they were against all Coercion Bills for the
future. If they had confined themselves to the first of their two   25
propositions they would have been on impregnable ground. In
truth the real necessity for the Crimes Bill arises from the Irish
not being under equal laws with the English and Scotch. If an
Englishman or a Scotchman commits murder, or mutilates animals, or cuts off a girl's hair and tars her head, he can with   30
certainty be punished; an Irishman, at present, cannot. It is to
make the convictions and sentences of the criminal law reach
the Irish criminal as they reach the English or Scotch criminal,
that a Crimes Act is at present necessary. If the Conservatives
stuck obstinately to their second proposition, they would be   35
making it impossible to give effect to their first. They do well,
therefore, to confess that their essential proposition was their
first one, and that their second, which they imagined to mean

but the same thing as their first, was a mistake. The country
did not commit their mistake, and can have no difficulty in
concluding that if the Irish ought, as certainly they ought, to
live under equal laws with the English and Scotch, and to have
5 impunity for crime no more than we have, a Crimes Act may
under the present circumstances be necessary, and to this conclusion the country will, I believe, certainly come.

I myself could have wished that the government had seen its
way to act administratively, and by the common law, with
10 much more vigour than it did. My opinion that it was in their
power to do so counts for very little, but it is an opinion held
also, I know, by men well entitled to judge. How much a
government can do administratively, under the common law,
in such a state of things as that which prevails in Ireland, has
15 never fairly been tried. It needs resolution to try it, but to try
it might have been well, and might have shown government
that it had much more strength than it supposed. 'The laws,'
says Burke with his usual wisdom, 'reach but a very little way.
Constitute government how you please, infinitely the greater
20 part of it must depend upon the exercise of the powers which
are left at large to the prudence and uprightness of ministers of
state.'

Our ministers, however, instead of boldly using the large
powers given to them by the common law to prevent crime and
25 outrage, prefer to proceed by statute. Their preference is
natural enough. They have Great Britain in view, where the
state of affairs and the temper of the people are not revolutionary, and where to proceed regularly by statute gives all the
security needful. But the state of affairs and the temper of the
30 people in a large part of Ireland is revolutionary. If we suppose
parts of Great Britain in the same state, it would be preferable
here also to act with vigour administratively, rather than to
proceed by special statute. Administrative action is what certain emergencies require. The French republican government
35 the other day did not prosecute the municipality of Marseilles
for glorifying the Commune: it dissolved it.

In certain emergencies, therefore, vigorous administrative
action may be required in some parts of one whole country

under the same laws, although in other parts it is not required. Does such an emergency present itself in parts of Ireland? Is the state of affairs, the temper of the people, revolutionary there, and the law set at defiance? In Kerry, says Judge O'Brien, 'the law has ceased to exist: there is a state of war with authority 5 and with the institutions of civilised life.' In other parts, terrorism, we are told, is regnant; there is quiet, because the orders of the League are obeyed without resistance. If resistance is attempted, crime comes swiftly to punish it. 'I am not fastidious,' says a lieutenant of Mr. Parnell, 'as to the meth- 10 ods by which the cause may be advanced: I do not say you should alone use dynamite, or the knife, or the rifle, or parliamentary agitation; but I hold no Irishman true who will not use all and each as the opportunity presents itself.' If resistance has made it necessary to 'advance the cause' by crime, convic- 15 tions for crime can no longer be obtained. As to the law's being set at defiance in parts of Ireland, this will surely suffice.

Then as to the temper of revolution, Mr. Parnell declared his programme, with entire candour, some time ago in America. 'None of us, whether we are in America or in Ireland or 20 wherever we may be, will be satisfied until we have destroyed the last link that keeps Ireland bound to England.' But since then, he and his followers have consented, we are told, to be satisfied with Ireland's having the control of her own local affairs only, and for imperial affairs they will let her remain 25 subject to the Crown and to the Imperial Parliament. And Mr. Godkin is angry with me for not believing them. But only the other day comes another lieutenant of Mr. Parnell and cries: 'Ireland a nation! Strike a blow for Home Rule, the Irish nation, and the green flag of our people!' And another lieutenant 30 avows at Chicago—a place very favourable to plain speaking— that it is 'the duty of the League to make the government of Ireland by England an impossibility.' Another declares that 'any person entering Ireland officially commissioned by England to any administrative office *enters it at his peril.*' A priest 35 who refuses to give evidence in a court of justice is brought up for contempt of court, and a Board of Guardians, which has no concern whatever with the matter, publishes the following resolution: 'We condemn the brutal and tyrannical action of the authorities in arresting Father Kelleher, the respected and patriotic parish priest of Youghal.' Finally Mr. W. O'Brien, elate with his impunity at home, promises to his friends new worlds to conquer abroad: 'If Trench dares to lay a robber hand upon any honest man's home, we will hunt Lord Lansdowne with execrations out of Canada.'

This is the revolutionary temper and language which Mr. Gladstone formerly described as that of men 'marching through rapine to the disintegration of the Empire,' but which, since the last election, he and his friends prefer to call 'the disorder inevitable while the responsibility for the maintenance of order is withdrawn from the leaders chosen by the majority of the Irish people.' With them, with the very holders, therefore, of the language just quoted, are 'the influences of moderation and legality' which will give us all that we want, if we do but surrender Ireland to Mr. Parnell and his lieutenants. And I suppose it is in order to enable us to believe this the more readily that Mr. Dillon says: 'The magistrates and police know perfectly well that Mr. Parnell will be their master, as he will be the master of this country, within a very short time.' One can feel the balmy 'influences of moderation' beginning to breathe already. And Mr. Morley is shocked that people should be prevented from saying the 'disagreeable' things which have been above quoted. He and Mr. Gladstone are shocked that we should even call them 'revolutionary,' and talk of repressing them, when they proceed from 'the representatives of Ireland.' If they proceeded from the representatives of Yorkshire they would alike be revolutionary, alike need repression. I wonder how far Mr. Morley's indulgence would extend. I believe he is kindly disposed to me, as I am sure I am kindly disposed to him; yet I should not like to be brought before him, as president of a Committee of Public Safety, on a charge of *incivism*. I suspect he would be capable of passing a pretty sharp sentence with 'sombre acquiescence.' At any rate the 'disagreeable' sayings and doings which in his Irish friends he cannot bear to check would in any other country of Europe infallibly bring down upon the performers the 'state of siege.'

For they are really and truly the sayings and doings of revolution, as different as possible from those of lawful political agitation familiar in this country. The latter may be a safety-valve; the former is an incendiary fire. Its kindlers and feeders do not exhale their passion by what they are doing and saying: they heighten it. By holding such furious language as theirs, a man in Great Britain finds that he diminishes his importance, and stops; in Ireland he finds that he increases it, and therefore proceeds more hotly than ever. 'What you make it men's interest to do,' says Burke, 'that they will do.' The more they have free play, the more do the sayers of such things as I have been quoting get drunk with rage and hatred themselves, and make their followers drunk with them also.

It is of no use deceiving ourselves, and holding insincere language. I regretted to see Mr. Balfour congratulating himself on the number of meetings which had been held without hindrance. Perhaps he congratulates himself, too, on the Dublin municipality being undissolved, or the *resolving* board of guardians. Perhaps Mr. Forster congratulated himself on *United Ireland* appearing quite regularly. I suppose being in Parliament debauches the mind and makes it lose all sense that make-believe of this kind is not only insincere but absurd. Else Mr. Gladstone would not gravely tell us that such debates as have of late gone on in the House of Commons were 'protracted discussion which was required,' and that he 'can conceive no greater calamity to the House of Commons' than the frequent cutting-short of such debates by the closure. Sir George Trevelyan would not tell us that 'the real defect' of the Crimes Bill is that 'it is directed against the written and spoken expression of opinion.' As if all that chooses to call itself debate and discussion were really such! As if, because in general the expression of opinion should be free, you must allow the expression of *all* opinion, at all times, and under all circumstances! This is adopting Professor Huxley's theory of the *summum bonum* with a vengeance. In the present state of Ireland, is Mr. Parnell's 'None of us will be satisfied until we have destroyed the last link that keeps Ireland bound to England;' is Mr. Harris's 'If the tenant farmers shot down landlords as partridges are

shot down in September, Matt Harris never would say one
word against them;' is Mr. W. O'Brien's 'If Trench dares to
lay a robber hand upon any honest man's home, we will hunt
Lord Lansdowne with execrations out of Canada,' *expression of*
5   *opinion* which it is wise to permit, and with which it is *a real*
defect in the Government to interfere? A man must surely have
deluged his mind with make-believe before he can think or even
say so. Anywhere else in Europe, as I have said, such *expression*
of opinion, and what is now going on in Ireland, would be met
10   by the state of siege. For the sake of the Irish themselves it is
wrong and cruel to let it continue. The whole force of reasonable opinion in this country will go with the Government in
stopping it. Whether Government should have proceeded administratively or by special statute may be a question; but the
15   important thing is to stop the state of things and the language
now prevailing in parts of Ireland, and as the Government have
elected to proceed by statute, they should be supported. And
with regard to details of the statute, the end to be attained
should be steadily kept in view. A man may dislike, for in-
20   stance, the change of venue, but he must keep in mind the end
to be attained, conviction on clear proof of guilt. Can a conviction for murder, even on clear proof, be now secured without change of venue? If not, the Government ought to be supported in changing it. But the real mind of the country, if the
25   Government will be frank with it and trust it, may be relied
upon, I hope, much more than politicians, for not being led
off from the real aim by cries and pretexts.

I hope so, and I believe so too; and therefore merely to ex-
hort reasonable people, who are happily a great force in this
30   country, to be steady as they have hitherto been, to brush insincerities aside, to keep in clear view the dangerous features of
disorder in Ireland at present, and to support the Government
in quelling it, I should not now be writing. It is what is to come
after quelling it that has the great interest for me. I am not
35   afraid of a refusal by the reasonable people of this country for
the powers necessary to quell disorder; I am only afraid of their
not insisting strongly enough on a further thing—how much,
after it is quelled, will still require to be done. Not that they

do not sincerely desire to give Ireland the due control of her own affairs. I am convinced that the great body of reasonable people in this country do, as I have repeatedly said, sincerely desire and intend two things: one, to defeat Mr. Gladstone's dangerous plan of Home Rule; the other, to remove all just 5 cause of Irish complaint, and to give to the people of Ireland the due control of their own local affairs. But how large and far-reaching are the measures required to do this, I am afraid many of us do not adequately conceive. Yet, if these measures are not forthcoming, Mr. Gladstone's Home Rule will certainly 10 arrive.

The Gladstonian contention is now, as we all know, that for the disordered state of Ireland 'no remedy is possible until the national aspirations of the Irish people are gratified.' The cry of the Irish people is, 'Ireland a nation! Strike a blow for Home 15 Rule, the Irish nation, and the green flag of our people!' The Gladstonian cry is, 'A separate Parliament and separate Executive for Ireland.' Both cries lead in the end to the same thing, and a thing full of mischief and danger both for Great Britain and Ireland—a separate Ireland. 20

To this they lead, as the great body of reasonable people in England perceived instinctively, and as no reasonable person who has not an interest in being insincere with himself can fail to perceive. It would not be possible for Ireland to possess, without using it for getting more, such a vantage-ground as a 25 separate Parliament and Executive would give her, any more than it would have been possible for the Americans of the South to possess, without using it for getting more, such a vantage-ground as a separate Southern Congress and Executive would have supplied. Such is the nature of things. In the case of 30 Ireland we have our warning, not only from the nature of things, but from the express words of the Irish themselves, who when they are free to speak their real mind tell us that they 'will not be satisfied until they have destroyed the last link that keeps Ireland bound to England,' and that what they want is 35 'Ireland a nation, and the green flag of our people.' I can understand Mr. Gladstone shutting his eyes to what is sure to happen, because he can shut or open his eyes to whatever he pleases, and

has his mind full of a great piece of parliamentary management which will insure to him the solid Irish vote and seat him firmly again in power. I can understand his partisans shutting their eyes to it, some out of fidelity to his person, some out of
5   fidelity to their party, others from reasons which I will not now stay to draw out. But that any reasonable man, letting his mind have fair play, should doubt that Mr. Gladstone's 'separate Parliament and Executive for Ireland' leads by a rapid incline to Mr. W. O'Brien's 'Ireland a nation, and the green flag
10 of our people,' I cannot understand. Nor can I understand his doubting that this has danger.

    We confuse ourselves with analogies from distant and unlike countries, which have no application. Let us take our analogy from close at hand, where the political incorporation has been,
15 and is, the same as that of Ireland with England. Provence was once a nation, the *Nation Provençale*, as down to the end of the last century it was still called. A sagacious lawyer, Portalis, remonstrating in 1789 against a uniform legislation for France, declared that France was a country *composé de divers peuples*,
20 'composed of different peoples,' and it was for Provence, in particular, that Portalis spoke. Whatever Ireland had to make her a nation, that Provence had also. Ireland's troubled history can show one beautiful and civilising period in the far past; but Provence founded modern literature. It had its own Estates and
25 Parliament; it had the greatest of French orators, Mirabeau. Well, if Provence were discontented to-day, and demanded back its separate Estates and nationality, what should we think of a French statesman, a French political party, which declared that for the discontent of Provence there was 'no remedy pos-
30 sible until the national aspirations of the Provençal people are gratified?' We should say they were lunatics. If they went on to inflame and infuriate the discontent by all the means in their power, calling the incorporation with France 'disgraceful,' and expatiating on the 'infamy and corruption' through which it
35 had been brought about, we should say they were criminal lunatics.

    As for Provence being a nation, we should say that she was indeed a nation poetically, but not now politically, and that to make her now a nation politically would be suicide both for France and herself. And if some well-meaning ex-prefect, like Lord Spencer, were to plead as a reason for making Provence a nation politically, that 'repressive measures, accompanied though they had been by remedial measures, had not suc- 5 ceeded,' and that therefore 'they ought to use the Provençal spirit of nationality, having failed in the past from not having sufficiently consulted the wishes of Provence in that respect,' what should we say? We should say he was a most extraordinary reasoner. We should say that if his remedial measures had 10 not succeeded, that was probably because they were bad and insufficient; and not till the right remedial measures had been sought and applied far more seriously than hitherto, need France think of committing suicide by erecting Provence, and probably this and that other part of France afterwards, follow- 15 ing the example of Provence, into a separate nation again. In fact, means have been found, without 'using the Provençal spirit of nationality,' to make Provence perfectly contented in her incorporation with France. And so they have to be found, and may be found, for Ireland. 20

It is a consolation for us in the troublous times through which we are passing, that we have public men who appear to possess, distributed amongst them, the powers requisite for discerning and treating all the capital facts of the situation: one having the powers needed for dealing with one branch of such 25 facts, another with another. Mr. Gladstone is no doubt a source of danger. The historian will some day say of him what was said by the preacher of an eccentric funeral sermon in Mayfair Chapel on Frederick, Prince of Wales: 'He had great virtues; indeed they degenerated into vices; he was very generous, but 30 I hear his generosity has ruined a great many people; and then his condescension was such that he kept very bad company.' But as a compensation for our dangers from Mr. Gladstone, we have in Lord Hartington a statesman who has shown that he thoroughly grasps the meaning of Gladstonian Home Rule, sees 35 where the proposal to give Ireland a separate Parliament and Executive leads, and is staunch in rejecting it, clear and keen in judging fallacious securities offered with it. Such a security is

the retention of the Irish members at Westminster. Their retention, if their brethren wielded the legislature and executive
of Ireland, would but double, as Lord Hartington truly saw,
our dangers and difficulties.

5   All Lord Hartington's firmness will be needed. It has suited
Mr. Gladstone and his friends to launch their new doctrine that
no constraint must be put upon the Irish, and that there is no
remedy for the disorder there until the national aspirations of
the Irish are gratified. I have said that no reasonable man, who

10   thinks fairly and seriously, can doubt that to gratify these aspirations by reconstituting Ireland as a nation politically, is
full of dangers. But we have to consider the new voters, the
democracy, as people are fond of calling them. They have
many merits, but among them is not that of being, in general,

15   reasonable persons who think fairly and seriously. We have had
opportunities of observing a new journalism which a clever
and energetic man has lately invented. It has much to recommend it; it is full of ability, novelty, variety, sensation, sympathy, generous instincts; its one great fault is that it is *feather-

20   brained.* It throws out assertions at a venture because it wishes
them true; does not correct either them or itself, if they are
false; and to get at the state of things as they truly are seems to
feel no concern whatever. Well, the democracy, with abundance of life, movement, sympathy, good instincts, is disposed

25   to be, like this journalism, feather-brained; just as the upper
class is disposed to be selfish in its politics, and the middle
class narrow. The many restraints of their life particularly incline the democracy to believe with Mr. Fox that if people very
much desire a thing they ought to have it, and that, therefore,

30   the national aspirations of the Irish ought to be gratified. They
do not look to the end and forecast consequences. When they
are told that if we satisfy the national aspirations of the Irish
the Irish will love us, and that all will thenceforth go well, they
believe it because they wish to believe it. If they are told that

35   the Bill for dealing with disorder in Ireland is savage and odious beyond precedent, they believe it, because to think this
of a restraining measure is agreeable to them. The democracy
is by its nature feather-brained; the English nation is not; and

the democracy will in England work itself, probably, at last clear. But at present, even here, in England, and above all in those industrial centres where it is most left to itself, and least in contact with other classes, it is disposed to be feather-brained. This makes the strength of Mr. Gladstone. The great body of reasonable opinion in England is against him on Home Rule, and in Lord Hartington we have a leader convinced and firm; but we must not deceive ourselves. The democracy is being plied with fierce stimulants, and is agitated and chafing. If we cannot remove all just cause of complaint in Ireland, cannot produce, for local government there and for the land, a plan manifestly reasonable and good, the democracy will burst irresistibly in, bearing Mr. Gladstone in triumph back to power, and Home Rule along with him.

Lord Salisbury has declared his belief that 'remedial measures, and remedial measures of a very far-reaching tendency, are strongly called for by the condition of things in Ireland.' Undoubtedly they are, and to hug ourselves in the belief that they are not, but that all which is required is to put down disorder, is fatal. Some people say Ireland has no more cause of complaint than England or Scotland. One of these gentlemen wrote the other day to a newspaper saying that Ireland had even less, because she has not an established church. This is like congratulating Mr. Gladstone on living under the blessings of a Divorce Act, or Mr. Beresford Hope on having the prospect of soon being allowed to marry his deceased wife's sister.

A man peculiarly well informed on the matter, Mr. Edwin Chadwick, asserts that in several important branches of local government (he mentions the Poor Law system in especial) Ireland has the advantage of England. No doubt he is right. But this advantage is something devised and conferred by superior authority: the question is whether the call of the community itself for a thing desired by it and fairly reasonable, is not more likely to be thwarted in Ireland than in Great Britain. Most certainly it is. Let me take a single instance in illustration: I will be as brief as possible. I believe that public aid was desired for a Catholic training school for elementary teachers in Ireland, and that Lord Spencer thought the desire reasonable, and wished

it to be complied with. Denominational training schools, as we call them, have in Great Britain, and have long had, the bulk of their expense supplied from public funds. But the moment the members from northern Ireland got wind of the matter, they
5   were indignant, and protested against the project. Probably the northern members would have had the support of British Nonconformity and secularism: 'the Liberal party has emphatically condemned religious endowment.' At any rate Lord Spencer foresaw a storm, and the project was not persisted in. But how
10 reasonable and permissible a thing, how entirely a thing within the fair scope of a community's wishes, to have in a part of Ireland, where the vast bulk of the community is Catholic, a Catholic training school with public aid; and how irritating to find that in Great Britain there are denominational training
15 schools with public aid, because the community wishes it; but in Ireland, although the community may wish it, it cannot have them!

I have often said that·one has no need to go beyond Church and education to see how completely Great Britain, while talk-
20 ing pompously of 'the tolerance of the British Constitution,' has had two sets of weights and measures, one for itself and another for Ireland. The tolerance of the British Constitution consists in letting Irish revolutionists say whatever they like; a liberty often extremely bad for them. But in complying with the fair
25 wishes of the Catholic community in Ireland the tolerance of the British Constitution utterly disappears. I feel the more strongly on this matter because of what I have seen abroad, in acquainting myself with the humble but everywhere present public service of popular education. There indeed there is ab-
30 solute equality of treatment; there indeed there is not a double set of weights and measures; there you will never find a Protestant community indulged with a training school of its own, while a Catholic community is denied one. Goethe used to pray: 'God give us clear notions of the consequences of things.'
35 If the British Philistine could ever frame such a prayer and have it granted, he would come to understand how completely Archbishop Walsh and Archbishop Croke are the consequences of things of our own doing. No doubt the Vatican disapproves

their action; but how must the Vatican at the same time secretly feel that it serves us right!

It is undeniable that a fairly reasonable wish of the community in Ireland is more likely to be thwarted than in England
and Scotland. That is a reason against leaving the Imperial Par- 5
liament to go on controlling Irish local affairs. But who, with
Colonel Saunderson and Mr. Sexton present to his mind, will
believe that in the present state of tempers the Catholic Irish
in an Irish Parliament would duly entertain reasonable wishes
of the Protestants of the north, or the Protestant Irish those of 10
Catholics of the south? This is an objection to Mr. Gladstone's
Home Rule not from an imperial point of view any longer, but
from a purely Irish one. The fairly reasonable wishes of the
community, in the respective parts of Ireland, ought to be made
possible of attainment by the community. 'Ireland a nation, 15
and the green flag of our people,' is not a fairly reasonable wish.
But a Catholic training school is.

Whoever has had occasion to learn the course of public
business in foreign countries, knows what we lose for want of
proper local government in Great Britain. The House of Com- 20
mons is far too large; a quantity of business comes before it
which it should not have to discharge. Of our numerous House
of Commons very many men are members, and unfit for such a
position, who would be excellently fitted for local assemblies,
which do not, however, exist to receive them. The best thing I 25
have observed in New England is the effect of the training in
local government upon the average citizen there. With us,
little is known of systems of local government, and there is
no cry for the thing; to discredit it, to throw out the scoff of
the Heptarchy, is easy enough. But it is unpatriotic and unwise. 30
Infinitely more unpatriotic and unwise is the neglect of this
remedy in Ireland, where the want of it has had special bad
consequences which it has not had in Great Britain, and which
are full of danger. It should be made as serious, important, and
strong there, as possible. 35

The county is too small a basis to take even in rich and
populous England, except in a very few cases. Certainly it is
too small a basis to take in Ireland. Every one sees how the

province in Ireland affords a larger unit at once convenient and
natural. I do not know what arrangements might be the best in
the interests simply of local business. But it is important to remark that *politically* there could be no objection to resolving
5   the provincial assemblies of Ireland into two only, one for the
Catholic South and another for the Protestant North. The formidable political danger of Mr. Gladstone's one Parliament and
Executive for all Ireland is that such a power would most surely
be tempted, so far as we can at present foresee, to pose as a sep-
10 arate nation with a policy contrary to that of Great Britain.
But an assembly for a part only of Ireland cannot so pose; the
assembly and government of the Catholic South will be balanced by those of the Protestant North, which is smaller, indeed, in extent and numbers, but superior in wealth, energy,
15 and organisation. The governments would balance one another
politically, and administratively would each do simply their
own business, which in the furious conflicts of a joint assembly
would often suffer or be left undone. Many men who now
have no trade but agitation would become good and useful citi-
20 zens in the field of activity opened by these assemblies and their
business. The flower of the political talent of Ireland would
find its place in the Imperial Parliament.

Mr. Reginald Brett says that no other Irish policy is possible
than Mr. Gladstone's, 'which was *right in principle, but faulty
25 in vital details.*' This is in the sacred language of the practical
politicians, to which a plain outsider has not the key. But let
us hope that the plan of two assemblies may be sufficiently like
Mr. Gladstone's to pass with Mr. Brett as Gladstonian in principle, possible, and desirable.

30 The reason of the country judged Mr. Gladstone's Home
Rule dangerous. It perceives, however, the need of local government for Ireland, and leaves the plan of it to the Government; only let us insist that what is done shall be effectual. Happily we have in Mr. Goschen a statesman as fit for planning
35 local government as Lord Hartington is for combating Gladstonian Home Rule.

Finally, there is the land question. Mr. Gladstone's mission-
aries are sent out to cry that all the Conservative Government

wants is to enable the landlords to extort their unjust rents. Of course some danger there is that the Conservative party may not be stringent enough in dealing with landlords. But evidently something has to be done. It is confessed that the Bill for admitting leaseholders to the benefit of the Act of 1881, and for preventing harsh evictions, is a measure of temporary relief only. The Act of 1881 has failed, as it was likely to fail. I may say so, for I said so in 1881, provoking somewhat, I may add, my friend Mr. John Morley by my want of faith. By that Act, I said, 'ownership and tenure will be made quite a different thing in Ireland from that which they are in England, and in countries of our sort of civilisation generally, and this is surely a disadvantage.'[1] An adumbration of dual ownership there was in Irish land-tenure already; such an ownership, with such parties to it, had elements of trouble; the thing was to get rid of it. Instead of getting rid of it, the Act of 1881 developed and strengthened it. What we all now see to be desirable, is to have one owner, and that owner, as far as possible, the cultivator.

The reason of the country supports the Government in quelling revolutionary anarchy in Ireland, and in restoring the rule of law and order there. Here it is as conservative as the Conservative party. But it has no landlord bias, and in its judgment on Irish landlords it is disposed to be severe. 'Mere land-merchants,' too many of them, says their own friend Croker; 'from their neglect of their duties springs their difficulty with their rents, and the general misery and distraction.' Often 'insolent' besides; an offence which the Irish peasant resents more even than oppression. It is a terrible indictment; and there are landlords still against whom it might justly be brought. The Land Purchase Commissioner of the government 'has known rack-renting prevail to an extent simply shocking;' Sir Redvers Buller desires 'a court with a very strong coercive power on a bad landlord.'

Landlordism, as we know it in these islands, has disappeared from most countries. It depends on the consent of the com-

[1] *Irish Essays*, p. 29.

munity. In England, as I have often said, it has kept this consent partly through the moderation of the people, but above all through that of the landlords themselves. It has become impossible to maintain by the force of England the system of
5   landlordism where it has not, as in England itself, the consent of the community; and this the reason and conscience of England begin to feel more and more. Mr. Chamberlain, I believe, is the statesman who might be proctor for the real mind of the country on this matter, as Lord Hartington might be proctor
10   for it on the matter of Home Rule, and Mr. Goschen on that of local government. It seems admitted, however, that if we organise local government in Ireland, we yet cannot leave, as would be natural, the community itself to deal with the landlords there: the Government of the Catholic South with the
15   landlords of the South, that of the Protestant North with those of the North. England and its Government are partly accountable for the faults of the landlords and for their present position. The Imperial Parliament must therefore help in solving the land question. But Mr. Gladstone's twenty years' purchase
20   all round is as little pleasing to the mind of the country as his Home Rule. No solution will satisfy the mind and conscience of the country which does not regard equity, discriminate between the good landlord and the bad, and lance the deep imposthume of moral grievance.
25   Sir George Trevelyan adheres to his passionate love for the Liberal party, his passionate grief at its not being in power. I am too old for these romantic attachments. Sir George Trevelyan himself confesses that 'it is impossible for young politicians to have any idea of the half-heartedness of the Liberal politics
30   of the past.' I confess that I am not sanguine about those of the near future. Why then should we be so very eager to take up again with 'the tabernacle of Moloch,' Mr. Gladstone's old umbrella, or 'the star of our god Remphan,' the genial countenance of Sir William Harcourt, merely in order to pass forty
35   years in the wilderness of the Deceased Wife's Sister? If the

Conservative Government will quell anarchy in Ireland, give us a sound plan of local government there, and deal effectually with the land question, we may be well satisfied to allow them the lease of power requisite for this, and I believe the country will let them have it.

5

Schools in the
Reign of Queen Victoria

I have to speak of the progress of schools in England during the present reign, and I begin with elementary schools—schools for the great bulk of the people.

First grants for elementary schools. The first grant of public money for these schools dates from 1833, four years before the accession of her Majesty. This grant was administered by the Treasury, and was not accompanied by the right of inspection. The first rudiments of an Education Department appear in 1839, the third year of her Majesty's reign. On the 12th of February in that year, Lord John Russell laid upon the table of the House of Commons a letter which he had addressed by her Majesty's command to Lord Lansdowne, the President of the Council. The letter began as follows:

'My Lord,—I have received her Majesty's command to make a communication to your lordship upon a subject of the greatest importance. Her Majesty has observed, with deep concern, the want of instruction which is still observable among the poorer classes of her subjects. All the inquiries which have been made show a deficiency in the general education of the people, which is not in accordance with the character of a civilised and Christian nation.'

The letter goes on to mention the want of qualified teachers, better methods of instruction, and adequate inspection of the schools; it then touches on the 'wide, or apparently wide, difference of opinion with respect to religious instruction,' and on the difficulties which this difference creates, and concludes as follows:

'On this subject I need only say, that it is her Majesty's wish that the youth of this kingdom should be religiously brought up, and that the rights of conscience should be respected.'

In pursuance of this letter, a Committee of Council on Education was appointed on April 10, 1839, consisting of the Lord President and four other of the Queen's Ministers. The Committee took over from the Treasury the superintendence of the application of any sums voted by Parliament for the promotion 5 of public education. But it established, as a condition of its grants, the right of inspection, and it appointed inspectors. It is the beginning, therefore, of our Department of Public Education.

Sir James Shuttleworth. Sir James Kay-Shuttleworth was, in 10 fact, its founder. He it was who did most to interest Ministers in the effort to be made for bringing State help to schools for the people, and who chiefly devised the plans of proceeding. Sir James Shuttleworth, as I shall throughout call him, although in 1839 he did not yet bear that name, has never had full jus- 15 tice done to him. This doctor of medicine (in 1839 he was Dr. Kay), who in his professional practice for some ten years observed closely the condition of the labouring population in great cities—Edinburgh, Dublin, Manchester—and who became convinced that for the barbarism which he found there 20 the school was the natural and true cure, that this cure would conquer barbarism slowly but would conquer it in the end, was a most remarkable man. He was not a man of high cultivation, and he was not a good writer. I am told that he might easily have become a powerful speaker, and I can well believe it; but 25 he was not in Parliament, and his work was not to be done on the platform. As an administrator, when he had become Secretary to the Committee of Council on Education, he did not attract by person and manner; his temper was not smooth or genial, and he left on many persons the impression of a man 30 managing and designing, if not an intriguer. But the faith in popular education which animated him was no intriguer's passion. It was heroic, it was a gift planted by nature, and truly and earnestly followed, cultivated, and obeyed. And he who had this clear vision of the road to be pursued, had a clear vision 35 also of the means toward the end. By no other means than those adopted by him could a system of public education have been then introduced in this country. Moreover, in laying out popular education he showed in general an instinct wonderfully sound—he grasped the subject more thoroughly, made fewer 40

mistakes, than any of his successors. He was, too, a religious
man, though both Church and Dissent distrusted him. He sincerely desired to make religious instruction a power in schools;
he believed as firmly as Butler, that of education what is called
5 *information* is really the least part. Only, the problem how at
present to supply an effectual religious instruction seemed to
him simpler than it is. As to programmes of secular instruction,
he had acquired full knowledge of what was done in the good
schools established on the Continent, and he applied this knowl-
10 edge judiciously. I have already said that he did not attract, that
he had faults; that both the clergy and the sects disliked and
distrusted him. The general public was indifferent; it needed a
statesman to see his value. Statesmen like Lord Lansdowne and
Lord John Russell appreciated him justly; they followed his
15 suggestions, and founded by them the public education of the
people of this country. When at last the system of that education comes to stand full and fairly formed, Shuttleworth will
have a statue.

    Sunday-schools. The Reformation did not in England, as in
20 Scotland and on the Continent, create a system of elementary
schools. The endowed schools founded in the reign of Edward
VI. and Elizabeth were ill adapted to meet the wants of the
poor, and, being ill-managed and without any effective supervision, became more and more unserviceable as time went on.
25 Even the catechetical instruction of the children of the poor,
for which provision is made by the 79th Canon, had come in
the eighteenth century to be much neglected. Towards the
end of that century, however, a movement in religion awakened a new sense of responsibility, and Sunday-schools were
30 founded. They were of invaluable service. Up to 1839 a large
part of the population owed to these schools not only their
religious instruction, but their power, whatever it was, to write
and read. The promoters of the Sunday-school, having seized
the fruitful idea that the school is an inseparable element of the
35 organisation of a Christian congregation, were naturally led to
give more extension to this idea, and to institute the day-school.
In the early years of the present century the National Society
and the British and Foreign School Society were founded, in

order by association to obtain the means of better reaching the
end in view. The National Society was to promote schools in
connexion with the Church of England, and in which the
catechism and doctrines of that Church were taught; the British
and Foreign School Society was to offer to all Protestant con-   5
gregations a common school, where the Bible was read, but no
catechism admitted.

Condition of the lower classes. From that time forward until
1839 these great societies were the chief and almost the sole
agents for improving popular education in this country. Prob-   10
ably even before they existed there were scattered over the
country a certain number of good schools, created and maintained by the zeal of individuals. But certainly from the time
when the two societies came to reinforce individual efforts,
schools of high merit were brought into existence. I am sure   15
that my memory does not deceive me as to the merit of certain
National schools which I remember to have seen in my youth.
They were thoroughly good schools, schools which would be
called good even now. Later I have visited, as an inspector,
British schools which did not avail themselves of the annual   20
grants from Government, and had remained therefore British
schools of the old-fashioned type; some of these, too, I found
to be thoroughly good schools, with certain merits of their
own which modern schools do not, I think, reproduce. But undoubtedly the monitorial system, which all these old schools   25
had to employ, required almost a man of genius as head teacher
to work it profitably. Moreover, the means at the disposal of
the great societies and of individual promoters of education
were wholly insufficient. Immense and formidable gaps in the
supply of schools presented themselves; whole regions were in   30
a state of ignorance and barbarism, and there was no power of
reaching them. Riots and rick-burning in the agricultural districts, sedition and outrage in the manufacturing towns, compelled attention to the neglected condition of the people. Inquiry followed inquiry; the returns given were in many cases   35
inaccurate and misleading, but enough of the truth became visible to prove the urgent need for some action on the part of the
Government. I have myself heard from those who, before the

Reform Bill, visited Lancashire to inquire into the state of the manufacturing population, that in the town of Oldham they found it a common practice for men to run races through the streets naked, and in another large town they found that less
5   than one hundred, of all the children of school age there, were at school.

But no one has drawn so striking a picture as Sir James Shuttleworth himself of the parents and scholars with whom, in London, the agricultural counties, and the manufacturing dis-
10 tricts respectively, the schools, when the Government first took them in hand, had very frequently to deal. The picture of the London 'street Arab' is familiar, and I need not here repeat it. Of the parents in the pauperised rural counties of the South of England he says:
15 'They were in a state resembling helotry. They were largely dependent on the poor-rate. There were few or no schools. The population was ignorant and demoralised; it had the craft of the pauper, or of the pensioner on parochial doles, of the poacher and the squatter on the common.'
20 And he says of the children, even those who attend some school:
'The very early labour of the children on the farms, and the interference of successive harvest and seed-time, make school attendance so brief, and interrupt it by such long intervals, that
25 the child's poor capacity for school-work and his learning are subject to constant drawbacks. Moreover, there is no help at home. His parents, though they may be skilful in farm work, are unlettered, and in all other respects ignorant.'
Most striking of all is the picture of the school-children of
30 immigrant families feeding the manufacturing districts of the northern counties:
'A family enters a manufacturing village; the children are at various school ages, from seven to eleven. They probably have never lived but in a hovel; have never been in the street
35 of a village or a town; are unacquainted with common usages of social life; perhaps never saw a book; are bewildered by the rapid motion of crowds, confused in an assemblage of school-

children. They have to be taught to stand upright, to walk without a slouching gait, to sit without crouching like a sheep-dog. They have to learn some decency in their skin, hair, and dress. They are commonly either cowed and sullen, or wild, fierce, and obstinate. They are probably classed with scholars 5 some years younger than themselves. They have no habits of attention; the effort of abstraction required to connect a sound with a letter is at first impossible to them. Their parents are almost equally brutish. They have lived solitary lives in some wild region, where the husband has been a shepherd, or hind, or 10 quarryman, or miner, or turfcutter, or has won a precarious livelihood as a carrier, driver of loaded lime ponies, or poacher. The pressing wants of a growing family have induced them to accept the offer of some agent from a mill. From personal experience of many years, I know that such children as these 15 form a large portion of the scholars whom the schools of the cotton and woollen districts have to civilise and Christianise.'

Want of good teachers. The half-time system in factories, and the rule that no child under eight shall be employed in them, date from about the same time as the formation of the 20 Committee of Council on Education. Without them the school could have produced little effect on a population such as that which has just been described. But there was another hindrance to the work of the school which half-time Acts could not touch—a hindrance prevailing not in the manufacturing dis- 25 tricts only, but all over England—the want of good teachers. There were no training-schools; almost the only teachers whom the Committee of Council found at its disposal in 1839 were 'either untrained men who, from some defect of body or health, had been driven from the rougher struggles of life and mus- 30 cular toil; or self-taught Sunday-school teachers, trained for three or six months in some central model school'—such, for instance, as the British and Foreign School Society had established in the Borough Road.

Opposition to the proposed normal school. The Treasury 35 grant of 20,000*l.* a year, from 1833 to 1839, was distributed through the National Society and the British and Foreign

School Society, for the purpose of building schoolhouses, and for that purpose only. When the Committee of Council was formed, the grant, of the same amount as before, was meant to provide also a system of inspection for schools, and to provide,
5   above all, a normal school for the training of teachers, with a model or practising school attached to it. The system of inspection was established, and has been in operation ever since. The projected normal school met with keen opposition from the bishops and clergy of the Church of England, and was
10 abandoned. Students of different religious confessions were to have been combined in it, and the religious instruction was to have been of two kinds, general and special—the general instruction to embrace all the students, and to be given by the headmaster of the school; the special to be given by the clergy and
15 ministers of religion, at hours set apart for the purpose, to members of their own confession. It was at once assumed that the Government proposed to extend this plan of combined religious instruction to all the elementary schools of the country. In the storm which the Church raised, the newly launched
20 Committee of Council very nearly suffered shipwreck. It escaped, however, but it had to throw overboard its projected normal school. It continued to distribute its grants through the two great societies, as the Treasury had done; securing, however, that guarantee of inspection for which the Treasury had
25 neither established the means nor formulated the demand.

Government inspection. The third regulation of the Committee of Council's Minutes, presented to Parliament in 1840, was as follows:

'The right of inspection will be required by the Committee
30 in all cases. Inspectors authorised by her Majesty will be appointed from time to time, to visit schools to be henceforth aided by public money; the inspectors will not interfere with the religious instruction or discipline or management of the schools, it being their object to collect facts and information,
35 and to report the result of their inspection to the Committee of Council on Education.'

Much apprehension was felt lest the interference of the new inspectors should be vexatious, and the instructions to them

were judiciously drawn so as to allay these apprehensions. The inspectors were to be careful to explain to school-managers that the object of the Government was not to supersede them, but to co-operate with them; not to control them, but to afford them assistance; to assist them in efforts for school-improve-   5
ment in which they might want aid. 'You are in no respect,' the inspectors were told, 'to interfere with the instruction, manage-ment, or discipline of the school, or press upon the managers any suggestions which they may be disinclined to receive.'

As a proof of the sincere desire to work harmoniously with   10
the managers, the Government undertook to appoint different classes of inspectors. The authorities of the Church of England desired that the inspectors should examine into the religious instruction of schools, and report upon it. This was agreed to, and the Government undertook to appoint no inspector of   15
Church of England schools in whom the archbishops had not confidence, and to retain no inspector from whom that con-fidence had been withdrawn. Moreover, the inspector's report on the discipline and instruction was to be in duplicate, one copy of it for the Committee of Council and one for the arch-   20
bishop of the province. Only clergymen were appointed as in-spectors of Church of England schools. The British and For-eign School Society preferred that the inspectors of their schools should not examine into the religious instruction given there. These schools were therefore inspected by laymen; but   25
here, again, the Committee of Council undertook to communi-cate to the Society the name of any proposed inspector, and not to press his appointment if he did not possess the Society's con-fidence.

A Minute of 1839 declared that, if a school in England ap-   30
plying for aid were not in connection with either the National Society or the British and Foreign School Society, the appli-cation would not be entertained, except under special circum-stances. In the schools of the two societies there was religious instruction; and it was held that no school could be admitted   35
to aid in which the Bible was not read. With this condition Wesleyan, Catholic, and Jewish schools could of course com-ply; and, as time went on, these schools were admitted to aid.

Secular schools, which could not comply with this condition, were excluded.

The first training-school. The opposition of the bishops had prevented the establishment of a State normal school, yet a normal school was indispensable. The indefatigable man who was founding our public education determined to start a normal school himself, and to show how such an institution worked. In conjunction with his friend Mr. Edward Carleton Tufnell, who not long ago closed a long life of public-spirited labour, he took at Battersea the manor-house by the Thames, which is now known as the oldest and most distinguished of Church of England training-schools. The name of Mr. Robert Eden, afterwards Lord Auckland, at that time vicar of Battersea, should be remembered as that of a helper in the good work. It was his cordial encouragement which drew to Battersea the founders of the training-school, and he placed his parochial schools at their disposal as practising schools for the students.

The design was at first merely to provide a supply of trained teachers for workhouse schools. In these schools the rudiments of the pupil-teacher system, a system which was found at work at this time in Holland, had already appeared. The emergence of the first English pupil-teacher deserves record. A good school had been formed in the Gressenhall workhouse in Norfolk. The master of this school, an active and intelligent man, fell ill. Among his scholars was a forward lad called William Rush, who had risen rapidly to the top of the school. When the master suddenly fell ill, this boy of thirteen years old took, of his own accord, the charge of the school, carried forward the prescribed routine, not only of the schoolroom, but of the school garden and workshop as well, and with such success that the guardians were summoned to see. They authorised Rush to continue his work, and invited Sir James Shuttleworth, who as Dr. Kay was then employed in Norfolk to administer the new Poor Law, to visit the school. Dr. Kay came, and, having seen the boy's work, engaged him to remain as appointed assistant to the master, who soon recovered. Rush was afterwards moved to the School of Industry at Norwood, for the sake of the ampler teaching and training to be obtained there, and afterwards to Battersea. Meanwhile the hint had been taken, and promising boys engaged as apprentices in several workhouse schools.

Work began at Battersea in February 1840. The first pupils 5 were brought there from Norwood—boys like Rush, who were thought likely to form a class of serviceable apprentices. In a year's time their number grew to twenty-four. Friends of the founders aided the new institution by sending to it boys in whom they were interested, and paying 20*l.* a year towards 10 their support. But, besides the pupil-teachers, there was a smaller class of young men, sent in the same way by benevolent persons wishing to train them to be schoolmasters. The number in this class amounted at the end of the first year to nine.

Sir James Shuttleworth lived in the house, and superintended 15 the whole working of the new institution. Two departments were formed, for each of which a master was appointed. The life of the pupils was to be plain, and the work was to be both bodily and mental; how plain the life, and the work how severe, let the training-school students of to-day learn with awe: 20

'The whole school rose at half-past five. The household work occupied the pupil-teachers altogether, and the students partially, till a quarter to seven o'clock (there were no servants kept except a cook). At a quarter to seven they marched into the garden and worked till a quarter to eight, when they were 25 summoned to prayers. They then marched to the tool-house, deposited their implements, washed, and assembled at prayers at eight o'clock. At half-past eight they breakfasted. From nine to twelve they were in school. They worked at the garden from twelve to one, when they dined. They resumed their 30 labour in the garden at two, and returned to their classes at three, where they were engaged till five, when they worked another hour in the garden. At six they supped, and spent from seven till nine in their classes. At nine evening prayers were read, and immediately afterwards they retired to rest.' 35

The meals were 'frugal or even coarse; it was thought desirable that their diet should be as frugal as was consistent with

constant activity of mind and some hours of steady and vigorous labour, and that it should not pamper the appetite by its
quality or its variety.'

This severe regimen was found trying by several weakly
5   pupils at first, but presently they were braced and invigorated
by it. 'They rapidly gained strength; the most delicate soon
lost all their ailments.'

Both in the management and in the instruction of the Battersea school was felt the influence of the normal and orphan
10 schools of Switzerland, and of the admirable men—Pestalozzi,
Fellenberg, Vehrli—who had worked in them. Of these men
or their methods Sir James Shuttleworth had made a close and
careful study, with the happiest fruit for his own plans. To prepare him for laying out the instruction for the future teachers
15 of popular schools, he could not have come under better influence than Pestalozzi's. A Pestalozzian he always remained.

He and Mr. Tufnell, with the aid of some subscriptions from
friends of their scheme, had borne the expense of the training-
school during its first year. But he had solicited permission from
20 the Government to have the periodical examinations entrusted
to the newly appointed inspectors of schools, and he had always hoped that when his normal school was started and doing
work, the Government would, if not adopt it, at least aid it.

The expectation was not disappointed. The Committee of
25 Council granted in 1842 the sum of 1,000*l.* towards the expenses
of the Battersea Training School, and in the following year a
further sum of 2,200*l.* to enlarge and improve the school prem-
ises. To this second grant was attached the condition that satisfactory arrangements should be made for the future support of
30 the institution. Its founders had meanwhile made an important
change in their plan. They had come to the conclusion that
boys could not with advantage be trained in a normal school,
had raised the age of admission, and proposed henceforth to
train adult students only. But the school had grown until it re-
35 quired for its maintenance resources greater than those of its
original founders. At the same time, they felt that their original
design of training masters for workhouse schools only might
with advantage give place to the wider design of supplying

with teachers the elementary schools of the country. Accordingly, with the consent of the Government, they made over, at the end of 1843, the Battersea Normal School to the National Society, in whose hands it has ever since remained. The founders of the school retired from its management.   5

But they had accomplished a great work. Their example had speedily been followed. The British and Foreign School Society established a normal school in connexion with their model school in the Borough Road; the Church established others; and Great Britain, which at the date of the Battersea experiment did   10 not possess a single normal school, could show eight normal schools four or five years after it.

Defects of elementary schools. Meanwhile the reports of the inspectors drew attention to the defects of the elementary schools, although, the Parliamentary grant being then in aid of   15 building only, they had no power to bring help towards the maintenance of schools and the improvement of their teaching. They gave advice and recommendations to managers which the managers had no means for following; the reports, however, made it manifest that progress was impossible unless something   20 more was done. The number of school-houses had considerably increased since 1833, but they were in general ill-furnished, ill-warmed, ill-supplied with books and apparatus. Above all, the condition of the teacher was deplorable. 'He has often an income very little greater than that of an agricultural labourer,   25 and very rarely equal to that of a moderately skilful mechanic. Even this income is to a great degree contingent on the weekly pittances paid from the earnings of his poor neighbours, and liable to be reduced by bad harvests, want of employment, strikes, sickness among the school-children, or his own ill-   30 health.' He had monitors for his assistants; but 'the monitors usually employed are under twelve years of age, some of them as young as eight or nine, and they are in general very ignorant, rude, and unskilful.'

Religious difficulties. In 1843 the Government of Sir Robert   35 Peel attempted to deal with the education of at least the manufacturing districts. Sir James Graham's famous education clauses in the Factories Act provided for the establishment and

support of schools in those districts. The religious instruction
was to be that of the Church of England, but the exemption of
Dissenters' children from this instruction, at the parent's wish,
was secured. Now came the turn of the Dissenters to stop the
5   way, as the bishops had stopped it in 1839. A fierce agitation
was raised against the preference to be given to the Church of
England. Mr. Henry Dunn, the acute and accomplished secretary of the British and Foreign School Society, who took part
with great energy in that agitation, told me himself that what
10 he had seen of tempers and motives while prosecuting it had so
shocked him that he had registered a vow never to be induced
to take part in a religious agitation again. The Whig leaders of
the Opposition behaved well. The clauses could have been carried, but the fire which had been kindled over them would have
15 continued to rage around the schools which they were to establish. No friend of education could like such a prospect. The
Government therefore withdrew the clauses, and as the bishops
had triumphed in 1839, so the Dissenters triumphed in 1843.

Solely concerned for the school, perfectly incapable of sacri-
20 ficing it to the interest of either Church or Dissent, Sir James
Shuttleworth took note of the situation, and of the possibilities
created by it. There were extreme men on both sides who
could not be conciliated. There were Dissenters who argued
that the school was a religious institution, that the State could
25 not touch religion without profaning it, and that with the
school, therefore, the State should have nothing to do. On the
other side, the attitude of Archdeacon Denison and men like
him is well known. I myself once received a letter from a
clergyman, then trustee of a school which I proposed to visit on
30 account of a building grant made to it some years previously,
who told me that he 'would never permit an emissary of Lord
John Russell, or any other Turkish Bashaw, to enter the school.'
But there were a great many worthy people on both sides who
were concerned that the cause of popular education should
35 suffer a check, perhaps a little ashamed that it might be said that
the check was owing to their religious disputes. The great body
of promoters of Church of England schools were in this case;

so were the majority of the Wesleyans and of the supporters of the British and Foreign School Society.

The Parliamentary grant for school building and school inspecting had risen in 1846 to 100,000*l*. By the Minutes of that year the Government of Lord John Russell, who had now returned to office, took a great and decisive step in advance. It was determined, instead of striving to establish schools of a new kind, to try a system capable of adapting itself to schools of the kind already existing, so as to encourage voluntary contributions for their support, to stimulate the activity of their management, and to promote their efficiency by rendering it one of the conditions on which aid should be awarded.

Sir James Shuttleworth had now become Secretary to the Committee of Council on Education, and the Minutes of 1846 were his work. An arrangement for aiding existing schools must of necessity benefit Church schools principally, because these were by far the most numerous. The Dissenters had not forgotten their recent victory. In the session of 1847 the new Minutes were attacked with great acrimony. Macaulay made a celebrated and highly rhetorical speech in their favour. A most vigorous speech by Mr. Bright against them deserves preservation, as a specimen both of his powers as a speaker and of the temper of political Dissent. Mr. Bright was very indignant at being asked 'to aggrandise a Church by whose act his forefathers had languished in prison.' But the author of the Minutes had judged the situation rightly, and they were carried by a majority of 325.

Pupil-teachers. The points of weakness to which the Minutes of 1846 addressed themselves were the teachers and the monitors. As to the monitors, it had been observed that schoolmasters succeeded in making monitorial schools efficient exactly in proportion as they were enabled by local circumstances to retain the monitors beyond the age of thirteen, or were permitted by the trustees to pay them a small weekly stipend, giving them at the same time the advantage of some separate instruction. By the Minutes of 1846 boys and girls of thirteen could be engaged for five years as pupil-teachers, with a stipend from the Gov-

ernment rising from 10*l.* a year to 20*l.*, and with daily separate
instruction from the master and mistress, an instruction to
which the Government attached a gratuity.

The training-schools were suffering because the supply of
5   candidates for admission was poor in quality and insufficient in
quantity. In the pupil-teachers they would have a natural supply of better prepared candidates. To enable the pupil-teacher
to enter them, the Minutes of 1846 offered scholarships of 25*l.*,
to be supplemented by a further payment of 20*l.* at the end of
10 the first year's residence in the training-school if a certificate
examination were then passed successfully, 25*l.* at the end of the
second year, and 30*l.* at the end of the third, on the same condition. Four-fifths of the expense of the student's first year at
the training-school would thus, it was calculated, be defrayed
15 by the Government, and one-half of his expense in the years
following. Here was help indeed to the struggling training-
schools.

Not only had monitors been inefficient and normal schools
suffering, but the salaries of schoolmasters and schoolmistresses
20 had been in general miserably low. The Minutes of 1846 offered
to students who, after passing the certificate examination, became teachers, a grant in augmentation of their salary varying
from 15*l.* to 30*l.* a year, according to their degree of merit in
the examination. But this augmentation grant was accompanied
25 by the conditions that the managers should provide its recipient
with a house rent-free, and with a further salary equal to twice
the amount of the grant. Thus not only did the Government
in itself better the teacher's position, it obliged the managers
also, on their part, to better it.

30   These provisions were such as to secure a supply of better-
instructed and better-paid teachers in the future. Meanwhile,
however, the actual teachers would have been unaffected by
them. But it was added, as an incentive to actual teachers to
improve their qualifications, that untrained teachers might be
35 admitted to an examination for certificates corresponding with
those granted in the normal schools, and that the augmentation
grant annexed to such certificates would be extended to these
teachers also.

We have thus in the Minutes of 1846 a source of improvement of monitors, normal schools, and teachers. The Minutes likewise improved the fittings and material of the elementary school by stipulating that a school which received grants should be well furnished and well supplied with books and apparatus.

There were other provisions in the Minutes of 1846, provisions for very real needs of any complete system of popular education—for pensioning teachers, for establishing school gardens, school workshops, school kitchens, and laundries—which either failed of realisation or were realised but imperfectly. The provisions for the institution of pupil-teachers, for the support of training-schools, for the augmentation of teachers' salaries, were realised fully; and the good done by them, and which to this day continues to operate, cannot be exaggerated.

Everybody can understand the utility of supporting training-schools and of bettering the position of teachers. The system of pupil-teacher apprenticeship has now many adversaries. Yet the institution of this system was undoubtedly the grand and chief merit of the Minutes of 1846. It provided a class of efficient schoolmasters and schoolmistresses more quickly than they could have been provided in any other way; it interested the population in the schools, it caused the teacher's profession to be generally regarded as a promising one, instead of as a refuge for the poor, the halt, and the maimed. I will add that the English schoolmaster has proved himself to have a remarkable aptitude for managing boy helpers, and not by any means an equal aptitude for managing adult helpers. Of course the introduction of the adult assistant was a necessity which soon made itself felt, and the pupil-teachers, moreover, were too numerous, were chosen at an age when their vocation could not clearly be discerned, and were not weeded, as they ought to have been, when after two or three years a youth's want of vocation became apparent. Had Sir James Shuttleworth not been forced by the failure of his health to leave the Education Department before the Minutes of 1846 had been five years in operation, he would, I am convinced, have seen the danger in his pupil-teacher system and have provided against it. As it was, all the pupil-teachers, bad and good, once caught in the scho-

lastic net, were as a rule kept there, and drawn to land finally in the training-school; many issued from it unserviceable teachers, who had been unserviceable apprentices long before they entered it. But the abolition of the system would be a
5   real misfortune. In point of fact, in spite of the attacks upon it, it is extending; what is to be desired is that it should be maintained for those who prove to have a genuine vocation, and that others should after a time be strictly eliminated.

Sir James Shuttleworth's work in 1846 was a truly states-
10   manlike one; he did all that was possible at the time. This, however, is in itself no great achievement; but what he did was not only possible to be done at the time, it was likewise destined to grow and to bear much fruit in the future. Throughout the country, moderate Churchmen and moderate Dissenters were,
15   in general, favourable to the new work; the working population, for whose especial benefit the improved schools would act, began to feel interest in them. But the grant grew. It had begun at 20,000*l*. in 1833; in 1846 it had grown to 100,000*l*. The Minutes of that year caused it to swell much more. Opponents
20   predicted with horror that it would rise to a million and a half. Three years after the Minutes appeared there were 681 certificated teachers, and 3,580 pupil-teachers; ten years later, in 1859, the number of certificated teachers had risen to 6,878, of pupil-teachers to 15,224.

25   *The Duke of Newcastle's Commission.* The appointment of the Commission 'to inquire into the present state of popular education in England,' commonly known as the Duke of Newcastle's Commission, was due to the apprehensions caused by the rapid growth of the Parliamentary grant. The Commission
30   reported in 1861. By a large majority, the Commissioners decided on recommending the continuance of public aid on an unreduced scale to both normal and elementary schools. They enounced the opinion, however, that the actual system of grants was too complicated and that it threatened to become unman-
35   ageable by the central office, and they proposed to transfer to the local rates a considerable part of the charge. The grant then stood at about three-quarters of a million. The Commissioners proposed to lay on the county rates a charge calculated at

428,000*l.* a year for the present. Moreover, they had convinced themselves that insufficient attention was paid to junior classes in elementary schools; that the teachers were tempted to be too ambitious, and to concentrate their attention on a showy upper class, while the bulk of the scholars were comparatively neglected and failed to acquire instruction in 'the most necessary part of what they came to learn,' reading, writing, and arithmetic, in which only one-fourth of the school-children, it was alleged, attained any tolerable knowledge. But the Commissioners thought that, even under the present conditions of age and attendance, it would be possible, if the teachers had a strong motive to make them bring the thing about, for at least three-fifths of the children on the books of the schools—the three-fifths who were shown to attend one hundred days and upwards—'to read and write without conscious difficulty, and to perform such arithmetical operations as occur in the common business of life.' To supply the teachers with the requisite motive, therefore, the grant from the county rates was to take the form of a capitation grant, dependent on the number of scholars who could pass an examination in reading, writing, and arithmetic.

The Revised Code. The Vice-President of the Education Department in 1861 was Lord Sherbrooke, then Mr. Lowe, an acute and brilliant man to whom pretentiousness with unsoundness was very distasteful and comtemptible. The permanent secretary was one of the best and most faithful of public servants, the present Lord Lingen, who saw with apprehension the growth of school grants with the complication attending them, and was also inclined to doubt whether Government had not sufficiently done its work, and the schools might not now be trusted to go alone. These powerful officials seized upon the statements and proposals of the Commissioners, and produced, as a consequence of them, the Revised Code. But they went far beyond the Commissioners. The training-schools were to lose their lecturers' salaries, the stipends of pupil-teachers and the augmentation grants of masters and mistresses were to be discontinued; everything was to be capitation grant, dependent on the ability of the individual scholars to pass an

examination in reading, writing, and arithmetic, an examination
for which they were to be arranged in four groups according to
their age. The system of bounties and protection, said Mr.
Lowe, had been tried and had failed; now another system
should be tried, a system under which he would promise that
popular education, if not efficient, should at least be cheap, and
if not cheap, should be efficient.

There was a great outcry. It was said that, if the Government
grant had increased, so had voluntary contributions; the one-
third of the cost of popular education which the State contributed had called forth two-thirds from local and private
sources to meet it, and this resource it was now proposed to
discourage and endanger. The improved schools had been but
a dozen years at work; they had had to civilise the children as
well as to instruct them; reading, writing, and ciphering were
not the whole of education; people who were so impatient because so many of the children failed to read, write, and cipher
correctly did not know what the children were when they
came to school, or what were the conditions of the problem
which their educators had to solve. Sir James Shuttleworth
maintained that, so far from its being true that all the children
who had been at school for one hundred days and upwards
in the year preceding the examination ought to be able to pass
in reading, writing, and arithmetic, only those of them who
had attended more than two years were fit subjects for the
examination proposed.

The impossibility of preparing the bulk of the children to
pass the examination proposed was no doubt exaggerated. We
have seen what can be accomplished in this line by preparers.
On the other hand, I have always thought that the Commissioners, finding in the state of the junior classes and of the elementary matters of instruction a point easy to be made and
strikingly effective, naturally made it with some excess of energy and pressed it too hard. I knew the English schools well in
this period between 1850 and 1860, and at the end of it I was
enabled to compare them with schools abroad. Some preventible neglect of the junior classes, some preventible shortcoming
in the elementary instruction, there was; but not nearly so

much as was imagined. What there was would have been sufficiently met by a capitation grant on individual examination,
not for the whole school, but for the children between seven or
eight years old and nine or ten, a grant which would then have
been subsidiary, not principal. General 'payment by results' has   5
been a remedy worse than the disease which it was meant to
cure.

The opposition to Mr. Lowe's Revised Code of 1862 so
far prevailed that it was agreed to pay one-third of the Government grant on attendance, and but two-thirds on examination.   10
Moreover, the grouping by age was abandoned, and the arrangement of the children in six classes, or standards, as they
have come to be called, was substituted for it. The teacher
presented the child in the standard for which he thought him
fit; he must present him the next time, however, in a standard   15
above that.

Defects of the Revised Code. The capitation grant on attendance was four shillings; that on examination was twice that
amount, one-third of which was forfeited for a failure in reading or writing or arithmetic. This latter grant has governed   20
the instruction and inspection of our elementary schools ever
since. I have never wavered in the opinion—most unacceptable
to my official chiefs—that such a consequence of the Revised
Code was inevitable, and also harmful. To a clever Minister and
an austere Secretary, to the House of Commons and the news-   25
papers, the scheme of 'payment by results,' and those results
reading, writing, and arithmetic, 'the most necessary part of
what children come to school to learn'—a scheme which should
make public education 'if not efficient, cheap, and if not cheap,
efficient'—was, of course, attractive. It was intelligible, plausi-   30
ble, likely to be carried, likely to be maintainable after it had
been carried. That, by concentrating the teacher's attention
upon enabling his scholars to pass in the three elementary matters, it must injure the teaching, narrow it, and make it mechanical, was an educator's objection easily brushed aside by our   35
public men. It was urged by Sir James Shuttleworth, but this
was attributed to a parent's partiality for the Minutes of 1846
and the Old Code founded on them—a code which the Revised

Code had superseded. But the objection did really occur to him
and weigh with him, because he was a born educator, and had
seen and studied the work of the great Swiss educators,
Pestalozzi, Fellenberg, Vehrli. It occurred to me because I
5   had seen the foreign schools. No serious and well-informed
student of education, judging freely and without bias, will approve the Revised Code. In other countries no such plan is
followed. It is said that the State must have the security of such
a plan, when State aid to schools rises so high as it has risen in
10 England; but in France, where the State is taking upon itself
almost the whole charge for the popular schools, no such plan
is adopted or contemplated. That is because the serious and
well-informed opinion of educators has more influence on
school regulation abroad than it has in England. In England
15 it has little or none. The uneasiness and resistance of the teachers, hampered by a false system, will at last perhaps give the
'purchase' for upsetting the Revised Code which the opinion of
educators is too weak here to supply. Meanwhile our schools,
with many merits, are undeniably less intelligent than those of
20 the Continent; and this their inferiority is due in great part, although not entirely, to the Revised Code.

Mr. Forster's Elementary Education Bill. A far more real
fault of the system on which the Duke of Newcastle's Commission reported than its alleged neglect of the junior classes
25 was its failure to meet more than partially the needs of the
country. It reached not more than half of the children requiring education. The Revised Code did nothing to make good
the old system's deficiencies in this respect. It dropped the proposal of the Newcastle Commission to throw on the rates a
30 part of the public charge for schools, and kept the whole of it
on the Consolidated Fund. During the eight years which followed the revision of the Code, several attempts were made to
introduce a general system with support from the rates, but
without success. At last, in February 1870, Mr. Forster pro-
35 duced his Elementary Education Bill. He proposed no interference with the existing aided schools. But he asked for powers
to ascertain what in each locality was the supply of efficient elementary schools in proportion to the wants of the population,

and, where the supply was deficient, to require the borough or parish where this was the case to make good the deficiency. The new schools needed were to be provided out of the rates, and a school board was to exercise the functions which in voluntary schools appertain to their promoters and managers. Mr. Forster at first intended that the town councils and vestries should nominate the school boards, and that these should have the power both of aiding existing schools and of appointing at their discretion, subject to a conscience clause, the religious instruction in the new Board schools. Compulsory attendance, to which Mr. Forster had until lately been opposed, the school boards were to have the power of establishing by by-laws, if they thought fit.

The speech of Mr. Forster in introducing his measure, and the measure itself, made a most favourable impression, and at first all seemed going smoothly. Presently a storm sprang up. Dissenters and secularists seized upon the provisions enabling school boards to aid existing schools and to admit in Board schools what religious instruction they might think proper. Undoubtedly these provisions would in many cases have led to the establishment and support of Church of England schools out of the rates. To many this seemed intolerable; and, in resisting a provision favourable to the Church of England, the further question was raised whether in schools supported by public money there ought to be any religious instruction at all.

The country would not at that time have accepted—I doubt whether it would accept now—a system of secular public schools. As to the special religious instruction of Church of England schools, it is not, in my opinion, their best and most attractive feature. I prefer, it is true, the management and personal influences of a good Church school to those of a good Board school. In secular instruction I think the two kinds of school are about equal; but I have always thought that the Biblical instruction which the school boards have adopted, with some improvement, from the old British schools, was the religious instruction fittest on the whole to meet the desires of the population of this country and to do them good. To promote, in preference to such an instruction, the teaching of the

catechism and special doctrines of the Church of England in
elementary schools, was certainly not Mr. Forster's desire. But
he was a man with a feeling heart and great fairness of mind;
he was deeply sensible of the labours and sacrifices of the
5   clergy for popular education, and if the localities chose to mark
their sense of these by establishing Church schools, he would
have permitted them.

Credit due to the clergy. In truth, if there is a class in English
society whose record in regard to popular education is honour-
10 able, it is the clergy. Every inquiry has brought this out. I will
give only one illustration, but it is an illustration indeed. The
Newcastle Commission investigated the sources from which a
sum of 4,518*l*. raised for schools in a particular district was derived. It appeared that the main contributors were the land-
15 owners and the clergy; the contributions from other sources
were trifling. The landowners contributed 5*l*. 6*s*. per head, their
rental from the district being estimated at 650,000*l*. a year. The
clergy contributed ten guineas per head. The Newcastle Commission, with facts like this before it, did full justice to the
20 clergy. 'The landowners as a class,' the report of the Commission adds, 'especially those who are non-resident (though
there are many honourable exceptions), do not do their duty in
the support of popular education; and they allow others, who
are far less able to afford it, to bear the burden of their neglect.'
25 The clergy, therefore, well deserved consideration from Mr.
Forster, and perhaps the best arrangement would have been one
by which Church schools should have been aidable by rate,
but a larger and simpler religious instruction given in them than
at present. To admit a solution of this kind neither the clergy
30 nor their adversaries had then moderation enough. The battle
raged fiercely over Mr. Forster's Bill; he showed admirable
skill and patience, and without them would never have saved
it. He admitted several changes. The aid from the Parliamentary grant to voluntary schools was continued, but these schools
35 had to submit to what is called 'a time-table conscience clause,'
assigning the religious instruction to the beginning or the end
of the school-time, and enabling the school-children to be withdrawn both from that and from the Sunday-school. In the new

schools to be aided from the rates religious instruction might be given, but with the same 'time-table conscience clause' in force; and in the religious instruction of these schools no religious catechism or distinctive formularies were to be used. The school boards were not to be nominated by the town councils and vestries, but elected by the ratepayers. These changes in Mr. Forster's original plan are none of them to be regretted; the great object of his Bill, to provide means for supplying the whole country with efficient schools, and for filling them, was attained.

Mr. Forster too, like Sir James Shuttleworth, deserves the praise of having discerned and done what was possible to be done at the time, and what would grow and bear much fruit in the future. For the extension of our popular instruction, he was able to do much more than Sir James Shuttleworth. He made this instruction for the first time national. He had also a high estimate of the teacher's calling, was the sincere well-wisher and friend of the teachers; they have gratefully recognised him as such, and he fully deserves their gratitude. But Mr. Forster was not, like Sir James Shuttleworth, a born educator, an earnest student of methods and problems of education; neither was he a Minister like Guizot or Wilhelm von Humboldt, with a philosophical mind trained and interested to weigh all questions of teaching, and well fitted to judge and decide them. The false direction given by the Revised Code to teaching, Mr. Forster did not correct; 'payment by results' he left as he found it. I doubt whether he even took its faults and fallacies into his mind at all. Other and great work for popular education, however, he found to do, and he did it with his might.

Hitherto throughout this sketch I have designedly been very sparing of figures; but now, in order to show what has been accomplished since Mr. Forster carried his Education Act in 1870, to figures I must have recourse. The Newcastle Commission reported that in 1860 the annual public grants promoted the education of about 920,000 children, while they left unaffected the education of 1,250,000 others of the same class. The public grant was at that time about 750,000*l.*, and, to meet this sum voted by Parliament, there were raised by voluntary contributions and school-fees 1,250,000*l.*

In 1870, when Mr. Forster's Act was passed, there were in average attendance in day-schools aided by public grants 1,152,389 children. Fifteen years later, in 1885, there were in average attendance 3,371,325. There were 12,467 certificated teachers in 1870; in 1885 there were 40,706.

It is calculated that 20 per cent. of the population are children of a class and age to require elementary schools. The public schools in 1870 were sufficient for only 8·75 of the population; in 1885 they were sufficient for 18·18 per cent.

But the annual Government grants, which in 1860 were about 750,000*l.*, and of which the imagined possible rise to 1,500,000*l.* caused dismay, had risen in 1885 to nearly 3,000,000*l.* Rates, which are but another form of public aid, produced 1,140,964*l.* Voluntary contributions and school-pence produced over 2,500,000*l.* We have a total expenditure, in 1885, on public elementary schools, of more than 6,500,000*l.*, of which more than 4,000,000*l.* are from Parliamentary grants and from rates.

The proportion of public to private aid has indeed wonderfully changed since the Newcastle Commission reported in 1861. It was then estimated that, of the expenditure for the support of public elementary schools, one-third was supplied by the Parliamentary grant and the remaining two-thirds came from voluntary contributions and school-fees. Sir James Shuttleworth thought that he saw his way to the establishment of a constantly increasing proportion of private support, a constantly diminishing proportion of public. 'The force,' he said, 'which will ultimately transform the whole, will be the result of education itself. When the people know that they have even more interest in the education of their children than their rulers have, they will more and more take charge of it. They now bear two-thirds of the burden; but that third which they do not pay has given value to what before was of little worth, and has thus created a transient power destined to pass from the Government into the hands of those who will take the charge. The transference of administrative power

to the local managers and the parents, will attend the gradual assumption by them of the payment of pupil-teachers
and of the whole of the stipends of the certificated teachers,
consequent on the effects of education on some generations of
parents and on the middle classes.' But all calculations were   5
changed by the nation's resolve in 1870 to provide at once efficient popular schools for the whole country. It is remarkable,
not that the amount of private support from fees and subscriptions should not now be larger than it is, but that with rates and
a national system it should still be so large.   10

Although 20 per cent. of the population are supposed to be
subjects for the elementary school, there were in average attendance there, in 1885, only 12·26 per cent. The attendance
will become better than this; but this, compared with the attendance in 1870 (but 5·5 per cent. of the population), and   15
compared with what is found elsewhere, affords plenty of
cause for satisfaction. The number of juvenile criminals, moreover, has diminished and is diminishing; it is impossible not to
connect this diminution with the growth of schooling.

There had been established in England and Wales, up to the   20
beginning of April in last year, 2,203 school boards. The powers
of school boards to enforce attendance were given by the
original Act. Extensions of that Act have provided for the appointment of a school attendance committee for every borough
and parish in which a school board has not been elected.   25

'*Payment by results.*' Ever since the establishment of the Revised Code in 1862, attempts have been made to palliate the
evil effects of 'payment by results,' of concentrating the teacher's efforts upon the securing of the greatest possible number of
passes in the three elementary matters. By no Vice-President   30
have such attempts been so zealously prosecuted as by Mr.
Mundella. Of the Government grant, a considerably larger proportion than formerly now depends upon the average attendance; plans have been devised for obtaining more uniformity
in the inspectors' judgments of 'results;' grant-earning matters   35
other than the three elementary matters have been multiplied,
and more latitude in the choice of them given to the school-
managers. By the 'merit-grant,' the encouragement of results

more general than those which are measured by the other grants has been attempted. Unfortunately, the whole system is vicious, and the truly useful Minister will be he who, instead of patching it, clears it away. To support your popular schools by appraising so many matters at so much each, then setting your inspectors to appraise the amounts earned by the children's performance, adding the totals and paying to the school the sum given, is fatal to instruction, fatal (though that is a much smaller matter) to inspection. It is a plan prohibitive of a good programme of study, and productive of mechanical teaching. A boy who leaves a town school in Germany has in his school course been taught eleven or twelve matters, whereas an English boy leaving a like school has been taught but six or seven; and all the German boy's matters of study, except perhaps handwriting, have in general been better taught than the English boy's. Ours is a plan, I repeat, which no serious educator would entertain, and it has been entertained here because we have no provision whatever for bringing the influence of serious educators to bear permanently upon our school legislation.

Necessity of technical schools. Mr. Mundella, however, has shown by his utterances respecting technical and secondary instruction that his thoughts are moving on the line which alone will conduct us to fruitful reforms. Technical schools are needed, and in elementary schools manual training should be given; yet it is undesirable to bestow in the elementary school too much prominence on this training, to turn the elementary school itself too much into a technical school. The technical school is, in fact, a secondary school, to follow the elementary school, after some manual training has there been acquired. But our secondary instruction is a chaos; unless, therefore, we organise the technical school within the sphere of our primary instruction, which is not desirable, we have no means of organising [it] at all. Mr. Mundella sees the difficulty; he sees that there are problems of instruction for primary schools which we can only solve by having public secondary schools. There are problems of expense also. The school-rate for London was in 1885 over eightpence in the pound, for the whole of England and Wales over sixpence-halfpenny. Mr. Forster,

in introducing his Bill in 1870, estimated that the rate could not exceed threepence. The cost for each Board school child in London was, in 1885, 3*l.* 7*s.* 10¾*d.;* in England as a whole, 2*l.* 6*s.* 2¼*d.* This is a very heavy rate of charge. If necessary, it must be continued; but the question is, How far is it neces-   5
sary? We shall never know, so long as our elementary edu-cation stands as at present isolated, our one service of public schools. Then only can the expense of our primary schools be rightly adjusted, when an organic connexion between all our schools, primary, intermediate, and higher, supplies us with   10
a scale of proportion for expense, as well as with a graded series of means for teaching.

[SECONDARY SCHOOLS]

Defective secondary education. The first year of her Maj-esty's reign found English elementary education a chaos; the fiftieth finds it, with whatever imperfections of detail, at any   15
rate a national system. But English secondary education, like-wise a chaos when her Majesty's reign began, remains a chaos still.

I have said so much on this subject that I prefer now to let any one rather than myself speak of it. The invaluable report   20
of the Schools Inquiry Commission of 1865 sums up thus the state of secondary schools in England:

'There is no public inspector to investigate the educational condition of a school by direct examination of the scholars, no public board to give advice on educational difficulties, no   25
public rewards given directly to promote educational progress except those distributed by the Science and Art Department, hardly a single mastership in the gift of the Crown, not a single payment from the central government to the support of a secondary school, not a single certificate of capacity for teach-   30
ing given by public authority professedly to teachers in schools above the primary schools. In any of these senses there is no public school and no public education for the middle and upper classes. The State might give test, stimulus, advice, dignity; it withholds them all.'   35

This account holds good to the present day. If we had accurate and complete information of the supply and quality at the present time of our secondary schools, such as they are, we should have taken the first step towards introducing order into
5   their chaos, and should be on the way to improvement. But we have not. Let me recount the principal data we have, and the conclusions to be gathered from them.

In 1837, the first year of the present reign, the Charity Commission concluded its inquiries, begun in 1818, into the chari-
10 table trusts in England and Wales. In 1842 a digest of the reports of this Commission was published. It showed 705 endowed grammar schools at that time in England and Wales, and nearly 2,200 other endowed schools which the Commission designated as 'non-classical.' No further classification of the en-
15 dowed schools was given, and no estimate of their state of instruction.

Public Schools Act. In 1862 nine of the 705 grammar schools were subjected to a very thorough inquiry by the Public Schools Commission, of which Lord Clarendon was chairman.
20 Two other great secondary schools not classed among endowed schools answered so fully questions addressed to them by the Commission, that of eleven chief secondary schools we may be said to have acquired, through the report of the Commission of 1862, sufficient information. The schools were Eton, Win-
25 chester, Westminster, Harrow, Rugby, Shrewsbury, Charterhouse, St. Paul's, Merchant Taylors', Marlborough, and Wellington. Seven of the eleven became in 1868 the subject of an Act of Parliament—the Public Schools Act—which, in conformity with recommendations of the Commission, altered
30 their constitution and established for them new governing bodies.

All the eleven schools, however, were previously in the public eye—were known and important, attracted much interest and criticism. In this way they gave a solid guarantee. About
35 twenty others might be added to them which gave a guarantee not so imposing, but perhaps adequate—the guarantee of a considerable, though more restricted, interest and publicity. All these schools gave guarantees, and were undoubtedly the best

secondary schools of the country, and schools doing very good work. Dr. Arnold's son is not the fittest person to enlarge on what Dr. Arnold accomplished at Rugby before his death in 1842, and on the fruit so widely borne by his labours. The spirit in which many a chief teacher, and many and many an assistant teacher, have striven to do their duty in our great public schools during the last forty years, and not in our oldest and greatest schools only, but also in schools such as Clifton, the City of London, Repton, Uppingham, cannot be too highly honoured, or the good done by such labours be too highly prized. Still, the schools in question must all be regarded as points, more or less bright, emergent from a general darkness. Unillumined, around and beyond them, lay chaos; and unillumined, after the report of the Clarendon Commission, it still continued to lie.

Lord Taunton's Commission. A far more important Commission was that of 1865, of which Lord Taunton was chairman, and in which the masculine character, strong sense, and thorough experience of Dr. Temple, now Bishop of London, exercised, I think, and most happily and usefully exercised, a leading influence. This Commission had to deal with the schools between the nine of the Clarendon Commission and the elementary schools—with the real body and mass, therefore, so little observed and known hitherto, of our secondary education. The report, published just twenty years ago, in 1867, is a mine of valuable information and sound and judicious comment. Twenty years have elapsed since it appeared, and nobody reads Blue-books; but if that report—or, at any rate, the first, second, third, sixth, and seventh chapters of it—could be republished now as an ordinary book, at the price of sixpence or a shilling, it would, I believe, have a wide circulation and do great good.

The Schools Inquiry Commission found that, of the endowed schools designated as 'non-classical' by the Charity Commission, a certain number were secondary schools, and that the endowed secondary schools of the country were therefore nearly eight hundred in number. Into the condition of all of these, except the reserved nine, they inquired fully. The proprietary

schools they found to be in number about eighty, and they inquired fully into the condition of these also. Finally, of the
numerous private schools existing throughout the country, and
amounting, it appeared, to more than ten thousand in number,
5   they examined specimens.

It is calculated that about twelve and one-half boys in every
thousand of our population ought to be attending secondary
schools. As the population stood in 1865, the Schools Inquiry
Commission estimated the number of boys coming within the
10 scope of their inquiry at about 255,000. The number of boys in
England and Wales at the present moment who require secondary schools would, at the same rate of calculation, be about
320,000.

The report of the Schools Inquiry Commission appeared at
15 the end of 1867. The Commissioners reported that the secondary schools, 'whether public or private, which are thoroughly satisfactory, are few in proportion to the need.' As to
the endowed schools, 'there are few endowments applicable to
secondary education which are put to the best use, and very
20 many which are working to little or bad use.' Moreover, 'in at
least two-thirds of the towns in England there is no public
school at all above the primary schools, and in the remaining
third the school is often insufficient in size or in quality.' Proprietary schools have in certain places been established to meet
25 the need felt, but though 'educationally they have very largely
succeeded, commercially the majority have not succeeded.'
Whatever their success, they, like the endowed schools, educate but comparatively few of those requiring secondary education. 'The total number of boys in endowed and proprietary
30 schools for secondary education appears to be 52,000. If the
total number of boys requiring secondary education be 255,000,
nearly 80 per cent. of the whole are educated in private schools,
or at home, or not at all.' In fact, the immense majority of these
are brought up in private schools. But 'the state of the private
35 academies, though not wholly without hopeful features, is lam-
entably unsatisfactory.' There are 'excellent private schools of
the more expensive sort,' but 'we find a rapid deterioration as
we descend in the scale of price, and most of those which we

should reckon as belonging to the third grade are quite unequal
to the task which they have undertaken.' On the whole, the
Commissioners sum up thus: 'The result of our inquiry has
been to show that there are very many English parents who,
though they are willing to pay the fair price of their children's   5
education, yet have no suitable schools within their reach where
they can be sure of efficient teaching, and that, consequently,
great numbers of the youth of the middle class, and especially
of its lower divisions, are insufficiently prepared for the duties
of life, or for the ready and intelligent acquisition of that tech-   10
nical instruction the want of which is alleged to threaten such
injurious consequences to some of our great industrial interests.
We believe that schools, above most other institutions, require
thorough concert among themselves for their requisite efficiency; but there is in this country neither organisation, nor sup-   15
ervision, nor even effective tests to distinguish the incompetent
from the truly successful; and we cannot but regard this state
of things as alike unjust to all good schools and schoolmasters,
and discreditable and injurious to the country itself.'

The Commissioners recommended a plan for bringing about   20
the resettlement of educational trusts, so many of which were
'working to little or bad use;' for bringing about, also, that
supervision, those effective tests for distinguishing the incompetent schools and teachers from the capable, and, with time,
that general organisation and concert, which they considered   25
so desirable for English secondary schools, and so grievously
lacking to them. They had in view an organisation of secondary
schools in three grades—the third and lowest to carry the
scholar to the age of fourteen, the second to the age of sixteen,
the highest to the age of eighteen or nineteen. 'The most urgent   30
educational need of the country,' they said, 'is that of good
schools of the third grade.'

In my opinion, the Commissioners erred in treating these
third-grade schools as establishments for secondary education,
and I suppose every one well acquainted with German schools   35
must have shared that opinion. The Commissioners might very
properly have insisted on the need in elementary education of
such schools, but they should not, I think, have imported them

into secondary. However, the Elementary Education Act and
its developments have now made it sufficiently clear that to elementary education the third-grade schools belong, and I believe that in official schemes dealing with endowments for sec-
5   ondary instruction the third-grade school now rarely or never
appears.

The Endowed Schools Act. With this single exception, the
views and recommendations of the Commissioners were excellent. In 1869 the Endowed Schools Act provided for the re-
10 settlement of educational trusts by a Commission which has
since been blended with the Charity Commission. An Endowed
Schools Act No. 2 was to have provided for the supervision,
the testing, the gradual co-ordering of our secondary schools.
This Bill was dropped, and all the projected machinery of edu-
15 cational council, provincial authority, inspectors, examiners,
disappeared. Ten years later, in 1879, Sir Lyon Playfair introduced a Bill for registering teachers engaged in intermediate
education. To be on the register, future teachers must, after the
Bill had become law, submit to an examination; and here, for
20 the future at any rate, was an effective test for distinguishing
the incompetent from the qualified teacher. But this Bill likewise was dropped.

What has been gained, then, since the Schools Inquiry Commission reported in 1867, has been a very extensive resettle-
25 ment, for the benefit of secondary education, of charitable
trusts. Many additional endowed schools, with schemes adapting them to present local wants, have thus come into existence.
Proprietary schools, likewise, have multiplied considerably.
The ten thousand private schools of 1867 may also undoubtedly
30 be taken to have multiplied, although information in regard to
this entire class of schools is greatly wanting.

Secondary education improved: Those who find in all our
history for the last fifty years nothing but glorious progress,
and cause for jubilee, will say that, during that time, the im-
35 mense development of the industrial and commercial energies
of the country has been accompanied by the spread of modern
studies and natural science in our secondary schools; that there
is hardly now a provincial town of importance without its

college of science or school of art; that the City guilds are powerfully aiding the movement; that companies provide day-schools for both girls and boys; that the examinations of the College of Preceptors ever since 1854, the Oxford and Cambridge local examinations ever since 1858, have afforded to our   5 secondary education the tests and supervision requisite.

But still very defective. But whoever is not carried away by the torrent of jubilee, whoever has well observed our secondary schools and compared them with those of the Continent, knows that we have indeed broken up our old type of second-   10 ary instruction, but not yet founded a new one of any soundness and worth; that our provision of secondary schools is utterly incoherent and inadequate; that the local examinations supply us with neither the tests nor the supervision really requisite; that the bulk of the middle class in this country is   15 worse educated than the corresponding class in Germany, Switzerland, Holland, Belgium, or even the United States; that it is brought up on an inferior plane, in schools both of lower standing and worse taught. The reason why no effective remedy is applied to this serious evil is simply, as I have often said, be-   20 cause the upper class amongst us do not want to be disturbed in their preponderance, or the middle class in their vulgarity. People call this an epigram; alas, it is much rather a scientific formula truly and closely summarising the facts. That many who cling to their preponderance or to their vulgarity, cling   25 to them unconsciously, makes no difference. Their action is the same, and its hurtful consequence.

Registration of teachers. I ask myself what seems at present possible in this great work of which Parliament and the nation so little grasp the scope and importance, the work of reforming   30 our secondary education. I think it might be possible to get powers to ascertain, as was done for elementary education in 1870, the actual supply and its character. It would also be possible, I think, to carry a Registration Bill like Sir Lyon Playfair's, or even a better one. By that Bill every existing teacher   35 was to have been recognised for the purposes of registration; it would be sufficient, surely, if every existing teacher over fifty years of age were so recognised. But younger teachers should

not be so recognised; they should either produce their titles or
pass an examination. If we abstain from bearing hardly on old
practitioners, the public mind is ripe, I cannot but believe, for
admitting that, in general, just as an apothecary ought not to
5   practise without being registered and supplying proof of com-
petency, so neither ought a schoolmaster. With more doubt I
add, that it might be possible also to constitute the College of
Preceptors, under proper conditions, as a public normal school
for secondary teachers—the true function for that useful Col-
10   lege, and a most valuable and far-reaching one.

Need of a Minister of Education. I have spoken on this subject of middle-class education much and often. By too great
persistency the advocate of a cause may indispose the public
to it, and I would avoid that danger. Probably I shall never re-
15   turn to the subject again; let me for the last time, therefore,
insist on the mischief to be cured and on the impossibility of
curing it by makeshifts and half-measures. Uneasiness is felt as
to the state and prospects of our industry, trade, and commerce;
the blame is commonly thrown on defects of the working-class,
20   and a remedy is by many people thought to lie in giving to this
class more of technical instruction. The instruction of our elementary schools does indeed require, as I have said, to become
more intelligent; but this will not be accomplished by making
it more technical. Let the child have good primary schooling,
25   with the rudiments of manual training, till the age of thirteen;
let the technical school, for those who are fit to profit by it,
come later. But the failure, after all, and the menace to the
future of our industry and commerce, lies far more in the defects of mind and training of our middle class than of our
30   lower—yet to those defects hardly any one will as yet open his
eyes. The middle class in England has merits which the middle
classes elsewhere do not possess; but it has peculiar disadvantages, and its disadvantages are at this moment very prominent.
It has not the training which local government affords to the
35   corresponding classes abroad, and it has a school-education
markedly inferior to theirs and formative for good neither of
the mind nor of the character. Its religion has done much for
it, its schools have done little or nothing. Unformed itself, it

exercises on the great democratic class, rising up beneath or rather around it, no formative influence; and this class, too, loses means of training both natural for it and most wholesome. May we live to see the coming of a state of things more promising! Throughout the country good elementary schools, taking the child to the age of thirteen; then good secondary schools, taking him to sixteen, with good classical high schools and commercial high schools, taking him on further to eighteen or nineteen; with good technical and special schools, for those who require them, parallel with the secondary and high schools—this is what is to be aimed at. Without system, and concert, and thought, it cannot be attained: and these, again, are impossible without a Minister of Education as a centre in which to fix responsibility, and an Educational Council to advise the Minister and keep him in touch with the tendencies, needs, and school-movement of the time. May the founding of such a system signalise the latter years of her Majesty's reign, as the founding of public elementary instruction has signalised its earlier years!

From Easter to August

The Session is ending. Whatever we may have wished, whatever we may have conjectured, when the Session began, as to
things likely to happen in it, it is ending now, and its facts can
speak for themselves. And for any one with his eyes open two
5 facts above all, at the closing of the present Session, stand out
clear and undeniable—the disappearance of the Gladstonian
plan of Home Rule, the weakening of the Government.

Whether the Liberal Unionists live or die, they have at any
rate rendered to their country this signal service—they have
10 compelled the abandonment and disappearance of the Gladstonian plan of Home Rule. The Land Bill which was to be its
accompaniment and condition disappeared long ago. But the
scheme of a separate national Parliament and a separate national
Executive for Ireland remained, and was full of dangers. To
15 give to the people of Ireland the due control of their own local
affairs was, as I said a year ago, an object approved by all reasonable people in this country, and professed by every Liberal
Unionist, by Mr. Bright and by Mr. Chamberlain as much as by
Mr. Gladstone. But what gave to Mr. Gladstone's scheme its
20 essential character was the withdrawal of the Irish members
from Westminster and their establishment as a national power
in Dublin, with an executive and justice and police of their
own. It is now conceded that the Irish members shall be retained at Westminster. Nor is there to be at Dublin any national
25 Parliament or Executive for Ireland. An assembly and executive
for the northern province is conceded; and so Ireland will have,
at any rate, not a national Parliament and national Executive
single, but an assembly and government for northern or British
Ireland on the one hand, and an assembly and government for

southern or Celtic Ireland on the other. Finally, assurances appear to have been given with respect to the control of justice and police which to Sir George Trevelyan, at all events, are satisfactory.

The Liberal Unionists, I say, may survive or they may be extinguished, but they have saved their country from a great peril, they have converted the Gladstonian scheme of Home Rule from a most dangerous to a comparatively safe one. Not a single Gladstonian candidate who now wins an election wins it as a supporter of Mr. Gladstone's old unconverted plan. The plan converted, or to be converted, is the one he adopts and upholds; and the conversion of the plan has been brought about by the opposition of the Liberal Unionists to the surrender originally offered by Mr. Gladstone.

On the other hand, the Government is weaker than when the Session began. It has been losing, not gaining, in credit and consideration. I speak of home affairs only. The Leader of the House of Commons has qualities which win every one's good word; he has filled his difficult position far better than people in general expected, and on the whole with success. Mr. Balfour, who did not begin happily, has since shown himself to possess great vigour and resource. The Government has carried and applied the closure, which the country, I am convinced, heartily wished to be carried and applied; it has also carried the Crimes Bill, which its adversaries loudly and confidently defied it to carry. Still it is at the present time visibly, I am sorry to say, declined and declining in consideration, credit, and power. True it has actually lost only four seats, but the change indicated by the voting at those and other elections is grave. Nor can the Government show any important gain, except in one constituency, to set on the other side. It is manifest that the democracy, in whose impulses lies the Government's danger, is beginning to move; while, on the other hand, the great body of quiet reasonable people, in whose support lies the Government's strength, are somewhat discouraged and disconcerted.

Let me recall two warnings which I was moved to give (it is so easy to give warnings!), one of them in a letter to the

Times more than a year ago, the other in this Review just before the present Session began. In the *Times*, after a misunderstood and unfortunate speech by Lord Salisbury, I urged that however necessary restraining measures for Ireland might be,
5 still for the Government to rely on restraining measures merely was to play the game of their adversaries and to deliver us over to Cleon and his democracy. In this Review I urged, when the Session was about to begin, that of fumbling and failure the country has had more than enough, that people are become impatient of seeing the efforts of Government turn awry and our
10 affairs go amiss; that *success*, clear and broad success, is what the general sentiment earnestly demands from the Government and its measures.

Now it is evident that, if the first of these two warnings was
15 sound, the Government could not expect that the Crimes Bill, a purely restraining measure, would be sufficient alone. It might be accepted, and I am convinced it *was* accepted, by the great body of quiet reasonable people as a necessity, and as such approved, but with the understanding that fit remedial measures
20 would follow it. By the democracy, by the new electorate, any Crimes Bill was sure to be regarded with impatience and misgiving. It might be just tolerated, in the hope of better things immediately to follow it; it could not be approved. Everything depended upon what came after. What came after was the
25 Bodyke evictions, a repetition of the scenes enacted at Woodford and Glen Beigh. Mr. Balfour said he 'thought it his duty' to enable the Bodyke evictions to take place. Mr. Balfour is a brilliant man, but his 'thinking it his duty' to carry into execution, at that juncture, the Bodyke evictions, reminded me painfully of a saying of Goethe's: *The English are pedants!* It was
30 pedantry at that juncture, in a revolutionary state of things, with a bad case, and with a Crimes Bill before Parliament, so to construe his duty. And heavily indeed was Mr. Balfour's stroke of pedantry punished. The evictions were conducted, like the
35 preceding cases of the kind, in a manner to bring ridicule and contempt upon the police and soldiery, and upon the Government which was behind them. Some of the evictions were of a character to raise the temper of the democracy, already im-

patient and annoyed at the Crimes Bill, to a white heat of indignation. Rude but moving pictures of the harshest passages in the
evictions were hawked about through the villages; mob orators
used with all their might the opportunity given to them. 'It is
to perpetuate scenes like this,' they kept crying, 'that the   5
Government pass a Crimes Bill!' Quiet, reasonable people, out
of the reach of mob orators, and well knowing that even in
harsh evictions the fault is not always all on the side of the
evictors, were yet seriously shocked and disquieted.

In this untoward condition of things, it was of the utmost   10
importance that the next proceeding of the Government should
be beyond all question frank, firm, simple, and healing. Success
is what is demanded, and the first conditions of success for the
measures of a government are frankness and firmness. It was
necessary, further, that their proceeding should be simple, be-   15
cause the time was short, and healing, because after the Crimes
Bill the turn for a healing measure was come, and was announcing itself imperiously. Under these circumstances the Government appeared with their Land Bill in the House of Commons.
The measure was neither frank, firm, simple, nor healing. The   20
promise of a complete Land Bill at the beginning of next Session, and a short bill staying evictions in the meantime, would
no doubt have produced a far better and more satisfying effect
upon the mind of the country. But to take this course was
thought impossible. A course, however, less calculated to   25
weaken the Government than the course actually followed by
them might surely have been found. When something healing
has to be done, it is surely weak statesmanship to seek to do it
by a bill fashioned at first in the House of Lords so as to suit the
landlords, then gravely altered in the House of Commons at   30
the instigation of the Liberal Unionists, but with a burning
question, that of arrears, left unprovided for; subsequently
again altered in the House of Lords in such a manner as to
create fresh dissatisfaction and delay. I will not pronounce an
opinion upon a single clause of the bill, it is not necessary to do   35
so in order to be convinced that this intended measure of healing has been managed most unhappily. The main alterations
made by the House of Lords have finally been adopted, but to

the bitter disappointment of the Ulster Unionists and at the
cost of much heart-burning and friction; so that, instead of the
Government having derived any advantage from this their
first attempt at a healing measure, the positive weakening of the
5 Government is, I fear, the capital and serious fact at the close
of the Session.

Plainly, then, Conservatism is not now any longer at its zenith. It ought to be added that this is in no degree by the fault
of the Conservative party in the House of Commons. That
10 party has behaved admirably. Readers of the Fathers, if there
are any such readers left, may possibly remember a passage in a
homily at the end of St. Cyprian's works: *Incredibilis res est
pastores pati posse aliquid a pecore.* The homilist puts it too
strongly; the shepherd has sometimes cause to complain of the
15 flock. But certainly of their *pecus*, the Conservative flock in the
House of Commons, the Ministerial shepherds have no cause
to complain. Never was there a body of followers more steady,
more willing, more self-sacrificing. Mr. Courtney has spoken
severely of the demeanour of some of their younger members;
20 but Mr. Courtney, like myself, has come to an age when one
is liable to attacks of a sort of irritable antipathy towards white
waistcoats, and when one has to be on one's guard against the
moroseness of old age. From all I have myself seen, or can learn
from others, I should say that any impartial observer who re-
25 calls the interruptions prevalent and victorious in the House of
Commons of former days, and who witnesses the provocation
offered by many of the Irish members now, would be inclined
to pronounce the parliamentary demeanour of the whole Conservative party at present, young as well as old, almost angelic.
30 At any rate, of the staunchness, fidelity, patience, and reasonableness of this party towards its leaders there can be no doubt.
Nor has the staunchness of the Liberal Unionist members been
less exemplary. Their course has been that of men sincerely
anxious to save the Government from committing errors, to
35 help the Government out of difficulties, not to make capital out
of those errors and difficulties for themselves. Their position is
in many respects a harassing one, a position to cause restlessness;
but only two of them have been unsettled and carried away

by restlessness, Mr. Winterbotham and Sir George Trevelyan. The majority behind the Government has, I repeat, done its duty perfectly. But the fortunes of the Government decline, and those of the majority cannot but decline with them.

Before the Session began, I inquired what the Government should do in order to retain the goodwill of that great body of quiet, reasonable people throughout the country, who thought the course attempted by Mr. Gladstone and his followers a false and dangerous one, and had placed the Conservatives in power in order to stop it. And I answered my own inquiry by saying, as I have mentioned above, that what the Government had to do was to take, on the great questions of the Session, a course not dubious, fumbling, and failing, but frank, firm, and successful. At Easter I inquired how things stood at the moment to which we were then come; what had been accomplished, what still remained to be accomplished; what was likely to lead to final success, what to failure. And again I answered my own inquiry, and said that reasonable people were glad to see the closure carried, and would be glad to see the Crimes Bill carried, but that there was perhaps a danger of quiet people not insisting strongly enough upon a further thing: how much, after the Crimes Bill was carried, would still require to be done. I said that I believed them to desire and intend most sincerely both to defeat Mr. Gladstone's dangerous plan of Home Rule, and also to remove all just cause of Irish complaint, but that I feared we did not all of us adequately conceive how large and far-reaching were the measures required in order to effect the latter purpose. I added that it was the more necessary for reasonable people to acquire an adequate conception of this, and to make the Government act upon it, because the democracy, the new voters, were feather-brained, were unapt to understand the dangers of such a plan of Home Rule as Mr. Gladstone's, were by nature inclined to dislike a restraining measure such as the Crimes Bill, were being plied with fierce stimulants by Mr. Gladstone and his followers, were agitated and chafing, and if nothing effective was done for removing cause of complaint in Ireland as well as repressing crime there, were likely to burst irresistibly in, bearing Mr. Gladstone back to power.

What I feared has in great measure come to pass. The democ-
cracy has not yet indeed borne Mr. Gladstone back in triumph
to power, but in the Northwich division it has broken irresistibly in, carrying in triumph on its shoulders Mr. Brunner, who
5   adopts his leader's watchword of *Masses against classes!* and
proclaims his election to be a signal victory in that war. Mr.
Gladstone and his followers are superbly elate, they will ply
the democracy with fiercer stimulants than ever; if things continue to go as they are now going, the agitation will grow hot-
10 ter and hotter; at election after election will be raised the cry of
Masses against classes! and a perpetual series of Mr. Brunners
will win by it, until at last there is nothing left for them except to devour one another.

The end of the Session will give us a little breathing time. At
15 Easter I said that the prospects of a final happy issue were favourable, if the great force of quiet reasonable opinion throughout the country—the force which defeated Mr. Gladstone at the
last election—remained active and watchful. At the end of the
Session, in spite of all that has happened, I still say the same
20 thing. The Government is weaker. But the dangerous parts of
the Gladstonian plan of Home Rule have been dropped and
abandoned by its authors. To plain people outside of the rivalry
of parties it will seem of little matter which party settles the
Irish question so long as the settlement is a safe and good one.
25 But it may be said that the passions they have fomented, the
tempers they have raised, the feather-brained democracy to
which they appeal, may compel Mr. Gladstone and his lieutenants to withdraw concessions which he had been compelled
to make, and to recur to a scheme of Home Rule bad and un-
30 safe. And this is no doubt a possible danger. Only in one way
can it be averted. Only in one way can either the present weak
Government be strengthened so as to endure and so as to
achieve a settlement of the Irish question, or Mr. Gladstone be
controlled and influenced so as to adhere to his present con-
35 cessions, and to adopt a settlement of the Irish question, if to
him it falls to settle it, safe and reasonable. Either thing can
come about only by the force of quiet reasonable opinion in the
country continuing active and watchful—nay, increasing its

activity and watchfulness. And it is in one direction above all
that its activity and watchfulness have to be directed: to secure
the full and frank removal, now that power has been taken
for quelling disorder, of all just cause of complaint in Ireland;
and with this object, to habituate itself to consider, more ade-   5
quately perhaps than it has yet considered, what large and far-
reaching measures are required for that purpose, and to make
its insistence on such measures as operative as its approval of a
Crimes Bill has been.

Nor, in doing this, need our friends go back in the very   10
slightest degree from their approval of the closure and the
Crimes Act. To them, indeed, to brush away the claptrap and
insincerities, with which the politician inflames the feather-
brained democracy, is not difficult. In 'the present deplorable
Session, which must make every Englishman blush, or weep, or   15
both,' cries Mr. Gladstone, 'the closure imposes upon the de-
liberations of your free Parliament restraints hitherto totally
unknown.' But in the eyes of reasonable people the present Session is deplorable not because too much restraint has been put
upon the barren obstructive talk which Mr. Gladstone is   20
pleased to call deliberation, but because too little has been put
upon it. 'The liberties of the House of Commons,' he cries
again, 'have been sacrificed to the causeless, wanton, mischievous, insidious coercion of Ireland.' But a Judge declares to us
that in parts of Ireland 'the law has ceased to exist; there is a   25
state of war with authority and with the institutions of civilised
life.' Mr. Dillon boasts that 'there are hundreds of farms in
Kerry on which no person dares lay his foot.' The *Tuam News*
reports: 'Hugh Baldwin was summoned to attend the meeting
of the Kiltartan branch of the National League, the charge of   30
associating with a notorious anti-Nationalist being brought
against him. He assured some members of the Committee before the meeting that he did not know what he was doing, and
that it would not happen again.' If these things are so, if there
is this paralysis of the law, this intimidation and terrorism, and   35
if the offenders either cannot be brought to justice, or if they
are brought to justice cannot be convicted, what reasonable
quiet man will call it 'causeless, wanton, mischievous, insidious

coercion' to strengthen the ordinary law so as to enable it to reach them? 'No coercion, but a vigorous enforcement of the ordinary law!' cries the feather-brained journalism of the democracy. This is as much as to say, 'No enforcement of the law, but a vigorous enforcement of it!' It is because the ordinary law cannot be enforced that it needs strengthening. Every reasonable man must surely see that the strengthening of the power of the ordinary law is here no case for crying out against 'causeless, wanton coercion,' but rather for applying the excellent Bible text: 'Do that which is good, and thou shalt not be afraid of the power.'

Or, again, when Sir George Trevelyan asserts that 'the real defect' of the Crimes Bill is that 'it is directed against the written and spoken expression of opinion,' and Mr. Labouchere complains that it will 'crush out the legitimate expression of opinion in Ireland,' and Professor Stuart admonishes us that 'whatever may be the opinions of any body of persons, it is for the public detriment that those opinions should not be fully expressed,' reasonable people will surely take the trouble to ask what is really the sort of *opinion* which all this fine talk is to cover and license. And they will find that it is such opinion as this of Mr. Wm. O'Brien's: 'If Trench dares to lay a robber hand upon any honest man's house in Ireland, we will hunt Lord Lansdowne with execrations out of Canada.' And reasonable people will surely think that to permit, in the present state of things in Ireland, the free expression of this sort of 'opinion,' is good neither for Ireland, England, Canada, nor Mr. O'Brien. No one would call this 'the legitimate expression of opinion' except a political agitator; and he would himself expect no one except a feather-brained democracy to take him seriously.

The coercion, then, is not causeless in the present instance. Is it mischievous? Reasonable people in this country, if they have no bias, will not think so. The democracy, with a life full of restraints, naturally thinks restraint a curse, and doing as one likes the height of felicity. The Americans in general think so too. Mr. Godkin reports that 'go where you will in the United States, you will find that popular feeling, however ignorant about the facts of the case, runs in favour of the Irish.' It runs

in their favour because of the opinion, so prevalent in the
United States, that 'any measures of coercion are not only unjust, but nugatory.' Perhaps in a country like America, with
society in an early and simple stage, even reasonable people
may easily enough come to hold this opinion. I do not say   5
that it does them no harm, but at any rate they have little practical experience of its unsoundness and danger; they have not
yet reached that corporate stage when its falsehood is manifest.
Senator Riddleberger is thrown into prison in Virginia for some
contempt of court. His friends are indignant, and these plain   10
citizens, in their unsophisticated stage of life, after a repast of
fishballs, no doubt, and a drink of iced water, march to the
prison with ladders and take Senator Riddleberger out. And
what is characteristic of American society in its present stage
is, that then the citizens go away, one to his farm, another to his   15
merchandise, and no disturbance follows. But reflecting people
in our artificial European world would be inexcusable if they
expected here a like termination to a like case. Suppose Mr.
Labouchere were unlucky enough to be cast into prison, and
that the democracy of Northampton, when the tocsin sounded   20
from all the Nonconformist chapels, could go with ladders
and take him out; we all know that here this would mean
riot, roughs, drink, fires, and bloodshed. And Macaulay used
to contemplate with sadness, as we know, the sure coming of
a time when in America too it would, alas, be the same.   25

The Irish themselves are the worse, not the better, for the license which they claim for themselves, and of which their
friends say it is wrong to deprive them. Democratic journalism
reproaches the Conservatives with want of chivalry in not
sparing men who are down, as the Irish are. Mr. Parnell's threat   30
that his countrymen will 'look to methods outside the Constitution,' Mr. O'Brien's threat, 'If Trench dares to lay a robber
hand upon any honest man's home, we will hunt Lord Lansdowne with execrations out of Canada,' is scarcely the language
of men who are down. In fact the extraordinary impunity   35
which the Irish enjoy has generated in them a temper of audacity and defiance as mischievous to themselves as it is to England. Misgovernment—for the misgovernment must never be

denied or put out of sight—has begotten alienation, impunity in violent language and proceedings has begotten defiance. The Irish have many fine qualities, but they have also qualities which render them prone to be reckless and defiant, and which make 5 excess of this kind peculiarly baneful to them. A penetrating moralist has observed that of ordinary human nature itself 'the ground is seditious, insolent, refractory, inclined to contradict and contemn whatever lays claim to rule over it; consequently opposed to order, ungovernable, and negative.' Certainly this 10 is no inaccurate description of the temper which has grown up, whosesoever the fault may be, in Ireland, and which at present is in possession of the Irish nature. And it is a fatal temper; the *radicale Böse*, as our moralist goes on to say, of Kant; a temper which makes not only government impossible, but all order, 15 progress, and happiness. Until the Irish are convinced that the law is stronger than they or we, until they have had to re-nounce and forgo this temper of 'insolence, refractoriness, de-fiance,' not only they cannot be governed, they cannot be sane, they cannot be settled, they cannot be happy.

20   Both Lord Spencer and Sir George Trevelyan have used an argument, intended to embarrass the Unionists, which may usefully be noticed in this connexion. They reproach the Un-ionists with believing and countenancing certain grave charges against Mr. Parnell and others of his party, and they say: 'You 25 yourselves propose to bestow on Ireland local government, to give to the Irish, not indeed Mr. Gladstone's Home Rule, but the due control of their own local affairs; and how can you reconcile it with your conscience to put the local government of Ireland into the hands of men against whom such charges 30 as these are admitted by you?' Now of the charges here spoken of I say nothing; I have never relied upon them in the discus-sion of the Irish question—never, I believe, mentioned them. But this I will say to Lord Spencer and to Sir George Trevel-yan: To put the local government of Ireland into the hands 35 of men in whom their present temper of insolence, refractori-ness, defiance is rampant, would indeed be to invite failure and misery. Not until their temper has yielded, not until Irish-men have convinced themselves that the law is stronger than they, that it is vain and foolish for them to talk of making the

government of Ireland impossible and of driving Lord Lansdowne with execrations out of Canada, not until then can a
system of local government work well in Ireland. And surely
all reasonable people will see that this is an irrefragable argument for the Crimes Bill.   5

Whether or no it is expedient to suppress the National
League, or any particular branches of it, must depend, reasonable men will think, upon whether or no this refractory temper
of outrageous defiance yields or is broken down without such
suppression. If not, all reasonable people will wish the League   10
suppressed. But they will wish it suppressed simply to break
this malign temper, and not to comply with any clamour or
hatred; as, on the other hand, they will wish its not being suppressed, if suppressed it is not, to be because this temper is
suppled and reduced, not because the Government is nervous   15
about an election, apprehensive of enraging the democracy.
And if any branch of the League is to be suppressed they will
wish it suppressed firmly, not in a hesitating and fumbling
manner; because proceedings taken in a hesitating and fumbling manner never succeed. Meanwhile all reasonable people   20
must rejoice, I should have thought, that the League has been,
at any rate, proclaimed.

I have said that any Crimes Bill will be distasteful to the
democracy, because a measure of this kind is a restraining one;
and the proclamation of the League is likely to be distasteful for 25
the same reason. But I believe that the new electors, who have
a root of the English good sense and moderation in them, and
who not only hear Irish stump orators but begin also to read
newspapers, and newspapers not all on one side only—I believe
that the new electors might have been brought to understand   30
the necessity for a Crimes Bill, and even for the proclamation
of the National League. They might be disposed to judge
severely men who had told them they would never vote for a
Crimes Bill, and then went and voted for one. But neither
would this have been decisive with them. What was decisive   35
with them was, I repeat, the evictions, the continuing evictions,
the harsh and inhuman evictions of suffering people. The plea
that the landlord had no other course left to him; that the
same thing is done elsewhere; that the sufferers are much to

blame—the kind of unction which the propertied and satisfied
classes lay to their souls so readily—had and could have no
power upon the democracy at all. These evictions were brought
home to their imagination, feeling, senses; they thought them
5   horribly harsh and inhuman, and that was decisive. It cannot be
too often repeated: Mr. Balfour's 'thinking it his duty' to allow
the Bodyke evictions to take place was the crying, fatal fault
in the Government's proceedings this Session. It has made it
almost impossible for the democracy either to see the Crimes
10   Bill, or to see the proclamation of the League, as reasonable
people see it.

Of course the dangers of Mr. Gladstone's plan of Home Rule
the democracy was not likely to see; of course the grievances
alleged as a reason for it the democracy was likely to see
15   readily, and readily to admit the separatist constitution prescribed as a cure for them. To the mass of mankind nothing can
sound more plausibly than a cry for Home Rule; nothing needs
more training and reflexion than to appreciate rightly the
character and tendencies of the Home Rule proposed. Let me
20   ask Mr. Godkin (it is a pleasure to converse with him even in
the pages of a Review), whether he has sufficiently understood
how small was the number of persons I meant, when I said that
all the highly instructed and widely informed people I met in
America, except himself, thought Mr. Gladstone's scheme of
25   Home Rule injudicious. Mr. Godkin begins by quoting my
words accurately enough; but presently he makes me speak of
'intelligent' Americans, as if that were the same thing as 'highly
instructed and widely informed' Americans. Now the whole
American nation may be called 'intelligent,' that is to say,
30   quick; and certainly I never meant to dispute that, as Mr. Godkin asserts, 'go where you will in the United States, popular
feeling is in favour of the Irish demand.' I fully admit that this
is so, that such is the feeling of the mass of 'intelligent Americans' as they are called; only I add, with Mr. Godkin himself,
35   that these intelligent Americans are for the most part 'ignorant
of the facts of the case.' But I said that when I came across
highly instructed and widely informed Americans, I found
them of opinion that Mr. Gladstone's Irish policy was a mis-

take. I say the same thing still. I say it of the Continent of Europe as well as of the United States of America; I say it of what Mr. Gladstone calls 'the civilised world.' Mr. Gladstone sometimes appears to think that the civilised world is on his side if it agrees that Ireland has been misgoverned. But what I maintain is, that throughout the civilised world, so far as my experience goes, the highly instructed and widely informed people, while strongly thinking that Ireland has been misgoverned, think at the same time that Mr. Gladstone's plan of Home Rule, with its national Parliament and national Executive for Ireland, was a mistake. But indeed he has now abandoned the plan himself, although apparently without any just conception, even now, of its intrinsic character and of its dangers.

Yet Mr. Gladstone is a highly instructed and widely informed person. So is Mr. John Morley, so is Mr. Godkin. But in each and all of these cases there is a bias. Mr. Gladstone is biassed by his longing to command the eighty-five Parnellite votes, and so to be master of the House of Commons and of power. Mr. John Morley is so convinced of the stupidity and stiffness of the English nation, that he despairs of its ever managing Ireland properly. Mr. Godkin has the alienated feelings of so many of his Irish countrymen. All the three men, having this bias, use arguments, take a line, which without bias such men would never employ.

I always invite Americans, who call out for Irish Home Rule, to consider how they would themselves like to have not a number of Southern States each with its own Legislature and Executive, but one South with a national Southern Congress and a national Southern Executive. No one has ever cried, that I know of, *Alabama a nation!* as the Irish cry, *Ireland a nation, and the green flag of our people!* But there has been in America, as we well know, the cry, *The South a nation, and the flag of the Confederate States!* Would the Americans concede that nationality—would they not recognise its danger? I can myself imagine but one answer from them. Yet I seem to remember that Mr. Godkin, in his zeal to parry the argument against Home Rule which this illustration of mine conveys, was capable of maintaining in his newspaper that if the South had chosen to insist on their own Congress and Executive they might have had it.

Mr. Gladstone too—how, without a bias, could a man of Mr. Gladstone's training and knowledge, who has learnt how hard
5 and slow a labour is the grand work of building a nation, how mischievously the jealousies and pretensions of 'our parish' interfere with it—how could such a man go about the country evoking and envenoming provincial discontents everywhere, and thus not only vexing the present, but sowing also, so far as
10 in him lies, the certain seeds of trouble for the future? Without a bias how could Mr. John Morley taunt the Ulstermen with being bad Irishmen if they hold aloof from the national Parliament and Executive in Dublin? As if the height of political virtue for the Irishman was to feel allegiance to his island, not to
15 the Empire! As if a Breton who stood aloof from a separatist movement in Brittany, and said that he placed his pride in being a citizen not of Brittany but of France, was to be called a bad patriot! Yet a Breton is no more a Frank than an Irishman is an Angle.

20 Reasonable people have no cause to waver in their judgment that Ireland, like Brittany or Wales, is and must be now a nation poetically only, not politically, and that all projects for making it a nation politically are disastrous and pregnant with danger. A project of the kind their firm resistance has baffled.
25 Let them be watchful and zealous to prevent any reappearance either of that project or of a second project fraught with like dangers.

But Home Rule is not the pressing question for the moment; the pressing question for the moment is the question of the
30 land and the landlords. The greatest possible service, which the body of quiet reasonable people in England can now render to their country, is to set their face like a flint against all paltering with this question, to insist on a thorough and equitable settlement of it. I am convinced that they are sincerely bent on
35 doing right as to the land, no less than on quelling disorder. Their body is not aristocratical in its composition; if it were, it would have but a very small part of its present strength. The Conservative Government is aristocratical in its composition,

and inevitably contracts weakness from this cause; it leans to
the landlords; it imagines solidity where there is none; above
all, it has not the popular fibre, the instinct for what will please
or offend the feelings and imagination of men in general. The
present Conservative Prime Minister, Lord Salisbury, is even 5
conspicuously devoid of this instinct. His Jubilee honours afforded a good measure of his popular fibre. As seriously as if
he had been celebrating the Jubilee by assigning to Phidias or to
Socrates a public maintenance in the Prytaneum, he celebrated
it by investing Mr. Eaton with a purple robe, and lost the 10
Coventry seat for his party in consequence.

The body of quiet reasonable people throughout England
is not a feather-brained democracy, but it has popular fibre
enough to be shocked by such evictions as some of those which
we have seen, to feel the madness of permitting them, to insist 15
on their ceasing. And it does not lean to the landlords. On the
contrary, it judges them with entire freedom. As I said in January: 'If Lord Clanricarde's tenants are evicted, the general
opinion of reasonable people wishes them evicted without rioting; but it has its own thoughts about Lord Clanricarde.' 20

The Irish landlords complain that they are being sacrificed,
that they are treated differently from other landlords, that the
faults of the past are visited upon them, that no account is taken
of their amendment. And indeed their case is peculiar. Everywhere the propertied and satisfied classes have to face an as- 25
pect of things which is new and unfamiliar to them; everywhere a change is preparing; everywhere the word *equity* is
acquiring a force and an extension hitherto unknown; everywhere it becomes plainer that he who thinks it enough to say,
May I not do what I will with my own? will no longer be suf- 30
fered to have the last word. But for the Irish landlords we cannot but see that, above and beyond this general and gradual
law of change, an epoch has indeed come, what the Bible calls
a *crisis*, the close of a period, of a whole state of things. In
such an epoch, even the amendment of individuals and the ef- 35
forts of their friends are powerless to avert the end which is
inevitable. We may and must insist on the morality of a crisis
of this sort by calling to mind the faults committed and the

warnings given. And that is why it is well to repeat again and
again that impressive expostulation of Croker, an Irishman and
a Conservative, with the Irish landlords: 'A landlord is not
mere land merchant; he has duties to perform as well as rents to
5 receive, and from his neglect of the former springs his difficulty
in the latter, and the general misery and distraction.' It is well
to recall the words of Henry Drummond, an English country
gentleman and high Tory: 'I much err if the enemies to the
happiness of the Irish people are not the Irish gentlemen and
10 nobility; but this is a truth which well-conditioned people
dare not utter.' Even at the present hour, though amendment
there has undoubtedly been, the evictions which have recently
caused so much scandal have shown us still existing and powerful for mischief the three types of landlord which have been
15 the bane of Ireland: the insolent landlord, the exacting landlord, the beggared landlord in the hands of mortgagees and
attorneys. But we need not dwell on the faults of living individuals, or deny the amendment in the class of Irish landlords.
What we have to do is to recognise and acknowledge that great
20 law of human affairs, which makes amendment, after a certain
lapse of time and course of conduct, too late, and the crisis and
fall inevitable. Butler's profound and solemn sentences utter
the stern truth which is fulfilling itself in Ireland to-day:—

Though, after men have been guilty of folly and of extrava-
25 gance *up to a certain degree*, it is often in their power to retrieve
their affairs, at least in good measure, yet real reformation is, in
many cases, of no avail at all towards preventing the miseries
naturally annexed to folly and extravagance *exceeding that degree*.[1] There is a certain bound to imprudence and misbehaviour,
30 which being transgressed, there remains no place for repentance
in the natural course of things. It is further very much to be
remarked, that neglects from inconsiderateness, want of attention,
not looking about us to see what we have to do, are often attended
with consequences altogether as dreadful as any active misbehav-
35 iour from the most extravagant passion.

[1] The italics are Butler's own.

It is by steadily directing their minds to the necessity for
great and far-reaching changes in the land system of Ireland
that the body of quiet reasonable people will keep abreast of
events, and can now be of most service to their country. By
bringing the Government to recognise that necessity they will   5
be of service to the Government. For the Government everything now depends upon their producing an adequate Land
Bill next Session. I say that everything depends upon this, pre-
suming, of course, that in the meanwhile Mr. Balfour will not
'think it his duty' to authorise any more ,evictions such as those   10
of Bodyke.

Not impossibly, however, we may have tb traverse a time
when the quiet reasonable people will be swept away, and their
influence quenched for the time and annulled; when the Liberals of the nadir and the new democracy will pass over their   15
body. It is not for nothing that a stump orator of Mr. Gladstone's calibre proclaims the divorce between the masses and
the classes, and invites every province and platform to consider
its wrongs. The masses are stirred, tempers are kindled, a torrent of insincere and envenomed declamation feeds the flame.   20
Mr. Gladstone's powers of self-deception are so inexhaustible
that he is never insincere. But how is it possible for Sir William
Harcourt or Mr. John Morley, if, as I suppose, they are sincerely desirous to get judicial rents in Ireland revised, to
imagine that they further this object by covering the Govern-   25
ment with scorn, contumely, and insult for adopting it?

This is probably the last time that I shall speak on these political subjects; certainly, if I follow my own inclination, it will
be the last time. In ending, therefore, let me fortify the quiet
reasonable people, with whom all along I have supposed my-   30
self conversing, by reminding them that even if, as seems not
altogether improbable, they should have to traverse bad times,
to see their wishes thwarted, and to be for a while powerless,
yet the temper of fairness and moderation, which makes their
force, is not to be the less kept up and prized by them, but on   35
the contrary is to be still cultivated by them in the highest
degree. In the first place, its time is sure to come again, it will

not be powerless always, or even for very long; in the second
place, it is its own exceeding great reward. It is hardly possible
to exaggerate the comfort and consolation which this temper
is capable of producing, even in view of characters and pro-
5   ceedings obnoxious to us. The Irish members are extremely provoking; but the provocation is far less acute when we have the
fairness to remember that these men are impulsive natures to
start with, pariahs in the House of Commons, with no hand in
the regular administration of their country, and that country
10 long and grievously mismanaged; that they are men, finally,
maddened by the stolid self-delusion of a number of worthy
people in Great Britain that the Irish have nothing to complain
of, but are treated just like the English and Scotch. Again, it is
painful to see the new democracy inflaming itself by feeding
15 greedily on the declamation of stump orators who to a man of
training and reflexion are intolerable; but here again it is tran-
quillising to make oneself consider that here may be the first
beginnings, however crude, of a new life and new interests
among men full of good stuff, and who are by skill and patience
20 to be brought to listen by-and-by to the counsels of reason and
moderation. Mr. Gladstone makes us indignant with his *masses
and classes;* but what peace of mind comes from the spirit of
mildness and indulgence which makes us own that to lose
power after so many years of it is for a public man a sore trial,
25 and the re-acquisition of it through the popular vote a mighty
temptation! Mr. John Morley's pessimism, his conviction that
his countrymen are too stupid and stiffnecked ever to manage
Ireland, shocks us, and we condemn it; but I for my part find
a positive satisfaction in forcing myself fairly to admit at the
30 same time, that our countrymen, with a thousand good qualities, are really, perhaps, a good deal wanting in lucidity and
flexibility. Therefore let the body of quiet reasonable people
take heart and keep up their spirits, even though the line of Mr.
Brunners should stretch out to the crack of doom. To be a
35 quiet reasonable person always answers, always makes for happiness; there is always profit in being, as Horace says the poets
are, a counter-influence to asperity, envy, and anger—

Asperitatis et invidiæ corrector et iræ.

Amiel[1]

It is somewhat late to speak of Amiel, but I was late in reading him. Goethe says that in seasons of cholera one should read no books but such as are tonic, and certainly in the season of old age this precaution is as salutary as in seasons of cholera. From what I heard I could clearly make out that Amiel's Journal was not a tonic book: the extracts from it which here and there I fell in with did not much please me; and for a good while I left the book unread.

But what M. Edmond Scherer writes I do not easily resist reading, and I found that M. Scherer had prefixed to Amiel's Journal a long and important introduction. This I read; and was not less charmed by the *mitis sapientia*, the understanding kindness and tenderness, with which the character of Amiel himself, whom M. Scherer had known in youth, was handled, than interested by the criticism on the Journal. Then I read Mrs. Humphry Ward's interesting notice, and then—for all biography is attractive, and of Amiel's life and circumstances I had by this time become desirous of knowing more—the *Étude Biographique* of Mademoiselle Berthe Vadier.

Of Amiel's cultivation, refinement, and high feeling, of his singular graces of spirit and character, there could be no doubt. But the specimens of his work given by his critics left me hesitating. A poetess herself, Mademoiselle Berthe Vadier is much occupied with Amiel's poetry, and quotes it abundantly. Even Victor Hugo's poetry leaves me cold, I am so unhappy as not to be able to admire *Olympio;* what am I to say, then, to Amiel's

[1] Published in *Macmillan's Magazine*, September 1887.

'Journée
Illuminée,
Riant soleil d'avril,
En quel songe
5   Se plonge
Mon cœur, et que veut-il'?

But M. Scherer and other critics, who do not require us to admire Amiel's poetry, maintain that in his Journal he has left 'a
book which will not die,' a book describing a malady of which
10   'the secret is sublime and the expression wonderful'; a marvel
of 'speculative intuition,' a 'psychological experience of the
utmost value.' M. Scherer and Mrs. Humphry Ward give
Amiel's Journal very decidedly the preference over the letters
of an old friend of mine, Obermann. The quotations made from
15   Amiel's Journal by his critics failed, I say, to enable me quite
to understand this high praise. But I remember the time when
a new publication by George Sand or by Sainte-Beuve was an
event bringing to me a shock of pleasure, and a French book
capable of renewing that sensation is seldom produced now. If
20   Amiel's Journal was of the high quality alleged, what a pleasure
to make acquaintance with it, what a loss to miss it! In spite,
therefore, of the unfitness of old age to bear atonic influences,
I at last read Amiel's Journal,—read it carefully through. Tonic
it is not; but it is to be read with profit, and shows, moreover,
25   powers of great force and value, though not quite, I am inclined
to think, in the exact line which his critics with one consent
indicate.

In speaking of Amiel at present, after so much has been written about him, I may assume that the main outlines of his life
30   are known to my readers: that they know him to have been
born in 1821 and to have died in 1881, to have passed the three
or four best years of his youth at the University of Berlin, and
the remainder of his life mostly at Geneva, as a professor, first
of æsthetics, afterwards of philosophy. They know that his
35   publications and lectures, during his lifetime, disappointed his
friends, who expected much from his acquirements, talents, and
vivacity; and that his fame rests upon two volumes of extracts

from many thousand pages of a private journal, *Journal Intime*, extending over more than thirty years, from 1848 to 1881, which he left behind him at his death. This Journal explains his sterility; and displays in explaining it, say his critics, such sincerity, with such gifts of expression and eloquence, of pro- 5 found analysis and speculative intuition, as to make it most surely 'one of those books which will not die.'

The sincerity is unquestionable. As to the gifts of eloquence and expression, what are we to say? M. Scherer speaks of an 'ever new eloquence' pouring itself in the pages of the Journal: 10 M. Paul Bourget, of 'marvellous pages' where the feeling for nature finds an expression worthy of Shelley or Wordsworth: Mrs. Humphry Ward, of 'magic of style,' of 'glow and splendour of expression,' of the 'poet and artist' who fascinates us in Amiel's prose. I cannot quite agree. Obermann has been men- 15 tioned: it seems to me that we have only to place a passage from Senancour beside a passage from Amiel, to perceive the difference between a feeling for nature which gives magic to style and one which does not. Here and throughout I am to use as far as possible Mrs. Humphry Ward's translation, at once spirited 20 and faithful, of Amiel's Journal. I will take a passage where Amiel has evidently some reminiscence of Senancour (whose work he knew well), is inspired by Senancour—a passage which has been extolled by M. Paul Bourget:—

'Shall I ever enjoy again those marvellous reveries of past days, 25 —as, for instance, once, when I was still quite a youth in the early dawn sitting amongst the ruins of the castle of Faucigny; another time in the mountains above Lancy, under the mid-day sun, lying under a tree and visited by three butterflies; and again another night on the sandy shore of the North Sea, stretched full length 30 upon the beach, my eyes wandering over the Milky Way? Will they ever return to me, those grandiose, immortal, cosmogonic dreams in which one seems to carry the world in one's breast, to touch the stars, to possess the infinite? Divine moments, hours of ecstasy, when thought flies from world to world, penetrates 35 the great enigma, breathes with a respiration large, tranquil, and profound like that of the ocean, and hovers serene and boundless like the blue heaven! Visits from the Muse Urania, who traces

around the foreheads of those she loves the phosphorescent nim-
bus of contemplative power, and who pours into their hearts the
tranquil intoxication, if not the authority of genius,—moments of
irresistible intuition in which a man feels himself great as the
universe and calm like God! . . . What hours, what memories!'

And now for Obermann's turn, Obermann by the Lake of
Bienne:—

'My path lay beside the green waters of the Thiele. Feeling inclined to muse, and finding the night so warm that there was no
hardship in being all night out of doors, I took the road to Saint
Blaise. I descended a steep bank, and got upon the shore of the
lake where its ripple came up and expired. The air was calm;
every one was at rest; I remained there for hours. Towards morning the moon shed over the earth and waters the ineffable melancholy of her last gleams. Nature seems unspeakably grand, when,
plunged in a long reverie, one hears the rippling of the waters
upon a solitary strand, in the calm of a night still enkindled and
luminous with the setting moon.

'Sensibility beyond utterance, charm and torment of our vain
years; vast consciousness of a nature everywhere greater than we
are, and everywhere impenetrable; all-embracing passion, ripened
wisdom, delicious self-abandonment—everything that a mortal
heart can contain of life-weariness and yearning, I felt it all, I
experienced it all, in this memorable night. I have made a grave
step towards the age of decline, I have swallowed up ten years
of life at once. Happy the simple, whose heart is always young!'

No translation can render adequately the cadence of diction,
the 'dying fall' of reveries like those of Senancour or Rousseau.
But even in a translation we must surely perceive that the
magic of style is with Senancour's feeling for nature, not
Amiel's; and in the original this is far more manifest still.

Magic of style is creative: its possessor himself creates, and
he inspires and enables his reader in some sort to create after
him. And creation gives the sense of life and joy; hence its extraordinary value. But eloquence may exist without magic of
style, and this eloquence, accompanying thoughts of rare
worth and depth, may heighten their effect greatly. And M.

Scherer says that Amiel's speculative philosophy is 'on a far other scale of vastness' than Senancour's, and therefore he gives the preference to the eloquence of Amiel, which clothes and conveys this vaster philosophy. Amiel was no doubt greatly Senancour's superior in culture and instruction generally; in philosophical reading and what is called philosophical thought he was immensely his superior. My sense for philosophy, I know, is as far from satisfying Mr. Frederic Harrison as my sense for Hugo's poetry is from satisfying Mr. Swinburne. But I am too old to change and too hardened to hide what I think; and when I am presented with philosophical speculations and told that they are 'on a high scale of vastness,' I persist in looking closely at them and in honestly asking myself what I find to be their positive value. And we get from Amiel's powers of 'speculative intuition' things like this—

'Created spirits in the accomplishment of their destinies tend, so to speak, to form constellations and milky ways within the empyrean of the divinity; in becoming gods, they surround the throne of the sovereign with a sparkling court.'

Or this—

'Is not mind the universal virtuality, the universe latent? If so, its zero would be the germ of the infinite, which is expressed mathematically by the double zero (oo).'

Or, to let our philosopher develop himself at more length, let us take this return to the zero, which Mrs. Humphry Ward prefers here to render by *nothingness:*—

'This psychological reinvolution is an anticipation of death; it represents the life beyond the grave, the return to Sheol, the soul fading into the world of ghosts or descending into the region of *Die Mütter;* it implies the simplification of the individual who, allowing all the accidents of personality to evaporate, exists henceforward only in the indivisible state, the state of point, of potentiality, of pregnant nothingness. Is not this the true definition of mind? is not mind, dissociated from space and time, just this? Its development, past or future, is contained in it just as a curve is contained in its algebraical formula. This nothing is an all. This *punctum* without dimensions is a *punctum saliens.*'

French critics throw up their hands in dismay at the violence which the Germanised Amiel, propounding his speculative philosophy, often does to the French language. My objection is rather that such speculative philosophy as that of which I have been quoting specimens has no value, is perfectly futile. And Amiel's Journal contains far too much of it.

What is futile we may throw aside; but when Amiel tells us of his 'protean nature essentially metamorphosable, polarisable, and virtual,' when he tells us of his longing for 'totality,' we must listen, although these phrases may in France, as M. Paul Bourget says, 'raise a shudder in a humanist trained on Livy and Pascal.' But these phrases stood for ideas which did practically rule, in a great degree, Amiel's life, which he often develops not only with great subtlety, but also with force, clearness, and eloquence, making it both easy and interesting to us to follow him. But still, when we have the ideas present before us, I shall ask, what is their value, what does Amiel obtain in them for the service of either himself or other people?

Let us take first what, adopting his own phrase, we may call his 'bedazzlement with the infinite,' his thirst for 'totality.' *Omnis determinatio est negatio.* Amiel has the gift and the bent for making his soul 'the capacity for all form, not *a* soul but *the* soul.' He finds it easier and more natural 'to be *man* than *a* man.' His permanent instinct is to be 'a subtle and fugitive spirit which no base can absorb or fix entirely.' It costs him an effort to affirm his own personality: 'the infinite draws me to it, the *Henosis* of Plotinus intoxicates me like a philtre.'

It intoxicates him until the thought of absorption and extinction, the *Nirvâna* of Buddhism, becomes his thought of refuge:—

'The individual life is a nothing ignorant of itself, and as soon as this nothing knows itself, individual life is abolished in principle. For as soon as the illusion vanishes, Nothingness resumes its eternal sway, the suffering of life is over, error has disappeared, time and form have for this enfranchised individuality ceased to be; the coloured air-bubble has burst in the infinite space, and the misery of thought has sunk to rest in the changeless repose of all-embracing Nothing.'

With this bedazzlement with the infinite and this drift towards Buddhism comes the impatience with all production, with even poetry and art themselves, because of their necessary limits and imperfection:—

'Composition demands a concentration, decision, and pliancy which I no longer possess. I cannot fuse together materials and ideas. If we are to give anything a form we must, so to speak, be the tyrants of it. We must treat our subject brutally and not be always trembling lest we should be doing it a wrong. We must be able to transmute and absorb it into our own substance. This sort of confident effrontery is beyond me; my whole nature tends to that impersonality which respects and subordinates itself to the object; it is love of truth which holds me back from concluding and deciding.'

The desire for the all, the impatience with what is partial and limited, the fascination of the infinite, are the topics of page after page in the Journal. It is a prosaic mind which has never been in contact with ideas of this sort, never felt their charm. They lend themselves well to poetry, but what are we to say of their value as ideas to be lived with, dilated on, made the governing ideas of life? Except for use in passing, and with the power to dismiss them again, they are unprofitable. Shelley's

> 'Life like a dome of many-coloured glass
> Stains the white radiance of eternity
> Until death tramples it to fragments'

has value as a splendid image nobly introduced in a beautiful and impassioned poem. But Amiel's 'coloured air-bubble,' as a positive piece of 'speculative intuition,' has no value whatever.

Nay, the thoughts which have positive truth and value, the thoughts to be lived with and dwelt upon, the thoughts which are a real acquisition for our minds, are precisely thoughts which counteract the 'vague aspiration and indeterminate de-
5 sire' possessing Amiel and filling his Journal: they are thoughts insisting on the need of limit, the feasibility of performance. Goethe says admirably—

> 'Wer grosses will muss sich zusammenraffen:
> In der Beschränkung zeigt sich erst der Meister.'

10 'He who will do great things must pull himself together: it is in working within limits that the master comes out.' Buffon says not less admirably—

> 'Tout sujet est un; et quelque vaste qu'il soit, il peut être renfermé dans un seul discours.'

15 'Every subject is one, and however vast it may be is capable of being contained in a single discourse.' The ideas to live with, the ideas of sterling value to us, are, I repeat, ideas of this kind: ideas staunchly counteracting and reducing the power of the infinite and indeterminate, not paralysing us with it.
20   And indeed we have not to go beyond Amiel himself for proof of this. Amiel was paralysed by living in these ideas of 'vague aspiration and indeterminate desire,' of 'confounding his personal life in the general life,' by feeding on these ideas, treating them as august and precious, and filling hundreds of pages
25 of Journal with them. He was paralysed by it, he became impotent and miserable. And he knew it, and tells us of it himself with a power of analysis and with a sad eloquence which to me are much more interesting and valuable than his philosophy of Maïa and the Great Wheel. 'By your natural tend-
30 ency,' he says to himself, 'you arrive at disgust with life, despair, pessimism.' And again: 'Melancholy outlook on all sides. Disgust with myself.' And again: 'I cannot deceive myself as to the fate in store for me: increasing isolation, inward disappointment, enduring regrets, a melancholy neither to be con-

soled nor confessed, a mournful old age, a slow agony, a death in the desert.' And all this misery by his own fault, his own mistakes. 'To live is to conquer incessantly; one must have the courage to be happy. I turn in a vicious circle; I have never had clear sight of my true vocation.'

I cannot, therefore, fall in with that particular line of admiration which critics, praising Amiel's Journal, have commonly followed. I cannot join in celebrating his prodigies of speculative intuition, the glow and splendour of his beatific vision of absolute knowledge, the marvellous pages in which his deep and vast philosophic thought is laid bare, the secret of his sublime malady is expressed. I hesitate to admit that all this part of the Journal has even a very profound psychological interest: its interest is rather pathological. In reading it we are not so much pursuing a study of psychology as a study of morbid pathology.

But the Journal reveals a side in Amiel which his critics, so far as I have seen, have hardly noticed, a side of real power, originality, and value. He says himself that he never had clear sight of his true vocation: well, his true vocation, it seems to me, was that of a literary critic. Here he is admirable: M. Scherer was a true friend when he offered to introduce him to an editor, and suggested an article on Uhland. There is hardly a literary criticism in these two volumes which is not masterly, and which does not make one desire more of the same kind. And not Amiel's literary criticism only, but his criticism of society, politics, national character, religion, is in general well informed, just, and penetrating in an eminent degree. Any one single page of this criticism is worth, in my opinion, a hundred of Amiel's pages about the Infinite Illusion and the Great Wheel. It is to this side in Amiel that I desire now to draw attention. I would have abstained from writing about him if I had only to disparage and to find fault, only to say that he had been overpraised, and that his dealings with Maïa seemed to me profitable neither for himself nor for others.

Let me first take Amiel as a critic of literature, and of the literature which he naturally knew best, French literature. Hear

him as critic on that best of critics, Sainte-Beuve, of whose
death (1869) he had just heard:—

> 'The fact is, Sainte-Beuve leaves a greater void behind him
> than either Béranger or Lamartine; their greatness was already
> 5   distant, historical; he was still helping us to think. The true critic
> supplies all the world with a basis. He represents the public judg-
> ment, that is to say, the public reason, the touchstone, the scales,
> the crucible, which tests the value of each man and the merit of
> each work. Infallibility of judgment is perhaps rarer than any-
> 10   thing else, so fine a balance of qualities does it demand—qualities
> both natural and acquired, qualities of both mind and heart.
> What years of labour, what study and comparison, are needed
> to bring the critical judgment to maturity! Like Plato's sage,
> it is only at fifty that the critic is risen to the true height of his
> 15   literary priesthood, or, to put it less pompously, of his social
> function. Not till then has he compassed all modes of being, and
> made every shade of appreciation his own. And Sainte-Beuve
> joined to this infinitely refined culture a prodigious memory and
> an incredible multitude of facts and anecdotes stored up for the
> 20   service of his thought.'

The criticism is so sound, so admirably put, and so charming,
that one wishes Sainte-Beuve could have read it himself.

Try Amiel next on the touchstone afforded by that 'half
genius, half charlatan,' Victor Hugo:—

> 25   'I have been again looking through Victor Hugo's *Paris* (1867).
> For ten years event after event has given the lie to the prophet,
> but the confidence of the prophet in his own imaginings is not
> therefore a whit diminished. Humility and common sense are
> only fit for Lilliputians. Victor Hugo superbly ignores everything
> 30   which he has not foreseen. He does not know that pride limits
> the mind, and that a limitless pride is a littleness of soul. If he
> could but learn to rank himself with other men and France with
> other nations, he would see things more truly, and would not fall
> into his insane exaggerations, his extravagant oracles. But propor-
> 35   tion and justness his chords will never know. He is vowed to the
> Titanic; his gold is always mixed with lead, his insight with child-

ishness, his reason with madness. He cannot be simple; like the blaze of a house on fire, his light is blinding. In short, he astonishes but provokes, he stirs but annoys. His note is always half or two-thirds false, and that is why he perpetually makes us feel uncomfortable. The great poet in him cannot get clear of the charlatan. A few pricks of Voltaire's irony would have made the inflation of this genius collapse, and rendered him stronger by rendering him saner. It is a public misfortune that the most powerful poet of France should not have better understood his *rôle*, and that, unlike the Hebrew prophets who chastised because they loved, he flatters his fellow-citizens from system and from pride. France is the world, Paris is France, Hugo is Paris. Bow down and worship, ye nations!'

Finally, we will hear Amiel on a consummate and supreme French classic, as perfect as Hugo is flawed, La Fontaine:—

'Went through my La Fontaine yesterday, and remarked his omissions. . . . He has not an echo of chivalry haunting him. His French history dates from Louis XIV. His geography extends in reality but a few square miles, and reaches neither the Rhine nor the Loire, neither the mountains nor the sea. He never invents his subjects, but indolently takes them ready-made from elsewhere. But with all this, what an adorable writer, what a painter, what an observer, what a master of the comic and the satirical, what a teller of a story! I am never tired of him, though I know half his fables by heart. In the matter of vocabulary, turns of expression, tones, idioms, his language is perhaps the richest of the great period, for it combines skilfully the archaic with the classical, the Gaulish element with what is French. Variety, finesse, sly fun, sensibility, rapidity, conciseness, suavity, grace, gaiety—when necessary nobleness, seriousness, grandeur—you find everything in our fabulist. And the happy epithets, and the telling proverbs, and the sketches dashed off, and the unexpected audacities, and the point driven well home! One cannot say what he has not, so many diverse aptitudes he has.

'Compare his *Woodcutter and Death* with Boileau's, and you can measure the prodigious difference between the artist and the critic who wanted to teach him better. La Fontaine brings visibly before you the poor peasant under the monarchy, Boileau but exhibits a drudge sweating under his load. The first is a historic witness, the second a school-versifier. La Fontaine enables you to reconstruct the whole society of his age; the pleasant old soul from Champagne, with his animals, turns out to be the one and only Homer of France.

'His weak side is his epicureanism, with its tinge of grossness. This, no doubt, was what made Lamartine dislike him. The religious string is wanting to his lyre, he has nothing which shows him to have known either Christianity or the high tragedies of the soul. Kind Nature is his goddess, Horace his prophet, and Montaigne his gospel. In other words, his horizon is that of the Renascence. This islet of paganism in the midst of a Catholic society is very curious; the paganism is perfectly simple and frank.'

These are but notes, jottings in his Journal, and Amiel passed from them to broodings over the infinite, and personality, and totality. Probably the literary criticism which he did so well, and for which he shows a true vocation, gave him nevertheless but little pleasure because he did it thus fragmentarily and by fits and starts. To do it thoroughly, to make his fragments into wholes, to fit them for coming before the public, composition with its toils and limits was necessary. Toils and limits composition indeed has; yet all composition is a kind of creation, creation gives, as I have already said, pleasure, and, when successful and sustained, more than pleasure, joy. Amiel, had he tried the experiment with literary criticism, where lay his true vocation, would have found it so. Sainte-Beuve, whom he so much admires, would have been the most miserable of men if his production had been but a volume or two of middling poems and a journal. But Sainte-Beuve's motto, as Amiel himself notices, was that of the Emperor Severus: *Laboremus*. 'Work,' Sainte-Beuve confesses to a friend, 'is my sore burden, but it is also my great resource. I eat my heart out when I am not up to the neck in work; there you have the secret of the life I lead.' If M. Scherer's introduction to the *Revue Germanique* could but have been used, if Amiel could but have written the article on Uhland, and followed it up by plenty of articles more!

I have quoted largely from Amiel's literary criticism, because this side of him has, so far as I have observed, received so little attention, and yet deserves attention so eminently. But his more general criticism, too, shows, as I have said, the same high qualities as his criticism of authors and books. I must quote one or two of his aphorisms: *L'esprit sert bien à tout, mais il ne suffit à rien:* 'Wits are of use for everything, sufficient for nothing.' *Une société vit de sa foi et se développe par la science:* 'A society lives on its faith and develops itself by science.' *L'État libéral est irréalisable avec une religion antilibérale, et presque irréalisable avec l'absence de religion:* 'Liberal communities are impossible with an anti-liberal religion, and almost impossible with the absence of religion.' But epigrammatic sentences of this sort are perhaps not so very difficult to produce, in French at any rate. Let us take Amiel when he has room and verge enough to show what he can really say which is important about society, religion, national life and character. We have seen what an influence his years passed in Germany had upon him: we have seen how severely he judges Victor Hugo's faults: the faults of the French nation at large he judges with a like severity. But what a fine and just perception does the following passage show of the deficiencies of Germany, the advantage which the western nations have in their more finished civilisation:—

'It is in the novel that the average vulgarity of German society, and its inferiority to the societies of France and England, are most clearly visible. The notion of a thing's *jarring on the taste* is wanting to German æsthetics. Their elegance knows nothing of grace; they have no sense of the enormous distance between distinction (gentlemanly, ladylike) and their stiff *Vornehmlichkeit.* Their imagination lacks style, training, education, and knowledge of the world; it is stamped with an ill-bred air even in its Sunday clothes. The race is poetical and intelligent, but common and ill-mannered. Ease, amiability, manners, wit, animation, dignity, charm, are qualities which belong to others.

'Will that inner freedom of soul, that profound harmony of all the faculties, which I have so often observed among the best Germans, ever come to the surface? Will the conquerors of to-day ever civilise their forms of life? It is by their future novels that we shall be able to judge. As soon as the German novel can

give us quite good society, the Germans will be in the raw stage
no longer.'

And this pupil of Berlin, this devourer of German books,
this victim, say the French critics, to the contagion of German
5   style, after three hours, one day, of a *Geschichte der Æsthetik
in Deutschland*, breaks out:—

'Learning and even thought are not everything. A little *esprit*,
point, vivacity, imagination, grace, would do no harm. Do these
pedantic books leave a single image or sentence, a single striking
10   or new fact, in the memory when one lays them down? No,
nothing but fatigue and confusion. Oh, for clearness, terseness,
brevity! Diderot, Voltaire, or even Galiani! A short article by
Sainte-Beuve, Scherer, Renan, Victor Cherbuliez, gives one more
pleasure, and makes one ponder and reflect more, than a thousand
15   of these German pages crammed to the margin and showing the
work itself rather than its result. The Germans heap the faggots
for the pile, the French bring the fire. Spare me your lucubra-
tions, give me facts or ideas. Keep your vats, your must, your
dregs, to yourselves; I want wine fully made, wine which will
20   sparkle in the glass and kindle my spirits instead of oppressing them.'

Amiel may have been led away *deteriora sequi:* he may have
Germanised until he has become capable of the verb *déperson-
naliser* and the noun *réimplication;* but after all, his heart is in
25   the right place: *videt meliora probatque*. He remains at bottom
the man who said: *Le livre serait mon ambition*. He adds, to be
sure, that it would be *son ambition,* 'if ambition were not
vanity, and vanity of vanities.'
Yet this disenchanted brooder, 'full of a tranquil disgust at
30   the futility of our ambitions, the void of our existence,' be-
dazzled with the infinite, can observe the world and society
with consummate keenness and shrewdness, and at the same
time with a delicacy which to the man of the world is in general wanting. Is it possible to analyse *le grand monde*, high
35   society, as the Old World knows it and America knows it not,
more acutely than Amiel does in what follows?—

'In society people are expected to behave as if they lived on ambrosia and concerned themselves with no interests but such as are noble. Care, need, passion, do not exist. All realism is suppressed as brutal. In a word, what is called *le grand monde* gives itself for the moment the flattering illusion that it is moving in an ethereal atmosphere and breathing the air of the gods. For this reason all vehemence, any cry of nature, all real suffering, all heedless familiarity, any genuine sign of passion, are startling and distasteful in this delicate *milieu*, and at once destroy the collective work, the cloud-palace, the imposing architectural creation raised by common consent. It is like the shrill cock-crow which breaks the spell of all enchantments, and puts the fairies to flight. These select gatherings produce without intending it a sort of concert for eye and ear, an improvised work of art. By the instinctive collaboration of everybody concerned, wit and taste hold festival, and the associations of reality are exchanged for the associations of imagination. So understood, society is a form of poetry; the cultivated classes deliberately recompose the idyll of the past, and the buried world of Astræa. Paradox or not, I believe that these fugitive attempts to reconstruct a dream, whose only end is beauty, represent confused reminiscences of an age of gold haunting the human heart; or rather, aspirations towards a harmony of things which every-day reality denies to us, and of which art alone gives us a glimpse.'

I remember reading in an American newspaper a solemn letter by an excellent republican, asking what were a shopman's or a labourer's feelings when he walked through Eaton or Chatsworth. Amiel will tell him: they are 'reminiscences of an age of gold haunting the human heart, aspirations towards a harmony of things which every-day reality denies to us.' I appeal to my friend the author of *Triumphant Democracy* himself, to say whether these are to be had in walking through Pittsburgh.

Indeed it is by contrast with American life that *Nirvâna* appears to Amiel so desirable:—

'For the Americans, life means devouring, incessant activity. They must win gold, predominance, power; they must crush rivals, subdue nature. They have their heart set on the means,

and never for an instant think of the end. They confound being
with individual being, and the expansion of self with happiness.
This means that they do not live by the soul, that they ignore the
immutable and eternal, bustle at the circumference of their exis-
5   tence because they cannot penetrate to its center. They are restless, eager, positive, because they are superficial. To what end
all this stir, noise, greed, struggle? It is all a mere being stunned
and deafened!'

Space is failing me, but I must yet find room for a less indi-
10   rect criticism of democracy than the foregoing remarks on
American life:—

'*Each function to the most worthy:* this maxim is the professed
rule of all constitutions, and serves to test them. Democracy is
not forbidden to apply it; but Democracy rarely does apply it,
15   because she holds, for example, that the most worthy man is the
man who pleases her, whereas he who pleases her is not always
the most worthy; and because she supposes that reason guides the
masses, whereas in reality they are most commonly led by passion.
And in the end every falsehood has to be expiated, for truth
20   always takes its revenge.'

What publicists and politicians have to learn is, that 'the ulti-
mate ground upon which every civilisation rests is the average
morality of the masses and a sufficient amount of practical
righteousness.' But where does duty find its inspiration and
25   sanctions? In religion. And what does Amiel think of the traditional religion of Christendom, the Christianity of the
Churches? He tells us repeatedly; but a month or two before
his death, with death in full view, he tells us with peculiar im-
pressiveness:—

30   'The whole Semitic dramaturgy has come to seem to me a
work of the imagination. The apostolic documents have changed
in value and meaning to my eyes. The distinction between belief
and truth has grown clearer and clearer to me. Religious psychology has become a simple phenomenon, and has lost its fixed and
35   absolute value. The apologetics of Pascal, Leibnitz, Secrétan, appear to me no more convincing than those of the Middle Age,

for they assume that which is in question—a revealed doctrine, a definite and unchangeable Christianity.'

Is it possible, he asks, to receive at this day the common doctrine of a Divine Providence directing all the circumstances of our life, and consequently inflicting upon us our miseries as 5 means of education?

'Is this heroic faith compatible with our actual knowledge of the laws of nature? Hardly. But what this faith makes objective we may take subjectively. The moral being may moralise his sufferings in turning the natural fact to account for the education 10 of his inner man. What he cannot change he calls the will of God, and to will what God wills brings him peace.'

But can a religion, Amiel asks again, without miracles, without unverifiable mystery, be efficacious, have influence with the many? And again he answers:— 15

'Pious fiction is still fiction. Truth has superior rights. The world must adapt itself to truth, not truth to the world. Copernicus upset the astronomy of the Middle Age; so much the worse for the astronomy. The Everlasting Gospel is revolutionising the Churches; what does it matter?' 20

This is water to our mill, as the Germans say, indeed. But I have come even thus late in the day to speak of Amiel, not because I found him supplying water for any particular mill, either mine or any other, but because it seemed to me that by a whole important side he was eminently worth knowing, and 25 that to this side of him the public, here in England at any rate, had not had its attention sufficiently drawn. If in the seventeen thousand pages of the Journal there are many pages still unpublished in which Amiel exercises his true vocation of critic, of literary critic more especially, let his friends give them to 30 us, let M. Scherer introduce them to us, let Mrs. Humphry Ward translate them for us. But *sat patriæ Priamoque datum*: Maïa has had her full share of space already: I will not ask for a word more about the infinite illusion, or the double zero, or the Great Wheel. 35

Count Leo Tolstoi[1]

In reviewing at the time of its first publication, thirty years
ago, Flaubert's remarkable novel of *Madame Bovary*, Sainte-
Beuve observed that in Flaubert we come to another manner,
another kind of inspiration, from those which had prevailed
hitherto; we find ourselves dealing, he said, with a man of a
new and different generation from novelists like George Sand.
The ideal has ceased, the lyric vein is dried up; the new men are
cured of lyricism and the ideal; 'a severe and pitiless truth has
made its entry, as the last word of experience, even into art itself.' The characters of the new literature of fiction are 'science, a spirit of observation, maturity, force, a touch of hardness.' *L'idéal a cessé, le lyrique est tari.*

The spirit of observation and the touch of hardness (let us
retain these mild and inoffensive terms) have since been carried in the French novel very far. So far have they been carried, indeed, that in spite of the advantage which the French
language, familiar to the cultivated classes everywhere, con-
fers on the French novel, this novel has lost much of its attraction for those classes; it no longer commands their attention as it did formerly. The famous English novelists have
passed away, and have left no successors of like fame. It is not
the English novel, therefore, which has inherited the vogue
lost by the French novel. It is the novel of a country new to
literature, or at any rate unregarded, till lately, by the general
public of readers: it is the novel of Russia. The Russian novel
has now the vogue, and deserves to have it. If fresh literary

1 Published in the *Fortnightly Review*, December 1887.

productions maintain this vogue and enhance it, we shall all
be learning Russian.

The Slav nature, or at any rate the Russian nature, the Russian nature as it shows itself in the Russian novels, seems marked
by an extreme sensitiveness, a consciousness most quick and   5
acute both for what the man's self is experiencing, and also for
what others in contact with him are thinking and feeling. In a
nation full of life, but young, and newly in contact with an old
and powerful civilisation, this sensitiveness and self-consciousness are prompt to appear. In the Americans, as well as in the   10
Russians, we see them active in a high degree. They are somewhat agitating and disquieting agents to their possessor, but
they have, if they get fair play, great powers for evoking and
enriching a literature. But the Americans, as we know, are apt
to set them at rest in the manner of my friend Colonel Higgin-   15
son of Boston. 'As I take it, Nature said, some years since:
"Thus far the English is my best race; but we have had Englishmen enough; we need something with a little more buoyancy
than the Englishman; let us lighten the structure, even at some
peril in the process. Put in one drop more of nervous fluid, and 20
make the American." With that drop, a new range of promise
opened on the human race, and a lighter, finer, more highly
organised type of mankind was born.' People who by this sort
of thing give rest to their sensitive and busy self-consciousness
may very well, perhaps, be on their way to great material pros-   25
perity, to great political power; but they are scarcely on the
right way to a great literature, a serious art.

The Russian does not assuage his sensitiveness in this fashion.
The Russian man of letters does not make Nature say: 'The
Russian is my best race.' He finds relief to his sensitiveness in   30
letting his perceptions have perfectly free play, and in recording their reports with perfect fidelity. The sincereness with
which the reports are given has even something childlike and
touching. In the novel of which I am going to speak there is
not a line, not a trait, brought in for the glorification of Russia, 35
or to feed vanity; things and characters go as nature takes
them, and the author is absorbed in seeing how nature takes
them and in relating it. But we have here a condition of

things which is highly favourable to the production of good literature, of good art. We have great sensitiveness, subtlety, and finesse, addressing themselves with entire disinterestedness and simplicity to the representation of human life. The Russian novelist is thus master of a spell to which the secrets of human nature—both what is external and what is internal, gesture and manner no less than thought and feeling—willingly make themselves known. The crown of literature is poetry, and the Russians have not yet had a great poet. But in that form of imaginative literature which in our day is the most popular and the most possible, the Russians at the present moment seem to me to hold, as Mr. Gladstone would say, the field. They have great novelists, and of one of their great novelists I wish now to speak.

Count Leo Tolstoi is about sixty years old, and tells us that he shall write novels no more. He is now occupied with religion and with the Christian life. His writings concerning these great matters are not allowed, I believe, to obtain publication in Russia, but instalments of them in French and English reach us from time to time. I find them very interesting, but I find his novel of *Anna Karénine* more interesting still. I believe that many readers prefer to *Anna Karénine* Count Tolstoi's other great novel, *La Guerre et la Paix*. But in the novel one prefers, I think, to have the novelist dealing with the life which he knows from having lived it, rather than with the life which he knows from books or hearsay. If one has to choose a representative work of Thackeray, it is *Vanity Fair* which one would take rather than *The Virginians*. In like manner I take *Anna Karénine* as the novel best representing Count Tolstoi. I use the French translation; in general, as I long ago said, work of this kind is better done in France than in England, and *Anna Karénine* is perhaps also a novel which goes better into French than into English, just as Fredrika Bremer's *Home* goes into English better than into French. After I have done with *Anna Karénine* I must say something of Count Tolstoi's religious writings. Of these too I use the French translation, so far as it is available. The English translation, however, which came into my hands late, seems to be in general clear and good. Let me say in passing that it has neither the same arrangement, nor the same titles, nor altogether the same contents, with the French translation.

There are many characters in *Anna Karénine*—too many if we look in it for a work of art in which the action shall be vigorously one, and to that one action everything shall converge. There are even two main actions extending throughout the book, and we keep passing from one of them to the other—from the affairs of Anna and Wronsky to the affairs of Kitty and Levine. People appear in connection with these two main actions whose appearance and proceedings do not in the least contribute to develop them; incidents are multiplied which we expect are to lead to something important, but which do not. What, for instance, does the episode of Kitty's friend Warinka and Levine's brother Serge Ivanitch, their inclination for one another and its failure to come to anything, contribute to the development of either the character or the fortunes of Kitty and Levine? What does the incident of Levine's long delay in getting to church to be married, a delay which as we read of it seems to have significance, really import? It turns out to import absolutely nothing, and to be introduced solely to give the author the pleasure of telling us that all Levine's shirts had been packed up.

But the truth is we are not to take *Anna Karénine* as a work of art; we are to take it as a piece of life. A piece of life it is. The author has not invented and combined it, he has seen it; it has all happened before his inward eye, and it was in this wise that it happened. Levine's shirts were packed up, and he was late for his wedding in consequence; Warinka and Serge Ivanitch met at Levine's country-house and went out walking together; Serge was very near proposing, but did not. The author saw it all happening so—saw it, and therefore relates it; and what his novel in this way loses in art it gains in reality.

For this is the result which, by his extraordinary fineness of perception, and by his sincere fidelity to it, the author achieves; he works in us a sense of the absolute reality of his personages and their doings. Anna's shoulders, and masses of hair, and half-shut eyes; Alexis Karénine's updrawn eyebrows, and tired

smile, and cracking finger-joints; Stiva's eyes suffused with facile moisture—these are as real to us as any of those outward peculiarities which in our own circle of acquaintance we are noticing daily, while the inner man of our own circle of ac-
5   quaintance, happily or unhappily, lies a great deal less clearly revealed to us than that of Count Tolstoi's creations.

I must speak of only a few of these creations, the chief personages and no more. The book opens with 'Stiva,' and who that has once made Stiva's acquaintance will ever forget him?
10 We are living, in Count Tolstoi's novel, among the great people of Moscow and St. Petersburg, the nobles and the high functionaries, the governing class of Russia. Stépane Arcadiévitch— 'Stiva'—is Prince Oblonsky, and descended from Rurik, although to think of him as anything except 'Stiva' is difficult.
15 His *air souriant*, his good looks, his satisfaction; his 'ray,' which made the Tartar waiter at the club joyful in contemplating it; his pleasure in oysters and champagne, his pleasure in making people happy and in rendering services; his need of money, his attachment to the French governess, his distress at his wife's
20 distress, his affection for her and the children; his emotion and suffused eyes, while he quite dismisses the care of providing funds for household expenses and education; and the French attachment, contritely given up to-day only to be succeeded by some other attachment to-morrow—no, never, certainly,
25 shall we come to forget Stiva. Anna, the heroine, is Stiva's sister. His wife Dolly (these English diminutives are common among Count Tolstoi's ladies) is daughter of the Prince and Princess Cherbatzky, grandees who show us Russian high life by its most respectable side; the Prince, in particular, is excel-
30 lent—simple, sensible, right-feeling; a man of dignity and honour. His daughters, Dolly and Kitty, are charming. Dolly, Stiva's wife, is sorely tried by her husband, full of anxieties for the children, with no money to spend on them or herself, poorly dressed, worn and aged before her time. She has mo-
35 ments of despairing doubt whether the gay people may not be after all in the right, whether virtue and principle answer; whether happiness does not dwell with adventuresses and

profligates, brilliant and perfectly dressed adventuresses and profligates, in a land flowing with roubles and champagne. But in a quarter of an hour she comes right again and is herself—a nature straight, honest, faithful, loving, sound to the core; such she is and such she remains; she can be no other. Her sister Kitty is at bottom of the same temper, but she has her experience to get, while Dolly, when the book begins, has already acquired hers. Kitty is adored by Levine, in whom we are told that many traits are to be found of the character and history of Count Tolstoi himself. Levine belongs to the world of great people by his birth and property, but he is not at all a man of the world. He has been a reader and thinker, he has a conscience, he has public spirit and would ameliorate the condition of the people, he lives on his estate in the country, and occupies himself zealously with local business, schools, and agriculture. But he is shy, apt to suspect and to take offence, somewhat impracticable, out of his element in the gay world of Moscow. Kitty likes him, but her fancy has been taken by a brilliant guardsman, Count Wronsky, who has paid her attentions. Wronsky is described to us by Stiva; he is 'one of the finest specimens of the *jeunesse dorée* of St. Petersburg; immensely rich, handsome, aide-de-camp to the emperor, great interest at his back, and a good fellow notwithstanding; more than a good fellow, intelligent besides and well read—a man who has a splendid career before him.' Let us complete the picture by adding that Wronsky is a powerful man, over thirty, bald at the top of his head, with irreproachable manners, cool and calm, but a little haughty. A hero, one murmurs to oneself, too much of the Guy Livingstone type, though without the bravado and exaggeration. And such is, justly enough perhaps, the first impression, an impression which continues all through the first volume; but Wronsky, as we shall see, improves towards the end.

Kitty discourages Levine, who retires in misery and confusion. But Wronsky is attracted by Anna Karénine, and ceases his attentions to Kitty. The impression made on her heart by Wronsky was not deep; but she is so keenly mortified with

herself, so ashamed, and so upset, that she falls ill, and is sent
with her family to winter abroad. There she regains health and
mental composure, and discovers at the same time that her
liking for Levine was deeper than she knew, that it was a
5   genuine feeling, a strong and lasting one. On her return they
meet, their hearts come together, they are married; and in
spite of Levine's waywardness, irritability, and unsettlement of
mind, of which I shall have more to say presently, they are
profoundly happy. Well, and who could help being happy
10 with Kitty? So I find myself adding impatiently. Count Tolstoi's heroines are really so living and charming that one takes
them, fiction though they are, too seriously.

But the interest of the book centres in Anna Karénine. She
is Stiva's sister, married to a high official at St. Petersburg,
15 Alexis Karénine. She has been married to him nine years, and
has one child, a boy named Serge. The marriage had not
brought happiness to her, she had found in it no satisfaction to
her heart and soul, she had a sense of want and isolation; but
she is devoted to her boy, occupied, calm. The charm of her
20 personality is felt even before she appears, from the moment
when we hear of her being sent for as the good angel to reconcile Dolly with Stiva. Then she arrives at the Moscow station
from St. Petersburg, and we see the gray eyes with their long
eyelashes, the graceful carriage, the gentle and caressing smile
25 on the fresh lips, the vivacity restrained but waiting to break
through, the fulness of life, the softness and strength joined,
the harmony, the bloom, the charm. She goes to Dolly, and
achieves, with infinite tact and tenderness, the task of recon-
ciliation. At a ball a few days later, we add to our first impres-
30 sion of Anna's beauty, dark hair, a quantity of little curls over
her temples and at the back of her neck, sculptural shoulders,
firm throat, and beautiful arms. She is in a plain dress of black
velvet with a pearl necklace, a bunch of forget-me-nots in the
front of her dress, another in her hair. This is Anna Karénine.

35 She had travelled from St. Petersburg with Wronsky's
mother; had seen him at the Moscow station, where he came
to meet his mother, had been struck with his looks and manner, and touched by his behaviour in an accident which hap-

pened while they were in the station to a poor workman crushed by a train. At the ball she meets him again; she is fascinated by him and he by her. She had been told of Kitty's fancy, and had gone to the ball meaning to help Kitty; but Kitty is forgotten, or at any rate neglected; the spell which draws Wronsky and Anna is irresistible. Kitty finds herself opposite to them in a quadrille together:—

'She seemed to remark in Anna the symptoms of an overexcitement which she herself knew from experience—that of success. Anna appeared to her as if intoxicated with it. Kitty knew to what to attribute that brilliant and animated look, that happy and triumphant smile, those half-parted lips, those movements full of grace and harmony.'

Anna returns to St. Petersburg, and Wronsky returns there at the same time; they meet on the journey, they keep meeting in society, and Anna begins to find her husband, who before had not been sympathetic, intolerable. Alexis Karénine is much older than herself, a bureaucrat, a formalist, a poor creature; he has conscience, there is a root of goodness in him, but on the surface and until deeply stirred he is tiresome, pedantic, vain, exasperating. The change in Anna is not in the slightest degree comprehended by him; he sees nothing which an intelligent man might in such a case see, and does nothing which an intelligent man would do. Anna abandons herself to her passion for Wronsky.

I remember M. Nisard saying to me many years ago at the École Normale in Paris, that he respected the English because they are *une nation qui sait se gêner*—people who can put constraint on themselves and go through what is disagreeable. Perhaps in the Slav nature this valuable faculty is somewhat wanting; a very strong impulse is too much regarded as irresistible, too little as what can be resisted and ought to be resisted, however difficult and disagreeable the resistance may be. In our high society with its pleasure and dissipation, laxer notions may to some extent prevail; but in general an English mind will be startled by Anna's suffering herself to be so overwhelmed and irretrievably carried away by her passion, by her almost at once regarding it, apparently, as something which it was hopeless to fight against. And this I say irrespectively of the worth of her lover. Wronsky's gifts and graces hardly qualify him, one might think, to be the object of so instantaneous and mighty a passion on the part of a woman like Anna. But that is not the question. Let us allow that these passions are incalculable; let us allow that one of the male sex scarcely does justice, perhaps, to the powerful and handsome guardsman and his attractions. But if Wronsky had been even such a lover as Alcibiades or the Master of Ravenswood, still that Anna, being what she is and her circumstances being what they are, should show not a hope, hardly a thought, of conquering her passion, of escaping from its fatal power, is to our notions strange and a little bewildering.

I state the objection; let me add that it is the triumph of Anna's charm that it remains paramount for us nevertheless; that throughout her course, with its failures, errors, and miseries, still the impression of her large, fresh, rich, generous, delightful nature, never leaves us—keeps our sympathy, keeps even, I had almost said, our respect.

To return to the story. Soon enough poor Anna begins to experience the truth of what the Wise Man told us long ago, that 'the way of transgressors is hard.' Her agitation at a steeplechase where Wronsky is in danger attracts her husband's notice and provokes his remonstrance. He is bitter and contemptuous. In a transport of passion Anna declares to him that she is his wife no longer; that she loves Wronsky, belongs to Wronsky. Hard at first, formal, cruel, thinking only of himself, Karénine, who, as I have said, has a conscience, is touched by grace at the moment when Anna's troubles reach their height. He returns to her to find her with a child just born to her and Wronsky, the lover in the house and Anna apparently dying. Karénine has words of kindness and forgiveness only. The noble and victorious effort transfigures him, and all that her husband gains in the eyes of Anna, her lover Wronsky loses. Wronsky comes to Anna's bedside, and standing there by Karénine, buries his face in his hands. Anna says to him, in the hurried voice of fever:—

   ' "Uncover your face; look at that man; he is a saint. Yes, uncover your face; uncover it," she repeated with an angry air. "Alexis, uncover his face; I want to see him."
   'Alexis took the hands of Wronsky and uncovered his face, disfigured by suffering and humiliation.
   ' "Give him your hand; pardon him."
   'Alexis stretched out his hand without even seeking to restrain his tears.
   ' "Thank God, thank God!" she said; "all is ready now. How ugly those flowers are," she went on, pointing to the wall-paper; "they are not a bit like violets. My God, my God! when will all this end? Give me morphine, doctor—I want morphine. Oh, my God, my God!" '

She seems dying, and Wronsky rushes out and shoots himself. And so, in a common novel, the story would end. Anna would die, Wronsky would commit suicide, Karénine would survive, in possession of our admiration and sympathy. But the story does not always end so in life; neither does it end so in Count Tolstoi's novel. Anna recovers from her fever, Wronsky from his wound. Anna's passion for Wronsky reawakens, her estrangement from Karénine returns. Nor does Karénine remain at the height at which in the forgiveness scene we saw him. He is formal, pedantic, irritating. Alas! even if he were not all these, perhaps even his *pince-nez*, and his rising eyebrows, and his cracking finger-joints, would have been provocation enough. Anna and Wronsky depart together. They stay for a time in Italy, then return to Russia. But her position is false, her disquietude incessant, and happiness is impossible for her. She takes opium every night, only to find that 'not poppy nor mandragora shall ever medicine her to that sweet sleep which she owed yesterday.' Jealousy and irritability grow upon her; she tortures Wronsky, she tortures herself. Under these trials Wronsky, it must be said, comes out well, and rises in our esteem. His love for Anna endures; he behaves, as our English phrase is, 'like a gentleman'; his patience is in general exemplary. But then Anna, let us remember, is to the last, through all the fret and misery, still Anna; always with something which charms; nay, with something, even, something in her nature, which consoles and does good. Her life, however, was becoming impossible under its existing conditions. A trifling misunderstanding brought the inevitable end. After a quarrel with Anna, Wronsky had gone one morning into the country to see his mother; Anna summons him by telegraph to return at once, and receives an answer from him that he cannot return before ten at night. She follows him to his mother's place in the country, and at the station hears what leads her to believe that he is not coming back. Maddened with jealousy and misery, she descends the platform and throws herself under the wheels of a goods train passing through the station. It is over—the graceful head is untouched, but all the rest is a crushed, formless heap. Poor Anna!

We have been in a world which misconducts itself nearly as much as the world of a French novel all palpitating with 'modernity.' But there are two things in which the Russian novel— Count Tolstoi's novel at any rate—is very advantageously distinguished from the type of novel now so much in request in France. In the first place, there is no fine sentiment, at once tiresome and false. We are not told to believe, for example, that Anna is wonderfully exalted and ennobled by her passion for Wronsky. The English reader is thus saved from many a groan of impatience. The other thing is yet more important. Our Russian novelist deals abundantly with criminal passion and with adultery, but he does not seem to feel himself owing any service to the goddess Lubricity, or bound to put in touches at this goddess's dictation. Much in *Anna Karénine* is painful, much is unpleasant, but nothing is of a nature to trouble the senses, or to please those who wish their senses troubled. This taint is wholly absent. In the French novels where it is so abundantly present its baneful effects do not end with itself. Burns long ago remarked with deep truth that it *petrifies feeling*. Let us revert for a moment to the powerful novel of which I spoke at the outset, *Madame Bovary*. Undoubtedly the taint in question is present in *Madame Bovary*, although to a much less degree than in more recent French novels, which will be in every one's mind. But *Madame Bovary*, with this taint, is a work of *petrified feeling;* over it hangs an atmosphere of bitterness, irony, impotence; not a personage in the book to rejoice or console us; the springs of freshness and feeling are not there to create such personages. Emma Bovary follows a course in some respects like that of Anna, but where, in Emma Bovary, is Anna's charm? The treasures of compassion, tenderness, insight, which alone, amid such guilt and misery, can enable charm to subsist and to emerge, are wanting to Flaubert. He is cruel, with the cruelty of petrified feeling, to his poor heroine; he pursues her without pity or pause, as with malignity; he is harder upon her himself than any reader ever, I think, will be inclined to be.

But where the springs of feeling have carried Count Tolstoi, since he created Anna ten or twelve years ago, we have now to see.

We must return to Constantine Dmitrich Levine. Levine, as I have already said, thinks. Between the age of twenty and that of thirty-five he had lost, he tells us, the Christian belief in which he had been brought up, a loss of which examples nowadays abound certainly everywhere, but which in Russia, as in France, is among all young men of the upper and cultivated classes more a matter of course, perhaps, more universal, more avowed, than it is with us. Levine had adopted the scientific notions current all round him; talked of cells, organisms, the indestructibility of matter, the conservation of force, and was of opinion, with his comrades of the university, that religion no longer existed. But he was of a serious nature, and the question what his life meant, whence it came, whither it tended, presented themselves to him in moments of crisis and affliction with irresistible importunity, and getting no answer, haunted him, tortured him, made him think of suicide.

Two things, meanwhile, he noticed. One was, that he and his university friends had been mistaken in supposing that Christian belief no longer existed; they had lost it, but they were not all the world. Levine observed that the persons to whom he was most attached, his own wife Kitty amongst the number, retained it and drew comfort from it; that the women generally, and almost the whole of the Russian common people, retained it and drew comfort from it. The other was, that his scientific friends, though not troubled like himself by questionings about the meaning of human life, were untroubled by such questionings, not because they had got an answer to them, but because, entertaining themselves intellectually with the consideration of the cell theory, and evolution, and the indestructibility of matter, and the conservation of force, and the like, they were satisfied with this entertainment, and did not perplex themselves with investigating the meaning and object of their own life at all.

But Levine noticed further that he himself did not actually proceed to commit suicide; on the contrary, he lived on his lands as his father had done before him, busied himself with all the duties of his station, married Kitty, was delighted when a son was born to him. Nevertheless he was indubitably not happy at bottom, restless and disquieted, his disquietude sometimes amounting to agony.

Now on one of his bad days he was in the field with his peasants, and one of them happened to say to him, in answer to a question from Levine why one farmer should in a certain case act more humanely than another: 'Men are not all alike; one man lives for his belly, like Mitiovuck, another for his soul, for God, like old Plato.'[1] 'What do you call,' cried Levine, 'living for his soul, for God?' The peasant answered: 'It's quite simple —living by the rule of God, of the truth. All men are not the same, that's certain. You yourself, for instance, Constantine Dmitrich, you wouldn't do wrong by a poor man.' Levine gave no answer, but turned away with the phrase, *living by the rule of God, of the truth*, sounding in his ears.

Then he reflected that he had been born of parents professing this rule, as their parents again had professed it before them; that he had sucked it in with his mother's milk; that some sense of it, some strength and nourishment from it, had been ever

[1] A common name among Russian peasants.

with him although he knew it not; that if he had tried to do the duties of his station it was by help of the secret support ministered by this rule; that if in his moments of despairing restlessness and agony, when he was driven to think of suicide, he had yet not committed suicide, it was because this rule had silently enabled him to do his duty in some degree, and had given him some hold upon life and happiness in consequence.

The words came to him as a clue of which he could never again lose sight, and which with full consciousness and strenuous endeavour he must henceforth follow. He sees his nephews and nieces throwing their milk at one another and scolded by Dolly for it. He says to himself that these children are wasting their subsistence because they have not to earn it for themselves and do not know its value, and he exclaims inwardly: 'I, a Christian, brought up in the faith, my life filled with the benefits of Christianity, living on these benefits without being conscious of it, I, like these children, I have been trying to destroy what makes and builds up my life.' But now the feeling has been borne in upon him, clear and precious, that what he has to do is to *be good;* he has 'cried to *Him.*' What will come of it?

'I shall probably continue to get out of temper with my coachman, to go into useless arguments, to air my ideas unseasonably; I shall always feel a barrier between the sanctuary of my soul and the soul of other people, even that of my wife; I shall always be holding her responsible for my annoyances and feeling sorry for it directly afterwards. I shall continue to pray without being able to explain to myself why I pray; but my inner life has won its liberty; it will no longer be at the mercy of events, and every minute of my existence will have a meaning sure and profound which it will be in my power to impress on every single one of my actions, that of *being good.'*

With these words the novel of *Anna Karénine* ends. But in Levine's religious experiences Count Tolstoi was relating his own, and the history is continued in three autobiographical works translated from him, which have within the last two or three years been published in Paris: *Ma Confession, Ma Reli-*

gion, and *Que Faire.* Our author announces further, 'two great works,' on which he has spent six years: one a criticism of dogmatic theology, the other a new translation of the four Gospels, with a concordance of his own arranging. The results which he
5 claims to have established in these two works are, however, indicated sufficiently in the three published volumes which I have named above.

These autobiographical volumes show the same extraordinary penetration, the same perfect sincerity, which are ex-
10 hibited in the author's novel. As autobiography they are of profound interest, and they are full, moreover, of acute and fruitful remarks. I have spoken of the advantages which the Russian genius possesses for imaginative literature. Perhaps for Biblical exegesis, for the criticism of religion and its docu-
15 ments, the advantage lies more with the older nations of the West. They will have more of the experience, width of knowledge, patience, sobriety, requisite for these studies; they may probably be less impulsive, less heady.

Count Tolstoi regards the change accomplished in himself
20 during the last half-dozen years, he regards his recent studies and the ideas which he has acquired through them, as epochmaking in his life and of capital importance:—

'Five years ago faith came to me; I believed in the doctrine of Jesus, and all my life suddenly changed. I ceased to desire that
25 which previously I desired, and, on the other hand, I took to desiring what I had never desired before. That which formerly used to appear good in my eyes appeared evil, that which used to appear evil appeared good.'

The novel of *Anna Karénine* belongs to that past which
30 Count Tolstoi has left behind him; his new studies and the works founded on them are what is important; light and salvation are there. Yet I will venture to express my doubt whether these works contain, as their contribution to the cause of religion and to the establishment of the true mind and mes-
35 sage of Jesus, much that had not already been given or indicated by Count Tolstoi in relating, in *Anna Karénine*, Levine's mental history. Points raised in that history are developed and

enforced; there is an abundant and admirable exhibition of
knowledge of human nature, penetrating insight, fearless sincerity, wit, sarcasm, eloquence, style. And we have too the
direct autobiography of a man not only interesting to us from
his soul and talent, but highly interesting also from his nation- 5
ality, position, and course of proceeding. But to light and salvation in the Christian religion we are not, I think, brought
very much nearer than in Levine's history. I ought to add that
what was already present in that history seems to me of high
importance and value. Let us see what it amounts to. 10

I must be general and I must be brief; neither my limits nor
my purpose permit the introduction of what is abstract. But in
Count Tolstoi's religious philosophy there is very little which
is abstract, arid. The idea of *life* is his master idea in studying
and establishing religion. He speaks impatiently of St. Paul as 15
a source, in common with the Fathers and the Reformers, of
that ecclesiastical theology which misses the essential and fails
to present Christ's Gospel aright. Yet Paul's 'law of the spirit
of life in Christ Jesus freeing me from the law of sin and death'
is the pith and ground of all Count Tolstoi's theology. Moral 20
life is the gift of God, is God, and this true life, this union with
God to which we aspire, we reach through Jesus. We reach it
through union with Jesus and by adopting his life. This doctrine is proved true for us by the life in God, to be acquired
through Jesus, being what our nature feels after and moves to, 25
by the warning of misery if we are severed from it, the sanction
of happiness if we find it. Of the access for *us*, at any rate, to
the spirit of life, us who are born in Christendom, are in touch,
conscious or unconscious, with Christianity, this is the true account. Questions over which the churches spend so much 30
labour and time—questions about the Trinity, about the god-
head of Christ, about the procession of the Holy Ghost, are not
vital; what is vital is the doctrine of access to the spirit of life
through Jesus.

Sound and saving doctrine, in my opinion, this is. It may be 35
gathered in a great degree from what Count Tolstoi had already given us in the novel of *Anna Karénine*. But of course it
is greatly developed in the special works which have followed.

Many of these developments are, I will repeat, of striking force, interest, and value. In *Anna Karénine* we had been told of the scepticism of the upper and educated classes in Russia. But what reality is added by such an anecdote as the following from *Ma Confession:—*

'I remember that when I was about eleven years old we had a visit one Sunday from a boy, since dead, who announced to my brother and me, as great news, a discovery just made at his public school. This discovery was to the effect that God had no existence, and that everything which we were taught about Him was pure invention.'

Count Tolstoi touched, in *Anna Karénine*, on the failure of science to tell a man what his life means. Many a sharp stroke does he add in his latter writings:—

'Development is going on, and there are laws which guide it. You yourself are a part of the whole. Having come to understand the whole so far as is possible, and having comprehended the law of development, you will comprehend also your place in that whole, you will understand yourself.

'In spite of all the shame the confession costs me, there was a time, I declare, when I tried to look as if I was satisfied with this sort of thing!'

But the men of science may take comfort from hearing that Count Tolstoi treats the men of letters no better than them, although he is a man of letters himself:—

'The judgment which my literary companions passed on life was to the effect that life in general is in a state of progress, and that in this development we, the men of letters, take the principal part. The vocation of us artists and poets is to instruct the world; and to prevent my coming out with the natural question, "What am I, and what am I to teach?" it was explained to me that it was useless to know that, and that the artist and the poet taught without perceiving how. I passed for a superb artist, a great poet, and consequently it was but natural I should appropriate this theory. I, the artist, the poet—I wrote, I taught, without myself

knowing what. I was paid for what I did. I had everything: splendid fare and lodging, women, society; I had *la gloire*. Consequently, what I taught was very good. This faith in the importance of poetry and of the development of life was a religion, and
I was one of its priests—a very agreeable and advantageous office. 5
'And I lived ever so long in this belief, never doubting but
that it was true!'

The adepts of this literary and scientific religion are not
numerous, to be sure, in comparison with the mass of the people, and the mass of the people, as Levine had remarked, find 10
comfort still in the old religion of Christendom; but of the mass
of the people our literary and scientific instructors make no
account. Like Solomon and Schopenhauer, these gentlemen,
and 'society' along with them, are, moreover, apt to say that
life is, after all, vanity: but then they all know of no life except 15
their own.

'It used to appear to me that the small number of cultivated,
rich, and idle men, of whom I was one, composed the whole of
humanity, and that the millions and millions of other men who
had lived and are still living were not in reality men at all. In- 20
comprehensible as it now seems to me, that I should have gone
on considering life without seeing the life which was surrounding me on all sides, the life of humanity; strange as it is to think
that I should have been so mistaken, and have fancied my life,
the life of the Solomons and the Schopenhauers, to be the ver- 25
itable and normal life, while the life of the masses was but a
matter of no importance—strangely odd as this seems to me now,
so it was, notwithstanding.'

And this pretentious minority, who call themselves 'society,'
'the world,' and to whom their own life, the life of 'the world,' 30
seems the only life worth naming, are all the while miserable!
Our author found it so in his own experience:—

'In my life, an exceptionally happy one from a worldly point
of view, I can number such a quantity of sufferings endured for
the sake of "the world," that they would be enough to furnish 35
a martyr for Jesus. All the most painful passages in my life, be-

ginning with the orgies and duels of my student days, the wars
I have been in, the illnesses, and the abnormal and unbearable
conditions in which I am living now—all this is but one martyr-
dom endured in the name of the doctrine of the world. Yes, and
5   I speak of my own life, exceptionally happy from the world's
point of view.

'Let any sincere man pass his life in review, and he will perceive that never, not once, has he suffered through practising the
doctrine of Jesus; the chief part of the miseries of his life have
10   proceeded solely from his following, contrary to his inclination,
the spell of the doctrine of the world.'

On the other hand, the simple, the multitudes, outside of this
spell, are comparatively contented:—

'In opposition to what I saw in our circle, where life without
15   faith is possible, and where I doubt whether one in a thousand
would confess himself a believer, I conceive that among the people (in Russia) there is not one sceptic to many thousands of be-
lievers. Just contrary to what I saw in our circle, where life
passes in idleness, amusements, and discontent with life, I saw
20   that of these men of the people the whole life was passed in
severe labour, and yet they were contented with life. Instead of
complaining like the persons in our world of the hardship of
their lot, these poor people received sickness and disappointments
without any revolt, without opposition, but with a firm and
25   tranquil confidence that so it was to be, that it could not be otherwise, and that it was all right.'

All this is but development, sometimes rather surprising, but
always powerful and interesting, of what we have already had
in the pages of *Anna Karénine*. And like Levine in that novel,
30   Count Tolstoi was driven by his inward struggle and misery
very near to suicide. What is new in the recent books is the
solution and cure announced. Levine had accepted a provisional
solution of the difficulties oppressing him; he had lived right on,
so to speak, obeying his conscience, but not asking how far all
35   his actions hung together and were consistent:—

'He advanced money to a peasant to get him out of the clutches
of a money-lender, but did not give up the arrears due to him-

self; he punished thefts of wood strictly, but would have scrupled
to impound a peasant's cattle trespassing on his fields; he did not
pay the wages of a labourer whose father's death caused him to
leave work in the middle of harvest, but he pensioned and maintained his old servants; he let his peasants wait while he went   5
to give his wife a kiss after he came home, but would not have
made them wait while he went to visit his bees.'

Count Tolstoi has since advanced to a far more definite and
stringent rule of life—the positive doctrine, he thinks, of Jesus.
It is the determination and promulgation of this rule which is   10
the novelty in our author's recent works. He extracts this essential doctrine, or rule of Jesus, from the Sermon on the
Mount, and presents it in a body of commandments—Christ's
commandments; the pith, he says, of the New Testament, as
the Decalogue is the pith of the Old. These all-important com-   15
mandments of Christ are 'commandments of peace,' and five in
number. The first commandment is: 'Live in peace with all
men; treat no one as contemptible and beneath you. Not only
allow yourself no anger, but do not rest until you have dissi-
pated even unreasonable anger in others against yourself.' The   20
second is: 'No libertinage and no divorce; let every man have
one wife and every woman one husband.' The third: 'Never
on any pretext take an oath of service of any kind; all such
oaths are imposed for a bad purpose.' The fourth: 'Never employ force against the evil-doer; bear whatever wrong is done   25
to you without opposing the wrong-doer or seeking to have
him punished.' The fifth and last: 'Renounce all distinction of
nationality; do not admit that men of another nation may ever
be treated by you as enemies; love all men alike as alike near
to you; do good to all alike.'   30
If these five commandments were generally observed, says
Count Tolstoi, all men would become brothers. Certainly the
actual society in which we live would be changed and dissolved. Armies and wars would be renounced; courts of justice, police, property, would be renounced also. And whatever   35
the rest of us may do, Count Tolstoi at least will do his duty
and follow Christ's commandments sincerely. He has given up
rank, office, and property, and earns his bread by the labour

of his own hands. 'I believe in Christ's commandments,' he says, 'and this faith changes my whole former estimate of what is good and great, bad and low, in human life.' At present—

'Everything which I used to think bad and low—the rusticity of
5 the peasant, the plainness of lodging, food, clothing, manners—
all this has become good and great in my eyes. At present I can
no longer contribute to anything which raises me externally
above others, which separates me from them. I cannot, as formerly, recognise either in my own case or in that of others any
10 title, rank, or quality beyond the title and quality of man. I cannot seek fame and praise; I cannot seek a culture which separates
me from men. I cannot refrain from seeking in my whole existence—in my lodging, my food, my clothing, and my ways of
going on with people—whatever, far from separating me from
15 the mass of mankind, draws me nearer to them.'

Whatever else we have or have not in Count Tolstoi, we have at least a great soul and a great writer. In his Biblical exegesis, in the criticism by which he extracts and constructs his Five Commandments of Christ which are to be the rule
20 of our lives, I find much which is questionable along with much which is ingenious and powerful. But I have neither space, nor, indeed, inclination, to criticise his exegesis here. The right moment, besides, for criticising this will come when the 'two great works,' which are in preparation, shall have
25 appeared.

For the present I limit myself to a single criticism only—a general one. Christianity cannot be packed into any set of commandments. As I have somewhere or other said, 'Christian-ity is a *source;* no one supply of water and refreshment that
30 comes from it can be called the sum of Christianity. It is a mistake, and may lead to much error, to exhibit any series of maxims, even those of the Sermon on the Mount, as the ulti-mate sum and formula into which Christianity may be run up.'

And the reason mainly lies in the character of the Founder
35 of Christianity and in the nature of his utterances. Not less important than the teachings given by Jesus is the *temper* of their giver, his temper of sweetness and reasonableness, of

epieikeia. Goethe calls him a *Schwärmer*, a fanatic; he may much more rightly be called an opportunist. But he is an opportunist of an opposite kind from those who in politics, that 'wild and dreamlike trade' of insincerity, give themselves this name. They push or slacken, press their points hard or let them be, as may best suit the interests of their self-aggrandisement and of their party. Jesus has in view simply 'the rule of God, of the truth.' But this is served by waiting as well as by hasting forward, and sometimes served better.

Count Tolstoi sees rightly that whatever the propertied and satisfied classes may think, the world, ever since Jesus Christ came, is judged; 'a new earth' is in prospect. It was ever in prospect with Jesus, and should be ever in prospect with his followers. And the ideal in prospect has to be realised. 'If ye know these things, happy are ye if ye do them.' But they are to be done through a great and widespread and long-continued change, and a change of the inner man to begin with. The most important and fruitful utterances of Jesus, therefore, are not things which can be drawn up as a table of stiff and stark external commands, but the things which have most soul in them; because these can best sink down into our soul, work there, set up an influence, form habits of conduct, and prepare the future. The Beatitudes are on this account more helpful than the utterances from which Count Tolstoi builds up his Five Commandments. The very *secret* of Jesus, 'He that loveth his life shall lose it, he that will lose his life shall save it,' does not give us a command to be taken and followed in the letter, but an idea to work in our mind and soul, and of inexhaustible value there.

Jesus paid tribute to the government and dined with the publicans, although neither the empire of Rome nor the high finance of Judea were compatible with his ideal and with the 'new earth' which that ideal must in the end create. Perhaps Levine's provisional solution, in a society like ours, was nearer to 'the rule of God, of the truth,' than the more trenchant solution which Count Tolstoi has adopted for himself since. It seems calculated to be of more use. I do not know how it is in Russia, but in an English village the determination of 'our circle' to earn their bread by the work of their hands would produce only dismay, not fraternal joy, amongst that 'majority' who are so earning it already. 'There are plenty of us to compete as things stand,' the gardeners, carpenters, and smiths would say; 'pray stick to your articles, your poetry, and nonsense; in manual labour you will interfere with us, and be taking the bread out of our mouths.'

So I arrive at the conclusion that Count Tolstoi has perhaps not done well in abandoning the work of the poet and artist, and that he might with advantage return to it. But whatever he may do in the future, the work which he has already done, and his work in religion as well as his work in imaginative literature, is more than sufficient to signalise him as one of the most marking, interesting, and sympathy-inspiring men of our time— an honour, I must add, to Russia, although he forbids us to heed nationality.

Shelley[1]

Nowadays all things appear in print sooner or later; but I have heard from a lady who knew Mrs. Shelley a story of her which, so far as I know, has not appeared in print hitherto. Mrs. Shelley was choosing a school for her son, and asked the advice of this lady, who gave for advice—to use her own words to me— 'Just the sort of banality, you know, one does come out with: Oh, send him somewhere where they will teach him to think for himself!' I have had far too long a training as a school inspector to presume to call an utterance of this kind a *banality;* however, it is not on this advice that I now wish to lay stress, but upon Mrs. Shelley's reply to it. Mrs. Shelley answered: 'Teach him to think for himself? Oh, my God, teach him rather to think like other people!'

To the lips of many and many a reader of Professor Dowden's volumes a cry of this sort will surely rise, called forth by Shelley's life as there delineated. I have read those volumes with the deepest interest, but I regret their publication, and am surprised, I confess, that Shelley's family should have desired or assisted it. For my own part, at any rate, I would gladly have been left with the impression, the ineffaceable impression, made upon me by Mrs. Shelley's first edition of her husband's collected poems. Medwin and Hogg and Trelawny had done little to change the impression made by those four delightful volumes of the original edition of 1839. The text of the poems has in some places been mended since; but Shelley is not a classic, whose various readings are to be noted with earnest attention. The charm of the poems flowed in upon us from that

[1] Published in *The Nineteenth Century*, January 1888.

edition, and the charm of the character. Mrs. Shelley had done
her work admirably; her introductions to the poems of each
year, with Shelley's prefaces and passages from his letters, supplied the very picture of Shelley to be desired. Somewhat
5   idealised by tender regret and exalted memory Mrs. Shelley's
representation no doubt was. But without sharing her conviction that Shelley's character, impartially judged, 'would stand in
fairer and brighter light than that of any contemporary,' we
learned from her to know the soul of affection, of 'gentle and
10 cordial goodness,' of eagerness and ardour for human happiness,
which was in this rare spirit—so mere a monster unto many.
Mrs. Shelley said in her general preface to her husband's poems:
'I abstain from any remark on the occurrences of his private
life, except inasmuch as the passions which they engendered
15 inspired his poetry; this is not the time to relate the truth.' I for
my part could wish, I repeat, that that time had never come.

   But come it has, and Professor Dowden has given us the
Life of Percy Bysshe Shelley in two very thick volumes. If the
work was to be done, Professor Dowden has indeed done it
20 thoroughly. One or two things in his biography of Shelley I
could wish different, even waiving the question whether it was
desirable to relate in full the occurrences of Shelley's private
life. Professor Dowden holds a brief for Shelley; he pleads for
Shelley as an advocate pleads for his client, and this strain of
25 pleading, united with an attitude of adoration which in Mrs.
Shelley had its charm, but which Professor Dowden was not
bound to adopt from her, is unserviceable to Shelley, nay, injurious to him, because it inevitably begets, in many readers of
the story which Professor Dowden has to tell, impatience and
30 revolt. Further, let me remark that the biography before us is of
prodigious length, although its hero died before he was thirty
years old, and that it might have been considerably shortened
if it had been more plainly and simply written. I see that one
of Professor Dowden's critics, while praising his style for 'a
35 certain poetic quality of fervour and picturesqueness,' laments
that in some important passages Professor Dowden 'fritters
away great opportunities for sustained and impassioned narra-
tive.' I am inclined much rather to lament that Professor Dow-

den has not steadily kept his poetic quality of fervour and picturesqueness more under control. Is it that the Home Rulers have so loaded the language that even an Irishman who is not one of them catches something of their full habit of style? No, it is rather, I believe, that Professor Dowden, of poetic nature himself, and dealing with a poetic nature like Shelley, is so steeped in sentiment by his subject that in almost every page of the biography the sentiment runs over. A curious note of his style, suffused with sentiment, is that it seems incapable of using the common word *child*. A great many births are mentioned in the biography, but always it is a poetic *babe* that is born, not a prosaic *child*. And so, again, André Chénier is, not guillotined, but 'too foully done to death.' Again, Shelley after his runaway marriage with Harriet Westbrook was in Edinburgh without money and full of anxieties for the future, and complained of his hard lot in being unable to get away, in being 'chained to the filth and commerce of Edinburgh.' Natural enough; but why should Professor Dowden improve the occasion as follows? 'The most romantic of northern cities could lay no spell upon his spirit. His eye was not fascinated by the presences of mountains and the sea, by the fantastic outlines of aërial piles seen amid the wreathing smoke of Auld Reekie, by the gloom of the Canongate illuminated with shafts of sunlight streaming from its intersecting wynds and alleys; nor was his imagination kindled by storied house or palace, and the voices of old, forgotten, far-off things, which haunt their walls.' If Professor Dowden, writing a book in prose, could have brought himself to eschew poetic excursions of this kind and to tell his story in a plain way, lovers of simplicity, of whom there are some still left in the world, would have been gratified, and at the same time his book would have been the shorter by scores of pages.

These reserves being made, I have little except praise for the manner in which Professor Dowden has performed his task; whether it was a task which ought to be performed at all, probably did not lie with him to decide. His ample materials are used with order and judgment; the history of Shelley's life develops itself clearly before our eyes; the documents of im-

portance for it are given with sufficient fulness, nothing essential seems to have been kept back, although I would gladly, I confess, have seen more of Miss Clairmont's journal, whatever arrangement she may in her later life have chosen to exercise
5   upon it. In general all documents are so fairly and fully cited, that Professor Dowden's pleadings for Shelley, though they may sometimes indispose and irritate the reader, produce no obscuring of the truth; the documents manifest it of themselves. Last but not least of Professor Dowden's merits, he has pro-
10   vided his book with an excellent index.

Undoubtedly this biography, with its full account of the occurrences of Shelley's private life, compels one to review one's former impression of him. Undoubtedly the brilliant and attaching rebel who in thinking for himself had of old our sym-
15   pathy so passionately with him, when we come to read his full biography makes us often and often inclined to cry out: 'My God! he had far better have thought like other people.' There is a passage in Hogg's capitally written and most interesting account of Shelley which I wrote down when I first read it and
20   have borne in mind ever since; so beautifully it seemed to render the true Shelley. Hogg has been speaking of the intellectual expression of Shelley's features, and he goes on: 'Nor was the moral expression less beautiful than the intellectual; for there was a softness, a delicacy, a gentleness, and especially (though
25   this will surprise many) that air of profound religious veneration that characterises the best works and chiefly the frescoes (and into these they infused their whole souls) of the great masters of Florence and of Rome.' What we have of Shelley in poetry and prose suited with this charming picture of him;
30   Mrs. Shelley's account suited with it; it was a possession which one would gladly have kept unimpaired. It still subsists, I must now add; it subsists even after one has read the present biography; it subsists, but so as by fire. It subsists with many a scar and stain; never again will it have the same pureness and beauty
35   which it had formerly. I regret this, as I have said, and I confess I do not see what has been gained. Our ideal Shelley was the true Shelley after all; what has been gained by making us at moments doubt it? What has been gained by forcing upon

us much in him which is ridiculous and odious, by compelling
any fair mind, if it is to retain with a good conscience its ideal
Shelley, to do that which I propose to do now? I propose to
mark firmly what is ridiculous and odious in the Shelley
brought to our knowledge by the new materials, and then to   5
show that our former beautiful and lovable Shelley nevertheless survives.

Almost everybody knows the main outline of the events of
Shelley's life. It will be necessary for me, however, up to the
date of his second marriage, to go through them here. Percy   10
Bysshe Shelley was born at Field Place, near Horsham, in Sussex, on the 4th of August 1792. He was of an old family of
country gentlemen, and the heir to a baronetcy. He had one
brother and five sisters, but the brother so much younger than
himself as to be no companion for him in his boyhood at home,   15
and after he was separated from home and England he never
saw him. Shelley was brought up at Field Place with his sisters.
At ten years old he was sent to a private school at Isleworth,
where he read Mrs. Radcliffe's romances and was fascinated by
a popular scientific lecturer. After two years of private school   20
he went in 1804 to Eton. Here he took no part in cricket or
football, refused to fag, was known as 'mad Shelley' and much
tormented; when tormented beyond endurance he could be
dangerous. Certainly he was not happy at Eton; but he had
friends, he boated, he rambled about the country. His school   25
lessons were easy to him, and his reading extended far beyond
them; he read books on chemistry, he read Pliny's *Natural History*, Godwin's *Political Justice*, Lucretius, Franklin, Condorcet. It is said he was called 'atheist Shelley' at Eton, but this
is not so well established as his having been called 'mad Shelley.'   30
He was full, at any rate, of new and revolutionary ideas, and he
declared at a later time that he was twice expelled from the
school but recalled through the interference of his father.
In the spring of 1810 Shelley, now in his eighteenth year,
entered University College, Oxford, as an exhibitioner. He had   35
already written novels and poems; a poem on the Wandering
Jew, in seven or eight cantos, he sent to Campbell, and was

told by Campbell that there were but two good lines in it. He
had solicited the correspondence of Mrs. Hemans, then Felicia
Browne and unmarried; he had fallen in love with a charming
cousin, Harriet Grove. In the autumn of 1810 he found a pub-
5   lisher for his verse; he also found a friend in a very clever and
free-minded commoner of his college, Thomas Jefferson Hogg,
who has admirably described the Shelley of those Oxford days,
with his chemistry, his eccentric habits, his charm of look and
character, his conversation, his shrill discordant voice. Shelley
10   read incessantly. Hume's *Essays* produced a powerful impression on him; his free speculation led him to what his father, and
worse still his cousin Harriet, thought 'detestable principles';
his cousin and his family became estranged from him. He, on
his part, became more and more incensed against the 'bigotry'
15   and 'intolerance' which produced such estrangement. 'Here I
swear, and as I break my oaths, may Infinity, Eternity, blast
me—here I swear that never will I forgive intolerance.' At the
beginning of 1811 he prepared and published what he called a
'leaflet for letters,' having for its title *The Necessity of Atheism.*
20   He sent copies to all the bishops, to the Vice-Chancellor of Oxford, and to the heads of houses. On Lady Day he was summoned before the authorities of his College, refused to answer
the question whether he had written *The Necessity of Atheism,* told the Master and Fellows that 'their proceedings would
25   become a court of inquisitors but not free men in a free
country,' and was expelled for contumacy. Hogg wrote a letter
of remonstrance to the authorities, was in his turn summoned
before them and questioned as to his share in the 'leaflet,' and,
refusing to answer, he also was expelled.
30   Shelley settled with Hogg in lodgings in London. His father,
excusably indignant, was not a wise man and managed his son
ill. His plan of recommending Shelley to read Paley's *Natural
Theology,* and of *reading it with him himself,* makes us smile.
Shelley, who about this time wrote of his younger sister, then
35   at school at Clapham, 'There are some hopes of this dear little
girl, she would be a divine little scion of infidelity if I could
get hold of her,' was not to have been cured by Paley's *Natural
Theology* administered through Mr. Timothy Shelley. But by

the middle of May Shelley's father had agreed to allow him two hundred pounds a year. Meanwhile in visiting his sisters at their school in Clapham, Shelley made the acquaintance of a schoolfellow of theirs, Harriet Westbrook. She was a beautiful and lively girl, with a father who had kept a tavern in Mount Street, but had now retired from business, and one sister much older than herself, who encouraged in every possible way the acquaintance of her sister of sixteen with the heir to a baronetcy and a great estate. Soon Shelley heard that Harriet met with cold looks at her school for associating with an atheist; his generosity and his ready indignation against 'intolerance' were roused. In the summer Harriet wrote to him that she was persecuted not at school only but at home also, that she was lonely and miserable, and would gladly put an end to her life. Shelley went to see her; she owned her love for him, and he engaged himself to her. He told his cousin Charles Grove that his happiness had been blighted when the other Harriet, Charles's sister, cast him off; that now the only thing worth living for was self-sacrifice. Harriet's persecutors became yet more troublesome, and Shelley, at the end of August, went off with her to Edinburgh and they were married. The entry in the register is this:—

> '*August 28, 1811.*—Percy Bysshe Shelley, farmer, Sussex, and Miss Harriet Westbrook, St. Andrew Church Parish, daughter of Mr. John Westbrook, London.'

After five weeks in Edinburgh the young farmer and his wife came southwards and took lodgings at York, under the shadow of what Shelley calls that 'gigantic pile of superstition,' the Minster. But his friend Hogg was in a lawyer's office in York, and Hogg's society made the Minster endurable. Mr. Timothy Shelley's happiness in his son was naturally not increased by the runaway marriage; he stopped his allowance, and Shelley determined to visit 'this thoughtless man,' as he calls his parent, and to 'try the force of truth' upon him. Nothing could be effected; Shelley's mother, too, was now against him. He returned to York to find that in his absence his friend Hogg had been making love to Harriet, who had indignantly re-

pulsed him. Shelley was shocked, but after a 'terrible day' of explanation from Hogg, he 'fully, freely pardoned him,' promised to retain him still as 'his friend, his bosom friend,' and 'hoped soon to convince him how lovely virtue was.' But for
5   the present it seemed better to separate. In November he and Harriet, with her sister Eliza, took a cottage at Keswick. Shelley was now in great straits for money; the great Sussex neighbour of the Shelleys, the Duke of Norfolk, interposed in his favour, and his father and grandfather seem to have offered
10 him at this time an income of £2000 a year, if he would consent to entail the family estate. Shelley indignantly refused to 'forswear his principles,' by accepting 'a proposal so insultingly hateful.' But in December his father agreed, though with an ill grace, to grant him his allowance of £200 a year again, and Mr.
15 Westbrook promised to allow a like sum to his daughter. So after four months of marriage the Shelleys began 1812 with an income of £400 a year.

Early in February they left Keswick and proceeded to Dublin, where Shelley, who had prepared an address to the
20 Catholics, meant to 'devote himself towards forwarding the great ends of virtue and happiness in Ireland.' Before leaving Keswick he wrote to William Godwin, 'the regulator and former of his mind,' making profession of his mental obligations to him, of his respect and veneration, and soliciting Godwin's
25 friendship. A correspondence followed; Godwin pronounced his young disciple's plans for 'disseminating the doctrines of philanthropy and freedom' in Ireland to be unwise; Shelley bowed to his mentor's decision and gave up his Irish campaign, quitting Dublin on the 4th of April 1812. He and Harriet
30 wandered first to Nant-Gwillt in South Wales, near the upper Wye, and from thence after a month or two to Lynmouth in North Devon, where he busied himself with his poem of *Queen Mab*, and with sending to sea boxes and bottles containing a *Declaration of Rights* by him, in the hope that the winds and
35 waves might carry his doctrines where they would do good. But his Irish servant, bearing the prophetic name of Healy, posted the *Declaration* on the walls of Barnstaple and was taken up; Shelley found himself watched and no longer able to

enjoy Lynmouth in peace. He moved in September 1812 to
Tremadoc, in North Wales, where he threw himself ardently
into an enterprise for recovering a great stretch of drowned
land from the sea. But at the beginning of October he and Harriet visited London, and Shelley grasped Godwin by the hand   5
at last. At once an intimacy arose, but the future Mary Shelley—
Godwin's daughter by his first wife, Mary Wollstonecraft—was
absent on a visit in Scotland when the Shelleys arrived in London. They became acquainted, however, with the second Mrs.
Godwin, on whom we have Charles Lamb's friendly comment: 10
'A very disgusting woman, and wears green spectacles!' with
the amiable Fanny, Mary Wollstonecraft's daughter by Imlay,
before her marriage with Godwin; and probably also with Jane
Clairmont, the second Mrs. Godwin's daughter by a first marriage, and herself afterwards the mother of Byron's Allegra.   15
Complicated relationships, as in the Theban story! and there
will be not wanting, presently, something of the Theban horrors. During this visit of six weeks to London Shelley renewed
his intimacy with Hogg; in the middle of November he returned to Tremadoc. There he remained until the end of Feb-   20
ruary 1813, perfectly happy with Harriet, reading widely, and
working at his *Queen Mab* and at the notes to that poem. On
the 26th of February an attempt was made, or so he fancied, to
assassinate him, and in high nervous excitement he hurriedly
left Tremadoc and repaired with Harriet to Dublin again. On   25
this visit to Ireland he saw Killarney, but early in April he and
Harriet were back again in London.

There in June 1813 their daughter Ianthe was born; at the
end of July they moved to Bracknell, in Berkshire. They had   30
for neighbours there a Mrs. Boinville and her married daughter,
whom Shelley found to be fascinating women, with a culture
which to his wife was altogether wanting. Cornelia Turner,
Mrs. Boinville's daughter, was melancholy, required consolation, and found it, Hogg tells us, in Petrarch's poetry; 'Bysshe   35
entered at once fully into her views and caught the soft infec-
tion, breathing the tenderest and sweetest melancholy as every
true poet ought.' Peacock, a man of keen and cultivated mind,
joined the circle at Bracknell. He and Harriet, not yet eighteen,

used sometimes to laugh at the gushing sentiment and enthusiasm of the Bracknell circle; Harriet had also given offence to
Shelley by getting a wet-nurse for her child; in Professor Dowden's words, 'the beauty of Harriet's motherly relation to her
babe was marred in Shelley's eyes by the introduction into his
home of a hireling nurse to whom was delegated the mother's
tenderest office.' But in September Shelley wrote a sonnet to
his child which expresses his deep love for the mother also, to
whom in March 1814 he was remarried in London, lest the
Scotch marriage should prove to have been in any point irregular. Harriet's sister Eliza, however, whom Shelley had at
first treated with excessive deference, had now become hateful
to him. And in the very month of the London marriage we
find him writing to Hogg that he is staying with the Boinvilles,
having 'escaped, in the society of all that philosophy and friendship combine, from the dismaying solitude of myself.' Cornelia
Turner, he adds, whom he once thought cold and reserved, 'is
the reverse of this, as she is the reverse of everything bad; she
inherits all the divinity of her mother.' Then comes a stanza,
beginning

> 'Thy dewy looks sink in my breast,
>   Thy gentle words stir poison there.'

It has no meaning, he says; it is only written in thought. 'It is
evident from this pathetic letter,' says Professor Dowden, 'that
Shelley's happiness in his home had been fatally stricken.' This
is a curious way of putting the matter. To me what is evident
is rather that Shelley had, to use Professor Dowden's words
again—for in these things of high sentiment I gladly let him
speak for me—'a too vivid sense that here (in the society of the
Boinville family) were peace and joy and gentleness and love.'
In April come some more verses to the Boinvilles, which contain the first good stanza that Shelley wrote. In May comes a
poem to Harriet, of which Professor Dowden's prose analysis
is as poetic as the poem itself. 'If she has something to endure
(from the Boinville attachment), it is not much, and all her
husband's weal hangs upon her loving endurance, for see how

pale and wildered anguish has made him!' Harriet, uncon-
vinced, seems to have gone off to Bath in resentment, from
whence, however, she kept up a constant correspondence with
Shelley, who was now of age, and busy in London raising
money on post-obit bonds for his own wants and those of the   5
friend and former of his mind, Godwin.

And now, indeed, it was to become true that if from the inflammable Shelley's devotion to the Boinville family poor Harriet had had 'something to endure,' yet this was 'not much'
compared with what was to follow. At Godwin's house Shelley   10
met Mary Wollstonecraft Godwin, his future wife, then in her
seventeenth year. She was a gifted person, but, as Professor
Dowden says, she 'had breathed during her entire life an atmosphere of free thought.' On the 8th of June Hogg called at Godwin's with Shelley; Godwin was out, but 'a door was partially   15
and softly opened, a thrilling voice called "Shelley!" a thrilling
voice answered "Mary!"' Shelley's summoner was 'a very
young female, fair and fair-haired, pale indeed, and with a
piercing look, wearing a frock of tartan.' Already they were
'Shelley' and 'Mary' to one another; 'before the close of June   20
they knew and felt,' says Professor Dowden, 'that each was to
the other inexpressibly dear.' The churchyard of St. Pancras,
where her mother was buried, became 'a place now doubly
sacred to Mary, since on one eventful day Bysshe here poured
forth his griefs, his hopes, his love, and she, in sign of everlasting 25
union, placed her hand in his.' In July Shelley gave her a copy
of *Queen Mab*, printed but not published, and under the tender
dedication to Harriet he wrote: 'Count Slobendorf was about to
marry a woman who, attracted solely by his fortune, proved
her selfishness by deserting him in prison.' Mary added an in-   30
scription on her part: 'I love the author beyond all powers of
expression . . . by that love we have promised to each other,
although I may not be yours I can never be another's,'—and a
good deal more to the same effect.

Amid these excitements Shelley was for some days without   35
writing to Harriet, who applied to Hookham the publisher to
know what had happened. She was expecting her confinement;
'I always fancy something dreadful has happened,' she wrote, 'if

I do not hear from him. . . . I cannot endure this dreadful state of suspense.' Shelley then wrote to her, begging her to come to London; and when she arrived there, he told her the state of his feelings, and proposed separation. The shock made Harriet ill; and Shelley, says Peacock, 'between his old feelings towards Harriet, and his new passion for Mary, showed in his looks, in his gestures, in his speech, the state of a mind "suffering, like a little kingdom, the nature of an insurrection."' Godwin grew uneasy about his daughter, and after a serious talk with her, wrote to Shelley. Under such circumstances, Professor Dowden tells us, 'to youth, swift and decisive measures seem the best.' In the early morning of the 28th of July 1814 'Mary Godwin stepped across her father's threshold into the summer air,' she and Shelley went off together in a post-chaise to Dover, and from thence crossed to the Continent.

On the 14th of August the fugitives were at Troyes on their way to Switzerland. From Troyes Shelley addressed a letter to Harriet, of which the best description I can give is that it is precisely the letter which a man in the writer's circumstances should not have written.

'My dearest Harriet (he begins).—I write to you from this detestable town; I write to show that I do not forget you; I write to urge you to come to Switzerland, where you will at last find one firm and constant friend to whom your interests will be always dear—by whom your feelings will never wilfully be injured. From none can you expect this but me—all else are either unfeeling or selfish, or have beloved friends of their own.'

Then follows a description of his journey with Mary from Paris, 'through a fertile country, neither interesting from the character of its inhabitants nor the beauty of the scenery, with a mule to carry our baggage, as Mary, who has not been sufficiently well to walk, fears the fatigue of walking.' Like St. Paul to Timothy, he ends with commissions:—

'I wish you to bring with you the two deeds which Tahourdin has to prepare for you, as also a copy of the settlement. Do not

part with any of your money. But what shall be done about the
books? You can consult on the spot. With love to my sweet little
Ianthe, ever most affectionately yours,   S.
   'I write in great haste; we depart directly.'

Professor Dowden's flow of sentiment is here so agitating,   5
that I relieve myself by resorting to a drier word. Certainly my
comment on this letter shall not be his, that it 'assures Harriet
that her interests were still dear to Shelley, though now their
lives had moved apart.' But neither will I call the letter an odious letter, a hideous letter. I prefer to call it, applying an un-   10
translatable French word, a *bête* letter. And it is *bête* from
what is the signal, the disastrous want and weakness of Shelley,
with all his fine intellectual gifts—his utter deficiency in humour.

Harriet did not accept Shelley's invitation to join him and   15
Mary in Switzerland. Money difficulties drove the travellers
back to England in September. Godwin would not see Shelley,
but he sorely needed, continually demanded and eagerly accepted, pecuniary help from his erring 'spiritual son.' Between
Godwin's wants and his own, Shelley was hard pressed. He got   20
from Harriet, who still believed that he would return to her,
twenty pounds which remained in her hands. In November she
was confined; a son and heir was born to Shelley. He went to
see Harriet, but 'the interview left husband and wife each em-
bittered against the other.' Friends were severe; 'when Mrs.   25
Boinville wrote, her letter seemed cold and even sarcastic,' says
Professor Dowden. 'Solitude,' he continues, 'unharassed by
debts and duns, with Mary's companionship, the society of a
few friends, and the delights of study and authorship, would
have made these winter months to Shelley months of unusual   30
happiness and calm.' But, alas! creditors were pestering, and
even Harriet gave trouble. In January 1815 Mary had to write
in her journal this entry: 'Harriet sends her creditors here;
nasty woman. Now we must change our lodgings.'

One day about this time Shelley asked Peacock, 'Do you   35
think Wordsworth could have written such poetry if he ever
had dealings with money-lenders?' Not only had Shelley deal-

ings with money-lenders, he now had dealings with bailiffs also. But still he continued to read largely. In January 1815 his grandfather, Sir Bysshe Shelley, died. Shelley went down into Sussex; his father would not suffer him to enter the house, but

5 he sat outside the door and read *Comus*, while the reading of his grandfather's will went on inside. In February was born Mary's first child, a girl, who lived but a few days. All the spring Shelley was ill and harassed, but by June it was settled that he should have an allowance from his father of £1000 a

10 year, and that his debts (including £1200 promised by him to Godwin) should be paid. He on his part paid Harriet's debts and allowed her £200 a year. In August he took a house on the borders of Windsor Park, and made a boating excursion up the Thames as far as Lechlade, an excursion which produced his

15 first entire poem of value, the beautiful *Stanzas in Lechlade Churchyard*. They were followed, later in the autumn, by *Alastor*. Henceforth, from this winter of 1815 until he was drowned between Leghorn and Spezzia in July 1822, Shelley's literary history is sufficiently given in the delightful intro-

20 ductions prefixed by Mrs. Shelley to the poems of each year. Much of the history of his life is there given also; but with some of those 'occurrences of his private life' on which Mrs. Shelley forbore to touch, and which are now made known to us in Professor Dowden's book, we have still to deal.

25 Mary's first son, William, was born in January 1816, and in February we find Shelley declaring himself 'strongly urged, by the perpetual experience of neglect or enmity from almost every one but those who are supported by my resources, to desert my native country, hiding myself and Mary from the

30 contempt which we so unjustly endure.' Early in May he left England with Mary and Miss Clairmont; they met Lord Byron at Geneva and passed the summer by the Lake of Geneva in his company. Miss Clairmont had already in London, without the knowledge of the Shelleys, made Byron's acquaintance and be-

35 come his mistress. Shelley determined, in the course of the summer, to go back to England, and, after all, 'to make that most excellent of nations my perpetual resting-place.' In September he and his ladies returned; Miss Clairmont was then

expecting her confinement. Of her being Byron's mistress the Shelleys were now aware; but 'the moral indignation,' says Professor Dowden, 'which Byron's act might justly arouse, seems to have been felt by neither Shelley nor Mary.' If Byron and Claire Clairmont, as she was now called, loved and were happy, all was well.

The eldest daughter of the Godwin household, the amiable Fanny, was unhappy at home and in deep dejection of spirits. Godwin was, as usual, in terrible straits for money. The Shelleys and Miss Clairmont settled themselves at Bath; early in October Fanny Godwin passed through Bath without their knowing it, travelled on to Swansea, took a bedroom at the hotel there, and was found in the morning dead, with a bottle of laudanum on the table beside her and these words in her handwriting:—

'I have long determined that the best thing I could do was to put an end to the existence of a being whose birth was unfortu- nate,[1] and whose life has only been a series of pain to those persons who have hurt their health in endeavouring to promote her welfare. Perhaps to hear of my death will give you pain, but you will soon have the blessing of forgetting that such a creature ever existed as . . .'

There is no signature.

A sterner tragedy followed. On the 9th of November 1816 Harriet Shelley left the house in Brompton where she was then living, and did not return. On the 10th of December her body was found in the Serpentine; she had drowned herself. In one respect Professor Dowden resembles Providence: his ways are inscrutable. His comment on Harriet's death is: 'There is no doubt she wandered from the ways of upright living.' But, he adds: 'That no act of Shelley's, during the two years which im- mediately preceded her death, tended to cause the rash act which brought her life to its close, seems certain.' Shelley had been living with Mary all the time; only that!

[1] She was Mary Wollstonecraft's natural daughter by Imlay.

On the 30th of December 1816 Mary Godwin and Shelley were married. I shall pursue 'the occurrences of Shelley's private life' no further. For the five years and a half which remain, Professor Dowden's book adds to our knowledge of Shelley's
5   life much that is interesting; but what was chiefly important we knew already. The new and grave matter which we did not know, or knew in the vaguest way only, but which Shelley's family and Professor Dowden have now thought it well to give us in full, ends with Shelley's second marriage.
10   I regret, I say once more, that it has been given. It is a sore trial for our love of Shelley. What a set! what a world! is the exclamation that breaks from us as we come to an end of this history of 'the occurrences of Shelley's private life.' I used the French word *bête* for a letter of Shelley's; for the world in
15   which we find him I can only use another French word, *sale*. Godwin's house of sordid horror, and Godwin preaching and holding the hat, and the green-spectacled Mrs. Godwin, and Hogg the faithful friend, and Hunt the Horace of this precious world, and, to go up higher, Sir Timothy Shelley, a great
20   country gentleman, feeling himself safe while 'the exalted mind of the Duke of Norfolk [the drinking Duke] protects me with the world,' and Lord Byron with his deep grain of coarseness and commonness, his affectation, his brutal selfishness—what a set! The history carries us to Oxford, and I think
25   of the clerical and respectable Oxford of those old times, the Oxford of Copleston and the Kebles and Hawkins, and a hundred more, with the relief Keble declares himself to experience from Izaak Walton,

'When, wearied with the tale thy times disclose,
30   The eye first finds thee out in thy secure repose.'

I am not only thinking of morals and the house of Godwin, I am thinking also of tone, bearing, dignity. I appeal to Cardinal Newman, if perchance he does me the honour to read these words, is it possible to imagine Copleston or Hawkins declaring
35   himself safe 'while the exalted mind of the Duke of Norfolk protects me with the world'?

Mrs. Shelley, after her marriage and during Shelley's closing years, becomes attractive; up to her marriage her letters and journal do not please. Her ability is manifest, but she is not attractive. In the world discovered to us by Professor Dowden as surrounding Shelley up to 1817, the most pleasing figure is poor Fanny Godwin; after Fanny Godwin, the most pleasing figure is Harriet Shelley herself.

Professor Dowden's treatment of Harriet is not worthy—so much he must allow me in all kindness, but also in all seriousness, to say—of either his taste or his judgment. His pleading for Shelley is constant, and he does more harm than good to Shelley by it. But here his championship of Shelley makes him very unjust to a cruelly used and unhappy girl. For several pages he balances the question whether or not Harriet was unfaithful to Shelley before he left her for Mary, and he leaves the question unsettled. As usual Professor Dowden (and it is his signal merit) supplies the evidence decisive against himself. Thornton Hunt, not well disposed to Harriet, Hogg, Peacock, Trelawny, Hookham, and a member of Godwin's own family, are all clear in their evidence that up to her parting from Shelley Harriet was perfectly innocent. But that precious witness, Godwin, wrote in 1817 that 'she had proved herself unfaithful to her husband before their separation. . . . Peace be to her shade!' Why, Godwin was the father of Harriet's successor. But Mary believed the same thing. She was Harriet's successor. But Shelley believed it too. He had it from Godwin. But he was convinced of it earlier. The evidence for this is, that, in writing to Southey in 1820, Shelley declares that 'the single passage out of a life, otherwise not only spotless but spent in an impassioned pursuit of virtue, which looks like a blot,' bears that appearance 'merely because I regulated my domestic arrangements without deferring to the notions of the vulgar, although I might have done so quite as conveniently had I descended to their base thoughts.' From this Professor Dowden concludes that Shelley believed he could have got a divorce from Harriet had he so wished. The conclusion is not clear. But even were the evidence perfectly clear that Shelley believed Harriet unfaithful when he parted from her, we should have to take into account Mrs. Shelley's most true sentence in her introduction to *Alastor:* 'In all Shelley did, he, at the time of doing it, believed himself justified to his own conscience.'

Shelley's asserting a thing vehemently does not prove more than that he chose to believe it and did believe it. His extreme and violent changes of opinion about people show this sufficiently. Eliza Westbrook is at one time 'a diamond not so large' as her sister Harriet but 'more highly polished'; and then: 'I certainly hate her with all my heart and soul. I sometimes feel faint with the fatigue of checking the overflowings of my unbounded abhorrence for this miserable wretch.' The antipathy, Hogg tells us, was as unreasonable as the former excess of deference. To his friend Miss Hitchener he says: 'Never shall that intercourse cease, which has been the day-dawn of my existence, the sun which has shed warmth on the cold drear length of the anticipated prospect of life.' A little later, and she has become 'the Brown Demon, a woman of desperate views and dreadful passions, but of cool and undeviating revenge.' Even Professor Dowden admits that this is absurd; that the real Miss Hitchener was not seen by Shelley, either when he adored or when he detested.

Shelley's power of persuading himself was equal to any occasion; but would not his conscientiousness and high feeling have prevented his exerting this power at poor Harriet's expense? To abandon her as he did, must he not have known her to be false? Professor Dowden insists always on Shelley's 'conscientiousness.' Shelley himself speaks of his 'impassioned pursuit of virtue.' Leigh Hunt compared his life to that of 'Plato himself, or, still more, a Pythagorean,' and added that he 'never met a being who came nearer, perhaps so near, to the height of humanity,' to being an 'angel of charity.' In many respects Shelley really resembled both a Pythagorean and an angel of charity. He loved high thoughts, he cared nothing for sumptuous lodging, fare, and raiment, he was poignantly afflicted at the sight of misery, he would have given away his last farthing, would have suffered in his own person, to relieve it. But in one important point he was like neither a Pythagorean nor an angel: he was extremely inflammable. Professor Dowden leaves no doubt on the matter. After reading his book, one feels sickened for ever of the subject of irregular relations; God forbid that I should go into the scandals about Shelley's 'Neapolitan charge,' about Shelley and Emilia Viviani, about Shelley and Miss Clair-

mont, and the rest of it! I will say only that it is visible enough
that when the passion of love was aroused in Shelley (and it
was aroused easily) one could not be sure of him, his friends
could not trust him. We have seen him with the Boinville family. With Emilia Viviani he is the same. If he is left much alone 5
with Miss Clairmont, he evidently makes Mary uneasy; nay, he
makes Professor Dowden himself uneasy. And I conclude that
an entirely human inflammability, joined to an inhuman want
of humour and a superhuman power of self-deception, are the
causes which chiefly explain Shelley's abandonment of Harriet 10
in the first place, and then his behaviour to her and his defence
of himself afterwards.

His misconduct to Harriet, his want of humour, his self-
deception, are fully brought before us for the first time by Professor Dowden's book. Good morals and good criticism alike 15
forbid that when all this is laid bare to us we should deny, or
hide, or extenuate it. Nevertheless I go back after all to what I
said at the beginning; still our ideal Shelley, the angelic Shelley,
subsists. Unhappily the data for this Shelley we had and knew
long ago, while the data for the unattractive Shelley are fresh; 20
and what is fresh is likely to fix our attention more than what
is familiar. But Professor Dowden's volumes, which give so
much, which give too much, also afford data for picturing anew
the Shelley who delights, as well as for picturing for the first
time a Shelley who, to speak plainly, disgusts; and with what 25
may renew and restore our impression of the delightful Shelley
I shall end.

The winter at Marlow, and the ophthalmia caught among
the cottages of the poor, we knew, but we have from Professor
Dowden more details of this winter and of Shelley's work 30
among the poor; we have above all, for the first time I believe,
a line of verse of Shelley's own which sums up truly and perfectly this most attractive side of him—

'I am the friend of the unfriended poor.'

But that in Shelley on which I would especially dwell is that 35
in him which contrasts most with the ignobleness of the world
in which we have seen him living, and with the pernicious non-

sense which we have found him talking. The Shelley of 'marvellous gentleness,' of feminine refinement, with gracious and considerate manners, 'a perfect gentleman, entirely without arrogance or aggressive egotism,' completely devoid of the proverbial and ferocious vanity of authors and poets, always disposed to make little of his own work and to prefer that of others, of reverent enthusiasm for the great and wise, of high and tender seriousness, of heroic generosity, and of a delicacy in rendering services which was equal to his generosity—the Shelley who was all this is the Shelley with whom I wish to end. He may talk nonsense about tyrants and priests, but what a high and noble ring in such a sentence as the following, written by a young man who is refusing £2000 a year rather than consent to entail a great property!

'That I should entail £120,000 of command over labour, of power to remit this, to employ it for benevolent purposes, on one whom I know not—who might, instead of being the benefactor of mankind, be its bane, or use this for the worst purposes, which the real delegates of my chance-given property might convert into a most useful instrument of benevolence! No! this you will not suspect me of.'

And again:—

'I desire money because I think I know the use of it. It commands labour, it gives leisure; and to give leisure to those who will employ it in the forwarding of truth is the noblest present an individual can make to the whole.'

If there is extravagance here, it is extravagance of a beautiful and rare sort, like Shelley's 'underhand ways' also, which differed singularly, the cynic Hogg tells us, from the underhand ways of other people; 'the latter were concealed because they were mean, selfish, sordid; Shelley's secrets, on the contrary (kindnesses done by stealth), were hidden through modesty, delicacy, generosity, refinement of soul.'

His forbearance to Godwin, to Godwin lecturing and renouncing him and at the same time holding out, as I have said, his hat to him for alms, is wonderful; but the dignity with which he at last, in a letter perfect for propriety of tone, reads a lesson to his ignoble father-in-law, is in the best possible style:—

'Perhaps it is well that you should be informed that I consider your last letter to be written in a style of haughtiness and encroachment which neither awes nor imposes on me; but I have no desire to transgress the limits which you place to our intercourse, nor in any future instance will I make any remarks but such as arise from the strict question in discussion.'

And again:—

'My astonishment, and, I will confess, when I have been treated with most harshness and cruelty by you, my indignation, has been extreme, that, knowing as you do my nature, any considerations should have prevailed on you to have been thus harsh and cruel. I lamented also over my ruined hopes of all that your genius once taught me to expect from your virtue, when I found that for yourself, your family, and your creditors, you would submit to that communication with me which you once rejected and abhorred, and which no pity for my poverty or sufferings, assumed willingly for you, could avail to extort.'

Moreover, though Shelley has no humour, he can show as quick and sharp a tact as the most practised man of the world. He has been with Byron and the Countess Guiccioli, and he writes of the latter:—

'La Guiccioli is a very pretty, sentimental, innocent Italian, who has sacrificed an immense fortune for the sake of Lord Byron, and who, if I know anything of my friend, of her, and of human nature, will hereafter have plenty of opportunity to repent her rashness.'

Tact also, and something better than tact, he shows in his dealings, in order to befriend Leigh Hunt, with Lord Byron. He writes to Hunt:—

'Particular circumstances, or rather, I should say, particular dispositions in Lord Byron's character, render the close and exclusive intimacy with him in which I find myself intolerable to me; thus much, my best friend, I will confess and confide to you.
5   No feelings of my own shall injure or interfere with what is now nearest to them—your interest; and I will take care to preserve the little influence I may have over this Proteus, in whom such strange extremes are reconciled, until we meet.'

And so we have come back again, at last, to our original
10 Shelley—to the Shelley of the lovely and well-known picture, to the Shelley with 'flushed, feminine, artless face,' the Shelley 'blushing like a girl,' of Trelawny. Professor Dowden gives us some further attempts at portraiture. One by a Miss Rose, of Shelley at Marlow:—

15   'He was the most interesting figure I ever saw; his eyes like a deer's, bright but rather wild; his white throat unfettered; his slender but to me almost faultless shape; his brown long coat with curling lambs' wool collar and cuffs—in fact, his whole appearance—are as fresh in my recollection as an occurrence of
20   yesterday.'

Feminine enthusiasm may be deemed suspicious, but a Captain Kennedy must surely be able to keep his head. Captain Kennedy was quartered at Horsham in 1813, and saw Shelley when he was on a stolen visit, in his father's absence, at Field
25 Place:—

'He received me with frankness and kindliness, as if he had known me from childhood, and at once won my heart. I fancy I see him now as he sate by the window, and hear his voice, the tones of which impressed me with his sincerity and simplicity.
30   His resemblance to his sister Elizabeth was as striking as if they had been twins. His eyes were most expressive; his complexion beautifully fair, his features exquisitely fine; his hair was dark, and no peculiar attention to its arrangement was manifest. In person he was slender and gentlemanlike, but inclined to stoop; his
35   gait was decidedly not military. The general appearance indicated great delicacy of constitution. One would at once pro-

nounce of him that he was different from other men. There was an earnestness in his manner and such perfect gentleness of breeding and freedom from everything artificial as charmed every one. I never met a man who so immediately won upon me.'

Mrs. Gisborne's son, who knew Shelley well at Leghorn, declared Captain Kennedy's description of him to be 'the best and most truthful I have ever seen.'

To all this we have to add the charm of the man's writings—of Shelley's poetry. It is his poetry, above everything else, which for many people establishes that he is an angel. Of his poetry I have not space now to speak. But let no one suppose that a want of humour and a self-delusion such as Shelley's have no effect upon a man's poetry. The man Shelley, in very truth, is not entirely sane, and Shelley's poetry is not entirely sane either. The Shelley of actual life is a vision of beauty and radiance, indeed, but availing nothing, effecting nothing. And in poetry, no less than in life, he is 'a beautiful *and ineffectual* angel, beating in the void his luminous wings in vain.'

Milton[1]

The most eloquent voice of our century uttered, shortly before
leaving the world, a warning cry against 'the Anglo-Saxon contagion.' The tendencies and aims, the view of life and the social
economy of the ever-multiplying and spreading Anglo-Saxon
race, would be found congenial, this prophet feared, by all the
prose, all the vulgarity amongst mankind, and would invade and
overpower all nations. The true ideal would be lost, a general
sterility of mind and heart would set in.

The prophet had in view, no doubt, in the warning thus
given, us and our colonies, but the United States still more.
There the Anglo-Saxon race is already most numerous, there
it increases fastest; there material interests are most absorbing
and pursued with most energy; there the ideal, the saving ideal,
of a high and rare excellence, seems perhaps to suffer most
danger of being obscured and lost. Whatever one may think
of the general danger to the world from the Anglo-Saxon contagion, it appears to me difficult to deny that the growing greatness and influence of the United States does bring with it some
danger to the ideal of a high and rare excellence. The *average
man* is too much a religion there; his performance is unduly
magnified, his shortcomings are not duly seen and admitted. A
lady in the State of Ohio sent to me only the other day a volume on American authors; the praise given throughout was of
such high pitch that in thanking her I could not forbear saying
that for only one or two of the authors named was such a strain
of praise admissible, and that we lost all real standard of excel-

[1] An address delivered in St. Margaret's Church, Westminster, on the
18th of February 1888, at the unveiling of a Memorial Window presented by Mr. George W. Childs of Philadelphia.

lence by praising so uniformly and immoderately. She answered me with charming good temper, that very likely I was
quite right, but it was pleasant to her to think that excellence
was common and abundant. But excellence is not common and
abundant; on the contrary, as the Greek poet long ago said, 5
excellence dwells among rocks hardly accessible, and a man
must almost wear his heart out before he can reach her. Whoever talks of excellence as common and abundant, is on the way
to lose all right standard of excellence. And when the right
standard of excellence is lost, it is not likely that much which 10
is excellent will be produced.

To habituate ourselves, therefore, to approve, as the Bible
says, things that are really excellent, is of the highest importance. And some apprehension may justly be caused by a tendency in Americans to take, or, at any rate, attempt to take, 15
profess to take, the average man and his performances too seriously, to over-rate and over-praise what is not really superior.

But we have met here to-day to witness the unveiling of a
gift in Milton's honour, and a gift bestowed by an American,
Mr. Childs of Philadelphia; whose cordial hospitality so many 20
Englishmen, I myself among the number, have experienced in
America. It was only last autumn that Stratford-upon-Avon
celebrated the reception of a gift from the same generous donor
in honour of Shakespeare. Shakespeare and Milton—he who
wishes to keep his standard of excellence high, cannot choose 25
two better objects of regard and honour. And it is an American
who has chosen them, and whose beautiful gift in honour of
one of them, Milton, with Mr. Whittier's simple and true lines
inscribed upon it, is unveiled to-day. Perhaps this gift in honour
of Milton, of which I am asked to speak, is, even more than the 30
gift in honour of Shakespeare, one to suggest edifying reflections to us.

Like Mr. Whittier, I treat the gift of Mr. Childs as a gift in
honour of Milton, although the window given is in memory of
his second wife, Catherine Woodcock, the 'late espoused saint' 35
of the famous sonnet, who died in child-bed at the end of the
first year of her marriage with Milton, and who lies buried
here with her infant. Milton is buried in Cripplegate, but he

lived for a good while in this parish of St. Margaret's, West-minster, and here he composed part of *Paradise Lost*, and the whole of *Paradise Regained* and *Samson Agonistes*. When death deprived him of the Catherine whom the new window com-

5 memorates, Milton had still some eighteen years to live, and Cromwell, his 'chief of men,' was yet ruling England. But the Restoration, with its 'Sons of Belial,' was not far off; and in the meantime Milton's heavy affliction had laid fast hold upon him, his eyesight had failed totally, he was blind. In what remained

10 to him of life he had the consolation of producing the *Paradise Lost* and the *Samson Agonistes*, and such a consolation we may indeed count as no slight one. But the daily life of happiness in common things and in domestic affections—a life of which, to Milton as to Dante, too small a share was given—he seems to

15 have known most, if not only, in his one married year with the wife who is here buried. Her form 'vested all in white,' as in his sonnet he relates that after her death she appeared to him, her face veiled, but with 'love, sweetness, and goodness' shining in her person,—this fair and gentle daughter of the rigid sectarist

20 of Hackney, this lovable companion with whom Milton had rest and happiness one year, is a part of Milton indeed, and in calling up her memory, we call up his.

And in calling up Milton's memory we call up, let me say, a memory upon which, in prospect of the Anglo-Saxon con-

25 tagion and of its dangers supposed and real, it may be well to lay stress even more than upon Shakespeare's. If to our English race an inadequate sense for perfection of work is a real danger, if the discipline of respect for a high and flawless excellence is peculiarly needed by us, Milton is of all our gifted men the

30 best lesson, the most salutary influence. In the sure and flawless perfection of his rhythm and diction he is as admirable as Virgil or Dante, and in this respect he is unique amongst us. No one else in English literature and art possesses the like distinction.

Thomson, Cowper, Wordsworth, all of them good poets

35 who have studied Milton, followed Milton, adopted his form, fail in their diction and rhythm if we try them by that high standard of excellence maintained by Milton constantly. From style really high and pure Milton never departs; their depar-tures from it are frequent.

Shakespeare is divinely strong, rich, and attractive. But sureness of perfect style Shakespeare himself does not possess. I have heard a politician express wonder at the treasures of political wisdom in a certain celebrated scene of *Troilus and Cressida;* for my part I am at least equally moved to wonder at the fantastic and false diction in which Shakespeare has in that scene clothed them. Milton, from one end of *Paradise Lost* to the other, is in his diction and rhythm constantly a great artist in the great style. Whatever may be said as to the subject of his poem, as to the conditions under which he received his subject and treated it, that praise, at any rate, is assured to him.

For the rest, justice is not at present done, in my opinion, to Milton's management of the inevitable matter of a Puritan epic, a matter full of difficulties for a poet. Justice is not done to the *architectonics*, as Goethe would have called them, of *Paradise Lost;* in these, too, the power of Milton's art is remarkable. But this may be a proposition which requires discussion and development for establishing it, and they are impossible on an occasion like the present.

That Milton, of all our English race, is by his diction and rhythm the one artist of the highest rank in the great style whom we have; this I take as requiring no discussion, this I take as certain.

The mighty power of poetry and art is generally admitted. But where the soul of this power, of this power at its best, chiefly resides, very many of us fail to see. It resides chiefly in the refining and elevation wrought in us by the high and rare excellence of the great style. We may feel the effect without being able to give ourselves clear account of its cause, but the thing is so. Now, no race needs the influences mentioned, the influences of refining and elevation, more than ours; and in poetry and art our grand source for them is Milton.

To what does he owe this supreme distinction? To nature first and foremost, to that bent of nature for inequality which to the worshippers of the average man is so unacceptable; to a gift, a divine favour. 'The older one grows,' says Goethe, 'the more one prizes natural gifts, because by no possibility can they be procured and stuck on.' Nature formed Milton to be a great poet. But what other poet has shown so sincere a sense of

the grandeur of his vocation, and a moral effort so constant and sublime to make and keep himself worthy of it? The Milton of religious and political controversy, and perhaps of domestic life also, is not seldom disfigured by want of amenity, by
5   acerbity. The Milton of poetry, on the other hand, is one of those great men 'who are modest'—to quote a fine remark of Leopardi, that gifted and stricken young Italian, who in his sense for poetic style is worthy to be named with Dante and Milton—'who are modest, because they continually compare
10 themselves, not with other men, but with that idea of the perfect which they have before their mind.' The Milton of poetry is the man, in his own magnificent phrase, of 'devout prayer to that Eternal Spirit that can enrich with all utterance and knowledge, and sends out his Seraphim with the hallowed fire
15 of his altar, to touch and purify the lips of whom he pleases.' And finally, the Milton of poetry is, in his own words again, the man of 'industrious and select reading.' Continually he lived in companionship with high and rare excellence, with the great Hebrew poets and prophets, with the great poets of
20 Greece and Rome. The Hebrew compositions were not in verse, and can be not inadequately represented by the grand, measured prose of our English Bible. The verse of the poets of Greece and Rome no translation can adequately reproduce. Prose cannot have the power of verse; verse-translation may
25 give whatever of charm is in the soul and talent of the translator himself, but never the specific charm of the verse and poet translated. In our race are thousands of readers, presently there will be millions, who know not a word of Greek and Latin, and will never learn those languages. If this host of
30 readers are ever to gain any sense of the power and charm of the great poets of antiquity, their way to gain it is not through translations of the ancients, but through the original poetry of Milton, who has the like power and charm, because he has the like great style.
35   Through Milton they may gain it, for, in conclusion, Milton is English; this master in the great style of the ancients is English. Virgil, whom Milton loved and honoured, has at the end of the *Æneid* a noble passage, where Juno, seeing the defeat of

Turnus and the Italians imminent, the victory of the Trojan
invaders assured, entreats Jupiter that Italy may nevertheless
survive and be herself still, may retain her own mind, manners,
and language, and not adopt those of the conqueror.

> 'Sit Latium, sint Albani per secula reges!   5

Jupiter grants the prayer; he promises perpetuity and the future
to Italy—Italy reinforced by whatever virtue the Trojan race
has, but Italy, not Troy. This we may take as a sort of parable
suiting ourselves. All the Anglo-Saxon contagion, all the flood
of Anglo-Saxon commonness, beats vainly against the great   10
style but cannot shake it, and has to accept its triumph. But it
triumphs in Milton, in one of our own race, tongue, faith, and
morals. Milton has made the great style no longer an exotic
here; he has made it an inmate amongst us, a leaven, and a
power. Nevertheless he, and his hearers on both sides of the   15
Atlantic, are English, and will remain English—

> 'Sermonem Ausonii patrium moresque tenebunt.'

The English race overspreads the world, and at the same time
the ideal of an excellence the most high and the most rare abides
a possession with it for ever.   20

Disestablishment in Wales

A good while ago I said I would write no more on religion, and up to the present time I have kept my word pretty faithfully. About six months ago I declared that on politics, too, I would write no more; and now here I find myself with a subject where
5   both politics and religion are concerned, and which I cannot treat without doubly breaking my word. A casuist might say that a promise not to write on religion, or a promise not to write on politics, was no promise not to write on a conjunction of the two together. But instead of resorting to casuistry, I will
10   say, what is the truth, that I have been led to depart from my intention by the temper of openness and moderation which is at present visible in so many members of the Conservative Party and in their main organs. To see this temper may well raise the spirits and the hopes of all quiet reasonable people who
15   simply desire the good of their country; the wish to turn this happy and wholesome temper to advantage, in a question which especially needs the exercise of such a temper, is my motive for returning, yet this once, to subjects which I had quitted.

I have frequently lamented the narrow aims and the bitter
20   temper of those whom, since they dislike the name of political Dissenters, I will call religious Liberals. Vinet's cry on issuing from a disestablishment debate in Canton Vaud has often risen to my mind as I watched them: *"O religion de Jésus Christ! ô culte en esprit! ô paisible et silencieux asile des âmes!"* The
25   secular Liberals are not narrow; they are free enough. But they, on the other hand, have spokesmen who always make me think of Voltaire's delicious comment on a young friend who was extolled as being *libre*, free. *"C'est déjà quelque chose; mais malheureusement cette bonne qualité, quand elle est seule, devi-*

ent un furieux vice." Where religion is concerned, their good
quality of freedom stands so entirely alone, that it "becomes a
furious vice." The difficulty to be feared is, that in confronting
the religious and the secular Liberals on questions where religion and the Church are concerned, one may have only a party 5
of impracticable Conservatives. The moment Conservatives
show themselves equitable and moderate in temper, open and
reasonable in mind, this difficulty vanishes, and a good deal of
danger along with it.

In England, an old country full of anomalies, and where the 10
national characteristics, as has often been said, are energy and
honesty rather than lucidity and logic, it is not enough recognized that a thing's being absurd is really an objection to it. As
long as the political party charged naturally with the interests
of conservation and permanence fails to recognize this, so long 15
the party charged with the interests of demolition and change
goes on and prospers, sure of succeeding in the end, whatever
resistance it may have to overcome, however it may be checked
for a time. The guiding spirits of this party do not want to
mend, they want to demolish; they think demolishing *is* mend- 20
ing. To suggest to them ways of mending is therefore waste of
time. To have suggested, for instance, to the Liberal Party in
1868 ways of mending the Irish Church Establishment would
have been waste of time; their desire and resolve was simply
to destroy it. And so long as the Conservatives, too, on their 25
side, will not really entertain the notion of mending things, but
seek simply to keep them as they are, while their adversaries
seek simply to destroy them, it is of no use to suggest ways of
mending a thing to Conservatives any more than to Liberals.

The case, however, is quite altered when the minds of the 30
Conservative party open, and that party brings itself to recognize that a thing's absurdity puts the thing in danger, makes it
indefensible as it now stands; and that the thing must be, not
necessarily destroyed, but certainly altered and mended so as
to get rid of this source of danger. 35

The Stoics, with whom the great matter was adherence to the
moral will and purpose, the living, as we commonly express it,
by principle, used to tell their pupils to say to themselves,

whenever they found themselves desiring a thing: "This I desire; *and also to keep my principle*." And so, too, the Conservatives should learn to say to themselves—and learning to say to themselves they do seem now to be: "We desire government, order and stability; *and also to get rid of what is indefensible and absurd*." With regard to Ireland they should say: "We desire to see the Crimes Act put resolutely in force; *and also to get rid of Lord Clanricarde*." With regard to the Church of England they should say: "We desire to keep a National and Established Church; *and also to get rid of Lord Lonsdale*." I mean, of course, of Lord Lonsdale as the patron of forty English livings, and of Lord Clanricarde as the owner of fifty thousand Irish acres; not of Lord Lonsdale and Lord Clanricarde as men passing their little hour above ground like the rest of us.

The moment the notion of mending an absurd and indefensible thing is fairly entertained, the question arises, how best to mend it. And for arriving at an answer to this question, it is well to know what is done elsewhere in the matters wherein our practice is alleged to be absurd and indefensible. The establishment, as at present existing, of the Anglican Church in Wales is alleged to be absurd and indefensible, and to be a grievance. If it is so, there seems good hope that the Conservative party will now be disposed to correct the absurdity and to remove the grievance. But, in doing this, Conservatives may naturally look for some help from knowing what happens elsewhere, where religion is publicly endowed and established, and yet all religionists are not of one confession. The United States can teach us nothing here, for the United States, founded by Separatists and with separation in their people's blood, have no public endowment and establishment of religion. But on the Continent of Europe the public endowment and establishment of religion is general. What happens there?—so I can imagine a Conservative asking himself when he has to deal with the case of Wales—what happens on the Continent, where there is public endowment for religion, and yet the religionists are of different religious confessions? Now it happens that in going repeatedly about among elementary schools on the Continent, I have seen also a good deal of the provision for churches and ministers there, what it is, and how it works. I could hardly help seeing it, the school system has so many connexions with the parish system. Therefore, when I see the case of Wales, I think naturally of what I have seen on the Continent; and Conservatives, too, may perhaps be glad to look there with me, and to see what is there done.

Now the Anglican form was settled and imposed by law, in the belief that all might unite in it. In England the majority did unite in it, and are united in it now; but in Scotland, Ireland, and Wales it has not been so. For Scotland and Ireland other arrangements have been made, but not for Wales; Wales remains with its churches and church property confined to the Anglican form, which has not been accepted by the majority of the inhabitants of the principality. A different religious form is preferred and used by that majority. And it may be said, that never has the preference of the people been regarded in disposing of the churches and church property in Wales, but it was taken for granted that the people would acquiesce in the form chosen for them, and would come to use it; and they have not. I put the thing in the simplest and most informal language I can find, because it is my object, not to seek technicalities on which an argument may be founded, but to present the matter as it really presents itself to plain people. I shall use language of the same kind in describing what happens on the Continent. I will confine myself to countries whose example will most interest us. We shall not find in France or Germany one form of religion chosen by the legislature as suitable to the whole nation, and entitled to the sole possession of the churches and church property accordingly. We shall find public endowment of religion, but what the law has done is not to select one form of religion and establish it, but to follow the preference of the people; to ascertain the main forms actually existing among the people, and to endow these main forms. Thus in France the Catholic form of Christianity, the Lutheran form, and the Calvinistic form, all receive support from public funds. The example of Germany interests us more nearly than that of France, because Germany was the country of the Reformation, and has never been revolutionized. In Germany the settlement of 1648, after the Thirty Years' War—the settlement by the treaties of Westphalia—took for its basis just this fact of the forms of religion actually existing among the German people, and preferred by them. It took a particular year, the year 1624, as an *annus normalis*, and provided that the churches and church property, in German territories, should remain with the religious party which had possessed them on the 1st day of January in that year. These great parties in religion, whom the settlement of 1648 thus established as corporations in possession, were the Catholic, the Lutheran, and the Zwinglian or Reformed, the more Calvinistic Protestant party. And so things remain to this day, except that in Prussia the Lutheran and the Reformed churches were united by a measure due to Frederick William III., in the present century, and are now a united corporation with the name of the Evangelical Church. To one or other corporation the churches belong, and in each parish the church established is maintained from its own property, and from the contributions of its members—contributions supplemented, in cases of necessity, by grants from the State.

The further sects and sub-divisions into which Protestantism is apt to break up are not regarded. There are Baptists, Wesleyans, Plymouth Brethren, Irvingites, found in Lutheran parishes in Germany, and these sects have the free exercise of their worship, but they are not endowed and established. The establishment of the main form of Lutheranism is held to be sufficient. Attempts have been made to establish the old Catholics in some Catholic territories of Germany. But these attempts have not succeeded; the main form of Catholicism holds, as we say now, the field.

People may call it a grievance not to have sects and sub-divisions of religious parties established, as well as the main bodies. And perhaps the German governments and legislatures are not ready enough and flexible enough in making changes which might more thoroughly adapt the settlement of 1648 to the wants of the present day. But the tendency to multiply sects is a misfortune to Protestantism; it may become a disease; it would not be possible for establishment to follow it into all the varieties it produces, and would not be desirable if even it were possible. Some main forms must be chosen for establishment, if establishment there is to be. In Germany the somewhat un-elastic settlement inherited from the seventeeth century does not, so far as I can learn, cause any serious dissatisfaction, al-though there are many Dissenters for whom it does not pro-vide; no one talks or thinks of altering it.

But the case is different where, as formerly in Ireland and now in Wales, the form of religion established is one which was not that followed in those localities at the outset, and has not been adopted by more than a minority of the people there since. A grievance in this case there certainly is, and it will be felt to be a grievance, will provoke complaints. In Ireland it was removed by disestablishment; the question now is as to the grievance in Wales. People dispute as to the numbers of the majority outside of the Establishment; some say that they are diminishing, and that the established form will win over the majority in time. The Dissenters have prevented hitherto the taking of a religious census; such a census would be of very great convenience, and its refusal is indefensible; it is to be hoped that the Conservative majority will procure its being taken. In its absence no one can say with certainty what are the numbers, in Wales, of the majority outside of the Establish-ment; but, at any rate, a considerable majority is outside of it. In some districts of Wales almost the whole population is out-side of it; in other districts the Establishment has many adher-ents, and they are increasing in number. But I am talking to Conservatives, and considering what is the line for them, in their present temper of fairness and moderation, to follow as to the Establishment in Wales. Let them take it, then, that the ma-jority outside of the Establishment is certainly considerable; and do not let them be deceived into thinking, that to uphold the Establishment as it is, is the way to win the majority over to the Establishment, and thus to solve the question peaceably and happily. The Church has, in the last thirty or forty years, been much more active than formerly, and has, accordingly, gained much ground, especially in localities where it has circumstances in its favour. But it is not to know human nature to imagine

that with the Establishment upheld just as it is the Church will
ever absorb dissent in Wales, or the minority be converted
into the majority. Above all, this will not happen in times like
ours, democratic times when the masses are keen to spy a
5   grievance, to attack a grievance, and when the Welsh Dissenters
have leaders whose temper and character are what they are—
eager to encourage battle, averse from composing or preventing
it.

I feel sure that if the Conservatives enter on the battle with
10 the resolve to uphold in Wales the Establishment just as it is,
the Establishment in Wales is lost. The Conservatives are strong
now, as they deserve to be strong; they may defeat those who
attack the Church in Wales, they may put off the evil day of
its disestablishment; but its disestablishment will have been
15 rendered certain, and will soon come. The battle will have been
engaged on terms which make impossible any other solution of
the question at issue. And, undoubtedly, this will bring the
Establishment into some danger in England also. It will be said:
"Where there are several forms of religion present, none of
20 them ought to have any support from public funds. It is unfair that one form should have all the support, and no mode
of concurrent endowment is found practicable. The case of
Wales proves it. It was quite clear that the Church of the
minority could not continue to take all the endowments, and
25 the friends of the Church had nothing else to suggest. Disestablishment is the only solution."

It is not the religious argument that Christian Churches suffer spiritually through not being independent of the State, and
that Jesus Christ enjoined that independence when he said: "My
30 kingdom is not of this world"—it is not this argument which
endangers the Establishment, either in Wales or elsewhere. I see
the *Guardian* thinks the strength and prevalence of that argument under-estimated, and the attention of Churchmen not
directed to it enough. I know that it is very prevalent among
35 Dissenters at the present day, but I do not think it requires any
great attention, because really there is very little in it. Dissenters use it, I admit, with entire sincerity, and believe that it ut-
ters a genuine religious conviction with them; but they did

not entertain it originally and naturally, they were led to it by circumstances which made it of irresistible convenience to them, and they have given it a firm and central place in their minds because of that convenience. Anyone who reflects seriously will perceive that there is very little in it. An established Church may be unspiritual; so may a free church also. It is neither the freedom nor the establishment which makes the unspirituality. On the other hand, religion exciting the strong affection which it does, religious people, when circumstances favoured, gladly had honour done to their religion by making it a thing of public institution, and this honour they will be reluctant to withdraw from it. And they are right. Who will deny that religion has gained in England through the hold of the Church of England upon the upper and cultivated classes, and that its being *the Church of England* has made this hold stronger? Who will deny that in modern democratic times a great and imposing institution, if it can be had, for the higher spiritual life and culture of the nation, becomes more desirable rather than less? If its friends are grasping and unreasonable, it cannot be had; but if their minds open and their tempers soften, it can. I said not very long ago that Professor Goldwin Smith was too bitter against the Church; in an admirable letter he has told me that against *the Church* he had never meant to be bitter, and that he now no longer urges Disestablishment, but Church Reform. For the times have changed, and the possibilities widened.

Arguments from religious theory against established Churches will not destroy the Establishment in Wales. What will destroy it, if it comes to be destroyed, is the sense of grievance; of grievance not redressed, grievance which the friends of the Church will not attempt to redress, will not recognize. Let the Conservatives put themselves in the place of the dissident majority in Wales. I altogether agree with Lord Selborne in wishing to preserve the Establishment there. I agree with him that a man who takes land binds himself to pay the tithe upon it just as much as to pay the rent. I am ready to admit that tithe was not imposed on Wales by any English laws; that in Wales, as elsewhere, tithe arose out of a sense of religious propriety.

But the grievance is that this tithe, arising out of a sense of religious propriety, is not applied to meet the religious needs acknowledged by those who pay it, but to meet some other sort of religious needs. It is true that the tithe is as much the property of *somebody* as any land which the law secures to an individual, and that this somebody is by law the clergyman; but the hardship is that in Wales, throughout Wales, the clergyman, and the clergyman alone, it should be. And in Wales now, as in Ireland formerly, those who can allege this hardship will very easily bring themselves to dispute and deny the obligation of tithe.

Let the Conservatives beware of plausibilities, of arguments which may well enough do duty for reasons with men who have made up their mind to keep things as they are, but which cannot possibly have the smallest effect in convincing or satisfying the man whom the shoe pinches. I have mentioned Lord Selborne, for whom I entertain a great respect. Lord Selborne adopts an argument, used with effect, it appears, by Mr. Gladstone formerly in the House of Commons; the argument that "there is a complete ecclesiastical, constitutional, legal, and I may add, for every practical purpose, historical identity between the Church in Wales and the rest of the Church of England." Well? afterwards? This argument is of that unreal sort so abundantly provided in the House of Commons, and which made me once say that the banquet for the mind there was to any serious taste a banquet of Thyestes. If the Establishment in Wales is on its present footing a grievance, why should it be kept because between the Church in Wales and the rest of England there is complete identity ecclesiastical, constitutional, and so on? If the four Welsh dioceses were suppressed, the Church of England would have four dioceses the less, just as from time to time it acquires dioceses additional; if the dioceses survive, but with arrangements somewhat altered, the Church of England will have those four dioceses with their arrangements somewhat altered. Is the danger that we may then be called upon to do for other parts of England what we have done for Wales? Well, if in other large well-defined territories, as large and as well defined as Wales, there is inflicted by the actual

establishment a grievance similar to the grievance inflicted in
Wales, certainly we should act by those territories as we should
act by Wales. But in Wales, as formerly in Ireland, the large
majority is admittedly dissident. Is there in England any other
territory, well-defined and considerable as Wales, where the   5
large majority is admittedly dissident as in Wales? There is
none. We have not at present the statistics, for the Dissenters
have prevented our getting them; but I believe that in every
one of the large divisions of England, except Wales, the adher-
ents of the Church will be found to outnumber the Dissenters.   10
In Wales the contrary is clearly the case, and statistics are not
needed to establish it; we will talk about the other large divisions of England when we get the statistics. But let me again
say beforehand, that if in any one of these divisions the case
was proved to be as in Wales, the Conservatives would be very   15
ill advised in refusing to modify the Establishment there.

The Conservatives cannot maintain the Establishment in
Wales on its present footing; of that they may be certain. The
Church will not be suffered to try the experiment whether,
continuing in sole possession of the churches and church prop-   20
erty as at present, it cannot, in the course of another century,
absorb the Dissenters. I feel sure it could not, but it will not
be suffered to try. I believe the power of attraction in the
Church of England, indeed, to be great and increasing; I believe the establishment of the Church adds to its force and   25
efficiency, and I wish it to remain established in Wales, though
not established sole; I feel confident that its powers of attraction
will continue to operate after it has ceased to be established
sole, and to operate more efficaciously than at present because
they will no longer have the angry sense of grievance to coun-   30
teract them. But at any rate the Establishment in Wales will not
be long allowed to endure on exactly its present footing; so
much, I say, is certain.

Conservatives may perfectly well refuse to enter upon the
question of altering the Establishment in Wales during this   35
present Session of Parliament. This Session has its own work
already laid out for it, and the Welsh question will gain by
being deliberately and fairly thought over before it is ap-

proached in the House of Commons. What is important is that
the Conservatives should show themselves capable of an equitable treatment of it; that they should recognize the grievance
which exists, and should be prepared to do for its redress some-
5   thing which may satisfy the moral feeling in men, something
which answers to men's desire for justice, which their conscience can rest upon.

To lay out in detail measures for politicians to adopt is not
my business; to attempt such a thing would, in me, be pedantic,
10   officious, and nugatory. But what a man in my position may,
perhaps, usefully do, is to indicate the sort of plan which a
Government and politicians, bent on a Conservative but equitable solution of this Welsh question, would do well to keep
before their mind as desirable, as the kind of solution to be
15   aimed at, because it can satisfy, and may, therefore, succeed.

Now what is done elsewhere, where there is an establishment of religion, may surely afford us some guidance, supposing that this which is done elsewhere works smoothly, as it
does, and gives satisfaction to those concerned. Establishment
20   there, instead of dictating a religious form, follows the main
religious form prevalent. Now there are districts of Cardigan-
shire and Caermarthenshire in which, as I suppose no one will
deny, almost every soul is a Dissenter; yet the religious establishment there takes no account of this, but offers to the people
25   a religious form not theirs, and that form only. But the people,
it will be said, are divided into so many sects! True; but all
their important sects follow one form of worship, the Genevan
form as it used to be called, but which is now best understood
if we speak of it as the Presbyterian form, because we have
30   most of us seen this form in the churches of Presbyterian Scotland, if not here. This all the considerable sects follow; and to
this main form of the religious worship of Protestant Dissenters, not to the Anglican and Episcopalian form, the churches
and tithe, in such districts as those I just now mentioned, ought
35   surely to be given. The churches and tithe should remain to
the Church of England in districts on whose population the
Church has laid firm hold; and the Church should, moreover,
retain the Cathedrals, which followers of the Episcopalian

form prize more and turn to greater account than followers of the Presbyterian form do.

Patronage, in so far as this change is concerned, might remain as it is; only, in Presbyterian districts, ministers of the Presbyterian form must be appointed, and everywhere the parish should have a power which, I think, throughout Protestant Germany the parishes possess—the power of a *suffragium negativum*, or veto. This power would be a safeguard against the appointment of a minister, following the Presbyterian form indeed, but of a sect at variance with the religious persuasion of the majority.

But how are the districts to be adjusted? Why, if once the equity of the case were brought home to people's minds, and there were a disposition and resolve to make things conform to it, an adjustment of the districts might be accomplished with very little difficulty. It is a matter to be referred to fair and intelligent men, of whom, happily, we have plenty whom one could quite trust to carry honestly into effect a distribution of which the principle was understood and accepted by them. The counties I mentioned above are in South Wales. To take, then, South Wales: I have no doubt whatever that if Lord Cawdor and the Bishop of Llandaff on the one part, Lord Aberdare and Mr. Henry Richard on the other, were commissioned to make an equitable division of South Wales into districts of the Presbyterian and of the Anglican form (the Cathedrals being reserved to the Anglicans), so that establishment might follow that division, they could do it admirably and to the full satisfaction of the Principality.

Between this kind of arrangement and disestablishment the Conservatives have at present the option. Keep things just as they are they cannot. The case is in a remarkable degree parallel to that which presents itself to the Conservatives in dealing with Ireland. In Wales, as in Ireland, much that the Conservatives propose to themselves is right and expedient, much that the Liberals propose to themselves is wrong and dangerous. In Ireland the Conservatives propose to themselves to restore law and order; in Wales to maintain an establishment of religion. Both objects are, in my opinion, excellent. Still, if the Conservatives confine themselves to these objects, if they cannot, in addition, discover and propose, to remedy the state of things now existing, something which may satisfy the moral feeling in men, something which answers to men's desire for justice, something which men's conscience can rest upon, the Conservatives will suffer defeat; the policy proposed by the Liberals, however wrong and dangerous it may be, will prevail.

In Ireland there is, as again and again I have urged, a moral grievance which has never yet been met. The Land Act did not meet it, and that was the great defect of the Land Act, a defect on which I kept insisting so long as the Land Act was under consideration. The Land Act created a condition of intense complication and entanglement; it enabled Mr. Shaw-Lefevre to speak of Lord Clanricarde's tenants as his "co-owners"—a promising and blessed state of things, indeed, for Lord Clanricarde's litigious and discontented tenantry! But the Land Act did not meet the moral grievance which had mainly prevented Ireland's settling down into tranquillity, and which constituted permanent danger to public order—the grievance Ireland had and has in its bad landlords. Lord Clanricarde, at the recent trial in Dublin, showed the world what they can be. The Land Act did not touch that grievance, did not stay disorder. The disorder continued, convictions for crime and outrage could not be obtained, and we had a judge telling us that "the law has ceased to exist," and Mr. Dillon boasting that "there are hundreds of farms on which no man dare set his foot." Mr. Parnell's original declaration, that "none of us will be satisfied until we have destroyed the last link that keeps Ireland bound to England," has been re-uttered again and again by his followers whenever they had no pressing motive to disguise their real thoughts; it was re-uttered only the other day. The Government passed a Crimes Act, and they did well. Mr. Balfour has won praise for putting it in force with determination and vigour, and he deserves praise. To a sane mind the sayings and doings of that "victim" of the Crimes Act, Mr. William O'Brien, appear, not fine and impressive, but pitiful, ridiculous. Still, the disorder continues.

The Liberals propose remedies certain to secure to them the support of the Irish vote, and which they hope will be approved also by the democracy, feather-headed and passionate, of Great Britain. They propose to repeal the Crimes Act. Lord Rosebery says that Ireland is in a revolutionary state, in a state of what may be called civil war; and Mr. Redmond supplements this by explaining that what exists in Ireland is, more precisely, "a state of rebellion tempered by scarcity of fire-arms." Then Lord Rosebery goes on to ask how we, in England, should like to be deprived of those three grand liberties, liberty of speech, liberty of publishing, liberty of meeting, and complains that from the Irish these liberties are, in part at any rate, withheld. How extraordinary that so clever a man should not perceive that if England were, unfortunately, in "a state of rebellion tempered by scarcity of fire-arms," in a state of civil war, these liberties would most certainly be suspended in England too; perhaps he may even one day see his Radical friends suspending them. Ireland is not in a state of civil war because those liberties are suspended; they are suspended because she is in a state of civil war.

Then the Liberals have the remedy of a national Irish Parliament. Mr. Gladstone talks now constantly of the "national aspirations" of Ireland; he asks if anyone believes that they can long be left ungratified. Mr. John Morley feels himself "deeply moved to see the representatives of cities like Cork and Limerick and Kilkenny still bearing aloft the national flag, and bent on showing that the old national aspiration survives and is cherished by them as warmly as in any past century." This is statesmanship, indeed! When one thinks what an old, highly-organized country, such as France or our own country, is, to talk with this satisfaction of the persistence, in such a country, of rival and disintegrating nationalities, to encourage them, to promise them help in establishing themselves more fully! It is as if a French statesman congratulated himself on the persisting "particularism" of La Vendée, and proposed to give La Vendée a separate Parliament. The "particularism" may be inflamed and angry, but this is owing to injudicious treatment; it is to be

suppled and reduced, not further inflamed. Who would think
that a Liberal statesman needed to be taught this? But at this
time the Liberal leaders are not serious statesmen. Serious parti-
zans they all are; serious politicians some of them are; but a
5   serious statesman not one of them is.

Nevertheless, because the Liberals insist now on that moral
grievance of Ireland, the bad landlords, they will win, as I have
repeatedly prophesied, and now prophesy for the last time—
they will win, if the Conservatives think it enough to put firmly
10 in force the Crimes Act, and do not touch the moral grievance.
The measures proposed by the Liberals are in a high degree unwise and dangerous; but they do insist on that moral grievance,
and they appeal to a mass of untrained and ardent minds. A
Land Court with power to expropriate bad landlords would be
15 a far more efficacious cure for the grievance than the elaborate
Liberal Land Act turning the tenants of all landlords alike, bad
and good, into *co-owners;* and a far safer cure than an Irish
Parliament. Even safe and much-needed measures of local government for Ireland may quite properly be deferred until the
20 country is less inflamed and disorderly. But some sign of wishing to deal with the moral grievance there must be; there must
be some satisfaction given to men's sense of impatience under it.
I fear that Mr. Balfour, with all his talents and all his energy
and courage, does not see this clearly enough. The Irish agita-
25 tors and Separatists have never been in such danger of defeat
as at the moment when Sir Michael Hicks-Beach firmly drew
his line of distinction between evictions which are permissible
and aidable, and evictions which are not. His step may have
been revolutionary, but Ireland is, as Lord Rosebery truly says,
30 in a revolutionary state. Mr. Balfour damaged the Unionist
cause last year by thinking it his duty to support harsh and fair
evictions indifferently. If the moral grievance in Ireland continues to find him without any sense or resource for it, the
trouble will not die away, but the satisfaction with his spirit
35 and courage will. He will fail, the Liberals will win, and for a
time, at any rate, the Unionist cause will be lost.

Let us come back to Wales. There, also, is found a moral
grievance—the moral grievance of the establishment of the

minority's Church sole. There, too, the Liberals have only a
mischievous remedy to propose, the remedy of Disestablishment. There, too, there is danger of the Conservatives imagin-
ing they have nothing to do but to stand on the defensive, and
to uphold things as they are. If they do no more than this, the   5
Liberals will win, and disestablishment will arrive. It is a stupid
remedy; a mere work of destruction; an abandonment of means
and influences very valuable. But the Conservatives cannot prevent it by a mere negative; they can prevent it only by having
some satisfaction to offer to the moral feeling and the sense of   10
justice with which the actual arrangement conflicts. Let them
be ready with such satisfaction; a good deal is at stake. There is
no doubt that disestablishment in Ireland lessened the security
of the Church in England, and that disestablishment in Wales
would lessen it still more. It would further familiarize people   15
with the idea of disestablishment as inevitable, as the only solution possible wherever there is complaint. By offering a better
solution in Wales, the Conservatives will benefit not only
Wales, but England. By failing to offer it they will weaken the
Church of England, and that they may indeed well be loth to   20
do.

> Who lets so fair a house fall to decay,
> Which husbandry in honour might uphold
> Against the stormy gusts of winter's day,
> And barren rage of death's eternal cold?   25

Civilisation in the United States

Two or three years ago I spoke in this Review on the subject
of America; and after considering the institutions and the social
condition of the people of the United States, I said that what,
in the jargon of the present day, is called 'the political and
social problem,' does seem to be solved there with remarkable
success. I pointed out the contrast which in this respect the
United States offer to our own country, a contrast, in several
ways, much to their advantage. But I added that the solution of
the political and social problem, as it is called, ought not so to
absorb us as to make us forget the human problem; and that it
remained to ask how the human problem is solved in the United
States. It happened that Sir Lepel Griffin, a very acute and distinguished Indian official, had just then been travelling in the
United States, and had published his opinion, from what he saw
of the life there, that there is no country calling itself civilised
where one would not rather live than in America, except Russia.
Certainly then, I said, one cannot rest satisfied, when one finds
such a judgment passed on the United States as this, with admiring their institutions and their solid social condition, their
freedom and equality, their power, energy, and wealth. One
must, further, go on to examine what is done there towards
solving the human problem, and must see what Sir Lepel Griffin's objection comes to.

And this examination I promised that I would one day make.
However, it is so delicate a matter to discuss how a sensitive nation solves the human problem, that I found myself inclined to
follow the example of the Greek moralist Theophrastus, who
waited, before composing his famous *Characters*, until he was
ninety-nine years old. I thought I had perhaps better wait until

I was about that age, before I discussed the success of the
Americans in solving the human problem. But ninety-nine is a
great age; it is probable that I may never reach it, or even come
near it. So I have determined, finally, to face the question without any such long delay, and thus I come to offer to the readers   5
of this Review the remarks following. With the same frankness with which I discussed here the solution of the political
and social problem by the people of the United States, I shall
discuss their success in solving the human problem.

Perhaps it is not likely that any one will now remember what   10
I said three years ago here about the success of the Americans
in solving the political and social problem. I will sum it up in
the briefest possible manner. I said that the United States had
constituted themselves in a modern age; that their institutions
complied well with the form and pressure of those circum-   15
stances and conditions which a modern age presents. Quite
apart from all question how much of the merit for this may be
due to the wisdom and virtue of the American people, and how
much to their good fortune, it is undeniable that their institutions do work well and happily. The play of their institutions   20
suggests, I said, the image of a man in a suit of clothes which
fits him to perfection, leaving all his movements unimpeded and
easy; a suit of clothes loose where it ought to be loose, and
sitting close where its sitting close is an advantage; a suit of
clothes able, moreover, to adapt itself naturally to the wearer's   25
growth, and to admit of all enlargements as they successively
arise.

So much as to the solution, by the United States, of the political problem. As to the social problem, I observed that the people of the United States were a community singularly free from   30
the distinction of classes, singularly homogeneous; that the
division between rich and poor was consequently less profound
there than in countries where the distinction of classes accentu-
ates that division. I added that I believed there was exaggeration
in the reports of their administrative and judicial corruption;   35
and altogether, I concluded, the United States, politically and
socially, are a country living prosperously in a natural modern
condition, and conscious of living prosperously in such a con-

dition. And being in this healthy case, and having this healthy consciousness, the community there uses its understanding with the soundness of health; it in general, as to its own political and social concerns, sees clear and thinks straight. Comparing the United States with ourselves, I said that while they are in this natural and healthy condition, we on the contrary are so little homogeneous, we are living with a system of classes so intense, with institutions and a society so little modern, so unnaturally complicated, that the whole action of our minds is hampered and falsened by it; we are in consequence wanting in lucidity, we do not see clear or think straight, and the Americans have here much the advantage of us.

Yet we find an acute and experienced Englishman saying that there is no country, calling itself civilised, where one would not rather live than in the United States, except Russia! The civilisation of the United States must somehow, if an able man can think thus, have shortcomings, in spite of the country's success and prosperity. What is civilisation? It is the humanisation of man in society, the satisfaction for him, in society, of the true law of human nature. Man's study, says Plato, is to discover the right answer to the question *how to live?* our aim, he says, is very and true life. We are more or less civilised as we come more or less near to this aim, in that social state which the pursuit of our aim essentially demands. But several elements or powers, as I have often insisted, go to build up a complete human life. There is the power of conduct, the power of intellect and knowledge, the power of beauty, the power of social life and manners; we have instincts responding to them all, requiring them all. And we are perfectly civilised only when all these instincts in our nature, all these elements in our civilisation, have been adequately recognised and satisfied. But of course this adequate recognition and satisfaction of all the elements in question is impossible; some of them are recognised more than others, some of them more in one community, some in another; and the satisfactions found are more or less worthy.

And meanwhile, people use the term *civilisation* in the loosest possible way, for the most part attaching to it, however, in their own mind some meaning connected with their own preferences and experiences. The most common meaning thus attached to

it is perhaps that of a satisfaction, not of all the main demands
of human nature, but of the demand for the comforts and conveniences of life, and of this demand as made by the sort of
person who uses the term.

Now we should always attend to the common and prevalent 5
use of an important term. Probably Sir Lepel Griffin had this
notion of the comforts and conveniences of life much in his
thoughts when he reproached American civilisation with its
shortcomings. For men of his kind, and for all that large number of men, so prominent in this country and who make their 10
voice so much heard, men who have been at the public schools
and universities, men of the professional and official class, men
who do the most part of our literature and our journalism,
America is not a comfortable place of abode. A man of this sort
has in England everything in his favour; society appears orga- 15
nised expressly for his advantage. A Rothschild or a Vanderbilt
can buy his way anywhere, and can have what comforts and
luxuries he likes whether in America or in England. But it is in
England that an income of from three or four to fourteen or
fifteen hundred a year does so much for its possessor, enables 20
him to live with so many of the conveniences of far richer
people. For his benefit, his benefit above all, clubs are organised
and hansom cabs ply; service is abundant, porters stand waiting
at the railway stations. In America all luxuries are dear except
oysters and ice; service is in general scarce and bad; a club is a 25
most expensive luxury; the cab-rates are prohibitive—more than
half of the people who in England would use cabs must in
America use the horse-cars, the tram. The charges of tailors
and mercers are about a third higher than they are with us. I
mention only a few striking points as to which there can be no 30
dispute, and in which a man of Sir Lepel Griffin's class would
feel the great difference between America and England in the
conveniences at his command. There are a hundred other points
one might mention, where he would feel the same thing. When
a man is passing judgment on a country's civilisation, points of 35
this kind crowd to his memory, and determine his sentence.

On the other hand, for that immense class of people, the great
bulk of the community, the class of people whose income is
less than three or four hundred a year, things in America are

favourable. It is easier for them there than in the Old World
to rise and to make their fortune; but I am not now speaking of
that. Even without making their fortune, even with their income below three or four hundred a year, things are favourable
to them in America, society seems organised there for their
benefit. To begin with, the humbler kind of work is better
paid in America than with us, the higher kind worse. The official, for instance, gets less, his office-keeper gets more. The
public ways are abominably cut up by rails and blocked with
horse-cars; but the inconvenience is for those who use private
carriages and cabs, the convenience is for the bulk of the community who but for the horse-cars would have to walk. The
ordinary railway cars are not delightful, but they are cheap,
and they are better furnished and in winter are warmer than
third-class carriages in England. Luxuries are, as I have said,
very dear—above all, European luxuries; but a working man's
clothing is nearly as cheap as in England, and plain food is on
the whole cheaper. Even luxuries of a certain kind are within a
labouring man's easy reach. I have mentioned ice, I will mention
fruit also. The abundance and cheapness of fruit is a great boon
to people of small incomes in America. Do not believe the
Americans when they extol their peaches as equal to any in the
world, or better than any in the world; they are not to be compared to peaches grown under glass. Do not believe that the
American Newtown pippins appear in the New York and
Boston fruit-shops as they appear in those of London and Liverpool; or that the Americans have any pear to give you like the
Marie Louise. But what labourer, or artisan, or small clerk, ever
gets hot-house peaches, or Newtown pippins, or Marie Louise
pears? Not such good pears, apples, and peaches as those,
but pears, apples, and peaches by no means to be despised, such
people and their families do in America get in plenty.

Well, now, what would a philosopher or a philanthropist
say in this case? which would he say was the more civilised
condition—that of the country where the balance of advantage,
as to the comforts and conveniences of life, is greatly in favour
of the people with incomes below three hundred a year, or that
of the country where it is greatly in favour of those with incomes above that sum?

Many people will be ready to give an answer to that question without the smallest hesitation. They will say that they are, and that all of us ought to be, for the greatest happiness of the greatest number. However, the question is not one which I feel bound now to discuss and answer. Of course, if happiness and civilisation consist in being plentifully supplied with the comforts and conveniences of life, the question presents little difficulty. But I believe neither that happiness consists, merely or mainly, in being plentifully supplied with the comforts and conveniences of life, nor that civilisation consists in being so supplied; therefore I leave the question unanswered.

I prefer to seek for some other and better tests by which to try the civilisation of the United States. I have often insisted on the need of more equality in our own country, and on the mischiefs caused by inequality over here. In the United States there is not our intense division of classes, our inequality; there is great equality. Let me mention two points in the system of social life and manners over there in which this equality seems to me to have done good. The first is a mere point of form, but it has its significance. Every one knows it is the established habit with us in England, if we write to people supposed to belong to the class of gentlemen, of addressing them by the title of *Esquire*, while we keep *Mr.* for people not supposed to belong to that class. If we think of it, could one easily find a habit more ridiculous, more offensive? The title of *Esquire*, like most of our titles, comes out of the great frippery shop of the Middle Age; it is alien to the sound taste and manner of antiquity, when men said *Pericles* and *Camillus*. But unlike other titles, it is applied or withheld quite arbitrarily. Surely, where a man has no specific title proper to him, the one plain title of *Master* or *Mr.* is enough, and we need not be encumbered with a second title of *Esquire*, now quite unmeaning, to draw an invidious and impossible line of distinction between those who are gentlemen and those who are not; as if we actually wished to provide a source of embarrassment for the sender of a letter, and of mortification for the receiver of it.

The French, those great authorities in social life and manners, find *Mr.* enough, and the Americans are more and more, I am glad to say, following the French example. I only hope they will persevere, and not be seduced by *Esquire* being 'so English, you know.' And I do hope, moreover, that we shall one day take the same course and drop our absurd *Esquire*.

The other point goes deeper. Much may be said against the voices and intonation of American women. But almost every one acknowledges that there is a charm in American women—a charm which you find in almost all of them, wherever you go. It is the charm of a natural manner, a manner not self-conscious, artificial, and constrained. It may not be a beautiful manner always, but it is almost always a natural manner, a free and happy manner; and this gives pleasure. Here we have, undoubtedly, a note of civilisation, and an evidence, at the same time, of the good effect of equality upon social life and manners. I have often heard it observed that a perfectly natural manner is as rare among Englishwomen of the middle classes as it is general among American women of like condition with them. And so far as the observation is true, the reason of its truth no doubt is, that the Englishwoman is living in presence of an upper class, as it is called—in presence, that is, of a class of women recognised as being the right thing in style and manner, and whom she imagines criticising *her* style and manner, finding this or that to be amiss with it, this or that to be vulgar. Hence self-consciousness and constraint in her. The American woman lives in presence of no such class; there may be circles trying to pass themselves off as such a class, giving themselves airs as such, but they command no recognition, no authority. The American woman in general is perfectly unconcerned about their opinion, is herself, enjoys her existence, and has consequently a manner happy and natural. It is her great charm; and it is moreover, as I have said, a real note of civilisation, and one which has to be reckoned to the credit of American life, and of its equality.

But we must get nearer still to the heart of the question raised as to the character and worth of American civilisation. I have said how much the word civilisation really means—the humanisation of man in society; his making progress there towards his true and full humanity. Partial and material achievement is always being put forward as civilisation. We hear a nation called highly civilised by reason of its industry, commerce, and wealth, or by reason of its liberty or equality, or by reason of its numerous churches, schools, libraries, and newspapers. But there is something in human nature, some instinct of growth, some law of perfection, which rebels against this narrow account of the matter. And perhaps what human nature demands in civilisation, over and above all those obvious things which first occur to our thoughts—what human nature, I say, demands in civilisation, if it is to stand as a high and satisfying civilisation, is best described by the word *interesting*. Here is the extraordinary charm of the old Greek civilisation—that it is so *interesting*. Do not tell me only, says human nature, of the magnitude of your industry and commerce; of the beneficence of your institutions, your freedom, your equality; of the great and growing number of your churches and schools, libraries and newspapers; tell me also if your civilisation—which is the grand name you give to all this development—tell me if your civilisation is *interesting*.

An American friend of mine, Professor Norton, has lately published the early letters of Carlyle. If any one wants a good antidote to the unpleasant effect left by Mr. Froude's *Life of Carlyle*, let him read those letters. Not only of Carlyle will those letters make him think kindly, but they will also fill him with admiring esteem for the qualities, character, and family life, as there delineated, of the Scottish peasant. Well, the Carlyle family were numerous, poor, and struggling. Thomas Carlyle, the eldest son, a young man in wretched health and worse spirits, was fighting his way in Edinburgh. One of his younger brothers talked of emigrating. 'The very best thing he could do!' we should all say. Carlyle dissuades him. 'You shall never,' he writes, 'you shall never seriously meditate crossing the great Salt Pool to plant yourself in the Yankee-land. That is a miserable fate for any one, at best; never dream of it. Could you banish yourself from all that is interesting to your mind, forget the history, the glorious institutions, the noble principles of old Scotland—that you might eat a better dinner, perhaps?'

There is our word launched—the word *interesting*. I am not saying that Carlyle's advice was good, or that young men should not emigrate. I do but take note, in the word *interesting*, of a requirement, a cry of aspiration, a cry not sounding in the imaginative Carlyle's own breast only, but sure of a response in his brother's breast also, and in human nature.

Amiel, that contemplative Swiss whose journals the world has been reading lately, tells us that 'the human heart is, as it were, haunted by confused reminiscences of an age of gold; or rather, by aspirations towards a harmony of things which everyday reality denies to us.' He says that the splendour and refinement of high life is an attempt by the rich and cultivated classes to realise this ideal, and is 'a form of poetry.' And the interest which this attempt awakens in the classes which are not rich or cultivated, their indestructible interest in the pageant and fairy tale, as to them it appears, of the life in castles and palaces, the life of the great, bears witness to a like imaginative strain in them also, a strain tending after the elevated and the beautiful. In short, what Goethe describes as 'was uns alle bändigt, *das Gemeine*—that which holds us all in bondage, the common and ignoble,' is, notwithstanding its admitted prevalence, contrary to a deep-seated instinct of human nature and repelled by it. Of civilisation, which is to humanise us in society, we demand, before we will consent to be satisfied with it—we demand, however much else it may give us, that it shall give us, too, the *interesting*.

Now, the great sources of the *interesting* are distinction and beauty: that which is elevated, and that which is beautiful. Let us take the beautiful first, and consider how far it is present in American civilisation. Evidently this is that civilisation's weak side. There is little to nourish and delight the sense of beauty there. In the long-settled States east of the Alleghanies the landscape in general is not interesting, the climate harsh and in extremes. The Americans are restless, eager to better themselves and to make fortunes; the inhabitant does not strike his roots lovingly down into the soil, as in rural England. In the valley of the Connecticut you will find farm after farm which the Yankee settler has abandoned in order to go West, leaving the farm to some new Irish immigrant. The charm of beauty which comes from ancientness and permanence of rural life the country could not yet have in a high degree, but it has it in an

even less degree than might be expected. Then the Americans
come originally, for the most part, from that great class in English society amongst whom the sense for conduct and business
is much more strongly developed than the sense for beauty. If
we in England were without the cathedrals, parish churches,   5
and castles of the catholic and feudal age, and without the
houses of the Elizabethan age, but had only the towns and
buildings which the rise of our middle class has created in the
modern age, we should be in much the same case as the Americans. We should be living with much the same absence of train-   10
ing for the sense of beauty through the eye, from the aspect of
outward things. The American cities have hardly anything to
please a trained or a natural sense for beauty. They have buildings which cost a great deal of money and produce a certain
effect—buildings, shall I say, such as our Midland Station at St.   15
Pancras; but nothing such as Somerset House or Whitehall.
One architect of genius they had—Richardson. I had the pleasure to know him; he is dead, alas! Much of his work was injured by the conditions under which he was obliged to execute
it; I can recall but one building, and that of no great impor-   20
tance, where he seems to have had his own way, to be fully himself; but that is indeed excellent. In general, where the Americans succeed best in their architecture—in that art so indicative
and educative of a people's sense for beauty—is in the fashion of
their villa-cottages in wood. These are often original and at the   25
same time very pleasing, but they are pretty and coquettish, not
beautiful. Of the really beautiful in the other arts, and in literature, very little has been produced there as yet. I asked a German portrait-painter, whom I found painting and prospering in
America, how he liked the country? 'How *can* an artist like it?'   30
was his answer. The American artists live chiefly in Europe; all
Americans of cultivation and wealth visit Europe more and
more constantly. The mere nomenclature of the country acts
upon a cultivated person like the incessant pricking of pins.
What people in whom the sense for beauty and fitness was   35
quick could have invented, or could tolerate, the hideous names
ending in *ville*, the Briggsvilles, Higginsvilles, Jacksonvilles, rife
from Maine to Florida; the jumble of unnatural and inappro-

priate names everywhere? On the line from Albany to Buffalo
you have, in one part, half the names in the classical dictionary
to designate the stations; it is said that the folly is due to a surveyor who, when the country was laid out, happened to possess
5   a classical dictionary; but a people with any artist-sense would
have put down that surveyor. The Americans meekly retain
his names; and indeed his strange Marcellus or Syracuse is perhaps not much worse than their congenital Briggsville.

So much as to beauty, and as to the provision, in the United
10   States, for the sense of beauty. As to distinction, and the interest which human nature seeks from enjoying the effect made
upon it by what is elevated, the case is much the same. There
is very little to create such an effect, very much to thwart it.
Goethe says somewhere that 'the thrill of awe is the best thing
15   humanity has':—

Das Schaudern ist der Menschheit bestes Theil.

But, if there be a discipline in which the Americans are wanting,
it is the discipline of awe and respect. An austere and intense
religion imposed on their Puritan founders the discipline of re-
20   spect, and so provided for them the thrill of awe; but this religion is dying out. The Americans have produced plenty of men
strong, shrewd, upright, able, effective; very few who are
highly distinguished. Alexander Hamilton is indeed a man of
rare distinction; Washington, though he has not the high men-
25   tal distinction of Pericles or Cæsar, has true distinction of style
and character. But these men belong to the pre-American age.
Lincoln's recent American biographers declare that Washington is but an Englishman, an English officer; the typical American, they say, is Abraham Lincoln. Now Lincoln is shrewd,
30   sagacious, humorous, honest, courageous, firm; he is a man
with qualities deserving the most sincere esteem and praise, but
he has not distinction.

In truth everything is against distinction in America, and
against the sense of elevation to be gained through admiring
35   and respecting it. The glorification of 'the average man,' who
is quite a religion with statesmen and publicists there, is against

it. The addiction to 'the funny man,' who is a national misfortune there, is against it. Above all, the newspapers are against it.

It is often said that every nation has the government it deserves. What is much more certain is that every nation has the newspapers it deserves. The newspaper is the direct product of the want felt; the supply answers closely and inevitably to the demand. I suppose no one knows what the American newspapers are, who has not been obliged, for some length of time, to read either those newspapers or none at all. Powerful and valuable contributions occur scattered about in them. But on the whole, and taking the total impression and effect made by them, I should say that if one were searching for the best means to efface and kill in a whole nation the discipline of respect, the feeling for what is elevated, one could not do better than take the American newspapers. The absence of truth and soberness in them, the poverty in serious interest, the personality and sensation-mongering, are beyond belief. There are a few newspapers which are in whole, or in part, exceptions. The *New York Nation*, a weekly paper, may be paralleled with the *Saturday Review* as it was in its old and good days; but the *New York Nation* is conducted by a foreigner, and has an extremely small sale. In general, the daily papers are such that when one returns home one is moved to admiration and thankfulness not only at the great London papers, like the *Times* or the *Standard*, but quite as much at the great provincial newspapers too—papers like the *Leeds Mercury* and the *Yorkshire Post* in the north of England, like the *Scotsman* and the *Glasgow Herald* in Scotland.

The Americans used to say to me that what they valued was news, and that this their newspapers gave them. I at last made the reply: 'Yes, news for the servants' hall!' I remember that a New York newspaper, one of the first I saw after landing in the country, had a long account, with the prominence we should give to the illness of the German Emperor or the arrest of the Lord Mayor of Dublin, of a young woman who had married a man who was a bag of bones, as we say, and who used to exhibit himself as a skeleton; of her growing horror in living with this man, and finally of her death. All this in the most minute detail, and described with all the writer's powers of rhetoric. This has always remained by me as a specimen of what the Americans call news.

5   You must have lived amongst their newspapers to know what they are. If I relate some of my own experiences, it is because these will give a clear enough notion of what the newspapers over there are, and one remembers more definitely what has happened to oneself. Soon after arriving in Boston, I opened a

10   Boston newspaper and came upon a column headed: 'Tickings.' By *tickings* we are to understand news conveyed through the tickings of the telegraph. The first 'ticking' was: 'Matthew Arnold is sixty-two years old'—an age, I must just say in passing, which I had not then reached. The second 'ticking' was:

15   'Wales says, Mary is a darling;' the meaning being, that the Prince of Wales expressed great admiration for Miss Mary Anderson. This was at Boston, the American Athens. I proceeded to Chicago. An evening paper was given me soon after I arrived; I opened it, and found under a large-type heading,

20   '*We have seen him arrive,*' the following picture of myself: 'He has harsh features, supercilious manners, parts his hair down the middle, wears a single eyeglass and ill-fitting clothes.' Notwithstanding this rather unfavourable introduction I was most kindly and hospitably received at Chicago. It happened that I

25   had a letter for Mr. Medill, an elderly gentleman of Scotch descent, the editor of the chief newspaper in those parts, the *Chicago Tribune*. I called on him, and we conversed amicably together. Some time afterwards, when I had gone back to England, a New York paper published a criticism of Chicago and

30   its people, purporting to have been contributed by me to the *Pall Mall Gazette* over here. It was a poor hoax, but many people were taken in and were excusably angry, Mr. Medill of the *Chicago Tribune* amongst the number. A friend telegraphed to me to know if I had written the criticism. I, of course, in-

35   stantly telegraphed back that I had not written a syllable of it. Then a Chicago paper is sent to me; and what I have the pleasure of reading, as the result of my contradiction, is this: 'Ar-

nold denies; Mr. Medill [my old friend] refuses to accept Arnold's disclaimer; says Arnold is a cur.'

I once declared that in England the born lover of ideas and of light could not but feel that the sky over his head is of brass and iron. And so I say that, in America, he who craves for the 5 *interesting* in civilisation, he who requires from what surrounds him satisfaction for his sense of beauty, his sense for elevation, will feel the sky over his head to be of brass and iron. The human problem, then, is as yet solved in the United States most imperfectly; a great void exists in the civilisation over there: a 10 want of what is elevated and beautiful, of what is interesting.

The want is grave; it was probably, though he does not exactly bring it out, influencing Sir Lepel Griffin's feelings when he said that America is one of the last countries in which one would like to live. The want is such as to make any edu- 15 cated man feel that many countries, much less free and prosperous than the United States, are yet more truly civilised; have more which is interesting, have more to say to the soul; are countries, therefore, in which one would rather live.

The want is graver because it is so little recognised by the 20 mass of Americans; nay, so loudly denied by them. If the community over there perceived the want and regretted it, sought for the right ways of remedying it, and resolved that remedied it should be; if they said, or even if a number of leading spirits amongst them said: 'Yes, we see what is wanting to our civilisa- 25 tion, we see that the average man is a danger, we see that our newspapers are a scandal, that bondage to the common and ignoble is our snare; but under the circumstances our civilisation could not well have been expected to begin differently. What you see are *beginnings*, they are crude, they are too 30 predominantly material, they omit much, leave much to be desired—but they could not have been otherwise, they have been inevitable, and we will rise above them;' if the Americans frankly said this, one would have not a word to bring against it. One would *then* insist on no shortcoming, one would ac- 35 cept their admission that the human problem is at present quite insufficiently solved by them, and would press the matter no

further. One would congratulate them on having solved the
political problem and the social problem so successfully, and
only remark, as I have said already, that in seeing clear and
thinking straight on *our* political and social questions, we have
5   great need to follow the example they set us on theirs.

But now the Americans seem, in certain matters, to have
agreed, as a people, to deceive themselves, to persuade themselves that they have what they have not, to cover the defects
in their civilisation by boasting, to fancy that they well and
10   truly solve, not only the political and social problem, but the
human problem too. One would say that they do really hope
to find in tall talk and inflated sentiment a substitute for that
real sense of elevation which human nature, as I have said, instinctively craves—and a substitute which may do as well as the
15   genuine article. The thrill of awe, which Goethe pronounces to
be the best thing humanity has, they would fain create by proclaiming themselves at the top of their voices to be 'the greatest nation upon earth,' by assuring one another, in the language
of their national historian, that American democracy proceeds
20   in its ascent 'as uniformly and majestically as the laws of being,
and is as certain as the decrees of eternity.'

Or, again, far from admitting that their newspapers are a
scandal, they assure one another that their newspaper press is
one of their most signal distinctions. Far from admitting that in
25   literature they have as yet produced little that is important,
they play at treating American literature as if it were a great
independent power; they reform the spelling of the English
language by the insight of their average man. For every English
writer they have an American writer to match. And him good
30   Americans read; the Western States are at this moment being
nourished and formed, we hear, on the novels of a native author
called Roe, instead of those of Scott and Dickens. Far from admitting that their average man is a danger, and that his predominance has brought about a plentiful lack of refinement,
35   distinction, and beauty, they declare in the words of my friend
Colonel Higginson, a prominent critic at Boston, that 'Nature
said, some years since: "Thus far the English is my best race,
but we have had Englishmen enough; put in one drop more of

nervous fluid and make the American." And with that drop a
new range of promise opened on the human race, and a lighter,
finer, more highly organised type of mankind was born.' Far
from admitting that the American accent, as the pressure of
their climate and of their average man has made it, is a thing to   5
be striven against, they assure one another that it is the right
accent, the standard English speech of the future. It reminds
me of a thing in Smollet's dinner-party of authors. Seated by
'the philosopher who is writing a most orthodox refutation of
Bolingbroke, but in the meantime has just been presented to the   10
Grand Jury as a public nuisance for having blasphemed in an
alehouse on the Lord's day'—seated by this philosopher is 'the
Scotchman who is giving lectures on the pronunciation of the
English language.'

The worst of it is, that all this tall talk and self-glorification   15
meets with hardly any rebuke from sane criticism over there.
I will mention, in regard to this, a thing which struck me a
good deal. A Scotchman who has made a great fortune at Pittsburgh, a kind friend of mine, one of the most hospitable and
generous of men, Mr. Andrew Carnegie, published a year or   20
two ago a book called *Triumphant Democracy*, a most splendid
picture of American progress. The book is full of valuable information, but religious people thought that it insisted too much
on mere material progress, and did not enough set forth America's deficiencies and dangers. And a friendly clergyman in   25
Massachusetts, telling me how he regretted this, and how apt
the Americans are to shut their eyes to their own dangers, put
into my hands a volume written by a leading minister among
the Congregationalists, a very prominent man, which he said
supplied a good antidote to my friend Mr. Carnegie's book.   30
The volume is entitled *Our Country*. I read it through. The
author finds in evangelical Protestantism, as the orthodox Protestant sects present it, the grand remedy for the deficiencies
and dangers of America. On this I offer no criticism; what
struck me, and that on which I wish to lay stress, is, the writer's   35
entire failure to perceive that such self-glorification and self-
deception as I have been mentioning is one of America's dangers, or even that it *is* self-deception at all. He himself shares in

all the self-deception of the average man among his countrymen, he flatters it. In the very points where a serious critic
would find the Americans most wanting he finds them superior;
only they require to have a good dose of evangelical Protes-
5   tantism still added. 'Ours is the elect nation,' preaches this reformer of American faults—'ours is the elect nation for the age
to come. We are the chosen people.' Already, says he, we are
taller and heavier than other men, longer lived than other men,
richer and more energetic than other men, above all, 'of finer
10   nervous organisation' than other men. Yes, this people, who
endure to have the American newspaper for their daily reading,
and to have their habitation in Briggsville, Jacksonville, and
Marcellus—this people is of finer, more delicate nervous organisation than other nations! It is Colonel Higginson's 'drop more
15   of nervous fluid,' over again. This 'drop' plays a stupendous part
in the American rhapsody of self-praise. Undoubtedly the
Americans are highly nervous, both the men and the women. A
great Paris physician says that he notes a distinct new form of
nervous disease, produced in American women by worry
20   about servants. But this nervousness, developed in the race out
there by worry, overwork, want of exercise, injudicious diet,
and a most trying climate—this morbid nervousness our friends
ticket as the fine susceptibility of genius, and cite it as a proof
of their distinction, of their superior capacity for civilisation!
25   'The roots of civilisation are the nerves,' says our Congregation-
alist instructor again; 'and, other things being equal, the finest
nervous organisation will produce the highest civilisation. Now,
the finest nervous organisation is ours.'

The new West promises to beat in the game of brag even the
30   stout champions I have been quoting. Those belong to the old
Eastern States; and the other day there was sent to me a Cali-
fornian newspaper which calls all the Easterners 'the unhappy
denizens of a forbidding clime,' and adds: 'The time will surely
come when all roads will lead to California. Here will be the
35   home of art, science, literature, and profound knowledge.'

Common-sense criticism, I repeat, of all this hollow stuff
there is in America next to none. There are plenty of cultivated, judicious, delightful individuals there. They are our hope

and America's hope; it is through their means that improvement must come. They know perfectly well how false and hollow the boastful stuff talked is; but they let the storm of self-laudation rage, and say nothing. For political opponents and their doings there are in America hard words to be heard in abundance; for the real faults in American civilisation, and for the foolish boasting which prolongs them, there is hardly a word of regret or blame, at least in public. Even in private, many of the most cultivated Americans shrink from the subject, are irritable and thin-skinned when it is canvassed. Public treatment of it, in a cool and sane spirit of criticism, there is none. In vain I might plead that I had set a good example of frankness, in confessing over here, that, so far from solving our problems successfully, we in England find ourselves with an upper class materialised, a middle class vulgarised, and a lower class brutalised. But it seems that nothing will embolden an American critic to say firmly and aloud to his countrymen and to his newspapers, that in America they do not solve the human problem successfully, and that with their present methods they never can. Consequently the masses of the American people do really come to believe all they hear about their finer nervous organisation, and the rightness of the American accent, and the importance of American literature; that is to say, they see things not as they are, but as they would like them to be; they deceive themselves totally. And by such self-deception they shut against themselves the door to improvement, and do their best to make the reign of *das Gemeine* eternal. In what concerns the solving of the political and social problem they see clear and think straight; in what concerns the higher civilisation they live in a fool's paradise. This it is which makes a famous French critic speak of 'the hard unintelligence of the people of the United States'—*la dure inintelligence des Américains du Nord*—of the very people who in general pass for being specially intelligent—and so, within certain limits, they are. But they have been so plied with nonsense and boasting that outside those limits, and where it is a question of things in which their civilisation is weak, they seem, very many of them, as if in such things they had no power of perception whatever, no idea of a proper scale, no sense of the difference between good and bad. And at this rate they can never, after solving the political and social problem with success, go on to solve happily the human problem too, and thus at last to make their civilisation full and interesting.

To sum up, then. What really dissatisfies in American civilisation is the want of the *interesting*, a want due chiefly to the want of those two great elements of the interesting, which are elevation and beauty. And the want of these elements is increased and prolonged by the Americans being assured that they have them when they have them not. And it seems to me that what the Americans now most urgently require, is not so much a vast additional development of orthodox Protestantism, but rather a steady exhibition of cool and sane criticism by their men of light and leading over there. And perhaps the very first step of such men should be to insist on having for America, and to create if need be, better newspapers.

To us, too, the future of the United States is of incalculable importance. Already we feel their influence much, and we shall feel it more. We have a good deal to learn from them; we shall find in them, also, many things to beware of, many points in which it is to be hoped our democracy may not be like theirs. As our country becomes more democratic, the malady here may no longer be that we have an upper class materialised, a middle class vulgarised, and a lower class brutalised. But the predominance of the common and ignoble, born of the predominance of the average man, is a malady too. That the common and ignoble is human nature's enemy, that, of true human nature, distinction and beauty are needs, that a civilisation is insufficient where these needs are not satisfied, faulty where they are thwarted, is an instruction of which we, as well as the Americans, may greatly require to take fast hold, and not to let go. We may greatly require to keep, as if it were our life, the doctrine that we are failures after all, if we cannot eschew vain boasting and vain imaginations, eschew what flatters in us the common and ignoble, and approve things that are truly excellent.

I have mentioned evangelical Protestantism. There is a text which evangelical Protestantism—and for that matter Catholicism too—translates wrong and takes in a sense too narrow. The text is that well-known one: 'Except a man be born again he cannot see the kingdom of God.' Instead of *again*, we ought to translate *from above;* and instead of taking the kingdom of God in the sense of a life in Heaven above, we ought to take it, as its speaker meant it, in the sense of the reign of saints, a renovated and perfected human society on earth, the ideal society of the future. In the life of such a society, in the life *from above*, the life born of inspiration or *the spirit*—in that life elevation and beauty are not everything; but they are much, and they are indispensable. Humanity cannot reach its ideal while it lacks them: 'Except a man be born *from above*, he cannot have part in the society of the future.'

Appendix I

Reports of Public Lectures and
Brief Notes in the Press

[ROYAL ACADEMY BANQUET (1881)]

[On Saturday evening, April 30, 1881, the anniversary banquet
of the Royal Academy of Arts was held at Burlington House to
signal the opening of the annual exhibition. Sir Frederick
Leighton, president of the Academy, presided. After toasts to
5 the Queen and the Royal family, the Army and the Navy, and
Her Majesty's Government, the president said:] "No task is
more congenial to the occupant of this chair, be he who he
may, than that of proposing the toast which custom places
next on our list—the toast in which we do homage to Science
10 and Literature. . . . In response to Literature, I, a lover of form,
gladly call on a writer to whom form is peculiarly dear, and
who has for this response a twofold qualification. He is a most
happy poet, and withal a critic not to be surpassed, if he be
equalled, in the subtle felicities of his insight (cheers); a writer
15 in whom a keen and Attic spirit finds utterance in speech more
than usually chastened, bright and supple—a seeker after light,
the foe of all Philistines—Matthew Arnold." (Cheers.) [After
Sir William Grove responded for Science,]

Mr. M. ARNOLD, who was cheered, said,—Sir Frederick
20 Leighton, your Royal Highnesses, my Lords, and Gentlemen,—
I have to thank you for doing honour to the toast of "Literature," and I have to thank you, Mr. President, for the kind
way in which you have joined with the toast my name. I suppose everybody must be in some degree conscious that the gen-
25 eral estimate of literature, of its powers and value, is not at
present quite what it once was. The French divide the matters
taught in their primary schools into obligatory and facultative.

I cannot but be conscious, when this toast of "Science and Literature" is given, that in what tends to become the popular view it is Sir William Grove and Science who are obligatory; it is I and Literature who are facultative. Science is necessary, and of literature, the newspapers; the rest—all that you and I, Mr. President, understand by literature—is a facultative extra, more or less interesting and ornamental. I am not now, of course, going to combat this estimate; I only say that it prevails, and that it makes, perhaps, the task of speaking for Literature a little depressing. But there is one consoling thought which in this Royal Academy of Arts can hardly fail to visit the man of letters; it is that we and you are, if I may venture to say so, in the same boat. Whatever polite things Sir William Grove may say to you, you and we are in the same boat. Before their sister, Science, now so full of promise and pride, was born, there were Art and Literature, like twins together, innocently believing in their own necessity, as eager in the pursuit of the eternal and unseizable shadow, beauty, as if they were pursuing something positive. If we are not necessary, you are not necessary. From you, at least, when Science is bidding us stand on one side, we may hope for sympathy. And the same thought of your sympathy comes to my aid, too, when I turn to your other guests, even more splendid than the men of science; when I survey this brilliant company of Princes, Ministers of State, noble and wealthy patrons of art, whom you have collected round you, and wonder what can have induced you to import among them such an inutility as a poor man of letters. After all, with us you have sympathies which you cannot have with these grander guests. Their functions are high and honourable, their sympathy with art and literature is refining and precious; yet how remote is their experience and career from ours. Take one point only. Our struggle—yours and ours—what do they know of it? What do they know of it, these favourites of fortune, for whom existence, at any rate, has been always secure and easy, and who, so far as the great first needs of our poor mortality are concerned—lodging, food, and raiment—never passed an anxious hour; what do they know of the struggle through which even the most gifted and successful artists and

authors have often to pass at the outset, and from which many
and many a one among us never emerges? What do they know,
by the sharp experience of themselves or of those dear to them,
of all that tragical history of

5   "the fear that kills,
                          "And hope that is unwilling to be fed;
                          "Cold, pain, and labour, and all fleshly ills,
                          "And mighty poets in their misery dead?"

They know nothing of it, they can know nothing of it. But as
10   long as art and literature exist, so long will the artist and the
man of letters have an indestructible bond of sympathy in the
common experience of that stern apprenticeship which both
must so often traverse. And with this sympathy between us,
however august the company which you collect around you,
15   even the humblest man of letters may feel, as I do to-night, that
at your table he is at the table of friends, and that your welcome to him is not less cordial than it is courteous. (Cheers.)
                    —*The Times*, *Monday*, May 2, 1881, p. 13, cols. 3–4

[THE BEST HUNDRED BOOKS]

"Lists such as Sir John Lubbock's," [Mr. Matthew Arnold]
20   writes, "are interesting things to look at, but I feel no disposition to make one." Mr. Matthew Arnold is busy with educational work of another kind—and, besides, has he not told us
already "who prop in these bad days his mind"—Homer, to wit,
and Epictetus and Sophocles?
25   —*Pall Mall Gazette*, January 29, 1886, p. 4

[MR. MATTHEW ARNOLD INSTRUCTING
AMERICANS ON THE IRISH QUESTION]

At a recent meeting of a body calling itself "the American
Branch of the Irish Loyal and Patriotic Union" of New York,
the following characteristic letter from Mr. Matthew Arnold
was read:—

The Buffalo Club, Buffalo, June 28, 1886

To J. C. O'Connor, Esq., Jun.:

My dear Sir,—I cannot possibly attend your meeting to-morrow, but I am glad you are going to hold it. I hope you will make clear one point in especial. Mr. Gladstone says that he insists on the "principle of giving Ireland an effective government by Irishmen," and would gladly have the world believe that all his opponents are hostile to this principle. On the contrary, all the best of them are favourable to it. But they think his proposed mode of giving effect to it a bad and dangerous one. Mr. Bright is as favourable as Mr. Gladstone to "the principle of permitting Ireland, with proper limitations, to govern herself." But the question is what these proper limitations are. Mr. Bright believes, and the best of the Liberal party believe, that a national Irish Parliament would be a sure source of trouble in the future, and that some plan for Irish self-government must be found which does not involve the establishment of such a Parliament. If Mr. Gladstone were twenty, or perhaps only ten, years younger, he would think and say the same. But he is in a hurry; he wants to settle the Irish question at once, and he thinks he sees his way to settling it for the moment by securing the Parnellite vote, which can be secured only by conceding a national Irish Parliament. The trouble in the future he will not live to see.

Let Americans ask themselves what they would have thought of a statesman who assumed that the only way of giving the Southern States an effective government by Southerners was to create a general Southern Congress at Richmond. With the talents which the Southern men have for politics and oratory, such a Congress would inevitably have grown into a power confronting the Washington Congress and embarrassing it, however sincerely the Southern men might have professed, in first asking for it, that into this it should never grow. So as to Ireland. The very talents of the Irish for politics and oratory will inevitably make an Irish Parliament grow into a power confronting the Imperial Parliament and embarrassing it, however sincerely the Irish may now profess that they do not mean their Parliament to grow into anything of the kind. I by no means blame them for asking for such a Parliament. But I say that an English Minister who concedes it may be a dexterous politician and parliamentary manager, but is no statesman.

Let, however, "the principle of giving Ireland an effective 5 Government by Irishmen" be your principle as firmly as it is Mr. Gladstone's.—Very faithfully yours, MATTHEW ARNOLD. —*Pall Mall Gazette*, July 19, 1886, p. 4

[THIRTY-FIVE YEARS OF SCHOOL INSPECTING: MR. MATTHEW ARNOLD'S FAREWELL]

[A testimonial was given to Arnold on the evening of November 12, 1886, upon his retirement from the inspectorship of 10 schools for the Westminster District, after service of thirty-five years. He made the following speech in acknowledgment:]

Ladies and gentlemen, I thank you with all my heart. I remember many years ago, and perhaps my friend, Mr. Healing, behind me will remember it too, that once, after we had been 15 inspecting a school in the north of London, we were entertained at luncheon by one of the managers, who said so many kind things about me that at last, growing embarrassed, I cut it short by saying, "Nobody can say I am a punctual inspector." (Laughter.) You have praised me so much that I feel almost 20 disposed to say something disparaging of myself now. The truth is, my path as an inspector has been made very smooth for me. Everywhere I have found kindness; everywhere I have favours to acknowledge and obligations to express. I hardly know where to begin.

25 I will begin where my obligations are least. To Government I owe nothing. (Cheers and laughter.) But then I have always remembered that under our Parliamentary system the Government probably takes little interest in such work, whatever it is, as I have been able to do in the public service, and even perhaps 30 knows nothing at all about it. And, ladies and gentlemen, we must take the evils of our system along with the good. Abroad probably a Minister might have known more about my performances. But then abroad I doubt whether I should ever

have survived to perform them. (Laughter.) Under the strict bureaucratic system abroad I feel pretty sure I should have been dismissed ten times over for the freedom with which on various occasions I have expressed myself on matters of religion and politics. (Laughter.) Our Government here in England takes a large and liberal view of what it considers a man's private affairs, and so I have been enabled to survive as an inspector for 35 years; and to the Government I at least owe this—to have been allowed to survive for 35 years.

When I pass from Government this somewhat bounded kind of obligation ceases, and my obligation becomes ample and full indeed. As to the permanent officials, past and present, of the Education Department, whether I take the living, Lord Lingen, Sir Francis Sandford (hear, hear), Mr. Cumin, or recall the names of the dead—Chester, Bowstead, Clough—I find only friends and friendliness to remember. Most of them have been my personal friends at the time of life when friendship has an intimacy and a savour which it can hardly acquire afterwards; but all the officials of the department with whom I have had to do have lightened for me the troubles of an inspector's life instead of aggravating them. I suppose the permanent officials are sometimes found by an inspector to be harsh and trying, but in that case I am like the dairymaid in the rustic poem, who found the dun cow that was vicious to others gentle to her. (Laughter.) If there is any viciousness in the breasts of permanent officials I never felt it; they have left with me no feelings for them but feelings of gratitude and affection. My colleagues the inspectors I have found always friendly and ready to help; we have had no quarrels nor an approach to one. Often and often I have admired work and qualities of theirs, and I rejoice to see succeeding me in my district one of them, for whom I have a special esteem—Mr. Sharpe. (Cheers.) Then my assistants—how my assistants have smoothed my path for me. I know it is thought at the office that an inspector's path is often too much smoothed for him by his assistant. (Laughter.) My rule was—and I think it a good one—to let my assistant do whatever he could do as well or better than I could myself. I found that to be a considerable quantity, I confess. But I do not

think my assistants felt themselves to be unfairly put upon.
(Hear, hear.) At any rate, they did not work for me as if they
did. What I owe to the assiduity, good sense, and cheerful good
temper of Mr. Healing, whom I have known ever since I ap-
5   prenticed him, a smooth-headed little boy in the Wesleyan
school at Cheltenham, I can never forget, and never tire of
acknowledging. Mr. Myhill was with me for a much shorter
time, but he, too, has left me full of regard and gratitude for
his zeal and trustworthiness. Lastly, I come to the managers and
10   teachers. From the time when the authorities of the Borough-
road and the Wesleyan Education Committee acquiesced in my
appointment, though it was made, let me tell you, irregularly
and with neglect of their right of veto, down to the other day,
when Canon Fleming insisted on entertaining from the Confer-
15   ence quite an unreasonably large party of us, the managers, too,
have been my kind friends. And the teachers! When I think of
their good will, their confidence in me, their alacrity to comply with my wishes—when I think of all this, crowned finally
by our meeting to-night and by their beautiful gift—I am in-
20   deed disposed to say with Wordsworth that it is the gratitude
of man which leaves one mourning.

I ask myself with astonishment to what I owe this confidence,
this favour. I assure you I am not at all a harsh judge of myself.
But I know perfectly well that there have been much better
25   inspectors than I; I could enumerate and I have seen in my
colleagues dozens of merits which I do not possess. Whence,
then, all this favour and confidence towards me? Well, one
cause of it was certainly that I was my father's son (cheers);
another cause has been, I think, that I am more or less known
30   to the public as an author (hear, hear), and I have been always
touched to see how the teachers—so often reproached with
being fault-finders and overweening—are disposed to defer to
their inspector on the score of any repute he may have as an
author (hear, hear), although, undoubtedly, an author of repute
35   may be but a bad inspector. However, I do not mean to say
that I think I have been altogether a bad inspector. (Cheers.) I
think I have had two qualifications for the post. One is that of
having a serious sense of the nature and function of criticism. I
from the first sought to see the schools as they really were. Thus

it was soon felt that I was fair (hear, hear), and that the
teachers had not to apprehend from me crotchets, pedantries,
humours, favouritism, and prejudices. (Cheers.)

That was one qualification. Another was that I got the habit,
very early in my time, of trying to put myself in the place of
the teachers whom I was inspecting. I will tell you how that
came about. Though I am a schoolmaster's son I confess that
school teaching or school inspecting is not the line of life I
should naturally have chosen. I adopted it in order to marry a
lady who is here to-night, and who feels the kindness as warmly
and gratefully as I do. (Cheers.) My wife and I had a wandering life of it at first. There were but three lay inspectors for all
England. My district went right across from Pembroke Dock
to Great Yarmouth. We had no home; one of our children was
born in a lodging at Derby, with a workhouse, if I recollect
right, behind and a penitentiary in front. (Laughter.) But the
irksomeness of my new duties was what I felt most, and during
the first year or so this was sometimes almost insupportable.
But I met daily in the schools with men and women discharging
duties akin to mine, duties as irksome as mine, duties less well
paid than mine, and I asked myself, Are they on roses? Would
not they by nature prefer, many of them, to go where they
liked and do what they liked, instead of being shut up in
school? I saw them making the best of it; I saw the cheerfulness
and efficiency with which they did their work, and I asked
myself again, How do they do it? Gradually it grew into a
habit with me to put myself into their places, to try and enter
into their feelings, to represent to myself their life, and I assure you I got many lessons from them. This placed me in
sympathy with them. Seeing people once a year is not much,
but when you have come into sympathy with them they do
not fade from your mind, and I find myself able to recall, and
almost daily recalling, names and faces and circumstances of
teachers whom I have not seen for years. That is because I have
been in sympathy with them. I will not accept all the praise
you have given me, but I will accept this—I have been fair and
I have been sympathetic. (Cheers.)

And now, my kind friends of many years, before we come
to the word which, as Byron tells us, must be and hath been, al-

though it makes us linger, the word farewell, let me say that
I had hoped to come round and take leave of you all in your
schools before meeting you here. I have not been able quite
to accomplish this yet, but those of you whom I have not al-
5   ready visited at your schools I hope to visit there shortly.
(Cheers.) And before we now part I wish to give a counsel
and to make a reflection. First, the counsel. You have a very
strong association, the Elementary Teachers' Union. Some people would say it was too strong. I do not think so (hear, hear);
10   but I wish it would concentrate its strength in one object in the
first place, and let other objects be until this one is gained. Insist on having a Minister for Education. (Cheers.) I know the
Duke of Richmond told the House of Lords that, as Lord President, he was Minister of Education (laughter); but really the
15   Duke of Richmond's sense of humour must have been slumber-
ing when he told the House of Lords that. A man is not Minister of Education by taking the name, but by doing the functions. (Cheers.) To do the functions he must put his mind to
the subject of education; and so long as Lord Presidents are
20   what they are, and education is what it is, a Lord President will
not be a man who puts his mind to the subject of education. A
Vice-President is not—on the Lord President's own showing—
and cannot be, Minister for Education; he cannot, therefore, be
made responsible for mistakes and neglects. Now, what we
25   want in a Minister for Education is this—a centre where we
can fix the responsibility. Insist, therefore—as you, the chief
sufferers by mistakes and neglects in the management of education, have a right to insist—insist on having a Minister for Education.

30   There is my counsel; now for my reflection. My reflection
is one to comfort and cheer myself, and I hope others, at this
our parting. We are entering upon new times, where many
influences, once potent to guide and restrain, are failing. Some
people think the prospect of the reign of democracy, as they
35   call it, very gloomy. This is unwise, but no one can regard it
quite without anxiety. It is nearly 150 years since the wisest of
English clergymen told the Lord Mayor and Sheriffs of London in a hospital sermon that the poor are very much what the
rich make them. (Hear, hear.) That is profoundly true, though

perhaps it rather startles us to hear it. On the other hand, it is almost a commonplace that children are very much what their teachers make them. I will not ask what our masses are likely to be if the rich have the making of them. I prefer to ask what they are likely to be so far as the teachers have the making of 5 them. And on the whole—and here is the consoling reflection with which I shall end—though the teachers have, of course, their faults as individuals, though they have also their faults as a class, yet, on the whole, their action is, I do think and believe, powerful for good. (Hear, hear.) And not in England 10 only, but in other countries as well, countries where the teachers have been much spoken against, I have found it so. I find plenty of deleterious and detestable influences at work, but they are influences of journalism in one place, in another influences of politicians, in some places both the one and the 15 other; they are not influences of teachers. The influence of the elementary teacher, so far as my observation extends, is for good; it helps morality and virtue. I do not give the teacher too much praise for this; the child in his hands so appeals to his conscience, his responsibility is so direct and palpable. But the 20 fact is none the less consoling, and the fact is, I believe, as I have stated it. Burke speaks of the ancient and inbred integrity and piety of the English people; where should this influence of the teachers for good be so strong and sustained as here? Thus, in conclusion, we are carried beyond and above the question of 25 my personal gratitude, although that, too, is very deep and real. I love to think of the elementary teachers, to whom I owe so much and am so grateful, as more and more proving themselves to deserve, and more and more coming to possess, in the days which are now at hand for us, the esteem and gratitude of 30 the entire country. (Cheers.)

—*The Times*, November 13, 1886, p. 5, cols. 5–6

[ENGLISH AT THE UNIVERSITIES]

We have received the following communication from Mr. Matthew Arnold:—

I have no difficulty in saying that I should like to see standard 35 English authors joined to the standard authors of Greek and

Latin literature who have to be taken up for a pass, or for
honours, at the Universities.

I should be sorry to see a separate School, with degrees and
honours, for the modern languages as such, although it is de-
5   sirable that the professors and teachers of those languages
should give certificates of fitness to teach them.

I would add no literature except that of our own country to
the classical literature taken up for the degree, whether with
or without honours, in Arts.

10   These seem to me to be elementary propositions, when one
is laying down what is desirable in respect to the University
degree in Arts. The omission of the mother tongue and its
literature in school and University instruction is peculiar, so
far as I know, to England. You do a good work in urging us
15   to repair that omission.

But I will not conceal from you that I have no confidence
in those who at the Universities regulate studies, degrees, and
honours. To regulate these matters great experience of the
world, steadiness, simplicity, breadth of view, are desirable; I
20   do not see how those who actually regulate them can well have
these qualifications; I am sure that in what they have done in
the last forty years they have not shown them. Restlessness, a
disposition to try experiments and to multiply studies and
schools, are what they have shown, and what they will prob-
25   ably continue to show—and this though personally many of
them may be very able and distinguished men. I fear, therefore,
that while you are seeking an object altogether good—the completing of the old and great degree in Arts—you may obtain
something which will not only not be that, but will be a posi-
30   tive hindrance to it.

                                   —*Pall Mall Budget*, January 6, 1887, p. 14
                                   —*Pall Mall Gazette*, January 7, 1887, pp. 1–2

[FINE PASSAGES IN VERSE AND PROSE;
SELECTED BY LIVING MEN OF LETTERS]

Mr. Matthew Arnold writes:—
Acts of mental judgment attempted in compliance with a sud-

den call like yours, are difficult and untrustworthy. I should
not like to pronounce on the spur of the moment, what work or
what passage, in prose and poetry, I think the best of those
known to me. But independently of any such weighing, comparing, and judging as is needed for this, we have a positive 5
test of the degree in which *passages* at any rate, have moved
and pleased us, from the force with which such passages have
lodged themselves in our mind and memory. Applying this
test, I should say that no passages have moved and pleased me
more than, in poetry, the lines describing the pity of Zeus for 10
the horses of Achilles (*Iliad*, xvii. 441–447), and the famous
stanza of Horace, "Linquenda tellus," &c [*Odes* II, xiv, 21–24];
in prose, Bossuet's passage on St. Paul and Plato, quoted at
p. 72 of my *Essays in Criticism*, and Burke's tribute to John
Howard, the prison reformer. . . . 15

Passages from the Bible I leave out of account. Things like
"Foxes have holes," &c., comply with the test mentioned as
much as anything in the world, but in their case the conditions
are somewhat different.

—Fortnightly Review, XLVIII, 299 (August, 1887) 20

[AN OLIVE BRANCH FROM AMERICA: AN ANGLO-AMERICAN COPYRIGHT]

From Mr. Matthew Arnold.

Pain's Hill, Cobham

As to copyright . . . I have read Mr. Pearsall Smith; his plan
is not favourable to the British author. I am not prepared to
accept his assertion that of the difference between the cost 25
price and the price paid by the buyer the trade gets seven-
eighths and the author only one-eighth. I believe that I get from
Macmillan for the American edition of my books a larger share
of the profit than Mr. Pearsall Smith's plan would give me.
When therefore he says 'a privilege that is obtainable,' &c., I 30
must meet him by a strong doubt whether what he offers me
is a privilege. If it were a privilege, however, I should still at
present decline the discussion of it. 'Congress,' he says, 'will always find it difficult to resist the pressure of numberless con-

stituents against the suppression of the cheap reprints so long
in use.' It will indeed. America is governed, as Mr. Hawley says,
'by and for the average man;' and so long as this average man, in
America, is what he is, he will not give to the British author
5   copyright. As I have said somewhere or other, he has not *delicacy* enough to feel the author's claims; he feels only that he
himself has 'a good thing' and had better keep it. A similar ruling power here in England would do just as the American
people does. Perhaps in France and Italy *the people* might be
10   trusted to feel with the author and artist, but nowhere else. The
standard must be higher in America generally, not here and
there only, before we shall get copyright.
                    —*Nineteenth Century*, XXII, 619 (November, 1887)

[REMARKS AT UNIVERSITY COLLEGE, BRISTOL]

[At the Victoria Rooms, Clifton, Bristol, on the evening of
15   March 8, 1888, Arnold lectured on "Life in America" in aid of
the Bristol University College Students' Endowment Fund to
set up chairs of English Literature and History and of Classical
History and Literature. After a vote of thanks to the lecturer,
carried amid applause,]
20   "Mr. Arnold, in returning thanks, said it was a great pleasure to him to be able to do anything for University College,
Bristol, especially because of its connection with Balliol, Oxford, where he had spent three of the happiest years of his life.
He hoped the College would get over the difficulties that were
25   besetting it, and if anything could be done to induce the
Government to give aid to Colleges of this sort, one of the endeavours of his life would be gratified, and a very great benefit would be conferred on the whole of the community (applause)."
30   —*The Bristol Times and Mirror*,
                               Friday, March 9, 1888, p. 8, col. 4

Appendix II

Prefatory Note
[TO *Essays in Criticism, Second Series*]

The collection of Essays contained in this volume was made by
Mr. Arnold himself, and they are, therefore, in the opinion of
a critic, at once competent and severe, worthy to be collected
and preserved. Severe is perhaps hardly an epithet ever properly applicable to Mr. Arnold; but his judgment was as serene   5
and unbiassed in regard to his own compositions as in regard
to those of any author whom from time to time he criticised.
But it was further characteristic of him to be content to say
one thing at one time; and he has been accused, not perhaps entirely without reason, of repeating the same thing in the same   10
words, sometimes almost to the weariness of the reader. This
habit, however, had at least the effect of fixing in the mind the
phrases, and therefore the thoughts or ideas which the phrases
conveyed, and with which for the moment he was concerned.
But in order to gather the mind of Mr. Arnold on the whole   15
of any subject, literary, political, or religious, it is often necessary to read more than one paper, because in each paper he
frequently deals with one aspect of a subject only, which requires, for sound and complete judgment, to be supplemented
or completed by another. It is especially necessary to bear this   20
in mind in reading what has become his last utterance on Shelley. In Shelley's case he is known to have intended to write
something more; not, indeed, to alter or to qualify what he
said, but to say something else which he thought also true, and
which needed saying.   25
    This is not the place to attempt a character of Mr. Arnold,
even as a critic or an essayist. A preface would expand into a
volume if it attempted to indicate even the materials for
thought on such subjects, handled by Mr. Arnold, as Poetry,

Gray, Keats, Shelley, Byron, Wordsworth (to name no others),
which are the subjects of some of the Essays here collected.
This is the last volume he ever put together, and it contains
some of his ripest, best, most interesting writing.

5   Perhaps it is well to add that these few words are contributed
at the request of others. *Inane munus* indeed, but all that a
friend can do!

C.

[John Duke, Lord Coleridge]

Appendix III

Advertisement
[TO DR. THOMAS ARNOLD'S *Fragment on the Church*]

10   The following pages are a part of a much larger work which
Dr. Arnold contemplated, but which was interrupted by his
early death.

The executors having kindly allowed me to fulfil my wishes
as to this fragment, I have felt it a duty not to withhold what
15   remains from his pen on the subject which so greatly occupied
his thoughts.

The references, which it was not his habit to make till after
the work for which they were required was completed, have
been in part supplied.

20   Before he began the work in the more historical form in
which it appears in these pages, he had already, on two occasions, approached the question of Church and State. These
fragmentary essays—for they are scarcely more—it is intended
to include in a volume containing some of his miscellaneous
25   works.

M. A.

Fox How, October 5, 1844

Critical and Explanatory Notes

References in the following notes to Arnold's diary-notebooks are drawn from H. F. Lowry, K. Young, and W. H. Dunn, eds., *The Note-Books of Matthew Arnold* (London: Oxford University Press, 1952), supplemented by W. B. Guthrie, ed., *Matthew Arnold's Diaries: the Unpublished Items* (Ann Arbor: University Microfilms, 1959). Letters of Arnold, if their source is not sufficiently indicated in the notes, can usually be found with the help of A. K. Davis, Jr., *Matthew Arnold's Letters: a Descriptive Checklist* (Charlottesville: The University Press of Virginia, 1968), a listing in chronological order indexed also by the name of the correspondent. The largest published collection of Arnold's letters is that gathered by G. W. E. Russell seven years after Arnold's death. It is referred to in the notes merely by the editor's name and the date of the letter; since it was printed in various editions page references are not helpful.

[ELEMENTARY EDUCATION IN GERMANY, SWITZERLAND, AND FRANCE]

Arnold's third journey to the Continent to gather information was unlike the other two in that he was sent by the Education Department itself, not by a royal commission. And apparently the decision was a very sudden one, on short notice. On October 19, 1885, he returned to his inspectoral duties from a holiday, and that afternoon wrote to his son Richard: "I am just back from the Office, where the authorities had sent for me to ask if I would go to Berlin and Paris to get information for them as to Free Schools. I should like it very much, because on one of these official tours one has the opportunity of learning so much. They have to get the consent of the Treasury, but Lord Cranbrook [lord president of the Privy Council] is certain of obtaining that; and by the beginning of November I shall be off, as they want my report at Christmas, that they may acquaint themselves with the facts before Parliament meets. Won't this be news for mamma and Nelly tonight? I shall go to Berlin, which is an expensive and not delightful place, by myself; and then I hope they will meet me in Paris. I shall not be away more than six weeks."—*Letters*, ed. Russell. Then for more than a week he heard no more about the matter, and could talk of it only with his family. But the necessary permission was forthcoming. "This last touch of 'affairs' before I retire is rather pleasing to me, and I say with Solon: ['I grow old learning ever more things.']," he wrote to Humphry Ward on October 31. To A. J. Mundella he wrote on November 6: "I assure you I am going with a perfectly open mind. At the present time I am against the abolition of school fees in our country; but this is not for the sake of the voluntary schools at all."—W. F. Connell, *The Educational Thought and Influence of Matthew Arnold* (London: Routledge and Kegan Paul, 1950), p. 284. He set off on November 11, armed with letters from Cardinal Manning to open the doors of the Catholic schools in North Germany. He kept no record in his pocket diary, but from his letters one can place him in Berlin (after a night in Cologne) by the evening of November 13; from there he journeyed to Dresden on the 30th. There was a frosty excursion to Görlitz on December 12 to visit Baron Carl von Canitz. He returned to Berlin on December 17, spent three days there, stopped a day to see schools in Cologne, and was home on December 22.

The tour was resumed on January 21, 1886, when he travelled to Paris in the company of his wife and younger daughter, to spend about three weeks there. He went on alone to Lucerne, then to Zurich, and left the latter city for Munich on February 25. On March 5 he went to Nuremberg, on March 7 to Dresden, thence to Berlin, to Hamburg, to Cologne (for one night), to Paris, and on March 21 home.

Meanwhile the Conservative government before its defeat had set up a commission under the chairmanship of Richard Assheton Cross "to enquire into the working of the Elementary Education Acts, England and Wales." Arnold was called upon to testify on April 6 and 7, largely on the strength of his recent tour, but it should be emphasized that he was not sent abroad by the Cross

Commission. Mrs. Arnold and their younger daughter went out to New York to be with the older daughter at the birth of her first child, and Arnold was eager to join them. "The correcting my evidence given before the Commission, and given in the careless manner of conversation, is very hard work, and I wish it were over; it keeps me from my Report," he complained on April 21; his testimony was published in the first volume of the Commission's report. By May 22 he was on shipboard, his own report completed. Proofs followed him on June 1, reached New York on the 12th, and were waiting for him when he arrived there from Philadelphia and Washington on the 14th. The report, issued by the Stationery Office for the Education Department at the end of July, was described by the *Spectator* as "one of the most Arnoldian and readable of Parliamentary papers."—August 7, p. 1044. *The Times* praised it and summarized it at great length in a pair of articles on August 4 and 6 (p. 13, cols. 1–3 and p. 13, cols. 1–4). Arnold repeated the substance of his report in his Philadelphia lecture on "Common Schools Abroad" (pp. 88–105). The manuscript remains in the United States, in the Alderman Library of the University of Virginia. An interesting brief account of this and Arnold's other Continental tours of investigation may be found in P. H. Butterfield, "Aspects of the Work of Matthew Arnold for Royal Commissions," *British Journal of Educational Studies* XV, 284–91 (October, 1967).

The Education Reform League, which republished the report a year and a half later, was formed late in 1884 by Samuel Barnett, first warden of the newly-built Toynbee Hall (see Arnold's Whitechapel Address, *Prose Works*, ed. Super, X, 249–55). It aimed, among other things, at providing "equal opportunities for all children to attain their highest capability by continuity of training—technical, physical, and intellectual."—H. O. Barnett, *Canon Barnett, His Life, Work, and Friends* (London, 1918), I, 293–94. Arnold jotted in his pocket diary for February 23, 1888: "preface to report."

4:1. "I have been to see the Director of the Division for Elementary Schools at the Ministry to-day; very civil, and happily he speaks French, though bad French. But he can hardly bring himself to understand that one is in a hurry, or that one is not going to give a month to Berlin alone," wrote Arnold on November 18 of his first meeting with Schneider. And on November 29, "Yesterday . . . at nine Dr. Tyszka called for me—a sensible, pleasant man who speaks English, who took me to a country school six miles from Berlin—very interesting."—*Letters,* ed. Russell.

4:2–3. Karl Wilhelm Eichenberg (1840–99) became one of the original school inspectors under the Saxon Popular School Law in 1874; he served in Chemnitz from 1877 to 1885 and then moved to Dresden.

The Swiss schoolmen were Kaspar Küttel (1843–1912), director of the boys' school at Lucerne from 1870 to 1891, and Heinrich Paulus Hirzel (1831–1908), head of the schools of Zurich from 1874.

Ferdinand-Édouard Buisson (1841–1932) began as a school inspector and by 1879 was director of Primary Education. He was the principal collaborator of Jules Ferry (see p. 16:17) in formulating the laws that made elementary instruction free, lay, and compulsory. In his testimony before the Cross Commission, Arnold called him "a charming, excellent, and very able man."—*First Report of the Royal Commission* [*on*] *the Elementary Education Acts* (London, 1886), qu. 6154.

Gaillard was formerly an elementary schoolmaster in one of the poorer and laboring quarters of Paris, then an inspector, who was assigned to take Arnold round in Paris. See Arnold's testimony before the Cross Commission, qu. 5094.

7:22–35. Arnold's letters to his sister Frances on December 21 and 27, 1885, make the same statements: "My three days in Berlin were very interesting; I saw the Education Minister, Herr von Gossler, who gave me an account of what was going to happen as to free schooling in Prussia, quite different from what every one else had given me; I can only suppose that Prince Bismarck has made up his mind that so it shall be, and if he has made up his mind that so it shall be, so it probably will be." "My work is unusually interesting because it enables me to see and hear so many of the rank and file instead of merely the chiefs, who are all that a foreigner on a mission usually comes in contact with. If I only saw the Minister in Berlin I should report that a system of free schools would certainly be adopted throughout Prussia very shortly; as it is, I very much doubt whether it will be. But the question is being discussed throughout Germany, and this, with the great excellence of the schools, makes it so interesting to be there on an errand like mine. It is odd that while in this extraordinary England no one seems to think of connecting the elementary school question with the question of intermediate schools, though the case is ten thousand times stronger here than there, in Germany the constantly heard argument is: Why is it harder on an artisan with £50 a year to pay 4*s*. a year for his son's schooling than on an officer or functionary with £150 or £200 a year to pay 40*s*. a year for his? Lucky country, we might say, where the officer or functionary can get firstrate schooling for his son for 40*s*. a year, whatever may be done as to relieving other classes! I suppose if they have a Royal Commission that will at any rate give time for the question to be considered, and Chamberlain and his company will not be able to rush free schools in a session."—*Letters*, ed. Russell. Gustav von Gossler (1838–1902) became minister of Education for Prussia in 1881.

8:4. See p. 42:22–23n.

9:32. Karl Friedrich Wilhelm von Gerber (1823–91) became minister of Education for Saxony in 1871.

10:1–4. See letter of December 27, 1885, quoted at p. 7:22–35n.

11:12. "I had letters for the Mayor; . . . [he] showed me all over the Town Hall . . . [He] sent his secretary, a charming young man, to show me all over the [town]," Arnold wrote to his younger daughter from Nuremberg on March 6, 1886.—*Letters*, ed. Russell.

12:24–27. See p. 31:6–10n.

14:9–11. Dr. Victor N. Boutellier of Zurich identifies this industrialist for me as Hans Wunderly-von Muralt (1842–1921), whose firm (founded by Wunderly's kinsman, the "spinner-king" Heinrich Kunz; after 1893 Zollinger & Co.) was the largest cotton thread manufacturer in Switzerland. Wunderly had spent some time in England and France studying factories. He had two boys and a girl, the youngest about nine years old when Arnold visited Zurich. On February 24 (as he told his wife two days later) Arnold "went to dine (half past twelve) with the Wunderlys; an excellent dinner, and he produced real Johannisberg."—*Letters*, ed. Russell.

16:17. Jules-François-Camille Ferry (1832–93), a politician with wide range of interests, was minister of Public Instruction for most of the period from 1879 to 1883.

17:22. Charles-Frédéric Robert (1827–99), as secretary-general of the Ministry, was one of the best of the co-workers with Victor Duruy, minister of Public Instruction from 1863 to 1869 (for whom, see *Schools and Universities on the Continent, Prose Works*, ed. Super, IV, Index). Robert resigned when Duruy left office.

19:28–20:27. Arnold's district at the close of his inspectoral career was Westminster. See his testimony before the Cross Commission, qu. 5839.

27:39. The Royal Military Academy at Woolwich trained officers for the Royal Engineers and the Royal Artillery. See p. 147:8n.

29:3–5. Johann Amos Comenius (1592–1671), Moravian Protestant bishop and schoolmaster, was the most influential writer on pedagogy of his day. Arnold jotted a German version of this maxim in his pocket diaries at the beginning of 1881, 1882, 1883, and for March 8, 1882, as well as in one of his general notebooks.—*Note-Books*, ed. Lowry, pp. 350, 368, 371, 387, 523. He quoted it in English in his General Report for the Year 1880.—*Reports on Elementary Schools*, ed. F. Sandford (London, 1889), p. 233; ed. F. S. Marvin (London, 1908), p. 207. The words may be a paraphrase, not a quotation: "[Ich behaupte] dass alle, die als Menschen geboren sind, des Unterrichtes bedürfen." "[Es] soll in der Schule allen alles gelehrt werden, was den Menschen angeht."—Comenius, *Grosse Unterrichtslehre*, tr. and ed. Julius Beeger and Franz Doubek (3rd ed.; Leipzig: Siegismund & Volkening, n.d. [c. 1881]), pp. 48, 62.

29:15–17. See p. 93:13–15n.

29:31. Arnold was fond of Thucydides' expression that his history would be "a possession for all time."—I, xxii.

30:13–20. See p. 101:11–17n.

31:6–10. Still among Arnold's papers in his family is a 136-page pamphlet, *Zusammenstellung der eidgenössischen und kantonalen Verfassungs- und Gesetzesbestimmungen und Gesetz über das gesammte Unterrichtswesen des kantons Zürich* (Dielsdorf: Druck von Fritschi-Zinggeler, 1878).

31:12–13. For Humboldt and Guizot, see p. 233:22–23n. The philosopher Victor Cousin (1792–1867) was minister in 1840.

31:22. Sir James Mackintosh (1765–1832), philosopher, historian, journalist, and legal theorist, was regarded as having the most prodigious mind of his day. He was a Whig member of Parliament from 1813 until his death.

32:19. The École Turgot, oldest of the higher elementary schools in Paris, was founded in 1839. See Arnold's testimony before the Cross Commission, qu. 5881–85.

36:23–34. Arnold mentioned her in his testimony before the Cross Commission on April 6, qu. 5734. He himself visited the Paris Exhibition of 1878 as a tourist.

37:11–12. *Wallensteins Tod* was the third part of a historical trilogy by Schiller. See Arnold's testimony before the Cross Commission, qu. 5772.

37:14–15. The state (kingdom) of Bavaria was divided into eight provinces. "The *Staat* is the central government; then there is the province, the *Regierung;* and then there is the municipality, the *Gemeinde.* There are normal schools supported by all three, and there are some private ones too."–Arnold's testimony before the Cross Commission, qu. 5223.

39:30. Auteuil, a village between the Seine and the Bois de Boulogne, was annexed to Paris in 1860. The normal school in the Rue Molitor was only a few years old when Arnold visited it.

39:32. The new girls' normal school at Fontenay-aux-Roses, five kilometers south of Paris, was of course not the school Arnold saw in that village in 1865.

40:23. Félix Pécaut (1828–98) was appointed by Ferry in 1879 to organize the school at Fontenay-aux-Roses, and remained there until 1895. He too had been an inspector of primary schools. "You mention M. Pécaut," Arnold wrote to Ernest Fontanès on November 27, 1886; "if you see him, pray ascertain whether he received a copy of my *Report on Foreign Schools.* Much as I dislike the *jacobinisme autoritaire* of your Ministry of Education, I like and admire M. Pécaut, and have endeavoured to do justice to him in my Report."–*Letters,* ed. Russell.

41:25–27. Félix-Antoine-Philibert Dupanloup (1802–78), bishop of Orléans from 1849, was a liberal Catholic with a continuing interest in education. Arnold probably refers to his book *De l'Éducation* (1850), which had reached a tenth edition by 1881.

42:22–23. *Zeitschrift des königlich preussischen statistischen Bureaus.* Ergänzungsheft X: *Die öffentlichen Volksschulen in Preussen . . . im Jahre 1878.* Bearbeitet von A[lwin] Petersilie (Berlin: Verlag des Königlichen Statistischen Bureaus, 1882), p. xiv.

44:6–10. The school was at Görlsdorf bei Angermünde, northeast of Berlin, where Arnold was guest of Wilhelm, Count von Redern, on November 22–23. "His school [is] a little village school with not more than fifty children—a specimen of its class which I shall be glad to see, for, of course, the great town schools are what the officials will chiefly take me to. Count Redern is one of the greatest Prussian proprietors; they say he has £70,000 a year," Arnold wrote to his wife on November 23.–*Letters,* ed. Russell.

44:10–12. At Mittel Sohra, near Görlitz, where Arnold was guest of Baron Carl von Canitz on December 12–14.

44:25–30. On the afternoon of February 24, 1886, Arnold told his wife, "I drove over the slopes of the mountain behind Zurich to

Wytikon, a small village. . . . I took the school by surprise, and anything more creditable to Canton Zurich you cannot conceive. I had sent back the carriage, and the schoolmaster walked back to Zurich with me, three or four miles, but downhill; his parents live in Zurich, and he was going in to some choir singing."—*Letters*, ed. Russell.

48:4–5. Baron von Canitz; see p. 44:10–12n.

48:13. See p. 44:25–26.

53:11–13. See *The Popular Education of France* (1861), *Prose Works*, ed. Super, II, 90.

53:26. The secretary of the Education Department from 1884 to 1890 was Arnold's friend and Balliol contemporary Patrick Cumin.

[THE NADIR OF LIBERALISM]

After five years of government, Gladstone and his Liberal cabinet were forced to resign by a vote in the House of Commons on June 8, 1885. Lord Salisbury became prime minister, and the Conservative administration was confirmed by the country in a general election in November-December, the first to be held under the new and broad Liberal extension of the franchise. Arnold watched the reports of the voting with interest from the Continent, where he was on his schools mission. "I should never myself vote for a Tory," he wrote to his sister Frances on December 4; "but for the present I wish Lord Salisbury to stay in, the Liberals being so unripe. Lord Salisbury is an able man, and I think he improves and is capable of learning and growing."—*Letters*, ed. Russell. The election victory was won with the assistance of Parnell and the Irish, who had some expectation of a kind of home rule measure from Salisbury. Then on December 17 came the disclosure that Gladstone favored home rule, and from that moment the issue was strictly a party one: the Conservatives felt bound to oppose it, but Gladstone faced an insurmountable task in uniting his party behind it. "What a move is this of Gladstone's in the Irish matter! and what apprehensions it gives me," Arnold wrote to his sister from Cologne on December 21.—*Letters*, ed. Russell. Back at home in early January, 1886, he sent Lord Rosebery, a leading Liberal and husband of Lady de Rothschild's niece, a copy of *Culture and Anarchy*. "The preface contains a prophecy which has come quite wonderfully true," he wrote to his sister Frances on January 11. "If I had time I would write a last political article with the title of *The Nadir of Liberalism.* For all I have ever said of the Liberals calling *successes* not things which really succeed, but things which take with their friends, unite their party, embarrass their adversaries, and are carried—and how very, very far this is, in politics, from true success, has proved itself to a degree beyond which we shall not, it may be hoped, pass."—*Letters,* ed. Russell.

Lord Salisbury's government was defeated on January 27, and Gladstone formed his administration a few days later, committed to home rule, though in what form was still uncertain. "We are all against Gladstone's present policy," wrote Arnold of himself and some Englishmen with whom he had been talking in Paris on March 20. "I am glad to think it seems threatened with a check; but the mass of middle class Liberalism on which he relies is so enthusiastically devoted to him, and so ignorant, that I am not sure of his being frustrated until I see it happen."—*Letters,* ed. Russell.

On March 26 the first defections occurred when Gladstone announced his plan to the cabinet and two ministers resigned, Joseph Chamberlain and George Otto Trevelyan. On April 8 Gladstone introduced his bill in the House of Commons; he proposed to set up an Irish parliament and executive in Dublin which should have legislative powers and control over everything but such matters as peace and war, foreign affairs, customs and excise, trade, the post office, coinage, and matters affecting the Crown; and Ireland should no longer send members to the Imperial Parliament in Westminster. It was at this point that Arnold wrote his article. If he coined the title while the Conservatives were still in power, he became convinced that the Liberals sank even lower when they gained power: "In the last month of Mr. Gladstone's Government the Liberal party did indeed reach its lowest, its *nadir*," he told a French friend on November 27, 1886. "I had a severe week with my article last week," he wrote to his wife on April 21, "but it is all done now, and Knowles telegraphs to me that it is 'magnificent,' and that he means to open his number with it. So, at any rate, I continue to give satisfaction to the Editors."—*Letters,* ed. Russell. The article appeared in the May number of the *Nineteenth Century,* and Arnold was paid £50 for it. It has been republished in Fraser Neiman's *Essays, Letters, and Reviews by Matthew Arnold* (Cambridge, Mass.: Harvard University Press, 1960).

It was the first of five articles (in addition to two letters to *The Times*) that Arnold directed to the Irish question during the last two years of his life. In many ways they were, as he himself indicates, an extension of *Culture and Anarchy:* he was warmly sympathetic to the Irish cause, severely critical of English misrule, but at the same time distressed by riot and disorder and unalterably opposed to the separation of the two nations, a separation to which Gladstone's scheme seemed inexorably to point. Two useful studies of his position are William Robbins, "Matthew Arnold and Ireland," *University of Toronto Quarterly* XVII, 52–67 (October, 1947), and the sixth chapter of Patrick J. McCarthy, *Matthew Arnold and the Three Classes* (New York: Columbia University Press, 1964).

54:1–4. "Do thy diligence to come shortly unto me: For Demas hath forsaken me, having loved this present world, and is departed unto Thessalonica."–Paul to Timothy (II), 4:9–10.

54:4–14. In *Culture and Anarchy*, Conclusion (1868) and Preface (1869).–*Prose Works*, ed. Super, V, 227–28, 253–55.

55:1–15. Arnold travelled on the Continent for the Schools Inquiry Commission in 1865 and on his return published "My Countrymen" (1866), an essay reprinted at the end of *Friendship's Garland* in 1871 (hence no doubt Arnold's "fifteen years ago"). See *Prose Works*, ed. Super, V, 6, 16, 26–27. The newspaper quoted was *The Morning Star*, December 2, 1864, p. 4, col. 3, and the minister of state was Robert Lowe, in the House of Commons on May 3, 1865.

55:15. Arnold journeyed to the Continent on behalf of the Education Department in the winter of 1885–86. See pp. 385–86.

55:22–29. Quoted from de Retz's *Mémoires* by Sainte-Beuve, "Le Cardinal de Retz" (II), *Causeries du lundi* (3rd ed.; Paris, 1869), V, 247.

55:30–32. British policy in Egypt was confused beyond belief. After the bombing of Arabi Pasha's fortifications at Alexandria by the British fleet in July, 1882, General Sir Garnet Wolseley defeated Arabi at Tel-el-Kebir on September 13. A year later Sir Evelyn Baring, as British consul-general in Cairo, became in effect the governor of the country. But a revolt in the Sudan under the Mahdi led to the dispatch of Gordon to Khartoum in January, 1884. He was cut off there, and Wolseley's relief column reached Khartoum only on January 28, 1885, two days after the Mahdi's forces stormed the city and killed Gordon. Later that year Gladstone's uncertain policy led to the establishment of a six-power commission to administer the Egyptian debt, and placed Germany in the effective position of balancing the power. The difficulties in

Ireland were perennial, and her parliamentary representatives used the rules of the House ingeniously to obstruct government action.

55:32–36. A meeting sponsored by the Revolutionary Social Democratic Federation in Trafalgar Square on February 8, 1886—the very day the new Liberal home secretary took office—led to three days of disorder and the breaking of windows in the Pall Mall clubs and the west-end houses and shops. Four leaders—H. M. Hyndman, John Burns, H. H. Champion, and Jack Williams—were prosecuted, but were acquitted after a five-day trial on April 10. Meanwhile a monster meeting in Hyde Park on February 21 produced no serious disorder. The occurrences seemed like a repetition of those which nearly twenty years earlier led Arnold to write *Culture and Anarchy*.

55:37–56:14. This passage echoes a remark Arnold made in a letter to his sister Frances from Munich on March 1, 1886: "The real concern which people in Switzerland and here show about English affairs, and the critical period on which we seem to be entering, is remarkable; and is evidently not the affected and mortifying concern of enemies, but the true concern of those who at bottom like England and think her a great and useful force in the world."—*Letters*, ed. Russell.

56:20–26. "The Future of Liberalism" (1880), *Prose Works*, ed. Super, IX, 148.

56:35. I.e., Gladstone.

57:16–19. Sainte-Beuve, *Souvenirs et indiscrétions*, ed. Jules Troubat (nouv. éd.; Paris, 1880), p. 280. See p. 111:2–8.

57:25–26. In a speech at Leeds, March 23, 1886, reported in *The Times* next day, p. 9, col. 6. G. F. S. Robinson, Marquess of Ripon, was first lord of the Admiralty in Gladstone's cabinet of 1886.

57:26–28. Rogers was Liberal M.P. from Bermondsey and professor of statistics and economic science at King's College, London.

57:28–30. Letter to *The Times*, March 15, 1886, p. 12, col. 2. Brett, son of Viscount Esher, had been private secretary to the Marquess of Hartington.

57:30–33. Speaking at Chelmsford, Essex, on January 7, 1886; reported in *The Times* next day, p. 6, col. 2. Morley, a friend of Arnold's, former editor of the *Fortnightly Review* and *The Pall Mall Gazette*, was M.P. for Newcastle-on-Tyne and chief secretary for Ireland in Gladstone's cabinet of 1886.

57:33–37. Sir Horace Davey was appointed solicitor general in Gladstone's new administration, but having failed to secure reelection to Parliament was obliged to stand for a new constituency in a by-election. He made this remark at Ipswich on April 8, 1886.—*Times*, April 9, p. 10, col. 4. Six days later he finished at the bottom of the poll there.

58:4. Arnold used the term "success" in the same way as early as "My Countrymen" (1866), with Cavour as example.—*Prose Works*, ed. Super, V, 12, 14–15, etc.

58:28. The "May laws," passed by the Prussian legislature in May of 1873–74–75, gave the state large powers over the education and appointment of the clergy (both Protestant and Catholic), banned the religious orders, and aimed at destroying any religious power that seemed in conflict with the state. They were suspended in 1879 and repealed in 1886; in 1887 most religious orders were permitted to return. Bismarck entered public life in 1847 and became prime minister of Prussia in 1862.

59:1–14. In alliance with Austria, Bismarck's Prussia defeated Denmark in 1864 and annexed Schleswig-Holstein; then, by virtue of the overwhelming victory at Sadowa on July 3, 1866, Prussia defeated Austria in the seven-weeks' war.

59:15. Russian intervention destroyed the independent revolutionary Hungarian republic under Kossuth in 1849, and Hungary was restored to the Austrian Imperial crown.

59:28–29. Prussia defeated France in the Franco-German War of 1870–71 and annexed Alsace and Lorraine. The first consequence of the war was the unification of Germany under the Prussian crown.

60:9–15. "Sir H[enry] Maine on Popular Government," *Fortnightly Review* XLV, 171 (February, 1886).

60:21. The Crown Prince, husband of Queen Victoria's daughter, succeeded in 1888 to the German throne as Frederick III, but his reign was only a few months long. He and the Crown Princess invited Arnold to dine with them and their family in Berlin on November 26, 1885.

60:32–33. The Corn Laws, which provided an import duty on grain to protect home growers, were repealed by the Conservative government under Sir Robert Peel in 1846; their repeal led to repeal of further import duties and gave England some three-quarters of a century of free trade.

61:16–21. Arnold quoted *The Daily Telegraph* and Robert Lowe to this effect in the Preface to *Higher Schools and Universities in Germany* (1874) and in "Irish Catholicism and British Liberalism"

(1878), and Lowe's remark alone in "The Incompatibles" (1881).–
Prose Works, ed. Super, VII, 129; VIII, 321; IX, 238. Lowe made
his remark in a speech at Sheffield on September 4, 1873, reported
in *The Times* next day, p. 3, col. 3, and jotted in Arnold's pocket
diary for August 10, 1873.–*Note-Books*, ed. Lowry, p. 199.

61:21–28. *Prose Works*, ed. Super, V, 254. The (Episcopal)
Church of Ireland was disestablished by the Liberals in 1869, but
the Roman Catholic Church was barred from benefiting from its
endowments. Gladstone's home rule proposal likewise prohibited
the establishment of the Roman Catholic religion.

61:29. In "The Incompatibles" (1881) Arnold repeatedly referred to himself as "an insignificant person."–*Prose Works*, ed.
Super, IX, 238, etc.

61:34. Gladstone carried two acts for the reform of Irish land
tenure, in 1870 and 1881; Arnold alludes to the latter.

61:35–37. See p. 57:28–30.

62:2–4. Gladstone moved to set up a Select Committee on Procedure on February 22, almost immediately upon assuming power,
with a view to conducting the business of the House of Commons
more efficiently, and laid before it the government's proposals on
March 18. But procedure was not reformed; the Committee had
not yet reported when Arnold wrote.

62:10–12. See p. 57:27–28, 26, 30.

62:16–18. See p. 57:30–33.

62:36–37. In "The Function of Criticism at the Present Time"
(1864), Arnold described the long era of resistance in England to
the ideas of the French Revolution as an "epoch of concentration."
"But epochs of concentration cannot well endure for ever; epochs
of expansion, in the due course of things, follow them. Such an
epoch of expansion seems to be opening in this country."–*Prose
Works*, ed. Super, III, 266, 269. For his view of Burke in this context, see his letter to Ernest Fontanès, January 21, 1880.–*Letters*,
ed. Russell.

63:11. "*Morgue*" is arrogance.

63:14–16. James Robert Hope married Sir Walter Scott's
granddaughter Charlotte Lockhart in 1847 and in 1853, upon in-
heriting Abbotsford, took the name of Hope-Scott. Gladstone's
long letter to Hope-Scott's daughter Mary after his death in 1873
is printed as Appendix III in Robert Ornsby, *Memoirs of James
Robert Hope-Scott* (2nd ed.; London, 1884), II, 284–98. "I have
been reading in the new Quarterly the article on Hope Scott,

which is by somebody who knows; the man always interested me, but his life is too long and too out of date now in its ideas; but there is an account of Bunsen by Gladstone which is remarkably good," Arnold wrote to his sister Frances on April 29, 1884.

63:26–29. Perhaps on June 21, 1870, when the Marquess of Salisbury, as chancellor of the University of Oxford, conferred an honorary doctorate on Arnold. Salisbury had a seat in Conservative cabinets from 1866, but first became prime minister in June, 1885.

64:16–17. Gladstone's *Studies on Homer and the Homeric Age* (Oxford, 1858) was ridiculed, though not by name, in Arnold's first lecture *On Translating Homer* (1860).—*Prose Works*, ed. Super, I, 100. More recently Gladstone was engaged in a debate with Huxley and others over the book of Genesis; Gladstone published "Dawn of Creation and of Worship" and "Proem to Genesis: a Plea for a Fair Trial," *Nineteenth Century* XVIII, 685–706 (November, 1885) and XIX, 1–21 (January, 1886).

64:25. For "light and leading," see p. 368:15n.

64:36–38. Arnold's Continental tour took him to Zurich in February, 1886. See p. 14:9–10.

65:13–17. Slightly modified from "Our Venetian Constitution," *Fortnightly Review* VII, 276 (March, 1867), reprinted in Harrison's *Order and Progress* (London, 1875), and thence quoted by Morley in "Sir H[enry] Maine and Popular Government," p. 164. See note to p. 60:9–15.

65:28. In his final lecture from the chair of poetry at Oxford (later the first chapter of *Culture and Anarchy*) Arnold in 1867 said that certain "novel and untried ways, . . . the ways of Jacobinism," were "naturally alluring to the feet of democracy": "Violent indignation with the past, abstract systems of renovation applied wholesale, a new doctrine drawn up in black and white for elaborating down to the very smallest details a rational society of the future." "Two things . . . are the signal marks of Jacobinism,—its fierceness, and its addiction to an abstract system." And therefore he playfully imagined, in *Friendship's Garland*, that he had seen Harrison himself "furbishing up a guillotine."—*Prose Works*, ed. Super, V, 109, 76.

66:9–10. Arnold quoted some of the Nonconformist attacks on the idea of religious endowment in Ireland in *Culture and Anarchy* (1868).—*Prose Works*, ed. Super, V, 193–99 and notes.

66:11–12. "*I pede fausto*": "Go on and prosper."—Horace *Epistles* II, ii, 37.

66:17–18. Arnold coined this characterization of Charles James Fox, the Whig leader at the turn of the century, in "The Incompatibles" (1881).–*Prose Works*, ed. Super, IX, 246.

66:18–22. Madame Françoise Bertaut de Motteville, quoted by Sainte-Beuve, *Causeries du lundi* (3rd ed.; Paris, 1869), V, 187. The italics are Ste.-Beuve's. The passage begins "Quand les sujets," not "Quand les hommes."

67:28. "There is a Latin law-maxim which tells us that it is the business of a good judge to seek to extend his jurisdiction:–*Boni judicis est ampliare jurisdictionem.*"–"'Ecce, Convertimur ad Gentes,'" (1879), *Prose Works*, ed. Super, IX, 2.

68:1–3. On April 12, 1886, Samuel Whitbread, M. P. for Bedford, speaking in the home rule debate, distinguished between the opinions of the violent faction of American Irish, whom it would be base to heed, and the opinions of the thoughtful American and the thoughtful Irishman in America, whom it would be most unstatesmanlike to turn against the British by rejecting home rule.– Reported in *The Times* next day, p. 8, col. 4.

68:3–69:14. Arnold here repeats what he said in "A Word More about America" (1885), *Prose Works*, ed. Super, X, 209–11. Ireland's four provinces are historical; they had no political significance in Arnold's day, but retain an importance in the hearts of the people.

70:8–10. Quoted by Sainte-Beuve, "Mémoires du cardinal de Retz" (I), *Causeries du lundi* (3rd ed.; Paris, 1869), V, 54.

70:33–34. Alfred Illingworth was M.P. for Bradford (West) and Arnold's brother-in-law W. E. Forster was M.P. for Bradford (Central). James Stansfeld (1820–98), a dissenter, M.P. for Halifax from 1859 to 1895, gave up a promising career as cabinet minister to lead the agitation for repeal of the Contagious Diseases Acts, which provided for registering, licensing, and medically examining prostitutes in garrison and dockyard towns. After nine years of single-minded campaigning under his leadership the repealers in 1883 carried a resolution in the Commons and three years later the repeal was effected, only a few weeks before the publication of Arnold's article. Thereupon Stansfeld took Joseph Chamberlain's cabinet seat as president of the Local Government Board when Chamberlain resigned on the issue of home rule for Ireland.

70:35–71:2. "Irish Catholicism and British Liberalism" (1878), *Prose Works*, ed. Super, VIII, 327.

71:5–6. Arnold referred to the Liberals as "the party of movement," somewhat ironically, as early as "The Function of Criticism at the Present Time" (1864), *Prose Works*, ed. Super, III, 276:26.

71:18–20. A major revolt against the Revolutionary government of France broke out in the Vendée, in western France, in March, 1793. Initially a peasant rebellion against conscription, it was joined by royalist nobility and supported from England. It was finally put down in December of that year.

71:33–35. "To see things as they really are" and "the one thing needful" (the latter from Luke 10:42) are favorite expressions of Arnold's; see *On Translating Homer*, Lecture II (1860), "The Function of Criticism at the Present Time" (1864), and *On the Study of Celtic Literature* (1866) for the former, "A Courteous Explanation" (1866) and *Culture and Anarchy* (1868) for the latter.—*Prose Works*, ed. Super, I, 140; III, 258; 298–99; V, 34, 176.

71:35–72:2. Sermon VII, "Upon the Character of Balaam," ¶16; *Works*, ed. W. E. Gladstone (Oxford, 1896), II, 134. This sentence was quoted frequently by Arnold from the time of "Bishop Butler and the Zeit-Geist" (1876), *Prose Works*, ed. Super, VIII, 12.

72:8–12. In the speech at Chelmsford, January 7, 1886, quoted in *The Times* next day, p. 6, cols. 2, 1.

72:20–21. Charles Bradlaugh, radical M.P. for Northampton, closed his remarks on the Government of Ireland Bill on April 12, 1886, by saying: "The people were prepared to follow the Prime Minister even further than they could see (Opposition laughter), provided only his keen sight could see the end. (Hear, hear.) At any rate, they knew the other side was blind."—*Times*, April 13, p. 8, col. 1.

73:31–37. Arnold's source is probably R. W. Dale, *Impressions of America* (New York, 1879), p. 183. The First Amendment to the Constitution (1791) prohibited the establishment of any religion by the Federal government, and despite Arnold's statement no state would have exercised that power when Arnold was writing. Nevertheless Godkin, writing as editor of *The New York Post* in response to Arnold's published letter of June 28, 1886, said: "Any American State might . . . set up a State church." See p. 497.

74:22. James Lowther, first Earl of Lonsdale (1736–1802), "who was known throughout Cumberland and Westmoreland as the 'bad earl,' was a man of unenviable character and enormous wealth," described by Alexander Carlyle as "an intolerable tyrant over his tenants and dependents."—*D.N.B.* Among the creditors he declined to pay was Wordsworth's father, whom he had employed as his attorney at Cockermouth.

74:26. In "A Word More about America" (1885), Arnold alluded to such a statement of the Duke of Argyll as his article "On the Economic Condition of the Highlands of Scotland," *Nineteenth Century* XIII, 173–98 (February, 1883), in which the duke compared the prosperity of those regions where ruthless doctrines of "political economy" prevail with the distress of the areas where benevolence and reclamation have too much encouraged the growth of population.—*Prose Works*, ed. Super, X, 207 and n. In 1885 the duke engaged in a debate on Scottish land tenure through letters to *The Times*, September 29, p. 8, cols. 3–4, and October 12, p. 4, col. 3.

74:27. Johnson thus described the relation of landlord and tenant in the Highlands in 1773: "The laird is the original owner of the land, whose natural power must be very great, where no man lives but by agriculture. . . . The laird has all those in his power that live upon his farms. Kings can, for the most part, only exalt or degrade. The laird at pleasure can feed or starve, can give bread, or withhold it. . . . The chiefs, divested of their prerogatives, necessarily turned their thoughts to the improvement of their revenues, and expect more rent, as they have less homage. The tenant, who is far from perceiving that his condition is made better in the same proportion, as that of his landlord is made worse, does not immediately see why his industry is to be taxed more heavily than before. He refuses to pay the demand, and is ejected; the ground is then let to a stranger, who perhaps brings a larger stock, but who, taking the land at its full price, treats with the laird upon equal terms, and considers him not as a chief but as a trafficker in land. Thus the estate perhaps is improved, but the clan is broken. . . . There seems now, whatever be the cause, to be through a great part of the Highlands a general discontent."—*A Journey to the Western Islands of Scotland*, "Ostig in Sky," one-fifth and two-fifths through.

74:28. Walter Winans (1852–1920), grandson of the American railway magnate Ross Winans, purchased and leased large tracts of land in the north of Scotland in order to convert them into deer forest, and in enforcing his rights rode roughshod over the cotters in the area; he even took one of them, the cobbler Murdoch Macrae, to court in July, 1884, for grazing a pet lamb by the roadside. See "A Word More about America" (1885), *Prose Works,* ed. Super, X, 201 and note. The case was still in the public eye through the newspapers early in 1886.

74:36–75:4. "Letter to Richard Burke, Esq.," ¶25, 23, 21, quoted in "The Incompatibles" (1881), *Prose Works,* ed. Super, IX, 247.

75:7–13. *Analogy of Religion,* I, ii, ¶14, somewhat modified; *Works,* ed. Gladstone, I, 58.

75:24–27. First "Letter to Sir Hercules Langrishe, Bart.," halfway through; quoted in "The Incompatibles," *Prose Works,* ed. Super, IX, 247.

76:7–12. The Earl of Rosebery entered the cabinet for the first time as Gladstone's lord privy seal in March, 1885; he became foreign secretary in the cabinet of February, 1886, and was Gladstone's successor as prime minister in 1894. A Scottish landowner, married to Hannah Rothschild (the niece of Arnold's friend), and himself a personal acquaintance of Arnold's, he had taken a step in the direction of regional government by designing a new Scottish secretaryship, normally of cabinet rank, in 1885. "Lord Rosebery is very gay and 'smart,' and I like him much," Arnold told his older daughter on March 17, 1885, after meeting him at a large party at Lady de Rothschild's. The Marquess of Hartington, long a leader of the Liberals, declined office in Gladstone's cabinet of 1886 because of Gladstone's conversion to home rule. Macaulay's nephew George Otto Trevelyan and the Birmingham Nonconformist leader Joseph Chamberlain accepted cabinet posts but resigned them in the cabinet home rule debate of March. Hartington (as Duke of Devonshire) and Chamberlain ultimately held high office in Conservative governments.

76:20. First in "The Future of Liberalism" (1880), *Prose Works,* ed. Super, IX, 138.

77:6–8. Arnold arrived in Munich on February 25, and in a letter to his sister Frances five days later described a "long visit to Döllinger."—*Letters,* ed. Russell. Johann J. I. von Döllinger, theologian and church historian, broke with the Roman church over the issue of papal infallibility in 1871 and thereafter was associated, though not formally, with the Old Catholics.

77:10. The Irish Lord de Vesci was a leader of a bipartisan movement devoted to maintaining the Union. As such he had written to Gladstone, and Gladstone replied on February 12, 1886, that he would welcome "free communication of views from the various classes and sections most likely to supply full and authentic knowledge of the wants and wishes of the Irish people, I mean of all classes of Irish people, whether belonging to a majority or a minority, and whether they may be connected with the land industry or with property in general," in order to assist the government "in the difficult task of determining how we may best, at this important juncture, discharge our duties to Ireland and to the Empire."—*Times*, February 16, p. 6, col. 3.

77:12–14. When forced to summon the States-General, or national legislature, which had not been convened for many years, the French prime minister Loménie de Brienne in the summer of 1788 issued an invitation to thinkers to provide him, through discussion in the public press and in pamphlets, a plan for constituting that body. He fell from power a few weeks later. Carlyle ridicules the matter in *The French Revolution*, book III, chapt. viii.

77:14–16. Hector to Polydamas, *Iliad* XII, 243.

77:25–27. This description of the English character Arnold quoted frequently in his works and jotted frequently in his pocket diary. It comes from "A Letter to a Noble Lord," three-fifths through.

[THE POLITICAL CRISIS]

It was Arnold's fate to observe both of the early crises over Irish home rule from abroad. "It will be tantalizing to be on the sea during the crisis of the great debate, but probably I shall be too sick to care," he told Yates Thompson on May 17, 1886. On the eve of his departure for America, he addressed a letter to *The Times* which, as he wrote from Germantown (Philadelphia) on June 9, "has done good by drawing the distinction between giving to the Irish legislative control over their own local affairs, and giving to them *a single national legislative body* to exercise such control. They all here go off saying, 'Of course Ireland ought to have Home Rule just as all our States have,' and till the thing is pressed to their attention they do not see the difference between what their States have and what Gladstone proposes to do."—*Letters*, ed. Russell. Arnold's letter appeared in *The Times* for May 22. It has been republished, with the one following, in Fraser Neiman's *Essays, Letters, and Reviews by Matthew Arnold*.

78:1–2. Arnold sailed from Liverpool on May 22 (the day this letter was published) and landed in New York on May 30. Home rule was defeated in the House of Commons early in the morning of June 8 by thirty votes; some ninety-three were cast by Liberals against their leaders.

78:12. See p. 76:7–12n.

78:17. Henry Campbell-Bannerman, who had been chief secretary for Ireland in 1884–85, was secretary for war in Gladstone's cabinet of 1886 and remained staunchly loyal.

78:21–22. In his speech at the National Union of Conservative Associations on May 15, 1886 (see pp. 80:19–20, 86:29–38nn.), Lord Salisbury remarked that Parnell "said the other night that Ireland is a 'nation.'" James Stansfeld's "gushing" speech in the House of Commons on May 17, 1886, was a reply to Salisbury's speech.—*Times*, May 18, p. 7, col. 1.

79:11. The Austrian empire in 1867 was divided into the "dual monarchy" which gave Hungary a separate parliament under the Austrian crown. The entire structure collapsed as a sequel to the first World War, and by 1938 Austria's German provinces were indeed united with Germany (from which they became independent, however, after the second World War).

79:20–22. Playfair, formerly professor of chemistry at the University of Edinburgh, was vice-president of the Privy Council (and hence at the head of public education) in Gladstone's government. Arnold alludes to his speech in the House of Commons on May 18, 1886, reported in *The Times* next day, p. 10, col. 2.

79:22–24. James Bryce was under-secretary for foreign affairs. He used the analogy of the United States after the Civil War in the House of Commons on May 17, 1886; reported in *The Times* next day, p. 8, cols. 1–2.

79:33–37. A popular uprising in Brittany against new taxation, "the revolt of the stamped paper," is described in Mme. de Sévigné's letters of October 20–November 13, 1675.

80:3–6. Horace Walpole told this ancedote to Horace Mann in a letter of September 6, 1745, during the Scottish rebellion in favor of Bonnie Prince Charlie; jotted in Arnold's pocket diary for December 18, 1884, and January 6, 1886.—*Note-Books*, ed. Lowry, pp. 409, 423.

80:13–15, 19–20. In addressing the National Union of Conservative Associations at St. James's Hall, London, on May 15, 1886, Lord Salisbury advocated twenty years of the kind of rule that should enable the government of England to govern Ireland—"government that does not flinch, that does not vary." "Coercion means nothing else than forcing people to abstain from . . . propagating their political opinions" by shooting their landlord's agents or vivisecting his cows "because he does not agree with" them.— *Times*, May 17, p. 6, col. 5. Lord Randolph Churchill's political intriguing, especially with Parnell at the latest election, was constantly in the news in the early months of 1886.

80:23-25. The Marquess of Hartington, long a leader of the Liberals, broke with Gladstone on home rule. So too did George Joachim Goschen, a friend of Arnold's, who had had a seat in Gladstone's first cabinet. Goschen's special interest in local government had resulted in a bill as early as 1871 that was dropped through Gladstone's lack of support, but bore fruit in the Local Government (or County Councils) Act passed by the Salisbury government in 1888.

80:31-32. On March 5, 1886, Labouchere moved a resolution declaring it to be "inconsistent with the principles of representative government that any member of either House of the Legislature should derive his title to legislate by virtue of hereditary descent." The motion was negatived by the House of Commons, 202 to 166.— *Times*, March 6, pp. 8-9. "In all political matters the presumption is against the upper classes being right," said Labouchere in the House of Commons on May 18, 1886; reported in *The Times* next day, p. 9, col. 4. Arnold wrote to his wife from the hotel at Bellaggio on September 22, 1880: "At dinner I found myself by a man who made himself very pleasant—so pleasant that we sat on when the other people were gone," and then discovered from the amused comment of an acquaintance that he had been chatting with Henry Labouchere, the Northampton radical and proprietor of the weekly gossip journal *Truth*, which Arnold had ridiculed good-naturedly from time to time.—*Letters*, ed. Russell.

81:1-2. Cromwell conquered a rebellious Ireland in 1649 with great brutality and parcelled out the land among his veterans. Catholic Ireland supported James II against William III, who in 1690 defeated James at Boyne; thereupon England imposed stringent penal laws upon the Catholics that lasted more than a century.

[AFTER THE ELECTIONS]

As reports reached America of Liberal defeats in one after another of the constituencies in the general election (July 1-17, 1886) the Americans were astonished and bewildered. "My eyes are glad-

dened by the heading, 'The Liberal Defeat becomes a Rout,'" wrote
Arnold on July 8. "Smalley's despatches to the *Tribune* are our
only indication of there being any other opinion expressed in the
world except a pro-Gladstone one. Of course, the elections tell
their own tale, but not in speech. To-day we hear of Trevelyan's
defeat and Lord Hartington's return," Arnold wrote to his sister
from Stockbridge on July 11. "I shall perhaps write another letter
to the *Times,* as now comes the critical moment. Lord Salisbury
and Lord Hartington have an opportunity offered to them, and if
they miss it now, it will never return; and the worst of it is that the
English do not know how much more than other people—than
the French, the Germans, the Swiss, the Americans—they are without any system of local government of an effective kind themselves, and what they lose by being without it, so they can the less
understand the necessity of granting something of the kind to the
Irish, though they see in a dim way what a necessity there is."—
Letters, ed. Russell. This was in fact the controlling line of Arnold's
thought about the Irish question. "The Americans are fairly puzzled," he wrote on July 8; "they thought Parnell [i.e., the home
rule party] was going to win. You cannot make them understand
that his cause is not that of the local self government which is
universal here and works well. The truth is we have not their
local self government in England or Scotland any more than in
Ireland; Parliament has been at the same time local and national
legislature for those countries, as well as for Ireland. But as government in England and Scotland has been in accordance with the
wishes of the majority in the respective countries, the system has
worked well enough hitherto, though public business is now getting
too great for it. But in Ireland, where government has been conducted in accordance with the wishes of the minority and of the
British Philistine, the defects of the system have come into full
view. Therefore I am most anxious that the question of local
government should be in every one's mind; if it comes to be fairly
discussed, the Americans will be capable of seeing that there is no
more need for merging Ulster in Southern Ireland than for merging Massachusetts in New York State."—*Letters,* ed. Russell. This
was by no means a new doctrine for Arnold: he spoke vigorously
in favor of local government from the time of his earliest visits to
Continental schools, and more recently and explicitly in "'Ecce,
Convertimur ad Gentes'" (1879), and he applied it directly to the
Irish problem in "A Word More about America" (1885).—*Prose*

Works, ed. Super, IX, 12–13; X, 210–11. To M. E. Grant Duff in Madras he wrote on July 29: "The Elections are a great relief. What a power of solid political sense there is in the English nation still! And now, unless the Conservatives let things drift and miss their opportunity, we have a really interesting and fruitful political work before us—the establishment of a thorough system of local government. How different from the Wife's Sister, Church Rate and Disestablishment business familiar to modern Liberalism! I thought (and said in the *Times* six weeks before the election) that Gladstone would be beaten, but the majority against him exceeds my best hopes."—*Letters,* ed. Russell. Arnold was not a politician and his solution was never adopted. But neither was Gladstone's. The independent Ireland of today—further removed by far from the British crown than even Gladstone's bill proposed—is nevertheless not a united Ireland, but an Ireland without the larger part of Ulster. And Ulster is still represented at Westminster.

Arnold dated his letter on July 24, the day he returned from New York to Stockbridge after a round of visits in New Jersey and Pennsylvania. It was published in *The Times* on August 6. Until his sister forwarded a copy to him from England that reached him on August 23, he did not see it. "The state of things here is curious," he told her next day; "no part of the letter which spoke of the best American opinion being adverse to Gladstone's proceeding was given, but a telegraphic summary of part of the letter appeared with this heading—*Mr. M. A. favourable to Home Rule,* and so they go on. . . . I shall be sincerely glad to have done with the American newspapers."—*Letters,* ed. Russell.

82:11–12. After the defeat of his home rule proposal in the Commons, Gladstone appealed to the people and was soundly defeated: there were 316 Conservatives in the new Parliament to 191 Gladstonian Liberals, and the number of Irish Nationalists (85) was almost balanced by the dissident Liberal Unionists (78) who would vote with the Conservatives. And so Lord Salisbury formed a Conservative government.

82:14–15. Thomas Patrick Gill was M.P. for South Louth (Ireland). Arnold jotted this phrase, with an attribution to Gill, at the beginning of his pocket diary for 1886.—*Note-Books,* ed. Lowry, p. 422.

82:15–17. Speaking at Northampton on July 10, 1886 (when the results of the election were certain), Morley "prophesied that within a few months from the present time the measures which had been brought into Parliament would represent the accepted policy of the Parliament of Great Britain."—*Pall Mall Gazette*, July 12, p. 10; see *Times*, July 12, p. 8, col. 2.

82:17–18. At the beginning of his pocket diary for 1886, Arnold jotted, "We have with us the civilized world. Gladstone."—*Note-Books*, ed. Lowry, p. 422. See p. 259:3 and n.

83:13–15. E. L. Godkin, born in Ireland of English family, emigrated to the United States and there founded *The Nation*, a weekly newspaper Arnold regarded very highly. In 1881 he became editor of *The New York Evening Post*. Godkin refuted Arnold's representation of educated American opinion in a good-humored article a year later: "American Opinion on the Irish Question," *Nineteenth Century* XXII, 285–92 (August, 1887), and he also commented on the opinions Arnold expressed in a letter to the Irish-Americans from Buffalo; see pp. 496–97.

84:25–26. Henry Clay of Kentucky and John C. Calhoun of South Carolina were influential politicians in Congress before the Civil War.

86:12. Cleon became leader of Athens after the death of Pericles, during the Peloponnesian War. His portrait by Thucydides has made him for future historians, as for Arnold, the type of the vulgar demagogue. See Arnold's review of Curtius's *History of Greece* (1872), *Prose Works*, ed. Super, V, 283.

86:19–21. The opposite contingents of the Liberal dissentients were the Whigs, led by the Marquess of Hartington, and the radicals, led by Joseph Chamberlain. Neither man entered Salisbury's cabinet until 1895.

86:27. "Sufficient unto the day is the evil thereof."—Matthew 6:34.

86:29–38. Speaking rather too loosely to the National Union of Conservative Associations in London on May 15, 1886, Salisbury said: "You would not confide free representative institutions to the Hottentots, for instance. Nor, going higher up the scale, would you confide them to the Oriental nations whom you are governing in India. . . . I doubt whether you could confide representative institutions to the Russians with any great security. . . . [What] is called self-government . . . works admirably well when it is confided to people who are of Teutonic race, but . . . it does not work so well when people of other races are called upon to join in it. . . . My alternative policy is that Parliament should enable the Government of England to govern Ireland. Apply that recipe honestly, consistently, and resolutely for 20 years, and at the end of that time you will find that Ireland will be fit to accept any gifts in the way of local government or repeal of coercion laws that you may wish to give her."—*Times*, May 17, p. 6, cols. 4–5. Four days later Salisbury denied that he had urged twenty years of coercion—he had urged that good government supply the Irish with the conditions for peace, good order, moral advancement, and prosperity; but he was never allowed to forget the Hottentots.—*Times*, May 20, p. 8, cols. 1–2.

87:6. "Blessed are the poor in spirit."—Matthew 5:3.

87:11. Labouchere regarded the elections as a betrayal of the party by a few Liberals who supported the Tories. He himself was a home ruler and a radical who believed that these groups must not let themselves be dominated by the minority of the party.—*Truth*, July 29, 1886, pp. 177–79.

87:17–26. *The Pall Mall Gazette*, though strongly Gladstonian and in favor of home rule, on July 12, 1886, referred to the "many deplorable utterances in which [Gladstone] indulged during the campaign."—p. 1.

87:26. Matthew 11:19 (Luke 7:35).

[COMMON SCHOOLS ABROAD]

On Tuesday, June 8, only nine days after his arrival in America, Arnold lectured at the University of Pennsylvania on the substance of his observations of Continental education during his recent tour of investigation. The provost of the university, Dr. William Pepper, who introduced him to his audience of over six hundred crowded into the chapel, remarked in his diary, "What a good fellow—frank and easy in manner—strong fine figure, strong face." "My lecture did very well at Philadelphia," Arnold told his sister Jane on June 13; "I send you the letter with which the President of the University enclosed a cheque for 500 dollars—£100. The Century gives me £100 more for the right of printing it, and I daresay the Buffalo people will give me nearly as much more for hearing it; I have refused to give it anywhere else, as wherever I give it there is an attending ceremony of receptions and social business which in this hot weather is very tiring. But £300 will amply pay the expenses of our journey." Buffalo, however, paid him only £40 for his lecture there on June 26. The article was published in the *Century* for October, 1886, and though signed was unknown to Arnold bibliographers until very recently. It has been republished in Fraser Neiman's *Essays, Letters, and Reviews by Matthew Arnold.* The manuscript is at the University of Pennsylvania. An account of Arnold's visit is given by Neda Westlake, "Matthew Arnold at the University," *Library Chronicle* (University of Pennsylvania) XXV, 43–44 (Winter, 1959).

88:1–16. In "Equality" (1878), *Prose Works*, ed. Super, VIII, 287–88. Arnold was presented to Cardinal Antonelli, secretary of state to Pius IX, on June 6, 1865. He alluded to their conversation also in *Schools and Universities on the Continent* (1868), *Prose Works*, IV, 304.

88:21–25. See p. 29:3–5.

89:2–3. "Was uns alle bändigt, das Gemeine."–"Epilog zu Schillers Glocke," line 32; quoted in "The Literary Influence of Academies" (1864), the Preface to *Essays in Criticism* (1865), and "A Last Word on the Burials Bill" (1876).–*Prose Works*, ed. Super, III, 235, 290; VIII, 90.

89:7–11. Joseph Roswell Hawley (1826–1905) was senator from Connecticut from 1881 until the year of his death. On Christmas day, 1883, Hawley presented Arnold and his family to President Arthur at the White House. Arnold jotted this remark of Hawley's in his pocket diary for January 7, 1886.–*Note-Books*, ed. Lowry, p. 423.

91:21. Arnold alluded to this list of sects in "A Word about America" (1882); *Whitaker's Almanack*, an annual compendium of information that has been published since 1868 (for 1869), listed 175 sects in England and Wales in 1882.–*Prose Works*, ed. Super, X, 11 and note. See Arnold's testimony before the Cross Commission on April 6–7, 1886.–*First Report of the Royal Commission [on] the Elementary Education Acts* (London, 1886), qu. 5199–5203, 5803–9.

92:5. Presumably Eichenberg at Dresden; see p. 4:2 and n.

92:13–15. See Arnold's testimony before the Cross Commission, qu. 6105. Theodor Mommsen (1817–1903), historian of Rome and founding editor of the *Corpus inscriptionum*, was secretary to the Berlin Academy for over twenty years and professor of ancient history at the University of Berlin from 1858. Arnold spoke of the "charming crudity" of his inaugural address as rector (1874) in *God and the Bible*, *Prose Works*, ed. Super, VII, 280. Arnold carried a letter of introduction to him from Max Müller in 1885, and saw him on December 18: "He is quite white, and older than I expected;—in manner, mode of speech, and intellectual quality something between Voltaire and Newman," Arnold wrote to Charles J. Leaf later in the day.–*Letters*, ed. Russell.

92:24–27. A quatrain from "Zahme Xenien," sect. ix; Goethe, *Werke* (Weimar, 1893), V (1), 134. Arnold may have seen it in F. W. Riemer, *Mittheilungen über Goethe* (Berlin, 1841), I, 142; he jotted the first half in his pocket diary for November 14, 1869, and quoted it in *Literature and Dogma* (1871).–*Note-Books*, ed. Lowry, p. 112; *Prose Works*, ed. Super, VI, 177.

93:13–15. The reference is to Luther's explanation in the *Small Catechism* of the petition in the Lord's Prayer, "Lead us not into temptation."

93:27–28. In "Eugénie de Guérin" (1863), *On the Study of Celtic Literature* (1866), *Culture and Anarchy* (1868), *Literature and Dogma* (1871), and "A Last Word on the Burials Bill" (1876).–*Prose Works*, ed. Super, III, 98, 368–70; V, 184; VI, 191; VIII, 104–5.

94:26–31. In his testimony before the Cross Commission on April 7, Arnold remarked on the distinction between the State's regulations for religious instruction and the more explicitly atheistical regulations of the municipality of Paris. "The minister [of education] said in a speech which I heard that God and the spiritualist philosophy, a philosophy the glory of Descartes and the French nation, were in the syllabus, and so they are. . . . There is a book that was sanctioned, I think, by the Municipal Council which contains extravagant attacks on religion, but that has never been brought into use." "I have such a book of the worst character, which is professedly sanctioned for French schools," added Cardinal Manning, a member of the Commission.–qu. 5715, 5737–38.

95:6–8. See p. 17:32–34 and Arnold's testimony before the Cross Commission, qu. 5739–48.

95:13–14. Maria Edgeworth's *The Parent's Assistant; or, Stories for Children*, a collection of sixteen original moral stories first published in 1796, was perennially popular in the nineteenth century.

95:16–30. See p. 41:4–16.

95:37. See p. 39:32n.

96:6. See p. 40:23n. Pécaut, five or six years younger than Arnold, was not yet fifty-eight when Arnold saw Fontenay.

96:18–19. See p. 41:25–27n.

98:13–15. See p. 28:21–22.

98:30–31. This is Aristotle's way of determining the "mean" which is moral virtue.–*Nicomachean Ethics* 1107a. Arnold quoted it in "A French Critic on Goethe" (1878), *Prose Works*, ed. Super, VIII, 264.

101:7. Trachenberge is a suburb about three miles north of the center of Dresden.

101:11, 16–17. Both were very moralized ballads, "Der Sänger" (1795) of 42 lines, "Der Graf von Habsburg" (1803) of 120 lines.

102:1–4. See p. 31:6–12.

102:25. Arnold frequently uses the definition of the State which he ascribes to Burke: "the community [the people] in its [their] collective and corporate character." The conception is Burkean, but the precise definition apparently is not.

102:29–31. See p. 31:12–13, 233:22–23 and nn.

103:21. See p. 39:30n.

103:37. Arnold perpetually urged the establishment of an education minister in England, but the nearest thing to it at this time was the vice-president of the Committee of Council on Education, who was a member of the House of Commons.

104:9. "Payment by results," introduced by Robert Lowe in 1861, though somewhat modified over the years, made a substantial portion of the government grant to each school dependent on the number of its students who passed satisfactorily the state's examinations at the appropriate level. Arnold campaigned vigorously against it in the journals at the time it was proposed.

104:22. For Mackintosh, see p. 31:22n. Henry Hallam (1777–1859), historian of European institutions and letters, was influential in Whig intellectual circles but never entered practical politics.

105:17. The University of Pennsylvania, where Arnold delivered this address, claims descent from the Philadelphia Academy founded by Benjamin Franklin and others in 1753. Provost Pepper's wife was Franklin's great-great-granddaughter.

[SAINTE-BEUVE]

One of the happiest assignments an editor of an encyclopedia ever made was the invitation to Arnold to write the article on Sainte-Beuve for the ninth edition of the *Encyclopaedia Britannica;* presumably the decision was George Saintsbury's, as chief adviser to the *Britannica* on French literature. Arnold committed himself to having it done by the end of October, 1885 ("I have been living in his letters for the last few weeks," he told Humphry Ward on October 24); the volume containing it was published about a year later, the second week in November, 1886. On the 27th he wrote to his older daughter, "If you have access to the *Encyclopaedia Britannica,* read my article on Sainte Beuve in the last volume. He

would have been pleased by it himself, poor dear man, I think."—
Letters, ed. Russell. He had a few offprints of the article, one of
which he sent to John Churton Collins on December 4, another to
John Morley, who acknowledged it on December 12: "I read it
last night with lively pleasure and edification, as I do all that you
write and say outside of the Sahara of pure theology." Arnold received 12 gns. in payment. The French Swiss critic Edmond
Scherer was delighted that Arnold should have written it.—"Une
Histoire anglaise de la littérature française" (September, 1887),
Études sur la littérature contemporaine (Paris, 1895), X, 139. In his
obituary notice of Arnold in *Le Temps* (Paris) on April 18, 1888,
he concluded: "Je ne songe point à cacher ce qui se glisse de
personnel dans les regrets que j'exprime. Tous ces volumes d'Arnold, que j'ai là autour de moi, portent en tête la marque d'une
liaison qui datait déjà de loin. Je viens de retrouver le billet par
lequel Sainte-Beuve m'invitait, en 1866*, à un dîner à nous trois,
chez Véfour, 'dans un petit salon sur le jardin où nous causerons.'
Causeries reprises il n'y a que deux ans, chez Arnold lui-même,
dans les allées de sa petite campagne de Surrey. Nous y parlions de
ces auteurs français qu'il connaissait si bien et goûtait si vivement.
Telle était sa simplicité de bonhomie, qu'il fallait de la réflexion
pour se dire qu'on avait devant soi un si rare esprit."—p. 3, col. 2.

The Times (?Humphry Ward) said that the essay showed "all
the writer's well-known characteristics; it is, at the same time, a
good encyclopaedia article."—November 17, 1886, p. 9, col. 6. It
is one of the very finest of Arnold's essays in criticism, though
never published with those essays. Hardly a single phrase of it survives in the *Britannica*, but it was reprinted with notes in Kenneth
Allott, ed., *Five Uncollected Essays of Matthew Arnold* (Liverpool: University of Liverpool Press, 1953).

106:1–110:37. Arnold drew for his biographical data principally
on the posthumously published "Ma Biographie," with its commentary by Ste.-Beuve's secretary Jules Troubat.—Ste.-Beuve,
Souvenirs et indiscrétions, ed. Troubat (nouv. éd.; Paris, 1880),
pp. 1–120. He was clearly influenced also by the articles of d'Haussonville cited at p. 109:17–22n.

---

*In an article on "Documents in the Matthew Arnold–Sainte Beuve
Relationship," *Modern Philology* LX, 210 (February, 1963), the present
editor asserted that 1866 was an error for 1865; it was not. Arnold's diary
records a very brief visit to Paris in early May, 1866, which was not
apparent in his published letters.

106:8–10. In a poem "À M. Patin, après avoir suivi son cours de poésie latine," final 24 lines, published in *Pensées d'août* (1837); *Souvenirs et indiscrétions,* pp. 112–13.

106:19–20. Charles Neate (1806–79) was a fellow of Oriel College from 1828 until his death; Arnold was a fellow of the college from 1845 to 1852.

106:28. Paul-François Dubois (1793–1874).

107:3–4. *Le Globe,* January 2 and 9, 1827, reprinted in Sainte-Beuve, *Premiers Lundis* (Paris, 1874), I, 164–88. Goethe, a close follower and admirer of *The Globe,* commented on the former on January 4; J. P. Eckermann, *Gespräche mit Goethe,* ed. E. Castle (Berlin, 1916), I, 154. And Ste.-Beuve mentioned the comment in "Ma Biographie," pp. 32, 82. Ste.-Beuve began writing for *The Globe* in 1824 and gave up the study of medicine in 1827.

107:13–14. Reported in a letter of Ste.-Beuve's dated April 23, 1829; *Correspondance* (Paris, 1877), I, 16 and *Souvenirs et indiscrétions,* p. 178.

107:19–23. "Avertissement" to a new edition of *Les Consolations* (Paris, 1863), p. 2.

107:33. Port-Royal was an old Cistercian convent southwest of Paris which became a place of retreat and a center for schools in the Jansenist religious revival of the mid-seventeenth century. Pascal was closely associated with the community and the dramatist Jean Racine was educated in its schools.

108:2. The Bibliothèque Mazarine, the core of which was the collection of books bequeathed to the nation by Cardinal Mazarin in the mid-seventeenth century, is housed in the Palais de l'Institut de France, across the river from the Louvre.

108:6–7. *Souvenirs et indiscrétions,* p. iii (Preface by Charles Monselet).

108:10. *Ibid.,* pp. 138–40, 143–44.

108:25. Casimir Delavigne (1793–1843) was a dramatist and poet whom Ste.-Beuve admired enthusiastically in his own youth, but whose reputation has now vanished.

108:27–109:4. Ste.-Beuve tells the story in a prefatory note ("Avertissement") to *Chateaubriand et son groupe littéraire sous l'Empire* (nouv. éd.; Paris, 1889), I, 1–9; reprinted in *Correspondance,* I, 163n.

109:5–6. It was in this book that Ste.-Beuve published a translation of Arnold's poem "Obermann," largely done by Auguste Lacaussade.

109:12. Louis-Désiré Véron (1798–1867), who made a fortune with a patent medicine, was founder of the *Revue de Paris* and from 1844 proprietor of *Le Constitutionnel.*

109:15–17. *Souvenirs et indiscrétions,* p. 95.

109:17–22. Othenin d'Haussonville, "Écrivains contemporains: Charles-Augustin Sainte-Beuve," *Revue des deux mondes* XLV (3rd ser.), 121 (January 1, 1875), the first of three articles.

109:28–110:7. Ste.-Beuve gives a full account of these matters in a letter of July 13, 1863; *Correspondance,* I, 323–26. Hippolyte-Nicolas-Honoré Fortoul (1811–56), a warm adherent of the politics of Louis-Napoleon, was rewarded with the portfolio of Public Instruction on the morrow of the *coup d'état* of December 2, 1851, and held it until his death.

109:33–35. Letter of September 6, 1852; jotted in one of Arnold's "general notebooks."–Ste.-Beuve, *Nouvelle correspondance* (Paris, 1880), p. 133; Arnold, *Note-Books,* ed. Lowry, pp. 519–20. *Mollities frontis* is bashfulness (Pliny *Epistolae* VI, xxix, 6). As Arnold read further in *Nouvelle correspondance* he must have seen Ste.-Beuve's recommendation of "Obermann Once More" to Senancour's daughter.–p. 296 (August 12, 1868).

110:8–9. For his having refused twice under Louis-Philippe, see *Nouvelle correspondance,* p. 135n.

110:14–15. *Souvenirs et indiscrétions,* p. 186.

110:18–22. Letter of April 30, 1864; *Nouvelle correspondance,* p. 189.

110:28–29. The Princess Mathilde was daughter, the Prince Napoleon was son, of the first Napoleon's brother Jerome; they were therefore first cousins of Napoleon III. Both were patrons of literature and the arts.

110:34–37. *Souvenirs et indiscrétions,* pp. 15–16.

110:38–111:16. *Ibid.,* pp. 259–60, 224n.

111:6–9. *Ibid.,* pp. 249–51, 263, etc. Eugène Rouher (1814–84), an ardent Bonapartist, was the force that thrust the law restraining the freedom of the press through the Chambers on May 11, 1868. See p. 57:16–19. Ste.-Beuve for a second time had moved from the *Constitutionnel* to the *Moniteur* in September, 1867.

111:9–18. *Souvenirs et indiscrétions,* pp. 15–16, 313–14, 192.

111:18–25. *Ibid.,* pp. 328–29, 339–43.

111:28–30. *Ibid.,* p. 62 (conclusion of an autobiographical statement).

111:36–38. Letter of June 9, 1861, to a reviewer of the new edition of *Joseph Delorme; Correspondance*, I, 277.

112:1–4. Letter of mid-June, 1862; *ibid.*, I, 295.

112:6–7. Swinburne chiefly (in Arnold's view), and to a certain extent Saintsbury (see p. 118:29–31).

112:11–18. Letter of May 15, 1869; *Nouvelle correspondance*, pp. 352–53. Here Ste.-Beuve also refers to English poetry as "*la plus saine*," "the soundest."

112:18–23. Letter of March 26, 1861; *Correspondance*, I, 273.

112:25–27. Ste.-Beuve appended a number of critiques of the first edition when he published a new edition of *Les Consolations* (Paris, 1863). The reservations here cited were expressed by George Farcy and by Prosper Duvergier de Hauranne (pp. 125, 115).

112:33–36. Letter of March 31, 1848; *Correspondance*, I, 157 and *Souvenirs et indiscrétions*, pp. 206–7. The passage was jotted in Arnold's pocket diary at the end of 1872.—*Note-Books*, ed. Lowry, p. 188.

113:7–11. *Les Consolations* (1863), pp. 110, 115 (from *The Globe* of May 7, 1830).

113:18–21. *Ibid.*, p. 120. Ste.-Beuve quotes letters to himself on the poems from Béranger, Lamartine, Beyle ("Stendhal"), and, in the new edition of *Joseph Delorme* published at the same time, Jouffroy.

113:25. The first volume of *Critiques et portraits littéraires* was published in 1832; the work was expanded to five volumes in 1836–39. The essays were rearranged later as *Portraits littéraires, Portraits des femmes*, and *Portraits contemporains*.

113:30–31. Letter of 1838 (misdated 1839), *Nouvelle correspondance*, p. 59.

114:18–23. "Victor Hugo, 1831: 'Les Feuilles d'Automne,'" *Portraits contemporains* (nouv. éd.; Paris, 1881), I, 416–30. Arnold quotes from pp. 417 ("adorable"), 425 ("sublime"), 422 ("suprême"), 429.

114:24. Ste.-Beuve called his *Critiques et portraits littéraires* "une galerie de Portraits."—Letter of December 18, 1831; *Nouvelle correspondance*, p. 20. And the principal work of the popular and superficial critic George Gilfillan (1813–78) was his *Gallery of Literary Portraits* (1845–54).

114:24–31. "Victor Hugo, 1835; 'Les Chants du Crépuscule,'" *Portraits contemporains*, I, 446–63. Arnold quotes from pp. 449 ("de creux et de sonore"), 450 ("quelque chose d'artificiel, de voulu, d'acquis," "le théâtral"), 458 ("violent"), 457.

115:5–7. Arnold's phrases (derived from Ste.-Beuve) in "The Literary Influence of Academies" (1864), *Prose Works*, ed. Super, III, 246:20–21.

115:9–10. *Souvenirs et indiscrétions*, pp. v (Preface by Charles Monselet), 153.

115:17–20. Letter of May 30, 1830; *Nouvelle correspondance*, p. 17.

115:20–23. Letter of April 19, 1868; *Correspondance*, II, 284.

115:28–29. Letter of June 18, 1845; *Nouvelle correspondance*, p. 98. Louis-François Veuillot was a very militant conservative Catholic writer and journalist; Michelet and Quinet were anticlerical historians.

115:33–116:8. Letter of May 9, 1860; *Correspondance*, I, 252–53. Ste.-Beuve had been invited to write an article on *Les Girondins* of Adolphe Granier de Cassagnac.

116:11–14. Letter of February 9, 1862; *Correspondance*, I, 283.

116:17. "O you chorus of indolent reviewers," the opening line of one of Tennyson's "Experiments in Quantity," the hendecasyllabics.

116:18–29. Ste.-Beuve, *Correspondance*, I, 179–80.

117:1–3. Letter of June 13, 1857, perhaps to Lord Brougham; Louis J. Jennings, ed., *The Correspondence and Diaries of the Late . . . John Wilson Croker* (2nd ed.; London, 1885), III, 376.

117:6–9. "Oeuvres et correspondance de M. de Tocqueville," *Causeries du lundi* (3rd ed.; Paris, 1876), XV, 94. Arnold commented at greater length on this *Causerie* in his article on Ste.-Beuve's death (1869), *Prose Works*, ed. Super, V, 307–8.

117:11–14. *Souvenirs et indiscrétions*, p. 299.

117:17–18. "Je suis pour la gauche de l'Empire, et je suis presque seul."—Letter of January 6, 1869; *Correspondance*, II, 350 and *Souvenirs et indiscrétions*, p. 262.

117:21–23. Eckermann, *Gespräche mit Goethe*, ed. E. Castle, I, 140 (June 1, 1826).

117:29–30. See p. 282:11–12.

117:35–118:2. Letter of November 3, 1856; *Correspondance*, I, 218. A few years later Arnold himself received a similar letter from Ste.-Beuve. In "Maurice de Guérin" (1863) Arnold referred to him as "the first of living critics" (*Prose Works*, ed. Super, III, 12) and Ste.-Beuve demurred in a letter to Arnold on January 25: "Je ne peux ambitionner qu'un honneur, c'est d'être compté *parmi les critiques* qui ont leur coin d'originalité et qui savent leur métier: plus est trop et votre amitié ici va au-delà de ce qui peut être accordé par des indifférens."–A. F. Powell, "Sainte-Beuve and Matthew Arnold–an Unpublished Letter," *French Quarterly* III, 154 (September, 1921). Arnold replied: "Non, cher Monsieur, je n'en rabattrai rien; vous êtes le premier."–L. Bonnerot, *Matthew Arnold, poète* (Paris, 1947), p. 531. See "General Grant," p. 179:27.

118:4–10. Letter of June 18, 1845; *Nouvelle correspondance*, p. 98.

118:17. Arnold reread the fourth volume of the *Causeries* in 1885.–*Note-Books*, ed. Lowry, p. 618.

118:29–31. Arnold read George Saintsbury's *Primer of French Literature* (1880) and copied passages from it in his pocket diary for October 4–8, 1880.–*Note-Books*, ed. Lowry, p. 345. John P. Farrell discusses Arnold's view of this book in "Homeward Bound: Arnold's Late Criticism," *Victorian Studies* XVII, 197–99 (December, 1973).

[PREFACE TO MARY S. CLAUDE'S
Twilight Thoughts]

A few weeks after Arnold's much-publicized arrival in New York for his lecture tour of 1883–84, he was surprised by "getting a cordial letter from Louis Claude, entreating me 'as an old Ambleside boy' to come and visit him somewhere out on the way to St. Paul."–Letter to his sister Frances, Boston, November 8; *Letters*, ed. Russell. Since the lecture tour took Arnold no closer than Madison, Wisconsin, Claude (described in the Madison newspapers as "a retired merchant of some means") met him there on January 25, and in the intervals of a formal reception talked over old times.–C. H. Leonard, *Arnold in America* (Ann Arbor: University Microfilms, 1964), p. 217. Nearly three years later Arnold wrote to his sister Mrs. Forster on October 21, 1886: "You remember the Claudes: I promised, for the sake of old times, to give Louis Claude a few lines of preface for an edition of his sister's 'Twilight Thoughts' they are publishing in America; I have had to read the little book carefully through, and now to write two pages of preface gives me more trouble than you would imagine." On the 29th he told his daughter Lucy Whitridge that the preface was finished. "I don't think you know [the stories], but I wanted to do her brother a good turn, and about her I have a sentiment and her books as I remember them forty years ago and more."

Mary Sophia Claude, a year or two older than Arnold, moved to Ambleside with her three sisters, her brother, and her mother, after the death of her father, a Liverpool merchant, in the late 1820s. Except for the decade 1836–46, she lived in or near Ambleside until her death at the age of ninety-two on February 24, 1912. Both her parents were German born. She knew Clough and his sister Anne Jemima, and of course was acquainted with the Ambleside-Rydal-Grasmere society, which included the Arnolds seasonally from 1834 until Dr. Arnold's death in 1842, and permanently thereafter, when Fox How became Mrs. Arnold's home. Hartley Coleridge described her on April 10, 1847, as "still beautiful in face and person, though her bloom has been prematurely paled by pain and pensiveness—in mind she is *beautiful exceedingly.*"—*Letters*, ed. G. E. and E. L. Griggs (London: Oxford University Press, 1936), p. 289. On November 25, 1848, Arnold's younger sister Mary wrote to their brother Thomas in New Zealand a letter that has not survived, but Thomas commented to his mother, "[Mary's] account of Matt's romantic passion for the Cruel Invisible, Mary Claude, amused me beyond everything."—Thomas Arnold, *New Zealand Letters*, ed. James Bertram (Auckland: University of Auckland, 1966), pp. 119–20. Two brief articles have recently made public what is known of their relationship: Kenneth Allott, "Matthew Arnold and Mary Claude," *Notes and Queries* CCXIV, 209–11 (June, 1969), and Park Honan, "A Note on Matthew Arnold in Love," *Victorian Newsletter*, no. 39, pp. 11–15 (Spring, 1971).

Mary Claude's *Twilight Thoughts*, a dozen pleasant little rural stories for children published by Chapman and Hall in 1848, was one of several books for children she brought out under the initials "M. S. C." The Boston edition of 1887 added three stories, and is the only one of her books to give the author's name in full.

120:4. Hartley Coleridge returned to the Lakes in September, 1833, and died there on January 6, 1849. Wordsworth, who had only a little more than a year to live, was at his bedside the day before his death. As the body lay on the bed after death, Derwent Coleridge "saw a tall and beautiful woman come quietly into the room and, without noticing him, kneel down by the bedside in prayer, then pass like a dream silently away. That momentary apparition was Mary Claude."—H. D. Rawnsley, *Past and Present at the English Lakes* (Glasgow, 1916), p. 30. Hartley wrote a poem to Mary, visited the household frequently, and when they were away wrote to both mother and daughter.

120:8. The English edition had a quotation from Jean Paul as epigraph.

120:21–23. Robinson recalled this statement in a letter to Mrs. Wordsworth, March 7, 1848.—*Diary, Reminiscences, and Correspondence of Henry Crabb Robinson*, selected and edited by Thomas Sadler (London, 1869), III, 315.

[THE ZENITH OF CONSERVATISM]

When Arnold retired he was both relieved to be rid of his inspectoral duties and somewhat oppressed by the number of commitments he had already made for the services of his pen. An editor offered him £250 a year "for four articles on subjects of my own choice," he told his sister Jane on October 21, 1886; "this would make up the income I lose by resigning my professorship [*sic;* inspectorship?—he went on two-thirds pay with his retirement], but I have refused, because I want to keep myself free and not to make writing a trade." Politically, he thought there was hope. "Lord Randolph [Churchill] has *freshness*—a great thing. The fatal thing at this moment, as I have so often said, is drifting—and the stale old hacks always love to talk plausibly and to drift. I do not wish to have anarchy in Ireland, or to disestablish the Church of England. But Lord Clanricarde as an Irish landlord, and Lord Lonsdale as the patron of forty livings, have become impossible; they must be seriously dealt with; the old hacks want still to leave them as they are, to talk plausibly about them, and to drift; the same as to Winans in Scotland [See p. 74:28]. Lord Randolph, as I say, is *fresh;* he perceives that something serious must be done. Lord Salisbury's intellect is such that he perceives the same thing, perhaps with clearer and deeper view than Ld Randolph; but I doubt whether without Ld R.'s freshness and go to stimulate him, he would act. I shall probably write one political article for Knowles at Christmas, simply to try to be of use by keeping people's eyes fixed on main issues, and preventing their going off on side ones. I should like to write one political article a year—only one—and an article of this nature."—*Letters*, ed. Russell. Arnold had had some very serious warning signals from his heart during the visit to America, but he reported to Charles Eliot Norton on December 22, after completing this article and the first one on General Grant at the same time, "I found myself able to answer to the spur, and to produce my two articles under pressure, without any bad effects, and I think the stuff produced is of about the same quality as usual—not worse."—*Letters,* ed. Russell. One blow was yet in store—the hero of Arnold's article, Lord Randolph Churchill, resigned from the cabinet while Arnold's article was in proof. "Then came Chamberlain's speech also [on December 23], to change the posture of things still further. But I have made everything right, and think the article will do very well, and, I hope, be of use," Arnold told his sister on December 27. Knowles received the revised proof (which is now in the library of Balliol College, Oxford) at his home on December 28, took it himself to the printer, and it was published as the final article in the January number of the *Nineteenth Century.* Arnold was paid £50 for it. It has been republished in Neiman's *Essays, Letters, and Reviews by Matthew Arnold.*

122:18–21. In "The Nadir of Liberalism," pp. 54–77.

122:23–24. Lord Randolph Churchill, at thirty-seven the youngest chancellor of the exchequer since the younger Pitt nearly a century earlier, resigned on December 23 over a budget dispute in the cabinet, and the Conservatives thereby lost their leader in the House of Commons. Arnold and Churchill both spoke at the dinner on behalf of the Jews' Free School on May 21, 1884, when Arnold publicly praised Churchill.—*Prose Works,* ed. Super, X, 246. The latter, addressing his constituents after the election of July, 1886, claimed for himself Arnold's virtue of "lucidity."— *Pall Mall Gazette,* August 5, 1886, p. 3. Arnold's opinion of Churchill personally was another matter: "Few people like Ld Randolph Churchill less than I do, but I can see the need for having a vigorous and spirited personage to speak for the government in the H. of Commons, and one not likely to be overborne by Gladstone, Morley, Labouchere and the Irish," he wrote to his sister Jane on August 1, 1886.

122:25. The session of Parliament opened on January 27, 1887.

123:7–8. See p. 82:11–12n.

123:21–23. Chamberlain as a Liberal Unionist was unopposed for his seat for West Birmingham in the general election of 1886 and at the same time secured the defeat of the Gladstonian Liberal, William Cook, in East Birmingham in favor of the Conservative Henry Matthews. When Matthews accepted the home secretaryship, however, he was by custom obliged to resign and stand for reelection. The Chamberlain forces then entered into negotiation with Cook in the hope that they could sway him to the Unionist side, but were discontented with his publicly expressed views, declined their support on the eve of the election, and Cook withdrew at the last minute. See *The Times's* running account, especially August 6, p. 5, col. 5, August 11, p. 5, col. 6, and August 12, p. 6, cols. 3–4.

123:24–25. Trevelyan lost his seat for the Border Burghs to a Gladstonian Liberal in the general election of 1886, and was invited by the Liberal leaders at Brighton to stand for that constituency in late November. Rumors circulated that he had accepted the invitation, but he did not and the Conservative candidate was elected without opposition. Trevelyan was reconciled to Gladstone and won the Liberal seat at Bridgeton (Glasgow) in 1887.

123:25–32. Gladstone's proposal was made in a letter to Lord Wolverton published in *The Times*, November 10, 1886, p. 10, col. 4. Lord Hartington's rebuff was made from the chair of the Liberal Unionist Association meeting in London on December 7, reported in *The Times* next day, p. 6, col. 3.

123:33–37. Beginning of chapt. iii, jotted in Arnold's pocket diary for September 1, 1883.—*Note-Books*, ed. Lowry, p. 398.

124:8–9. Chamberlain, speaking to the Liberal Divisional Council of W. Birmingham (his constituency) on the day Churchill's resignation was announced, said: "I fear it is probable that the old Tory influences have gained the upper hand and that we may be face to face with a Tory Government whose proposals no consistent Liberal will be able to support." And so he laid stress on the vast number of points of agreement among Liberals, if only home rule were abandoned.—*Times*, December 24, p. 4, col. 5.

124:14–16. The Conservatives remained in power until July, 1892.

124:37–125:1. See pp. 55:30–32, 61:34, 62:2–4 and notes.

125:32–37. For Arnold's view of the actual achievement of the Conservatives, see "From Easter to August," pp. 246–64.

126:33–34. The first business of the Commons in January was the amendment of the rules to allow closure by a bare majority, provided the Speaker consented and at least two hundred members voted for the closure. Procedure was further tightened by putting a time limit on debate when the House was in committee. Arnold in 1882 expressed his preference for the form "closure" rather than "cloture."—*Prose Works*, ed. Super, X, 242.

127:1–5. In an important speech during the Parliamentary recess, Lord Randolph Churchill, government leader in the House of Commons, on October 2, 1886, insisted on the necessity of closure of debate by a bare majority. The newspapers contrasted that position with a speech Lord Randolph made in the Commons on November 1, 1882, as an opposition member, calling upon his party to "resort to all those forms and privileges which the minority still possessed" to oppose and defeat Gladstone's closure proposals.— *Pall Mall Gazette*, October 4, 1886, pp. 1, 11; October 6, p. 6.

127:5–9. Thomas Wilson, *Maxims of Piety and of Christianity*, ed. Frederic Relton (London, 1898), p. 44, jotted in Arnold's pocket diary for September 14, 1883, at the beginning of 1884, for January 10, 1885, and in one of his general notebooks, the last with the heading "The Thing to Remember."—*Note-Books*, ed. Lowry, pp. 399, 405, 413, 537. The *Saturday Review*, in an article on Arnold's retirement, good-naturedly expressed the hope that Arnold would spend his years of unofficial life avoiding the practical; that he would "finally forswear the ambition to settle the Irish question and to recast the Christian religion," and as for his reading list, "of two books, if we had the disposal of it, we can speak with certainty. We should lock up his Bishop Wilson and his Burke."—"Mr. Matthew Arnold," November 20, 1886, p. 676.

127:12. "The only nation-wide scheme of local authorities [in 1868] was that of the boards of guardians administering the 1834 Poor Law. For the rest, the counties were still ruled by the justices of the peace in quarter sessions; and in the urban areas responsibility for such primary services as paving, cleansing, lighting, or drainage devolved sometimes on a municipal corporation, sometimes on an improvement commission, sometimes on a local board, sometimes on a London vestry; not unfrequently being divided between two of these bodies. The 1868–74 [Liberal] government itself added yet another *ad hoc* authority—the school boards, which were set up in most areas under its 1870 Education Act. . . . The blind eye, which [Gladstone] consistently turned towards the importance of local government, . . . in its effect on history may be accounted a national misfortune."—R. C. K. Ensor, *England 1870–1914* (Oxford: Clarendon Press, 1936), p. 125.

128:2–4. Arnold described aspects of local government of schools in his report on *Elementary Education in Germany, &c.* (1886).

128:31–33. On September 15, 1886, in the House of Commons, Lord Randolph Churchill promised to remake Irish local government in accordance with Irish wishes. But as the new session approached, the Government announced that Ireland would not be included in its new Local Government Bill.—*Pall Mall Gazette*, September 16, p. 1 and December 15, p. 3.

128:34–35. On the eve of the Liberal Conference, John Morley, rising young star of the party, remarked in a letter published in *The Times* of November 3, 1886: "My own opinion is that the disestablishment of the Church in Wales . . . is a reform which cannot any longer be kept out of the active objects of the Liberal party."—p. 6, col. 5.

129:10–11. Voting in England became secret by the Liberals' Ballot Act of 1872; the franchise was democratized and constituencies were redistributed through a pair of bills passed under the Gladstone government in 1884–85 that raised the number of voters from about three million to about five million.

129:22–24. Harrison, "Leon Gambetta. A Positivist Discourse," *Contemporary Review* XLIII, 323 (March, 1883). For Trevelyan's return to the Liberal fold, see p. 123:24–25n.

129:27–28. "Mr. Willis' motion to remove the Bishops from the House of Lords was lost by 11 votes on the 21st of March, 1884."— G. W. E. Russell, *Matthew Arnold* (London, 1904), p. 123n.

130:1–3. First "Letter to Sir Hercules Langrishe . . . on the . . . Roman Catholics of Ireland," fifth paragraph from end; jotted in one of Arnold's general notebooks.—*Note-Books,* ed. Lowry, p. 512.

130:6–13. "The Function of Criticism at the Present Time" (1864), *Prose Works,* ed. Super, III, 265, 282.

130:13–14. See p. 62:36–37n.

130:19–22. In late September, 1886, the British light opera singer Violet Cameron arrived with her company in New York, bringing with her as business manager, financial backer, and intimate friend Hugh Cecil Lowther, fifth Earl of Lonsdale. The countess had remained behind, and Miss Cameron's husband arrived by another ship, threatening divorce. The American newspapers made the most of the scandalous and the ridiculous aspects of the affair.

131:24–25. See p. 86:12.

131:28. Quoted in Sainte-Beuve's essay on Sieyès, *Causeries du lundi* (3rd ed.; Paris, 1869), V, 209. The phrase is from Lucan *de Bello Civili* I, 509: "The mob rushes headlong, irrevocable."

131:38–132:1. See p. 141:31–32n.

132:32–37. Speaking at a Liberal conference at Leicester, November 25, 1886; reported in *The Times* next day, p. 6, col. 4. Lord Spencer was lord-lieutenant of Ireland in the Gladstone government.

133:36–134:1. George Berkeley, *The Querist* (1736), part ii, no. 253 (dropped from the version of 1750); quoted by Arnold in "The Incompatibles" (1881), *Prose Works*, ed. Super, IX, 285.

134:13–19. First "Letter to Langrishe," five-sixths through. Gladstone having often appealed to the authority of Burke, and an Irishman named H. de F. Montgomery having challenged him in a pamphlet, the Baron H. de Worms undertook to prove in a letter to *The Times* that Gladstone was wrong, and A. J. Mundella, quoting this passage from Arnold's *Selections from Burke*, wrote to prove Gladstone was right.—*Times*, December 8, 1886, p. 7, col. 6; December 10, p. 10, col. 4; December 14, p. 10, col. 2. The *Saturday Review* commented: "To quote Burke in reference to the present Irish controversy, is simply to show an absolute misunderstanding, and even a hopeless incapacity to understand, his habit of thought. His political doctrine was essentially that of circumstances. If anybody had suggested to him that he could express in 1797 an opinion worth anything in regard to the politics of 1886, he would have thought that he was talking to a fool. We cannot pretend to think that he would have been wrong."—"Polling Dead Men," December 18, 1886, p. 802.

134:33–35. "Letter on the Affairs of Ireland" (1797), ¶13, quoted in "The Incompatibles" (1881), *Prose Works*, ed. Super, IX, 249.

134:35–135:4. "Letter on the Affairs of Ireland," ¶14.

135:10–12. *Coriolanus*, I, i, 181–83.

135:13–16. See p. 66:21–22.

135:18–20. "I wonder whether any country that ever undertook to govern another could present so ignoble a table of vacillations, of hesitancies, and precipitations," said Morley in a speech at Edinburgh on December 2, 1886.—*Times*, December 3, p. 7, col. 3. Arnold's pocket diary on December 3 notes "Morley's speech (L.ᵈ Spencer)." "You are not sound on the Irish question, alas," wrote Morley to Arnold on December 12. "That is no reason why I should not rejoice if chance or design sh.ᵈ bring us face to face for an evening. I try to keep myself humane in the midst of the battle."

136:2–6. David Sheehy, William O'Brien, and John Dillon were all Irish members of Parliament, leaders of the "Plan of Campaign" (see p. 137:23). Sheehy's dialogue with the crowd took place at a meeting at Woodford on October 17, 1886, and was recalled in an article on the meeting in *The Pall Mall Gazette*, December 8, p. 2.

136:6–8. "[The English] are dealing with a nation that is like an army on the march. . . . [Our leader, Parnell,] will carry us . . . over the runis of landlordism and English domination in Ireland."–O'Brien in Chicago, August 18, 1886, reported in *The Times*, August 20, p. 5, col. 2.

136:8–10. At Castlereagh on December 6 Dillon said: "The time is at hand–and very close at hand too–when the police will be our servants. . . . I warn the men to-day who take their stand by the side of landlordism and signalize themselves as the enemies of the people that in the day of our power we will remember them."–*Times,* December 7, 1886, p. 6, col. 1.

136:10–12. Daniel O'Connell (whose son was with Bolivar in South America) was widely reported to have made this remark, but when the government brought charges against him none of the newspaper reporters could be persuaded to testify (one of them said he had fallen asleep at that point and had reported what he had been told by a neighbor). And so the bill was thrown out without a trial.

136:13–17. The tone, but not the language, of a leading article, "England's Trouble Ireland's Hope," *Pall Mall Gazette*, December 20, 1886, p. 1. "Nous avons changé tout cela," said Sganarelle in Molière's *Le Médecin malgré lui*, II, iv.

136:38–137:4. The scene was typical enough, but Arnold may have had in mind the fate of the bailiffs who failed in their attempt to evict Timothy Hurley from Castleview Farm, near Cork, on October 18, 1886.–*Times*, October 20, p. 6, col. 5. It is equally an account of the events on Lord Clanricarde's estate at Woodford in mid-August, 1886. See also p. 139:38–140:3.

137:9–11. Sir James Graham was home secretary in Peel's cabinet when the government in 1844 brought O'Connell to trial and won a verdict against him from a packed (all Protestant) jury. The verdict was overthrown by the House of Lords. (At that time the Irish secretary was subordinate to the home secretary.)

137:14. Mirabeau is said to have used this expression: "Administrer, c'est gouverner; gouverner, c'est régner; tout se réduit à cela."

137:20–21. A phrase from Morley's speech at Edinburgh, December 2, 1886, reported in *The Times* next day, p. 7, col. 3.

137:22–24, 29. When Parnell's Tenants' Relief Bill (see p. 142:12) failed to pass the Conservative House of Commons on September 21, 1886, and renewed evictions followed, the Irish leaders circulated throughout Ireland as a supplement to the newspaper *United*

Ireland on October 21 the "Plan of Campaign," which "called on the tenants of each estate to organize; to treat with the landlord as a united body, standing or falling together; and if their offers of rent were not accepted by him, to pay the money instead into a campaign fund."—Ensor, *England 1870–1914*, p. 179. Arnold quotes the language of the justices of the Queen's Bench, Dublin, on the trial of Dillon, December 14, 1886, reported in *The Times* next day, p. 6, cols. 3–4.

137:31–34. Arnold visited his brother-in-law W. E. Forster in Dublin from September 21 to October 1, 1881, while Forster was chief secretary for Ireland. On his return he wrote to Lord Coleridge: "The Irish press was a new thing to me: it is like the Jacobin press in the heat of the French Revolution. I don't see how Ireland is to settle down while such stimulants to the people's hatred and disaffection are applied every day. But our English pedants will continue to believe in the divine and saving effect, under all circumstances, of right of meeting, right of speaking, right of printing."—E. H. Coleridge, *Life & Correspondence of John Duke Lord Coleridge* (London, 1904), II, 307. The Nationalist newspaper *United Ireland*, weekly organ of the Land League, began publication under the editorship of William O'Brien on August 13, 1881; in the middle of October O'Brien was arrested under the powers of the Coercion Act of that year and for six months conducted the paper from Kilmainham Gaol.

138:3–6. Dillon's language in his own defense at the Dublin trial of December 14, 1886.—*Times*, December 15, p. 6, col. 3.

138:30–31. "The law bears, and must bear, with the vices and follies of men, until they actually strike at the root of order."—Burke, "Tracts on the Popery Laws," chapt. iii, pt. 2, ¶4, as quoted in "The Incompatibles" (1881), *Prose Works*, ed. Super, IX, 251.

138:33–139:6. Croker, letter to Lord Lonsdale, September 4, 1852, and "A Sketch of the State of Ireland, Past and Present" (1807), *The Croker Papers: The Correspondence and Diaries of . . . John Wilson Croker*, ed. Louis J. Jennings (2nd ed.; London, 1885), III, 259 and I, 456. Sir Arthur Wellesley, chief secretary for Ireland in 1807–9, became the Duke of Wellington.

139:27–33. Hubert George de Burgh Canning (1832–1916) became second Marquess of Clanricarde in 1874. "The rest of [his] life was spent in resisting the movement to limit the Irish landlord's power. His campaign was conducted at a distance, as he never visited his large property—some 56,000 acres—in East Galway, but lived continuously in the Albany, Piccadilly."—Stephen Gwynn in *D.N.B.*

139:38–140:3. See p. 136:38–137:4.

140:10–11. Goschen used the terms "pickpockets and garotters" in his speech at the Liberal Unionist Association's conference in London on December 7, 1886.—*Times*, December 8, p. 7, col. 3. Speaking at the City Conservative Club on December 8, 1886, Lord Salisbury said: "If my neighbour gives money to a mendicant on the roadside, and I refuse to do it, that is no excuse for the mendicant proceeding to highway robbery on me. But that is the sort of argument advanced on behalf of the Irish tenants."—*Pall Mall Gazette*, December 9, p. 11. The *Pall Mall*'s leading article that day linked Salisbury's remark with Goschen's.

140:15–16. Judges 16:25–30.

141:1–12. In "The Incompatibles" (1881), *Prose Works*, ed. Super, IX, 262–67, 257. The judge was Lord Coleridge, the philanthropist Samuel Morley.

141:12–16. Lord Spencer, viceroy of Ireland in the previous Gladstone administration and lord president of the Privy Council in that of 1886, during the cabinet debates of March, 1886, insisted that the Home Rule Bill be accompanied by a Land Purchase Bill if he were to support the former proposal. Accordingly, a week after Gladstone moved his Home Rule Bill, he moved a Land Purchase Bill (April 16, 1886) which fixed the normal price of the landlord's interest at the net rental of twenty years, purchase to be secured by the consolidated fund and to be optional with the landlord. This bill died when the Home Rule Bill was defeated at its second reading and Parliament was dissolved.

141:31–32. Hicks-Beach was chief secretary for Ireland in Disraeli's government of 1874 and again in Salisbury's cabinet of 1886. He was replaced by Salisbury's nephew A. J. Balfour in March, 1887. General Sir Redvers Buller was sent by the Salisbury government in August, 1886, (as a civilian) to restore order in Kerry through reorganizing the police, and became under-secretary for Ireland.

142:2. John Morley was chief secretary for Ireland in Gladstone's home rule cabinet of February–June, 1886.

142:12–13. On September 10, 1886, Parnell brought forward his Tenants' Relief (Ireland) Bill giving the land court power to suspend eviction proceedings if half the rent was paid, and to vary the judicial rent. It was supported by the Gladstonians, but defeated at the second reading on September 21.

142:32. Deuteronomy 31:6, 7, 23; Joshua 1:6, 9, 18; 10:25; I Chronicles 22:13, 28:20.

[GENERAL GRANT]

Arnold's American friends more than once threw him in with General U. S. Grant. On June 18, 1877, he was guest at a large breakfast given for Grant in London by G. W. Smalley. Grant was among those who attended the great reception given by Andrew Carnegie in Arnold's honor in New York on October 27, 1883, at the beginning of the American lecture tour, and he attended Arnold's first lecture, on "Numbers," on October 30. The story is told that, unable to hear the speaker in the crowded hall, Grant turned to his wife and said, "Well, wife, we have paid to see the British lion; we cannot hear him roar, so we had better go home."–J. B. Pond, *Eccentricities of Genius* (New York, 1900), p. 323. Next day, Grant indirectly paid his respects to Arnold: "Imagine General Grant calling at the Tribune Office to thank them for their good report of the main points of my lecture, as he had thought the line taken so very important, but had heard imperfectly," Arnold wrote to his sister on November 8. "Now I should not have suspected Grant of either knowing or caring anything whatever about me or my productions."–*Letters*, ed. Russell. Grant died before Arnold's visit to the United States in the summer of 1886, and his *Personal Memoirs* by that time had attracted much attention both for the number of copies published and for the magnitude of the royalty: they were indeed something of a sensation. When, therefore, Arnold's nephew Edward A. Arnold asked for an article for the first number of the new *Murray's Magazine* which he was editing, Arnold wrote to his older sister on October 21, 1886: "Ted is at me for his magazine; I think I shall do Gen! Grant's Memoirs for him: the Americans will like it, the book has hardly been noticed in England, and Grant is shown by this book to be one of the most solid men they have had; I prefer him to Lincoln; except Franklin, I know hardly any one so *selbst-ständig*, so broad and strong sighted, as well as firm-charactered, that they have had."–*Letters*, ed. Russell. A month later he wrote to his daughter in New York (November 27): "I have to write, rather against time, an article for Ted on General Grant's Life, of which not three hundred copies have been sold in England [but see p. 179:18–20]. That makes it all the better subject, as there are really materials in the book for a most interesting article, and no one has used them."–*Letters*, ed. Russell. His pocket diary makes no mention of the first part, but he worked at the second part from January 4 to 10; on the latter date he sent it off. He was paid £31.10.0 for each part, published in *Murray's Magazine* in January and February, 1887. The articles were republished in Boston in the same year as a 66-page pamphlet, *General Grant: An Estimate*, by Cupples, Upham; and by the same firm (now Cupples and Hurd) with Arnold's other essays on America, in the volume *Civilization in the United States*, shortly after Arnold's death in 1888. In fact, the Americans were not pleased with Arnold's essay. An account of its reception in the United States, together with a speech condemning it by Mark Twain (an investor in the firm that published the *Memoirs*), will be found in John Y. Simon, ed., *General Grant by Matthew Arnold with a Rejoinder by Mark Twain* (Carbondale and Edwardsville: Southern Illinois University Press, 1966).

144:1–5. The posthumous two-volume *Personal Memoirs of U. S. Grant* (New York: Charles L. Webster & Company, 1885–86) was composed by Grant in an attempt to recoup the financial disaster brought on by his son's and his own imprudent partnership with Ferdinand Ward (see p. 178:34n.). The first edition of 325,000 copies was "the largest first edition ever published." *The New York Times* on February 28, 1886 (p. 6, col. 7), reported that Mrs. Grant was paid $200,000 for the first volume and was promised another $250,000–$300,000 from the proceeds of the second. The two volumes were published in London by Sampson Low, Marston & Co. about December 1, 1885, and May 15, 1886, and were duly reviewed in *The Times* (December 1, May 19), *The Athenaeum* (May 29), and *The Saturday Review* (December 26, June 5). For Arnold's correction of his misstatement, see p. 179.

144:20. See headnote to "Civilisation in the United States," p. 487.

144:26–145:12. Arnold met Grant in London at a breakfast given on June 18, 1877, by George Washburn Smalley, correspondent for *The New York Tribune;* among other guests were Huxley, Trollope, Browning, and Thomas Hughes.–J. R. Young, *Around the World with General Grant* (New York, 1879), I, 28–29. Young's account suggests that Grant excited a great deal of attention in London.

145:17–18. Adam Badeau (1831–95), a clerk in the State Department when the Civil War broke out, became military secretary on Grant's staff on April 8, 1864, and retired with the rank of brigadier-general when Grant was inaugurated president in March,

1869. Thereafter he had various posts in the consular service until his resignation in 1884. He lived in Grant's house to assist the composition of the *Memoirs*.

145:25. Horace *Odes* III, iii, 2.

145:37. As a Latinist Arnold perceived "conscript" as itself a past passive participle; the English verb would be "to conscribe." But the use of "conscript" as a verb, which the *N.E.D.* traces to the United States in Civil War years, is now common enough.

146:18–147:6. *Personal Memoirs*, I, 21–22, 24–25.

147:8. The Royal Military College at Sandhurst, some thirty miles west of London, was the chief training college for British infantry and cavalry officers; the Royal Military Academy at Woolwich, a few miles below London on the Thames, trained officers for the Royal Engineers and the Royal Artillery. The two have now been amalgamated at Sandhurst.

147:11–37. *Personal Memoirs*, I, 25–27.

148:5–24. *Ibid.*, I, 29–30. Connecticut men, or Yankees, are proverbial for their cunning in business.

148:33–149:6. *Ibid.*, I, 32. The italics are Grant's. The United States Senator was Thomas Morris; Grant's Congressman, who actually nominated him for the Academy, was Thomas L. Hamer.

149:7–37. *Ibid.*, I, 34–35 (27), 37–40, 42–43.

150:1–11. *Ibid.*, I, 45–46, 51–52. Arnold liked to insist that "a public and high standing" was requisite for all good schools, and the lack of such public standing was his chief ground of complaint against all except a very few English secondary schools.

150:12–28. *Personal Memoirs*, I, 52–53, 56–58. "Filibustering" was raiding by irregular troops.

150:34–151:2. *Ibid.*, I, 53.

151:3–15. *Ibid.*, I, 54–55, 68. Grant wrote "sent to provoke a fight."

151:16–26. *Ibid.*, I, 89, 92, 161, 172.

151:27–152:9. *Ibid.*, I, 54, 56.

152:10–21. *Ibid.*, I, 158–59. "Voltigeurs" were light infantry or sharpshooters.

152:22–37. *Ibid.*, I, 193–94, 199, 202, 206, 210. The troop went by ship from New York to Aspinwall (Colon) on the Isthmus of Panama, then overland to the Pacific for shipment to San Francisco.

153:3–12. *Ibid.*, I, 210–12.

153:16–154:6. *Ibid.*, I, 213–15. John C. Fremont was the Republican candidate for president in 1856, the first year in which the party nominated such a candidate.

155:10–12. *Journal d'un voyageur pendant la guerre* (4th ed.; Paris, 1871), p. 20 (letter of September 23).

155:22–156:8. *Personal Memoirs*, I, 216, 222, 227–30. On April 6, a strong force of Confederates under General A. S. Johnston surprised Grant's encampment at Shiloh (Pittsburg Landing) on the Tennessee River, but the Confederates were driven back after a bloody two-day battle in which Johnston was killed. See p. 160. By the date of Lincoln's inauguration only seven states had seceded, but Grant's *Memoirs* are not clear on that point.

156:9–23. *Personal Memoirs*, I, 230–31.

156:24–157:19. *Ibid.*, I, 232–33, 239–43, 246–48.

157:29–31. "Hester," lines 29–31. Lamb's words are "When from thy cheerful eyes a ray | Hath struck a bliss upon the day, | A bliss that would not go away."

157:33–34. In his first collection of poems (1849), Arnold in a sonnet "To the Duke of Wellington" praised the Duke for "wit, | Which saw *one* clue to life and follow'd it," for becoming "Laborious, persevering, serious, firm."

157:35–36. Joseph Butler's expression, "a mind which sees things as they really are" (Sermon XV, ¶4) became a favorite phrase of Arnold's; in "The Function of Criticism at the Present Time" (1864) he defined the role of the critic as "in all branches of knowledge . . . to see the object as in itself it really is."—*Prose Works*, ed. Super, III, 258.

158:15–28. *Personal Memoirs*, I, 249–50.

158:29–159:8. *Ibid.*, I, 254, 256, 264–67, 269–80.

159:9–160:2. *Ibid.*, I, 284, 286–88, 294, 312, 314, 316–18.

160:3–23. *Ibid.*, I, 330, 354, 367, 370, 377, 379–81.

160:24–30. *Ibid.*, I, 382–83.

160:35–36. Arnold may have taken this expression from Sainte-Beuve, *Portraits littéraires* (nouv. éd.; Paris, 1864), III, 400. Alfred de Vigny had applied Mazarin's words to Charles-Guillaume Étienne in his address upon his reception into the Academy.

161:1–17. *Personal Memoirs*, I, 443. The italics were Grant's.

161:18–32. *Ibid.*, I, 392–94, 419–20.

162:1–29. *Ibid.*, I, 422–24, 432, 435.

162:30–163:18. *Ibid.*, I, 461, 437, 442–43, 441, 444, 458, 446.

163:18–164:8. *Ibid.*, I, 460, 466–68, 473, 461, 476–78.

164:9–15. *Ibid.*, I, 480.

164:16–165:21. *Ibid.*, I, 481, 483–84, 490–93, 495, 499–500, 506–7, 530–31, 563, 568.

165:22–26. *Ibid.*, I, 567–68.

165:31. "Bounce" is brash self-assertiveness.

165:32–38. *Memoirs*, I, 476. The italics are Arnold's.

166:3–33. *Ibid.*, I, 441–42, 546–47. The italics are Arnold's.

166:37–167:3, 7–15. *Ibid.*, I, 444, 458–59.

167:18–25. *Ibid.*, I, 570, 577.

167:33–34. Jean-Baptiste Carrier (1756–94) gained a reputation for atrocious cruelty by the system of wanton slaughter he instituted at Nantes in 1793 against those who had revolted against the Republic. Louis-Nicolas Davout (1770–1823), perhaps the best of Napoleon's field generals, was a strict disciplinarian who was much criticized for the stern measures he took to hold Hamburg against siege in 1813–14, even after the fall of Napoleon.

168:1–12. *Memoirs*, I, 507.

168:17–169:5. *Ibid.*, I, 459–60.

169:7–20. *Ibid.*, II, 18, 89, 98–100.

169:21–32. *Ibid.*, II, 101–2.

169:33–171:3. *Ibid.*, II, 114–18.

171:4–29. *Ibid.*, II, 119–20, 125, 122–23; Grant's italics.

172:7–173:20. *Ibid.*, II, 140, 126, 177–78, 241, 289, 298–99, 400–401, 335, 454, 456–58. Grant says he began with 116,000 men and had 115,000 at the crossing of the James River.

173:22–175:21. *Ibid.*, II, 483–85, 489–93, 495–96.

175:22–35. *Ibid.*, II, 517, 505, 508–9, 534–35. W. H. Seward, secretary of state, was wounded but not killed in the assassination plot.

175:37–176:11. *Memoirs*, II, 531 (paraphrased).

176:13–16. See pp. 117:37–118:2.

176:29–35. Arnold criticized Grimm's claims for Goethe in "A French Critic on Goethe" (1878) and repeated the criticism in "Emerson" (1883).—*Prose Works*, ed. Super, VIII, 254; X, 168.

177:1–4. "A Hunt for the Nightingale," *Century Magazine* XXVII (n.s. V), 776 (March, 1884); *The Writings of John Burroughs* (Boston, 1904), VI: *Fresh Fields*, p. 93. Frances Arnold sent her brother a volume of Burroughs for Christmas in 1886. "[He] is a good writer," Arnold commented. But after finishing the book on January 2, he wrote: "What a pity he has the American disease of always bringing into comparison his country and its things! They all do it, however, except you get a man like Emerson. He much overpraises the song of the American (so-called) robin."—*Letters*, ed. Russell.

177:7. "I was shown the Green River yesterday, the river 'immortalised by the American Wordsworth'—i.e. Bryant," Arnold wrote to Charles Eliot Norton from Stockbridge, August 27, 1886.

177:8. Charles Francis Richardson's *A Primer of American Literature* (Boston: Houghton, Osgood, 1878) was a very popular 117-page compendium that went through several revisions.

177:29–178:9. *Memoirs*, I, 471–72; II, 269.

178:13. See p. 160:35–36.

178:15–31. *Memoirs*, II, 548–49.

178:34–179:14. Grant's son Ulysses was a partner with Ferdinand Ward in a speculative and dishonest financial operation flamboyantly conducted by the latter. Grant himself became a silent partner by investing all his capital in the firm. In less than three years the firm collapsed and Ward decamped, leaving Grant without funds and indebted for $150,000 he had borrowed on his personal credit from W. H. Vanderbilt in the hope of relieving what he supposed were only temporary embarrassments of the firm. He composed his *Personal Memoirs* in order to pay off his debts; much of the work was done while he was suffering great pain from cancer of the throat. The book was completed in July, 1885, only fourteen months after the financial disaster, and Grant died a fortnight later. The friend Arnold quotes was probably George W. Childs, proprietor of the Philadelphia *Public Ledger*, whose summer home at Long Branch, New Jersey, adjoined Grant's, with no fence between. See p. 329:21–22n.

Arnold himself had undertaken his first American lecture tour in order to pay off the gambling debts of his only surviving son Richard—debts of over £1000.

179:30–31. The maxims of Poor Richard were apothegms composed by Benjamin Franklin as space-fillers in *Poor Richard's Almanack*, which he published in Philadelphia for a quarter of a century from 1733.

[A "FRIEND OF GOD"]

Arnold's commitment to review J. R. Morell's version of Tauler's *Following of Christ*, as an act of friendship to "a poor ex-colleague," was of long standing; he took the volume with him to America in the summer of 1886, and read it during his stay at Stockbridge with his daughter and granddaughter in July and August. It was an oppressive task: "There is that poor Morell who was dismissed; I have promised him four or five pages about a so-called work of Tauler which he has translated; this, if I do not take care, will be 'the sea to drink,'" he wrote to his sister Mrs.

Forster on October 21. The pressure of other commitments (including the revision of *St. Paul and Protestantism* for a "Popular Edition") was so great that it was not until March 14, 1887, that he could write to his daughter: "I have this week to perform the last of the promises I made before I retired—to write a short notice of Tauler, a German mystic before the Reformation, to help a poor man who has translated one of his works." His pocket diary shows him at work on the essay from March 14 to 19, 1887, and reading proofs of it on March 24. It was published in the *Nineteenth Century* in April, and Arnold received £18 in payment. It has been republished in Fraser Neiman's *Essays, Letters, and Reviews by Matthew Arnold*.

180:1–3. John Reynell Morell was a cousin of J. D. Morell, the author of widely-used textbooks of English grammar, who was for many years (1848–76) an inspector of schools. J. R. Morell's translation of the Tauler volume, in small octavo, was published about the middle of May, 1886, priced at 2*s. 6d.*

180:3–5. Morell describes the principal recent German editor of the work, Heinrich Denifle (1879), as "inclined to dispute the authorship of the 'Following' by Tauler."—p. xiii.

180:11–14. Johannes Tauler (c. 1300–1361), who entered the Dominican order at Strassburg at about the age of fifteen, was brought into close contact with the *Gottesfreunde*, or "Friends of God," during a five-year stay at Basel (1338–43) and exercised great influence on their teaching. The *Gottesfreunde* were a group of Rhineland and Swiss mystics who, though for the most part remaining within the Church, stressed the transforming personal union of their souls with God.—*Oxford Dictionary of the Christian Church*.

180:18–19. *Imitatio* I, v, 1.

180:26–181:3. This work is mentioned by Morell at the beginning of his Preface, p. v. "Miss Winkworth" is Susanna Winkworth, to whose translation of the anonymous mystical work *Theologia Germanica* (London, 1854) Arnold refers in line 8.

181:10–11. Luther, who had first published an edition of the *Theologia Germanica* in 1516, wrote a Preface for the second edition two years later in which he called it "a noble book," from which he had learned more of the nature of God and Christ, of man and all things, than from any other work except the Bible and St. Augustine. See Miss Winkworth's "Historical Introduction" to her translation.

181:17–19. Amos 8:11.

181:19–25. Tauler, pt. II, ¶11; tr. Morell, p. 162. Morell wrote "might well have helped."

181:29. *Imitatio* II, xii, 3.

181:35–37. Tauler, pt. I, ¶138; tr. Morell, p. 117.

182:1–3. Tauler, pt. I, ¶66; tr. Morell, p. 56.

182:4. The "real concern" of *Literature and Dogma* is "with the natural truth of Christianity."–Preface to the Popular Edition (1883). It is "all-important to insist on what I call the *natural truth* of Christianity."–Preface to *Last Essays* (1877); *Prose Works*, ed. Super, VI, 144; VII, 153.

182:7–11. Tauler, pt. I, ¶64; tr. Morell, p. 54.

182:12–15. Tauler, pt. I, ¶136, 138, 120; tr. Morell, pp. 116–17, 101.

182:19–22. Memorandum of October 5, 1821, summarized in Eugène Rambert, *Alexandre Vinet: Histoire de sa vie et de ses ouvrages* (3rd ed.; Lausanne, 1876), I, 102. Rambert's book is on Arnold's reading list for 1887.–*Note-Books*, ed. Lowry, p. 621.

182:33–34. *Commentarius . . . ad Galatos 3:13*, *Werke* (Weimar, 1911), XL (1), 442 (halfway through the discussion of this verse).

182:34–38. Martin Luther, *Table Talk*, trans. and ed. by William Hazlitt [the younger] (London: George Bell and Sons, 1902), pp. 147, 84 (nos. ccciv, cxcii). This translation was first published in 1848. See *St. Paul and Protestantism*, *Prose Works*, VI, 84:6–11.

183:3–4. Galatians 3:13.

183:7–21. *Werke*, XL (1), 437–38 (one-quarter through the discussion). Such justification, according to Luther, was granted to men through faith alone.

183:21–23. For the language, see *St. Paul and Protestantism* (1869; revised 1887), *Prose Works*, ed. Super, VI, 46:3–5.

183:24–25. *Ibid.*, p. 452 (near the end of the discussion).

183:32–33. Cronos, the father of Zeus, swallowed his children immediately after their birth in order to prevent their taking over his throne, but his wife concealed Zeus in a cave in Crete and gave Cronos a stone to swallow instead. Zeus, when he became chief of the gods, took the child Pallas Athene from the body of his wife before birth and concealed it in his own; in due course, she sprang fully armed from his head. Both stories are told in the eighth century (B.C.) *Theogony* of Hesiod. Cronos was commonly identified by the Romans with their god Saturn.

183:34. The "magnified and non-natural man" and his son were introduced by Arnold to illustrate the anthropomorphism of the traditional theological concept of the Christian God in *St. Paul and Protestantism*, *Prose Works*, ed. Super, VI, 60.

184:20. *Werke*, XL (1), 442.

184:24-25. The doctrine of election was central to the *Institutes* of Calvin, who held that certain persons are elected or chosen by God wholly without relation to faith or works.

185:7-8. The Salvation Army, first so called in 1878, was founded by William Booth. Revivalism is any religious movement (including the Salvation Army) that practices evangelical revivals, mass meetings designed to stimulate religious fervor through intensive preaching and prayer. Arnold probably alludes to the American revivalists Dwight Lyman Moody and Ira David Sankey, who toured Great Britain in 1873-75 and 1881-84. See the Conclusion to *God and the Bible* (version of 1884), *Prose Works*, ed. Super, VII, 372.

185:9-10. The Latitude Men were the Cambridge Platonists of the seventeenth century—Benjamin Whichcote, John Smith, Henry More, and others. Robert Leighton (1611-84) was archbishop of Glasgow under Charles II; his writings were quoted abundantly in Coleridge's *Aids to Reflection* (1825). Thomas Erskine (1788-1870) of Linlathen devoted his life to the study of theology; he was essentially liberal, and found the essence of Christianity to be its conformity with man's spiritual and ethical needs.

185:12. Joseph Butler (1692-1752), bishop of Durham and author of the *Analogy of Religion*, and Thomas Wilson (1663-1755), bishop of Sodor and Man and author of *Maxims of Piety and of Christianity*, were two of Arnold's favorite religious writers.

185:17-19. Sermon XV, "Upon the Ignorance of Man," ¶11; *Works*, ed. W. E. Gladstone (Oxford, 1896), II, 268. Butler wrote "make the dreadful experiment," not "commit the dreadful mistake."

185:21-22. See p. 181:35-37. The language is Tauler's, not Wilson's, and the *Maxims* do not allude to Tauler.

186:30-31. For example, "No: at all costs, it is to be prayed by all men that Shams may *cease*."—*Latter-Day Pamphlets*, I, "The Present Time," one-fourth through.

186:32-187:7. E.g., Tauler, pt. I, ¶15, 38; tr. Morell, pp. 10-11, 28-29. Arnold quotes Mark 10:23.

187:16-20. See p. 369:4-5n.

187:23. "The language of the Bible, then, is literary, not scientific language; language *thrown out* at an object of consciousness not fully grasped, which inspires emotion."—*Literature and Dogma* (1871), *Prose Works*, ed. Super, VI, 189.

187:33–188:2. Arnold harks back to his discussion of Jesus' "secret" and his "temper" in *Literature and Dogma, Prose Works*, ed. Super, VI, 291–301 *et passim*. The scriptural passage is a combination of John 12:25 and Luke 9:24 (Mark 8:35).

188:6–8. Arnold again harks back to his earlier religious writings: e.g., *St. Paul and Protestantism* (1869), *Prose Works*, ed. Super, VI, 28.

188:16–189:8. Tauler, pt. I, ¶136–38; tr. Morell, pp. 115–18. The Scriptural passage is Matthew 21:13. For "gone out from thyself," see ¶21, p. 16.

[UP TO EASTER]

The Irish question dominated the Parliamentary scene for the remaining months of Arnold's life. The Conservatives had no comprehensive plan to substitute for the defeated Gladstonian scheme of home rule, and the widening gap between the Liberals and their dissident faction, the Liberal Unionists, made the return of the Liberals to power increasingly unlikely. Arnold's friend George Joachim Goschen, who had been at Rugby and at Oriel College, Oxford, a former member of Gladstone's cabinet, replaced Lord Randolph Churchill as chancellor of the exchequer in Lord Salisbury's cabinet in January, 1887. Agrarian disorders and rioting in Ireland, commonly growing out of wholesale eviction, so stirred the passions of both sides that rational thought became well-nigh impossible. On March 7, 10, and 14 *The Times* published the first three of a series of articles on "Parnellism and Crime"—a series that began with the statement that when Arnold's brother-in-law W. E. Forster was chief secretary for Ireland, plots against his life grew up "under his very nose." Forster's adopted son, Arnold's nephew H. O. Arnold-Forster, who served with him in Ireland, was quoted for his memoranda on crime there. (As a Liberal Unionist he later became a member of a Conservative cabinet, and Arnold clearly believed that Forster, if he had lived, would have been for the preservation of the Union.) Arnold's diary for April 14–18, 1887, notes "work at article," and on April 19, "send article." "I . . . feel so relieved that I am ready to do whatever anybody asks me," he told his daughter Lucy when he sent it off. "Up to Easter" was published in the *Nineteenth Century* for May and brought Arnold £45.

On May 12 he wrote to his sister Jane (Mrs. Forster): "It is years since I was in the House, and I should like to see the corps of Irish members as they now are. I hope they will not be always what they are now. Of course, you are quite right in saying that local government with these men to administer it is no pleasant prospect. But I think if their violence and disorder were fairly confronted and broken, and at the same time good measures were introduced, there would be a change in them. However, very cautious proceeding is requisite. But the Castle and its system are as surely doomed as Protestant ascendency. Lord Emly has been greatly pleased with my article."—*Letters*, ed. Russell. Nevertheless, Arnold's writing on Irish matters grows increasingly unsatisfactory as he becomes mired in the particular and draws more and more heavily on the ephemera of Parliamentary debates and political speech-making. "Up to Easter" was republished in Neiman's *Essays, Letters, and Reviews by Matthew Arnold*.

190:1–3. Huxley, "Science and Pseudo-Science," *Nineteenth Century* XXI, 497 (April, 1887).

190:4. Dillon and O'Brien, Irish Members of Parliament, were leaders of the "Plan of Campaign"; see p. 137:22n.

190:6–8. Speaking at a meeting of the Council of the London Liberal and Radical Union, March 30, 1887; reported in *The Times* next day, p. 10, col. 2.

190:8–10. Compare p. 122:1–4.

190:26–27. Arnold made the same appeal to "plain reasonable people" (and see p. 122:28) against the professionals in his theological writings—e.g., in the Preface to *God and the Bible, Prose Works*, ed. Super, VII, 393.

191:12. See p. 123:3–20.

191:20. The House recessed at 3 p.m. on Thursday, April 7, 1887, and resumed its sittings on Tuesday afternoon, April 12.

191:24–32. The ministry announces its program for the session in the Queen's Speech, and the House formulates its reply in the Address to the Throne. The formulation of the Address of course gives the Opposition its first opportunity to express itself. The leader of the House of Commons is ordinarily the prime minister when he is a Commoner, but since the Conservative prime minister at this time was Lord Salisbury, another member of his cabinet had to serve as the government's leader in the Commons. This had been Lord Randolph Churchill until his resignation on December 23 (see p. 122:23–24); then W. H. Smith became first lord of the treasury and leader. In moving on February 17, 1887, to give

precedence to the discussion of the proposed rules of procedure,
Smith said: "I have some sense of pain and humiliation as a member
of this House in finding that it is necessary to ask the House to
place restrictions upon its own liberty of speech. . . . I have only
to point to the number of days [sixteen] that the discussion upon
the Address has this session already occupied."—*Times*, February
18, p. 7, col. 1.

191:37. "Qui diable est-ce donc qu'on trompe ici?" asked Don
Bazile in Beaumarchais' *Le Barbier de Séville*, III, xi.

192:5. See Acts 17:28.

192:9–10. Gladstone's article, "'Locksley Hall' and the Jubilee,"
is a very long list of the achievements of the nation between
"Locksley Hall" and "Locksley Hall Sixty Years After" to affirm
the proposition "that the laws and works of the half-century
[Tennyson] reviews are not bad but good."—*Nineteenth Century*
XXI, 1–18 (January, 1887).

192:12. The Closure Bill (see pp. 126:33, 191:24) was carried on
March 18 by a vote of 262 to 41, with less than half the House
present, and was made a standing order of procedure. It enabled the
government to force through its Crimes Bill.

192:33–35. The Conservative government's Land Bill was passed
first by the Lords, then came to the Commons on July 4. It was
preceded by the new Crimes Bill, that gave the lord lieutenant
power to suppress any associations and combinations "illegal in
their intent and operation." (See p. 195:8n.)

192:38–193:2. So called, for example, by Dillon in the House of
Commons on March 28, 1887, and by Labouchere on March 31.—
Times, March 29, p. 7, col. 3, and April 1, p. 7, col. 3.

193:8–12. Speaking to the University Liberal Club, Cambridge,
March 9, 1887; reported in *The Times* next day, p. 6, col. 2. Spencer
had been Gladstone's Irish Viceroy in 1868–74 and 1882–85.

193:21–22. "The resort to coercion will enormously reinforce
the Home Rule ranks. [Conservative] Ministers know well that at
least one half of their followers obtained their seats by virtue of
pledges that Ireland was to be governed like England. The Union,
they said, ought to bring with it united legislation. We are for one
throne, one Parliament, one law."—"Victory in Sight" (leading
article), *Pall Mall Gazette*, February 22, 1887, p. 1.

194:17–22. "Thoughts on the Cause of the Present Discontents,"
about one-third through.

194:34–36. When the Municipality of Marseilles on March 18,
1887, voted to adjourn in honor of the anniversary of the Paris

Commune of 1871, the French government dissolved the Municipality and ordered a new election.—*Times*, March 22, p. 5, col. 4.

195:4–6. Justice O'Brien, who had delivered the condemnation of the "Plan of Campaign" Arnold quoted on p. 137:23–24, made this remark before a Grand Jury at Kerry on March 10; reported in *The Times* next day, p. 8, col. 2.

195:8. The Irish Land League was formed on October 21, 1879, with Parnell as president, to agitate for agrarian reform in Ireland and in Parliament. It was succeeded by the much more aggressive National League of 1882, and the latter was outlawed under the provisions of the new Crimes Act of July 19, 1887.

195:9–14. Frank Byrne, an Irish Nationalist speaking in New York on July 2, 1883, and quoted in "Parnellism and Crime, II.—A Retrospect: America," *Times*, March 10, 1887, p. 8, col. 3. Byrne said "cause of liberty may" and "all and each method as."

195:18–22. "Parnellism and Crime, I.—A Retrospect: Ireland," *Times*, March 7, 1887, p. 8, col. 2. The remarks date from 1880.

195:26–27. See Godkin's reply to Arnold's published letter of June 28, 1886: p. 497.

195:27–30. The secretary for Ireland, A. J. Balfour, in Parliament on March 28, 1887, quoted these words from a speech made by W. H. K. Redmond at Castlereagh on December 7, 1886.—*Times*, March 29, p. 6, col. 6.

195:30–33. At the convention of the Irish National League of America in the Central Music Hall, Chicago—the same hall in which Arnold had lectured some two and one-half years earlier—John E. Redmond, M.P., one of Parnell's representatives, said on August 19, 1886, "I assert here to-day that the Government of Ireland by England is an impossibility. I believe it our duty to make it so."—*Times*, August 20, p. 5, cols. 3–4.

195:33–35. Resolution passed at the New York meeting of July 2, 1883; quoted in "Parnellism and Crime, II," *Times*, March 10, 1887, p. 8, col. 3.

195:35–196:3. Father Daniel Keller of Youghal ignored a summons to testify in a case before the Bankruptcy Court in Dublin and was committed to Kilmainham Gaol on March 19, 1887. Archbishop Croke expressed his warmest approval of Keller's action and Archbishop Walsh took his place beside Keller in court, then accompanied him on the ride to the gaol (see p. 204:37). The Midleton Board of [Poor Law] Guardians near Cork on the same day passed the resolution Arnold quotes.—*Times*, March 21, p. 7, cols. 1–3.

196:3–7. The fifth Marquess of Lansdowne, grandson of Arnold's patron nearly forty years earlier, was governor-general of Canada and an Irish landlord; Townsend Trench was his agent in Queen's County, Ireland. William O'Brien, M.P., spoke these words to a gathering of Lansdowne's tenants on January 23, 1887; when thirty-seven of them, acting on O'Brien's "Plan of Campaign," withheld their rents on the ground that their lands were not yielding the rent demanded, evictions began on March 22.—*Times,* March 22, p. 4, col. 5. O'Brien in May journeyed to Canada to agitate against Lansdowne.

196:8–10. Gladstone's earlier remark on the Land League was made before a committee of the Liverpool Liberal Association at Knowsley on October 27, 1881; reported in *The Times* next day, p. 8, col 3, and recalled in "Parnellism and Crime, III.—A Study in Contemporary Conspiracy," *Times,* March 14, 1887, p. 8, col. 3.

196:14–17. "What Mr. Gladstone chooses to consider the absence of outrage in Ireland . . . is dependent, we are told, on 'the influences of moderation and legality' now prevailing among Mr. Parnell's following."—Leading article on the debate on the Irish Crimes Bill, *Times,* March 30, 1887, p. 9, col. 2. Gladstone's language in the House of Commons on March 29 was not quite that.— p. 7, col. 3.

196:19–21. Addressing an open-air demonstration in Tipperary on March 13, 1887; reported in *The Times,* March 15, p. 10, col. 1.

196:23–28. See p. 190:6–8. Gladstone spoke warmly of "the representatives of Ireland" in the House of Commons on March 24, 1887; reported in *The Times* next day, p. 7, col. 1.

196:33. The nine-man *Comité de Salut public* (which Carlyle called the "Committee of Public Salvation") was established in late March, 1793, and soon gained supreme executive power in the French revolutionary government, with the guillotine as its right arm. "Incivisme" was the crime of disloyalty to the principles of the Revolution. On Easter Eve, 1887, Arnold wrote to his sister Jane: "Morley came and sate down at the table where I was lunching on Monday, and made himself very pleasant; he said he was going to dine alone with his wife and to read my poetry afterwards, as he constantly did. This could not but be pleasant to an author, but I think his speeches full of the real Jacobin temper."

197:9–10. Jotted in Arnold's pocket diary for January 31, 1886.— *Note-Books,* ed. Lowry, p. 424.

197:15. Balfour succeeded Sir Michael Hicks-Beach as chief secretary for Ireland on March 8, 1887.

197:19–20. See p. 137:31–34. Forster, Arnold's brother-in-law and one for whom he felt a very high regard, died on April 5, 1886; since he was chief secretary for Ireland in Gladstone's cabinet of 1880 Arnold here ironically implicates him in the current Gladstonian policies.

197:22–27. Speaking on the Crimes Bill (and incidentally on Closure) in the House of Commons on March 24, 1887; reported in *The Times* next day, pp. 6–7.

197:27–30. In a letter dated April 14, 1887, printed in *The Times* next day, p. 11, col. 5.

197:35–37. See p. 195:20–22.

197:37–198:2. Matthew Harris, M.P. for Galway East, speaking (with Parnell beside him) to his constituents on October 24, 1880; quoted in "Parnellism and Crime, I," *Times*, March 7, 1887, p. 8, col. 2.

198:20. Under the Crimes Act of 1887, cases that could not be tried fairly before an Irish jury might be transferred to England for trial.

199:13–14. Arnold quotes Wilfrid Scawen Blunt to this effect at the beginning of his pocket diary for 1886.—*Note-Books*, ed. Lowry, p. 422. But in "Disestablishment in Wales" (p. 347:22–23) he attributes the phrase to Gladstone himself, and the expression is common enough.

199:15–16, 200:9–10. See p. 195:27–30n.

200:15–21. From the thirteenth to the eighteenth centuries Provence had its own government, seated at Aix-en-Provence; from the fifteenth century this was closely linked to the government of France. At the end of 1789 the "Gouvernement" of Provence (like other ancient geographical divisions of France) was dissolved by the revolutionary government into geographical administrative units called "departements." Jean-Étienne-Marie Portalis (1746–1807) was himself a Provençal; for the expression *Nation provençale* and the argument Arnold quotes, see Sainte-Beuve, "Portalis, I," *Causeries du lundi* (3rd ed.; Paris, 1869), V, 450.

200:25. Honoré-Gabriel Riqueti, comte de Mirabeau (1749–91) was the principal leader of the Constituent Assembly from the outbreak of the French Revolution until his death. He was a superb parliamentary orator.

201:2–8. A paraphrase of Spencer's remarks of March 9 at Cambridge; see p. 193:8–12n.

201:27–32. The anecdote is told of an unnamed preacher by John Heneage Jesse, *Memoirs of the Court of England from the*

Revolution in 1688 to the Death of George the Second (London, 1843), III, 159. Frederick Louis, Prince of Wales (1707–51), was son of George II and father of George III.

202:12. The voters enfranchised by the Franchise Act of 1884; see p. 129:10–11.

202:16–20. John Morley's successor as editor of *The Pall Mall Gazette*, the sensational reforming journalist W. T. Stead (who spent several months in jail for too frankly exposing prostitution in London), published a pair of articles in the *Contemporary Review*, "Government by Journalism" and "The Future of Journalism" (XLIX, 653–74 [May, 1886]; L, 663–79 [November, 1886]). In the closing pages of the latter he twice casually used the expression "the new journalism." It is to this Arnold alludes. But Stead was so unaware of having used the phrase that in its obituary memoir of Arnold *The Pall Mall* said: "It was he who described [this paper] as the originator of the New Journalism, which he declared most accurately typified the democratic spirit of modern England."—April 16, 1888, p. 9. See Joseph O. Baylen, "Matthew Arnold and the *Pall Mall Gazette:* Some Unpublished Letters, 1884–1887," *South Atlantic Quarterly* LXVIII, 547–51 (Autumn, 1969). Stead replied to Arnold's remark here that no other newspaper was more concerned to find the truth of things or to correct its errors, and asserted that Arnold's own article better answered his description of the faults of the "New Journalism" than the newspaper.—*Pall Mall Gazette*, May 3, 1887, p. 4.

202:28. Gladstone, speaking to the Liberal Members for Yorkshire on March 17, 1887, cited the opposition of Fox to the Union by way of asserting that home rule was the historic position of the Liberal party.—*Times*, March 18, p. 10, col. 3. See also p. 73:20–22.

202:31. *Respice finem*—"Look to the end."—Latin proverb.

203:15–17. Speaking to the National Conservative Club on March 5, 1887; reported in *The Times*, March 7, p. 7, col. 2.

203:23–26. A. J. Beresford Hope was a staunch defender of the Church's prerogative and persistent opponent of the perennial efforts of the Nonconformist Liberals to repeal the statutory prohibition of a man's marriage to his deceased wife's sister. Arnold was equally ironic toward Hope's opposition to the Burials Bill in "Falkland" (1877), *Prose Works*, ed. Super, VIII, 205. Gladstone was the leading opponent of the Divorce Act of 1857.

203:27–30. Edwin Chadwick, "Mr. Gladstone's Claim as an Authority on Local Administration," *National Review* IX, 289

(April, 1887). Chadwick (1800–1890) was throughout his life an energetic sanitary reformer, with close knowledge of poor law administration and urban public health.

204:7–8. Arnold quoted the Liberal maxim on religious endowment in his 1874 Preface to *Higher Schools and Universities in Germany* and in "Irish Catholicism and British Liberalism" (1878), *Prose Works*, ed. Super, VII, 121–22; VIII, 325.

204:26–29. In 1859, 1865, and 1885–86.

204:33–34. F. W. Riemer, *Mittheilungen über Goethe* (Berlin, 1841), II, 95; jotted in Arnold's pocket diaries for 1871, 1872, 1873, 1875, and in one of his general notebooks.—*Note-Books*, ed. Lowry, pp. 152, 176, 191, 226, 522.

204:37. William John Walsh, archbishop of Dublin, and Thomas William Croke, archbishop of Cashel, were ardent advocates of tenants' rights. In May, 1883, Pope Leo XIII requested Croke to take a less active part in the land war, and in January, 1887, he sent instructions to the Irish bishops to act "with strict regard to legality" in the land question.—*Times*, January 25, 1887, p. 8, col. 2, and January 15, 1887, p. 5, col. 6.

205:7. Edward James Saunderson, M.P., an Ulster Protestant, had opposed Irish Church disestablishment in 1869 and now, a unionist, opposed Parnell. Thomas Sexton was one of the ablest of the Irish Nationalists in Parliament.

205:30. The "heptarchy" was the supposed seven kingdoms of the Angles and Saxons in Britain before 828. In his election address on June 19, 1886, Lord Randolph Churchill spoke of "this design for the separation of Ireland from Britain, this insane recurrence to heptarchical arrangements, this trafficking with treason, this condonation of crime," etc.—*Times*, June 21, p. 6, col. 1.

205:36–206:22. A repetition of Arnold's proposal in "The Nadir of Liberalism," pp. 68–69.

206:23–25. Reginald B. Brett, "The Liberal Unionists and Coercion," *Nineteenth Century* XXI, 621 (April, 1887). Brett (later Viscount Esher) had been private secretary to the Marquess of Hartington, 1878–85. Arnold met Brett and Balfour at the same party at Lady de Rothschild's on March 15, 1885, at which he met Lord Rosebery (see p. 76:7–12n.).

206:34–35. See p. 80:23–25n.

207:9–13. In "The Incompatibles" (1881), *Prose Works*, ed. Super, IX, 255.

207:24–27. See pp. 138:35–139:6.

207:30–32. Testifying before the Cowper Commission on the working of the Irish Land Act of 1881, John George McCarthy, one of the Commissioners who administered Lord Ashbourne's Land Purchase Act of 1885, said: "In my judicial experience, looking at the matter as a judge administering the Land Act, in Mayo, in Kerry, and in Clare, I found rack renting to prevail to an extent that I confess was simply shocking."—*Pall Mall Gazette*, March 12, 1887, p. 8.

207:32–34. Buller's testimony was quoted by Morley in the debate on the Crimes Bill, March 22, 1887, and again by Gladstone two days later; reported in *The Times*, March 23, p. 7, col. 1, and March 25, p. 7, col. 2.

208:7–9. Joseph Chamberlain, Birmingham Radical who broke with Gladstone on home rule, increasingly won Arnold's respect as a statesman. He was responsible (through his colleague Jesse Collings) for an English agricultural amendment to the Address which overthrew Salisbury's government on January 26, 1886. "I think the man with a future is Chamberlain," Arnold wrote on May 12, 1887.—*Letters*, ed. Russell. In a speech at Birmingham on January 29, 1887, Chamberlain outlined a principle of fair rents for Ireland which began with the tenant's receiving a reasonable return for his labor.—*Times*, January 31, p. 10, col. 2.

208:19–20. See p. 141:12–24.

208:25–30. Speech at a Liberal-Unionist luncheon at Liskeard on March 16, 1887; reported in *The Times* next day, p. 10, col. 6.

208:32–35. See Acts 7:42–43 (in reference to the Israelites of the Exodus under Moses). Sir William Vernon Harcourt was Gladstone's home secretary in 1880–85 and chancellor of the exchequer in the home rule cabinet of 1886. He was one of the few older Liberal leaders to support home rule, and made strenuous efforts to bring the Gladstonians and the dissidents together in mid-January, 1887.

[SCHOOLS IN THE REIGN
OF QUEEN VICTORIA]

Having succeeded so brilliantly in getting Arnold to write for his anthology of *The English Poets* in 1880, T. Humphry Ward turned to him again as he planned a two-volume survey by eminent hands of the first fifty years of Queen Victoria's reign. "I will undertake the Education Sketch on two conditions," Arnold told him on January 19, 1886: "one, that you never ask me to do anything for any of these infernal compilations again; the other, that I am not expected to begin upon it until I return from America in the autumn." A year later he had to fulfill his promise; his diaries show him busy with Kay-Shuttleworth's book, the reports of the Clarendon Commission and the Taunton Commission, etc., and he wrote to E. T. Cook on January 10, 1887: "I am so busy for the next 6 weeks with a horrid paper on Schools which I have promised to Humphry Ward's Jubilee Volume that I can undertake nothing whatever at present besides."—J. O. Baylen, "Matthew Arnold and the *Pall Mall Gazette*," *South Atlantic Quarterly* LXVIII, 554–55 (Autumn, 1969). Probably the entry "correct proofs" in Arnold's pocket diary for March 10 refers to this essay. The volume was published on June 15, and Arnold received £30 in payment. The essay is a valuable survey of a period in education most of which Arnold knew at first hand and in which he played a significant part. It has not hitherto been republished.

210:8–30. James Kay-Shuttleworth, *Four Periods of Public Education* (London, 1862), pp. 200, 445–46.

211:10. Sir James Kay-Shuttleworth (1804–77), born James Kay, took his M.D. at Edinburgh in 1827 and set up practice in Manchester, where as physician at a dispensary in a poor and populous district he could see disease and sanitation at their worst. He added the name "Shuttleworth" on his marriage to Janet Shuttleworth in 1842 and was created a baronet on his retirement from the secretaryship of the Committee of Council on Education in 1849.

212:4–5. "Information itself is really the least part of [education]; . . . it consists in endeavouring to put [children] into right dispositions of mind, and right habits of living."—"Six Sermons . . . upon Public Occasions," IV ("Children in Charity Schools"), ¶6; *Works*, ed. W. E. Gladstone (Oxford, 1896), II, 343; quoted in Arnold's Introduction to *Isaiah of Jerusalem* (1883), *Prose Works*, ed. Super, X, 100.

212:19–213:13. Kay-Shuttleworth, *Four Periods*, pp. 437–44. Canon 79 is quoted at pp. 438–39n. The Book of Canons consists of 141 canons adopted by the Church of England in 1604–6, the principal body of ecclesiastical legislation of that church.

213:17, 20–21. Prior to 1871, the National schools were inspected for government grants by their own inspectors, clergymen appointed with the concurrence of the respective archbishops; after the Education Act of 1870, denominational inspection was abandoned. Inspection was compulsory only for schools that received government grants.

213:25. Because of the shortage of teachers and money, both the National Society and the British and Foreign School Society depended on a system in which the schoolmaster taught the "monitors"—their most capable students—and the monitors then taught groups of their fellow students. Such instruction was inevitably mechanical.

214:1–2. Presumably the Reform Bill of 1832, after which Oldham sent two members to Parliament.

214:12. *Four Periods*, p. 584n.; see also pp. 491–92.

214:15–28. *Four Periods*, pp. 581 (with omission), 594 (with slight alterations).

214:32–215:17. *Four Periods*, pp. 583–84n., with omissions.

215:18–20. See p. 221:37–38n.

215:27–32. *Four Periods*, p. 582.

215:33–34. The Borough Road school, in Southwark, founded by Joseph Lancaster in 1798, adopted the monitorial system in 1803. In 1814 Lancaster and his associates founded the undenominational British and Foreign School Society. In due course the Borough Road establishment embodied, along with model schools for boys and girls, a training college for teachers of the British schools, which was periodically inspected by Arnold.

216:29–36. Shuttleworth, *Four Periods*, p. 458.

217:6–9. *Ibid.*, p. 459.

218:8–9. Tufnell's obituary appeared in *The Times* on July 12, 1886, p. 10, col. 2.

218:10–12. The Battersea Training College was founded by Tufnell and Shuttleworth out of their private resources in 1840. Shuttleworth at first lived in the house and superintended the institution himself. His account of the school is contained in two reports (January 1, 1841, and December 15, 1843), reprinted in his *Four Periods of Public Education*, pp. 293–431.

218:12–17. Robert John Eden (1799–1870) was vicar of Battersea from 1835 to 1847. He became bishop of Sodor and Man in 1847, inherited the barony of Auckland in 1849, and was translated to the see of Bath and Wells in 1854. See *Four Periods of Public Education*, p. 309.

218:20. The pupil-teacher was a paid apprentice who might, at the end of his term, seek admission to a training college. When Arnold began his inspectorship, the government gave grants to schools to augment the salaries of teachers who had completed the training college course, and gave them further augmentation for the pupil-teachers they trained.

218:21–219:4. Kay-Shuttleworth became an assistant poor law commissioner in 1835 (the year after the passage of the new poor law), and served first in Norfolk and Suffolk. Arnold draws the account of Rush from *Four Periods of Public Education*, pp. 287–89.

219:21–220:7. *Four Periods*, pp. 314–15 (312), 312, 314, 316.

220:10–11. Johann Heinrich Pestalozzi (1746–1827) won a European reputation for his methods of educating children at his school at Yverdon, Switzerland. Philipp Emanuel von Fellenberg (1771–1844), as a young man was associated with Pestalozzi, then founded a school at Hofwyl, near Bern, aimed at training the children of the poor. Johann Jakob Wehrli (or Vehrli) (1790–1855), formerly associated with Fellenberg at Hofwyl, became head of the Normal School at Kruitzlingen, on Lake Constance in Switzerland. Kay-Shuttleworth describes his visits to Fellenberg and Vehrli in 1839, prior to the opening of the training school at Battersea, in *Four Periods*, pp. 302–8.

220:17–221:12. *Four Periods*, pp. 370–71, 387, 397, 421, 427–30, 472–73.

221:13–23. *Four Periods*, pp. 472–73.

221:24–34. *Ibid.*, pp. 474, 477.

221:37–38. In 1843 Sir James Graham, Conservative home secretary, introduced a factory bill that both limited the hours of employment for children and required the provision of schools for them. The Protestant Dissenters and Roman Catholics, because they viewed these schools as merely a device to strengthen the power of the Church of England, flooded the table of the House of Commons with petitions against the bill and Graham withdrew it. The next year, when he reintroduced the bill, the education clauses had disappeared. Children between the ages of eight and thirteen might work in the textile mills no longer than six and a half hours a-day.—Spencer Walpole, *A History of England from ... 1815* (London, 1912), V, 72–79. Arnold alluded to this triumph of the Dissenters in *Friendship's Garland*, Letter VI (1867) and in *Culture and Anarchy* (1868); *Prose Works*, ed. Super, V, 69, 153 and n.

222:7. Henry Dunn (1800–78), secretary of the British and Foreign School Society until 1858, was an occasional correspondent of Arnold's and author of a pamphlet, *Facts, Not Fairy Tales:*

Brief Notes on . . . "Literature and Dogma" (London, 1873), upon which Arnold commented in *God and the Bible, Prose Works,* ed. Super, VII, 191–92.

222:27. George Anthony Denison (1805–96), archdeacon of Taunton, a belligerent high churchman, from the outset opposed regulation of parochial schools by the state and subsequently viewed the Education Act of 1870 with "unmitigated disgust."– *D.N.B.*

222:28–32. Arnold quoted this letter also in "'Ecce, Convertimur ad Gentes'" (1879), *Prose Works,* ed. Super, IX, 2. It was Lord John Russell who set up the Committee of Council on Education that instituted the system of inspection of schools that received parliamentary grants (see pp. 210–11).

223:19–27. Macaulay spoke on April 19 and Bright on April 20. At the division on April 22, there were 372 Ayes to 47 Noes. "My forefathers languished in prison by the acts of that Church which you now ask me to aggrandize," was Bright's peroration.–*Hansard's Parliamentary Debates,* 3rd ser., XCI, 1006–26, 1088–1100, 1235.

225:24. Luke 14:21.

226:25–227:21. House of Commons, *Accounts and Papers,* 1861, XXI, pt. i, pp. 1, 295–98, 327–47, 154, 174; see Shuttleworth, *Four Periods,* p. 580.

227:23. Robert Lowe (1811–92) became Viscount Sherbrooke in 1880.

227:27. Ralph R. W. Lingen (1819–1905), secretary of the Committee of Council from 1849 to 1869, became Baron Lingen in 1885.

228:3–7. Lowe, speaking on the Revised Code before the House of Commons on July 11, 1861, and February 13, 1862.–*Hansard's Parliamentary Debates,* 3rd ser., CLXIV, 736; CLXV, 229.

228:20–26. *Four Periods,* p. 588. This is a republication of the Shuttleworth *Letter to Earl Granville* that Arnold praised in his article on "The Twice-Revised Code" (1862).–*Prose Works,* ed. Super, II, 212.

230:29–31. Rates were local property taxes for local purposes; the Consolidated Fund was the source of monies for the parliamentary grant.

231:6. Vestries were elected governing bodies of Church of England parishes. Outside the boroughs they were the only form of local government for most purposes.

231:14. On February 17, 1870.

232:11–24. House of Commons, *Accounts and Papers*, 1861, XXI, pt. 1, pp. 77–78.

233:20. William E. Forster, Arnold's brother-in-law, died about a year before this was written, on April 5, 1886.

233:22–23. François Guizot (1787–1874), both a historian and a statesman, was minister of Public Instruction for most of the period from October 11, 1832, to April 15, 1837. He was Louis-Philippe's chief minister from 1841 until the Revolution of 1848. Arnold greatly admired the school law of June 28, 1833, promulgated by Guizot.—*The Popular Education of France, Prose Works*, ed. Super, II, 67–75. The philosopher and diplomatist Wilhelm von Humboldt (1767–1835) was first head of the Prussian Education Department, 1809–10. "It is from [his] accession to office . . . that the establishment of a fruitful relation between these two authorities, the schools and the central power, really dates."—*Schools and Universities on the Continent, Prose Works*, ed. Super, IV, 199.

233:34–234:2, 12–14. House of Commons, *Accounts and Papers*, 1861, XXI, pt. i, pp. 83, 20, 314.

234:29–235:5. Shuttleworth, *Four Periods*, pp. 569–70.

235:20–21. By the Education Act of 1870, the Education Department was empowered to cause the election of a local school board to establish schools only when it was determined that the schools in an area were otherwise insufficient for the population.

235:32. Anthony John Mundella (1825–97), a friend of Arnold's, was a warm supporter in Parliament of Forster's Education Act of 1870. He was vice-president of the Committee of Council on Education in Gladstone's administration of 1880–85.

237:9–10. See pp. 31:9–10, 102:2–4.

237:23–35. House of Commons, *Accounts and Papers*, 1867–68, XXVIII, pt. i, p. 107. The Science and Art Department, housed in South Kensington, an offshoot of the Great Exhibition of 1851, was set up in 1853 under the Committee of Council on Education.

238:8–14. House of Commons, *Accounts and Papers*, 1843, XVIII, 5–545, summarized by the Schools Inquiry Commission, *ibid.*, 1867–68, XXVIII, pt. i, pp. 4–5.

238:17–27. House of Commons, *Accounts and Papers*, 1867–68, XXVIII, pt. i, pp. 1, 5.

238:20. The two that were not subject to the inquiries of the Clarendon Commission were Marlborough and Wellington. These, with Merchant Taylors' and St. Paul's (the latter governed by the Mercers' Company, not associated with the cathedral) were excluded from the Public Schools Act of 1868.

239:19. Frederick Temple was headmaster of Rugby (1857–69), then bishop of Exeter (1869–85), bishop of London (1885–96), and after Arnold's death archbishop of Canterbury. Arnold wrote his *Schools and Universities on the Continent* (1868) as a part of the report of this Commission, which had sent him abroad, and he was especially pleased by Temple's reception of it.—*Prose Works*, ed. Super, IV, 350.

239:33–240:5. House of Commons, *Accounts and Papers*, 1867–68, XXVIII, pt. i, pp. 108–9, Appendix vi, and pp. 6–7. The Commission defined a "private" school as one conducted by the schoolmaster on his own account, a "proprietary" school as the property of an individual or company (including a religious organization) that appoints and supervises the schoolmaster.

240:6–10. *Ibid.*, p. 98.

240:14–241:19. *Ibid.*, pp. 104, 106, 102, 314, 434, 284–85, 660–61. 241:20–32. *Ibid.*, pp. 106, 15, 78.

242:11–13. The Endowed Schools (No. 2) Bill, which had been separated from the Endowed Schools Bill that passed its third reading in the Commons on June 18, 1869, provided for examining the scholars and certificating and registering the teachers in such schools. Like the bill of which it had been a part, it was sponsored by W. E. Forster and H. A. Bruce. It was withdrawn on August 7.

242:16–18. A Teachers Organization and Registration Bill for intermediate education, introduced by Playfair and others, had its first reading on March 13, 1879. It was withdrawn on July 30 without ever being debated. Lyon Playfair (1818–98), formerly professor of chemistry at the University of Edinburgh, was member for Edinburgh and St. Andrews Universities. He was knighted in 1883. Arnold spoke highly of this proposal in "'Porro Unum Est Necessarium'" (1878) and in a letter to Humphry Ward on October 26, 1878.—*Prose Works*, ed. Super, VIII, 364–65.

243:3–6. The College of Preceptors was an organization of secondary schoolmasters founded in 1846 and chartered in 1849. Its examinations, set for secondary school pupils, were voluntary with the individual pupils. The Oxford and Cambridge Middle Class (or "Local") Examinations were likewise voluntary with the pupils. Both aimed at influencing the studies and standards of secondary schools by testing the results, but they were in no way prescriptive.

243:15–19. This proposition Arnold repeatedly advanced, from *A French Eton* (1863–64) onward. "The great mass of the middle part of our community . . . are both badly taught, and are also brought up on a lower plane than is right, brought up ignobly."– "The Incompatibles" (1881), *Prose Works*, ed. Super, IX, 275.

244:34, 245:13. Arnold repeatedly advocated a system of local (or "municipal") government such as he found in France, and the creation of a ministry of education, but England had no such ministry until the mid-twentieth century.

[FROM EASTER TO AUGUST]

Arnold picked up his analysis of the Salisbury government with an essay he wrote in six days at Fox How in the summer of 1887– beginning it on August 16 (only ten days after sending off the essay on Amiel) and sending it to the *Nineteenth Century* on the 21st. It appeared in the September number, and brought him £40. "I do not know whether I shall do any more poetry, but it is something to be of use in prose, and by coming out from time to time as the organ of 'the body of quiet, reasonable people,' I believe I do some good."–*Letters*, ed. Russell. The essay has been republished in Neiman's *Essays, Letters, and Reviews by Matthew Arnold*.

246:1. The session of Parliament ended on September 16.

246:6–12. Gladstone's Home Rule Bill, providing for a separate Irish parliament and executive in Dublin with powers of legislation and control over all but certain reserved categories, and putting an end to Irish representation in the Imperial Parliament at Westminster, was defeated in the House of Commons on June 8, 1886, by a majority of 30, including some 93 Liberals. Many of these last formed a new Liberal Union party, allied with the Conservatives thenceforth against Gladstone. Parliament was dissolved and the combined Conservatives and Liberal Unionists swept the new elections of July, 1886. A bill for buying out the Irish landlords, an essential accompaniment of the home rule scheme, disappeared with the defeat of home rule.

246:16. See p. 86:13–18.

246:18. For Chamberlain's defections from Gladstone on home rule, see p. 76:7–12n. John Bright, one of the oldest and most popular of the Liberal leaders, came out against home rule a few days before the vote in the Commons of June 8, 1886.

246:25–26. Gladstone asserted that he was leaving "free and open . . . the question of granting to some portion of Ulster, if it should be desired, a separate system."—Speech in London, July 29, 1887, reported in *The Times* next day, p. 12, col. 3. A separate parliament and executive for Ulster had been Chamberlain's proposal. In the same speech, Gladstone left entirely open the question of retaining Irish representation in the Parliament at Westminster.

247:1–4. Speaking to the electors of the Bridgeton division of Glasgow on July 26, 1887, Trevelyan replied "to a question with regard to the appointment of Irish Judges and the control of the police being retained in the hands of the Imperial Parliament" by saying "that he had not the least doubt that when this question came up for settlement the Liberals in council with the Irish members would be able to arrive at a conclusion in this matter which would be safe for the unity of the Empire and yet not unacceptable to Ireland."—*Times*, July 27, p. 10, col. 1. Trevelyan, who a year earlier had split with the Gladstonians over home rule, returned to the fold and won the Glasgow by-election for the Gladstonians on August 2.

247:17–20. W. H. Smith; see p. 191:24–32n.

247:20–22. Balfour, Lord Salisbury's nephew, entered the cabinet as secretary for Scotland in November, 1886; he became secretary for Ireland in March, 1887, and piloted the Crimes Bill through the Commons.

247:22–26. Reform of the rules of procedure was accomplished on March 18; the Criminal Law Amendment (Ireland) Bill passed the Commons on July 8 and the Lords on July 18, then received the royal assent on July 19.

247:28–31. Gladstonian Liberals won seats held by Conservatives or Liberal Unionists in by-elections at Burnley on February 19, Lincolnshire (Spalding Division) on July 1, Coventry on July 9, and Cheshire (Northwich Division) on August 13, 1887. The Conservative majority was substantially increased in the by-election at Middlesex (Hornsey) on July 19.

247:37–248:13. See pp. 86:5–12 and 124:29–125:20.

248:24–27. While the Criminal Law Amendment (Ireland) Bill was in the committee stage in the Commons (where it passed its second reading on April 18), the tenants of Colonel John O'Callaghan at Bodyke, County Clare, were evicted by the constabulary, to the accompaniment of rioting and reports of brutality. The Irish members forced a discussion of the evictions in Commons on June 16; there Balfour asserted that the police had only been carrying out their undoubted duty, and that he himself, protesting "as earnestly as I can against the doctrine . . . that the remedy for a law which is in some cases harsh is to break that law," determined, "not cheerfully indeed, but with a firm resolve," to support O'Callaghan in these evictions.—*Times*, June 17, p. 7, col. 2. Evictions of defaulting tenants on the estate of Rowland Winn at Glenbeigh, County Kerry—an utterly impoverished tract of land—began on January 11, 1887; the houses were burned or demolished as soon as the tenants were forced out. The evictions on Lord Clanricarde's estate at Woodford in 1882 led to the imprisonment of seventy-five protesters and the murder in reprisal of Lord Clanricarde's agent and steward on June 29. There were new evictions there in 1886 (see p. 136:38n.). Parnell in the Commons on June 10, 1887, spoke of "the horrors of Glenbeigh and the infamies of Bodyke."—*Times*, June 11, p. 11, col. 2.

248:30. J. P. Eckermann, *Gespräche mit Goethe*, ed. E. Castle (Berlin, 1916), I, 149 (December 20, 1826), jotted in Arnold's pocket diary at the beginning of 1881 and in one of his general notebooks; quoted in "The Incompatibles" (1881).—*Note-Books*, ed. Lowry, pp. 350, 529; *Prose Works*, ed. Super, IX, 240, etc.

249:12. "Sir, it is proper to inform you, that our measures *must be healing*."—Burke, "Two Letters to Gentlemen in the City of Bristol" (1778), I, ¶6; quoted in "The Incompatibles" (1881), *Prose Works*, ed. Super, IX, 248.

249:29–250:6. The Irish Land Law Bill was first introduced in the House of Lords on March 31, 1887, and passed its third reading on July 4. That same day it was introduced in the Commons. Amended by the Commons, it passed its third reading there on August 6. The bill shuttled back and forth between the two houses until agreement was reached and it received the royal assent on August 23. It extended to 150,000 leaseholders the right to have their rents fixed judicially.

250:18–19. Courtney, as chairman of committees and deputy speaker, sat in the speaker's chair when the speaker was absent. "The behaviour of some Conservative members when the Irish are speaking is simply abominable. Mr. Courtney had to censure it the other day." "Latterly, after dinner, the Tories seated below the gangway have become very harassing and offensive in their interruption of Opposition speakers, . . . and . . . Mr. Courtney expressed a strong opinion as to the conduct of these noisy Conservatives." One of the Irish members spoke of them as being "in a half-drunken condition."—*Pall Mall Gazette*, May 21, 1887, pp. 3, 6, 8. Another incident while Courtney was in the chair on July 28 led *The Pall Mall* to remark, "The conduct of the young Tory 'bloods' after they are heated with alcohol is simply scandalous."—July 29, p. 1.

251:1. Arthur Brend Winterbotham, M.P. for Gloucestershire (Cirencester Division), and George Otto Trevelyan, M.P. for Hawick, though Liberals, both voted against home rule on June 7, 1886. Trevelyan lost his seat to a Gladstonian Liberal in the general election that followed. But he swung back more and more openly into the party fold, and on June 27, 1887, addressed a letter of warm support to the Liberal candidate for Spalding, a letter sharply critical of the Chamberlain group. On August 2 he was elected for Glasgow as a Gladstonian Liberal. Winterbotham voted consistently against the Conservative-Unionist coalition in the critical moments of the Coercion Bill debate in the spring of 1887 (e.g., on the second reading, April 18), and on other matters thereafter.

251:14–38. See pp. 198–200, 201–3.

252:3–6. The seat for the Northwich Division of Cheshire having fallen vacant by the death of the Liberal Unionist member, it was decisively won in a by-election on August 13, 1887, by John T. Brunner, a manufacturer of industrial chemicals and a Gladstonian liberal. When the result was announced, Brunner said, "For the first time that the issue had been made absolutely clear between the classes and masses, they had decided that they and not the aristocracy were to rule in that country," to which *The Times* replied: "Mr. Brunner, himself a millionaire, had the effrontery to assert . . . that the victory was that of the masses over the classes. Mr. Gladstone's celebrated piece of electoral claptrap has never been put to a more remarkable use than when this chemical Croesus told the labourers of Cheshire that in sending him to Parliament they were sending one of themselves."—*Times*, August 16, p. 5, col. 6 and p. 7, col. 2 (leading article).

253:14–18, 22–24. Gladstone at the meeting of the executive committee of the London Liberal and Radical Union, July 29, 1887, reported in *The Times* next day, p. 12, col. 4.

253:24–27. See p. 195:4–6.

253:27–28. In an article on "The Anti-Rent Policy Expounded by Its Authors," *The Times* quotes a speech by Dillon at Clough: "In the county of Kerry, there are three or four hundred farms on which no man dare lay his foot."—December 2, 1886, p. 12, col. 2.

253:28–34. This passage from *The Tuam News & Western Advertiser* of May 27, 1887, p. 3, col. 7, was quoted by Lord Ashbourne in moving the second reading of the Criminal Law Amendment Bill in the House of Lords on July 14, 1887.—*Times*, July 15, p. 6, col. 2. Tuam is a town in western Ireland, near Galway; *The Tuam News*, a four-page weekly nearly half of which was advertising, devoted its columns almost entirely to Irish agrarian problems—accounts of evictions, reports of National League meetings, etc.

254:2–4. In a leading article, "Why the Deserters Have Returned," *The Pall Mall Gazette* explained that the Unionist defectors from the Liberal party had pretended that they wished Ireland to be governed by equal laws. "Coercion was as unnecessary as Home Rule. The Ordinary Law was their rallying cry." The adherence of the Unionists to the Coercion Bill of the Conservatives was bringing many Liberal electors back to the Gladstonian fold.—July 11, 1887, p. 1. Earlier in the year, "No Coercion, and Why" set forth *The Pall Mall's* support of equal laws throughout the kingdom.—March 15, p. 1.

254:10–11. Romans 13:3, rearranged.

254:12–14. In a letter published in *The Times*, April 15, 1887, p. 11, col. 5.

254:14–16. Speaking at a Liberal meeting at High Wycombe on May 18, 1887.—*Pall Mall Gazette*, May 19, p. 6.

254:16–19. James Stuart (1843–1913), professor of Mechanism at Cambridge, was a Gladstonian Liberal M.P. for Shoreditch (Hoxton). He was protesting in Parliament on May 12, 1887, against police harassment of Socialist meetings.—*Times*, May 13, p. 7, col. 6.

254:22–24. See p. 196:3–7.

254:34. "Doing As One Likes" was a chapter heading in *Culture and Anarchy*, as revised in 1875.

254:36–255:3. E. L. Godkin, "American Opinion on the Irish Question," *Nineteenth Century* XXII, 291, 289 (August, 1887), the latter statement a quotation from an unnamed professor at Columbia College.

255:9–13. Harrison Holt Riddleberger (1844–90), U.S. Senator from Virginia, 1883–89, defended a man named J. W. Jones on a misdemeanor charge in the court of Shenandoah County in Woodstock on August 11, 1887. There was a good deal of squabbling in the courtroom, but the jury found Jones insane and discharged

him. Next day Riddleberger plied Jones with drink, placed him in
a wagon, and paid a lad $2 to draw him about town with the plac-
ard: "Verdict: Bill Jones not guilty, but insane; jury insane,
lawyers insane, court insane in the main." The judge ordered
Riddleberger brought into court, fined him $25 and sentenced him
to five days in jail for contempt. At two o'clock on the first night
of his imprisonment, he was freed by a mob of about a hundred of
his friends. After three days of freedom he returned to jail to serve
out his sentence, chatting with acquaintances on the verandah of
the jailhouse and wandering down the streets at will. "Friends of
the Senator say he is not in a condition to know what he is doing."—
New York Times, August 16, p. 5, col. 5 and August 17, p. 2, col.
5; see also August 13–14 and 18. The dates are so close to Arnold's
deadline for getting his article to the printer that he probably saw
only the incomplete version of the story in *The Times* (London),
August 15, p. 6, col. 2.

256:5–15. H. F. Amiel, *Journal intime*, ed. E. Scherer (4th ed.;
Geneva, 1885), II, 77, 76 (February 23, 1870); jotted in Arnold's
pocket diary for September 11, 18, 1887.—*Note-Books*, ed. Lowry,
p. 431.

256:20–30. Trevelyan, whose remarks Arnold summarizes, spoke
thus at a meeting of the Eighty Club on May 16, 1887.—*Pall Mall
Gazette*, May 17, p. 1; *Times*, May 17, p. 10, col. 2.

257:21–22. The National League (successor in 1882 to the Land
League) was proclaimed by the lord lieutenant of Ireland on September 20, 1887, to be a dangerous association within the terms of
the Crimes Act, and its meetings were suppressed in most of Ireland.

257:26. The "new electors" were those enfranchised by the
Reform Act of 1884.

258:25–36. Godkin, "American Opinion on the Irish Question,"
pp. 285, 291. Godkin is replying to Arnold's letter "After the
Elections," p. 83:6–15. Arnold wrote a long friendly letter to
Godkin on the Irish question on October 3, 1887.

259:3. In Cardiff on June 7, 1887, Gladstone affirmed that "the
voice of the civilized world," "the opinion of those great nations
who . . . outside ourselves constitute the civilized world" was
unanimously sympathetic to Ireland. A correspondent signing himself "Oxoniensis" a few days later pointed out that the expression
had been a favorite of Gladstone's from his days as an undergraduate debater.—*Times*, June 8, p. 12, col. 2; June 18, p. 8, col. 6. See
p. 82:17–18.

259:19–21. For Morley, see p. 135:18–20n.

259:22. Godkin was born in Ireland, though of an English family.

259:30–31. See p. 195:29–30.

259:35–260:2. Certainly not quite what Godkin said in *The New York Evening Post*, of which he was editor, in response to the letter Arnold wrote to J. C. O'Connor from Buffalo; see pp. 496–97.

260:15–19. See pp. 79:33–80:2.

260:32. "Therefore have I set my face like a flint."—Isaiah 50:7.

261:6–11. Professor Neiman quotes *The Spectator* on the honors list of June 21, 1887, for the Jubilee of Queen Victoria: "Six new peers have been created, . . . and nobody either knows a good reason for choosing any one of these gentlemen, or a good reason for blaming the selection."—June 25, p. 850. But when H. W. Eaton went to the House of Lords as Baron Cheylesmore, the Conservatives lost his seat for Coventry in the Commons to W. H. W. Ballantine, a Gladstonian Liberal. The Prytaneum was the official residence of the Archons, or magistrates of Athens, and the place where official hospitality was extended; purple was the color of the Roman emperor's and consul's robe.

261:17–20. See p. 140:8–10.

261:24–31. This echoes Arnold's remarks in Whitechapel on November 29, 1884; *Prose Works*, ed. Super, X, 249–55. "Is it not lawful for me to do what I will with mine own?" remarked a great English landowner, quoting Matthew 20:15, in a debate in the House of Lords earlier in the century.

261:34. The Greek "crisis" is translated as "judgment" in the Authorized Version, for example at Matthew 23:23 and John 5:22, 27, 30. See *Literature and Dogma, Prose Works*, ed. Super, VI, 304.

262:2–6. See p. 139:1–4.

262:7–11. Letter to Croker, February 26, 1825; *The Croker Papers: The Correspondence and Diaries of . . . John Wilson Croker*, ed. L. J. Jennings (2nd ed.; London, 1885), I, 284.

262:24–35. *Analogy of Religion*, I, ii, ¶14–15; *Works*, ed. W. E. Gladstone (Oxford, 1896), I, 58, somewhat abridged.

264:2. The Lord said to Abram, "I am thy shield, and thy exceeding great reward."—Genesis 15:1.

264:38. *Epistles* II, i, 129.

[AMIEL]

The last of the essays Arnold planned to write on his return to England from America in the autumn of 1886 (as he told his older daughter) was one on Amiel, "to fulfil a promise to Mary," his niece Mrs. Humphry Ward, whose translation of Amiel's *Journals* was published in mid-December, 1885.—*Letters*, ed. Russell. It was a promise of long standing. "I . . . shall take Amiel with me to read on the journey," he told Ward on October 24, 1885, as he planned his visit to Continental schools, but when he prepared for the second portion of that tour on January 19 he had to confess: "I have not yet read my Amiel. I see there is a Mlle. Vadier who ought to be read with him. I shall again take him with me." A year later, at the beginning of 1887, he was reading Berthe Vadier's biographical study of Amiel, but he was unable to turn to Amiel himself until the middle of June. On May 20, Alexander Macmillan wrote to Arnold, "I am sending you Mrs. Ward's translation of Amiel, and am delighted to hear of your coming article."— W. E. Buckler, *Matthew Arnold's Books* (Geneva: E. Droz, 1958), p. 75. He began to write the essay on July 27 and sent it off on August 6 for publication in the September number of *Macmillan's Magazine*, which paid him £25 for it. "Tell Mary I have at last done my promised notice of Amiel," he wrote to Ward on August 11. "As a philosopher he is unprofitable, I think; but I find him a quite excellent literary critic." A few months later he indicated the essay as one of the new series of *Essays in Criticism* he planned.

It was not only his niece who drew Arnold to Amiel, however; it was also Edmond Scherer, editor of the diaries in French. Indeed, Arnold was caught up in his reading of Scherer's essays early in 1887, and perhaps on that account was delayed in his work on this essay. Scherer was the "French critic" about whom Arnold wrote in two of his *Mixed Essays* ("A French Critic on Milton" and "A French Critic on Goethe"), and whose judgment of Byron he cited in his Introduction to his selections from Byron. For Scherer's tribute to Arnold in *Le Temps* when Arnold died, see the headnote to the article on Sainte-Beuve, p. 413.

Though Arnold began by using Mrs. Ward's translation in the passages he quoted, he gradually took to emending it, often extensively, and his alterations are instructive lessons in style; only one or two examples can be given in these notes. When she brought out a new edition of the *Journals* in 1889, Mrs. Ward followed none of his emendations.

265:10–11. Henri-Frédéric Amiel, *Fragments d'un journal intime*, précédés d'une étude par Edmond Scherer (4th ed.; Geneva, 1885). 2 vols. (The first edition appeared in 1882.) Scherer's introductory essay occupies I, ix–lxxv. Scherer, a friend of both Amiel and Arnold, is also described by Mrs. Ward in her Preface as "my friend and critic" in a paragraph acknowledging his "help and advice through the whole process of translation."—I, vii.

265:16. *Amiel's Journal. The Journal intime of Henri-Frédéric Amiel*, translated with an introduction and notes by Mrs. Humphry Ward (London, 1885). 2 vols. Mrs. Ward's "Introduction" occupies I, ix–lxxii. In her novel *Robert Elsmere*, published early in the year after this article of Arnold's, Mrs. Ward represented Amiel under the guise of Mr. Langham.

265:18–19. Berthe Vadier (Céleste Vitaline Benoît), *Henri-Frédéric Amiel, Étude biographique* (Paris, 1886).

265:25–26. "Tristesse d'Olympio" is a poem in *Les Rayons et les ombres* (1840) in which Hugo personifies himself as Olympio; thereafter he was often referred to by that name. To Swinburne's reiterated praises of Hugo, Arnold could after 1882 add George Saintsbury's pronouncement: "No one who cares for poetry at all, and who has mastered the preliminary necessity of acquaintance with the French language and French prosody, can read any of his better works without gradually rising to a condition of enthusiasm in which the possible defects of the matter are altogether lost sight of in the unsurpassed and dazzling excellence of the manner. This is the special test of poetry, and there is none other. . . . It may be asserted, without the least fear of contradiction, that Victor Hugo will hold to all posterity the position of the greatest poet and one of the greatest prose writers of France."—*A Short History of French Literature* (Oxford, 1882), pp. 524–25.

266:1–6. The stanza with which Amiel's "Printemps du nord" opens and closes; Vadier, pp. 73, 75.

266:8–10. Scherer, I, lxxv, quoted in Ward, "Introduction," p. xii.

266:10–12. "Nous assistons ici à des prodiges de la pensée spéculative." "L'annotation psychologique quotidienne dont rien ne surpasse l'intérêt."—Scherer, I, xli, l; the former quoted by Ward, "Introduction," p. xl.

266:12–14. See Scherer, I, xxxiv, and Ward, "Introduction," p. lxii. Arnold's "friendship" with Obermann was first expressed in "Stanzas in Memory of the Author of 'Obermann'" (1852).

266:30–267:3. Ward, "Introduction," pp. xvi, lvii, xxiv, xxxi, xi.

267:9–10. "Je retrouve la hantise des mêmes pensées, se présentant sous les mêmes images, mais s'exprimant avec une éloquence toujours nouvelle."—Scherer, I, xlii.

267:11–12. *Nouveaux essais de psychologie contemporaine* (Paris, 1886), pp. 285–86. The essay on Amiel was first published in the *Nouvelle Revue* for May 1, 1885.

267:13–15. Ward, "Introduction," pp. lx, lv, lxi.

267:25–268:5. *Journal*, tr. Ward, I, 39–40 (April 28, 1852). Amiel mentions his youthful reading of *Obermann* at II, 76 (December 8, 1869). See Bourget, *Nouveaux essais*, p. 285.

268:8–26. Senancour, *Oberman*, ed. A. Monglond (Paris, 1947), I, 24–25 (Letter 4), with omissions. Scherer quotes "vast consciousness . . . self-abandonment" in making the comparison between Amiel and Obermann.—I, xxxiii. Arnold himself quoted this passage in his essay on "Obermann" (1869) and here makes a few emendations in his translation. See *Prose Works*, ed. Super, V, 302.

268:28. "That strain again! it had a dying fall."—*Twelfth Night*, I, i, 4.

268:30. Arnold introduced the idea of "natural magic" (with an example from Senancour) in his essay on "Maurice de Guérin" (1863).—*Prose Works*, ed. Super, III, 13–14.

269:1–4. After discussing Rousseau, Maurice de Guérin and Obermann, Scherer remarks: "Amiel . . . dépasse à mon avis tous ces martyrs de la pensée. Sa philosophie spéculative est bien autrement vaste, sa psychologie morbide bien autrement curieuse, sa perplexité morale bien autrement pathétique."—I, xxxiv.

269:7–9. From the time Harrison published his "Culture: a Dialogue" (*Fortnightly Review* VIII, 608 [November, 1867]) in reply to Arnold's concluding lecture from the chair of poetry at Oxford, "Culture and Its Enemies," Arnold frequently alluded to Harrison's characterization of himself as without "a philosophy with coherent, interdependent, subordinate, and derivative principles." See *Culture and Anarchy* (1868), *Prose Works*, ed. Super, V, 126, 423–25. Swinburne publicly criticized Arnold's disparagement of Hugo in *A Study of Shakespeare* (1880), p. 158; see Arnold's *Prose Works*, IX, 351.

269:16–19. *Journal*, tr. Ward, I, 50 (August 12, 1852).

269:21–23. *Ibid.*, II, 263 (January 13, 1879).

269:27–270:3. *Ibid.*, II, 309 (September 9, 1880). "Sheol" is translated as "hell" in the Authorized Version, e.g., at Psalm 16:10. "Die Mütter" (the Mothers) are the mysterious goddesses, outside of space and time, of which Goethe's Faust gains a vision.—Part II, I, v.

270:4–6. See Ward, Preface, p. vi; "Introduction," p. xxv.

270:11–12. Scherer in his introductory essay quotes a passage from 1854 not printed in the text itself: "Nature de Protée, essentiellement métamorphosable, polarisable et virtuelle, qui aime la forme et n'en prend aucune définitive, esprit subtil et fugace qu'aucune base ne peut absorber ni fixer tout entier."–I, xxxix. See also: "Je me sens caméléon, caléidoscope, protée, muable et polarisable de toutes les façons, fluide, virtuel, par conséquent latent, même dans mes manifestations, absent, même dans ma représentation."–*Journal intime*, I, 234 (December 23, 1866).

270:13–15. Bourget, *Nouvelle Essais*, pp. 273–74.

270:22–27. In his introductory essay, Scherer speaks of Amiel's "éblouissement de l'infini," and cites as a recurrent expression in the *Journal* "le besoin de totalité." He quotes a passage from 1854 that he did not print in the text itself: "Mon âme est la capacité de toute forme; elle n'est pas âme, elle est l'âme. Tiraillé par mille possibilités, je puis être plus facilement l'homme qu'un homme."– I, xxx, xxxvi, xxxvii. Mrs. Ward speaks of "what he himself calls 'l'éblouissement de l'infini.'"–I, xlvii. See also: "Though I am less of *a* man, I am perhaps nearer to *the* man; perhaps rather more *man*."–*Journal*, tr. Ward, II, 67 (August 14, 1869), and II, 199–200 (August 28, 1875). The latter includes the quotation *Omnis determinatio est negatio*.

270:27–28. See p. 270:11–12n.

270:29–30. Quoted in Scherer's introductory essay from a passage of 1854 (?) not printed in the text.–I, xxxix.

270:34–271:5. *Journal*, tr. Ward, II, 94–95 (June 9, 1870).

271:10–19. *Ibid.*, II, 201 (September 1, 1875).

271:29–31. *Adonais*, lines 462–64.

272:4–5. "L'aspiration vague et le désir indéterminé," which Mrs. Ward translated "undefined desire."–*Journal*, II, 101 (July 22, 1870).

272:8–9. *Was wir bringen*, end of scene 19, *Werke* (Stuttgart, 1829), XI, 302; (Weimar, 1894), XIII (1), 84. Jotted in Arnold's pocket diary at the end of 1871 and for May 26, 1872.–*Note-Books*, ed. Lowry, pp. 164, 178.

272:11–14. "Discours sur le style" (1753), ¶6; ed. A. Rondelet (Paris, 1882), p. 18. Quoted by Ste.-Beuve, "Qu'est-ce qu'un classique?" *Causeries du lundi* (4th ed.; Paris, 1869), III, 45, and jotted in Arnold's pocket diary for June 3, 1883, and in one of his general notebooks.–*Note-Books*, ed. Lowry, pp. 395, 513.

272:22–23. "Notre penseur aspire à confondre sa vie personnelle dans la vie générale."–Scherer, I, xxxix.

272:28–29. "Mon instinct est d'accord avec le pessimisme de Bouddha et de Schopenhauer. . . . La nature est bien pour moi une Maïa." "Je sens, comme Bouddha, tourner la Grande Roue, la Roue de l'illusion universelle. . . . Je n'ose respirer, il me semble que je suis suspendu à un fil au-dessus de l'abîme insondable des destinées. Est-ce là un tête-à-tête avec l'infini, l'intuition de la grande mort?"—*Journal intime,* II, 70, 95–96 (August 31, 1869; July 22, 1870), the latter also quoted by Scherer in his Introduction, I, xliii.

272:29–31. *Journal,* tr. Ward, II, 3 (April 17, 1867).

272:31–32. "A Gloomy morning. On all sides a depressing outlook, and within, disgust with self."—*Journal,* tr. Ward, II, 33 (April 26, 1868).

272:32–273:2. "There is no deceiving myself as to the fate which awaits me:—increasing loneliness, mortification of spirit, long-continued regret, melancholy neither to be consoled nor confessed, a mournful old age, a slow decay, a death in the desert!"—*Ibid.,* II, 35 (August 26, 1868).

273:3–5. "Vivre, c'est donc triompher sans cesse." "Pour vivre . . . l'audace est nécessaire." "Au lieu de courir, je tourne en cercle." "Je n'ai jamais eu la vision distincte de ma vraie vocation."—*Journal intime,* I, 32 (December 2, 1851); I, lvi (Scherer's Introduction); II, 193 (September 1, 1875); I, liii (1858; Scherer's Introduction).

273:22–23. Scherer remarks that he himself left Geneva late in 1860. A year later Amiel wrote to ask if Scherer thought it was too late for him to begin writing for the public; Scherer knew that the editor of the *Revue germanique* would like nothing better than to have contributions from Amiel on philosophy or literature, "et, quelques temps après, dans une autre lettre, je lui proposais un article sur Uhland, comme un sujet admirablement adapté à son talent et à ses goûts." But it came to nothing.—I, xxii–xxv. Ludwig Uhland (1787–1862) was a German romantic poet.

274:3–20. *Journal,* tr. Ward, II, 75–76 (October 19, 1869). Mrs. Ward translates: "The fact is, that Sainte-Beuve leaves . . . ," "The true critic acts as a fulcrum for all the world," "scales, the refining rod, which tests the value of every one and the merit of every work," "of mind and heart," "that the critic rises to . . . ," "By then only can he hope for insight into all the modes of being, and for mastery of all possible shades of appreciation." Members of the ruling class in Plato's *Republic* complete their philosophic education by the age of thirty-five, serve in various posts in the military and civil service until they are fifty, then are free to spend most of the rest of their lives in study, though they must as a matter of duty take their turn as rulers.—VII, 540.

274:23–24. Arnold so described Hugo in his first essay on "George Sand" (1877), then again in "A Word about America" (1882).—*Prose Works*, ed. Super, VIII, 230; X, 14.

274:25–275:13. *Journal*, tr. Ward, II, 231–33 (April 26, 1877). Mrs. Ward translates: "I have been turning over again the *Paris* of Victor Hugo (1867)," "everything that he has not foreseen. He does not see that pride is a limitation of the mind, and that a pride without limitations is a littleness of soul," "learn to compare himself . . . ," "into these mad exaggerations, these extravagant judgments. But proportion and fairness will never be among the strings at his command," "simple; the only light he has to give blinds you like that of a fire. He astonishes a reader and provokes him, he moves him and annoys him. There is always some falsity of note in him, which accounts for the *malaise* he so constantly excites in me. The great poet in him cannot shake off the charlatan. A few shafts of Voltairean irony would have shrivelled the inflation of his genius and made it stronger by making it saner," "poet of a nation should not . . . ," "unlike those Hebrew prophets who scourged because they loved, he should devote himself proudly and systematically to the flattery of his countrymen," "Hugo is Paris; peoples, bow down!"

275:16–276:13. *Journal*, tr. Ward, II, 236–38 (July 17, 1877).

276:29–30. *Journal*, tr. Ward, II, 74 (October 16, 1869).

276:30–33. *Nouvelle correspondance* (Paris, 1880), pp. 182, 110 (letters of March 1, 1863, and November 26, 1846); jotted in Arnold's pocket diary for August 18 and 23, 1885.—*Note-Books*, ed. Lowry, p. 420.

277:4–7. *Journal intime*, II, 17 (February 16, 1868); II, 85 (May 7, 1870), the latter jotted in Arnold's pocket diary for August 21, 1887.—*Note-Books*, ed. Lowry, p. 431. See *Journal*, tr. Ward, II, 89.

277:8–9. "A liberal State is wholly incompatible with an anti-liberal religion, and almost equally incompatible with the absence of religion."—*Journal*, tr. Ward, II, 92–93 (May 9, 1870).

277:23–278:2. *Journal*, tr. Ward, II, 113–14 (February 7, 1871).

278:7–21. *Journal*, tr. Ward, II, 28 (April 9, 1868). Amiel had been reading Rudolf Hermann Lotze, *History of Aestheticism in Germany* (Munich, 1868).

278:22, 25. "Video meliora proboque, | deteriora sequor."—Ovid *Metamorphoses* VII, 20–21.

278:26–28. *Journal*, tr. Ward, II, 242 (July 30, 1877).

278:29–30. "The nothingness of our joys, the emptiness of our existence, and the futility of our ambitions, filled me with a quiet disgust."—*Journal*, tr. Ward, II, 51 (March 18, 1869).

279:1–24. *Journal*, tr. Ward, II, 116–17 (February 12, 1871). Astraea, goddess of Justice, withdrew from the world (according to Greek mythology) at the end of the golden age.

279:27–28. Eaton Hall, some four miles up the river Dee from Chester, was the vast seat of the dukes of Westminster, among the wealthiest men in England. It was built in 1867–80 and demolished in 1963. Chatsworth House, twenty-five miles from Derby, is the palatial seat of the dukes of Devonshire, dating back to 1687–1706.

279:30–33. See p. 365:18–22.

279:36–280:8. *Journal*, tr. Ward, II, 280–81 (January 2, 1880); Amiel contrasted this state of feeling with the "humble and yet voluptuous state" known only to the Yoghis and Soufis, "which combines the joys of being and of non-being, which is neither reflection nor will, which is above both the moral existence and the intellectual existence, which is the return to unity, . . .—Nirvana in its most attractive form."

280:12–20. *Journal*, tr. Ward, II, 104–5 (October 25, 1870).

280:21–24. *Journal*, tr. Ward, II, 107 (October 26, 1870).

280:30–281:2. *Journal*, tr. Ward, II, 330–31 (February 4, 1881). Charles Secrétan, a contemporary Swiss theologian, reviewed *Literature and Dogma* and was answered in *God and the Bible*.

281:3–12. *Journal*, tr. Ward, II, 184 (September 1, 1874). The concluding sentence paraphrases one of Arnold's touchstone passages in "The Study of Poetry" (1880): "In la sua volontade è nostra pace."—Dante, *Paradiso*, III, 85.

281:16–20. *Journal*, tr. Ward, II, 315 (December 27, 1880).

281:21. Arnold used this expression also in "A Liverpool Address" (1882), *Prose Works*, ed. Super, X, 76.

281:32. Vergil *Aeneid* II, 291.

[COUNT LEO TOLSTOI]

On May 14, 1861, Arnold mentioned hearing from "a Russian count who had been sent with a letter to me."—*Letters*, ed. Russell. The message was by that time several months old; its sender was Count Leo Tolstoy, who visited England in late February to look at the elementary schools. Arnold in a letter of March 11 bespoke for him the assistance of London school managers and may have conversed with him at the Athenaeum Club. Tolstoy read Arnold's critical and religious prose with great interest over the next quarter century, was especially pleased with *Literature and Dogma*, and sent a copy of the French version of *What I Believe* (*Ma Religion*, 1885) to Arnold by the hand of a friend. That book and *Que faire? Ma Confession*, and *Anna Karénine* (all in French) were on the reading list Arnold jotted at the end of his pocket diary for 1887.—*Note-Books*, ed. Lowry, pp. 621–22. The diary itself indicated that he was reading Tolstoi almost daily from February 3 to March 18, on August 22 and September 20, and *Que faire?* on October 4. No other progress is visible until the entry on November 15, "send Tolstoi." The essay appeared in the *Fortnightly Review* in December, 1887, and Arnold was paid £50 for it. "I had a special reason for writing about Tolstoi, because of his religious ideas," he told Florence Earle Coates on February 24, 1888; "in general I do not write about the literary performances of living contemporaries or contemporaries only recently dead. Therefore I am not likely to write about Tourguenieff, though I admire him greatly, and am going to read two of his novels this very year."—*Letters*, ed. Russell. Only a year later, a writer in the *Westminster* suggested that Arnold made Tolstoy's reputation in England, and twenty years later Aylmer Maude called the essay "one of the very best articles any one [had] written" on the subject.—*Westminster Review* CXXX, 278 (September, 1888); Maude, *The Life of Tolstoy: First Fifty Years* (London, 1908), p. 431. Tolstoy himself is said to have regarded the critique as "sound and just."—Maude, *Tolstoy and His Problems* (London, 1901), p. 39. The essay was designated by Arnold before his death for the second series of *Essays in Criticism*. Two illuminating short studies of the relations between the two authors are Marion Mainwaring, "Arnold and Tolstoi," *Nineteenth-Century Fiction* VI, 269–74 (March, 1952) and Victor O. Buyniak, "Leo Tolstoy and Matthew Arnold," *Wascana Review* III, no. 2, 63–71 (1968).

282:1–12. *Causeries du lundi* (Paris, 1858), XIII, 284, 297 (May 4, 1857).

282:20–21. Among the English novelists recently dead were Thackeray (1811–63), Dickens (1812–70), Trollope (1815–82), and George Eliot (1819–80).

283:15–23. Quoted also in "Civilisation in the United States" (1888), pp. 364–65.

284:12. "Mr. Gladstone Holds the Field" was a headline in *The Pall Mall Gazette* for October 25, 1887, p. 1. The article itself quotes *The Standard* (which it confutes): "Mr. Gladstone's substitute for a policy has not long been allowed to 'hold the field.'"

284:15–21. Tolstoy was born on August 28, 1828 (by the Russian calendar). *Anna Karenin* was published serially in Russia in 1875–77; a French translation appeared in 1885 and an English one by Nathan Haskell Dole in New York the next year. Almost immediately after its completion Tolstoy turned his attention to religious problems. *A Confession* was prohibited in Russia by the Spiritual Censor in the aftermath of the assassination of Alexander II in 1881, and the small private edition of *What I Believe* (1884) was seized by the authorities.

284:23. *War and Peace* (1867–69) was translated into French in 1884, into English in 1886.

284:26–28. *Vanity Fair* (1847–48) was set in nineteenth-century London, *The Virginians* (1857–59) in eighteenth-century England and America.

284:30–31. In "The Literary Influence of Academies" (1864) and, before that, in the anonymous review of a translation of Spinoza's *Tractatus* (1862).—*Prose Works*, ed. Super, III, 241–42, 58.

284:33–34. Fredrika Bremer's *Hemmet, eller familje-sorger och fröjder* (1839) was translated into English by Mary Howitt in 1843, into French by Mlle. R. Du Puget in 1853. The reading list in Arnold's pocket diary for the last year of his life (1888) includes *The Home.—Note-Books*, ed. Lowry, p. 625.

284:37. Arnold presumably refers to the volumes entitled *Christ's Christianity* (London: Kegan Paul, 1885) and *What I Believe*, tr. C. Popoff (London: Elliot Stock, 1885).

285:14–23. *Anna Karenin*, the early chapters of part VI and chapt. iii of part V.

285:27. The expression "inward eye" occurs three times in Wordsworth's poetry. Arnold may be echoing "They flash upon that inward eye" ("I Wandered Lonely as a Cloud," line 21), as perhaps he did many years earlier in the "Preface to *Poems* (1853)" (reprinted 1882): "by which the object is made to flash upon the eye of the mind."—*Prose Works*, ed. Super, I, 10:20.

286:35–36. "Les frivoles ont peut-être raison," Arnold quoted Renan in "Numbers" (1884).—*Prose Works*, ed. Super, X, 155, somewhat altering Renan's *Souvenirs d'enfance et de jeunesse* (Paris, 1883), pp. 149–50.

287:2. The Old Testament frequently refers to the land of the Canaanites as "a land flowing with milk and honey" (e.g., Exodus 3:8, 17).

287:20–25. Part I, chapt. xi.

287:29. George Alfred Lawrence's melodramatic novel, *Guy Livingstone, or, Thorough* (1857) was the story of a Guards officer of great prowess in sports, large, strong, handsome, very rich, and utterly unprincipled. The author was four years behind Arnold at Rugby and Balliol.

288:22–27, 29–34. Part I, chapts. xviii, xxii.

289:8–13. Part I, chapt. xxiii.

289:26–27. Désiré Nisard (1806–88) was director of the École normale supérieure from 1857 to 1867. Arnold mentions him several times in *Schools and Universities on the Continent* (1868), a book that grew out of his official tour of the Continent in 1865.

290:11. Alcibiades, the wayward Athenian leader of the expedition against Syracuse in the Peloponnesian War, dominates Plato's *Symposium* with his charm and vivacity. The Master of Ravenswood is the doom-ridden hero of Scott's *Bride of Lammermoor*, for love of whom Lucy Ashton goes mad. Eight of Scott's novels, including *The Bride*, were on Arnold's reading list for 1873.—*Note-Books*, ed. Lowry, p. 588.

290:23–24. Proverbs 13:15.

290:24–29. Part II, chapts. xxviii–xxix.

290:32–291:15. Part IV, chapt. xvii.

291:31–33. *Othello*, III, iii, 330, 332–33.

292:6–16. Part VII, chapts. xxvii–xxxi; part VIII, chapt. v.

292:29. The goddess Aselgeia, or Lubricity, was in Arnold's view the current deity of France and its literature; she figured largely in the lecture on "Numbers" which he delivered on his American tour of 1883–84.

292:31–33. Nevertheless, in his description of Anna's costume at the ball (p. 288:32–34), Arnold omits the word "low-necked."

292:36–37. In "Epistle to a Young Friend," line 48, a passage Arnold quoted in "The Study of Poetry" (1880).—*Prose Works*, ed. Super, IX, 184.

293:19–295:32. Part VIII, chapts. viii–xiii, xix.

293:31.   "And then he thinks he knows
            The hills where his life rose,
            And the sea where it goes."
                —Arnold, "The Buried Life" (1852).

296:1–4. *Ma Religion* (Paris: Librairie Fischbacher, n.d.), p. 5.

296:23–28. *Ibid.*, p. 1.

297:15–18. *Ibid.*, chapt. vii.

297:18–19. Romans 8:2.

297:31–32. The dogmas of the Nicene Creed, which declares that the Son is "very God of very God" and that the Holy Ghost "proceedeth from the Father and the Son."

298:6–11. *Ma Confession*, tr. "Zoria" (Paris: Albert Savine, 1887), p. 2.

298:15–22. *Ibid.*, pp. 72–73.

298:26–299:7. *Ibid.*, pp. 19–21.

299:13–15. "Vanity of vanities; all is vanity."— Ecclesiastes 1:2.

299:17–28. *Ma Confession*, pp. 134–35.

299:33–300:11. *Ma Religion*, pp. 185, 184–85.

300:14–26. *Ma Confession*, pp. 168–69.

300:36–301:7. *Anna Karenin*, part VIII, chapt. x.

301:11–30. *Ma Religion*, chapt. vi, pp. 81, 90, 95, 97, 106.

302:1–15. *Ibid.*, pp. 247, 257, 250–51.

302:28–33. *Literature and Dogma* (1873), chapt. vii, part 4 (Popular Edition, part 2).—*Prose Works*, ed. Super, VI, 299.

302:36–303:1. Arnold introduced this concept in *St. Paul and Protestantism* (1870) and *Literature and Dogma* (1873).—*Prose Works*, ed. Super, VI, 115, 299–301.

303:10–12. "The prince of this world is judged" (John 16:11) and "I saw a new heaven and a new earth" (Revelation 21:1) were both quoted in Arnold's address in Whitechapel on November 29, 1884.—*Prose Works*, ed. Super, X, 253–54.

303:14–15. John 13:17.

303:25–26. John 12:25, Luke 9:24, Mark 8:35. See *Literature and Dogma* (1873), *Prose Works*, ed. Super, VI, 291–99.

303:30–31. Matthew 9:10 (Mark 2:15, Luke 5:29); Matthew 17:24–25.

304:14. One is tempted to emend "marking" to "remarkable."

[SHELLEY]

When John Morley began to plan his biographical series, the "English Men of Letters," he was eager to have Arnold as one of his authors, and fancied he might choose Shelley.* But Arnold did not, and so Shelley was the only one of the great English

---

*Morley actually offered Arnold Shakespeare, which Arnold turned down after some days of indecision.

romantic poets of the beginning of the nineteenth century upon whom Arnold had not written when Edward Dowden published his two-volume *Life of Percy Bysshe Shelley* on November 26, 1886. (Perhaps one must make the reservation that "Joubert: or, a French Coleridge" was not concerned with Coleridge as a poet.) There was much in Shelley's life, moreover, that was close to Arnold. Thomas Arnold went up to Oxford as an undergraduate the year after Shelley; at Corpus Christi College with Thomas Arnold and John Keble was John Taylor Coleridge, nephew of S. T. C. and a contemporary of Shelley's at Eton. John Duke Coleridge, son of John Taylor, was a contemporary of Matthew Arnold's at Balliol and a close, lifelong friend (he wrote the Preface to the posthumous second series of *Essays in Criticism*). The senior dons at Oriel when Arnold was a young member of the Common Room in the late forties were Shelley's contemporaries. And so Arnold turned with some eagerness to the new book. As his essay too plainly shows, he was disappointed.

There is little about his work on the essay in his diary and correspondence; nevertheless word of his interest in the book got around early, for Percy W. Bunting, editor of the *Contemporary Review*, asked if he might have the essay: "I have promised Shelley elsewhere, if I do him at all in connexion with Dowden's book; but my doing him at all is doubtful," Arnold wrote Bunting on November 30, 1886.–R. L. Lowe, "Matthew Arnold and Percy William Bunting," *Studies in Bibliography* VII, 206 (1955). He jotted in his pocket diary two passages from the *Saturday Review*'s article on the book (December 18).–*Note-Books*, ed. Lowry, p. 424. It is more than a year later that his pocket diary notes, on December 13, 1887, "send Shelley." The essay was published in the *Nineteenth Century* for January, 1888, and brought Arnold £50. "In this article on Shelley I have spoken of his life, not his poetry," Arnold wrote to Lady de Rothschild on January 4. "Professor Dowden was too much for my patience."–*Letters*, ed. Russell. He was not displeased with the essay, for he recommended it to Florence Earle Coates late in February. Nevertheless, it was not what he really wanted to write about Shelley, and as he began planning a new collection of *Essays in Criticism* on January 20, his list included a second Shelley article to be devoted to the poetry.–W. E. Buckler, *Matthew Arnold's Books* (Geneva: E. Droz, 1958), p. 76. He did not live to write that essay, and the present one, by itself, is somewhat out of place in the collection; readers must bear firmly in mind that it is a review of a biography–

one more of Arnold's demolitions of humorless pedantry, but not an essay on poetry.

When he reviewed Arnold's *Letters* in 1895, Dowden remarked wistfully that it would have been pleasant had he been able to believe that anything he ever did had met with Arnold's approbation.—*Saturday Review* LXXX, 758 (December 7, 1895). Nevertheless, his own review of *Last Essays* (*Academy*, May 19, 1877, pp. 430–31) had been savage. Yeats in his *Autobiography* recalled a visit to Dowden with his father, when Dowden delighted him by reading some parts of the then unpublished biography. "I was chilled, however, when [Dowden] explained that he had lost his liking for Shelley and would not have written it but for an old promise to the Shelley family. When it was published, Matthew Arnold made sport of certain conventionalities and extravagances that were, my father and I had come to see, the violence or clumsiness of a conscientious man hiding from himself a lack of sympathy."—(New York, 1938), p. 78. George Saintsbury said of Arnold's essay: "From the moment of its appearance . . . this piece has been an unceasing joy to all who love literature with a sane devotion. . . . No English writer . . . has ever tempered such a blend of quiet contempt with perfect good-humour and perfect good-breeding."—*Matthew Arnold* (Edinburgh, 1899), p. 204. Dowden's book is still in print at the original publisher's.

305:1–13. Percy Florence Shelley (1819–89) was not quite three when his father died. A year later his mother took him back to England and in April, 1833, moved to Harrow so that she might send him to school there as a day boy (just as Arnold did for his sons in 1868). From 1846 until her death in 1851 she lived in Chester Square, London, where Arnold lived from 1858 to 1868. Dr. Marion Mainwaring has pointed out that Arnold had the story from the actress Fanny A. Kemble, whom he met at tea at the home of his neighbor Lady Grey in November, 1887.—Gertrude Lyster, ed., *A Family Chronicle. Derived from Notes and Letters Selected by Barbarina, the Hon. Lady Grey* (London, 1908), p. 333; Mainwaring, "Arnold on Shelley," *Modern Language Notes* LXVII, 122–23 (February, 1952). (Gertrude Lyster, Lady Grey's niece, tells the story as having been present at the conversation.)

305:8–9. Arnold was a school inspector for the Education Department from 1851 until his retirement in 1886.

305:14–19. Edward Dowden, *The Life of Percy Bysshe Shelley* (London: Kegan Paul, Trench & Co., 1886). 2 vols. Dowden in his Preface explains that Sir Henry Taylor in the summer of 1883 acted as ambassador between Sir Percy and Lady Shelley on the one hand and Dowden on the other, to commission the writing of the book. "I have had access to all the Shelley papers in their possession, and permission to make use of them without reserve."–I, v.

305: 21–24. Mary Shelley's four-volume edition of the poems first appeared in 1839. Shelley's cousin Thomas Medwin published his *Life of Percy Bysshe Shelley* in two volumes in 1847; Thomas Jefferson Hogg's two-volume *Life of Percy Bysshe Shelley* appeared in 1858. E. J. Trelawny in the latter year published his *Recollections of the Last Days of Shelley and Byron.*

306:6–15. In the first and second paragraphs of her Preface to the Collected Edition of 1839. Dowden quotes lines 7–8, 12–15 in his discussion of Shelley's separation from Harriet (*Shelley*, I, 427).

306:34–38. T. Hall Caine in *The Academy* (December 4, 1886), p. 371. Dowden's book contains about 1100 pages of text.

307:2–4. Dowden, born in Cork, was professor of English literature in the University of Dublin (Trinity College). "He disliked Irish nationalism and fought vigorously against Home Rule."– E. J. Gwynn in *DNB*.

307:10–13, 16–26. Dowden, *Shelley*, I, 375 and 465–66 and 513; 380; 181. "Old, unhappy, far-off things" is the expression from Wordsworth's "The Solitary Reaper."

308:18–28. I, 55–56, jotted (somewhat abbreviated) in Arnold's pocket diary for July 23, 1881, with the heading, "Hogg on Shelley."–*Note-Books*, ed. Lowry, p. 356. Dowden quotes this passage at I, 62.

309:8–33. Dowden, *Shelley*, I, 7, 9, 13, 17–18, 20, 23–25, 28–29, 221. Shelley's grandfather was made a baronet in 1806. The "popular scientific lecturer" was Adam Walker, who lectured both at Eton and at Sion House Academy, where Shelley was first a student.

309:35, 310:6. An "exhibitioner" is one who holds a stipend for his support from an endowment set up for the purpose; in American academic language an "exhibition" would be called a "scholarship." Shelley held the so-called "Leicester Exhibition," to which he had been nominated by his uncle, Sir John Shelley-Sidney of Penshurst. A "commoner" is a student not supported by funds from the college foundation.

309:36–310:4. Dowden, *Shelley*, I, 44–45, 48–50. Campbell singled out as the "only two good lines in the poem"

> It seemed as if some angel's sigh
> Had breathed the plaintive symphony.

Shelley's letters to the future Mrs. Hemans so alarmed the young lady's mother that she forbade further correspondence.

310:4–5. On September 18, 1810, John Joseph Stockdale of Pall Mall announced the publication of *Original Poems*, by "Victor and Cazire."–Dowden, *Shelley*, I, 50–51.

310:7–9. Quoted by Dowden, I, 61–66.

310:10–17. *Ibid.*, I, 75, 97–98, 101–2.

310:17–21. *Ibid.*, I, 116, 119. The "heads of houses" were the heads of the various Oxford colleges.

310:21–29. *Ibid.*, I, 119–21. Lady Day is March 25.

310:30–38. *Ibid.*, I, 127, 129, 148.

311:1–6. *Ibid.*, I, 150, 141–42, 145. Mount Street runs from Park Lane (the eastern end of Hyde Park, where Harriet later drowned) to the north end of Berkeley Square. When Arnold was private secretary to Lord Lansdowne (whose house was on Berkeley Square), he had lodgings on Mount Street.

311:9–19. Dowden, *Shelley*, I, 143, 168–69.

311: 23–25. *Ibid.*, I, 176.

311:27–29. *Ibid.*, I, 185–86.

311:33–34. *Ibid.*, I, 187, 189.

311:36–312:6. *Ibid.*, I, 191–92, 194.

312:11–15. *Ibid.*, I, 205, 208.

312:20–21. *Ibid.*, I, 233.

312:21–29. *Ibid.*, I, 217–19, 222, 249, 263.

312:29–313:1. *Ibid.*, I, 266–67, 279, 284–86, 292–93, 295–96. Timothy Michael Healy was one of the leaders of the vociferous Irish home rule party in Parliament after 1880.

313:1–8. *Ibid.*, I, 301–6.

313:10–11. Letter to John Rickman, September 16, 1801, quoted *Ibid.*, I, 305.

313:16. The story of Oedipus, who killed his father and married his mother.

313:18–32. Dowden, *Shelley*, I, 309, 317, 322, 338–41, 349, 359, 361, 375, 377. Bracknell is about nine miles southwest of Eton and twelve miles from Arnold's birthplace at Laleham.

313:32–37. Hogg, II, 383, quoted by Dowden, *Shelley*, I, 387.

313:38–314:11. Dowden, *Shelley*, I, 394, 405, 385–86, 402–3, 406–7.

314:13–25. *Ibid.*, I, 408–10.

314:29–315:1. *Ibid.*, I, 411, 413–14, 417. The former poem is entitled "Stanzas: April, 1814," and begins "Away! the moor is dark beneath the moon."

315:12–34. *Ibid.*, I, 418–21, 434, 415, 430.

315:35–316:15. *Ibid.*, I, 423, 431, 433–34, 430, 439, 435. The quotation is from *Julius Caesar*, II, i, 68–69.

316:16–317:9. *Ibid.*, I, 449–50. St. Paul ends the Second Epistle to Timothy with some very mundane commissions, such as the bringing of a cloak Paul had left behind him (4:13, 19–21). Lines 31–32, which Arnold quotes almost as Dowden gives them, should read "a mule to carry our baggage, & Mary who has not been sufficiently well to bear the fatigue of walking."

317:16–34. Dowden, *Shelley*, I, 461, 464–66.

317:35–318:17. *Ibid.*, I, 485, 507, 513, 511, 525–28.

318:25–30. *Ibid.*, I, 536, 546.

318:33–319:4. *Ibid.*, II, 5–6, 11, 26, 44–45.

319:7–23. *Ibid.*, II, 56–57. One might suppose that the note read "source of pain," but Arnold copies Dowden correctly.

319:24–33. *Ibid.*, II, 64–65.

320:20–22. Dowden, *Shelley*, I, 366. Dowden refers to the duke, an important Whig politician, as "a *bon vivant* surrounded by men who kept the table in a roar, and a famous trafficker in boroughs."— I, 133.

320:25–26. Edward Copleston (1776–1849) was fellow of Oriel College and vicar of St. Mary's, the University church, while Shelley was an undergraduate at University College; Shelley sent a copy of *The Necessity of Atheism* to him, and Dowden used him as characteristic of the intellectual tone of Oxford when Shelley went up (I, 125, 211, 55). He was provost (head) of Oriel when Thomas Arnold became fellow of the college (1815). Edward Hawkins (1789–1882) was an undergraduate at St. John's College, Oxford, when Shelley went up; he became fellow of Oriel in 1813 and was provost of the college when Matthew Arnold became a fellow in 1845. He was still provost, and Arnold's occasional host, when Arnold delivered his lectures from the chair of poetry in 1857–67. John Keble (1792–1866) became fellow of Oriel the year Shelley was expelled; he was Matthew Arnold's godfather. All three men were at Oriel when Newman became a fellow there in 1822 (three years after Thomas Arnold left the college), and all three figure in the *Apologia*, as does Keble's younger brother Thomas, who joined him at Corpus Christi College in 1808.

320:29–30. *The Christian Year*, Advent Sunday, lines 65–66.

321:11–39. Dowden, *Shelley*, I, 424–29; II, 338. Dowden quotes the sentence from the second paragraph of Mary Shelley's note to *Alastor*. Thornton Hunt was Leigh Hunt's son.

322:4–10. Dowden, *Shelley*, I, 156, 409; Hogg, II, 517. Arnold adapts the former passage; Shelley spoke of Harriet as "something more noble, yet not so cultivated as the elder—a larger diamond, yet not so highly polished."

322:10–18. Dowden, *Shelley*, I, 193, 313, 315.

322:25–28. *Ibid.*, II, 301, from one of Hunt's articles in *The Examiner* of September–October, 1819.

322:38–323:7. The "Neapolitan charge" was a female infant in whom Shelley was interested and whom gossips asserted to be his child by Claire Clairmont; she died in infancy.—Dowden, II, 251–53. Emilia Viviani, daughter of a Pisan nobleman who was residing in a convent until a suitable husband should be found for her, was subject of Shelley's enthusiastic affection in 1820–21 and inspired "Epipsychidion." For Mary Shelley's discomfort and Dowden's uneasiness over Claire, see II, 349–50.

323:28–34. Dowden, *Shelley*, II, 121–23; I, 318. The line of verse is the second last in the version of "On leaving London for Wales" printed by Dowden; "'I am the friend of the unfriended poor' was with Shelley a simple statement of fact," says Dowden.

324:1–4. Hogg, *Shelley*, I, 237, quoted by Dowden, I, 76; see also Dowden, I, 78, 83.

324:15–26. Dowden, *Shelley*, I, 205–6, 188–89.

324:28–33. Hogg, *Shelley*, I, 329–30, quoted by Dowden, I, 131–32.

325:5–21. Dowden, *Shelley*, I, 541, 551.

325:26–30, 326:1–8. *Ibid.*, II, 437, 459.

326:11–12. Trelawny, *Records of Shelley, Byron, and the Author* (1878), chapt. iii; quoted by Dowden, II, 460.

326:15–20. Dowden, *Shelley*, II, 120.

326:26–327:7. *Ibid.*, I, 388–89, 390n.

327:17–18. Arnold repeats his own description of Shelley from his essay on Byron (1881), *Prose Works*, ed. Super, IX, 237. The editor's note to that passage suggests certain elements that may have contributed to Arnold's famous characterization; to these one might add Pope, *Rape of the Lock*, II, 130: "While clogged he beats his silken wings in vain." Dowden had quoted and repudiated this language of Arnold's in "Last Words on Shelley," *Fortnightly Review* XLVIII, 470–72 (October, 1887).

[MILTON]

In July, 1886, Arnold and his daughter Eleanor spent a few days in Long Branch, on the New Jersey shore, with Mr. and Mrs. G. W.

Childs. "He owns the *Philadelphia Ledger,* and has entertained all the English who come over here," Arnold wrote to his sister on July 26.—*Letters,* ed. Russell. A year and a half later, when Childs had given a window in honor of Milton and his second wife to the parish church of St. Margaret's, Westminster (next to Westminster Abbey), Arnold's friend of many years, Archdeacon F. W. Farrar, who had instigated and arranged the gift, invited him to make the address at the unveiling. "You have made your request so charmingly that I cannot refuse it—but tell me of *what length* the discourse should be? I suppose it should not exceed a quarter of an hour or twenty minutes; and that, in that case, it is better read than spoken?" Arnold replied on January 4, 1888. The date was fixed for February 18; a week earlier Arnold wrote to Farrar from Cobham: "Childs has given the window; have you any other gifts from Americans in the *Church?* What are the gifts from Americans in the *Abbey?* Was it not a fountain Childs gave to Stratford? Is Whittier's quatrain good? will it be inscribed on the window? Is Lowell's on the Raleigh window? did the Americans give that, and the Caxton? . . . Did Milton ever actually live in the parish of St. Margaret's?" On February 17 Arnold wrote to his daughter Lucy Whitridge in New York that, in response to a telegram from her husband, he would send the address next day, after it was delivered, to R. W. Gilder, editor of the *Century Magazine.* "I hate delivering things, and I hate to have a subject found for me instead of occurring of itself to my mind; still, I think the Milton will read pretty well in print." His pocket diary records, "Work at Milton" on February 11 and 13, "Write out Milton" on the 14th. Admission to the ceremony, which was held in the vestry at 3:30, was by private invitation, and these were sent out late (to the dismay of Americans in London who would have liked to attend); Browning's was dated only the day before the lecture. "Only a few private friends will be present—among them, I hope, the Speaker [of the House of Commons, Arthur Wellesley Peel], the American Minister [Edward J. Phelps], Mr. Lecky, and others," Farrar told Browning; and of course Mrs. Arnold and their younger daughter. The address appeared in the *Century Magazine* for May (after Arnold's death). It was added, at the publisher's suggestion, to the collection of essays Arnold had been planning as *Essays in Criticism, Second Series;* in that company it is somewhat of a misfit.

328:1. Speculation on the identity of this eloquent voice began almost immediately after the publication of the essay. Goethe, Leopardi (whom Arnold was reading early in 1888), Emerson,

Carlyle have been suggested; to these one might add George Sand (whom Arnold was also reading strenuously about this time). But no one has yet found the phrase Arnold quotes, and Arnold does not seem to have identified the voice in his correspondence. (The tone of the reference to Leopardi on p. 332 would seem to preclude him.)

328:27–29. The stained glass window at the west end of the north aisle of St. Margaret's Church, Westminster, portrays scenes from *Paradise Lost* and Milton's life. It carries the legend: "To the glory of God and in memory of the immortal poet John Milton: whose wife and child lie buried here: this window is dedicated by George W. Childs of Philadelphia mdccclxxxviii." A full description of the window appears in *The Critic* (New York), n.s. IX, 94–95 (February 25, 1888); a lengthy account of the gift is given by L. Clarke Davis in George W. Childs, *Recollections* (Philadelphia, 1890), pp. 287–308.

329:4–7. Simonides of Ceos, fragment 58 (Bergk), 65 (Edmonds), or 37 (Diehl), based on Hesiod's *Works and Days* 289–91. Arnold cited this fragment in *Culture and Anarchy* (1868), *Prose Works*, ed. Super, V, 152.

329:12–13. Philippians 1:10.

329:21–22. At Childs' summer home in Elberon, near Long Branch, on the New Jersey shore, on July 17–18, 1886. See Arnold's letter to his sister Frances, July 26.—*Letters*, ed. Russell.

329:22–24. The pinnacled and ornate granite and stone fountain in the Rother Market, Stratford, given by Childs, was dedicated with great ceremony on October 17, 1887.

329:28. Whittier's lines are:

> "The New World honours him whose lofty plea
> For England's freedom made her own most sure
> Whose song immortal as its theme shall be
> Their common freehold while both worlds endure."

329:35–38. Katherine Woodcock married Milton on November 12, 1656, bore him a daughter on October 19, 1657, and died with the daughter on February 3, 1658. His Sonnet XIX, "Methought I saw my late espoused saint," was taken until recently to refer to her; now there is debate whether the poem may not refer to his first wife.

329:38–330:3. Milton lived in Petty France, Westminster (later 19 York Street, demolished 1877), where his garden opened on

St. James's Park, from December, 1651, to May, 1660. It is not certain when *Samson Agonistes* was written, but *Paradise Regained* cannot have been composed during the Westminster years.

330:6. Milton's Sonnet "To the Lord General Cromwell" (1652) begins "Cromwell, our chief of men."

330:7. "The sons | Of Belial, flown with insolence and wine" (*Paradise Lost* I, 501–2) is generally taken as Milton's characterization of the Restoration courtiers.

330:19–20. Though Katherine Woodcock was from Hackney, nothing is known of her parentage.

331:2–7. The council of the Greek leaders, Act I, scene iii, that includes Ulysses' famous speech on "degree." In the Preface to his *Poems* (1853), Arnold develops at greater length his criticism of Shakespeare's "extremely and faultily difficult, . . . artificial, . . . tortured" language.—*Prose Works*, ed. Super, I, 11.

331:15. In the same Preface (I, 9), Arnold cites a passage from Goethe on the power of architectonics that distinguishes the artist from the amateur.—"Über den sogenannten Dilettantismus" (1799), *Werke* (Stuttgart, 1833), XLIV, 262–63; (Weimar, 1896), XLVII, 326.

331:26–30. "In Sophocles what is valuable is not so much his contributions to psychology and the anatomy of sentiment, as the grand moral effects produced by *style*. For the style is the expression of the nobility of the poet's character, as the matter is the expression of the richness of his mind: but on men character produces as great an effect as mind," Arnold wrote to Clough about March 1, 1849.—*The Letters of Matthew Arnold to Arthur Hugh Clough*, ed. H. F. Lowry (London: Oxford University Press, 1932), p. 101.

332:6–11. *Pensieri*, no. lxiv. The *Pensieri* were on Arnold's reading lists for the last decade of his life, but he seems to have got to them only in 1887 and 1888.—*Note-Books*, ed. Lowry, pp. 435–37, 621, 624.

332:12–17. *The Reason of Church-government*, Book II, near the end of the prefatory remarks; *Works*, ed. H. M. Ayres et al. (New York: Columbia University Press, 1931), III (i), 241.

333:5, 17. *Aeneid* XII, 826, 834.

333:20. Thucydides described his history as written to be "a possession for all time" (I, xxii, 4), and Arnold quoted the expression in "An Eton Boy" (1882) and "Emerson" (1883).—*Prose Works*, ed. Super, X, 45, 165.

[DISESTABLISHMENT IN WALES]

The Liberals' disestablishment of the (Anglican) Church of Ireland in 1868 seemed to Arnold not an act of justice but an act of vindictiveness toward the Irish Catholics, since though it relieved a Catholic country of the burden of supporting a Protestant establishment it did nothing to supply the religious needs of the population, it left the church property in the hands of the Church of Ireland, and it even cut off the meager grant the government had formerly made to the education of Catholic priests; the question formed a substantial part of the concluding chapter of *Culture and Anarchy* ("Our Liberal Practitioners") and was the subject of the ironic "Recantation and Apology" a year later. Now the Nonconformists, who had united with the Anglicans against the granting of benefits to Irish Catholics, were united against the Anglicans in the move to disestablish the Church of Wales, since the population of the principality was almost entirely Presbyterian, Methodist, and Baptist. Arnold was eager that the mistakes of Ireland should not be repeated in Wales.

The opportunity of expressing himself came with an invitation from Alfred Austin, editor of the *National Review*, to which Arnold responded on October 28, 1887: "If I carry out a plan I have of saying something about disestablishment, you shall have it for the 'National' in February or March. Things are not looking agreeably, but the growing moderation and openness of mind in Conservatives is a ground for comfort and hope." On Christmas Eve, 1887, he wrote to Georg von Bunsen, son of his father's old friend Christian C. J. von Bunsen: "I know by experience how trustworthy your information is, and I want to fortify myself with it in a matter where I am rather vague. The editor of one of the Conservative reviews has begged me to give him an article on Disestablishment in Wales. A number of Conservatives are becoming very reasonable, and this editor thinks they will be willing to hear reason about the Establishment in Wales from me. The Liberal party has no idea beyond that of disestablishing the Church and secularizing its funds, the old-fashioned Tories have no idea beyond that of keeping things as they are. I am anxious that the endowments should remain for religion, that the Episcopalians should keep the cathedrals, since in the cathedral towns the Episcopalians are in a majority, but that the Nonconformists, who are all of the Presbyterian form of worship, should have the churches and endowments, for that Presbyterian form, where they are in majority, as in many of the country districts."—*Letters*, ed. Russell. There followed some specific questions about the handling of endowments, the determination of which religious body in any locality might claim official status, and the method of appointing the clergy, in Germany. As Bunsen's replies opened up new questions, Arnold wrote to him twice more to learn precisely what he wanted to know. "What is the latest day in February on which I may send my MS. to you?" Arnold asked Austin on January 22, 1888. "I shall not be long—15 or at most 16 pages. A horrid discourse at Hull, a horrid discourse in St Margaret's Church, and this paper for you." His pocket diary shows him at work on his article from February 15 to 20 (so busy, he told his older daughter, that he almost resolved to give up writing to her that week). It appeared in the March number of the *National Review*, and Arnold received £25 for it. It has been republished in Neiman's *Essays, Letters, and Reviews by Matthew Arnold*.

There is a great deal about Ireland in this article again, but the two problems had become well linked, especially by the Liberals, after a meeting of the Welsh members of the party at Aberystwyth on October 7, 1887, passed resolutions in favor of disestablishment of the State Church in Wales. But Welsh disestablishment did not come in Arnold's century: it became law in September, 1914, and took effect only after the end of the European War, in March, 1920.

334:1–4. In the Preface to *Last Essays on Church and Religion* (1877) and in "From Easter to August" (September, 1887).—*Prose Works*, ed. Super, VIII, 148, and XI, 263:27–29.

334:13. Among these "main organs," Arnold implies, was the *National Review*, in which the present article appeared.

334:20–21. Arnold used the term "political Dissenters," for example, in *God and the Bible* (1874), *Prose Works*, ed. Super, VII, 144:29. See "Schools in the Reign of Queen Victoria" (1887) p. 223:23, and "The Political Crisis" (1886), p. 80:30.

334:21–24. Eugène Rambert, *Alexandre Vinet* (3rd ed.; Lausanne, 1876), II, 245; quoted in Arnold's pocket diary for Whitsunday (May 29), 1887, and at the beginning of 1888.—*Note-Books*, ed. Lowry, pp. 430, 436.

334:27–335:1. Letter to N. C. Thieriot on the young Marquis d'Argens, September 11, 1735, *Oeuvres complètes* (Paris, 1880),

XXXIII, 527; jotted in Arnold's pocket diary for October 16, 1887.
—*Note-Books*, ed. Lowry, p. 432.

335:11–12. Arnold so characterized the English in "The Literary Influence of Academies" (1864), "My Countrymen" (1866), *On the Study of Celtic Literature* (1866), and more than once thereafter.—*Prose Works*, ed. Super, III, 237; V, 13; III, 341.

335:12–13. "A member of the House of Commons said to me the other day: 'That a thing is an anomaly, I consider to be no objection to it whatever.'"—"The Function of Criticism at the Present Time" (1864), *Prose Works*, ed. Super, III, 265.

335:22–25. One of the grounds of Arnold's criticism of the Liberals in *Culture and Anarchy* (1868), *Prose Works*, ed. Super, V, 193–99.

336:1–2. "Epictetus would have a philosopher in every particular action to say to himself, *Et hoc volo, et etiam institutum servare.*" —Bacon, *Advancement of Learning*, Book II, nearly five-sixths through. See Epictetus *Encheiridion* 4.

336:6–8. See pp. 139:29–33, 247:24–25 and nn.

336:9–10. See p. 130:21–22.

336:14. "Life's . . . a poor player, | That struts and frets his hour upon the stage."—*Macbeth*, V, v, 24–25.

336:37–38. Arnold paid official visits to elementary schools on the Continent for the Newcastle Commission in 1859 and for the Education Department in 1885–86; he visited higher schools and universities on the Continent for the Taunton Commission in 1865.

337:11–12. In Scotland, after a brief attempt to establish the episcopacy at the Restoration, the Presbyterian Church was established in 1690. In Ireland, the (Episcopal) Church of Ireland was disestablished by the Liberals in 1868, without endowing the Roman Catholic Church of the majority. A motion to disestablish the Church of Wales was rejected by the Commons on March 9, 1886, by a vote of 243 to 231.

338:13–16. In 1817. The union was also adopted in several other of the larger German states.

338:23. The Plymouth Brethren, a Puritan sect founded at Plymouth, England, by J. N. Darby in 1830, is conservative in its view of Scripture and of secular behavior, is millenarian in its doctrine, and lays great stress on the Breaking of the Bread each Sunday. The Irvingites are followers of Edward Irving in his Catholic Apostolic Church, founded about 1832 with headquarters in London; they too expect the Second Coming of Christ very soon.

338:27. The Old Catholic churches are national churches that have seceded at various times from Rome; they include the Church of Utrecht, which dates from 1724, and the German, Swiss, and Austrian churches that seceded over the dogma of Papal Infallibility as defined by the first Vatican Council in 1870.

338:29–30. See p. 284:12.

339:20–22. The inclusion of a question on religion in the census was debated every decade, but no such question was included in the 1891 census for England, Scotland, and Wales.

340:29–30. John 18:36.

341:21–25. In "A Word More about America" (1885), *Prose Works*, ed. Super, X, 215. Smith's reply, a letter dated August 17, 1885, is published in *A Selection from Goldwin Smith's Correspondence*, ed. Arnold Haultain (London, 1913), p. 176. To this Arnold answered on January 13, 1886: "I was particularly interested in what you said in your last letter to me about the Church of England: about your wish being at present for Church reform rather than Church abolition. Will you let me use those sentences in print if I ever touch the subject again?"—pp. 183–84.

341:33–38. Roundell Palmer, Lord Selborne, had been Gladstone's lord chancellor. Speaking at St. David's College, Lampeter, on October 28, 1887, he said: "The tithe was not imposed on Wales by any English law. In Wales, as elsewhere, it arose out of a sense of religious propriety, deepening into the idea of a religious duty. . . . Whoever bought or sold the land, [the tithe] was [from time immemorial] a charge upon it."—*Guardian*, November 2, p. 1675, col. 1; *Times*, October 29, p. 8, col. 2. Selborne replied to Arnold's essay in the *National Review* for May, 1888 (XI, 300–308).

342:18–23. Gladstone was so quoted in the weekly commentary of *The Guardian* on November 2, 1887 (p. 1649, col. 1) and by the Church Defence Institution in a memorandum (signed, among others, by the Earl of Selborne) published *Ibid.*, November 23, p. 1775, col. 2.

342:24–26. First in the Conclusion to *Culture and Anarchy* (1868), then in the Dedicatory Letter to *Friendship's Garland* (1871).—*Prose Works*, ed. Super, V, 227, 355.

345:21–23. John Frederick Vaughan Campbell, second Earl of Cawdor (1817–98), was of Scottish ancestry, but the family had its seat in Pembrokeshire, South Wales, for over two centuries, and Campbell, before succeeding to the peerage, was for twenty years M.P. for that county. His sister, Lady Ellesmere, was

Arnold's neighbor in Surrey. Richard Lewis (1821–1905) was the first Welshman in two centuries to hold the see of Llandaff (from 1883). Henry Austin Bruce (1815–95), also of Scottish family long settled in Wales, was vice-president of the Committee of Council on Education (1864–66), home secretary (1869–73), and after 1873 the first Baron Aberdare. He was Arnold's host at the Eisteddfod in Aberdare in 1885. Henry Richard (1812–88), Congregational minister, was elected to Parliament in 1868 and from the start was regarded as chief representative of the Welsh interest. He was a member of the Cross Commission on education, 1886.

346:9–12. Arnold's discussion of the shortcomings of Gladstone's Land Act of 1881 was fullest in "The Incompatibles" (1881), *Prose Works,* ed. Super, IX, 238–85. See his allusions to that essay in "The Zenith of Conservatism" (1887), p. 141:1–12 and "Up to Easter" (1887), p. 207:9–13.

346:13–15. The trial and conviction of Wilfrid Scawen Blunt in January, 1888, for exhorting the tenantry of the Marquess of Clanricarde to resist eviction led to frequent speeches against Clanricarde by Blunt's kinsman George John Shaw-Lefevre, who had been postmaster general in Gladstone's cabinet from 1883 to 1885. Respecting a tenant who had been evicted after raising a piece of land on Clanricarde's estate from a worthless bog to the value of £600, Shaw-Lefevre wrote to *The Times:* "The entire property of one co-owner, the tenant, has been confiscated by the other owner, the landlord."—January 16, 1888, p. 10, col. 6.

346:21. Francis Joyce, formerly agent of the Marquess of Clanricarde in Ireland, sued the Marquess for libel on the ground of letters the Marquess had published in *The Times* and *The Standard* on February 5, 1887. The trial was held on December 3–7. Clanricarde, on the witness stand on December 5, stated that he last visited the Woodford estate thirteen years earlier, on his father's death. The remarks of the presiding judge and of the counsel for the plaintiff upon Clanricarde's character were devastating.

346:24–25. See p. 195:4–6.

346:25–27. See p. 253:27–28.

346:27–29. See p. 195:20–22.

346:33–34. For example, "The Irish Executive have acted with promptitude and resolution in suppressing an audacious attempt to defy the law."—Leading article on the arrest of Blunt at Woodford, *Times,* October 24, 1887, p. 9, col. 1.

346:35–37. O'Brien, editor of *United Ireland*, was again imprisoned under the Crimes Act of 1887; his refusal to wear prison clothing was the subject of much jesting at the time, but his suffering in the cold prison, and that of his fellow prisoners (one of whom died a few months after release), was genuine and serious.

347:3. See p. 202:12–27.

347:4–6. Speaking at Ipswich, October 5, 1887.—*Pall Mall Gazette*, October 6, p. 6.

347:22–24. See p. 199:12–14.

347:24–28. John Morley and the Marquess of Ripon visited Dublin on February 1–4; they were warmly welcomed by large bodies of home rulers. Arnold's severe remark on Morley must be read in the context of their warm personal friendship. And despite their difference over home rule, Morley could say of Arnold, "His insight into the roots of the Irish case, and the strong persistence with which he pressed that case upon unwilling ears, were in some ways the most remarkable instance of his many-sided and penetrating vision."—*Recollections* (New York, 1917), I, 129.

347:34–36. See p. 71:18–20n.

348:26–32. See pp. 142:1, 248:26–27.

349:22–25. Shakespeare, Sonnet XIII, 9–12.

[CIVILISATION IN THE UNITED STATES]

Arnold composed his lecture on "Life in America" between January 20 and 27, 1888; it was, he told Lady de Rothschild, "a very ticklish subject." He delivered it three times: before the Literary and Philosophical Society at Hull on January 31, before the Philosophical Society at Bradford three days later, and at Bristol on March 8. He called at the office of the young editor of the Hull *Eastern Morning News*, J. A. Spender, to beg, "as one Balliol man to another," that the newspaper not take the bread out of his mouth by reporting the discourse, the publication of which in a magazine had been contracted for on condition of its not having previously appeared in print.—J. A. Spender, *Life, Journalism and Politics* (London, 1927), I, 41–42. "I never take a fee for lecturing in this country," he told R. H. Bourchier Nicholson, president of the society, on July 2, 1887, when he accepted the invitation to Hull. "In America, where it is fair that the Americans should repay me for pirating my books, it is different. All I shall ask of you is my fare to Hull and back." (At Bristol, where his lecture raised nearly £100 in aid of the endowment of two chairs at the University College, he declined to accept even his expenses.) "I found at Hull and Bradford that my American experience had made it quite easy for me to speak audibly in lecturing; but I also found lecturing a great bore, and determined henceforth to give it up, having discharged my positive promises," he wrote to his American daughter on February 17. The summaries of the lecture in the provincial newspapers indicate that the manuscript he sent to James Knowles on March 12 for publication in the April number of the *Nineteenth Century* was essentially unchanged. Payment—presumably the customary £45—was sent too late to be recorded in his diary.

The indignation Arnold felt toward the American newspapers had grown on him in the recent years. "Imagine our *Times* writing in this way about the editor of the *Standard*," he wrote of an attack by *The New York Times* upon the editor of *The New York Tribune* on October 22, 1885 ("We keep well within the bounds of moderation when we say that Mr. Whitelaw Reid is personally a sneak and in his newspaper an habitual liar."—p. 4, col. 5). "Say what Carnegie and others will, this is the civilisation of the Australian Colonies and not of Europe—distinctly inferior to that of Europe. It distresses me, because America is so deeply interesting to me, and to its social conditions we must more and more come here; but *these* social conditions!" From Stockbridge, Massachusetts, he wrote to his sister Frances on August 30, 1886: "The great relief [on coming home] will be to cease seeing the American newspapers. . . . Their badness and ignobleness are beyond belief. They are the worst feature in the life of the United States." —*Letters*, ed. Russell. And so it is not surprising that Arnold's article created a sensation in the American press. His long-time friend George W. Smalley, London correspondent of *The New York Tribune*, took him severely to task on the front page of that paper on April 1. Of what had seemed to Spender in Hull "precisely what a lecture should be, . . . full of telling phrases, delicate humour, and delightful English," to W. T. Stead in *The Pall Mall Gazette* "bright, lively, luminous," full of "Matthewarnoldism," Smalley remarked, "For my part, I never read anything which I thought more deplorable." Arnold's courteous explanation to Smalley was that he had been fully as critical of his own countrymen, and people to whom the criticism did not apply should not take offence. "But I was determined to say at some time what I thought of the newspapers over there and of the prevalent 'greatest nation upon earth' strain, and I am not without hope that it may do good. . . . I think you will end by judging this article of mine less unfavourably."–Smalley, *London Letters* (New York, 1891), I, 290; *New York Tribune*, May 6, 1888, p. 12, col. 1. Nevertheless, on the morning of his death, in what may have been the last letter he wrote, Arnold whimsically told G. W. E. Russell: "Smalley has written a letter full of shriekings and cursings about my innocent article; the Americans will get their notion of it from that, and I shall never be able to enter America again."–Russell, *Matthew Arnold* (London, 1904), p. 19. Walt Whitman, who in 1883 welcomed visitors like Lord Coleridge and Arnold ("Visits like theirs, . . . what divine solvents they are!"–*The Critic* III, 460 [November 17, 1883]), telegraphed to *The New York Herald* on Arnold's death, "I doubt whether America will miss Arnold at all." (April 18; see Horace Traubel, *With Walt Whitman in Camden* [Boston, 1906], [I,] 40–41, 45, 47.) In the same paper, E. C. Stedman remarked: "His comments on America are those of Lemuel Gulliver on the fair but colossal maidens of Brobdingnag. He saw its coarseness but could not measure its large beauty and distinction."–April 17, p. 5, col. 5. A future president of the United States, Theodore Roosevelt, writing for a magazine edited by Arnold's nephew, acknowledged the justice of some of Arnold's criticisms, but found him also guilty of some nonsense. "After all, taming a continent is nobler work than studying *belles lettres*."–"Some Recent Criticism of America," *Murray's Magazine* IV, 307 (September, 1888).

Within a month the essay was reprinted in Boston, along with "General Grant," "A Word about America," and "A Word More about America," in a little (presumably unauthorized) volume called *Civilization in the United States* (Boston: Cupples and Hurd, 1888), and that volume was translated into French by Edmond de Nevers, *Études sur les États-Unis*, par Matthew Arnold (Québec, 1902). The essay has been republished, with notes, in Kenneth Allott, ed., *Five Uncollected Essays of Matthew Arnold* (Liverpool: University Press, 1953).

350:1–24. In "A Word More about America" (1885), *Prose Works*, ed. Super, X, 198–217. Arnold concluded that essay by citing the opinion of Sir Lepel Griffin, "A Visit to Philistia," *Fort-*

nightly Review XLI, 50 (January, 1884), and by making the promise he here alludes to. The terms "human problem" and "social problem" were perhaps first suggested to him by George Sand; see *Prose Works*, VIII, 230, 279.

350:27–29. In the Prologue to the *Characters* the author speaks of having reached his ninety-ninth year—an exaggeration, since Theophrastus died at eighty-five and wrote his *Characters* some thirty years before his death.

351:3–4. About a fortnight after this article was published, Arnold died suddenly at the age of sixty-five.

352:18–20. Arnold thus defined "civilisation" in the essay on "Equality" (1878).—*Prose Works*, ed. Super, VIII, 286:10–11.

352:20–22. *Gorgias* 512 E or *Republic* I, 352 D.

352:24–29. Arnold first listed these powers in "Equality" (1878) and referred to them frequently thererafter, most recently in "A Word about America" (1882) and in one of his American lectures, "Literature and Science" (1882).—*Prose Works*, ed. Super, VIII, 287; X, 10, 12, 61–62.

353:16. Arnold was a close friend of Louisa, Lady de Rothschild, and in America he was entertained by a Vanderbilt. On October 28, 1883, he wrote to his sister Frances: "The wealth of New York strikes me very much. We dined with the [Elliott Fitch] Shepards on Friday. . . . Mrs. Shepard is a sister of Vanderbilt, who is said to be the richest man living, and the house was as splendid as a house of the Rothschilds."—*Letters*, ed. Russell. And to his sister Jane he wrote on November 15, 1883: "It is the best country for a Rothschild I ever knew."

353:19–20. Pounds, of course, not dollars. Arnold's annual income at this time was about £1,400–£1,600 (about $7,000–$8,000).

353:25. Ice cream, presumably.

353:28. Electric trams were still a few years away. "What it is in the towns, to have practically no cabs and to be obliged to use trams, you cannot imagine. It is as if in our Stockwell expedition we had had to get there by the tram, with two or three changes, and a walk at each end, and the chance of bad weather. And every one has to use these who has not a carriage."—Arnold to his sister Jane Forster from Hartford, Conn., November 15, 1883; *Letters*, ed. Russell.

354:25–28. Arnold was an amateur fruit-grower at his cottage in Cobham. "How I wish you could eat the Marie Louise pears! they are a perfect success," he wrote to his daughter in New York in November, 1885. "I [gave] Flu [his wife] . . . a Duchesse pear to take to Lady Ellesmere, who says she shall carry it to her gardener to show him how much finer pears are grown at the Cottage than at Burwood," he told his sister on October 29, 1886.—*Letters*, ed. Russell. Pippins are a variety of excellent dessert apples.

355:3–4. The axiomatic goal of society among the Utilitarians, and thence among the Liberals in general.

355:28. Camillus, the "second founder" of Rome, restored the city and its government after the invasion by the Gauls in 387–386 B.C.

356:3. The custom fell out of use in England only after the second World War. Arnold himself followed it when he addressed letters, even to Americans.

356:4–11. Arnold especially praised the American women in an interview published in *The Boston Herald* after his return to England in 1884; see *Prose Works*, ed. Super, X, 248.

357:18–21. J. A. Froude's *Thomas Carlyle, a History of His Life* was published in 1882 (vols. I and II) and 1884 (vols. III and IV). Charles Eliot Norton, a long time American friend of Arnold and Clough, whose edition of the Emerson-Carlyle correspondence gave Arnold much matter for his lecture on "Emerson" (1883), severely criticized Froude's work in his Preface to *Early Letters of Thomas Carlyle* (2 vols.; London, 1886). "Every one agrees with you as to Froude and Carlyle," Arnold wrote to Norton on August 31, 1887, "but there is no doubt that one of the bad effects of Froude's extraordinary proceedings has been to tire people of Carlyle, and disincline them from occupying themselves any more with him, for the present at any rate."—*Letters*, ed. Russell.

357:29–35. Thomas to Alexander Carlyle, February 22, 1822; *Early Letters*, II, 51–52.

358:4–10. See p. 279:17–24.

358:16–17. See p. 89:2–3n.

359:15–16. The St. Pancras Station in London (or rather the station hotel which gives it its façade) is a remarkable neo-Gothic red stone structure designed by Sir George Gilbert Scott in 1865; it is alternately ridiculed and revered. Somerset House, on The Strand, is a government office building, principally designed in the Palladian style by Sir William Chambers and constructed in 1777–86. Whitehall, the street that connects Trafalgar Square with the houses of Parliament, is lined by office buildings of the principal ministries of government, many dating from the eighteenth century.

359:17–22. Mariana Griswold van Rensselaer, who had just then completed a splendid monograph on the works of Henry Hobson Richardson (1838–86), challenged Arnold's proposition in a letter to the *Century Magazine* XXXVI, 314–16 (June, 1888). She was unable to guess which building "of no great importance" Arnold alluded to; Richardson himself, she said, wished most to be judged by the largest of them all, the courthouse in Pittsburgh, begun 1884. A somewhat earlier work of his was Trinity Church, Boston. On January 26, 1884, Arnold dined in Chicago with the merchant Franklin MacVeagh, for whom Richardson designed a house the next year.

359:25–27. Arnold reported on the summer colony at Cresson, Pennsylvania, after his visit there: "The railway company put the hotel there because of a beautiful and unfailing spring of water; it is a kind of toy hotel to look at, in wood and quite pretty; it holds 1000 people. It is common for the richer people to live in wooden cottages in the grounds and only to take their meals at the hotel. Carnegie does this, and we were at his cottage."—July 26, 1886; *Letters*, ed. Russell.

359:37–38. "When our race has built Bold Street, Liverpool, and pronounced it very good, it hurries across the Atlantic, and builds Nashville, and Jacksonville, and Milledgeville, and thinks it is fulfilling the designs of Providence in an incomparable manner."—*On the Study of Celtic Literature* (1866), *Prose Works*, ed. Super, III, 383. There were in 1874 two Briggsvilles (in Pennsylvania and Wisconsin), five Higginsvilles (in Illinois, Missouri, New York, Virginia, and West Virginia) and twenty-one Jacksonvilles in the United States.

360:1–8. Arnold's lecture tour in January, 1884, took him to or through Utica, Rome, Syracuse, and Aurora. There are at least two dozen other town names from the classical dictionary in up-state New York, including Marcellus and Camillus.

360:14–16. *Faust*, part II, act I, line 6272, jotted in Arnold's pocket diary at the beginning of 1886, of 1887, of 1888, and twice in one of his "general notebooks."—*Note-Books*, ed. Lowry, pp. 423, 427, 436, 493, 500.

361:22. See p. 83:13–15n.

361:27. After lecturing at Leeds on November 4, 1884, Arnold wrote to his sister Mrs. Forster (who had been in the audience) on November 7: "The Leeds Mercury was particularly amiable, both in its account of the lecture and in its occasional note."

361:32–362:4. A headline in *The Chicago Tribune* for January 19, 1884 (the day of Arnold's arrival in Chicago) reads: "A Skeleton's Bride. Two Days of Wedded Bliss Make Her a Maniac." The marriage was reported to have taken place in Philadelphia the preceding Tuesday, January 15.—p. 1, col. 5.

Asked by a reporter on the train en route to Chicago what he thought of American newspapers, Arnold replied: "Oh, they are smart," with a laugh. "But I think they have too much about the 'woman marrying the bony skeleton.' When I first came over I was very much interested in the story of a man turning out to be a woman, or something of that sort. I think there is too much of that sort of stuff with big, leaded headlines in your American newspapers; but I can't help but laugh at the racy way in which it is written about. . . . I think you make too much of the sort of news which is excluded from the English newspapers, and appears only in our *Police News*. . . . I have read the newspapers up and down, but little else."—*Chicago Tribune*, January 20, 1884, p. 14, col. 2.

361:35–36. The crown prince of Prussia (who had entertained Arnold on his visit to Berlin in 1885) fell ill of cancer of the throat in the winter of 1887–88, and his health was the subject of daily reports in the English papers (the crown princess was Queen Victoria's daughter). He ascended the Prussian (and German imperial) throne as Frederick III on March 9, 1888, and died ninety-nine days later. Timothy Daniel Sullivan, M.P. for Dublin and lord mayor of that city, on December 8, 1887, was imprisoned for two months under the Crimes Act for publishing in *The Nation* (Dublin) reports of the proceedings of suppressed branches of the National League.

362:14–17. The Prince and Princess of Wales attended the performance of Bulwer-Lytton's *The Lady of Lyons* by the American actress Mary Anderson at the Lyceum Theatre in London on October 27, 1883, and chatted with her after the performance. "The column of cablegram in the American papers every day is something wonderful," Arnold wrote to his sister from Stockbridge, Massachusetts, on July 11, 1886.—*Letters*, ed. Russell.

362:20–22. Arnold quoted this headline and description of himself, which he solemnly asserted was a fact, in a letter to Yates Thompson (owner of *The Pall Mall Gazette*) written from Bloomington, Illinois, on January 31, 1884.

362:25–27. Medill was three and a half months younger than Arnold.

362:28–33. About a month after Arnold returned to England from his lecture tour, *The New York Tribune* on April 6, 1884 (p. 4, col. 6) published under a London dateline a long article on culture in Chicago, purporting to be the first of a series on America being written by "Mr. Arnold" for *The Pall Mall Journal*. The article was wittily conceived, and though not markedly in Arnold's manner it bandied about phrases like "sweetness and light" and names like "Obermann." Newspapers throughout the United States instantly identified "Mr. Arnold" with Matthew Arnold, corrected the *Tribune*'s nonexistent *Pall Mall Journal* to *The Pall Mall Gazette*, and raised a loud cry of indignation, not very unlike the one stirred up by the present article in 1888. Most completely gulled was *The Chicago Tribune*, which printed as by "special cable" what it had merely appropriated from its New York namesake, identified the nameless business men and clergymen of the article, and interviewed them for their opinions of Arnold and his remarks. Many responded instantly and hostilely; only General A. C. McClurg, the bookseller who had been Arnold's host, maintained that there was something wrong with the story. Then there was an uncomfortable lull in the press, and *The New York Sun* revealed that its investigations through its London correspondent convicted the article of fraud. The backtracking was notable, but not uniform—there was some disposition, even in Chicago, to believe that this was what Arnold *would* have said if he had written about their city. On April 13 *The New York Tribune* devoted nearly a page to reprinting newspaper comments upon Arnold's supposed criticisms, from New England to New Orleans. The assertion that "Mr. Arnold's" article was planted in a single copy of *The New York Tribune* by the proprietor of *The Chicago Daily News* in order to entrap his Chicago rival is not true; the account given by Melville E. Stone, who claimed to have perpetrated the hoax and induced William Morton Payne to write the article, is not fully reliable.—*Fifty Years a Journalist* (New York, 1921), pp. 122–24. The spurious article is given in Chilson H. Leonard, *Arnold in America* (Yale University dissertation, 1932; Ann Arbor: University Microfilms, 1964), pp. 336–40.

362:33–34. Stone gives a facsimile of a cable of denial from Arnold to himself, dated April 9, 1884.

363:3–5. In "Heinrich Heine" (1863), *Prose Works*, ed. Super, III, 113. "Thy heaven that is over thy head shall be brass, and the earth that is under thee shall be iron."–Deuteronomy 28:23. "I will make your heaven as iron, and your earth as brass."–Leviticus 26:19.

364:19–21. George Bancroft, *History of the United States from the Discovery of the American Continent* (Boston, 1858), VII, 21 (chapt. i: May, 1774), quoted in "A Word More about America" (1885), *Prose Works*, ed. Super, X, 196. Arnold in fact drew his quotation indirectly from an anonymous article by Sir Henry Maine, "The Nature of Democracy," *Quarterly Review* CLVIII, 304 (October, 1884), and jotted it in his pocket diary for December 17, 1884.–*Note-Books*, ed. Lowry, p. 409.

364:32. Edward Payson Roe (1838–88), Presbyterian minister in upstate New York, was moved by the great Chicago fire to write his first novel, *Barriers Burned Away* (1872), published first serially in the *Evangelist*, then as a best-selling book. He published sixteen more novels which made for him a great deal of money and quickly enabled him to give up his pastorate.

364:35–365:3. This resembles, but is not, the passage from Thomas Wentworth Higginson's essay "On an Old Latin Text-Book" that Arnold jotted in his pocket diary for December 19–22, 1871.–*Atlantic Essays* (Boston, 1871), pp. 337–38, quoted in *Note-Books*, ed. Lowry, p. 163. There is a comparable passage in Higginson's "Americanism in Literature," *Atlantic Essays*, p. 57. See "Count Leo Tolstoi," p. 283:16–23.

365:4–7. Dr. William Pepper, provost of the University of Pennsylvania, noted of Arnold's speech there in June, 1886, "Terrible pronunciation of some words–'girls, geerls'!"

365:8–14. *The Expedition of Humphry Clinker*, ¶7 of the first letter of June 10. The letter is quoted at length as a footnote to the beginning of Thackeray's remarks on Smollett in his *English Humourists of the Eighteenth Century* (1853), a book Arnold read in 1887.–*Note-Books*, ed. Lowry, p. 622.

365:20–21. Andrew Carnegie, the Scottish-born Pittsburgh steel magnate, met the Arnolds on their arrival in New York on October 22, 1883, and gave a reception five days later to introduce them to some three hundred guests at the Hotel Windsor, where he had installed them. On July 19–23, 1886, Carnegie entertained Arnold and his younger daughter at his summer cottage at Cresson, Pennsylvania, and showed them Pittsburgh. On the 29th Arnold wrote to Grant Duff about Carnegie's *Triumphant Democracy, or, Fifty Years' March of the Republic* (New York, 1886): "The facts he has collected as to the material progress of this country are valuable, and I am told the book is having a great sale, being translated into French and German, etc. He and most Americans are simply unaware that nothing in the book touches the capital defect of life over here: namely, that compared with life in England it is so uninteresting, so without savour and without depth. Do they think to prove that it must have savour and depth by pointing to the number of public libraries, schools, and places of worship?"—*Letters*, ed. Russell. See also "Amiel" (1887), p. 279:31.

365:31. Josiah Strong, *Our Country: Its Possible Future and Its Present Crisis* (New York, 1885). Strong (1847–1916), minister of the Central Congregational Church in Cincinnati, became instantly famous for this book, with its warnings against the perils of immigration, Romanism, Mormonism, intemperance, socialism, wealth, and the city. Arnold himself was quoted twice, as saying "America holds the future" (p. 15) and that the republican form "is the only eventual form of government for all people" (p. 36).

366:5–10. Strong, *Our Country*, pp. 219 (quoting Prof. Phelps), 170, 168, 173, 168.

366:25–28. *Ibid.*, p. 169.

367:14–16. A description Arnold first used in "Equality" (1878), and frequently thereafter.—*Prose Works*, ed. Super, VIII, 299, 301–2.

367:23–24. For "seeing things as they are," see p. 71:33–35n.

367:31–33. Arnold attributed this expression to Michelet in a letter to Clough about February 24, 1848, and jotted it (without attribution) in his pocket diary for April 27, 1877. He quoted it in "A Word about America" (1882) as the word of an "acute French critic."—*Letters of Matthew Arnold to Arthur Hugh Clough*, ed. H. F. Lowry (London: Oxford University Press, 1932), p. 66; *Note-Books*, ed. Lowry, p. 276; *Prose Works*, ed. Super, X, 14.

368:15. "The men of England, the men, I mean, of light and leading in England."—Burke, *Reflections on the Revolution in France*, two-fifths through. On February 20, 1888, *The Pall Mall Gazette* had a headline: "The University of Oxford and Home Rule. 'Light and Leading' for Mr. Gladstone."—p. 8.

368:35. "Vain boasting" and "vain imaginations" are expressions used by St. Paul (II Corinthians 9:3; Romans 1:21). "Let him eschew evil" is I Peter 3:11. "That ye may approve things that are excellent" is Philippians 1:10.

369:4–5. John 3:3, the meaning of which Arnold discussed in *Literature and Dogma*, chapt. vi and Preface to the Popular Edition (1883).—*Prose Works*, ed. Super, VI, 261, 145–46. See also "A 'Friend of God,'" p. 187:16–20. The tone of the present paragraph is precisely that of the final paragraphs of *A French Eton* (1864), the Preface to *On the Study of Celtic Literature* (1867), the Preface to *Culture and Anarchy* (1869), and the Preface to *God and the Bible* (1875).—*Prose Works*, ed. Super, II, 324–25; III, 395; V, 255–56; VII, 397–98.

[ADDRESS AT THE ROYAL ACADEMY (1881)]

Arnold's diaries make no mention of this address, nor is it apparently recorded in any bibliography of his works. Nevertheless, it was recalled by a writer in *The World* who addressed Arnold on the eve of Arnold's lecture tour of America: "You have been the vogue in fashionable circles; but you have never failed to let the fine gentlemen and ladies with whom you have consorted clearly understand that you considered yourself their superior, and that your presence amongst them was an act of condescension on your part. There is, perhaps, no other man of letters now alive who would have had the intrepidity to make such a speech as you did a couple years ago in returning thanks for the toast of literature at the Academy dinner. The citizens of a Republic may well admire the attributes in you to which that speech testified."—September 13, 1882, pp. 5–7. Two years later Huxley gave the response for "Science" at the Academy banquet, and his remarks then were regarded in at least one quarter as a reply to Arnold's; if so, his hit was very oblique.—*Nature* XXVIII, 50–51 (May 17, 1883). When Huxley gave the Rede Lecture at Cambridge in June, 1883, a year after Arnold delivered "Literature and Science" there, he did not carry on the debate with Arnold. I am indebted to Mr. David A. Roos for calling Arnold's Academy address to my attention, and to his forthcoming article on Arnold and Huxley in *Modern Philology* for much of the substance of these notes.

370:20. The Royal Highnesses were the Prince of Wales and the Dukes of Cambridge and Connaught.

370:27. Arnold mentions the French term "facultative" in his General Report for 1880 as inspector of schools (written early 1881).—*Reports on Elementary Schools*, ed. F. Sandford (London, 1889), p. 234; ed. F. S. Marvin (London, 1908), p. 208. The report deals at some length with the value of literary studies in the schools. See also p. 40:10–11.

371:13. "We are all in the same boat,—all of us in whose school-ing the Greek and Latin classics fill the principal place."—"A Speech at Eton" (1879), *Prose Works,* ed. Super, IX, 21:14–16.

372:5–8. Wordsworth, "Resolution and Independence," lines 113–16.

[THE BEST HUNDRED BOOKS]

On January 9, 1886, Sir John Lubbock spoke on "The Pleasures of Reading" at the ceremony for the distribution of prizes and certifi-cates at the London Working Men's College in Great Ormond Street, and proposed a list of about a hundred books by way of an ideal curriculum for a liberal education. He "excluded (1) works by living authors, (2) science, and (3) history, with a very few exceptions, which I mentioned rather in their literary aspect."—*Pall Mall Gazette,* January 11, p. 4; January 12, p. 2. The acting editor of *The Pall Mall,* E. T. Cook (the editor, W. T. Stead, being then in jail) asked the leading literary figures in London for similar lists, and began publishing their replies on January 19. Ar-nold's letter appeared in the fourth installment. The entire col-lection was published as a *Pall Mall Extra,* no. 24, on February 22. Lubbock's own (corrected) list appeared at the conclusion of his article "On the Pleasure of Reading," *Contemporary Review* XLIX, 240–51 (February, 1886).

Arnold's letter to Cook was printed in facsimile in *The Pall Mall Budget* on April 19, 1888, p. 12. It was dated "Cobham Jan. 13ᵗʰ 1886" and continues: "Even if I did, I should have no time, for I am buried in documents about popular education in Germany, and am going abroad again almost immediately."

[MR. MATTHEW ARNOLD INSTRUCTING AMERICANS]

The Pall Mall Gazette reprinted Arnold's letter from the New York *Evening Post,* along with this comment by the *Post*'s editor, E. L. Godkin: "Mr. Arnold's letter is misleading, unintentionally of course, and the mysterious body called 'the American branch of the Irish Loyal and Patriotic Union' to which it is addressed, ought not to have given it out for publication, without adding some sort of correction in the interest of candour and fair play. Mr. Arnold gives the Mysterious Body to understand that Mr. Gladstone is endeavouring to do something in Ireland which would correspond to the setting up at the South of a Southern Congress, possessing powers like those of the Congress of the United States. Nothing could well be further from the truth. Mr. Gladstone's Irish Parliament would really have no more power than any Southern State now has. It could neither declare war, nor make peace, nor maintain an army or navy, nor make treaties with foreign Powers, nor levy import or export duties, nor coin money, nor punish offences against the law of nations, or offences on the high seas, or the crime of treason, nor legislate touching trade, navigation, or quarantine, lighthouses, copyright, or patent right, nor set up a State church (which any American State might do), nor impair the rights of any existing corporation. In fact, one would doubt whether Mr. Arnold had ever read Mr. Gladstone's bill if one did not hear Tory orators in England every day getting over its plain restrictions by the plea that the Irish would refuse to be bound by them. But then the fair way to put this argument is to say frankly that the bill is a good one, but that the Irish are such a pack of rascals that they cannot be trusted to live by it. This would, however, tell against any scheme of Home Rule."

[THIRTY-FIVE YEARS OF SCHOOL INSPECTING]

Arnold retired from his school inspectorship in April, 1886, after completing his report on his mission abroad, and sailed for New York on May 22. There remained, after his return to England on September 12, the tidying up of his affairs at the Education Office, and the ceremonials. On the evening of November 12, a large group of friends from his district (Westminster) assembled in St. Peter's School, Lower Belgrave Street, to do him honor. The chairman was E. T. Morgan, headmaster of St. James's School, Westminster. The teachers of the district had subscribed to present him with a silver claret jug and salver, the latter appropriately inscribed. After tributes from teachers who had worked with Arnold, the presentation, and Arnold's response, the Dean of Westminster, George Granville Bradley, a contemporary of Arnold's at Rugby, paid the tribute of nearly fifty years of friendship. *The Times* next morning in a leading article (p. 9, cols. 3–4) spoke in high terms of Arnold's work, especially in bringing the best of the Continental experience to the attention of the British public. "I have had a horrid week with my speech to the Westminster teachers," he wrote to his elder daughter. "You know how a thing of that kind worries me. However, last night it came off, and very well. The things they have given me are very beautiful. I was afraid of a tea service. . . . You can imagine the relief with which I have been going about the garden this morning and planting."—*Letters*, ed. Russell. The address is published in Fraser Neiman's *Essays, Letters, and Reviews by Matthew Arnold*.

374:13. Thomas Healing was one of Arnold's assistant inspectors. He wrote an account of Arnold's qualities as an inspector for Joshua G. Fitch, *Thomas and Matthew Arnold and Their Influence on English Education* (New York, 1897), pp. 173–75.

374:25–375:9. Two weeks later Arnold wrote to A. J. Mundella, who had been vice-president of the Committee of Council on Education from 1880 to 1885, to explain this passage: "One line to say that the *Minister* before my mind, who knew nothing about my work, was not you, but the man who gives preferment and opportunity—the Minister in the continental sense.

"Lord Ripon [Earl de Grey, lord president in Gladstone's cabinet, 1868–73] and Lord Aberdare [H. A. Bruce, vice-president from 1864 to 1866, and successor to Ripon as Lord president, 1873–74] both of them tried, in their time, to get opportunity given to me—but in their case, too, the politics and ignorance of the *Minister* stopped the way.

"However, no one made so strenuous an effort as you did, and I must some day make public acknowledgement of it.

"You are right, the permanent officials know I cared little about my performances; but all I meant to say of them was that in the routine work I had to do for them they were entirely friendly. The pension was expressly for literary and poetic performances, not educational. It is as a functionary of public education that I say I owe nothing to Governments. The recognition and opportunity which would have been useful to me they never gave me. It does not matter now. . . . Literature is henceforth my business, if at sixty-three it is not presumptuous to speak of having still a business."—W. F. Connell, *The Educational Thought and Influence of Matthew Arnold* (London: Routledge and Kegan Paul, 1950), p. 285.

375:8–9. When asked two months earlier to comment on his retirement, Arnold wrote on September 19: "I . . . have nothing to say at the end of my thirty-five years as school-inspector beyond the speech made by the man who had lived through the French

Revolution: 'J'ai vécu!'"—*Pall Mall Budget,* April 19, 1888, p. 12 (facsimile).

375:13–14. The successive secretaries of the Education Department during Arnold's inspectorate were R. R. W. Lingen (1849–69), Baron Lingen after 1885; Sir F. R. J. Sandford (1870–84), Baron Sandford after 1891; and Patrick Cumin (1884–90). All three, like Arnold and Clough, had ties with Balliol College, Oxford.

375:15. Harry Chester, who published a number of lectures and pamphlets on education, is described in one of them (1861) as "formerly an assistant-secretary of the Committee of Council on Education." Joseph Bowstead was an inspector of British and Foreign Schools whose long statement on education in South Wales in 1861 drew the fire of Connop Thirlwall, bishop of St. David's. Arnold's close friend Arthur Hugh Clough was an examiner at the Education Office from 1853 to 1861.

375:32. Arnold's successor was the Rev. T. W. Sharpe.

376:7. Some twenty of Arnold's letters to Charles Myhill survive.

376:10–13. In the Borough Road was the headquarters of the British and Foreign School Society. For the right of veto, see p. 217:26–29.

376:14. James Fleming (1830–1908), canon of York, was vicar of St. Michael, Chester Square, London, from 1874.

376:20–21. "Alas! the gratitude of men | Hath oftener left me mourning."—"Simon Lee," lines 95–96.

377:11–14. Arnold began as inspector for British, Wesleyan, and other Nonconformist schools in the midland district, which included the English counties of Lincoln, Nottingham, Derby, Stafford, Shropshire, Hereford, Worcester, Warwick, Leicester, Rutland, Northampton, Gloucester, and Monmouth, together with all of South Wales and all of North Wales except Flintshire and Denbyshire. Pembroke Dock is the southwestern corner of Wales, Great Yarmouth is on the North Sea in Norfolk. (When Norfolk was added to Arnold's district in 1853, however, South Wales was withdrawn.) Arnold became a senior inspector in 1871, a chief inspector in 1884. For the changes in his district, see Connell, *Educational Thought and Influence,* p. 229n.

377:14–15. Arnold's second son, Trevenen William ("Budge") was born in Derby on October 15, 1853; whether the lodging house was Mr. Sansom's, from which Arnold wrote to Wyndham Slade a year earlier, is uncertain.—*Times* (London), October 18, 1853, p. 10, col. 4; *Letters,* ed. Russell. The workhouse, then relatively new, accommodated 350 persons.

377:39–378:1. In the final stanza of *Childe Harold's Pilgrimage* (IV, 1666–67).

378:13–14. Charles Henry Gordon-Lennox, sixth Duke of Richmond, was lord president of the Privy Council in Disraeli's second administration (1874–80). In the Lords' debate on the Endowed Schools Acts Amendment Bill on August 3, 1874, he repudiated indignantly the charge made against him that though he "called himself the Minister of Education" he was more neglectful of education matters than he would have been of cases of cattle disease, Southdown sheep, or landlord-tenant relationships. (Diseases of cattle were the province of the lord president as well as the education of children.)

378:33–35. The Franchise Act of 1884 increased the electorate by some 60 percent; the first general election under that act was held in late November, 1885.

378:36–39. Joseph Butler, "Six Sermons Preached upon Public Occasions: II, ¶12," *Works,* ed. W. E. Gladstone (Oxford, 1896), II, 305.

379:22–23. "A Letter to a Noble Lord" (1796), three-fifths through. The quotation, a favorite of Arnold's, occurs repeatedly in his *Note-Books* and his prose works. For the *Saturday Review*'s comment, see p. 127:5–9n.

[ENGLISH AT THE UNIVERSITIES]

In October, 1886, John Churton Collins opened a vigorous campaign for the establishment of English literature as a regular university discipline by means of an anonymous article in the *Quarterly Review* that assailed the shallow "Dilettantism" with which English literature was then handled through a savage attack on the book *From Shakespeare to Pope* by Edmund Gosse, Clark Lecturer on English Literature at Cambridge. The campaign was continued in the pages of *The Pall Mall Gazette* through leading articles and through letters solicited from the intellectual leaders of the country, beginning with one from T. H. Huxley published on October 22. The questions to which the respondents were asked to address themselves were: (1) Was it desirable that the universities should provide systematic instruction in English literature? (2) Was it desirable that a distinction should be made between philology and literature, and that the instruction provided should be instruction in literature as distinguished from instruction in philology? (3) Was it desirable that the study of English literature should be indissolubly associated with the study of ancient Classical literature? Unfortunately, Collins in his characteristic way had given offence where he needed help: both Browning and Arnold knew Gosse and wanted no part of an attack on him. Arnold replied at first formally and briefly on October 24, a note Collins embedded in a second *Quarterly Review* article in January, 1887: "I should be glad to see at the Universities, not a new School established for Modern Literature or Modern Languages, but the great works of English Literature taken in conjunction with those of Greek and Latin Literature in the final Examination for honours in *Literae Humaniores*." Further negotiation produced the letter published in *The Pall Mall Budget* on January 6 and *The Pall Mall Gazette* on January 7, 1887. Collins gave an account of his movement in *The Study of English Literature* (London, 1891). The manuscript of Arnold's letter, dated from Pains Hill Cottage, Cobham, Surrey, December 29, 1886, is in the British Museum (Ashley A-25). This, with letters of October 24 and December 4, 1886, was printed in T. J. Wise's *Letters from Matthew Arnold to John Churton Collins* (London, 1910).

[FINE PASSAGES IN VERSE AND PROSE]

Frank Harris, editor of the *Fortnightly Review*, in 1887 conceived the notion of inviting his nation's and America's men and women of letters to choose "the one passage in all poetry which seems the finest, and also the one passage in prose which appears of its kind the best"—a request modified, because of his respondents' objections, to "such passages as had lodged themselves in the memory and had afforded the most continual delight." Tennyson, Browning, Cardinal Newman, and William Morris declined to answer; of the fifty-six replies Harris printed in August–November, 1887, Arnold's led all the rest (largely for alphabetical reasons). Only one contributor selected anything of Arnold's own: Thomas Bailey Aldrich (having chosen, as in duty bound, Lincoln's Gettysburg Address for prose) selected the last eighteen lines of "Sohrab and Rustum" for verse. Arnold's pocket diary records that he wrote to Harris on July 1 and 9.

381:12. In a little collection of "Pensées" at the end of the fifth volume of *Portraits contemporains*, Sainte-Beuve added one more item to Horace's list of things we must leave at death: "celle de lire Horace et les Anciens: un jour viendra bientôt, charmant poëte, où nous ne te lirons plus!"—(nouv. éd.; Paris, 1882), p. 468.

381:13-14. *Prose Works*, ed. Super, III, 246, from the "Panegyric of St. Paul," *Oeuvres choisies*, ed. J. Calvet (14th ed.; Paris: A. Hatier, 1947), p. 53.

381:14-15. From Burke's "Speech at Bristol Previous to the Election, 1780," about one-third through.

381:17. Luke 9:58; Matthew 8:20.

["AN OLIVE BRANCH FROM AMERICA"]

The editor of the *Nineteenth Century* in November, 1887, published, along with an article on "An Anglo-American Copyright" by the Philadelphian Robert Pearsall Smith, the comments on that article by eleven British men of letters known to have a lively interest in the question, and one British publishing firm. Smith's central proposal was that, since monopolistic copyright practices benefited the book trade far more than the author (in a ratio of seven to one, as he calculated), publishers be granted unrestricted right to reproduce copyright books upon payment to the author in advance of 10 percent of the retail price of the edition, the royalty to be signified by a stamp affixed to each copy and the price of the stamp to be added as a separate item to the final cost of the book (in the manner of a retail sales tax), not subject to trade discounts or wholesaler's discounts. (Two years earlier, in early December, 1885, Arnold had encountered Smith's twenty-year-old son in Dresden, and treated him kindly—an encounter amusingly recorded in Logan Pearsall Smith, *Unforgotten Years* [Boston: Little, Brown and Company, 1939], pp. 134-37.)

382:2-3. Arnold quoted Hawley's remark in "Common Schools Abroad," p. 89:9-11.

382:5-7. In his essay on "Copyright" (1880); *Prose Works*, ed. Super, IX, 131-33.

[PREFACE TO WORDSWORTH SELECTIONS]

Professor William Angus Knight, honorary secretary and founder of the Wordsworth Society, was indefatigable in his attempts to engage Arnold's pen. When he conceived the notion of publishing a little volume of selections from Wordsworth chosen by the members of the Society, he begged Arnold for a Preface. "I shall be much interested in seeing your selection," Arnold replied on November 17, 1886, "but I am not inclined to return to the criticism of our dear Poet, and I am sure it is better that in the Volume now in question I should not." Ten days later he told his daughter he had written "a short preliminary notice for an edition of Wordsworth."—*Letters*, ed. Russell. For whatever reason, *Selections from Wordsworth*, by William Knight and Other Members of the Wordsworth Society (London: Kegan Paul, Trench & Co., 1888), appeared late in the year of Arnold's death with no sign of a contribution from his pen.

[LORD COLERIDGE'S PREFACE TO *Essays in Criticism, Second Series*]

On January 18, 1888, George Lillie Craik, partner and business manager for the firm of Macmillan, wrote to Arnold, "Is it not time for you to make a volume of collected papers? You must have a great many Magazine articles that ought to be reprinted & we should much like to publish them." He seemed to be thinking of a miscellaneous volume like *Mixed Essays*, but Arnold replied on the 20th: "I have lately thought that a purely literary volume to go with 'Essays in Criticism' and to be called 'Essays in Criticism Second Series'—might do. I should like to include the Wordsworth and Byron Prefaces and the three Essays from Ward's book, then the Amiel, Tolstoi, two Shelley articles and one or two more literary articles which I hope to produce this year." (The last were presumably to be on Vauvenargues, on *Récit d'une Soeur*, and perhaps on George Sand and on Alexandre Vinet.—*Note-Books*, ed. Lowry, p. 626.) Craik was delighted; the volume might come out at Whitsuntide a year hence. Arnold's death on April 15 led Frederick Macmillan to approach Mrs. Arnold through her son Richard on April 30: "We shall be very glad to publish the projected book so far as it is complete. There are eight articles indicated by your father and these with the little address on Milton which might appropriately be included would be enough to form a volume which might be sold at 7/6. We shall be prepared to give £200 for an Edition of 2000 copies (for England) and £25 per 1000 for whatever copies we print for America." Six of the nine essays had previously been published in books by Macmillan or in their *Magazine;* they approached Gilder of the *Century Magazine* for permission to use the "Milton," and the Arnolds wrote to Knowles, who after some demur gave his consent to the use of "Shelley," and to the editor of the *Fortnightly* for "Count Leo Tolstoi." "It will not be necessary to trouble you with proofs," Frederick Macmillan wrote to Mrs. Arnold on May 29. "The printers will guarantee their accuracy, which is not difficult as they have printed copy to go by."

The Arnolds wished the publishers to consult with Lord Coleridge about the volume; the publishers, on their part, had sought John Morley's opinion on the order in which the articles should appear and thought Coleridge so busy he should hardly be troubled. But the Arnolds had already spoken to him. "It would certainly be a most excellent thing if Lord Coleridge would consent to write a few words of Introduction to the new volume of 'Essays in Criticism,'" wrote Frederick Macmillan to Mrs. Arnold on May 31. "If you have not already done so I do not think it is necessary to say anything to him about Mr. Morley having approved of the arrangement. I consulted him on my own responsibility and will answer for it that he will not feel annoyed at any changes Lord Coleridge may think fit to suggest." Morley's arrangement of the essays was adopted. Coleridge called at Macmillans and agreed to write the Introduction—but not for some weeks. "It is worth waiting for," wrote Macmillan. But when Mrs. Arnold saw it in mid-September, some changes were required. "So far as she knows," Frederick Macmillan wrote to Coleridge, "her husband had no intention of writing anything more about America. The article which was published in 'The Nineteenth Century' only a fortnight before his death was Mrs. Arnold believes the last word that he intended to say on the subject. He did intend, of course, to write another paper on Shelley—on Shelley's poetry—and he had formed the project of writing several other purely literary essays in the course of the year." And so Coleridge's note was revised accordingly; new proofs were sent to him on October 2 and returned on October 4. By the 26th Frederick Macmillan was able to send Mrs. Arnold advance copies of the book, which had a publication date of November 6.—William E. Buckler, *Matthew Arnold's Books* (Geneva: Droz, 1958), pp. 75–80. Lord Coleridge's "Prefatory Note" was signed simply with the initial "C."

The Second Series of *Essays in Criticism*, then, consists of "The Study of Poetry," "Milton," "Thomas Gray," "John Keats," "Wordsworth," "Byron," "Shelley," "Count Leo Tolstoi," and "Amiel." Four of these are published in the present volume of this edition, the other five have appeared in volume IX. It is tempting to regard the Second Series as one does the First Series, but they are very unlike in conception and intended audience. The First Series had its origin in Arnold's professorial lectures from the chair of poetry at Oxford; all the essays in the first edition were composed within a span of less than two years and even those that were not Oxford lectures were of the same sort as the lectures. The two latest were delivered after the book had been conceived and were composed with a view to tying the book together. The audience was a university community. The essays of the Second Series, on the other hand, had quite different purposes. Published over a ten-year span, five of them served as popular introductions to anthologies or selections of poetry, one was a ceremonial address, one was a book review, and only two were more general literary essays.

[ADVERTISEMENT TO
Fragment on the Church]

Dr. Thomas Arnold died on June 12, 1842, one day before his forty-seventh birthday. His oldest son was still an undergraduate at Balliol College, Oxford, twenty-one years old, when he wrote this "Advertisement" to the posthumous book on a subject which continued to interest him throughout his life. When in 1849 he sought a publisher for his first volume of poems, Matthew Arnold turned to the publisher of this fragment (and other of his father's works on church and theology), B. Fellowes of Ludgate Street, London. This brief piece should have appeared, of course, in the first and not the last volume of these collected prose works.

Textual Notes

[SPECIAL REPORT ON . . .
ELEMENTARY EDUCATION IN
GERMANY, SWITZERLAND, AND FRANCE]

86   Education Department. | [*short double rule*] | Special Report | on | Certain Points Connected with | Elementary Education in Germany, | Switzerland, and France. | [*double rule*] | Presented to both Houses of Parliament by Command of Her Majesty. | [*double rule*] | [*royal coat of arms*] | London: | Printed by Eyre and Spottiswoode. | [*short rule*] | . . . | [*short rule*] | 1886. | [C.–4752] *Price* 3½d.

88ed   Education Reform League | [*short rule*] | Special Report | on certain points connected with | Elementary Education | in | Germany, Switzerland, and France | by | Matthew Arnold | *with a prefatory note by the author* | Reprinted by | The Education Reform League | Toynbee Hall, Whitechapel, E. | 1888 | Price One Penny

MS   Manuscript in the Alderman Library, University of Virginia. 51 pp., with postmarked envelope. Not collated.

Pp. 1–2. *Preface and Note not in MS*, 86.
   2:8. the subjoined Preface 88ed, *where this note appears at the head of the Preface.*
6:35–38. *not in MS*
11:33. class 86, 88ed; classes *MS*
13:36–38. *not in MS*
14:8. prevails *MS*, 86; prevail 88ed

24:28. persons and events   *MS;* persons and points   86, 88ed

26:36. matters acquired for   *MS;* matters required for   86, 88ed

29:17. and of the intelligence and interest with which the children *MS,* 86

30:11. Trachenberg,   *MS,* 86, 88ed; *corrected by ed.*

30:19. Middle Age   *MS,* 86; Middle Ages   88ed

33:6. which I followed   *MS,* 86

33:34. schoolmistresses,   however,   takes   *MS;*   schoolmistresses, takes   86

38:32, 39:17, 20–21. religions   *mispr.* 86

40:30. the Ministry of   *MS,* 86

42:22. Petersilie's   *MS;* Petersilien's   *mispr.* 86, 88ed

42:27–31. At present ... £60.   *not in MS*

47:35. and on one occasion   *MS,* 86; and one occasion   *mispr.* 88ed

49:32–38.   *not in MS*

49:37–38.   scholars, receiving   *mispr.* 86

51:33. single master—was not their   *MS,* 86

52:11. peculiarly lending   *MS,* 86

[THE NADIR OF LIBERALISM]

Ninet.   "The Nadir of Liberalism," *Nineteenth Century* XIX, 645–63 (May, 1886).

Lit.   "The Nadir of Liberalism," Littell's Living Age CLXIX, 579–90 (June 5, 1886). Not collated.

Ecl.   "The Nadir of Liberalism," *Eclectic Magazine* XLIV n.s., 1–13 (July, 1886). Not collated.

63:34. stability and prominence   *Ninet.; corrected from p. 72:23.*

65:3–4. class ... class   *Ninet.; emended by ed.*

66:20. ils sont   *Ninet.; corrected from Ste.-Beuve.*

[THE POLITICAL CRISIS]

Times   "Mr. Matthew Arnold on the Political Crisis," *Times* (London), Saturday, May 22, 1886, p. 15, col. 6.

[AFTER THE ELECTIONS]

Times   "After the Elections," *Times* (London), Friday, August 6, 1886, p. 12, cols. 1–2.

[COMMON SCHOOLS ABROAD]

Cent. "Common Schools Abroad," *Century Magazine* (N.Y.) XXXII, 893–900 (October, 1886).

MS Manuscript in the Library of the University of Pennsylvania. 32 pp. Not collated.

100:1–2. in Brighton. [*altered to:*] in England. *MS*

101:7. Trachenberg, *MS, Cent.; corrected by ed.*

102:13–14. sees this University where I now speak, and Harvard, and [*altered to:*] sees colleges such as this, and Harvard, and *MS*

[SAINTE-BEUVE]

Brit. "Sainte-Beuve, Charles Augustin," *Encyclopaedia Britannica* (9th ed.; Edinburgh: Adam and Charles Black, 1886), vol. XXI, pp. 162–65. Signed "(M.A.)"

106:28. in 1827 *Brit.; corrected by ed.*

109:24. In 1857 *Brit.; corrected by ed.*

[PREFACE TO *Twilight Thoughts*]

Claude Twilight Thoughts | Stories for Children and Child-Lovers | by | Mary S. Claude | *Edited by Mary L. Avery, with a Preface by* | Matthew Arnold | Boston | Published by Ginn & Company | 1887

Preface, pp. 3–4, signed "Matthew Arnold."

[THE ZENITH OF CONSERVATISM]

Ninet. "The Zenith of Conservatism," *Nineteenth Century* XXI, 148–64 (January, 1887).

Proofs Page proofs, paginated 1–16, with Arnold's handwritten revisions, in the Library of Balliol College, Oxford. At the top of p. 1 is written "Press JTK [Knowles, the editor] but please be *very* careful about all corrections—which have been rendered necessary by the recent political changes—JTK."

Lit.   "The Zenith of Conservatism," *Littell's Living Age*
          CLXXII, 323–33 (February 5, 1887). Not collated.

122:5–6. to time I have criticised the action of our great political
parties, have said that to plain quiet people, who keep their heads
clear and their eyes open, this action seems far less valuable than
to our politicians themselves, seems wanting in candid [*ms revision:* fresh] and sound thought, dominated by stock phrases and
routine. The professional   *Proofs; ms revisions as in Ninet.*

123:10–11. would speedily dissolve, and how false, too, this prophesying has proved, and how firm the alliance still remains,
when one   *Proofs; ms revisions as in Ninet.*

123:19–21. that the Conservatives may be said to be now at their
zenith. ¶Certainly there have been and are appearances   *Proofs;
ms revisions as in Ninet.*

124:7–24. rather than national. And the majority will for the
present be unimpaired, and the Liberal Unionists staunch, if the
Conservatives, by their policy on one or two great questions,
carry the mind of the country with them. It placed them in
power, and it shows as yet no signs of withdrawing from them
its goodwill.
     So at the zenith we will say that the Conservatives now are;
and the question therefore for them, and for us who wish them
well, is how they are to remain there. The mind of the country
is favourable to them; that is, in my opinion, their present chief
strength, their paramount advantage. But how are they to keep
Proofs; ms revisions as in Ninet.

125:16–19. is most important ·for them to ascertain by what sort
of proceedings when Parliament meets, since   *Proofs; ms revisions as in Ninet.*

129:38. stability and prominence–   *Ninet.; corrected from p.
72:23.*

131:21–23. doubt or question; if they fumble and   *Proofs; ms revisions as in Ninet.*

131:27–28. All that … *vulgus.   ms addition on Proofs.*

140:23–26. some redress afforded.   *Proofs;* redress *altered to* relief
and The land … most true.   *ms addition on Proofs.*

140:34–36. wholly untouched. It recognised no difference   *Proofs;
ms revision as in Ninet.*

142:32–143:4. Let them … of the country.   *ms addition on Proofs.*

143:6–8. rather old, shall have to look forward to the Conservative
Ministry lasting   *Proofs; ms revision as in Ninet.*

[GENERAL GRANT]

Mur. "General Grant," *Murray's Magazine* I, 130–44, 150–66 (January, February, 1887).

87a Matthew Arnold | [*short rule*] | General Grant | *An Estimate* | Boston | Cupples, Upham & Co | Old Corner Bookstore | 1887
    This edition has no textual authority and is not collated.

88a Civilization | in the United States | First and Last Impressions | of America | by | Matthew Arnold | [*short rule*] | Boston | Cupples and Hurd | Publishers | 1888
    Contains "General Grant. An Estimate," "A Word about America," "A Word More about America," and "Civilization in the United States." This edition has no textual authority and is not collated.

146:13. completed the expression   *mispr. Mur.*
164:14. ever equalled, since I was   *Mur.; corrected from Grant.*
169:2. Captain Hellyer   *Mur.; corrected from Grant.*

[A "FRIEND OF GOD"]

Ninet. "A 'Friend of God,'" *Nineteenth Century* XXI, 499–506 (April, 1887).

188:4. are unceasingly   *Ninet.; emended by ed.*

[UP TO EASTER]

Ninet. "Up to Easter," *Nineteenth Century* XXI, 629–43 (May, 1887).

200:18. 1798   *Ninet.; corrected by ed.*
201:26. another of another.   *Ninet.; emended by ed.*

[SCHOOLS IN THE REIGN
OF QUEEN VICTORIA]

Ward The Reign | of | Queen Victoria | A Survey | of | Fifty Years of Progress | Edited by | Thomas Humphry Ward, M.A. | Late Fellow of Brasenose College, Oxford | In two

volumes | Vol. II. | London: Smith, Elder, & Co. | Philadel-
phia: J. B. Lippincott Co. | 1887
    "Schools," by Matthew Arnold, II, 238–79.

Marginal headings in Ward *have been placed in italics at the beginnings of paragraphs in the present text.*

210:9. 13th of   *Ward; corrected by ed.*
214:36. perhaps never seen a   *mispr.* Ward
215:4. cowed or sullen,   *Ward; corrected from Shuttleworth*
234:33. their rulers themselves have,   *Ward; corrected from
    Shuttleworth.*
236:33. of organising at all.   *Ward; emended by ed.*
237:24. by examination of   *Ward; corrected from Schools Inquiry
    Commission report.*
240:6–7. and one-half in every thousand boys of our   *Ward;
    emended by ed.*

[FROM EASTER TO AUGUST]

Ninet.   "From Easter to August," *Nineteenth Century* XXII, 310–
    24 (September, 1887).

253:38. invidious coercion   *mispr. Ninet.; see p. 253:24 and Times.*
262:3–4. not a mere   *Ninet.; corrected from Croker.*

[AMIEL]

Macm.   "Amiel," *Macmillan's Magazine* LVI, 321–29 (September,
       1887).
Lit.   "Amiel," *Littell's Living Age* CLXXV, 57–64 (October
       1–8, 1887). Not collated.
88.   Essays in Criticism | Second Series | by | Matthew Arnold |
       London | Macmillan and Co. | and New York | 1888 | *All
       rights reserved*
92.   Essays in Criticism | Second Series | by | Matthew Arnold |
       Copyright Edition. | Leipzig | Bernhard Tauchnitz | 1892.
       [Collection of British Authors Tauchnitz Edition. Vol.
       2859.]
           This edition has no textual authority and is not collated.
265:28.   *not in Macm.*

269:32. invisible state   *Macm.*, 88; *corrected from Amiel.*

271:6. bedazement with *Macm.*, 88; *corrected from French* éblouissement.

273:15–16. of morbid pathology.   *Macm.*, 88; of mental pathology. *later reprints of 88*

277:4. *mais ne   Macm.*, 88; *corrected from Amiel.*

277:31. practical and intelligent, *Macm.*, 88; *corrected from Amiel.*

281:9–10. suffering   *Macm.*, 88; *corrected from Amiel.*

281:34. infinite allusion,   *mispr.* 88

[COUNT LEO TOLSTOI]

Fortn.   "Count Leo Tolstoi," *Fortnightly Review* XLVIII (n.s. XLII), 783–99 (December, 1887).

Lit.   "Count Leo Tolstoi," *Littell's Living Age* CLXXVI, 82–92 (January 14, 1888). Not collated.
    Reprinted 88, 92 (not collated).

282:12. *lyrique a tari.   Fortn.*, 88; *corrected from Ste.-Beuve.*

282:27. *not in Fortn.*

293:15. even, I think,   *Fortn.*, 88; *emended by ed.*

[SHELLEY]

Ninet.   "Shelley," *Nineteenth Century* XXIII, 23–39 (January, 1888).

Lit.   "Shelley," *Littell's Living Age* CLXXVI, 323–33 (February 11, 1888). Not collated.

Ecl.   "Shelley," *Eclectic Magazine* XLVII n.s., 402–13 (March, 1888). Not collated.
    Reprinted 88, 92 (not collated).

305:28. *not in Ninet.*

307:24. its interesting wynds   *Ninet.*, 88; *corrected from Dowden.*

317:6. a drier world.   *Ninet.*, 88; *emended by ed.*

318:5. he sate outside   *Ninet.*

320:21. *The brackets are Arnold's.*

321:27. passage of a   *Ninet.*, 88; *corrected from Dowden.*

325:27. immense future   *Ninet.*, 88; *corrected from Dowden.*

326:28. he sate by   *Ninet.*, 88; he sat by   *Dowden.*

[MILTON]

Cent.   "Milton," *Century Magazine* (N.Y.) XXXVI, 53–55 (May, 1888).
    Reprinted 88, 92 (not collated).

328:28. 13th of   *Cent.*, 88; *corrected by ed.*

[DISESTABLISHMENT IN WALES]

Nat.   "Disestablishment in Wales," *National Review* XI, 1–13 (March, 1888).

342:22–23. and the rest of England." *Nat.; corrected from Guardian.*

[CIVILISATION IN THE UNITED STATES]

Ninet.   "Civilisation in the United States," *Nineteenth Century* XXIII, 481–96 (April, 1888).
Ecl.   "Civilization in the United States," *Eclectic Magazine* XLVII n.s., 689–99 (May, 1888). Not collated.
Lit.   "Civilization in the United States," *Littell's Living Age* CLXXVII, 285–93 (May 5, 1888). Not collated.
88a   (See p. 511.) This edition has no textual authority and is not collated.

358:7–8. every day   *Ninet.; corrected from Amiel.*
363:1. *The brackets are Arnold's.*

[THIRTY-FIVE YEARS OF SCHOOL INSPECTING]

The title and sub-title are taken from the abridged report in *The Pall Mall Gazette*, November 13, 1886, p. 6. The title of the report in *The Times* is "Mr. Matthew Arnold and the Westminster Teachers." There is no paragraphing in *The Times;* it has been supplied by the editor.

375:10. from Governments   *Times; emended by ed.*

[PREFATORY NOTE TO
Essays in Criticism, Second Series]

Printed in 88, 92 (not collated).

[ADVERTISEMENT TO
Fragment on the Church]

44 Fragment | on | the Church. | By | Thomas Arnold, D.D. | Late Head Master of Rugby School. | London: | B. Fellowes, Ludgate Street. | 1844.

   "Advertisement," p. [v], signed "M.A."

Additions and Corrections
Volumes I–X
*(Some of these have been introduced into the reprintings of
Volumes I and III)*

Text

27:28. *Read* for being set so near
111:5. *Read* powerful and delightful,
146:15. *Read* who heard the
210:15. *Read* quote the *Recluse*)
210:16. *Read* On man, on nature, and

Textual Notes

P. 255:4 (*and on pp. 257–58*). *For 65 read 65*a
17:6. wish 54, 57, 82, 91; wished 83m
27:28. for being so near *Macm.* (*corrected from Raleigh*)
P. 257, headnote to *On Translating Homer.* Arnold gave the following titles to his selections in 80: 102:20–24, "Key-Note to the Iliad"; 112:34–113:14, "Homer and the Elizabethans"; 137:26–138:24, "Homer and Scott"; 140:3–11, 13–33, "English Eccentricity"; 143:19–29, "Homer, Spenser, and Keats"; 155:29–156:12, "Homer and the Bible"; 168:7–22, "Genius of Homer"
111:5. power and delightful, *mispr.* 830, 96
146:15. who had the 61, 830, 96; *emended in deluxe ed., 1903.*
P. 258, headnote to *Last Words.* Arnold gave the following titles to his selections in 80: 171:37–172:16, "English Literary Opinion"; 206:2–27, "Simplicity and 'Simplesse'"; 210:8–212:1, "Homer and the Balladists"; 215:16–216:7, "Arthur Hugh Clough"
210:15. quote the *Excursion*) 62, 830, 96; *corrected by ed.*
210:16. On God, on Nature, and 62, 830, 96; *corrected by ed.*

Critical and Explanatory Notes

5:31–37, 6:23–24. Browning quoted these words as those of "an eloquent friend" in his Preface to *The Agamemnon of Aeschylus* (October 1, 1877).

8:12–15, 10:13–14. The article is by David Masson, not Ludlow.

10:20. Perhaps an echo of Wordsworth's "They flash upon that inward eye" ("I Wandered Lonely As a Cloud," line 21).

13:26–35. Professor DeLaura points to the similarity in tone between this passage and some remarks on poets like Alexander Smith in a current review of "Modern Poetry": "Instead of *writing* poetry, [these poets] talk about it. The age's want of a poet, what sort of a poet is wanted, what his mission is to be, how the age yearns for him, what are to be his characteristics, how he is to lead in the van of progress, and to guide men to an undreamed of perfection, are echoed from one to another."—*Christian Remembrancer* XXVI, 167 (July, 1853).

17:20–22. "To study models with a view to *emulate* them is not the same as to study them with a view to *imitate* them; the one is an invigorating—the other an enervating study. . . . Instead of Imitation we counsel Emulation; instead of following the mere fashions of Greek Art, follow no fashions but those which bear the general verdict of your age, and while learning from the Greeks the lessons they and all great artists have to teach, beware, above all things, of imitating them"—*Leader* IV, 1147, 1170 (November 26, December 3, 1853). This anonymous review was by G. H. Lewes. Arnold mentioned it in a letter to his sister Mrs. Forster.—*Unpublished Letters*, ed. A. Whitridge (New Haven: Yale University Press, 1923), p. 22.

18:2–4. (*Add:*) It was rather severely handled by a member of the audience in an undergraduate critical journal, especially for Arnold's dispraise of the Elizabethans and of Raleigh, who is not to be judged by his literary works alone. "The contemptuous laughter of [the Undergraduates' gallery in] the Oxford theatre will not outweigh the memory of a life, the noblest perhaps among the men of a great age."—*Undergraduate Papers* (Oxford), no. 1 (December 1, 1857), pp. 38–40. According to W. A. Knight, the author was Swinburne, then an undergraduate at Balliol.—*Memoir of John Nichol* (Glasgow, 1896), p. 157n.

18:25–19:10. (*Add:*) Arnold got it at second hand, however (as his spelling of "Pourna" indicates), from Jules Barthélemy

Saint-Hilaire, *Du Bouddhisme* (Paris, 1855), pp. 153–54, a book that was on his reading list for May, 1857.—*Note-Books*, ed. Lowry, p. 561. In January, 1858, he wrote to his sister Mrs. Forster: "I must ask you to send me back some day my Bouddhisme to make a reference for my next lecture—the book is now unprocurable."—*Unpublished Letters*, ed. Whitridge, p. 43.

23:13–15. "Although the exact words do not appear in the essay, the analogy between the life of the nation and the life of the individual is the dominant figure in Appendix I of Dr. Thomas Arnold's edition of Thucydides, *History of the Peloponnesian War* (2nd ed.; Oxford, 1840–42), I, 503."—Professor Neiman's note.

23:18–19. Thomas Arnold remarked: "We may learn also a more sensible division of history than that which is commonly adopted of ancient and modern. We shall see that there is in fact an ancient and a modern period in the history of every people: the ancient differing, and the modern in many essential points agreeing with that in which we now live. Thus the largest portion of that history which we commonly call ancient is practically modern, as it describes society in a stage analogous to that in which it now is; while, on the other hand, much of what is called modern history is practically ancient, as it relates to a state of things which has passed away. Thucydides and Xenophon, the orators of Athens, and the philosophers, speak a wisdom more applicable to us politically than the wisdom of even our own countrymen who lived in the middle ages; and their position, both intellectual and political, more nearly resembled our own." "The period to which the work of Thucydides refers belongs properly to modern and not to ancient history; and it is this circumstance, over and above the great ability of the historian himself, which makes it so peculiarly deserving of our study. The state of Greece from Pericles to Alexander . . . affords a political lesson perhaps more applicable to our own times, if taken all together, than any other portion of history which can be named anterior to the eighteenth century."—ed. of Thucydides, I, 522; III, xx.

24:30–33. The article was by Mark Pattison.

28:31–33. K. O. Mueller, *History of the Literature of Ancient Greece*, continued by J. W. Donaldson (London, 1858), I, 371.

29:10–15. "From this combination of a serious thought, by way of foundation, with the boldest creations of a riotous imagination, the *Ecclesiazusae* must be classed with the works [of Aristophanes] which appeared during the vigour of Attic comedy."–K. O. Mueller, *Literature of Ancient Greece*, II, 47.

36:30–31. Landor's phrase was applied to Arnold himself in the obituary tribute by G. W. E. Russell in *The Manchester Guardian*, April 17, 1888, p. 6, col. 2.

77:9. "I saw to-day at Arles on the Roman obelisk an inscription to Louis Napoleon with the simple words 'il nous a sauvés de l'Anarchie.'"–Arnold to his sister Jane Forster, May 22, 1859; *Unpublished Letters*, ed. Whitridge, p. 46.

91:9. "O most lame and impotent conclusion!"–*Othello*, II, i, 162.

147:29–30. *Hamlet*, V, i, 227.

156:8–12. *For* "Meyers" *read* "Myers." Walter Leaf was the son of Arnold's landlord in Cobham.

163:11. A Latin proverb: "You can judge the whole of Hercules merely by looking at his foot."

172:9–10. See note to I, 91:9 in these Additions and Corrections.

185:34. "For as Epictetus would have a philosopher in every particular action to say to himself, *Et hoc volo, et etiam institutum servare*, so a politic man in every thing should say to himself, *Et hoc volo, ac etiam aliquid addiscere*."–*Advancement of Learning*, book II, nearly five-sixths through. See note to "Disestablishment in Wales" (1888), XI, 336:1–2.

200:1–3. When Clovis presented himself to Saint Remigius for baptism on Christmas Day, 496, the Saint commanded him: "Gently bow thy neck, Sicambrian; adore what thou hast burned, burn what thou hast adored."–Gregory of Tours, *Historia Francorum*, II, 31. The expression was commonplace in nineteenth-century England.

215:16–216:7. Arnold sent a copy of *Last Words* to Emerson, as a valued friend of Clough's, so that he might see this passage.

Index

Insert: lucidity, 141
Cancel: Ludlow, *etc.*
Insert: Masson, David, 221, 223 [*see note to* I, 8:12–15 *in these Additions and Corrections*]
For Meyers *read* Myers
science, *insert* 177
simplicity, *insert* 177
Insert: spectacle, 17, 20–22, 173, 210
Insert: vivacity, 170

[VOLUME II: DEMOCRATIC EDUCATION]

Textual Notes

P. 398:7. *For* 65 *read* 65a

Critical and Explanatory Notes

31:9. (*Add:*) —*Prose Works,* ed. Super, X, 89–93.

136:17. An Athenian professor who developed a system of mnemonics offered to teach it to Themistocles, and promised that it would enable him to remember everything. Themistocles replied that he would be more grateful to the man if he could teach him to *forget* what he wished, rather than to remember.—Cicero *De Oratore* II, lxxiv, 299 and lxxxvi, 351. "Vain was the prayer of Themistocles for a talent of Forgetting," wrote Teufelsdröckh in Carlyle's *Sartor Resartus,* book I, chapter vii. Arnold referred to this wish also in *God and the Bible* (1875) and at the beginning of his Preface to Johnson's *Six Chief Lives of the Poets* (1878).—*Prose Works,* ed. Super, VII, 244; VIII, 306.

160:13–14. (*Add:*) (1864).—*Prose Works,* ed. Super, III, 232.

162:15–17. Macaulay, *History of England,* chapt. i (one-fourth through). Arnold repeated the statement in *Friendship's Garland,* Letter III (1866); *Prose Works,* ed. Super, V, 51.

211:5–22. "Nous aurions dû attendre, dit-il, cela est vrai. Mais nous avions raison, et il faut savoir hasarder quelque chose quand on a raison."—Adolphe Thiers, *Histoire du Consulat et de l'Empire* (Paris, 1845), III, 487 (halfway through book XIV).

223:5. *For* Chester *read* Cheshire

248:17–18. "Crowning the edifice" was an expression of the Emperor Napoleon III that had become a cliché; see *Prose Works*, ed. Super, V, 376–77.

P. 367. *Delete* the *from title*

P. 369:13. *After* writer *insert* (Matthew James Higgins)

262:1–5. *For the present note, substitute:* Matthew James Higgins, "Jacob Omnium," a friend of Thackeray's, whose three letters in the *Cornhill Magazine* on public school education were republished as a book over the signature "Paterfamilias" in 1861.

273:1. The Papal Nuncio at Paris in 1859 was Msgr. Sacconi.

Index

Protestant Dissent, *insert* 373
Protestantism, *delete* 373
Prussia, *delete* 160
Rocher, Rue de: *read* Rue du
securities, *for* 373 *read* 375
Insert: spectacle, 9, 25, 32, 161, 226
Spectator, for 370 *read* 371
Switzerland, education in, compulsion, *for* 168–69 *read* 168–72

[VOLUME III: LECTURES AND ESSAYS IN CRITICISM]

Text

3:18. *For* warm *read* warn
13:33. *For* cîme *read* cime
22:34, 35. *For* de la *read* de La
151:7. *For* shall *read* shalt
276:26. *For* party movement, *read* party of movement.
331:1. *For* and in "ey," Alderney, *read* and in "ey" for island, Alderney,
341:33. *for* perverseness; patient *read* perverseness; it is patient

Textual Notes

3:18. warm   *Fras., Martin; corrected from Wordsworth*
P. 519, editions of "Heinrich Heine," *insert:* 63a. Heinrich Heine. | By | Matthew Arnold. | Reprint from the Cornhill Magazine, (August, 1863.) | [*orn.*] | Philadelphia: | Frederick Leypoldt. | New York: F. W. Christern. | 1863. Not collated.
272:23. *The 75 reading is:* [¶] But neither Sir Charles Adderley . . . are by
276:26. *Add:* party movement, 75, 83e
P. 540, texts of *On the Study of Celtic Literature, insert:* MS National Library of Wales, Aberystwyth. Not collated.
297:7–8. farther and farther   *ms, 83o;* further and further   *Cornh., 67*
311:11. *Add:* frequent allusions   *ms;*
315:35. when a mediaeval   [*add*]   *ms,*
328:9. neither of them have yet   *ms*

331:1. "ey" for island, Alderney, [*add*] *ms;* [*delete "emended by Ed."*]

341:33. perverseness; it is patient   *ms;* perverseness; patient *Cornh.,* 67, 830

343:2. of his *douce* [*add*] *ms,*

345:25. stedfastness have kept the Celt   *ms*

348:11. in themselves, then, vital [*add*] *ms*

351:25–35, 352:35–39. *For* 35–39 *this reference should read* 35–38

363:25. to import style   *ms*

367:32. vexed question as   *ms*

385:35. *Add:* as matters of   *ms*

Critical and Explanatory Notes

P. 403:13. (*Insert:*) (For Goethe's use of the expression "daemonic element," see *Dichtung und Wahrheit,* book XX, one-third through.)

P. 404:16. (*Insert:*) On May 15, 1867, Étienne published an article in the *Revue des deux mondes* on "La Paganisme poétique en Angleterre: John Keats et Algernon Charles Swinburne."–2d pér., LXIX, 291–317.

P. 405:13. *For* 1962 *read* 1963

11:1–2. "I count all things but loss for the excellency of the knowledge of Christ Jesus my Lord."–Philippians 3:8.

13:31–32. (*Insert:*) William Sharp reports that when Arnold was accused of his misquotation from Keats he remarked, "I cannot believe it."–ed., *The Strayed Reveller, &c.* (London, 1896), p. xvii.

47:30. "The weaker vessel" comes from I Peter 3:7, where in an admonition to husbands it refers to the wife.

63:20–22. "Errare . . . malo cum Platone, . . . quam cum istis vera sentire."–Cicero *Tusculan Disputations* I, xvii, 39.

97:9. The dogma of the Immaculate Conception was defined by Pius IX in 1854.

P. 434:1. *For* 1848 *read* 1849

P. 434:8–9. (*Insert:*) V. E. Horn points out that Arnold's French phrase echoes the language of Gérard de Nerval's review of Heine's poetry in *Revue des deux mondes,* n.s. XXIII, 225 (July 15, 1848).–*Notes and Queries* CCXVI, 248–49 (July, 1971).

110:25. Professor Donald Hill points out that this sentence is the essence of Goethe's *Dichtung und Wahrheit,* book XII, ¶11; *Werke* (Weimar, 1890), XXVIII, 101–2.

111:38–112:1. (*Add:*) Also, "Respectability, with all her collected Gigs," in the penultimate paragraph of *The French Revolution, Works* (Centenary ed.), IV, 323.

124:3–4. (*Correct:*) From a poem by Eugénie de Guérin, *Journal*, p. 214 (entry for June 2, 1838); identified by L. Bonnerot, *Matthew Arnold, Poète* (Paris, 1947), p. 355n.

140:30. In his essay on Coleridge (1840; republished 1859), ¶5, J. S. Mill refers to "our enlightened age" (in quotation marks). Burke used the expression in *Reflections on the Revolution in France*, one-third through.

153:10. (*Add:*) Professor DeLaura suggests that Arnold's quoted phrase alludes to Pascal's *Pensées*, Article I; e.g., "Car enfin qu'est-ce que l'homme dans la nature? Un néant à l'égard de l'infini, un tout à l'égard du néant; un milieu entre rien et tout." —ed. Ernest Havet (nouv. éd.; Paris, 1883), p. 6.

196:36. *For* V, i, 199 *read* V, i, 227

P. 464, *fourth line from bottom. Read:* il faut

230:27–30. Professor DeLaura points out the similarity between this language and that of Clough on the age of Dryden (1851–52, but first published 1964): "It is a period, I confess, rather of the senses and the understanding than of the spirit and the imagination."—*Selected Prose Works of Arthur Hugh Clough*, ed. Buckner B. Trawick (University, Alabama: University of Alabama Press, 1964), p. 105.

230:32. Dr. V. N. Boutellier points out that the expression "Imaginative Reason" figures significantly in Bacon's *Advancement of Learning*, II, xii, 1, as characteristic of rhetorical expression.

243:1–6. In a footnote halfway through his essay on Coleridge (1840; republished 1859), J. S. Mill spoke of the "Cimmerian darkness still prevailing in England . . . concerning the very existence of the views of general history which have been received throughout the continent of Europe for the last twenty or thirty years," and mentioned a recent writer on ancient history in *Blackwood's* who had made "himself very ridiculous, and his country, so far as depends upon him, the laughing-stock of Europe."

256:33–34. In his first lecture *On Translating Homer* (1860), Arnold invokes the standard applied by Aristotle in his *Nicomachean Ethics* 1107a, "as the judicious would determine." —*Prose Works*, ed. Super, I, 99.

258:17–18. (*Add:*) Crabb Robinson read this essay on Arnold's recommendation and suspected it was Arnold's own, "though

I had not ascribed so much of the Wordsworth feeling to any of the Arnold race."—Robinson, *On Books and Their Writers*, ed. E. J. Morley (London, 1938), II, 812.

260–61. Arnold echoes Goethe's remarks to Eckermann on May 3, 1827 (part iii); "current" represents Goethe's "in Kurs."—ed. E. Castle (Berlin, 1916), II, 95–96.

268:7–10. (*Correct:*) In a memorial delivered to the States General of Holland on January 25, 1793, Auckland wrote: "It is not quite four years since certain unhappy and deluded persons, assuming the name of philosophers, have presumed to think themselves capable of establishing a new system of civil society."—*The Parliamentary History of England* (London: T. C. Hansard, 1817), XXX, 342.

270:1. (*Add:*) "Disinterestedness" was a favorite word of Bishop Joseph Butler's. And as so often, there is something Coleridgean in Arnold's doctrine: "It is a painful truth that not only individuals, but even whole nations, are ofttimes so enslaved to the habits of their education and immediate circumstances, as not to judge disinterestedly even on those subjects, the very pleasure arising from which consists in its disinterestedness, namely on subjects of taste and polite literature. Instead of deciding concerning their own modes and customs by any rule of reason, nothing appears rational, becoming, or beautiful to them, but what coincides with the peculiarities of their education."—Coleridge, "Shakespeare's Judgment Equal to his Genius," ¶4.

276:6. *For* V *read* VI

286:10. "He shall not strive, nor cry."—Matthew 12:19; "The will to neither strive nor cry, | The power to feel with others give!"—Arnold, "Lines Written in Kensington Gardens," lines 41–42.

386:14–15. According to a letter from Arnold to Clough about February 24, 1848, Michelet coined the expression "hard unintelligence" to describe the Americans. Arnold jotted it in his pocket diary for April 27, 1877, and used it of the Americans in "A Word about America" (1882) and "Civilisation in the United States" (1888).—*Letters of Matthew Arnold to Arthur Hugh Clough*, ed. H. F. Lowry (London: Oxford University Press, 1932), p. 66; *Note-Books*, ed. Lowry, p. 276; *Prose Works*, ed. Super, X, 14; XI, 367.

P. 493, *fifth line from bottom.* (*Add:*) Also in the audience for this fourth lecture was Gerard Manley Hopkins.—*Journals and Papers*, ed. Humphry House (London: Oxford University Press, 1959), p. 137.

299:2. Renan, to demonstrate the way in which various sciences might be brought to bear on the solution of a single problem such as the origins of humanity, raised the questions that might be resolved by ethnography, chronology, geography, physiology, psychology, and history, then added: "Je suis convaincu qu'il y a une science des origines de l'humanité qui sera construite un jour, non par la spéculation abstraite, mais par la recherche scientifique."—*L'Avenir de la science* (Paris, 1890), p. 163. The conception of science which dominates this book (parts of which had been published much earlier) clearly influenced Arnold's thought a great deal. The earliest quotation from it in his pocket diary dates from 1863.—*Note-Books*, ed. Lowry, p. 19.

303:15–16. *For* Caermarthan *read* Caermarthen

341:21. (*Add:*) and "My Countrymen," *Prose Works*, ed. Super, V, 13:7.

375:2–9. *For* ibid. *read* Mabinogion

377:34–36. (*Add:*) for "its folk" read "this folk."

395:13. Hebrews 6:1

Index

adequacy, *insert* 359

Canterbury, *insert* 415

culture, *insert* 128

curiosity, curious, *insert* 35, 64, 71, 96, 123, 143, 196, 215, 292, 359, 365

Insert: delicacy, 23, 30, 197, 211, 235, 250, 252, 342–43, 368, 390, 465

Insert: development, 77, 368

Essays and Reviews, insert 416

Goethe, *Faust, insert* 124

Guérin, Eugénie de, *insert* 124, 438 [*see note to III, 124:3–4 in these Additions and Corrections*]

Insert: justification by faith, 134

Kilhwch, *insert* 375

Paulinus, *for* G. *read* C.

perfection, *insert* 128, 355, 369

practical, practice, *insert* 44, 215

progress, *insert* 395
romanticism, *insert* 433, 451
Schleiermacher, *read* F. D. E.
science, *insert* 38, 44
Insert: spectacle, 16, 38, 154, 190, 381
Insert: tact, 368, 387

[VOLUME IV: SCHOOLS AND UNIVERSITIES ON THE CONTINENT]

Text

77:35. *For* 24 *read* 23
121:37. *For* 14 *mars read* 15 *mars*
128:20–21. *Transpose these lines*
137:38. *For* In *read* It

Textual Notes

77:35. 24 hours   68r, 68s; *corrected by ed.*
121:37. 14 *mars*   68r, 68s; *corrected by ed.*

Critical and Explanatory Notes

P. 337:6. *For* the published collection by *read* the collection edited by

P. 341:9. (*Add:*) —*Prose Works,* ed. Super, V, 488.

P. 345:25. *For* Newcastle Commission *read* Clarendon Commission

P. 351:22. (*Add:*) —*Prose Works,* V, 530–31.

P. 351:41. (*Add:*) —*Prose Works,* VII, 90–130.

P. 353:10. (*Add:*) —*Prose Works,* X, 53–73.

P. 353, *note to Epigraph:* (*Add:*) Arnold's source, Wiese, does not attribute this statement to Humboldt personally, merely to his ministry.

21:1–7. (*Add:*) —*Prose Works,* V, 126.

118:32–33. (*Add:*) —*Prose Works,* V, 505–6.

P. 370:15. (*Add:*) —*Prose Works,* VIII, 7–8.

186:21–26. (*Add:*) —*Prose Works,* X, 57.

P. 372:8. (*Add:*) —"German Letters on English Education," *Prose Works,* VIII, 208–15.

P. 385:32–33. *Cancel* nor in his surviving correspondence. (*Insert:*) Arnold wrote to his mother on June 2: "I have received today £3..13ˢ..6ᵈ for the page and a half on German Universities I wrote for the Pall Mall three weeks ago."

Index

[VOLUME V: CULTURE AND ANARCHY]

Text

6:16. *For* though *read* through
23:18. *For* receive *read* receives (*from ms*)
96:11. *For* indisputably joined *read* indissolubly joined (*from ms*)
122:14. *For* truthful *read* fruitful
183:5. *For* where *read* when (*from ms*)
184:27. *For* proves *read* pours (*from ms*)
189:4. *For* in a false *read* on a false (*from ms*)
197:21. *For* its sway *read* its way
228:4. *For* mean this, that *read* mean there, that (*from ms*)
231:3. *After* follows *insert* [i.e., precedes]
273:36. *For* of the States *read* of States

Textual Notes

P. 488. The ms of the *Cornhill* version of "My Countrymen" is in the library of Balliol College, Oxford.
30:16. developing itself! how they are shewing a quick   *ms*
30:19. and no other.   *ms*
P. 496. The second edition (75) was also issued with the imprint: Macmillan and Co. | New York | 1875
P. 497. The mss of the *Cornhill* versions of "Culture and Its Enemies" and parts III–V· of "Anarchy and Authority" (pp. 87–114, 163–229 in this edition) are in the library of Balliol College, Oxford. Each of these last is headed "Anarchy and Authority (Concluded)." The College also has corrected page proofs of the concluding pages of part IV (pp. 194:17–205:16 [variant version] in this edition).

87:19. *ms reads* a professor of

94:33, 95:25. an harmonious   *Cornh.;* a harmonious   *ms &c*

103:17. to ask the questioner: And   *ms*

105:25. generations of . . . are sacrificed.   *ms;* generation of . . .
are sacrificed.   *Cornh.*

108:36. *Read:* Tabernacle   *ms,* 69

113:15. make it operant outside   *ms*

164:30. exigences   *ms, Cornh.,* 69

167:37–38. beauty and naturalness   *ms*

175:25. habitual courses   *ms, Cornh.,* 69, 75, 80

178:13. the love of light,   *also ms*

179:26. culture, or the endeavour   *ms*

197:21. holding its way   *also ms*

212:5. *For* in *read* is

234:32–33. of Oxford, Lord Houghton, Mr. Gladstone   80

273:36. of the States   *PMG, Ward; corrected by ed.*

Critical and Explanatory Notes

14:20–22. "En même temps que les institutions et les coutumes,
la littérature anglaise passa le détroit et vint régner chez nous.
La poésie britannique nous révéla le doute incarné sous la figure
de Byron."–George Sand, Preface to Senancour's *Obermann,*
two-thirds through. She does not mention Scott.

P. 411:39. *For* pubished *read* published

90:21–22. *For* H. Marzials *read* F. T. Marzials

96:23–26. *Cancel the first sentence and read:* Two and a half
months after Arnold published this, the Paris . . .

106:25–26. Professor DeLaura points out that Goldwin Smith in
his Inaugural Lecture at Oxford, 1859, used the same language
to describe "that great storm of religious controversy through
which [the University] has just passed": it "has cast the wrecks
of her most gifted intellects on every shore."–*Lectures on
Modern History* (Oxford, 1861), p. 34.

111:5–10. (*Add:*) J. S. Mill spoke regretfully of this passage in
his essay on Bentham (1838; republished 1859), one-third
through.

117:18–22. John Bright on April 21, 1869, urged the House of
Commons "to affirm the principle . . . of personal liberty" for
those concerned, by "an emphatic vote" in favor of the Marriage with a Deceased Wife's Sister Bill.–*Times,* April 22,
p. 6, col. 5.

117:34–35. "The worth of a state in the long run is the worth of the individuals composing it."—Mill, *On Liberty*, final paragraph.

124:31–32. "An aristocracy has naturally a great respect for the established order of things, for the *fait accompli.—England and the Italian Question* (1859), *Prose Works*, ed. Super, I, 83.

127:1–2. (*Add:*) Arnold used this same pattern of "main basis," "defect," and "excellence" (without reference to Aristotle) in dealing with the Germanic, Celtic, and Norman genius in *On the Study of Celtic Literature* (1866), *Prose Works*, ed. Super, III, 351.

155:2–8. (*Add:*) On November 30, 1866, the Duke of Edinburgh, second son of Queen Victoria, laid the foundation stone of a new wing of the Licensed Victuallers' Asylum designed "for the reception of aged and decayed licensed victuallers," and was escorted by the children of the Licensed Victuallers' School in Kennington Lane.—*Times*, December 1, p. 9, col. 6 (Gregor). The school still exists.

169:8–18. Professor DeLaura points out that this idea is developed in Arnold's "Speech at Eton" (1879), *Prose Works*, ed. Super, IX, 31–35.

209:1–2. See *Macbeth*, V, iii, 40, and "Literature and Science" (1882), *Prose Works*, X, 69.

P. 447:12. *For* whch *read* which

232:37–233:4. See also *On the Study of Celtic Literature* (1866), *Prose Works*, ed. Super, III, 369.

P. 452. *For* 501:1–13 *read* 504:1–13

535:39 (p. 457). *For* 441 *read* 194:35.

P. 457:23. (*Insert:*) (Adolphus Ward's grandmother was Dr. Thomas Arnold's sister.)

259:34–38. *For* Arnold . . . period *read* He was a cousin of Arnold's and served briefly

283:33–284:12. *For Ibid., read History,*

288:16. "That dishonest victory | At Chaeronea, fatal to liberty." —Milton, Sonnet X ("To the Lady Margaret Ley"), lines 6–7.

313:26. *For* vol. X, Appendix *read* X, 245

315:23. Dr. Elsie Duncan-Jones suggests that "Jemima Bottles" became "Selina Bottles" from the name of Selina, Countess of Huntingdon, patroness of the Methodists in the eighteenth century.

324:1–2. *For* who advocated *read* who advocate. *For* vol. VI *read* VI, 101

P. 474:18. *For* through *read* though

328:19–21. *For* vol. VI *read* VI, 96–99

P. 477:3. For the original title of Letter X, "The Great Heart of England," see V, 17:10.

349:12. (*Insert after* "Oldenburg":) In an earlier dispatch Russell described in familiar terms a walk around Versailles with Bismarck.–October 22, 1870, p. 9, col. 6; see T. L. Williams, "Matthew Arnold and 'The Times,'" *Notes and Queries* CCXIV, 211–12 (June, 1969).

Index

delicacy, *insert* 266

disinterestedness, *insert* 521

energy, *insert* 135

Harrison, *insert* 126

Insert: Houghton, R. M. Milnes, Lord, 530 [*see textual note to V, 234:32–33 in these Additions and Corrections*]

For Marzials, H., *read* Marzials, F. T.

materialism, *insert* 22

Whitehurst, *for* 478 *read* 468

[VOLUME VI: DISSENT AND DOGMA]

Editor's Preface

vi:2. *For* from Dr. *read* from "Dr.

Text

210:32. *For posses read possess*

344:3. *For* yet *read* ye

Textual Notes

P. 505. The ms of the *Cornhill* version of "St. Paul and Protestantism," parts I and II (pp. 5–71 of this edition) is in the library of Balliol College, Oxford.

P. 506:28. [the method of   *ms*]

8:35. claims   *also ms*

9:11. as if he was   *also ms*

31:1. depend   *also ms*

43:34. immense tidal wave of   *ms*

59:7–10. (*Read:*) is as sentient beings we [is as beings *acted upon* and *influenced* that we 75, 83s] [is by an *influence,* and the emotion from it, that we 80] are saved! Well 70b, 75, 80, 83s

62:35. of Christ in man's stead *ms*

249:36–250:3. *For* 38li *read* 83li

353:4. (*not* 353:4–5)

361:23. *Insert* 80

Critical and Explanatory Notes

P. 419:9. *For* September 22 *read* September 8

3:16. (*Add:*) —*Prose Works,* ed. Super, XI, 54.

10:23. (*Add:*) Professor DeLaura adds, from Emerson's essay on "Art" (*Essays,* First Series), ¶10: "The real value of the Iliad or the Transfiguration [by Raphael] is as signs of power; billows or ripples they are of the stream of tendency; . . ."

19:6–9. The (Calvinistic) Heidelberg Catechism of 1563 asks this (Question 19) and gives as answer: "From the Holy Gospel, which God himself first revealed in Paradise, afterwards proclaimed by the holy Patriarchs and Prophets, and foreshadowed by the sacrifices and other ceremonies of the law, and finally fulfilled by his well-beloved Son."—Philip Schaff, *The Creeds of Christendom* (New York, 1877), III, 313.

26:13–14. (*Add:*) George Sand writes: "La source la plus vivante et la plus religieuse du progrès de l'esprit humain, c'est, pour parler la langue de mon temps, la notion de *solidarité.*"—*Histoire de ma vie* (Paris, 1879), I, 6 (part I, chapt. i). The book was first published in 1854.

32:5–6. *For* vol. IX *read* IX, 169

46:14–15. *For* vol. IX *read* IX, 237

80:31–33. Dr. Arnold referred to them thus: A. P. Stanley, *Life of Thomas Arnold* (4th ed.; London, 1845), II, 211. And William Chillingworth, in the Preface to his *Religion of Protestants,* said "I accept the Articles as articles of peace."

84:6–11. See note to *Prose Works,* ed. Super, XI, 182:34–38.

85:6. (*Add:*) Epiphanius's remark was made respecting, not primitive Christianity, but primitive humanity: "There was no heresy on the earth at that time, no difference of opinion. . . . Piety and impiety depended solely on natural law."—*Adversus haereses* I, i, 5; in Migne, *Patrologia Graeca,* XLI, 181–82.

93:4–16. Stephen's objection echoes that of J. S. Mill: "[Christianity] holds out the hope of heaven and the threat of hell, as the appointed and appropriate motives to a virtuous life: in this falling far below the best of the ancients, and doing what lies in it to give to human morality an essentially selfish character."—*On Liberty*, chapt. ii, ¶8 from end.

121:14–15. In "A Recantation and Apology," *Prose Works*, ed. Super, V, 322.

P. 458:1. *For* vol. VII *read* VII, 233

141:1. *For* vol. IX *read* IX, 114–35

142:6. *For* vol. VII *read* VII, 150–52

165:5–6. *For* vol. IX *read* IX, 272

176:26–31. Professor DeLaura calls attention to Arnold's essay on "Marcus Aurelius" (1863): "The paramount virtue of religion is, that it has *lighted up* morality."—*Prose Works*, ed. Super, III, 134:35–36.

183:38–39. *For* Brunschvigg *read* Brunschvicg

200:25. *For* vol. VII *read* VII, 396

231:12–13. "In this way of interpretation, any thing may be made of any thing."—*Analogy*, II, vii, ¶28n; *Works*, ed. Gladstone (1896), I, 326.

246:36. *For* vol. VII *read* VII, 110

256:19–21. *Read* For the single blind man, Mark 10:46–52; for the two, Matthew 20:29–34.

317:19. (*Add:*) And Carlyle uses "The Toiling Millions of Mankind."—*Past and Present*, book III, chapt. xiii.

325:7–10. *For* vol. VII *read* VII, 14–15

352:26. (*Add:*) Alban Butler speaks of her "extreme dread and abhorrence of the least shadow of detraction, insomuch that no one durst in the least reflect on any other person in her presence." Her rule was "to speak of [others] in the same manner she would desire others should speak of her."—*Lives of the Fathers, Martyrs, and Other Principal Saints* (Dublin, 1866), X, 307 (October 15). Arnold noted this passage in his pocket diary for April 1, 1871.—*Note-Books*, ed. Lowry, p. 152.

365:13. *For* vol. VIII *read* VIII, 49

407:4. (*Add:*) —*Prose Works*, ed. Super, VIII, 348–69.

Index

Insert: spectacle, 339

spirit, *insert* 25, 36

theology, *for* 9–12, 14–16, 18–19 *read* 9–19; *for* 156–57, 159 *read* 156–59; *insert* 317

theory, *insert* 296

world, *for* 91, 93–95 *read* 91–95; *delete* 145; *insert* 161; *for* 171 *read* 172

[VOLUME VII: GOD AND THE BIBLE]

Text

57:2. *For* subjects *read* subject

199:25. *For* every *read* ever

P. 303, head. *Insert: from*

329:19. *For* from Jesus *read* from John

341:3. *For* fourteenth verse of the twentieth *read* twentieth verse of the thirteenth

Textual Notes

329:19. from Jesus   *Cont.*, 75g, 83g, 84; *corrected from Arnold's pocket diary for 1883, p. 96*

341:3. fourteenth verse of the twentieth   *Cont.*, 75g, 83g; *corrected from Arnold's pocket diary for 1883, p. 96*

369:12. *Insert* 80

372:20. *Read* tale like that of Messrs. Moody and

Critical and Explanatory Notes

P. 401:2. *For* it is *read* is it

11:15–17. *For* vol. VIII, X *read* VIII, 292; X, 156.

P. 404:28–29. *For* on matters . . . Birmingham *read* on Church establishment.

92:13. *For* vol. X *read* X, 57; *for* sources *read* source

106:24–35. "National Education.—The 'Parental Conscience' Difficulty," letter signed "E.B.," *The Nonconformist*, January 29, 1873, p. 113; quoted again in "Irish Catholicism and British Liberalism" (1878), *Prose Works*, ed. Super, VIII, 326.

121:37–122:1. See p. 128:36n.

146:16–19. *For* vol. X *read* X, 183–84

148:15–18. (*Add:*) The reviewer of *Supernatural Religion* in

The Athenaeum referred to the author as "an earnest seeker after truth."—July 4, 1874, p. 15.

189:7. (*Add:*) Robespierre, at the Festival of the Supreme Being, said: "Français républicains! n'est-ce pas l'Être Suprême qui dès la commencement des temps décreta la République?"

209:27–28. *For* vol. IX *read* IX, 161

233:8–16. *For* vol. VIII *read* VIII, 11–62

244:38–245:1. *See note to II, 136:17 in these Additions and Corrections*

384:30–32. (*Add:*) In the case of Jenkins *v.* Cook, Sir Robert as Dean of Arches asserted on July 16, 1875, that "as to the existence and personality of the devil—the spiritual enemy who slandered God to man—we must receive that doctrine unless we impute error and deceit to the writers of the New Testament," and therefore he gave judgment that "the avowed and persistent denial of the existence and personality of the devil" constituted the promoter an "evil liver" in such sense as to warrant his vicar to deny him Holy Communion until he disavowed or withdrew his heretical opinion. See *The Times*, July 17, p. 13, cols. 3–4 and July 19, p. 9, cols. 2–3 (leading article).

Index

For Sécretan *read* Secrétan

[VOLUME VIII: ESSAYS
RELIGIOUS AND MIXED]

Text

159:31. *For* exhalt *read* exalt
218:32. *For* gaze *read* face [*from ms*]
224:23. *For* May *read* may [*from ms*]
225:2. *For* wild *read* wide [*from ms*]
225:8–9. *For* quotation *read* quatrain [*from ms*]
233:9. *For* life *read* hope [*from ms*]

Textual Notes

P. 504, "George Sand." MS, 28 pp., in the Beinecke Rare Book and Manuscript Library of Yale University, inscribed: "To

Lord Rosebery | From his friend, | John Morley. | 1888." Not collated

Critical and Explanatory Notes

12:30–32. *For* vol. X *read* X, 143

55:33–34. See Arnold's paraphrase of Spinoza: "The Bible contains much that is mere history, and, like all history, sometimes true, sometimes false."–*Prose Works*, ed. Super, III, 68, 166.

96:30. Arnold speaks in the Preface to *Culture and Anarchy* (1869) of "the recreative religion furnished on Sundays by my gifted acquaintance and others."–*Prose Works*, ed. Super, V, 231. An association that called themselves "Recreative Religionists" conducted "Sunday evenings for the people" in St. Martin's Hall, Longacre—meetings that consisted of discourses on social subjects or on science, with a view to instructing the audience and making science the handmaid of religion. Sacred music was performed by professional artists, but there was no public worship of the deity. See *Times*, November 20, 1868, p. 11, col. 3.

250:29–32. *For* vol. IX *read* IX, 48–50

287:14–16. *For* vol. X *read* X, 61–73

292:20–22. *For* vol. X *read* X, 156

322:29–32. *For* vol. IX *read* IX, 154

P. 468:1. *For* VI *read* VII

335:25–37. *For* vol. IX *read* IX, 295–311

348:1–3. Near the end of his review of Taine's *Histoire de la littérature anglaise,* Scherer quotes "le mot de [Nicolas] Chamfort: 'Le grand art, c'est de n'être dupe de rien.'"–*Études sur la littérature contemporaine* (nouv. éd.; Paris, 1894), VI, 134.

364:36. *Cancel* but the . . . 1879 *and see note to* "Schools in the Reign of Queen Victoria," XI, 242:16.

367:32–34. *For* After the first *read* After a first; *for* making them ascend *read* making them to ascend

P. 478:16–26. [*The World* alludes to Arnold's remarks at the Royal Academy banquet of April 30, 1881, not to these remarks of 1875; see *Prose Works*, ed. Super, XI, 370.]

Index

[VOLUME IX: ENGLISH LITERATURE
AND IRISH POLITICS]

Text

10:15. *For* than in others *read* than in any others
160:13. *Read* principles
165:7. *For* His *read* his   (*from ms, Ward*)
183:27. *For* touches; *read* touch;   (*from ms*)
186:26–27. *For* (this list *read* (the list
194:1. *Italicize* Cato
196:19. *For* from the great *read* from that great

Textual Notes

10:15. *Add:* in others,   83m
Pp. 442–43. The mss of "The Study of Poetry" and "Thomas Gray" are in the library of Balliol College, Oxford.
167:15. chaunt   *also ms*
171:11. is as given   *ms*
175:11, 181:4. in virginitee!'   *also ms*
186:26–27. (the list   *ms, Ward;* (this list   88
197:2. *Ms also misreads* light
266:16. *For* 82m *read* 83m

Critical and Explanatory Notes

2:33–36. *For* vol. XI *read* XI, 222
33:7–13. (*Add:*) quoted in Arnold's review of Curtius (1872), *Prose Works*, ed. Super, V, 283–84.
44:27–35. (*Add:*) Professor DeLaura points out that Arnold does not quote himself *verbatim;* he adds "of superiority," "under the conditions immutably fixed by the laws of poetic beauty and poetic truth," and "whatever it may be."
62:15–16. (*Add:*) "Man is a reasoning animal."–Seneca *Epistolae* xli, 8 (DeLaura).
P. 348:27, title. Dr. James Simpson points out that Goethe in *Über Kunst und Alterthum* published a two-page essay entitled "Französisches Schauspiel in Berlin."
P. 374, first note. *For* 145:8 *read* 145:9; *for* (see p. 146:30) *read* (see p. 146:31)
162:3–7. *For* (1800) *read* (1802 version)
P. 392:34. *For* ed id *read* et id

205:24. (*Add:*) Forman's unsigned article on Arnold in *Tinsley's Magazine* III, 146–55 (September, 1868) was an offensive and ill-mannered essay on the thesis that Arnold's "intense egotism has no sufficiently-rational basis." It was so rewritten as to be almost unrecognizable when Forman republished it in his book, *Our Living Poets* (London, 1871), and Arnold may never have seen it.

225:4–5. (*Add:*) Macaulay alludes to a comparable passage: "In one of his works . . . he compares the poetry of the eighteenth century to the Parthenon."–"Moore's Life of Byron," two-thirds through.

283:10–15. *For* vol. X *read* X, 183–84

[VOLUME X: PHILISTINISM IN
ENGLAND AND AMERICA]

Text

7:23. *For* midde *read* middle

112:33. *For* neighboring *read* neighbouring

242:17. *For* 1882 *read* 1884

257:24. *For* Council for *read* Council on

258:15. *For* appause *read* applause

432:22. *For* 4 *read* 5

Critical and Explanatory Notes

14:25–26. The characterization of Hugo is Arnold's own, in his first essay on George Sand (1877).–*Prose Works*, ed. Super, VIII, 230.

P. 464:11. (*Add:*) Even at the luncheon following Huxley's address, Professor Max Müller replied that "a true college of science could not live if it were to exclude the science of man. . . . Where can we study the science of thought, that most wonderful instance of development, except in the languages and literatures of the past?"–*Times*, October 5, p. 8, col. 3.

P. 466:4. *read* at the Opera House, Galesburg, Illinois;

P. 496:29. (*Add:*) Stephen Coleridge, son of Arnold's close friend, recalls Arnold's attendance at the performance of *Much Ado* at the Lyceum on December 13, 1882.–*Memories* (London, 1913), p. 151.

171:6–9. Arnold first used this figure in a letter to Gosse on August 11, 1882: "The Ode to Evening has not the evolution of Gray and of Simonides—like the rivers of central Asia, it loses itself in the sand." See *Prose Works*, ed. Super, IX, 387.

196:26–29. Bancroft's words are from an early version of his *History of the United States from the Discovery of the American Continent* (Boston, 1858), VII, 21 (chapt. i: May, 1774). Arnold jotted the expression in his pocket diary for December 17, 1884.—*Note-Books*, ed. Lowry, p. 409.

P. 528:3–4. *For* "sent . . . education there" *read* "called upon Arnold to testify as to his experience in English and Continental education."

P. 539:4–15. [A more accurate account of the hoax appears as the note to *Prose Works*, ed. Super, XI, 362:28–31. The spurious article appeared in all copies of *The New York Tribune* for April 6, 1884 (p. 4, col. 6) and trapped most American newspapers, not merely *The Chicago Tribune*.]

[CULTURE AND ITS ENEMIES]

[The manuscript of "Culture and Its Enemies" in the library of
Balliol College, Oxford, is that from which the printers set up the
essay as published in the *Cornhill Magazine* for July, 1867, the same
copy Arnold used as he delivered the lecture from the chair of
5   Poetry at Oxford on June 7. Most of the differences between the
manuscript and the *Cornhill* version are trifling and insignificant;
four substantial passages, however, were crossed out in the manuscript and never printed. There is no way of knowing whether they
were part of the lecture as delivered or not. The page references
10   below will serve to place them in the first chapter of *Culture and
Anarchy* in volume V of the present edition.]

92:22. Monsieur Sainte-Beuve's critical activity belongs chiefly to
a time of no great faith and ardour, a somewhat stationary time
coming [?] between an epoch of great effort and the present
15   which is promising in its turn to be an epoch of great effort again;
the intellectual horizon, which is now lifting and opening in all
directions, had for a good while before been comparatively firm
and bounded. No man can resist the influences of his time, and
Monsieur Sainte-Beuve's criticism and culture, coming at such a
20   time, inevitably took the character of a criticism and culture
founded mainly in curiosity,—curiosity here meaning a generous
and liberal zeal purely for knowing and for knowing right,—rather
than of a criticism and culture founded in a study of perfection.
Nay, at such a time it could not otherwise have had the hope, the
25   gaiety, the elasticity the vivacity needful to enable it to work in
many directions and to vary its point of view, but must probably
have become passionate, one-sided, and narrow. But the time has
now changed; and although the culture founded on curiosity, of
which Monsieur Sainte Beuve affords an eminent example, is an ob-
30   ject, if we consider it rightly, for esteem and praise, not, as its dis-
paragers imagine, for censure, although, too, I shall never be weary
of professing my own great obligations to Monsieur Sainte Beuve,
whom I think by far the best and most edifying critic whom we
have had amongst our contemporaries; yet it would be to give an
35   insufficient idea of the motive and value of culture at the present
moment, and an idea of which Monsieur Sainte-Beuve himself
would be the first to feel the insufficiency, if we were to consider

culture merely as we have seen it in him, or as having its motive in curiosity; and not rather as having its motive in quite another ground,–the study and pursuit of perfection.

[For now] And is not

93:26. [*no* ¶] That pure and admirable soul, Bishop Wilson, from whom I have taken the words which so well describe the office of true culture, Bishop Wilson has the strongest and most present sense of the dangers of curiosity and vanity; he takes care to remind the seeker of light that he must "avoid two rocks *curiosity* and *vainglory* either to amuse himself or be admired by others, the fault of too many men." But Bishop Wilson is careful to warn the seeker of light against this waste of his light, just that it may all be used "for no end but that he may better see and not miss his way"; just that it may all serve simply "to make reason and the will of God prevail." But knowledge and light are indispensable, and he sets his face against all disparagement of them. "After all," is his conclusion, "the better a man *knows* the grounds of his duty, the better he is prepared to practise it;" "nothing but innocency *and knowledge* can make the mind truly easy;" "zeal is no further commendable than as it is attended *with knowledge;*" "it is certain, from Holy Scripture, that we are to be judged for the faults of our understanding, as for any other crimes. If men 'hate knowledge,' if they 'despise wisdom and instruction,' if they take no heed of the light that is in them but let it turn into darkness, they will certainly be punished for their *ignorance*."

Religion has been apt so to lay stress upon emotion and affection as often to lose sight of the thought and reason which are necessary in order to guide emotion and affection and to give them their true object. But religion being undoubtedly the greatest, the deepest, the most important of the efforts by which the human race has manifested its impulse to perfect itself, and to draw near to the divine and incomprehensible life in which it exists and to be at one with it; religion being an endeavour through which the human race has on a far wider scale and with a far more intense earnestness sought to satisfy this impulse, than it has through art, or science, or poetry, all of them endeavours directed to the self-same end,– there is an advantage and a satisfaction in getting from religion, speaking by the witness of one of her truest children, sanction for the authenticity and necessity of the aim which is the great aim of culture, the aim of first seeing things as they are, of gaining a sense of how the universal order tends, what the will of God and reason prescribe, with the hope of giving to this knowledge, when gained, a practical influence for the direction of human life. And religion

97:14. [*no* ¶] Why, in a case such as I have fancied of England
5   being a hundred years hence looked back upon with perfectly disinterested eyes by the human race for the spectacle she might afford them, just as we now look back upon Greece or Rome, is it
not certain that even the England of 1815, that drunken Helot of
our modern liberals, would excite, as having successfully performed
10   a long, strenuous, splendid effort against a despotic power which
was weighing heavily on the world, more love interest and admiration, and would appear, therefore, invested with more signs of
greatness, than the England of the last 20 years, which has had in
its activity nothing so spiritual and so meant for the common good,
15   but has performed its prodigies with an aim to material advantage,
and that advantage its own? And yet, without culture, we fall into
such false notions that actually we make our greatness depend upon
our coal and iron.

99:30–32. poetry; and if to some people I have seemed to try
20   and use this chair too much for the general purposes of culture and
not enough for the particular criticism of poetry, this is my answer:
that culture and poetry have in view the same standard of human
perfection, and that in order to give poetry its full reach and to enable men to feel its real power, it is necessary to get this standard
25   of human perfection clear; for which end the varied and manifold
workings of culture are the best of disciplines. It is by culture, by
studying, with the disinterested aim of perfection in view, all the
great manifestations of our human nature—morality, philosophy,
history, art, religion, as well as poetry,—that we arrive at the
30   clearest sense of the worth of poetry, of its use for man's development, and of its function in the future. I have called religion the
greatest and the most important manifestation which has yet been
seen of human nature, and so it is; but it is so, religion conceived
as something wholly separate from poetry is so, only because the
35   rawness of the mass of mankind made them incapable of following
religion, conceived as something in harmony with poetry, incapable
of meeting the full demands on their spirit and powers which religion, conceived as something in harmony with poetry, would
impose; they were not ripe for religion as a conscious study of per-
40   fection, pursued with devout energy, for the whole of their being;
they could receive it but as a code of rules, and for one side of their

being only. In no other way could the animality of the mass of mankind be broken down, and the first beginnings of perfection be made by them. I have called

[ST. PAUL AND PROTESTANTISM]

[The first of the following passages appears uncancelled in the manuscript; since it did not appear in the *Cornhill Magazine* it presumably was removed at the proof stage. The second passage is crossed out in the manuscript. Page references will place them both in the text of volume VI of the present edition.]

16:23–25. day. Almost any hymn exhibits it:—

> We give immortal praise
> To God the Father's love
> For all our comforts here
> And better hopes above;
>   He sent his own
>   Eternal Son
>   To die for sin
>   That man had done.
>
> To God the Son belongs
> Immortal glory too,
> Who bought us with his blood
> From everlasting woe;
>   And now he lives
>   And now he reigns
>   And sees the fruit
>   Of all his pains.

Milton's lines exhibit it more classically. By
62:23. made. As the hymn says:

> Tell of our Redeemer's love
> Who for ever doth remove
> By his holy sacrifice
> All the guilt that on us lies.

[BIOGRAPHICAL SKETCHES OF GRAY AND KEATS]

[The biographical sketch of Thomas Gray, printed before Arnold's essay in Ward's *English Poets,* is a part of the manuscript of that

essay in Arnold's handwriting in the library of Balliol College. Passages here enclosed in brackets appear, uncancelled, in that manuscript but were not printed. Presumably the biographical sketch of
Keats in *The English Poets* (for which no manuscript is at present
5   known) is also Arnold's own. Neither biographical sketch was
printed in the second series of *Essays in Criticism*.]

(Thomas Gray was born in London on the 26th of December
1716. His father is described as 'a citizen and money-scrivener'; we
should say nowadays, he was on the stock-exchange. He appears
10 to have been a selfish, extravagant, and violent man. [The expense
of Gray's education was borne by his mother out of the proceeds of a business in which her small fortune was invested
before her marriage and of which the profits were secured to
her own use.] Mr Antrobus, Gray's uncle on the mother's side,
15 was one of the assistant masters at Eton, and at Eton, under his
care, Gray was brought up. At Eton he formed a friendship with
Horace Walpole, and with Richard West, whose father was Lord
Chancellor of Ireland. [Horace Walpole went from Eton to Cambridge, where his intimacy with Gray was continued; West went
20 to Oxford, but a correspondence and close friendship was kept up
between him and Gray until West's death in 1742.] At Cambridge
Gray did not read mathematics and took no degree. He occupied
himself with classical literature, history and modern languages;
several of his translations and Latin poems date from this time. He
25 intended to read law; but a few months after his leaving Cambridge,
Horace Walpole invited him to be his companion on a tour through
France and Italy. The friends visited Paris, Florence and Rome, and
remained abroad together more than two years. Gray saw and
noted much; on this journey were produced the best of his Latin
30 poems. Walpole, however, the son of the Prime Minister, and rich,
gave himself airs; a difference arose which made Gray separate
from him and return alone to England. He was reconciled with
Walpole a year or two later; but meanwhile his father died, in 1741;
his mother went to live at Stoke, near Windsor; and Gray, with a
35 narrow income of his own, gave up the law and settled himself in
college at Cambridge. [Between Cambridge and Stoke his time was
passed.] In 1742 he lost his friend West; the *Ode to the Spring* was
written just before West's death, the *Ode on the Prospect of Eton*,
the *Hymn to Adversity*, and the *Elegy written in a Country*
40 *Churchyard*, were written not long after. The first of Gray's poems

which appeared in print was the *Ode on the Prospect of Eton*, pub-lished in folio by Dodsley in 1747; 'little notice,' says Warton, 'was taken of it.' The *Elegy* was handed about in manuscript before its publication in 1750; it was popular instantly, and made Gray's repu-tation. In 1753 Gray lost his mother, to whom he owed everything, 5
and whom he devotedly loved [; "the careful tender mother" he says of her in her epitaph, "of many children, one of whom had the misfortune to survive her]. In 1755 *The Progress of Poesy* was finished, and *The Bard* begun. [The next year he moved from Peter-House in consequence of some annoyances he met with there, 10
and established himself at Pembroke Hall.] The post of Poet-Laureate was offered to Gray in 1757, and declined by him. [In 1759 the British Museum was opened to the public, and for two or three years Gray was much in London for the purpose of reading and transcribing manuscripts at the Museum.] He applied to Lord 15
Bute, in 1762, for the professorship of modern history at Cambridge, but in vain. Six years afterwards the professorship again became vacant, and the Duke of Grafton gave it to Gray without his apply-ing for it. The year afterwards the Duke of Grafton was elected Chancellor of the University, and Gray composed for his installa- 20
tion the well-known *Ode for Music*. It was the last of his works. He talked of giving lectures as professor of history, but his health was bad, and his spirits were low; Gray was the most temperate of men, but he was full of hereditary gout. Travelling amused and revived him; he had made with much enjoyment journeys to Scotland, 25
Wales, and the English Lakes, and in the last year of his life, 1771, he entertained a project of visiting Switzerland [, to visit his young friend Bonstetten to whom he was warmly attached]. But he was too unwell to make the attempt, and he remained at Cambridge. On the 24th of July, while at dinner in the College hall, he was seized 30
with illness; convulsions came on, and on the 30th of July, 1771, at the age of fifty-four, Gray died. He was never married.)

John Keats

(John Keats was born in London on the 29th of October, 1795. His father was in the employment of a livery-stable keeper in Moor-fields, whose daughter he married. Our poet was born prematurely. 35
He lost his father when he was nine years old, and his mother when he was fifteen. He and his brothers were sent to a good school at Enfield kept by Mr. Clarke, whose son, Charles Cowden Clarke, well known afterwards from his connexion with letters and literary

men, was a valuable friend to John Keats. As a schoolboy, Keats seems to have been at first remarked chiefly for his pugnacity and high spirit, but he soon showed a love of reading. On leaving school in 1810 he was apprenticed for five years to a surgeon at Edmonton;

5   he was thus still in the neighbourhood of the Clarkes, who continued to see him, took interest in his awakening powers, and lent him books,—amongst them the *Fairy Queen* of Spenser, the poet whose influence has left on the poetry of Keats so deep an impression. The young surgeon's apprentice took to verse-making; when

10   he went to London to walk the hospitals, he was introduced by the Clarkes to their literary friends there, and knew Leigh Hunt, Hazlitt, Basil Montagu, Haydon, Shelley, and Godwin. In 1817 he brought out his first volume of verse, and abandoned the profession of surgery, for which however, disagreeable though it was to

15   him, he had shown aptitude and dexterity. His first volume contained the *Epistles*, which we now read amongst his collected poems; it had no success. But his friends saluted his genius with warm admiration and confidence, and in 1818 he published his *Endymion*. It was mercilessly treated by *Blackwood's Edinburgh*

20   *Magazine* and by the *Quarterly Review*. Meanwhile Keats's small fortune was melting away, and signs of disease began to show themselves in him. Nevertheless, in the next year or two he produced his best poems; but his health and circumstances did not mend, while a passionate attachment, with which he was at this time

25   seized, added another cause of agitation. The seeds of consumption were in him, he had the temperament of the consumptive; his poetry fevered him, his embarrassments fretted him, his love-passion shook him to pieces. He had an attack of bleeding from the lungs; he got better, but it returned; change of climate was recommended,

30   and after publishing his third volume, *Lamia, Isabella, and other Poems*, he sailed for Italy in September 1820, accompanied by his friend Severn. Italy could not restore him. He established himself at Rome with Severn, but in spite of the devoted care and kindness of this admirable friend, he rapidly grew worse, and on the 23rd

35   of February, 1821, he died. He was twenty-five years old. John Keats was buried in the Protestant cemetery at Rome, and on his gravestone is the inscription which he himself told his friend to place there: *Here lies one whose name was writ in water*.)

Checklist of Manuscripts of
Arnold's Prose Works

"Anarchy and Authority," the *Cornhill Magazine* version of parts III–V (in this edition, V, 163–229). 108 pp. With 9 pp. of corrected page proofs of part IV (V, 194:17–205:16, *Cornhill* variants). In the library of Balliol College, Oxford.

"Common Schools Abroad," the *Century Magazine* version. 32 pp. In the library of the University of Pennsylvania.

Culture and Anarchy: see "Culture and Its Enemies," "Anarchy and Authority."

"Culture and Its Enemies," the *Cornhill Magazine* (Oxford lecture) version. 43 pp. In the library of Balliol College, Oxford.

"Emerson," the lecture version. 41 pp. With printed copy for use on the lecture platform, 32 pp., heavily corrected. In the Houghton Library of Harvard University.

"George Sand" (1877), the *Fortnightly Review* version, presented by its editor John Morley to Lord Rosebery in 1888. 28 pp. In the Beinecke Rare Book and Manuscript Library of Yale University.

"My Countrymen," the *Cornhill Magazine* version. 34 pp. In the library of Balliol College, Oxford.

"On the Study of Celtic Literature," the *Cornhill Magazine* (Oxford lecture) version, parts I–IV. 134 pp. Lacks III, 311:29–313:22. In the National Library of Wales, Aberystwyth.

"St. Paul and Protestantism," the *Cornhill Magazine* version, parts I–II. 79 pp. In the library of Balliol College, Oxford.

Special Report on . . . Elementary Education in Germany, &c, the Education Department version. 51 pp., with envelope addressed to Arnold from the Education Department, Whitehall. In the Alderman Library of the University of Virginia.

"The Study of Poetry," the *English Poets* version, headed "Preface." 36 pp. Given by Arnold's grandniece Miss Dorothy Ward on June 5, 1952, to the library of Balliol College, Oxford.

"Thomas Gray," the *English Poets* version, including biographical sketch; headed "Gray." 16 pp. Bound and given with "The Study of Poetry" to the library of Balliol College, Oxford.

"The Zenith of Conservatism," revised second proofs for the *Nineteenth Century*. 16 printed pp. (not manuscript). In the library of Balliol College, Oxford.

Index

A reference to a page of text should be taken to include the notes to that page.

Title Index to Arnold's Prose Works
Published in This Edition